22 MURDERS

22 MURDERS

INVESTIGATING THE
MASSACRES, COVER-UP AND
OBSTACLES TO JUSTICE
IN NOVA SCOTIA

PAUL PALANGO

RANDOM HOUSE CANADA

PUBLISHED BY RANDOM HOUSE CANADA

Copyright © 2022 Paul Palango

Library and Archives Canada Cataloguing in Publication

Title: 22 murders : investigating the massacres, cover-up and obstacles to justice in Nova Scotia / Paul Palango.
Other titles: Twenty-two murders
Names: Palango, Paul, 1950- author.
Identifiers: Canadiana (print) 20210256028 | Canadiana (ebook) 20210256060 | ISBN 9781039001275 (softcover) | ISBN 9781039001282 (EPUB)
Subjects: LCSH: Mass shootings—Nova Scotia—Portapique. | LCSH: Mass murder—Nova Scotia—Portapique. | LCSH: Mass murder investigation—Nova Scotia—Portapique. | LCSH: Mass murderers—Nova Scotia—Portapique.
Classification: LCC HV6536.6.C22 N67 2022 | DDC 364.152/340971612—dc23

Text design: Matthew Flute
Cover design: Matthew Flute
Image credits: (Country road) Grant Faint / Getty Images; (Police car) Andrew7726 / Dreamstime.com and Frank Wulfers

Printed in Canada

2 4 6 8 9 7 5 3 1

Penguin
Random House
RANDOM HOUSE CANADA

DEDICATED TO

The victims of the first massacre,
APRIL 18, 2020

Jamie Blair, Greg Blair, Lisa McCully, Corrie Ellison,
Frank Gulenchyn, Dawn Madsen Gulenchyn, John Zahl,
Elizabeth Joanne Thomas, Peter Bond, Joy Bond,
Aaron Tuck, Jolene Oliver and Emily Tuck

The victims of the second massacre,
APRIL 19, 2020

Sean McLeod, Alanna Jenkins, Tom Bagley,
Lillian Campbell Hyslop, Heather O'Brien, Constable Heidi
Stevenson, Joey Webber, Gina Goulet and Kristen Beaton . . .

and Kristen and Nick Beaton's unborn child

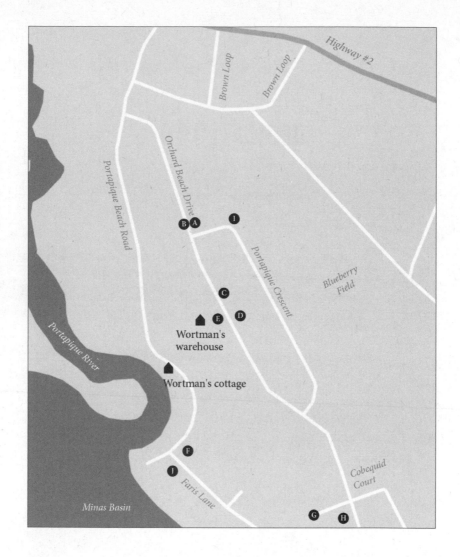

APRIL 18, PORTAPIQUE BEACH

Ⓐ Dawn and Frank Gulenchyn
Ⓑ Andrew MacDonald (injured)
Ⓒ Greg and Jamie Blair
Ⓓ Lisa McCully
Ⓔ Corrie Ellison
Ⓕ Elizabeth Joanne Thomas
  and John Zahl

Ⓖ Joy and Peter Bond
Ⓗ Aaron Tuck, Emily Tuck,
  and Jolene Oliver
Ⓘ Joudrey residence
Ⓙ Griffon residence

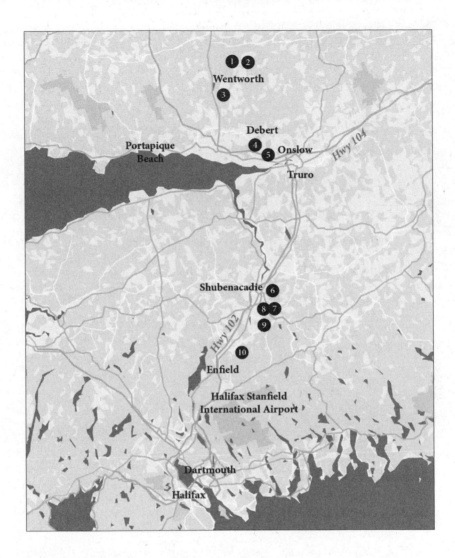

APRIL 19, NOVA SCOTIA

1. Alanna Jenkins
   and Sean McLeod
2. Tom Bagley
3. Lillian Campbell Hyslop
4. Kristin Beaton
5. Heather O'Brien

6. Chad Morrison (injured)
7. Heidi Stevenson
8. Joey Webber
9. Gina Goulet
10. Irving Big Stop

CONTENTS

PART ONE:
AN EPIC FAILURE IN POLICING

PART TWO:
THE SEARCH FOR THE TRUTH

PART ONE

AN EPIC FAILURE IN POLICING

1

CAPTAIN PORTAPIQUE

A few months before his beachfront village made international headlines, Gabriel Wortman began a winter's night where he often did, with drinks and a guest at the Black Bear Lodge. The name was emblazoned in block letters on an overturned green canoe that served as the roof of his ersatz tiki bar. He'd named it for a wild bear he had nurtured as a cub. He still hand-fed Tostitos to it, right out of the bag, whenever it showed up in his backyard, which overlooked picturesque Cobequid Bay in the Minas Basin, the easternmost arm of the mighty Bay of Fundy.

Black Bear Lodge couldn't be found by Google. It wasn't the resort by that name deep in the New Hampshire wilderness or the rehab facility near Fredericton, New Brunswick. Wortman's Black Bear Lodge was tucked inside his "warehouse" at 136 Orchard Beach Drive at Portapique Beach in Nova Scotia.

Portapique was the kind of place even Nova Scotians would need a map to find when it made the news that coming April. It was never a rich place. There used to be some money, years ago, and a lot of fun. It once had a dance hall with a two-acre parking lot that could hold 250 cars. Dance halls had been scattered throughout the province. The Kenwood in Mira Gut. The Birches in North Sydney. The Venetian Gardens in Sydney. The Shore Club in Hubbards. The Olympic Gardens in Halifax. And the Portapique Dance Hall, right on the edge of Cobequid Bay. One by one they nearly all disappeared. The Portapique Dance Hall and its massive parking lot were finally gobbled up by the ocean in the mid-seventies.

Wortman owned five properties in Portapique, three personally and two through a corporate entity. Three were vacant land. He had a beautiful, rustic log and stone cottage at 200 Portapique Beach Road. It was one of only two houses on the river side of the road; the other sat a half kilometre away. Wortman told people that after he died he wanted to be wrapped in a Hudson's Bay blanket and buried next door, at the old Portaupique Cemetery (an old spelling for the community). Any other property along that stretch of the road had washed away years ago as the red-mud shoreline collapsed in places under the enormous pressure of the tides. They are the highest tides in the world. Twice a day the water rushes in and rises more than 13 metres and then back out like a bathtub draining. Scientists say Nova Scotia tilts more than a centimetre every time this happens.

Wortman's cottage overlooked the mouth of the Portapique River where it empties into the bay. The worn-down foothills of the Appalachians stood off in the distance, the perfect setting for everyday sunsets. In a nod to American Appalachia, on the front porch near the steps to the deck, Wortman had placed a life-sized wood carving of a moonshiner, a single-barrelled shotgun in his right hand menacingly pointing out to the road while a jug of white lightning was clasped in his left.

Wortman also owned a large twenty-acre plot—287 Portapique Beach Road—that ran south, almost down to the water. It was nothing but a tangled tract of scrubby trees and bush. He had assembled two other adjacent parcels of land, which faced onto Orchard Beach Drive. He had visions of doing something big with it all someday.

On his fifth and final plot of land, Wortman had constructed his own entertainment centre, workshop and museum. The design was likely cribbed from a New England barn, complete with a cupola on top. It was a big building, fully covering a 3,200-square-foot concrete pad. It had a loft and bedroom upstairs. There were no grand vistas. No water views. The rising waters weren't going to get this building. In any direction all one could see were trees and more trees, not a majestic one in the bunch. It was his blind. His snug.

A banner touting Miller Genuine Draft hung behind the bar. It was framed by two diagonally mounted five-horsepower outboard boat motors—odd sentimental trophies. The dusty taxidermied head of a moose with a modest rack of antlers oversaw everything from its spot high above. The bar sat six. A bubble gum machine stood by for those who might want a chew after their brew. Off to the side a small blackboard read "Lisa's Bar," written in chalk.

Some of the locals who had seen the place up close described it as exquisite. One was truck driver Eddie Creelman. "It was really done up. It was beautiful in there. It had everything a man could ever want."

Beauty is in the eye of the beholder. Unfinished chipboard stuck out here and there. The bedroom was finished with drywall that hadn't been taped and mudded. Wortman fancied himself an accomplished carpenter and jack of all trades, but filling cracks in drywall defeated him, and he always wanted a better price than any professional would accept to clean up the mess he had made of the job.

Since childhood, Wortman had been obsessed with bikes, trikes and quads. He never stopped collecting and fiddling with them. Along its walls the warehouse was decorated with mini-bikes and dirt bikes that he'd been collecting since his early teens. He would regularly take them out for a spin to keep them fresh, ripping along the few roads that made up the neighbourhood as if he owned it.

Off in a corner downstairs sat Wortman's pride and joy: a replica Captain America–model Harley-Davidson from the classic 1969 movie *Easy Rider*. He had erected a makeshift shrine with the chopper posed in front of two crossed American flags. On the wall hung a leather jacket with an American flag on it. He had a colour-coordinated blue-and-white bandana, straight out of the movie, tied to one of the handlebars. An "authentic" helmet with the flag motif was perched on the extended sissy bar, as it's known, on the back of the bike. Finally, there was a photo of Wortman riding the bike somewhere, next to someone else riding what looks like the same bike.

The story of the bike and the movie it was featured in would provide eerie parallels to Wortman's own life. The original was created for *Easy Rider*, which debuted in 1969, the same year Wortman was born. The movie starred Peter Fonda, Dennis Hopper and a young Jack Nicholson, who stole the show, launching his fabulous acting career. Fonda and Hopper played two laid-back hippie drug smugglers, Wyatt and Billy, respectively. Wyatt and Billy were the personification of the new cool more than fifty years ago. Wortman wanted to be seen as cool, too, and in time the extent to which he leaned on Wyatt and Billy's examples to craft his own mystique would become clear. But for the most part, real life intruded. He made dentures for semi-empty mouths or those entirely devoid of teeth.

That night at the warehouse Wortman's guest was one of the local women. Her name was Cyndi. Years earlier he had told others how much he wanted to get into her pants—and those of her daughter, Ocean-Mist, as well. He was particularly fond of a series of photos posted by Ocean-Mist on Facebook, in which she is leaning provocatively over the hood of a car in an impossibly short skirt.

Cyndi and Wortman had been having a thing on the side for three years, though it was anything but exclusive. She wasn't the first to join him at the Black Bear Lodge, but she was certainly one of the last.

She was a troubled soul, a middle-aged Jesus freak who had careered between God and the bottle, with a lot of sex in between. She had spent some time in jail and had gone through rehab for alcoholism. Wortman was good at reeling in women like her. He had a surprisingly successful way with certain women, who felt they had lost a step or two and craved occasional and enthusiastic confirmation of their allure. He could be soft-spoken and engaging, a cuddler whom some called enchanting, others mesmerizing. He advertised his vasectomy, as if it were his key to opening any woman's door. He made them feel special, and they loved him for it even if he didn't really love them back. It was always transactional for him. Tit for tat. Scratch my back, I'll scratch yours. No woman ever called him a rapist, but he was clearly a satyr, constantly on the hunt.

He was a long-time fan of strip clubs. His favourite was near where he had grown up. It was Angie's Show Palace in Dieppe, a suburb of Moncton, New Brunswick, about an hour's drive west of Portapique. Another of his obsessions was the Royal Canadian Mounted Police. He had three relatives who were Mounties. Over the years he had collected RCMP items and memorabilia.

Once in the past, he combined the two interests and had Cyndi do a striptease in the red serge RCMP dress uniform. On her tiny frame the uniform was overwhelming. With its high-neck collar and navy-blue epaulettes, the tunic hung closer to her knees than her waist. The sleeves extended beyond her fingertips. The riding boots rode up to nearly meet the tunic. Her head disappeared into the Stetson hat. The striptease was going well, getting down to the part Wortman loved the most—the panties, which had to be sexy and never something comfortable. The spell broke when she ripped open the tunic and sent buttons skittering across the floor. It was a painful moment for Wortman. She wasn't going to be doing that again.

Now, on this winter's night, they were both drunk again. It was her first night back on the bottle after having dried out for a long while. It began with a beer and then another and then out came the Grey Goose. The vodka always pushed her over the top. She had once worked in a sex shop and had supplied Wortman with all kinds of S&M and bondage toys—dog collars, hog ties and even handcuffs that had a safety release on them so that they could easily be removed. They had done all that. It was time for something new, something a little crazy.

She wanted to dance on his special car. It would be a good war story for her, she thought, but her recent bout of sobriety had made her a little uncomfortable about being alone with Wortman. She wasn't planning on a striptease, this time. She called her daughter to come over and she did, bringing a female friend along with her. Wortman was in his element: three women and him.

Cyndi took off her shoes to avoid damaging the paint job and climbed up onto the roof of the car. She began making some of the moves she knew he'd find seductive. The roof of the car could handle her weight, being reinforced. That's the way Ford Taurus Police Interceptors are made. Each vehicle is rugged and tough, built to withstand the weight of all the equipment and banging around that is the life of such vehicles.

Cyndi danced as gracefully as she could around the light bar running across the middle of the roof. Her audience was in stitches, cheering her on. When her show-stopping performance was done, she slid down the windshield and onto the hood, coming to a stop with her feet resting on the push bar at the front of the car.

The front doors of the car were decorated with the distinctive buffalo head logo of the Royal Canadian Mounted Police, resting under a stylized crown. Throughout all the commotion above, the buffalo never flinched, staring as always into the distance. Circling the buffalo's head was a nearly untranslatable motto: "Maintiens le Droit." Some say it means "Uphold the Right," which might mean enforce the law. Others say it really means "Never Do Anything to Tarnish the Buffalo."

Whatever it means, Wortman had just christened his own picture-perfect RCMP cruiser, an easily passable counterfeit.

He had even created a fake fleet number for it: 28B11.

It was his self-styled Captain Portapique car.

2

A WHISPER IN THE NIGHT

It was Saturday Night Fever of a different kind—more like Cabin Fever—that April 18, 2020. People had been locked up for more than a month. Ever since the Golden Age of Piracy, three centuries before, Saturday nights had been a loud and raucous tradition in the Maritime province. But now, there was little likelihood of a bust 'em up party breaking out anytime soon.

Two weeks earlier, at an April 3 press conference, Premier Stephen McNeil had laid down the law about the importance of physical distancing. Until that moment, McNeil had been rated by a large margin as the least-popular premier in Canada in the annual DART Insight and Communications poll. COVID saved his bacon.

"We don't need online graphs to tell us what we need to do. We need to stay the blazes home. The virus will find you," an angry McNeil said. "Then it finds your loved ones. And then it finds your neighbour-hoods. And then we have community spread. And then everyone is putting pressure on the public health to solve it, our health care system to deal with it, and government to pay for it, when all we have to do is stay the blazes home." Within days, songs, memes, T-shirts and mugs were flooding the market.

McNeil's tirade would serve the province well in the long run, but he couldn't wave a magic wand and make the virus disappear. Fear was the watchword. Paranoia city. Don't touch anything, the public was told. Supermarket clerks didn't dare handle your environmentally friendly cloth bag. Plastic bags were back. In public spaces it was as if some invisible force were propelling people away from each other. Get too close and the nearest person would edge away and hover backwards over the bananas to let you pass. Bars were closed. The streets were empty. The airport was all but shut down. No one could visit anyone indoors.

The two road connections linking Nova Scotia with mainland North America had checkpoints. Nobody without a good reason was allowed in or out. Nova Scotia was a near-hermetically-sealed bubble. The COVID-19 pandemic was entering a second month of provincial lockdown. Many believed the whole pandemic thing—this novel coronavirus—was overblown, but the situation was clearly deteriorating.

The day before, Friday, April 17, three seniors had died at Northwood Manor in Halifax, almost doubling the total deaths in the Maritime province to seven. The virus was spreading, especially within the confines of Northwood, where more than fifty would eventually die. But Nova Scotia was one of the safest places to be, all things considered. It was worse almost everywhere else. Earlier that Friday, Prime Minister Justin Trudeau had announced that the border between Canada and the United States would be closed for another thirty days. Snowbirds were rushing home from their winter digs in Florida and Arizona.

In spite of the lockdown, something was going on. That Friday night the RCMP were handing out awards online. One of the big winners was Glen Byrne. The RCMP sent out a tweet alerting the world to his accolade:

Glen Byrne, Commander of the RCMPNS Operational Communications Centre, has been awarded the 2020 National OCC Award for OCC Commander of the Year! The award recognizes consistent excellence at work and alignment with the RCMP's core values. Congratulations, Glen!

A day later, with all that in mind—the COVID lockdown, the empty streets and an award-winning RCMP communications structure—Saturday was looking like the perfect night to be a police officer, especially for the handful of Mounties on duty at the Colchester County detachment in Bible Hill in central Nova Scotia. It's a suburb, as it were, of the town of Truro, population pushing 13,000.

If any of those Mounties needed help that night, they could call on the other 28 to 33 members (as the force calls its officers) stationed at Bible Hill. The numbers aren't precise because the Mounties keep that a secret, even from government overseers who pay the bills. There were another 36 well-trained municipal officers next door in Truro, and almost 800 more Mounties at detachments across Nova Scotia. If it got really knotty, there were more than 500 Halifax municipal police an hour away in the provincial capital. But what could possibly go so wrong that they'd need all of them?

More than a year earlier, the RCMP had begun promoting #9PMROUTINE, a program developed in 2017 by the Pasco County Sheriff's Office in Florida. At 9 p.m. every night the Mounties sent out a tweet or a Facebook post encouraging people to avoid becoming victims of crime by locking and securing their cars, homes and garages.

At 9 p.m. that night, the provincial RCMP looked like it was tucking itself into bed, notifying the world through a message on its Twitter feed, @RCMPNS. The tweet was decorated with an amusing GIF depicting a sleepy grey tabby cat lying on a bed and waving goodnight.

> It's Saturday and our #9PMROUTINE is complete! That means we get to relax for the evening and sleep in tomorrow. Are you done your #lockup? When you are share this post!

The tweet had no sooner been posted when evil began to break out in an obscure corner of the province. Portapique Beach is about a thirty-minute drive west of Bible Hill on the four-lane Highway 104—the Trans-Canada—and then the old two-lane Highway 2.

The locals call Highway 2 "the paved highway." Take it about five or six minutes west of Great Village, which isn't all that great these days, and every so often the farmland on the left gives way to the waters of Cobequid Bay. Up ahead is a tired old community centre, its horizontal white clapboard siding peeling away. It used to be part of the church property, but the church is long gone, as is the veneer of prosperity, such as it was. The big industry in Portapique had been pickling shad, a cousin of herring, and sending it to market down the coast in Boston. But a bony fish like shad couldn't compete with meaty, succulent scrod as the appetites of Bostonians began moving up the food chain after the First World War. Now the big market for shad is as bait for lobster.

On the last leg of the journey to Portapique Beach, there are two notable openings on the left, the south side. One is all but invisible, lost in the brush and trees. You would have to be looking for it to see it. It's the eastern end of Brown Loop, a rutty dirt semicircle of a road. About 150 metres farther down Highway 2 is the western end of Brown Loop.

Drive past Brown Loop and the green and white road sign announces Portapique. The name is a bastardization of the Acadian word *porc-epic*. We know it better as porcupine, the large rodent known to fire barbed quills at perceived enemies.

Portapique Beach Road is the next left. The locals call it PBR. It's the only way in and out of the little community. Well, the only official way, that is. PBR is a winding gravel road that runs for more than a kilometre down to the waterfront.

Just down Portapique Beach Road from the intersection with the paved highway is a row of community mailboxes on the left side. Going a little farther, there are two properties on the same side of the road, sitting on the typical 1.5 acres of lots in the area. The neighbourhood may be on the seashore, but it's no Palm Beach. It's a working-class getaway for most, a cheap home for a few. There are about fifty dwellings in the neighbourhood, including many trailers and shacks. The majority are seasonal. During the summer, about 250 people might call Portapique Beach home, but only about fifteen houses are occupied this early in the spring.

About the length of a football field south on PBR, there is a fork in the road. To the left is Orchard Beach Drive. It runs parallel to PBR for about a kilometre, down to the water. The two roads connect only this once, with thick, tangled, almost impassable woods and undergrowth between them.

Normally, in this age of twenty-four-hour cable news, the world knows about a spectacular atrocity within minutes, often before the families of the victims. Not this time. Caught flat-footed or asleep at the switch, the RCMP struggled to alert the world about what was unfolding in Portapique.

When it came to planning for disasters like this one, the RCMP had commissioned study after study, and by 2020 was regularly inviting the public to tune in to its Twitter feed and Facebook pages to stay up to date with the latest information. Social media became the RCMP's whistles, bullhorn and sirens all rolled into one. But it forgot one part of the equation: Who pays attention to the RCMP's Twitter feed? Its own records for that night show it had 119,800 followers. Impressive? The followers could be anywhere in the world. One would reasonably suspect the majority were RCMP members themselves, or their families, friends and associates. In rural Nova Scotia, other studies have shown, a third of people, at best, used Twitter sometime during the day. In the middle of the night? Zero or close to zero. As a public-alert system, updates on Twitter or Facebook were a whisper in the night.

After posting the grey tabby GIF at 9 p.m., the RCMP's first reference to the evolving tragedy under way in Portapique was in this tweet at 11:32 p.m.:

> #RCMPNS is responding to a firearms complaint in the #Portapique area. (Portapique Beach Rd, Bay Shore Rd and Five Houses Rd.) The public is asked to avoid the area and stay in their homes with doors locked at this time.

Sounds like the beginning of what's going on, doesn't it? Keep that time in mind: 11:32 p.m.

Back to the geography. When last on Highway 2, the paved highway, we turned left at Portapique Road, the only official entrance into the beach neighbourhood. If instead we continued straight on the paved highway, we would travel about 500 metres before crossing over Portapique River. Another 400 metres and we would come to Bay Shore Road on the left. It runs parallel to Portapique Beach Road, west of the river, down to the edge of the bay, and then arcs to the west along the water's edge to the tiny community of Five Houses. There are more than five houses there. Five Houses Road runs north from the hamlet to Highway 2, roughly parallel to Bay Shore Road to the east. It is almost a kilometre from Portapique Beach Road to Five Houses Road.

By the time the RCMP put out its first tweet, residents from the areas around Bay Shore Road and Five Houses Road who were still awake at that late hour were already out investigating signs that something was very wrong. Some were on social media capturing a little of the unfolding chaos. Others were using police scanner apps on their cellphones. Most RCMP operations are carried out using encrypted communications systems that cannot be captured by traditional scanner technology, but ambulances in Nova Scotia use an old-style analog system. Those channels can be heard by anyone who has a scanner or scanner app with the ability to monitor them.

One of the early investigators was Autumn Doucette, a mother of two who stands barely five feet tall. Fires, smoke and the sounds of gunshots and explosions caught her attention sometime around 10:30 p.m.

Doucette got into her car and drove two kilometres east to Portapique Beach Road to check out the situation. She saw no police cars on Highway 2 west of the river at that time. The first Mountie cruisers she found were congregated at the top of Portapique Beach Road, near the mailboxes south of the paved highway.

She made the trip back and forth twice. Around 10:50 p.m. she went to an area called Shady Nook, on the west side of Portapique River. From 10:56 p.m. to 11:17 p.m. she took photos and videos of what looked like two fires, one white hot, blazing across the river. She posted a few of them on the Firefighters of Nova Scotia website, which had a limited audience. Then she saw someone with a flashlight coming through the bush. When that person apparently saw her, the flashlight went dark. Frightened, Doucette left the scene and returned to her house nearby. As she did, she noticed the RCMP presence in her neighbourhood. The flashing lights of RCMP patrol cars were strewn all along Highway 2, west from Portapique toward Bass River and beyond. Based on her observations, the RCMP arrived well before 11:32 p.m. and the fires had been going since well before their arrival.

Doucette's impression was corroborated by one of her neighbours, Laurie George, who did much the same thing. George drove to Portapique, returned to the west side of the river and took time-stamped photos of a fire that appeared to be of Gabriel Wortman's cottage well involved in flames. The time of his first photo was 10:40 p.m.

At 11:08 p.m. this dispatch was sent from an EMS attendant at Portapique, a conversation first reported by the *Halifax Examiner*.

> So there's a structure fire. There's a person down there with a gun. They're still looking for him. The patient we have got shot by him. He was just down there observing the fire, checking out the fire, so there could be other patients around the fire that could be gone already, but we're not sure. Police are stationed at the end of the road there on the 2, not letting anybody down any further but it's very vague what's going on down there, but there is for sure multiple patients down there.

The transmission was captured on scanners twenty-four minutes before the RCMP's tweet. Some people heard it and chatted about it on social media, news in its rawest, thinnest form. There were still no mainstream media reports. No context. Maybe it was just another run-of-the-mill local fracas, soon to be forgotten.

At 11:22 p.m. a Facebook poster, Cindymike Ryan, seemed to put that notion to rest: "Anyone have a scanner and tell me what is happening on Portaupiqe [*sic*] beach road? 3 fires and multiple explosions!! It's not good."

By the time the RCMP tweeted at 11:32 p.m. that it was "respond-ing to a firearms complaint," the public in the immediate vicinity knew something much bigger than a firearms complaint was going on. What was it, though?

On Facebook, Holly Grue made what would be an important observation shortly after midnight. Grue was driving home when she came across police cars along Highway 2. She posted this at 12:44 a.m.:

> On my way home to Bass River (30min ago) there's 2 massive fires down portapique beach rd and about 5 rcmp cars at the rd entrance. Up the road, the entrance to shady nook is blocked off by 2 rcmp cars. When you get to Five Houses Rd. There's 2 SUVs blocking hwy 2 and five houses, 2 more cars up highway 2 further blocking traffic the other way. 2 or 3 more cars are parked in between. When I got to the SUV an officer ran up to me with a rifle around his chest and told me to turn around as fast as I possibly can. That's when I noticed 4 more officers in the area with their rifles out. The bass river fire department has their trucks out and ready to go to the fires. Obviously the shooter is still at large and they can't go until it's safe. Take Maple ave./Montrose rd if you have to go through that area tonight.

By Grue's count there were at least fourteen or fifteen police cars posted along the highway. There were likely others down the vari-ous roads, as well. It looked like a sufficient response to whatever the problem might be.

The Facebook chatter inside the tiny neighbourhood bubble con-tinued for hours.

Doucette told Adele Hart: "Swat team was driving around an hour ago."

Hart replied: "We have three cop vehicles outside now."

Pam Osborne interjected: "Are you okay?"

Hart replied: "Yes, thank you. Two cop cars outside our place stop-ping traffic. So scary and reassuring."

It looked "reassuring," but looks can be deceiving. Throughout the overnight hours, the RCMP's social media outlets went silent. The Firefighters of Nova Scotia website was doing its best to keep the public informed. At 2 a.m. it published this update:

> This is still an active situation. Lockdown remains in place. Reports are indicating that the police have locked down the area in a very large perimeter. As noted elsewhere, there have been reports of multiple fires throughout the night. Please remain in your houses with doors locked until directed otherwise by the RCMP on scene.

When the early risers among Nova Scotians woke up the next morning, most had no clue what was transpiring in Colchester County. The story still hadn't hit the news. The first inkling came at 8:02 a.m., when the RCMP blurted out this message:

> #RCMPNS remains on scene in #Portapique. This is an active shooter situation. Residents in the area, stay inside your homes & lock your doors. Call 911 if there is anyone on your property. You may not see the RCMP but we are there with you. #Portapique

Reassuring, again. The RCMP was telling the public: Don't worry, folks, we got it. Yet it was also saying: We don't have a clue where the shooter is. Anyone scrolling back through their feed would see that the situation had existed since the previous night.

At 8:54 a.m. the RCMP followed up with its first truly frightening tweet. The highlight was a photo of a suspect:

> 51-year-old Gabriel Wortman is the suspect in our active shooter investigation in #Portapique. There are several victims. He is considered armed & dangerous. If you see him, call 911. DO NOT approach. He's described as a white man, bald, 6'2-6'3 with green eyes.

Judging from his picture, Wortman looked like an innocuous sort of fellow. He was wearing a baseball cap. He had a bit of a weak smile.

At 9:18 a.m., in response to a query from someone referring to a story about Wortman in the past, the RCMP tweeted:

> That article is from 2013. We are still looking for Gabriel Wortman. #Portapique #RCMPNS

It was at this point that my wife, Sharon, called up to me, still lazing in bed on a beautiful spring Sunday morning. After making herself a coffee, she typically checks Facebook for messages from our daughter, who lives in the South Pacific. That day, Sharon couldn't help but stumble onto a trickle of disturbing information posted by others in her circle. It was confusing. It appeared something terrible had occurred and was still occurring in a place called Portapique.

"Since when?" I asked.

"Last night."

"Any details?

"No. Some people are saying he might be driving an RCMP vehicle," she said.

"That would be a huge story, if true." I made myself a coffee and headed to my office to read in.

"Reading in" is what newspaper editors do when they come in for their shift. Thirty years out of newspapers and I still start almost every day that way. I catch up with events and opinions, flitting from here to there, bringing myself up to speed. The local papers. CNN. The *New York Times*. The *Washington Post*. Maybe the CBC, the *Globe and Mail*, the *National Post* and a couple of random others such as *Vanity Fair* or Politico or the *New Yorker*.

I googled Portapique and studied the roads. There were not that many ways in and out of the area. A few roadblocks and the entire province could be shut down. Then I read the recent RCMP tweets.

"I think it's bad."

"You always think it's bad," Sharon replied.

"No, I've got a really sick feeling about this," I told her, drawing on my experiences as an author who had written about the RCMP for twenty-seven years. "There's something really wrong here. This is not going the way it should."

I googled Gabriel Wortman. He was a denturist. A denturist? This was getting weird. Having never had a cavity in my life, I'm not all that familiar with the inner workings of dental professions. I googled denturists. They manufacture and fit dentures. As it turned out, Nova Scotia is one of the few places in North America where denturists are licensed to deal directly with the public. Most everywhere else they are subcontractors employed by dentists. The thinking in Nova Scotia and those few places that license denturists is that they will provide a less-expensive service for the public, but it doesn't always work out that way.

There was still no RCMP confirmation that Wortman was driving a police car, as some on social media were saying.

Shortly before 10 a.m., the US Consulate in Halifax took notice and sprang into action. It sent an e-mail to American citizens who might be in harm's way:

Event: Royal Canadian Mounted Police (RCMP) are investigating an active shooter event in Portapique, Nova Scotia, on Sunday, April 19. The public is asked to avoid Portapique Beach Road, Bay Shore Road, Five Houses Road, and the surrounding areas and stay in their homes with doors locked at this time for their safety. Please follow instructions from local authorities and monitor local media for updates.

Actions to Take:
  · Avoid the Portapique Beach Road, Bay Shore Road,
    Five Houses Road, and surrounding areas.
  · Remain at home with doors locked.
  · Keep a low profile and be aware of your surroundings.
  · Review your personal security plans.

- Follow instructions from local authorities and monitor local media.
- Stay alert in public places, including schools, hospitals, churches, tourist locations, and transportation hubs.

Another security service, using the Peak app, minutes afterwards sent messages to thousands of international university students in Halifax and across Nova Scotia, warning them about the possible danger. Local students weren't so lucky.

Facebook groups were lighting up. But no one had facts to share, only supposition and conjecture, enough for one's imagination to explode with dire possibilities. This Wortman guy appeared to be roaming at will. How was he getting around the police roadblocks? There must be roadblocks. The danger was clearly escalating and members of the public were at risk, yet there was still no public alert coming from either the Mounties or the provincial government. The previous week, on April 10, the provincial government had used the two-year-old Alert Ready for the first time when it issued an emergency alert about COVID-19.

> Covid-19 is deadly. Stop the spread now. STAY HOME. Only leave for essential groceries, prescriptions or medical appointments. Ignoring public health direction endangers lives. STAY HOME. Protect yourself and others.

With the RCMP relying almost exclusively on Twitter, Facebook groups were front-running the story. A video was posted of a white-coated Wortman hawking his denture services while treating a satisfied young male customer. It was hard to believe that this regular guy had suddenly transformed into Mr. Mayhem.

Television news finally caught on, but it needed pictures. Newsworld, the CBC's twenty-four-hour station, set up in Great Village. Its first video showed heavily armed Mounties and some ambulances congregated around the fire hall. Then two all-black RCMP vehicles—a Suburban and a pickup truck with a cap—careered around a bend in the road with sirens wailing. They were coming from Portapique and headed somewhere east of there. It was an action shot, a scene that would be looped all day, but it also seemed incongruous, even perplexing. Before the two trucks roared through the village, there seemed to be no sense of panic or urgency among the assembled officers. One was helping firefighters casually roll up hose. Another was pacing back and forth, a Colt C8 tactical rifle strapped to his shoulder. He looked bored. What was going on in Great Village didn't look right to me.

A new post reported a fire somewhere in Wentworth. Back to the map. Wentworth is north of Portapique, the next big expanse of land north of Highway 104 heading into the mountains. Nova Scotia's largest ski resort is there. What was going on? A slow-motion Armageddon? Then came the first news of a death, a body appearing near Highway 4, also in Wentworth. Was this Wortman's work, too? Or was it a group of associates—like-minded terrorists? Nova Scotia would be the perfect target to put a scare into the world. Ordinary people living ordinary lives. It couldn't get much scarier than that. The RCMP continued to be mute.

To reiterate, there were almost 1,000 Mounties in Nova Scotia in various capacities and another 800 or so non-RCMP municipal police. It seemed a certainty that the entire province would be locked down. There are only two expressways in that part of western Nova Scotia, Highway 102 and Highway 104. The abundance of sea and fresh water in Nova Scotia, combined with the hilly terrain, allow for only a handful of secondary and tertiary roads. Yet this Wortman was still on the loose. How?

After more than an hour of silence, at 10:04 a.m. the RCMP tweet machine kicked into action again:

#RCMPNS is advising people to avoid Hwy 4 near Hidden Hilltop Campground in #Glenholme. Gabriel Wortman is in the area. Please stay inside your homes and lock your doors. #Portapique

Glenholme was a twelve-minute drive from Portapique. This was getting even more worrisome. We lived a ninety-minute drive away, on the South Shore, west of Halifax, but the imprecise descriptions and the lack of timely detail from the RCMP were making even us edgy. Social media kept saying that Wortman was driving what appeared to be a real police car on an unprecedented violent spree. It would have been helpful for the police to confirm this, since we were all potential victims. Nova Scotians across the province had to have been worried about him coming up their road or stopping at their house. We were.

It was around this time that I dared venture out of our house and take the 200-step walk to our glass studio. Our two rock star cats, Bono and Cyndi Lauper, needed to be fed and let out for the day. That short walk was a little too scary, and I'm not afraid of a lot. What would I do if I saw a police car coming up the road? How would we know if the driver was a real police officer or Wortman? If we had to hide, what place would be safe enough? Should I run (more like a moderately fast walk these days) to the workshop and lock myself in? What about Sharon? Would I have enough time to call her and warn her to lock up and hide? Maybe we should've bought ourselves a gun or two after we moved to the end of a dead-end road.

When I returned to the house and got back on the computer, the Mounties had been hashtagging the various communities the elusive Wortman was passing through, like some perverse travelogue. They appeared no closer to capturing him.

Facebook participants were now reporting a body being found on Plains Road in Debert and, moments later, possibly another one, not far away from the first. At 10:13 a.m. social media reports appeared of a two-car collision with people possibly trapped inside cars near 1760 Plains Road in Debert. Was this all related? Where were the Mounties?

At 10:17 the RCMP finally confirmed what had been swirling around in cyberspace:

#Colchester: Gabriel Wortman may be driving what appears to be an RCMP vehicle & may be wearing an RCMP uniform. There's

1 difference btwn his car and our RCMP vehicles. the car #. The suspect's car is 28B11, behind rear passenger window. If you see 28B11 call 911 immediately.

The tweet included a photo of the car, obviously taken inside a garage or building, and the questions just kept coming. Who had taken the photo? How did the RCMP get it so quickly? Did Stephen King write the script for this real-life horror?

Four minutes later, at 10:21, the RCMP was back:

> Gabriel Wortman is currently in the #CentralOnslow #Debert area in a vehicle that may resemble what appears to be an RCMP vehicle & may be wearing what appears to be an RCMP uniform. Please stay inside and avoid the area. #RCMPNS

The RCMP tweets were now coming fast and furious, at least faster than they had been. At 10:39 a.m. the RCMP put out this "helpful" message in the midst of all the chaos:

> Please stay tuned to our Twitter account for the latest information on the active shooter investigation where Gabriel Wortman is the suspect

Followed by:

> Thank you for your understanding as we work to provide the most updated information while addressing public and officer safety. #Portapique #Central Onslow #Debert #Glenholme #Colchester

At 11:01, in a reply to four people asking about Wortman's police car, the RCMP tweeted:

> We don't know if it's still there right now. The best identifier for this car is the 28B11 on the C pillar or behind the rear passenger door.

This was getting scarier and scarier. The RCMP was admitting that it didn't know where he was. Where were the roadblocks? The helicopter? If he was in Onslow, then he was just north of Truro. If the Mounties didn't get him, the Truro police surely would. But the next tweet from the Mounties had Wortman already on the other side of Truro, heading toward Halifax.

At 11:04 the RCMP tweeted:

> Gabriel Wortman, suspect in active shooter investigation, last seen travelling southbound on Hwy #102 from #Brookfield area in what appears to be RCMP vehicle & may be wearing RCMP uniform. Suspect's car is 28B11, behind rear passenger window. If you see 28B11 call 911.

How could he possibly have gotten through Truro? Police had been at this for almost twelve hours. It shouldn't have come as a surprise that he would have to go through Truro, and getting from Onslow to Truro meant crossing one of only three bridges over the Salmon River, including the major one on Highway 102.

Even from the far side of the province, I could sense everything was speeding up, getting faster and more furious.

Two minutes later, at 11:06 a.m., the RCMP tweeted:

> Gabriel Wortman, suspect in active shooter investigation, now believed to be driving small silver Chevrolet SUV. Travelling southbound on Highway #102 from #Brookfield area. If seen, call 911.

He'd changed cars? That suggested at the very least that he had carjacked someone, but Facebook was telling another more chilling story. A police car, maybe two of them, was on fire near Shubenacadie. If that was Wortman's work, he'd have to already be well south of Brookfield. Sitting at my computer, I calculated that Wortman had driven roughly 200 kilometres from Portapique to Wentworth back to Debert, and now he was heading toward Halifax. In the middle of this incredible rampage, he continued to manage to avoid being spotted by the police.

How was he doing that?

At 11:24 the RCMP provided another update on Twitter:

> Confirmed suspect vehicle is silver Chevy Tracker. Last seen #Milford. If seen, call 911.

He was getting closer to Halifax. Whatever was happening was building to a terrible climax.

At 11:35 the RCMP put out a message that showed just how far behind Wortman it was:

> To clarify, the suspect in our active shooter investigation, Gabriel Wortman, is NOT employed by the RCMP but he may be wearing an RCMP uniform. He is considered armed and dangerous. If you see him, do NOT approach and call 911 immediately.

Shane Millmore, the first person to comment on the tweet, wrote back: "Any update on the reports of him being at Irving Big Stop in Endfield [sic]?"

Irving Big Stops can be found all through the Maritime provinces, Quebec and Maine. Gas stations and rest stops, they are the go-to meeting and dining halls in many rural communities. The one in Enfield was at Exit 7 on Highway 102, a few kilometres north of Halifax Stanfield International Airport.

Five minutes later, the RCMP tweeted:

> Gabriel Wortman, suspect in active shooter investigation, is now in custody. More information will be released when available. Thank you for your cooperation and support. #Colchester

The wild ride was over. What a relief. The Mounties had finally made the big stop at the Big Stop. It was a strange ending in an even stranger place. Was he heading to the airport to shoot people there . . . or, at least in his mind, to flee the country? And why stop to fill up with gas? None of it made much sense, but who cared. We could breathe again, even though we all knew there was terrible news ahead. Many people must have been killed. Many more must have been injured.

Later that day various news agencies reported a different outcome for Wortman's "capture," complete with photos of what appeared to be Wortman's body lying beside a vehicle at the Irving gas pumps. At 3:45 p.m., a little more than four hours after the bullets must have been fired, the RCMP issued a terse statement confirming that an unnamed RCMP officer was dead, and that the Mounties had shot and killed Wortman at the Irving Big Stop.

What the hell was going on?

3

A SUNDAY STROLL...
BACK INTO JOURNALISM

The "inside" story about what was going on in Portapique was the buzz throughout Nova Scotia that morning. Jan Melvin, who managed the store Sharon and I owned in Chester, called and relayed a little of what she had heard on the grapevine.

"I'm told that there was a party and things got crazy. The husband got mad at his wife and her new boyfriend or her ex or something like that. He had a gun and tied them both to a tree and shot them and then he went back to the party and killed some of the people there," she said.

"What? How would you know that?" I asked incredulously, then remembered that she had a relative in the justice system.

"Someone told me," she said. "That's all I can say."

By noon Gabriel Wortman's body was lying dead on the pavement between the gas pumps at the Irving Big Stop. It was finally safe to go outside.

Coming up the road for his daily walk was our neighbour Doug Spafford. He is a retired child welfare worker from Ottawa who, like us, had moved to the Atlantic seacoast to enjoy a quieter and more affordable life in a beautiful location. He jokingly refers to himself as "a student of the social condition." We met by the magnificent hundreds-year-old oak tree that stood by the road at the edge of the studio property.

Take a few steps to the south out of the forest and what pops into view is the kind of scenery for which Nova Scotia is so famous. We have a panoramic view of Mahone Bay, filled with its many islands, including Oak Island, slightly to the southwest. The History Channel has made the island world-famous with its eight-season-long television series *The Curse of Oak Island*. The channel has devoted more than 120 episodes to the latest hunt for buried treasure at Oak Island. In 225 years, nothing of consequence has ever been found, but the search goes on. Investigative journalists and treasure hunters have much in common, so I can sympathize with the impulse. Once the digging starts, it's all but impossible to stop.

"I see they finally got him," I said to Spafford. "It's fucking unbelievable."

"I hear it was a real shit show up there," he replied. "I'm told he went through them around Onslow," he continued. "They had some kind of roadblock there or something. He just drove right through."

My mind was racing. First Jan Melvin and now Doug Spafford. Was everyone in the loop but me?

"What else did you hear?"

"He went into the gas station on one side of the highway and saw all the cops, so he went across to the other side of the highway. Wortman pulled into the pumps and some cops were there filling up," Spafford said in a matter-of-fact tone. "One of them thought he recognized him, but the others weren't so sure. I think there was a bit of an argument, mainly because Wortman was driving a different car than the one they said he had."

He must have noticed my mouth drop. He continued.

"Eventually, the canine guy and an ERT member confronted him and shot him."

The detail about the dog handler and the Emergency Response Team seemed too specific to be mere gossip. It had the kind of colour only eyes could see. You couldn't make that up.

"My son has a friend who was there. He saw it all. He said it was like there was no one in charge. It was a shit show," he reiterated. "He said they just happened to run into him. It was all an accident that they caught him."

There it was. Wortman's body was still warm. At this early hour, the RCMP hadn't even publicly admitted that he was dead, and Jan Melvin and Doug Spafford of Chester Basin, Lunenburg County, apparently already knew the dirty details. Time would tell if they were correct.

Welcome to Nova Scotia. It's one of those places where everyone you meet knows someone you know, and stories travel at the speed of light. Sometimes they arrive intact.

◆

Nova Scotia looks like a small place on the map when compared to the rest of Canada, but as they say here, "It has some size to it." The land runs about 600 kilometres from Meat Cove in the northeast to Clark's Harbour in the southwest. On the same relative footprint in the United States sit all the cities from Boston to Washington—56 million people. There are slightly less than 1 million residents in the province, and a higher percentage of Nova Scotians live in rural areas than anywhere else in Canada. The only "big city" is Halifax, population 440,000, the financial hub of the Canadian Maritimes.

That it is in Canada makes Nova Scotia generally a safe place to live, but Canada is not immune to mass killings. In January 2017, six men were murdered in a terrorist attack on a mosque in Quebec City; and in 2018, two separate attacks in Toronto, four months apart, left thirteen dead. On a larger scale, on July 8, 1965, Canadian Pacific Airlines Flight 21, a DC-6B was brought down by a bomb near 100 Mile House in interior British Columbia, killing all fifty-two people on board. The crime was never solved. Almost exactly twenty years later, on June 23, 1985, Air India Flight 182 exploded in mid-air over the Atlantic Ocean off the coast of Ireland by a Sikh terrorist bomb placed on it in Vancouver. All 329 people on board were killed. Most of them were Canadian citizens. Much closer to home, the city of Montreal has been the site of three sickening rampages. On December 6, 1989, Marc Lépine shot and killed thirteen young women at the École Polytechnique de Montréal. Less than three years later, former engineering professor Valery Fabrikant launched an attack at another school, Concordia University, and killed four people. A third event on September 13, 2006, at Dawson College left one student dead and nineteen injured.

In Nova Scotia, however, when people died en masse it usually had something to do with the ocean or being underground. The worst disaster, of course, was the Halifax Explosion on December 6, 1917, the result of a collision between the explosives-laden SS *Mont-Blanc* and the SS *Imo* in the Narrows of Halifax Harbour. It was the largest man-made blast before the atomic bomb was created. The north end of Halifax was flattened and 1,782 people were killed. About 9,000 were injured, many of them blinded by glass. Prior to that the White Star Line's SS *Atlantic*, a predecessor of the *Titanic*, went down on April 1, 1873, in Terrance Bay, just west of Halifax, after getting lost in the fog at 3 a.m. and crashing into Meagher's Rock. At least 535 people drowned that night.

On September 2, 1997, Swissair Flight 111, headed to Geneva from New York's JFK International Airport, crashed near Peggy's Cove, not far from the SS *Atlantic* crash site, killing 229 people. The official investigation declared it an accident. Some people close to the investigation say it wasn't. The debate continues.

One of the most dangerous jobs in Canada is commercial fishing, long a backbone of the Nova Scotia economy. At the Fishermen's Memorial in Lunenburg, the names of all the local deceased mariners are noted. Approximately 138 local South Shore men were killed in two separate hurricanes in 1926 and 1927, known as the August Gales. In all, more than 175 men were killed in the storms, some from nearby US ports in Maine or Massachusetts. In the winter of 2021, six scallopers died when their dragger, the *Chief William Saulis*, capsized in the Bay of Fundy. There were no parades or moments of silence for any of them.

The last of too many mining disasters in the province occurred on May 9, 1992, when twenty-six miners died in a methane explosion at the Westray Mine near Plymouth, about a fifty-minute drive east of Portapique. To compare a coal mining disaster to a violent crime might appear to be a case of apples to horse-drawn carriages. The point is to illustrate what has happened in the past when the RCMP has been called in to investigate politically sensitive matters. When there is a real or perceived threat to the office of the prime minister, the federal or provincial governments, powerful business interests or sacred institutions (like the RCMP itself), the Mounties have an established pattern of fumbling cases before they even get close to the door of a courtroom or public inquiry. One such matter involved an investigation into the Westray disaster.

The Westray Mine had long been closed. Deep mining of coal veins in Nova Scotia was a treacherous undertaking that had cost more than 2,500 miners their lives over 150 years. Curragh Inc. arrived with a plan to reopen the mine and lobbied the Nova Scotia government to approve it. The government fully supported the effort. Public concern about reopening the mine was countered by those determined to create more jobs in the economically beleaguered province.

Prior to the mine's reopening on September 11, 1991, a letter was sent to Nova Scotia's Progressive Conservative government by lawyer Bernie Boudreau, then a Liberal member of the province's legislative assembly. Boudreau described the Westray Mine as "potentially one of the most dangerous in the world." Soon after Westray began clawing out the coal, a number of collapses and unsafe procedures by the company were made public. The provincial government ignored all of them.

Eight months later a methane explosion killed the twenty-six miners.

"The promise of new jobs, rich profits and political rewards left those warnings and others unheeded," the Canadian Labour Congress reported years later. "A provincial inquiry lead [sic] by Mr. Justice Peter Richard found 'The Westray story is a complex mosaic of actions, omissions, mistakes, incompetence, apathy, cynicism, stupidity and neglect.'"

The RCMP investigated. The public expected that the Mounties would get to the bottom of the scandalous dealings. Justice would be served. And indeed, the RCMP laid fifty-two non-criminal charges against the company and four officials. Further, two managers faced twenty-six counts each of manslaughter and criminal negligence. The families of the dead miners and labour activists were excited to believe that someone would finally be held accountable. Newspapers and other media crowed that the Mounties were on the case. But over the next months and years, the cases eroded away until the Crown eventually withdrew all charges. The lingering question for the public and the media became: Did the RCMP botch the investigation, or was there political interference in the prosecution? Or was it a little of both?

Among the disturbing facts was the revelation in February 1995, twenty-eight months after the disaster, that the Crown had been sitting on evidence it was refusing to disclose. The Crown even tried to have the judge in the case removed. The judge eventually stayed the case because the Crown had refused to disclose pertinent evidence.

Amid all the legal shenanigans, the province set up a public inquiry, the salve applied to so many Canadian conflicts. Holding a public inquiry under an esteemed judge sounds like a perfect solution to overcoming poor investigations and politically sensitive conflicts. But in the Westray matter, Nova Scotia chief justice Constance Glube ruled that the inquiry was unconstitutional. She said it could continue only once the criminal charges were resolved. When the inquiry finally was held, Clifford Frame, the founder, shareholder, developer, chairman and chief executive officer of Curragh Inc., which owned Westray, refused to take the stand. His manager refused, as well.

What started out looking like a full-fledged effort—a massive police investigation and public inquiry—was actually a mirage, a manipulation so clumsy and obvious any observer could see the puppet's wires.

At the end of the day, the public didn't much care. The government had stretched everything out, and by the time it was all done, just about everyone had moved on. After all, there was no one to whom the decisions and outcomes could be appealed. It's a well-practised art in Canadian politics.

Once again, welcome to Nova Scotia—and to Canada.

◆

That Sunday afternoon, I was hooked by what Jan Melvin and Doug Spafford had told me. If there was even an ounce of truth to the rumours, there was much more going on in this disturbing Gabriel Wortman story than almost anyone could possibly imagine.

It was time to kick off the cobwebs, re-engage my journalist brain and start sniffing around. Maybe I could help out some young journo by offering context and background. I dug out my old contact lists and started calling around. Over the years I had kept in touch with a few people who were in the know about the latest developments inside the RCMP. I called them and others.

"I hear it was total chaos," one extremely reliable and tapped-in source in Ontario said. "A shit show, for sure."

There was no way this guy had been talking to Spafford's source, but the "shit show" description was rising on the charts.

"Wanna go on the record?"

"No, I couldn't do that, Paul," the ex-Mountie told me. "I still do a lot of business with the force."

Self-preservation is big among police and former police. With rare exceptions, police will never criticize other police, whether from their own department or a distant one. Just like the criminals they are paid to pursue, cops don't like rats in their ranks—the *omertà* of the thin blue line.

"This could be the worst day in the history of the RCMP," another former senior RCMP executive said to me. "I don't know all the facts, but it looks to me like it never got escalated to the top. I don't think there was really anyone in charge. They clearly were not ready."

Not ready. It's a damning term in policing circles. To be ready means preparedness, practice and execution. It means having the right people in the right positions doing the right things when the time comes. The RCMP clearly had not been ready.

The RCMP had promised to hold a press briefing at 6 p.m. at its spacious new headquarters at 80 Garland Avenue in the north end of Dartmouth, across the harbour from Halifax. This event had been unfolding since the previous evening. What could possibly be the explanation for such a delay?

To my eye, it looked like the RCMP might be in a jam. In the past, when it was in similar straits, the force typically stalled, deflected and took its sweet time in order to establish its preferred narrative. Knowing that, I too will take the time and space I need to tell my story in its entirety. The facts and intrigue will come in due course, but first it is my duty to provide a necessary foundation, hopefully making it easier for you to understand all the competing forces at play in this terrible tragedy.

Before we see the Mounties face the music, it would be useful to learn a little about the policing environment in Nova Scotia.

4

THE VAGABOND COPPERS

If just about everyone you meet in Nova Scotia knows someone you know, there is a group of important people who are virtually unknown—the leaders of the Royal Canadian Mounted Police. The commanding officers of the force in the province are strangers to the public they are paid to protect. It's the RCMP way. Senior Mounties are essentially vagabond police officers, flitting around Canada in one of the most unusual policing arrangements in the world. It is called contract policing.

Until the 1930s, the ten Canadian provinces each had their own police force. With the onset of the Depression, the poorer provinces could not afford their own policing services. The federal government cut them a deal. If the provinces agreed to hire the federal force, the RCMP, to provide provincial and municipal policing, Ottawa would subsidize the cost by 10 to 30 percent. Every province but the three largest—Ontario, Quebec and British Columbia—took up the deal. Those three kept their provincial police. In 1950, British Columbia disbanded its provincial police force and hired the Mounties.

The result is that the Mounties have spent nearly a century policing hundreds of municipalities across Canada. The US equivalent would be FBI agents driving marked FBI cruisers handing out speeding tickets in Oklahoma. The provinces that hire the Mounties have little, if any, control over the force. Even though the Mounties are technically working under provincial laws and statutes, the force reports to its own masters in Ottawa and is subject to federal laws and regulations.

Canadians are renowned for their deference to authority, a trait that has served the RCMP well. No matter how many mistakes it makes or how great the latest outrage, the Mounties have been given the benefit of the doubt. In an $80,000 survey commissioned by the force in 2020, 95 percent of the 2,988 respondents (1,671 of whom participated online) agreed that "the RCMP is a recognized symbol of Canada." The RCMP touts such surveys as proof of its popularity, but it's what it doesn't tell the public that undermines the claim. All federal employees, including Mounties, sign a non-disparagement clause that prohibits them from saying anything negative about the federal government or its departments, including the RCMP. The rules of the game have been rigged so that any criticism of the RCMP is tantamount to attacking the country itself: Canada is the RCMP and the Mounties are Canada.

I've been to dozens of public meetings over the years and watched politicians of every rank and stripe melt in the presence of Mounties, all but tugging their forelocks in subservience or basking in the reflected glow of being next to a real live Mountie. There have always been reasons to hold the force accountable for its actions, but few politicians seem eager to try. Too often, avoidance is the Canadian way.

All of which brings us to the question of who was going to be speaking for the RCMP at the 6 p.m. press briefing. There were really only a few choices.

Mark Furey was the Nova Scotia attorney general and minister of justice, the elected official in charge of just about everything to do with the law in the province, including policing. He was the chief judge, jury and prosecutor, wielding a combination of powers that most democratic jurisdictions find unseemly.

Before Furey entered politics in 2013, he spent thirty-two years in the RCMP, reaching the rank of staff sergeant, one notch short of the coveted inspector's job and the white shirt that comes with being anointed to the force's inner circle of managers. Furey had the power to hold the RCMP's feet to the fire, if he chose to exercise it. But would he? I had my doubts.

All police in modern democratic countries swear allegiance to their respective country. That is the way of the world, except when it comes to the RCMP: its members also swear an oath of allegiance to the RCMP. It reads: "I (_____ _____) solemnly swear that I will faithfully, diligently and impartially execute and perform the duties required of me as a member of the Royal Canadian Mounted Police, and will well and truly obey and perform all lawful orders and instructions which I receive as such, without fear, favour or affection of or towards any person or party. So help me God." The oath to the RCMP has a powerful effect on members and all too often takes precedence, former members have told me.

Furey may well have been the justice minister, but he left the RCMP as a staff sergeant. Any important dealings he would have with the force would involve his former betters—and they all knew it. The potential for blind eyes was evident. If not Furey, who would hold the RCMP accountable in Nova Scotia? Liberal premier Stephen McNeil didn't see a problem with Furey being a cabinet minister. But then again, McNeil had his own potential conflict of interest. He had five brothers who were police officers, some in the RCMP and others in municipal forces in Halifax and Annapolis Royal. Regardless, the question remained: If the Mounties had screwed up, who would hold the force accountable?

Perhaps the unusually long delay in holding the press briefing was because Brenda Lucki, the commissioner of the RCMP, would be coming to Halifax on the 100-minute flight from Ottawa to speak for the force. That's what previous commissioners had often done in times of crisis. She had been commissioner for two years and three days, and had inherited command of a force that for five decades had been careering from disaster to disaster, far too many to enumerate.

Some were counter-intelligence failures, such as the barn burnings in Quebec in 1972 and the strange Maher Arar case in 2001, when a

Syrian Canadian was caught up in the post-9/11 anti-terrorism sweeps and imprisoned for a year in Syria. In British Columbia, the RCMP failed to identify and capture serial killer Robert Pickton until after he had murdered dozens of women near Vancouver. The 2005 murders of four Mounties at Mayerthorpe, Alberta, were still fresh in the public's mind fifteen years later, as was the death of mentally disturbed Polish tourist Robert Dziekanski, who was repeatedly tasered by Mounties at Vancouver Airport in 2007. Three more Mounties were gunned down in Moncton, New Brunswick, in 2014 after the force failed to implement recommendations made following the Mayerthorpe debacle. In Nova Scotia itself, there was an ongoing controversy over the deliberate destruction of evidence by the RCMP that would have exonerated convicted murderer Glenn Assoun, who spent seventeen years in prison for a murder he didn't commit.

Other cases were less well known. Some were mired in complexity and others were entirely hidden. These include the repeated failures of the force in politically connected and white-collar crimes and money-laundering investigations. Failure is baked into the RCMP system of investigation, where the operating philosophy is essentially this: anyone can do any job.

The federal government has tried over the years to identify the source of endemic failure in the force. In various commissioned reviews and reports—more than fifteen of them—by both Ottawa and the RCMP, the force has variously been described, among other things, as being "dysfunctional," "a broken culture," "insular," "politicized," "unaccountable," "cultish," "stuck in the past," "resistant to change," "misogynistic," "poorly managed," "unsustainable," "deceitful," "incompetent," "unmanageable," "archaic," "nepotistic," "racist" and so on.

More than 200 recommendations have been made in recent years. Few have been implemented. Rather than tangle with the force and its supporters, when confronted with demands to reform the national police service, politicians of every stripe over the decades have uttered a few platitudes and then called the same play: appoint a new commissioner. It's a Hail Mary pass that never gets caught.

Scandal-plagued prime minister Brian Mulroney appointed Norman Inkster in 1987. Inkster made several moves that would further weaken the RCMP. He insisted that the force keep the government informed about politically sensitive investigations. It was a blueprint for corruption. Among other things, Inkster gave temporary "special constables" a career path inside the force where their accumulated seniority counted toward promotion. Taking the emphasis off merit when considering members for promotion helped weaken the DNA of the force. And in 1993, Inkster closed the RCMP Ontario headquarters on Jarvis Street in downtown Toronto and broke it into three different operations, spread across the deep suburbs west, north and east of the city, where the cost of living was more affordable. The move was ostensibly intended to make life easier on the pocketbooks of Mounties assigned to the area, but the net effect was to make the Mounties invisible in the country's largest financial market. Organized criminals and stock-fraud artists couldn't have been any happier.

In 1994 Prime Minister Jean Chrétien appointed Philip Murray to replace Inkster. Murray had been in charge of VIP and airport security for a number of years prior to entering the force's elite. When he got to the top, Murray was the kind of leader who wanted everyone to like him. Bowing to political pressures, he chased approval from politicians by trying to run the force as if it were a business—the growing fad that had been pushed by the Mulroney government. Suddenly RCMP leaders were mindlessly spouting business jargon at every turn: "total quality," "core values," "empowerment," "partnerships," "excellence," "risk-taking," "conflict resolution," "ownership" and "user-pay systems." The RCMP was being transformed from a police force to something more politically palatable—a police service.

Murray infused the force with client-partnership concepts. He solicited sponsorships from businesses at the local and national level, an unseemly notion for a police officer if ever there was one. The RCMP entered a licensing agreement for its images with Disney Corp. Murray decentralized operations so that field commanders were put

in place away from Ottawa, causing the force to lose influence in
the capital, while regional force leaders got closer to provincial and
municipal politicians.

The move to "empower" individual officers was, perhaps, the most
disturbing concept of them all. Murray pushed responsibility and
authority to the lowest-ranking members, upending the command-
and-control structure of a typical police force. This philosophy seemed
to miss a key point: police officers already are empowered. They have
guns and the power of arrest. They don't need more independence, but
better supervision.

"The people at the top say they are trying to run the force like a
business, but the RCMP is not a business. No police force is a business.
It's a public trust," former assistant commissioner Michel Thivierge
told me for my second book, *The Last Guardians*. "Most of these people clearly don't know what they're doing. They fundamentally do not
understand what it is that a police force is supposed to be doing in a
democratic society. They all see themselves as technocrats, trying to
manage away problems, but they are not addressing the deep underlying problems. They're not getting to the roots. There is no real vision.
They're just lurching from one thing to another, with no real long-term
solutions and no deep understanding of the implications for both the
force and society."

Another Murray invention was an "ethics officer" for the entire
force.

"I remember arguing that it was stupid idea," said one former deputy commissioner. "Mine was not a popular position to take inside
the force. The RCMP had 20,000 officers. Each one of them should be
his own ethics officer. By creating an ethics officer, the force was saying: 'Ethics? That department is down on the first floor.' It was completely wrong-headed. Upper management took their hands off the
steering wheel back then. Is it any wonder the RCMP has so many
problems today?"

By 2000 Chrétien was up to his beltline in alligators with corruption issues. To replace Murray, he chose a fellow Quebecker, Giuliano
Zaccardelli, who had been running "J" Division in New Brunswick.

The cocky and colourful Zaccardelli swarmed into Ottawa with his "J Division mafia," as they were nicknamed, and took over the RCMP. His reign ended in ignominy in December 2006 with fallout from the Maher Arar case and other unrelated but serious matters. Insiders say Zaccardelli left an RCMP upper-management structure even more incompetent than the one he had inherited from Murray. Talented and disheartened Mounties had left the force in droves, only to be replaced by Zaccardelli's minions.

Conservative prime minister Stephen Harper next tapped civilian William Elliott, who had strong ties to the counter-intelligence world. He was a civilian in name only. Elliott was a bust, his choice of lieutenants further eroding competence in the executive suite. Having not learned his lesson with Elliott, Harper next sought out a disciplinarian, former soldier and long-time Mountie Robert Paulson. An RCMP insider spoke to me about Paulson at the first news of his appointment. "He won't change anything," the Mountie said. "Paulson has a military mindset. If the outfit is good enough for him, he thinks that it should be good enough for everyone else." That's precisely what happened.

Paulson consolidated power in the commissioner's office while also expanding Philip Murray's destructive decentralization program by giving more power to the far-flung regional leaders. Everyone was in charge and no one was in charge. Dreaded code of conduct cases soared during Paulson's reign, as did several thousand long-term disability cases. Thousands of Mounties were being paid to sit at home, burned out, stressed out and, many of them, disgusted with the force.

Paulson pushed his own favourites to the top who, mixed with Zaccardelli's and Elliott's flubs, crippled upper management for the foreseeable future. Paulson's stated number one priority as commissioner was to destroy the Hells Angels in Canada. He didn't.

The precarity of the situation was obvious to anyone who cared to look, but the new Justin Trudeau government declined to undertake substantive changes. People were appointed inside the RCMP to be "agents of change," but no amount of fiddling could change the structure of the organization—the genesis of all that ailed it. The RCMP had been assigned too many different, incompatible roles in its multiple jurisdictions. That resulted in a promotions system that had been a source of problems for decades. The wrong people—be they men or women—were all too often reaching the top with questionable relevant experience.

The superb US television series *The Wire* captured this dynamic with its usual elegance. "He be natural poe-leese," Detectives Lester Freamon and Bunk Moreland would occasionally say to describe a fellow officer who had either instinctively or courageously done an outstanding job in an unsung fashion. Those who weren't natural poe-leese were described as "house cats." As the decades passed, the proportion of house cats within the RCMP grew.

If you think a more cultured approach to management has served to make the force more progressive, think again. Since the first woman graduated from Depot—the RCMP training academy, in Regina, Saskatchewan—in 1975, the RCMP has struggled to keep women in its ranks. The high-water mark has never risen above 24 percent of all officers, and it has been a continuing struggle to maintain even that level. As far as the top job goes, Beverley Busson once served as commissioner on an interim basis for seven months after Zaccardelli was forced to resign in December 2006. And now, more than a decade later, the Liberal government thought ensconcing a woman at the top would be a grand gesture and a political winner. Prime Minister Justin Trudeau made Brenda Lucki the twenty-fourth commissioner of the force and the first woman appointed to the position. She assumed her post on April 16, 2018.

Inside the RCMP, some were privately critical of the choice. "She was in my class at Depot," said one former Mountie who asked me for anonymity. "There were at least four others in the class who I thought would have been better choices, and a couple of them were women."

Other RCMP sources say Lucki was ranked sixth in qualifications on the selection chart, behind at least one other woman. That was highly regarded Deputy Commissioner Jennifer Strachan, who was in charge of the RCMP in British Columbia, where one-third of all Mounties were stationed. So why Lucki?

Like so many Mounties who get to the top, Lucki's career in the force was relatively unblemished; then again, she wasn't often in positions where her reputation could get scuffed. Lucki's first posting in 1986 was in Granby, in Quebec's Eastern Townships, just north of the Vermont border. It was a federal job, which meant no street policing but rather drug and customs investigations. Next, she went overseas on a United Nations mission to the former Yugoslavia. The RCMP does a lot of that in the name of Canada. Mounties chalk up big points on their CVs for foreign service. After that, Lucki returned to Ottawa, where she trained peacekeepers. As she did this, Lucki advanced through the ranks until she was appointed an acting detachment commander in Manitoba, a position she held for four years.

After seventeen years in the force, in 2003 Lucki made the bump to inspector and was placed in charge of traffic services in Saskatchewan. She soon rose to other white-shirted command positions in Manitoba and northwest Alberta before being promoted to chief superintendent. In 2016 she took command of Depot.

Two years after Lucki was appointed to commissioner, the top job in the force, the onslaught of bad news continued. In February 2020 two former male members launched a $1.1-billion class-action lawsuit alleging bullying and harassment. This came on the heels of two other payouts in 2016 and 2019, together totalling more than $300 million to more than 3,000 female members and civilian workers who had complained about sexual harassment.

The seemingly never-ending nightmare would continue well after Wortman's killing spree when in 2021 Supreme Court of Canada justice Michel Bastarache tabled a report titled *Broken Dreams, Broken Lives.* He found that sexual harassment continued to be rampant within the walls of the RCMP. Bastarache wrote that the problems faced by women in the RCMP had been known to the force and to the government for at least three decades.

"Culture eats Policy every time," Bastarache wrote. "It's time to discuss the need to make fundamental changes to the RCMP and federal policing. I am of the opinion that the culture change is highly unlikely to come from within the RCMP. The latter has had many years to proceed, has been the subject of numerous reports and recommendations, and yet unacceptable behaviour continues to occur." Among Bastarache's other findings was the fact that not only did the RCMP like to hide information (a point made urgently by a special report to Parliament in 2020 from federal Information Commissioner Caroline Maynard) but also the force was prone to hiding individual Mounties who got into ethical or legal trouble. "Like the Catholic Church, they just move them to another parish," Bastarache wrote. "I have a list [of RCMP officers] who have been found guilty up to 15 times. Those people have been promoted."

Once again, Trudeau and Lucki promised to remediate the situation. It was the cycle of life for the RCMP: a report was commissioned; mountains of evidence were provided, pointing out significant issues; RCMP leaders feigned outrage and concern; the government promised to look into it; nothing got done.

Another notable bump in the road came in June 2020, when Lucki stated publicly that she did not believe that systemic racism (another issue noted in Bastarache's scathing report) existed inside the force. She attempted to correct herself a few days later after calls were made for her to resign. Lucki was simply not the kind of person to speak truth to power, RCMP sources believed. "It's not in her DNA," one insider said. "She's the commissioner. It's a big deal to her. She would do nothing that might jeopardize that."

Lucki was committed to doing what Trudeau wanted, appointing numerous women to key positions at the upper levels of the RCMP. In short order Lucki ensconced female assistant commissioners in five of the ten provincial divisions. Among them, Lee Bergerman was already stationed in Nova Scotia before her promotion. Assistant commissioner might sound like a lofty position, but Bergerman became one of twenty-eight across the country. There were five deputy commissioners above her, as well. If that sounds right for a force of 30,000 employees, consider that 10,000 are civilians, many working in areas such as the force's respected forensic laboratories. Of the remaining 20,000, Statistics Canada, which keeps track of these things, says only 11,000 are constables. Even then, the number of uniformed members available on any given day is much lower due to unfilled positions, secret assignments or short- and long-term disability leave, which sideline thousands of Mounties at a time. In real terms, the RCMP has about half the number of uniformed officers, up to and including staff sergeants, as the slightly larger New York Police Department, which employs about 33,500 officers in equivalent on-the-street positions. That's a lot of brass and bureaucrats, and not so many people actually wearing boots to work.

Bergerman went through Depot in 1986, the same year as Lucki. Her first assignment was Thompson, Manitoba, 761 kilometres north of Winnipeg. Bergerman soon became involved in undercover work, a favoured use of female Mounties. In 1995, she was transferred to British Columbia and moved into the Criminal Intelligence and Serious Crime units. She worked for seven years on unsolved homicides. By most accounts she was a solid copper, but her nickname in British Columbia—"the Blade"—suggested that she was more than adept at office politics.

Most of Bergerman's career was in federal policing in Ontario and British Columbia, where organized crime was a priority, especially in the Greater Vancouver area. The Lower Mainland of BC, as it is known, is home to more than 100 competing criminal organizations, including the Hells Angels and a variety of gangs with monikers like the Big Circle, Red Scorpions and United Nations. To combat these threats, the police devised a new strategy, an integrated anti-gang unit: the Combined Forces Special Enforcement Unit (CFSEU). Its more than 400 members came from the RCMP, the Canadian Border Services Agency and every other federal, provincial or municipal police force in the province. Its mandate was "to target, investigate, prosecute, disrupt, and dismantle the organized crime groups and individuals that pose the highest risk to public safety during their involvement in gang violence."

Bergerman's husband, Mike Butcher, was once an RCMP staff sergeant and is considered one of the best undercover agents in the history of the force. He served for twenty-eight years in the RCMP and another five and a half years in provincial enforcement in

British Columbia. As such, Butcher had spent many years in the CFSEU orbit. He had been working as a civilian employee of the RCMP since 2009, mostly moving around the country following his upwardly mobile wife, but also working on files as a "disclosure" specialist, in the force's description.

Bergerman was named RCMP Officer of the Year in 2007, an unofficial award bestowed upon designated leaders relatively early in their career.

"Once you are named officer of the year, your shit doesn't stink anymore," said former RCMP Sergeant Tom Juby. "Some of the worst Mounties I have dealt with in terms of ability were former Officers of the Year."

Another Mountie, who asked not to be named, was well aware of the award. At one point in his career he was designated to write glowing commendations for colleagues nominated for it. The Mountie described the award as a symptom of the force's business-like thinking, which he said is a large part of the overall problems bedevilling today's RCMP.

"It used to be that those who rose to the top had deep experience and were respected for that," the Mountie said. "They had seen it all and they knew what they were doing. They were leaders in the truest sense of the word. Over the past 30 years, members have been selected for advancement because of their perceived managerial skills. They are identified early and literally being cited for merely doing their jobs. They are no better than anyone else, but their careers are curated. They are given a dusting of experience here and there to fill out their resumé and pushed to the top. It's all resumé building. To an outsider they might look deeply experienced, but everyone inside knows the truth. These people, for the most part, are not experienced at anything. They don't stay in one place long enough to learn anything. Most of them tend to have no command ability. They are managers, not leaders. When a difficult situation comes along, they don't know what to do. They don't have the intuitive touch because they don't have true experience in the field. The worst thing of all is that the system has taught them that they are the best of the best. Most of them are completely oblivious to their weaknesses. Over the past thirty years none of them have ever been held accountable for their mistakes. They just get transferred or retire, and the same four letters—RCMP—pays the price every time."

In 2016, Bergerman and Butcher moved across the country. She became the officer in charge of Halifax District in Nova Scotia. The RCMP operation in Halifax was a unique one. The city has its own municipal force. The RCMP polices the more rural areas. The two forces work together on major crimes, a unit controlled by the RCMP.

Moving Bergerman and Butcher eastward was the beginning of a near mass transfer of high-level Mounties, many of them husband-and-wife teams with CFSEU credentials, from British Columbia to Nova Scotia. In August 2018, a second RCMP power couple emigrated from BC to the East Coast. Superintendent Julie Moss was placed in charge of the Southwest Nova District. Moss had long been seen as favoured by then commissioner Paulson. She came from a line of former Mounties and was named Officer of the Year in 2016. She had worked in unsolved homicides and professional standards before being made executive assistant to Deputy Commissioner Craig Callens, who ran "E" Division in British Columbia. She was promoted to inspector and briefly took command of plainclothes officers in Kelowna. There she was involved in a personnel case where her credibility was called into question, but she got promoted out and sent to Nova Scotia. Moss's husband is Sergeant Terry Faulkner. He was part of the CFSEU program on the West Coast and joined his wife in the Annapolis Valley, where he was appointed head of the major crimes unit.

For the government to move a homeowner, it costs taxpayers about $35,000 plus moving charges. It's a little cheaper to move renters, since there are no real estate transaction fees. Moving soldiers, civil servants and Mounties costs the public purse $500 million a year. It's a big business for Brookfield Global Relocation Services, which won the federal government contract in 2006, even after the auditor general reported that government employees had rigged the bidding so that Brookfield would win the competition over another corporation.

The transfers came as the RCMP was under extreme political pressure on the West Coast. It was on the verge of losing the contract for its largest detachment in the country, Surrey (which dropped the RCMP in favour of its own 800-member force in 2021). Issues there included erratic staffing, uneven performance and accountability issues. Despite the CFSEU structure and the claims that it had gang violence under control, the people of Surrey and the rest of the province knew other-wise—"Gang wars are on the rise," the BC Liberal Party touted as late as October 2020.

After years of escalating criticism, the RCMP's fall from grace in BC began at the hands of one of its own, a former highly regarded deputy commissioner named Peter German. Many in the force believed German would have been a perfect choice for commissioner, but along the way he had become embroiled in controversy, a normal outcome in hard-nosed police work but unacceptable for a potential commissioner.

German, who was considered to be a legitimate expert in financial crime investigation, authored a report in 2018 in which he described casinos as laundromats for criminals to wash their illegally gotten gains. A second report by him in 2019 detailed how the real estate and luxury car markets were being used for the same purposes. A separate provincial expert panel corroborated German's findings. It found that an estimated $5 billion in criminal cash was funnelled through BC's real estate market in a single year.

German's findings provided substance to some long-standing com-plaints about the force. The RCMP controlled all serious policing because of its CFSEU and other joint-forces operations. It also con-trolled the national forensic labs and would use access to them as a way of bullying any force that threatened to step out of line. A provincial inquiry headed by BC associate chief justice Austin Cullen was empan-elled on May 15, 2019, to hold public hearings into the issues raised by German. With the excrement about to hit the fan, the RCMP moved some of its valued white shirts out of the line of fire. That same month, Lucki promoted Bergerman to the officer in charge of Nova Scotia.

The RCMP could rationalize that the East Coast was the perfect place to send Bergerman and others from CFSEU out west. The region faced a persistent threat from the Hells Angels, who for years had been openly growing its footprint in the Maritimes under its own name and through puppet motorcycle clubs. With its 13,300 kilometres of coastline and its large international container ports in Halifax and Sydney, Nova Scotia has always been a smuggler's haven. With many of the new RCMP arrivals having had undercover operations experience in British Columbia, Bergerman and the gang looked like a good fit. Over the next few years, they took over RCMP headquarters in Dartmouth and several of the larger detachments around the province.

Two who didn't have that experience took over their Nova Scotia posts in September 2019. One was Superintendent Darren Campbell, who arrived from British Columbia via a stint in Ottawa. Campbell became the officer in charge of support services for Criminal Operations in Nova Scotia. The other was his second wife, Inspector Erin Pepper, a forensic identification and blood-splatter expert, who took over management and administrative services for the Nova Scotia Mounties.

Campbell's was a special case. His first wife was Catherine Galliford, another Mountie. Galliford went from being a high-profile, highly regarded spokesperson for the RCMP's Missing Women's Task Force to a pariah. Her cardinal sin was to come forward in 2011 with allegations of sexual harassment and misconduct within the force. She also argued that the force had neglected its duties and allowed serial killer Robert Pickton to continue killing women for three years before he was finally arrested. Pickton was convicted of six murders on his pig farm but suspected of murdering as many as forty-nine women. Galliford suffered significant psychological damage for taking that stand. Still, she dug in and was eventually credited with being the inspiration behind a class-action sexual harassment lawsuit by 400 female Mounties that resulted in one of the $100-million-plus payouts by the force. Galliford was eventually granted a medical discharge.

While Galliford's career disintegrated, Campbell's soared. As a sergeant on the Emergency Response Team in the Lower Mainland (and a former homicide detective), Campbell and three other Mounties tracked down and captured an armed killer on a murder spree. For their efforts, the four Mounties were recognized for meritorious service at BC's 2013 Police Honours Night. Two years later, in 2015, Campbell was promoted to the coveted position of corps sergeant major (CSM) in Ottawa, the highest-ranking sergeant in the force, a heartbeat away from a white shirt. In that position, Campbell was part of the elite inner circle of the commissioner's office. As the RCMP puts it, he was "responsible for dress, deportment, ceremonial protocols and RCMP traditions. He is also responsible for maintaining a high standard of leadership, mentorship and accountability among the members of the RCMP's non-commissioned ranks (below Inspector)." In other words, in the cult-like atmosphere of the RCMP, he was the anointed keeper of the Kool-Aid dispenser.

Campbell was what the Mounties call a generational member. His father, Lionel, from New Waterford on Cape Breton, had risen in the RCMP ranks to staff sergeant, serving mostly in Manitoba, then Fredericton and finally Ottawa before retiring in 1994. Darren Campbell went to high school in Fredericton and then studied at the University of New Brunswick at the same time that Gabriel Wortman went there. It's not known if they ever met.

Critics of the RCMP had long accused it of being nepotistic. Instead of correcting that perception, the RCMP embraced family ties because drafting kin was a necessity—it was having trouble recruiting new officers. In his capacity as CSM, Campbell created a maple leaf insignia to be worn on the right lapel. Each maple leaf insignia symbolized a prior generation of service in the family of the Mountie wearing it. Introduced in November 2016, the insignia also helped new Mounties identify the dyed-in-the-wool members among them.

Next on Brookfield's moving manifest was Chief Superintendent Janis Gray, Officer of the Year in 2019. She arrived on October 19 of that year to become the officer in charge of Halifax District. Her rise was typical of a Mountie. After finishing high school in Belleville, Ontario, Gray joined the Mounties and amassed a laundry list of accomplishments from Newfoundland to the West Coast and places in between, including surveillance and undercover, and culminating with a couple of cushy appointments. She was the director of the RCMP's Canadian Air Carrier Protective Program and also chair of the International

In-Flight Security Officer Committee. Today, many Mounties remember her for quite another reason: her treatment of Catherine Galliford.

After Galliford settled with the force, a non-disclosure, non-disparagement agreement was signed. When Galliford was hailed as a hero on social media, Gray weighed in with some snarky comments that were taken by many in the force as a continuation of the harassment Galliford had complained about.

"I, too, know Catherine and this entire situation very well. It's unfortunate that some choose to write articles based on rumour and one side only," Gray wrote.

Former Mountie Leo Knight publicly slapped Gray for her comments: "Janis Gray, Cate went to you and you dismissed her. Shame on you."

Gray was promoted and moved to Halifax to run the Halifax District RCMP, the same job her boss, Assistant Commissioner Lee Bergerman, had before moving to the top of the heap in Nova Scotia.

Then there was Gray's husband, John Robin, another decorated Mountie from the West Coast, who was Officer of the Year in 2010. Robin had already had a complete career with the Delta, BC, municipal force and retired from that force as an inspector. Desperate for help, the RCMP lured Robin out of retirement and offered him his old rank. This was unusual for the Mounties, bringing an outsider directly into the inner circle. What really raised eyebrows was when the brass put Robin in charge of the Integrated Homicide Investigation Team (IHIT), the RCMP's only murder unit in British Columbia and the largest such unit in Canada.

One of his first cases was the infamous Surrey Six murders in October 2007. A gang hit in the Vancouver suburb ended up as a bloodbath when the shooters killed their target and five witnesses. Robin was in charge of the subsequent investigation, which turned into a debacle, well described in a February 2019 article, "Frat Boys and Egos Gone Wild," by Pete Cross, a former IHIT team leader. Some of the investigating officers had gone wild with partying, logging $800 bar bills and clocking endless overtime. Two had sexual relationships with the girlfriends of gang members being targeted for the murders. Several officers were either dismissed from the force or charged.

While the public might well have seen all this as a case of Mounties gone bad, inside the force many saw what happened as an example of poor leadership. "The girlfriends of gang members are usually the most beautiful women you will ever meet," said one Mountie familiar with what happened in Surrey. "These guys were sent out to mingle and get close to those women. They were in their twenties. The Mounties were balding guys in their forties. What did they think was going to happen? All those Mounties were at the end of their rope. They were crying for help, but they were totally ignored. When things went south, they all got hung out to dry. There needed to be strict supervision of what was going on, and there wasn't. At the end of the day, John Robin got a bump."

Before long he was a superintendent and then a chief superintendent. When his wife was moved to Nova Scotia, Robin did not join her. He was already in Ottawa. In 2015 he had been working at RCMP headquarters in Technical Investigation Services (TIS). That department includes the national research/policy centres responsible for lawful access to technology, covert physical surveillance, technical analysis and audiovisual forensic units of the RCMP. Two years later he was appointed director general of Covert Operations and Operational Information Management.

As Corporal Chris Marshall of the Nova Scotia RCMP described it: "Covert Operations is the RCMP policy centre for undercover operations, tactical open source and human source management. Operational Information Management is responsible for operational information intake and management, as well as coordination of priorities for federal investigations undertaken by the RCMP."

What that means in English is that Robin oversaw every confidential informant or police informant or agent in the country. He knew who the agents were and what they were doing. This would become a factor in the events to come. If the Nova Scotia RCMP was up to anything spooky, Robin's wife, Janis Gray, might be involved as part of her duties, or would at least be in the know.

Shortly after the Portapique massacres, one of my best inside sources told me: "Keep an eye on John Robin. At some point he will likely surface in this case." I tucked the advice into the appropriate compartment deep inside my brain.

A tight-knit group of RCMP all-stars—most with deep family ties inside the force—had been installed in Halifax, with significant ties to Ottawa headquarters. Until relatively recently, married couples had not been allowed to work in the same areas. Now it was not unusual to have one spouse reporting to the other. Not everyone saw this as a good thing. "They're all watching each other's back," said a former deputy commissioner, echoing the thoughts of many others. "It's too tight. There's no room for other views or accountability. Most corporations or institutions would not allow that to happen."

Another Mountie took a harsher tack that says a lot about how these changes have left many members feeling: "Some of that group are very good at what they do, while others are several ranks above their true ability. The bottom line is that 'H' Division seems like more of an ex-'E' Division girls club. It is who you know that gets you brought in . . . a core group based on alliances and gender rather than competence and relevance. Good old police work and promotion on merits is dead."

In September 2019, the final piece of the puzzle arrived in Halifax.

5

CHIEF SUPERINTENDENT CHRIS LEATHER

In his formative years in policing in the early 1990s, Chris Leather pushed a municipal patrol car around York Region, the sprawling suburbs north and east of the city of Toronto. York Regional Police divided the community into five districts. Leather worked out of Markham, a city in the region's east, but his usual assignment was Stouffville (rhymes with Slowville), then a town of about 10,000. Stouffville was a typical low-crime Canadian place—a one-man job.

"We called him 'the Sheriff of Stouffville,'" said Tim Kavanagh, a former York Regional Police detective. "Nothing ever happened in Stouffville that Chris didn't know about. All the punks respected him."

The first words that came to Kavanagh's mind when asked about Leather were: "Intelligent. Make that super-intelligent. Meticulous. He worked his ass off. He was a solid, hard-working and reliable officer. He could do it all. He was a complete stand-up guy."

One might think he fit the term "natural poe-leese," as Lester Freamon and Bunk Moreland put it in *The Wire*, but there was a major difference. In the grand tradition of cop shows, the police officers might

be dogged investigators, but the job came with an abundance of carous
ing, drinking and womanizing—and the bending of a rule or two.

"He was not like the other cops," Kavanagh said. "He was all about
family. Family was everything to him."

Leather was already married to his wife, Audra Goeree, when he
arrived at York Regional Police. Goeree soon landed herself a job on the
force as a civilian, working in the property room, where evidence and
confiscated items are stored. The two had a number of children together.

"No matter how many times we asked him to go out for beers after
work," said Kavanagh, "he would never come."

Leather got involved in community efforts, making a name for himself as a basketball coach. He spent about six years in uniform and
then began to move up the ranks, becoming involved in intelligence
gathering. The most evident criminal issue in Southern Ontario at the
time was the seemingly explosive growth of outlaw motorcycle gangs.
Leather became immersed in that world, which brought him into the
earliest Toronto-area joint-forces operations, overseen by the RCMP.

Kavanagh himself was seconded for years to the RCMP Proceeds
of Crime Unit in Newmarket, Ontario, just a little farther north. He
remained a York Regional Police detective, but for four years he got to
see inside the RCMP tent. He enjoyed the work, but saw things about
the RCMP that concerned him.

Before hooking up with the Mounties, Kavanagh and his now
deceased partner, Dave Carnell, had worked on a huge, volatile international fraud and money-laundering case with connections to Sinclair
Stevens, a businessman, lawyer and powerful former federal cabinet
minister. I first met Kavanagh and Carnell in the mid-1990s while
reporting on that case, and spent almost two years getting to know
them. The RCMP had been brought in and had worked the file but had
not told Kavanagh and Carnell what they had found, if anything. Once
inside the RCMP, Kavanagh went hunting for the file, only to learn that
it had disappeared and had likely been destroyed.

After his stint with the RCMP, Kavanagh was seconded to the
Ontario Provincial Police and worked out of a covert operations centre
near Toronto Pearson International Airport.

"I was doing a Hells Angels case, which I thought was a big deal," Kavanagh said in an interview. "Then I found out that there were four other Hells Angels projects going on at the same time. This was the era of killers like [Hells Angels national president] Walter Stadnick and Donald Stockford of Hamilton, and [Maurice] 'Mom' Boucher [then president of the Montreal charter of the Hells Angels]. Together they orchestrated the brutal biker wars in Quebec, in which dozens were murdered. [Our] thinking was 'Let's get rid of them now before they get a foothold here.' We took the whole group off the table in Ontario, but all they did was move west and east to the coast."

While the government and the police crowed about their successes against outlaw bikers, Kavanagh could see disturbing holes in the RCMP's methods and credibility. Strange things were happening.

"We had a whole storefront operation going in a money-laundering operation," Kavanagh said. "We played the launderers and were dealing with $2 million a shot, maybe $8 million in all. When the last transaction's ready to be made, the bad guys don't show up. It happened a couple of times. They somehow knew what we were doing." It wasn't the first or last time that leaks killed an RCMP-related investigation.

Unlike Kavanagh, who dabbled with the RCMP, Leather joined the Mounties' intelligence unit permanently in 2004. The force was desperate to fill jobs in the Greater Toronto Area. Moving Toronto headquarters to the suburbs had not helped attract members, as intended. The region was just too expensive. Hiring a local who was already established made sense.

"I haven't talked to him for years, but I considered Chris to be a good friend," Kavanagh said. "He was such a hard worker and I know that he got pissed off at the YRP brass. In his mind I think he believed he wasn't being recognized for how smart he was and the good things he had been doing. That's why he jumped to the RCMP."

Leather was one of the rarest of birds in that he entered the RCMP as an officer and was given his white shirt as an inspector in 2014. He was named Officer of the Year in 2015. He, Audra and the family moved to British Columbia to join Bergerman and the others in the organized crime fight there. Leather became the operations officer in charge of the Integrated National Security Enforcement Team. Three years later, in 2017, he was made a superintendent. Brookfield got the call to move him back to Toronto, where he became the commander of Serious and Organized Crime and the Combined Special Forces Unit in the Greater Toronto Area. That group included the RCMP, Ontario Provincial Police, Toronto police and municipal forces from adjacent York and Peel regions.

On September 12, 2019, Leather quietly arrived in Halifax with Goeree in tow. He had been promoted again and was now Chief Superintendent Leather. As CROPs (Criminal Operations) officer, as the job is known, he took over command of all RCMP operations in the province and was second only to Bergerman. No public announcement was made about this appointment until two months later.

Goeree was given a job at RCMP headquarters at 80 Garland Avenue, in the Burnside Industrial Park, across the harbour in the north end of Dartmouth. She was placed in charge of the one department many Mounties can't wait to hear from: Honours and Recognition. She helped identify, vet and hand out awards to deserving Mounties and others.

The November 19, 2019, press release announcing Chris Leather's posting to Nova Scotia made special note of the fact that he was a long-time basketball coach in the Toronto area and had been active with youth in the community and the Special Olympics. "I will aspire to lead by instilling hope for success in our members and a belief in themselves," Leather said in the press release. "I am committed to supporting the members of the RCMP in Nova Scotia and the public I serve." Leather had already been on the job since September 12.

I made a mental note to see what I could dig up about Chris Leather's background, but all it took was a couple of well-placed phone calls before a package arrived.

◆

When the RCMP undertakes a criminal investigation project, a working title is assigned to it. The first part of that title is the RCMP

Division. "O" stands for Ontario, just as "H" stands for Nova Scotia, "A" for Ottawa and "B" for Newfoundland. There is no apparent rhyme or reason to the letters. The file is then given a distinctive code name, which usually has a tongue-in-cheek meaning. Project O'Busbar was a joint-forces investigation into drug trafficking moving through Toronto Pearson International Airport. A busbar is "a system of electrical conductors in a generating or receiving station on which power is concentrated for distribution," according to the *Oxford Dictionary*. The airport appeared to be the connector—the busbar—in the matters at hand.

There is only one reference to the project on the Internet. It can be found in a "revised agenda" of a January 30, 2019, meeting of the Regional Municipality of York Police Services Board. In Appendix B on page 9 of the "2017–2019 Business Plan Year Two Status Report Community Focus," there are brief descriptions of active investigative projects "in progress" in which the York Regional Police are somehow involved. One was a joint-forces investigation with the Hamilton Police Service and others into the murders of mobster Angelo Musitano and Mila Barberi, an accidental victim of Musitano's shooting. There is a reference to Project Switch by the Asian organized crime task force. And then "Project O'BUSBAR—Toronto Airport Drug Enforcement Unit." That was it. Nothing else.

The sordid details of Project O'Busbar were not that difficult for me to find—and not much of a surprise once I did. It was an RCMP-led initiative into drug trafficking between the Dominican Republic and Toronto. It involved not only the usual array of Southern Ontario police forces but also the FBI. It began sometime in 2018 and was headed by then superintendent Chris Leather.

The investigation, which began in the summer of 2018, centred around a paid FBI undercover agent with connections to Colombian drug cartels. Much of the operation was conducted in the Dominican Republic. It would be fair to say it was conducted in a manner that was contrary to established protocols and procedures, according to a document obtained for this book: "The RCMP project members were required to use their personal 'blue' passports for entry and exit into the

Dominican Republic, to avoid exposure of the project, even though the Liaison Officer suggested members use green passports as the purpose in the Dominican Republic was to work and not to vacation, and the green passports would provide more protection to members in the event of problems. Members were also directed to lie when entering the Dominican Republic, and to CBSA [Canada Border Services Agency] after arriving into Canada from the Dominican Republic, if they were pulled into secondary examination and questioned about the purpose of their travel."

While in the Dominican Republic, the investigators used their own easily monitored cellphones and the WhatsApp communications app to conduct conversations, instead of government-provided secure devices. Just about everything was loosey-goosey. According to some RCMP sources aware of the investigation, the FBI paid agent went wild in the Dominican. Wine, women and plush accommodations were regularly on the menu. After months of unproductive investigation, hundreds of thousands of dollars were headed down the drain, along with a reputation or two.

From January 10 to 15, 2019, the investigating officers were back in Canada, staying at a York Region hotel. The FBI paid agent was in a hotel room with RCMP constable Antonio Castrillon, who was working twelve-hour overnight shifts. At this point, I must clarify that I have had no contact whatsoever with Castrillon, directly or indirectly, and he has no knowledge of and has made no contributions to what I am about to write.

Castrillon had "expertise in drug investigations," whatever that means inside the RCMP, and had spent much time in the Dominican Republic with the FBI agent. During that time, they had struck up a friendship. Castrillon's involvement in the case was simply a matter of expedience. He was of Colombian ancestry and spoke Spanish. The downside was that Castrillon had no RCMP training in the procedures and handling of undercover agents, situations and scenarios. After months of flitting back and forth between Canada and the Caribbean, the RCMP had all but exhausted its trained handlers. It needed someone to babysit the FBI paid agent, so Castrillon got the job.

On January 14, 2019, the FBI paid agent said he didn't want to get out of bed that day and go to work. He partially covered his face and posed with a blanket over his face up to his eyes, as Castrillon jokingly aimed his cellphone camera at him and then snapped off a shot. There was another Mountie in the room. All three realized immediately that taking photos of a police agent was a no-no, a very serious breach. Castrillon deleted the photo and thought no more of it.

Three days later, while on vacation, Castrillon was called in to the RCMP and asked by Inspector Jonathan Ko about the photo. He told Ko it had been deleted. Castrillon showed Ko that there was no such photo on his phone, but the inspector took control of the phone. The FBI and the RCMP suspected that Castrillon might have been working for the criminals, even though there was no such evidence.

Before he knew what hit him, Castrillon was suspended without pay by Superintendent Leather. His career looked like it was over before it had even begun. The FBI had stopped co-operating with the RCMP on the case and wouldn't allow their paid agent to be interviewed about what had taken place in the hotel room.

Castrillon was distraught. Some of his fellow RCMP members had seen all this before. Botched operations were nothing new in the RCMP. In my first book about the RCMP, *Above the Law*, published in 1994, I wrote about how the force was great at building files, but not cases. Nothing had changed since. Junior Mounties were often sacrificed so that the white shirts could live to realize another promotion. Castrillon sought legal advice. For more than four months, the RCMP fought him tooth and nail before reinstating his pay, but he was kept off the job.

The matter of Castrillon was inherited by Assistant Commissioner Jodie Boudreau, who had been appointed by Lucki as the chief of the Ontario Division on October 3, 2018, but who hadn't formally moved into "O" Division headquarters until April 17, 2019. Boudreau had been a Mountie for eighteen years—riding a rocket ship to the top—and had the typical credentials for the job. Not only had she worked in drug enforcement and undercover, she had served as aide-de-camp to

Alberta's lieutenant-governor. Hobnobbing with the elite rarely hurt an upwardly mobile Mountie's career.

At the change-of-command ceremony, Lucki described Boudreau: "Time and time again, Jodie has proven to be a respected, accountable leader. Her people-first mentality and diverse experience will serve the RCMP and the citizens of Ontario very well."

The RCMP kept its boot on Castrillon's neck, fighting him at every turn in his attempts to clear his name and get his job back. One of the weapons the Mounties wield against their own members is internal prosecution under the force's highly discretionary code of conduct. To be "coded" is the great fear of Mounties, because the process is often used to bully, intimidate or drum undesirables out of the force. Castrillon beat one code of conduct charge against him when it was dismissed, but the force would try again with a second in January 2021. Meanwhile, Chris Leather was promoted to chief superintendent and sent hurtling to Nova Scotia with his family.

Fast-forward to April 19, 2020. The question remained that Sunday afternoon: Who was going to show up at the press briefing and explain what Gabriel Wortman had done in Nova Scotia? It was likely going to be messy, which would rule out a politician like Justice Minister Mark Furey.

Who would it be: Brenda Lucki herself, Lee "the Blade" Bergerman, Chris "Sheriff of Stouffville" Leather or even Darren "Keeper of the Kool-Aid" Campbell?

6

A MOUNTIE DIES

While everyone waited for the RCMP's press briefing to begin, the horrific scope of Wortman's rampage was coming into sharper view for the public.

At 3:45 p.m., the CBC confirmed social media rumours that a Mountie had been shot and killed near Shubenacadie, north of Halifax Stanfield International Airport. Sensational photos of the burning police vehicles were flooding media around the world. The first unconfirmed reports were that the officer had rammed Wortman's fake police car with their own cruiser and then had engaged him in a gun battle before losing their life. A mere twenty-seven minutes after the CBC story ran, Prime Minister Trudeau tweeted his condolences to "the Portapique community," and added later:

> I was saddened to learn about the senseless violence in Nova Scotia, which claimed the lives of multiple people, including one member of the Royal Canadian Mounted Police, Constable Heidi Stevenson, a 23-year veteran of the Force.

Word soon came that another Mountie, Constable Chad Morrison, an eleven-year veteran who worked out of headquarters in Dartmouth, had also been shot, near where Stevenson was murdered. Morrison had been waiting in a marked SUV for Stevenson to arrive. He was parked on Highway 224, about 100 metres east of the T intersection at Highway 2. The two highways then run together south for a few hundred metres to what is known as Cloverleaf Circle, an old-fashioned interchange connecting the pair of two-lane highways. To continue north on Highway 2 past Cloverleaf Circle, one must exit to the right and take a descending ramp down to the continuation of Highway 2.

Two witnesses saw Morrison standing outside his vehicle and putting on a bulletproof vest. Actually, the RCMP revealed later, he already had on a hard vest and was putting a softer one over it. That suggests Morrison was told about Wortman being in the neighbourhood only after he got to Highway 224, where he was waiting for Stevenson.

The same witnesses soon passed Wortman driving south on Highway 2 from Brookfield and Truro. Heidi Stevenson radioed Morrison and told him she was almost at their predetermined meeting spot. Morrison got back into his marked SUV and pulled up just short of the stop sign at Highway 2. There was no way Wortman could have seen Morrison's vehicle tucked in behind the trees, but he somehow seemed to be aware of Morrison's location. Wortman made the left turn. As he did, Morrison noticed the push bar, or ram package, on the front of Wortman's car, but its significance didn't register. He thought it was Stevenson, even though no RCMP car in Nova Scotia was equipped with a ram package. Wortman pulled up beside him— door to door—maybe two feet away. He raised a handgun, and as he squeezed the trigger, a red laser painted Morrison's head. Morrison ducked and hit the gas. Wortman fired three or four shots. One bullet hit Morrison in the arm. Another shattered his rear passenger-side window. Morrison sped across the highway but couldn't quite make the turn and slammed his right bumper into the guardrail. He straightened the car out and headed south across the Shubenacadie River bridge, to the Cloverleaf Circle. He either took the ramp down to the continuation of Highway 2 or went straight and onto Highway 224.

At some point he hit the Emergency Request to Talk, or 10-33 (Officer Needs Help), button. It appears to have bonked out, as the Mounties say, because of too much traffic on the channel. It took him about four minutes to reach the EMS ambulance station in Milford Station.

Morrison had just missed Heidi Stevenson coming up the ramp from the lower stretch of Highway 2. Wortman, meanwhile, had turned his vehicle around and arrived at Cloverleaf Circle at the same time as Stevenson. She had driven north on Highway 2 from the RCMP detachment at Enfield. She should have heard Morrison's call that he had been shot, but may not have. She was emerging at the top of the arced ramp to Wortman's left. If Wortman was driving normally, there was little chance he could have seen Stevenson's vehicle until the last second, yet he seemed to know she was there. He veered across the centre line and rammed her vehicle. He had a push bar. She didn't.

Wortman's damaged car ended up parallel to the guardrail heading the wrong way—into traffic coming up the ramp. Its front hood was crumpled back. The driver's door was opened just enough for a person to squeeze out. Stevenson's vehicle was close behind, with its front end smashed against the guardrail overlooking Rex McCoul Park, which was set inside the eastern side of the cloverleaf.

On social media, video showed the scene as captured from different angles and at different times. In some there was no fire. In others, one of the cars was engulfed in flames. In yet another, a frantic young couple came upon the scene and used a phone to capture images of RCMP Emergency Response Team (ERT) members in a black Chevrolet Suburban arriving just in front of them. The ERT members dragged what appeared to be a dead police officer away from the cruiser that was nosed into the guardrail. The fire was growing in Wortman's vehicle, and then it leapt to Stevenson's.

Another photo was of a man in a camouflage coat with his hands up in Rex McCoul Park as two ERT members confronted him. The man's name was Craig Vanderkooi, a sixty-year-old handyman. His house was on the other side of the small park. He had been sitting in his living room trying to catch any new developments in the Portapique situation when he heard what he thought were three shots fired.

"I wasn't sure what it was, so I got off the couch and looked out the picture window," Vanderkooi remembered. "Then I heard three more—*boom*, *boom*, *boom*. It sounded like a shotgun or something. There was a real thud. I went to the kitchen window and I could see this cop at the front of [Wortman's] car near the driver's side headlight, right beside the guardrail. He squatted down and then he bobbed around. He was looking through his windshield at the other police car. He kept bobbing up and down. The cop in the other police car was just sitting there. Then I saw a silver vehicle pull up."

Vanderkooi went upstairs to get a better view. "A man in a hoodie got out of the car and walked right up to the police cars. He had his hand in his pocket. He wasn't panicking, just walking," he said. "He was going back to his car, and I could see that the cop told him to get into the back of his cruiser." At that point Vanderkooi went downstairs to grab his Nikon Coolpix digital camera. As he did, he heard shots. "There was one or two more shots. Then I didn't see the man in the hoodie or Wortman. I took a couple of pictures. You can see Heidi sitting behind the steering wheel still wearing her sunglasses. She looked like she was already dead to me. Then Wortman got out of his car and walked over to Heidi's car. He reached in and pulled something out. It looked like a backpack to me. He closed her car door. He stood there for a few seconds, then went back to the passenger side of his vehicle. I zoomed in but I couldn't see what he pulled out."

Vanderkooi grabbed his binoculars for a closer look. As he scoured the scene, he saw a foot and a pant leg. He realized it wasn't a backpack but a policer officer.

"It was right around then that a buddy sent me a text. It was the photo of Gabriel Wortman," Vanderkooi said. "I caught the guy's face in the binoculars. It was him! You'd think he'd be in a hurry, but he wasn't. He went back to his vehicle and opened the trunk and then went back to Heidi's car.

"My buddy was on the phone by now. While I was talking to him, I could see Wortman peek around the rear corner of her car like he was checking to see if she was dead. He did that twice. She never moved. Then he walked back to his car, lit something and tossed it into the trunk of his car. Then he took off the green vest he was wearing and tossed it into the trunk. I didn't see where the guy with the hoodie went. Wortman got in [that guy's] car and drove away down the 224."

There were no other police there yet. Vanderkooi thought he'd better do something, so he quickly dressed in a camouflage coat and boots and headed out across Rex McCoul Park to tend to the fallen officer. "I had no choice," he said. "I had to do something."

Darcy Sack and a friend came upon the scene from another angle. Sack, who was from Shubenacadie, said she heard two gunshots and then saw Wortman, who struck her as surprisingly calm in the circumstances. She told the CBC that Wortman seemed unworried and "looked like he wasn't in any type of rush."

Vanderkooi, meanwhile, made his way across the field as the first ERT truck arrived. A Mountie ordered him to put his hands up. Vanderkooi noticed an unidentified young woman up on the ramp trying to tend to Stevenson and heard an ERT member say something like "Fuck. Fuck." The cop told the woman to get down and get away from the body. Stevenson was dragged several feet away to the guardrail. As the fire in Wortman's car grew, Vanderkooi noticed the police did nothing to put it out.

"One Mountie went over and closed the trunk of Wortman's car like he was hoping to smother the fire," Vanderkooi recalled. "They didn't even try to use a fire extinguisher on it. I'm not the sharpest knife in the drawer, but I'm not that stupid, either. You'd think they'd be trying to save evidence. They did nothing. They wouldn't even let the fire trucks near those cars. They just let them burn."

As the fires burned, drivers at the scene tried to leave. One young woman backed her vehicle down the ramp and met Vanderkooi at the bottom. Police had let him go, and he and the woman had a brief chat. Her name was Kaitlyn Keddy.

That morning, Keddy, a twenty-six-year-old caregiver, was taking Earl, a seventy-two-year-old handicapped senior, for his regular Sunday morning drive. Earl, wearing his favourite bright-yellow safety glasses, was strapped into the front seat of the community centre work van that Keddy was driving. Her employer was the Confederacy of Mainland Mi'kmaq, the dominant Indigenous tribe in the northeastern United States and Canada. Their route that day took them north on Highway 2 past Barney's Brook and Milford toward Shubenacadie. As they approached Cloverleaf Circle and took the ramp to continue northward, the vehicle in front of Keddy slowed down. When she looked ahead to see what the problem might be, she was stunned. Two police cars were crashed beside each other against the guardrail.

"It was so bizarre," Keddy said in an interview. "I was saying 'Oh, my God, what's happening?' We have the news on at the centre all the time, but I hadn't heard anything. If I had known what was going on, I wouldn't have taken Earl out for his drive."

Keddy then picked up the phone and called 911. Her conversation with the emergency operator haunts her to this day. As she recollects it, the conversation suggests that Stevenson may not have known or fully appreciated the danger she was in.

"I told the 911 operator that there were two police cars that had crashed. I still hadn't seen any smoke coming from the cars. The 911 operator was absolutely calm, even nonchalant. She asked me if I could get out of my car and go up to the police cars and tell me what number was on the side of each one. It's like she didn't know what was going on. She gave me no warning. Even as I was hanging up the phone, she didn't tell me to go to safety. I could have kept driving up to the burning car, been nosy and tried to save someone, but I just had a gut feeling and knew that wasn't the right thing to do. I'm that person who will do anything, but it wasn't just about me, it was about Earl. I had to think of him," Keddy said. "I had to be calm for Earl."

At about 5:30 p.m., mainstream and social media were flooded with images of a procession of RCMP cruisers escorting a coroner's vehicle carrying Stevenson's body along Garland Avenue. She was being taken for an autopsy at the Dr. William D. Finn Centre for Forensic Medicine, across the street from RCMP headquarters.

The public still had no idea how many people had been killed by Wortman or if he had killed anyone after Stevenson, but she instantly became the face of the massacre. It was a sad and powerful image.

A popular photo showed her dressed in her red serge ceremonial uniform, with cavalry riding breeches and campaign Stetson hat, leading children across a crosswalk. The photo had been taken in 2015 as part of a back-to-school safety awareness program. At the time Stevenson was working as a school liaison officer in the Halifax suburb of Cole Harbour, home of hockey greats Sidney Crosby and Nathan MacKinnon. Many Nova Scotians already knew who Stevenson was, as she had also spent time as an RCMP spokesperson.

As the police of small-town Canada, the Mounties have historically drawn their members from that same population. Becoming a Mountie is a ticket to better paydays, cushy benefits and fatter pensions than most jobs offer in small communities. Stevenson came from Antigonish, Nova Scotia, where she grew up as Heidi Burkholder, a member of the local 4-H club. Her family described her as an avid reader and baker in her youth. She graduated with a bachelor of science from Acadia University in Wolfville, one of the province's most beautiful communities, also situated on the Minas Basin. Four years later, she passed through Depot and was accepted into the RCMP.

Former Mountie Cathy Mansley, another small-town Nova Scotia girl, met Stevenson at Depot. "Heidi was my pit partner. She was in the bed next to me in the dorm, seven months of living six feet away from her. Because we both worked in the Halifax area at the end, I used to cross paths with her here and there. She was a really nice girl."

Assigned back to Nova Scotia, Stevenson met her husband, Dean, a schoolteacher, and they and their two children settled in Cole Harbour. Her murder generated an explosion of kind words and tears. She was called a hero, and even in those earliest moments people were making plans to honour her. Her obituary captured what most people admired about her: her creativity and perseverance.

There was no doubt in her mind when she graduated from Acadia that her next step was going to be the RCMP. Reaching that goal wasn't always easy but her incredibly strong work ethic, driven personality and resilient nature got her to exactly where she wanted to be. . . . She loved her time working at headquarters as a Drug

Recognition expert and was especially proud of her expertise in that area and the respect the judges had for her professionalism in court. Whether it was general duty, community policing, communications or training, Heidi dedicated herself to her role, turned her colleagues into friends and was a role model for many in the communities she served. . . . Even with her extensive list of accomplishments in both career and life, Heidi found her one true calling when she became a Mom. She cherished Connor and Ava and they cherished her.

As fresh a tragedy as Stevenson's death was, something struck me. We didn't yet know many facts, but it was abundantly clear that Gabriel Wortman had been on a rampage for more than twelve hours. He was killing people on the roads leading south past Truro to Shubenacadie. The 911 operator who talked to Kaitlyn Keddy even asked her to go check the numbers on the cars. Keddy was smart enough not to do as asked. What if she had found one of the cars to be 28B11, and what if Wortman was still lingering in the vicinity? Was the RCMP that unaware of the danger? Was their communication system broken? Or was the force deliberately hiding something even from its own members?

◆

That Sunday morning, Heidi Stevenson had made the 35-kilometre, twenty-five-minute drive from her home to the RCMP's Enfield detachment, one exit north of the airport. She had been reassigned recently from the detachment in Cole Harbour, where she lived. At the age of forty-seven, she was doing general patrol as a traffic cop. Almost from the moment she was reported to have been murdered, rumours began flying on the Internet that she had filed a complaint against a superior at Cole Harbour. The force had only recently paid out roughly $300 million in settlements for harassment claims. So, even if unverified, such rumours were anything but fanciful, and the people making the allegations about Stevenson's complaint were persistent. The RCMP would not confirm or deny, which came as no surprise.

Stevenson's personnel history in the RCMP, as described by her family in her obituary, could be taken two ways. It depicted a well-rounded woman who not only succeeded in her chosen career but also never lost sight of the little things that were important to her. On the other hand, her curriculum vitae was a map depicting the very elements that made the RCMP such a treacherous and unsafe place to work.

The force continues to perceive itself as a cavalry even though soldiers on horseback became obsolete about 100 years ago. When ERT members get out of their armoured vehicle at a site, they still say they are "dismounting." And until recently, any new cadet entering the RCMP at Depot in Regina spent a large portion of their training devoted to "banging your bum on a saddle," as one former senior RCMP executive put it.

Every year the Musical Ride mounts shows across Canada and into the United States that are devoted to reinforcing an iconic impression of the force's good old days. Picture twenty-eight Mounties in red serge on horseback doing what is effectively four-legged square dancing to canned music on the dirt floor of a hockey arena. The climax of the show—"Get your cameras ready, folks!"—is "the Charge." The horses line up in two rows inside the blue line at one end of the arena and then charge to the other end. It's not much of a spectacle. The front row of horses cannot even get out of first gear since they have to start slowing down at the next blue line—maybe 15 metres from where they started. People pay to see this, and the public's fond memories of the Musical Ride are, the RCMP hopes, a powerful counterbalance to controversy and turmoil.

Heidi Stevenson didn't know how to ride a horse when she enlisted. So the force taught her, and that's what she did for thirteen of her twenty-three years as a Mountie. Borrowing on her undergraduate science degree, she spent some time as a drug recognition expert. As she went on to become a school liaison officer and then a press relations officer, she was in and out of patrol cars. In her final days, assigned to traffic patrol in Enfield, it seems unlikely that she drove toward Gabriel Wortman fully informed of the lethal danger ahead—and unlikely that she was properly prepared to face it.

"I went through Depot with Heidi," said former RCMP officer Chris Williams. "She was a wonderful person. I liked her a lot. She was a good police officer. I had tactical training. I was on an ERT team You never know when you are going to get into a life-and-death situation. At times like that you have to have that killer instinct. As much as I liked her, Heidi . . . didn't have an ounce of killer instinct."

Stevenson spent much of her career in positions that had nothing to do with street policing. She likely never gained enough experience to develop the Spidey sense cops rely on to both detect criminality and protect themselves and the public. The RCMP have denied this and will continue to do so. The force argues that Mounties are all trained to the same high standard, but they are not. Some ride horses for their pay. Others sit in police cars being de facto security guards, protecting government buildings, embassies and the Governor General. Still others weave their way through the hierarchy without ever gaining valuable street or court experience and the smarts that go with it. However, the force contends they all gain seniority equally and are functionally interchangeable parts, able to be plugged into any job. The reality of uniformed members working in those rural communities tells a different tale.

How dangerous is it to be a Mountie? Allow me to return to an earlier comparison between the RCMP and the NYPD. The NYPD has about twice as many members on the streets as the RCMP. New York City and its boroughs are a congested, densely populated urban jungle filled with guns and, in places, scary levels of violence. In other words, it's your basic American city, just with better entertainment, restaurants and culture. Today, in its contract policing roles, the RCMP patrols much of rural Canada outside of Ontario and Quebec. The only urban areas the RCMP patrols are some of the suburbs of Vancouver, smaller cities like Red Deer, Alberta, and Moncton, New Brunswick, and the outer suburbs of Halifax. Canada is one of the safest countries in the world. And yet, in the twenty years from 2000 to 2020, the RCMP lost the same number of members in the line of duty—thirty-six—as the NYPD. That's not including the NYPD officers who died during 9/11 or subsequently from 9/11-related maladies. That total includes only normal policing functions, and not even the two RCMP members killed in 2010 in Haiti during an earthquake.

No other Canadian police force comes close. A key reason for that is that other Canadian police forces have learned from their mistakes. Back in the mid-1980s, eight police officers were killed in and around the Greater Toronto Area over a period of several months. A number of them died because of poor training or procedures, like one who entered the site of a break-in before his backup arrived on the scene. Another two were killed when they pulled over an armed gunman on a spree by cutting off his vehicle from the front. They were sitting ducks. The police learned not to do that anymore.

As for the Mounties, well, the force has proven to be a slow learner. Historically, it has resisted attempts to change its culture and procedures. Now it will evade answering the question: Who sent an unprepared Heidi Stevenson to her death?

7

SAVE THE BUFFALO!

RCMP brass were getting ready at 80 Garland Avenue for the first press briefing. About twenty hours had passed since Wortman had begun his rampage. He'd been dead for more than six. The Mounties had remained mum, other than the news about Heidi Stevenson.

The Nova Scotia headquarters building was completed in 2013 at a cost of $113 million. The red-brick and glass building had been designed to consolidate all RCMP operations in the area. Like the force itself, the building looked enormous and solid, but from the day it opened, it was not as it seemed. For one thing, it was built on hard rock, a source of radon gas, the second-leading cause of lung cancer. High levels of radon were found in the building in 2019, although the RCMP said it had everything under control. The building was also bigger than required. To fill its cavernous new headquarters, the RCMP decided to consolidate all its communications operations there, which meant closing the backup facility in Bible Hill. This "business decision" went against the advice of emergency planners everywhere. Redundancy in emergency communications is critical in a crisis.

Television sets, mobile phones and computers were primed across the country, ready to receive the first official explanation for what had been happening in Nova Scotia. Rumours were circulating on social media about murders, perhaps many of them. Surely the RCMP would provide clarity and comfort.

The press conference promised to be a solemn affair, filled with grim details supported by photos and maps. There had been more than enough time to cobble together a respectable presentation and compel witnesses and experts to talk. Already it was evident that something was very different about the Wortman rampage. It certainly didn't fit the established pattern of a psychopathic shooter. The fact that it had spread over more than thirteen hours in so many disparate locations was unprecedented. How did one man evade police for so long?

A dais had been set up in the glassed-in pavilion at the front of the building. To the right was a large rendition of the RCMP buffalo head logo carved into the polished black marble wall. A pair of flags—Canada's and Nova Scotia's—stood to the left. Running the affair was Corporal Lisa Croteau.

There would be no red serge for the cameras, just the standard dark-blue RCMP uniform with the wide yellow stripe down each pant leg. Due to COVID-19 restrictions there was a limited number of reporters in the room—six at best. A couple wore masks. None of the police did. To accommodate the rest of the world, Croteau placed a cellphone on a knee-high table to the left of the dais.

In English Croteau introduced herself and then Assistant Commissioner Lee Bergerman and Chief Superintendent Chris Leather, the Criminal Operations officer. As she was repeating it all in French, a disembodied deadpan voice emanated via teleconference from the phone.

"Maurice Rees, the *Shoreline Journal*." Rees was the publisher of the monthly paper that served communities along the coast around Portapique. He said nothing more.

Croteau was distracted by Rees's unexplained interjection. She stumbled and combined the two surnames: ". . . Chris Leatherman."

Amid the occasional electronic crackle from the phone, Bergerman moved to the dais. Her hair was tied in a knot at the back of her head. She was wearing reading glasses—this was not going to be the place for extemporaneous, heartfelt meanderings.

"Today is a devastating day for Nova Scotia and it will remain etched in the minds for many years to come," Bergerman began flatly. "What has unfolded overnight and into this morning is incomprehensible and many families have experienced the loss of a loved one. That includes our own RCMP family. It is with tremendous sadness that I share with you that we have lost Constable Heidi Stevenson, a twenty-three-year veteran of the force, who was killed this morning while responding to an active shooter incident. Heidi answered the call of duty and lost her life while protecting those she cared for."

Many people appeared to have died, but the Mounties started where the Mounties pretty well always start: with themselves.

"Earlier this afternoon I met with Heidi's family and there are no words to describe the pain," she continued, flipping to the next page of her prepared text. She was occasionally distracted by the scratchy voices and electronic burbles from Croteau's phone. "Two children have lost their mother, and a husband has lost his wife. Parents have lost their daughter, and countless others have lost an incredible friend and colleague. Heidi's family is part of the RCMP family and we will embrace and support them in the days and weeks and months ahead," Bergerman read, choking up a little at one point and speeding up at others. She clearly couldn't wait to get out of there.

"Unfortunately," she continued, and this is where everyone must have thought the truly big bad news was coming, "I will also have to share that another one of our officers was injured and is in hospital receiving treatment with non-life-threatening injuries. He and his family will be supported, and we will be alongside him as he begins his road to recovery.

"This tragic incident has also resulted in many victims outside of the RCMP," Bergerman said, adding rather awkwardly. "Countless families are in mourning today. Each person who lost their family and friends—and they too will need their support. The impact of this incident will extend from one end of the province to the other."

She flipped to another page and concluded: "As Nova Scotians," she emphasized, "we have to do what we're known for. Come together in times of need and support each other."

As Nova Scotians? Bergerman had been in Nova Scotia for two years.

She called upon Leather to address the criminal investigation.

Leather is the kind of giant-sized cop they used to send into alleyways back in the day to mete out instant justice. He was not only extremely tall but also wide and thick. The Sheriff of Stouffville, indeed. It was easy to see why basketball was his favourite sport.

"Thank you, ma'am," Leather said to Bergerman. He looked flushed and stunned. Heidi Stevenson was lying in the morgue across the road, killed on his watch. Leather had escaped from Ontario and the ongoing but almost totally buried Project O'Busbar controversy. He had been in Nova Scotia, officially, for five months and unofficially for seven. Now the shit was beginning to hit the fan in public, and he was reduced to being an undercover specialist in desperate need of cover.

"I would like to offer my sincere condolences to the family of Constable Stevenson and the families of all the victims," Leather began. "I would also like to acknowledge the member who was injured and his family. As you can appreciate, this is an extremely difficult day for the RCMP and for the families who have been affected by these tragedies."

Leather cleared his throat. There was an air of uncertainty about him. The words came out slowly, deliberately, painfully, one at a time.

"We are in the early stages of an incredibly detailed and complex investigation that has forever changed countless lives and left multiple victims," Leather said, adding that the "focus right now is to gather all evidence and information about these incidents and to get answers to many unanswered questions."

When it looked as if he was finally ready to dole out some facts, he began to describe the events of the past twenty-four hours: "Last night, following multiple 911 calls, Nova Scotia RCMP responded to a firearms call to a Portapique residence in Colchester County. When the police arrived at the scene, members located several casualties inside and outside of a home. They did not however locate the suspect." Leather looked off to his left, into space. "This was a very quickly evolving situation and a chaotic scene. Many units responded, including Emergency Response Teams and police dog services. We also received support from other police services and continue to receive support from other police services, especially Halifax Regional Police.

"Our focus was the safety of the residents in the immediate area. We secured the area and began a search for the suspect. The initial search for the suspect led to multiple sites in the area, including structures that were on fire. The search continued overnight and into the morning. This morning we actively sought out the suspect through multiple communities throughout Nova Scotia. The search for the suspect ended this morning when the suspect was located, and I can confirm that he is deceased, and I can also confirm that the matter has been referred to SIRT [the Serious Incident Response Team].

"Again, this is still an early and very active investigation and involves multiple crime scenes and victims. We will have further updates as more information becomes available and we will let you know when that will be. There is an active investigation being conducted by the Serious Incident Response Team, so we are not able to provide any further details to some portions of the investigation. I want to thank the dedication and resilience of our members who worked tirelessly to locate the suspect. The coordination demonstrated by everyone involved was truly remarkable. We have reached out to all of our employees to make sure they have wellness resources available during this difficult time."

At less than four minutes, Leather's brevity and generalities couldn't help but arouse suspicion. The self-promotion, in particular, caught my ear: "the dedication and resilience of our members who worked tirelessly." It is a notable trait of the RCMP, a tic as it were, to grovel for public sympathy while simultaneously patting itself on the back, especially in the face of controversy, which I thought was certain to follow, because Leather's skimpy version of events didn't fit with information circulating on both social and mainstream media.

The world already knew that the RCMP had somehow allowed Wortman to roam for about 200 kilometres that morning while still killing people. None of this jibed with what Leather was saying, let alone what he seemed to be implying. Premier McNeil had ordered people to "stay the blazes home" two weeks earlier, but the RCMP

didn't do that. If the Mounties were working "tirelessly," where had this
work taken place? What had they actually done? It was as if Leather
was already laying the groundwork for some "alternative facts," like
some latter-day Chico Marx—"Who are you going to believe, me or
your own eyes?"

◆

In Edmonton, Tammy Oliver-McCurdie and her sister, Crystal
Mendiuk, had been on their phones with the RCMP all day trying to
track down three family members: their sister, Jolene Oliver; Jolene's
husband, Aaron Tuck; and Jolene and Aaron's seventeen-year-old
daughter, Emily Tuck. Jolene and her family lived at 41 Cobequid
Court in Portapique Beach. The house had been owned previously by
Aaron's father, Bruce. After he died, the Tucks pulled up stakes and
moved from Alberta to live at Portapique Beach. The ramshackle blue
house, at the intersection with Orchard Beach Drive, backed onto the
beach. It was one of the dozen or so neighbourhood homes occupied
that weekend.

As the two sisters and their mother tried to track down their family
members, they learned that Emily had been texting with her boyfriend
the night before. She had suddenly stopped at 10:07 p.m. Not returning calls and texts was not in character for any of them.

Oliver-McCurdie, who owns and operates an escape-rooms business, had been given the name of an RCMP constable, Wayne "Skipper"
Bent, who was acting as a liaison for many of the families of potential
victims. Oliver-McCurdie said Bent had informed them that a search
had been conducted and that her family members likely had got themselves out of the neighbourhood to safety.

"If they were okay, why couldn't we get in touch with them?"
Oliver-McCurdie wondered. "It wasn't like them. Where could they
possibly be?"

They persisted throughout the afternoon as the news reports grew
worse. Bent assured them that the force was meticulously going door
to door clearing residences. The facts suggest that the RCMP had not

checked the Tucks' house in person and was instead relying on an alternative method.

At 1:15 p.m. Sunday, Constable Bent had sent the following text to Aaron Tuck: "This is Cst. Bent with the RCMP. Looking for Aaron Tuck to call me ASAP. Important. Thank you."

The three Tucks at 41 Cobequid Court didn't answer.

Oliver-McCurdie, her sister and her mother kept calling. At one point they got Corporal Gerard Rose-Berthiaume on the line. They say he identified himself as the lead investigator in the matter. On most police forces, an inspector or higher would be in charge of such a serious incident, not a corporal.

"What's taking them so long?" Oliver-McCurdie and Mendiuk wondered. "What are they doing?"

Finally, Corporal Rose-Berthiaume texted Mendiuk and told her that they were on the way to 41 Cobequid Court. The time was 5:38 p.m.

The Mounties got to the Tucks' house around the time Bergerman and Leather were speaking to the press. The front door was open. Aaron Tuck's body was lying in the doorway. He had lacerations on his legs and hands as if he had been in a fight. He had been shot three times. Jolene was in the hallway behind him. One shot had gone through her upper arm and into her chest. A second was in the side of her head. It looked like she had been turning to go back into the house to protect her daughter. Emily was in the living room at the back. She had been executed, shot once, then again. Whoever had done this was leaving no witnesses.

Was it any wonder that Bergerman and Leather looked so discombobulated at their press briefing?

◆

Corporal Croteau finished reiterating Bergerman's and Leather's scripts in French and opened the "teleconference" to questions.

Michael Tutton of the Canadian Press news service popped the first obvious one, in the process mistakenly demoting the giant Mountie:

"Inspector Leather, Canadians would very much like to know how many people have died."

"I can tell you that in excess of ten people have been killed," Leather said somberly. It was sixteen minutes into the press briefing and the RCMP was only now giving its first hint about the scale of the horror. "The investigation is still ongoing, and I expect to have more details in that regard in the coming days."

Tutton, politely, pressed on: "Thank you very much, but can you please explain to me 'in excess of'?"

"I'm afraid, at this time, I can't elaborate any further," Leather said. "We are not fully aware of what that total may be, because as we stand here the investigation continues into areas that have not yet been explored across the province."

Across the province?

It was like trying to push a mule uphill. Every question was met with palpable resistance. Leather continued to speak softly, fiddling with his fingers. Bergerman stood to his left, her right hand clutching her left wrist as if she were monitoring her pulse. At one point she began to rock on her heels. Both she and Leather had risen to the top by avoiding moments like this.

"Are there locations, Inspector, besides Portapique, where people have died, besides the shooter?" Tutton continued. Leather looked like he was trying to formulate an answer, so Tutton reiterated. "Are there locations besides Portapique where people have died? Can you tell me the names of the locations? The names of the towns?"

"Yes, there are several locations across the province where a [sic] persons have been killed," Leather said nervously, his voice trailing off to a near whisper.

"Can you tell me the locations, the names of the towns?"

"I don't have those locations at my disposal," Leather replied. "Suffice to say there are several locations."

The names of some of the victims were already beginning to make their way into the media, but the RCMP wouldn't speak them. Why? In response to other questions, Leather said that "one person" was responsible for the killings and that "he alone" moved across the northern part of the province and committed several homicides. How were they so sure?

The voice of Maurice Rees of the *Shoreline Journal* popped out of nowhere again. "It's very unclear and hard to hear and understand," Rees said. "How many have been deceased?" Rees's frustration was understandable. Croteau's phone was at least two metres away from Leather, and the distance was aggravated by the fact that the Mountie was talking in an almost *sotto voce* tone of voice.

Leather looked bewildered. A man in his position is used to commanding respect and exerting control, and he was teetering on the edge of being pummelled. He leaned toward the phone on the table and tried to address Rees: "No, sir, I think we are still—"

Croteau rushed from her place against the marble wall and went around the statue-like Bergerman. Croteau leaned down to the low table and told Rees his turn would come. "We'll get to the teleconference in a few minutes. Just one second." It was a calamity.

When another reporter asked about a possible gun battle, Leather made this utterance: "At one point during the course of the evening there was an exchange of gunfire." But he didn't know where that had taken place.

There had been nothing on the news about a shootout. Was anyone else injured or killed? How did Wortman get away? How did he get a police uniform and a cruiser? Leather was the CROPs officer. He was supposed to know everything there was to know, and he didn't seem to know much of anything. And yet, despite the hundreds of questions that needed answers, the collected media weren't touching the number one issue on everyone's mind: Why hadn't the Mounties or the province put out a warning with the Alert Ready system?

The more Leather spoke, the weirder it got. He said at least ten people were dead but that no one was in the hospital. "It's quite possible victims checked themselves into area hospitals."

Shooting victims might have checked into a hospital and police didn't know about it? This was Colchester County, Nova Scotia. The only reasonable choice for any wounded person seeking emergency treatment was the Colchester East Hants Health Centre in Truro.

The alternative to this scenario—that there were no serious injuries because just about everyone shot had died—defied reason. If what Leather was saying was true, this was wildly out of the ordinary for any mass shooting. I couldn't get the idea out of my head.

CTV videographer Natasha Pace cut through the crackle on Croteau's cellphone, which the officer was now holding at waist level. Pace wanted to know more about Wortman being dressed like a police officer and driving what appeared to be a police car. It was the twenty-third minute of the briefing. The stress seemed to be getting to Bergerman. She licked her lips, bent over as if punched in the gut and then stared away from Leather and off into the distance to her left.

"I can confirm that at one point during the course of the evening hours he appears to have been wearing, if not all, a portion of a police uniform and that we believe that he was driving at one point a mock-up or a vehicle that was made to look like an RCMP police cruiser," Leather said. The camera angle shifted and the ghostly image of the carved buffalo on the marble wall was now behind Leather's right shoulder. Eerily, it appeared the marble beast was staring right through the Mountie as he answered Pace's follow-up question. "The fact that this individual had a uniform and a police car at his disposal certainly speaks to it not being a random act."

After fending off a few weak questions about whether it was possibly a hate crime and hiding behind privacy laws, Leather listened as Maurice Rees returned on Croteau's cellphone. Rees wanted to know specifics about the number of dead and where they were killed.

"Outside of the one village I mentioned earlier in my talking points, I can tell you that they were scattered across the province, and I don't have a list here to give you the specific locations or times because that is very much under investigation," Leather said. "Some of these crime scenes we have not even begun to process."

"Do you have an idea about how many are deceased?" Rees asked again.

"I spoke to that earlier," Leather said, getting a little testy. "Certainly, in excess of ten, but we don't have a final count."

Moments later, Corporal Croteau announced the end of the briefing. It had gone on for twenty-seven minutes and forty-one seconds. Bergerman scooped up her embossed briefing book, tucked it under her left arm, cut in front of Leather and exited stage right.

Although they hadn't said much, the door was now wide open to the scope of the disaster. There were going to be more bodies and they were going to be found just about everywhere in Nova Scotia, or so it seemed. Even the Mounties didn't seem to know where. Reporters wanted to ask more questions. Leather lingered for a moment, unsure of what to do, and then he headed for the exit, too.

For those watching, the press conference was confounding and unforgettable. RCMP insiders said their beloved force had never looked more unprofessional, uncertain or inept. "It was an absolute disaster," said one high-ranking former executive-level officer. "That was, perhaps, the most embarrassing moment in the history of the RCMP."

As dismal as the performance of the two Mounties was, the overly polite and somewhat laconic performance of the reporters was equally stunning—except, of course, for the timely interjections and comic relief supplied by Maurice Rees.

8

FRANK BY NAME, FRANK BY NATURE

Andrew Douglas started university playing jazz trumpet but eventually learned there wasn't much of a calling for jazz musicians in the Maritimes. When it comes to music in Nova Scotia, the mind leaps first to lively Celtic fiddlers such as the irascible Ashley MacIsaac and his cousin, Natalie MacMaster, but they are more of a Cape Breton thing. Country great Hank Snow hailed from Liverpool, on the South Shore. The province spawned international greats such as Anne Murray, Rita MacNeil and the Rankin Family. The late Dennis Doherty was a founder of the Mamas and the Papas in the sixties. Kevin MacMichael went to England and starred with Cutting Crew. Sloan became an internationally recognized grunge band, and then moved beyond that. Every year a festival is dedicated to the late influential folk artist and songwriter Stan Rogers. But jazz? Not so much.

So after years of listening to Howard Stern, Douglas thought he might instead try to follow in the shock jock's footsteps. He already had the deep, booming voice and dark, curly hair. Douglas enrolled in a radio course at Nova Scotia Community College in Kentville, where his Howard Stern ambitions soon gave way to an interest in radio news. He landed work at a few out-of-the-way stations. One was in Port Hawkesbury, the doorstep to Cape Breton Island, population 3,700 and shrinking fast. The next stop was down Highway 104 on the mainland at New Glasgow, where Douglas tripled his potential audience to 9,455. Finally, he landed a gig in a big Maritime city—Saint John, New Brunswick, population 68,000. The audiences were getting bigger, but New Brunswick wasn't the greatest place in the world to be a news reporter. The powerful Irving family controlled everything from the saplings in the forest to the oil in one's car and almost all the major media outlets.

The early-morning hours and the challenge of trying to do meaningful and impactful journalism got to Douglas. He saw a classified ad for a reporter at a magazine in Halifax. He applied and landed the job in 2005. For ten of the fifteen years since, Douglas had been the editor of that publication, *Frank*. Its motto: "Frank by Name, Frank by Nature."

That Sunday night in April Douglas was in his living room in the Halifax suburb of Spryfield, watching Bergerman and Leather on television. He hadn't gone to the RCMP briefing because he wasn't a fan of scrum or press-conference journalism. A scrum, or gaggle as they are called in the United States, is the practice of reporters gathering around a subject and conducting a rapid-fire question-and-answer session. As he watched the two hapless Mounties and the media do their stiff dance for those twenty-seven minutes and forty-one seconds, Douglas was appalled, screaming questions at his television: "What the fuck's going on? Ask them why there was no alert put out!"

Watching their near-tears demeanour, Douglas sensed that the RCMP was ragging the puck, as they say in hockey—just safely killing time. "The broad strokes from the RCMP were that this was not a good time for pressing questions. It's only a time for eulogizing their fallen officer," Douglas said in an interview for this book. "It took them a long time to even acknowledge how many civilians had died. If they were trying to open up criticism of the force, they were doing a good job of it."

Douglas thought the collective performance of the journalists covering the event was "a disgrace . . . If some arsehole, semi-outsider from *Frank* magazine was pushing hard, maybe it might lead some of the others to push harder."

Douglas's take was far from a journalistic stretch. *Frank* had a long and raucous history of terrorizing the boardrooms, political backrooms and historically somnolent newsrooms of the province with a precious weapon: facts. The magazine didn't normally cover breaking news, but rather trailed behind mainstream reporters, poring through court filings, divorce records and bankruptcy court trying to hold accountable governments and public institutions at all levels.

In 1990 *Frank* had uncovered evidence of a corrupt network that was secretly providing payments to four-term Progressive Conservative premier John Buchanan. Of course, the ever-charming Buchanan dodged prosecution when the RCMP declined to press charges, citing a lack of evidence. *Frank* then uncovered the sins of Buchanan's predecessor, Liberal Gerald Regan, who went on to serve at the federal level as a cabinet minister in the government of Pierre Elliott Trudeau. The RCMP charged Regan with nineteen criminal counts involving sexual misconduct with young girls. It looked like a slam-dunk case, but once again a miracle happened in a Nova Scotia court. Justice J. Michael MacDonald stayed the nine most serious charges against Regan, and he eventually beat the others (the stayed charges were reinstated years later after a ruling by the province's Court of Appeal, but were never prosecuted before Regan's death in 2019). More recently, *Frank* has broken the story of a funeral home inadvertently switching bodies in 2018 and caught a popular CTV personality in "an online flirtation with a hooker that goes sideways."

That *Frank* entered into the journalistic equation in the Portapique story is itself a commentary on the state of local journalism in North America, especially in smaller markets. The major existing newspaper in Nova Scotia is the Halifax *Chronicle Herald*. The paper, founded in 1874, is almost as old as Canada. It has been run by four generations of the upper-crust Dennis family. The current publisher is Sarah Dennis, who took over from her father, Graham, in 2010, after he had run it for fifty-seven years. In the clubby world of Canadian journalism, the paper has long been dubbed "the Chronically Horrid," largely due to its perpetually lax and incurious coverage of Halifax and Nova Scotia. Like most North American newspapers, its daily circulation has slumped in recent years, to slightly more than 100,000 copies per day.

The much-maligned but crucially important Canadian Broadcasting Corporation has a large cohort of reporters and editors in Nova Scotia, covering local, regional and national events for television, radio and online services. They can be counted on to do a solid, workman-like job of reporting. The CTV network and Global News also have a relatively high profile. But television news depends on solid print news to generate many of its stories. With a weak *Chronicle Herald*, the problem was obvious.

To fill the obvious gaps in news coverage, Halifax has enjoyed a long history of provocative alternative publications. From 1968 to 1978, the *Last Post*'s hard-nosed investigative journalism was a constant thorn in the side of the establishment. The unabashed left-wing magazine ruffled enough feathers in the Maritimes and Ottawa to become the subject of a clandestine surveillance effort from the RCMP Security Service—the national counter-intelligence service of the day. These were no ordinary rabblerousers. One of the *Last Post*'s co-founders, Mark Starowicz, went on to join the CBC in various capacities and was instrumental in the development of its top news and information shows.

As the *Last Post* withered away, another entity emerged in the Halifax suburbs, run by businessman David Bentley and his wife, Diana. Initially called the Great Eastern News Company Ltd., the business was run out of the Bentleys' house. In 1978, the couple purchased a press and before long were publishing a tabloid six days a week known as the *Bedford-Sackville Daily News*. They soon moved the paper into Halifax, where it became known as the *Daily News*, a scrappy newspaper that challenged the plodding *Chronicle Herald*, but not for long. The Bentleys' shares in the *Daily News* were bought out in 1987 by Newfoundland Capital Corporation, the operating company of the wealthy, powerful and politically connected Steele family.

Committed to the news business, the Bentleys poured some of their profits from the sale of the *Daily News* into the creation of *Frank*. Within two years, journalist Michael Bate set up a related *Frank* operation in Ottawa, which became relatively successful in Upper Canada. Both *Frank*s might best be described as a hybrid of the UK satirical magazine *Private Eye*, *Mad Magazine* and the old *Last Post*. Detractors dismiss it as a gossip rag, but its reporting on politicians, the business elite and journalism itself is often cutting edge and on the mark.

For a few brief years there was a semblance of competition during which ownership of the *Daily News* was flipped a number of times before Quebec-based TC Transcontinental, more a printer than a publisher, ran it into the ground, suddenly and unceremoniously shutting the paper down in 2008. The *Chronicle Herald* then did the modern thing. It made itself look bigger on its accounting ledgers by gobbling up its smaller competitors around the province and creating what it called the SaltWire Network, a near monopoly on mainstream print news coverage. The quality of coverage immediately declined.

The Bentleys eventually ceded controlling interest of *Frank* to one of its reporters, Cliff Boutilier, who had been with the magazine since its second month. He ran *Frank* for awhile before the Bentleys' daughter, Caroline Wood, took a hand at it. She eventually ceded control to another reporter, John Williams. No money had ever changed hands for the magazine until Williams decided to put it on the market in 2010. He offered it to then-reporter Andrew Douglas for $80,000.

A story about the possible sale of *Frank* was published in AllNovaScotia, the Bentleys' new online news site, where it caught the eye of a lawyer who worked for businessman Parker Rudderham. Originally from Sydney, Nova Scotia, Rudderham had made millions operating Pharmacy Wholesale Services Inc. in Montreal and owned or was a director in more than a dozen companies. Over the years Rudderham, a colourful character in his own right, had been "Franked," as it is called, on a number of occasions.

Hillary Windsor, a Halifax journalism student at the time, published this about Rudderham's interest in the magazine: "When he was considering the purchase, Rudderham hired a polling company in Montreal to conduct a telephone survey of some 1,200 households across Nova Scotia. On brand recognition, Rudderham says, *Frank* tested as high as internationally known companies such as General Motors. 'Whether you liked it or didn't like it,' he says, 'everybody knew *Frank*.'"

Rudderham bought the magazine in 2010 and installed Douglas as the editor. By 2020, after a controversial round of firings in 2011, *Frank* consisted of Douglas, Boutilier—"the institutional memory"—and Joan Weston, a long-time copy editor and layout editor. That core was supplemented by a revolving door of freelance reporters scattered hither and yon around the province. Together they put out a monthly print edition, with regular online updates and new stories hidden behind a paywall. You wouldn't think that so few could do so much journalistic damage, but as Joseph Pulitzer, the great nineteenth-century American newspaper publisher, put it so well in the language of the day: "An able, disinterested, public-spirited press, with trained intelligence to the right and courage to do it, can preserve that public virtue without which government is a sham and a mocker."

Pulitzer also had a much clearer message: "Newspapers should have no friends."

When the RCMP called another press briefing, Andrew Douglas felt he had no choice but to attend in person.

◆

By Monday condolences were pouring in from world leaders, even Pope Francis. Prime Minister Trudeau used the first few minutes of his daily national coronavirus update to speak about the tragedy. He solemnly read that eighteen were now confirmed dead and added: "I want to wish a full and speedy recovery to all those injured."

The RCMP had said earlier that no one had suffered life-threatening injuries or was in hospital. Everyone who was shot seemed to be dead, and it was suggested but not stated that some others were dead who may not have been shot but killed in some other way. Who were these injured people that Trudeau was talking about?

He acknowledged the death of Heidi Stevenson, and went on to wax eloquent about the risks, sacrifices and commitment to communities that are the hallmarks of all first responders. "They are all here for us," Trudeau said, then seemed to home in on the RCMP members on duty that night in Portapique. "These are exceptional circumstances, yet you did what you always do. You ran towards danger without pause, without hesitation. You put your life on the line on behalf of all Canadians. Thank you for your service."

Many might have found Trudeau's words and actions comforting, but I was not most people. I had seen it all before, and it was still not evident that, other than Stevenson and maybe Morrison, any rushing toward danger had actually happened. No matter what the Mounties did, though, the playbook was the same. It was like a Trumpian dog whistle. Political leaders at all levels of government summoned the general public to come to the defence of the RCMP. The prime minister tapped into emotions and reminded everyone that the Mounties needed their public support. Lawn signs would be planted: "We love our Mounties." People would don red. They would flood the media and shout down even the mildest of critics. I call these RCMP defenders Smurfs, not after the cartoon characters but after the money launderers who convert dirty money into clean at casinos and elsewhere. These Smurfs, though, weren't cleaning money; they were the powerful secret army of the RCMP, and they took any bad situation and used the power of the media to make it better.

◆

Chief Superintendent Chris Leather went solo in Monday's press conference. His boss, Assistant Commissioner Lee Bergerman, was nowhere to be seen. It was a full twenty-four hours since Wortman had been killed, and Leather said there were now nineteen victims. Once again, what was taking so long to get the facts straight? Were Aaron Tuck, Jolene Oliver and Emily Tuck included in the nineteen? No one knew.

A day after the perplexing performance he had given with Bergerman, I expected Leather to be a little crisper and more informative. But when he stepped in front of the camera, he was as flushed and uncomfortable as on Sunday.

"On Monday," Andrew Douglas said, "Leather was even more tone-deaf. His comments started by offering his condolences to Stevenson's family, friends and colleagues. He talked about how the public could extend their condolences on Twitter and Facebook. After all the condolences, he brightened up for a bit with some good news that injured Mountie Chad Morrison was going to be okay. Christ, it was sickening."

Corporal Croteau's cellphone—the teleconferencing system—was back on the knee-high table to the left of the dais. It was her job to work with the media, but she didn't seem to know all the players. She leaned down toward her phone and called for a question from Moira Warburton of Reuters. The name of the global wire service—among the world's biggest—is pronounced Roy-ters.

"We'll take a question from Moira Warburton of Rooters," Croteau said, mangling the reporter's first and last name as well as the name of the wire service. "Moira Warburton from Rooters."

There was a long pause.

"Hi, um, sorry about that," a somewhat frazzled Warburton said. "Can you hear me okay?"

"Yep, we can hear you," Croteau said.

"Oh, fuck," an exasperated Warburton said, as Croteau covered her own mouth and looked toward Leather.

There was an awkward pause before Leather told Croteau to move on to the next reporter. Douglas rolled his eyes.

About thirteen minutes into the briefing, Leather was fumbling around trying to answer another question about why the RCMP had used Twitter rather than the Alert Ready provincial warning system. "Perhaps my friend from communications could speak to that," Leather said, gesturing with his left hand and looking down toward Croteau for a lifeline. Before she could respond, he added: "I believe there was an Amber Alert that went out at some point."

"No," the bespectacled Croteau said, fighting to maintain her composure. "We used Twitter and Facebook because it was unfolding. We were in contact with the province about it. It"—meaning Alert Ready—"was never put into effect."

Like Bergerman the day before, Leather was grasping his right wrist as if it was some RCMP-approved position meant to communicate composure while in the act of pretending to know what one was talking about. He nervously flexed his index finger and left thumb. He licked his lips.

Douglas spotted an opening and pushed his way into the mix. "Follow-up to that," he interjected. "Is it possible to picture a better use of the emergency system than what was going on yesterday?"

Leather was frozen. He looked to be searching for a response when Croteau cut in. Her left hand gestured up and down. "I, we'll take questions," Croteau stumbled, "from the teleconference first." She leaned down to her cellphone and called out Raissa Tetanish from the *Tatamagouche Light*, a monthly publication.

The echo and garble made it difficult to decipher what Tetanish was saying, but then she said one of the most incredible phrases one could hear at a press conference of such magnitude, where there were a million unknowns.

"My question has already been asked," Tetanish said before disappearing into the ether.

Next Croteau called for "Robert Gillies from the Associated Press . . . Robert Gillies?" It was Ferris Bueller redux: "Bueller . . . Bueller . . . Bueller." Robert Gillies wasn't there. Maybe he was at a Cubs game.

Bill Martin from *Six Rivers News*, a Christian blog from Pugwash, Nova Scotia, got his shot at glory and, unbelievably, couldn't think of anything new to ask: "Thank you, but my question is also already asked," Martin said.

Croteau moved on to Nick Moore from the CTV Atlantic network. He wanted to know how many people were injured or still in hospital.

"Obviously our own member was injured, received medical attention and I believe is now home," Leather said, his left thumb twitching more than ever. "But we also had information that others may have been injured during the course of this shooting spree. However, that is yet to be confirmed. I don't have a fixed number for you, but that is something we are looking at."

The shootings took place on Saturday and Sunday. This was Monday.

Seventeen minutes into the press conference, the locally based reporters in the room were finally asked to line up at a microphone. They were the ones on the ground most capable of connecting the dots. Therefore, they were the most dangerous.

Tim Bousquet, publisher, editor and reporter from the five-year-old upstart online news site the *Halifax Examiner*, stepped up to the mike. "I don't think I heard an answer about why the emergency alert system was not activated. If not for this, what would be a good—"

"That's a good question," Leather said. "And I don't have an answer for you at this moment."

By this point it was difficult to tell if the carved marble buffalo staring out from the wall over Leather's right shoulder was embarrassed or pleased with Leather's stonewall performance. He had no answers. He couldn't even speak about the nature of any relationships between Wortman and his victims. It was a privacy issue. Wortman was the only suspect, he reiterated, but the investigation was continuing. He couldn't answer whether Wortman's spouse "had passed away." Privacy, again.

As for the use of Twitter, Leather reiterated: "We thought it was a superior way to communicate this threat."

Andrew Douglas reached the microphone. The day before, Leather had stated that there were three referrals to the Serious Incident Response Team, the civilian police-investigation unit in Nova Scotia. Since then, there had been no explanation by the RCMP of what had led to the three referrals. One was clearly the shooting of Wortman. Another might have been the shootings of Stevenson and Morrison, which were moments apart. What was the third? It was a good question.

"First of all, can you give us some basic detail on the two additional probes by SIRT, please?" Douglas asked.

Leather chose his words carefully. "So, the one additional probe that I referred to yesterday was the final takedown of the suspect. The other two have come to light pursuant to our investigation, uh, and we thought it was appropriate to make those referrals. Um, they're sensitive in nature, uh, I'm afraid I can't say anything more about those, uh, and, I, I, I would suggest and recommend that you direct those questions to SIRT. I don't believe they have commented on those two additional referrals and it wouldn't be fair for me to comment in that regard."

"Does it involve the police involvement in the injury and/or death of one of the victims? Is that fair to say?" Douglas pressed.

"Two separate instances," Leather responded. "Obviously two separate referrals, uh, with very different circumstances. Uh, and there was a use-of-force issue in both instances; however, I, I cannot speak to who was involved other than it was RCMP members in both those instances."

That was it. The local reporters had been given a total of nine minutes and two seconds with the chief superintendent responsible for what was already looking like one of the biggest massacres in the country's history—which had taken place in their backyard. And he'd said next to nothing.

Douglas was reminded why he didn't like press-conference journalism. It was show business.

◆

The first reviews of the performances by Bergerman and Leather began to roll in from around the country.

"That was an absolute disaster," said one former RCMP deputy commissioner. "I'm absolutely embarrassed for the force. I've never seen or experienced anything like it. They weren't ready for what happened. It looks as if he doesn't know what happened."

From his aerie back in Markham, Ontario, Leather's old friend, former detective Tim Kavanagh from York Regional Police, read the situation much differently. "You could tell he was so uncomfortable being up there. He doesn't like the spotlight. He's the kind of guy who says: 'Leave me alone in a backroom and let me do my work,'" Kavanagh said. "I don't think Chris Leather is dumb enough to be such an idiot.

He's a very intelligent guy. He was in a bad situation. He looked to me like he was being set up to be the fall guy. He didn't have the knowledge about what had happened. That makes more sense to me."

Chris Leather was supposed to know everything there was to know in Nova Scotia. RCMP protocol dictated that in a case like this one, with multiple crime scenes, he was to be alerted immediately about what happened at each of them. Two days later, he came across as not knowing even the basic details. If he was being made the fall guy, as Kavanagh suspected, who could possibly be pulling the strings, and why? It was an interesting thought, something to tuck away and pursue if the time ever came.

9

THE SHIFTING AND
SHIFTY NARRATIVE

On the evening of Tuesday, April 21, the RCMP announced that the total number of deceased victims had risen to twenty-two. The force still hadn't publicly identified all of them.

A makeshift memorial was being set up at the old community centre in Portapique with flowers and posters and tributes to the dead. Heidi Stevenson continued to be eulogized. Plans were afoot for a "Red Friday" celebration when all of Canada would wear red and stop work at noon for a minute to honour her.

Stories were flying every which way about Gabriel Wortman, his sordid past and the possible motives for the murder spree. People claimed he was abused as a child and abusive as an adult—a wife beater and a gold-card misogynist. He had duped a number of people out of their properties, even trying to pull a fast one on his uncle, who fought him off in court. He was a cigarette smuggler. He loved guns. He had been convicted of a minor assault on a young man. He had threatened to kill a cop about ten years earlier, and he had bragged about his ability to get rid of bodies, having had some experience with the dead while trying his hand for a few years in the 1990s apprenticing at a funeral home in Halifax. How mad was this mad man?

Then one person emerged with an utterly painful story that was not only riveting and memorable, but also seemed to contradict the RCMP's slender version of events.

A forlorn-looking and folksy-sounding Clinton Ellison was captured by CBC reporter and videojournalist Brett Ruskin standing at the intersection of Highway 2 and Portapique Beach Road. Ellison had returned to Portapique to pick up his car. It had been trapped behind police lines for two days. In Ruskin's report, two RCMP cars could be seen parked on the road behind Ellison, blocking traffic into the community. With his close-cropped hair and burly build, Ellison looked the epitome of rural everywhere. He was wearing a hooded hunting jacket with a woodsy camouflage pattern.

Ruskin's report was no montage of six-second sound bites. Rather, from the second Ellison started speaking, Ruskin received nine minutes of powerful testimony. Ellison gave the world a peek inside the overall crime scene at Portapique Beach, and it wasn't quite what most people expected. What follows borrows liberally from that unique CBC interview, which was written up by Emma Davie, Ruskin's fellow CBC videojournalist.

"Something right out of a horror movie, worse than a horror movie, a nightmare through hell," Ellison told Ruskin, reiterating and emphasizing: "It's a nightmare through hell."

Ellison lived in Halifax. He had picked up his forty-two-year-old brother, Corrie, in Truro and brought him to Portapique Beach so that Corrie could stay over Saturday night with their father, Richard, who lived near Wortman's warehouse at 136 Orchard Beach Drive. The Ellison property could be found at the end of a long laneway tucked away in the woods. An uncle and aunt lived there as well.

Corrie Ellison was the father of one child, but didn't work because of a visual impairment. Clinton rattled off a description of Corrie: "My brother was a really good guy. He would be the first to jump, go, run for help . . . He liked fishing and the outdoors."

Clinton said his father had gone up to bed around 10 p.m. The brothers were listening to music and talking when they heard a gunshot. "We didn't think anything of it," he said. In the Portapique Beach community, it wasn't unusual for residents sitting on their porch or deck draining a beer or two to pop off a couple of rounds at an unsuspecting rabbit.

Sometime later Corrie and Clinton stepped outside and noticed a large glow in the sky to the north, from what could only be a very large fire. Corrie wanted to walk up the road to see if he could lend a hand. Richard, now out of bed, told him not to go, but Corrie insisted. After he was gone for a bit, the Ellisons were getting worried, but Corrie finally called and let them know that Wortman's huge warehouse was on fire. "The fire's really bad. I'm taking pictures. Call the fire department."

When Corrie didn't come back and couldn't be contacted, Clinton grabbed a flashlight, and he and his father went looking for Corrie. Richard was wary and turned back for home, while Clinton moved up the dirt and gravel road. As he approached the steel gate of Wortman's property, Clinton stopped in his tracks.

"I could see a body laying on the side of the road. As I got closer, I could see it was my brother. I got one more step closer and I could see blood and he wasn't moving. I knew from the gunshots I had heard earlier that something was really wrong. I shut my flashlight off, I turned around and I ran for my life in the dark. I went up the first cottage road," he said, using his fingers to draw on the back of his left hand to describe what he called a bend. "I stopped there, and I was exhausted and out of breath. I turned around and looked down toward the road I had just run from to see a little flashlight flashing around looking for me. I ran so hard into the woods. I laid there for approximately, at least, for *four* hours," he said, emphasizing the time, "hoping and praying that the police would come, the police would come."

Four hours didn't seem possible. It must have just seemed like four hours. Leather had suggested that the RCMP had conducted a thorough search of the area. His exact words were: "I want to thank the dedication and resilience of our members who worked tirelessly to locate the suspect. The coordination demonstrated by everyone involved was truly remarkable." I looked at the map. It wasn't a big area. There weren't many houses, and few were occupied.

Ellison was dressed for the night, but the cold was pervasive and eating him up. He didn't dare move. "When I thought it was safe, I phoned my dad and told him, 'Phone the police, phone the police . . . Corrie's shot dead. Shut the lights off and hide . . . Don't call me back. I don't want my phone to light up.' I laid on the ground and I nearly froze to death."

Under gentle questioning from Ruskin, Ellison recounted hearing more gunshots and explosions while he hid in the woods for an hour without moving. "It was the most terrifyingest thing I have ever experienced in my life," he said, tears welling in his eyes and occasionally sniffling, "to walk up and find my brother dead and to be hunted by this fellow that killed all these people. I will be traumatized for the rest of my life. I'm having a really hard time with it . . . He liked to help people . . . but for him, going to help cost him his life."

Ruskin asked him if he knew the killer, and Ellison's answer was pure, overly polite, rural Nova Scotia to its core: "I did not know that gentleman. I did not know that man. I'm from Halifax." Ellison speculated that the ongoing lockdown might have played a role in Wortman's killings. He said people had been scared, adding: "A lot of people are living on edge."

The more Ellison rolled, the more his anger became evident, especially when the focus turned to the RCMP. "I was watching the news earlier; it really made me sick to my stomach that they didn't put the emergency alert out," he said. "If the police had have put the emergency alert out, I would have got it on my phone hiding in the woods and I would have known what was going on. And it could have saved some more lives."

He added: "The police could have handled this definitely a lot better. I hid in the woods for about four hours, staring up the sky, freezing to death, looking for red flashing lights that never came—that never came," he said. "Hours. Hours. People were in there burning to death and dying, and it took hours for a response. That's not right. That's not right at all."

Ellison was taken to the Great Village fire hall around 4 a.m. to be treated for mild hypothermia. He was stunned by what he saw there, confirming what the first CBC video from the location captured several hours later on Sunday morning: Mounties killing time, rolling up firehoses and looking bored, while Wortman remained at large. Ellison said there were more police personnel "than they knew what to do with. They were all standing around when people were dying. That's not right. That's not right. I get why you'd be scared and that, but your job is to serve and protect," he said into the camera, reiterating, "to serve and protect . . . not sit back and watch while people are being killed. You shouldn't wear that uniform," he said, gesturing with right hand to shoulder, "if you haven't got the guts to go in there and save people's lives. You shouldn't wear that uniform. I would have went in there. I went up looking for my brother. I didn't have a bulletproof vest, I never had a gun, but I went. They should have, too."

It was an unforgettable, decidedly un-Canadian television moment, particularly for the CBC, whose fairness guidelines dictate that both sides of a story must be given a chance to comment. When the CBC reached out to the RCMP for comment, sources say, Mounties, as is their way, gently pointed out that there are two sides to every story but that it couldn't tell its side because of the ongoing investigation.

Clinton Ellison's emotion-laden observations had cut a little too close to the Buffalo's bone. In a subsequent iteration of the CBC's Ellison interview, one minute of his harsh criticism was chopped from the video.

Almost 5,000 people logged on to the CBC's Facebook page to comment on the original broadcast. Some praised it and Ellison, who was a number of times described as having that "typically Canadian trait—he still refers to the vicious killer as 'the gentleman.'"

Stephen Gough wrote: "He appears to give a good account of what went on with the RCMP on the various locations mentioned. I hope they give a full account and pressure is put on them to do so. There is much more to this story than what's being told."

Elnora Green saw it for what it seemed to be: "When something bad like that happens, a person wants to share. Poor man he's shaking like a leaf Lord please just ease his pain and grief so much trauma."

But a surprising number of listeners castigated the CBC for the interview. The following brief sample captures the tone and substance of many of the collective concerns.

"This is a vulnerable person who should never have been put in front of a camera. Wrong choice, CBC," Alex Lassale complained.

Troy Jodriel said he had watched the full interview. "I am an avid CBC'er. I have no journalism training or experience and respect it must be very challenging to generate questions off the cuff in an interview. However, asking this poor individual who is clearly still in shock if he knew where his brother's body was now is 100% classless. You should be ashamed."

"Yes, they have milked this for all they can get," wrote Carole Clarke. "They do it as that is what people want unfortunately, the sensation. This man needs help not being taken advantage of."

Cherie Lascelle Hamilton declared: "Shame on the media! This man is in such shock and they continue to question him! My heart breaks for this man, his family and all those suffering."

Jackie King Sheppard added: "You guys should be ashamed of yourselves . . . This poor man told you several times he was traumatized and in shock. He told you 'I don't know what I'm doing.' Yet you continued to ask questions, some several times . . . Shame on you CBC. Shame on you."

#NovaScotiaStrong? Such slogans are a call for resilience and coming together, but there is an insidious side to them, as well. They are more about accepting the present, moving forward and forgetting what happened in the past. Toe the line. Don't ruffle feathers. Clinton Ellison got the message. He took to YouTube to recant his criticisms of the RCMP. Looking glum and puffy-faced, his eyelids were at half-mast. He was wearing a white T-shirt and looked uncomfortable as he addressed the camera.

"I've got to apologize to the RCMP. My comments on the news about you not running right in there . . . they were wrong. My condolences for your fallen comrade, and I appreciate you coming down there and saving my life. For everyone bashing that alert like I did on the news, stop. Would you have ran in there with that gunman with a fucking machine gun? I'd doubt it."

For almost fourteen minutes, sniffling here and there, he told a tale about the most intimate details of his life, his disappointments and all his failures.

He had apologized to the RCMP mainly because Mounties had contacted him and convinced him that he was never alone in the woods as he thought he was—the unseen men of the Buffalo had been everywhere protecting him.

◆

Andrew Douglas joined five other reporters in the pavilion at 80 Garland Avenue. The host of the Wednesday press conference was RCMP corporal Jennifer Clarke. Assistant Commissioner Bergerman's three-day sojourn from the public eye was over. She slowly walked up to the dais and took her place. For those in the television audience, the camera angle had changed. The ghostly carved buffalo on the wall was now just behind Bergerman's right shoulder, looking bigger and angrier than ever.

If the RCMP had hoped that Bergerman's previous performance was just a case of opening night jitters, they were in for a disappointment.

"What happened this weekend in our beautiful province can only be described as devastating," Bergerman read uneasily from her prepared text. "The sorrow in communities from coast to coast is palpable. I feel it, we feel it. We see candles lit in the windows and on the porches, the pain and heartache of all families and friends who have lost loved ones," she lamented, pointing out that the COVID-19 lockdown prevented people from coming together to provide comfort.

It had been almost four full days since the first 911 call had come in from Portapique and the RCMP still hadn't spoken the names of any victims other than that of Heidi Stevenson.

"I am very proud," Bergerman said with a quaver in her voice, "of the dedication of all employees in this division and their commitment to all Nova Scotians. This was never more on display than in our response this past weekend. From when our telecommunications received the 911 calls and we arrived in Portapique to do the extensive search for the suspect to when we stopped the gunman, our officers were there to protect Nova Scotians." She flipped to another page. "One of our jobs is to thoroughly investigate . . . this tragic incident, and we are doing just that . . . You can be assured that our investigative teams are working around the clock. Employees at every level are contributing to the investigation."

This was Wednesday afternoon. Thirteen murders had occurred on the previous Saturday evening. Nine more were committed Sunday morning. Bergerman was the top RCMP officer in the province. Combined with the two minutes and four seconds she had spoken on Sunday, Bergerman had now devoted an underwhelming five minutes and thirty-one seconds to communicating with the public about the biggest case of her lifetime. She turned the microphone over to Chief Superintendent Leather.

The mountainous Mountie expressed his condolence to the families. "This is a difficult time in our province. We all must find our own way to get through this. I want to assure all Nova Scotians that we are dedicating all the resources necessary to conduct a thorough investigation. This investigation is complex. This will take time, as we want to be as thorough as possible . . .

"There also have been several questions about why the emergency alert was not used. From that initial call, our response was dynamic and fluid, with members using their training to assess what was going on while encountering the unimaginable. Our Critical Incident Command staff were processing fast-changing information relating to what was unfolding in front of them and what they were being told of," Leather said.

Remember how the RCMP had sent out a tweet at 11:32 p.m. alerting its followers to the fact that it was responding to a firearms call in Portapique? At one point, the force said it had responded at 10:15 p.m. Leather had a new version: "We responded to a possible shooting at 10:26 p.m. on Saturday evening. It was determined to be a homicide and we immediately started searching the area and advising residents to stay inside. We used Twitter to alert residents that there was a firearms complaint in the Portapique area and to stay in. As we searched the Portapique area we found additional victims and several structure fires. We established a perimeter and our search continued into the evening and the early-morning hours of Sunday. In response to new information indicating that the suspect was not inside the secure perimeter, at 8:02 a.m. on Sunday the RCMP began providing real-time information from the Nova Scotia RCMP Twitter account. Twitter allowed our information to be shared, followed and broadcast by local, provincial and national news outlets. At 10:15 a.m. Nova Scotia local emergency-management officials contacted the RCMP to offer the use of the public emergency alerting system. We were in the process of preparing an alert when the gunman was shot and killed by the RCMP. As part of the investigation, we are now able to say that the shooter acted alone. We are continuing to investigate whether anyone may have assisted him leading up to the incident. That is still part of the active investigation. We are also looking for information from anyone who may know anything about what happened in the incidents on April 18 and April 19 . . . We have set up a tip line."

Clarke read everything again in French and then opened the floor and the teleconference to questions.

"How many were injured?" Shaina Luck of the CBC asked.

"I am not aware of any injured persons recovering in hospital," Leather replied. "I am aware of one injured person who sought medical attention in hospital but who has since been released."

"How and when did the RCMP become aware of someone with fake car and uniform?" Luck asked in her follow-up.

"Those details came in their totality to us early in the morning of Sunday after a key witness was located and interviewed," Leather said, choosing his words carefully and speaking in short bursts. "Prior to that time, we did not have all those details. The bulk of the details about our suspect came at that time . . . between seven and eight when that awareness came to the CIC [Critical Incident Command] commander."

No survivors but the officer, Morrison? How could that be? Had Wortman really killed everyone else he shot? The RCMP didn't know about the car until morning? It just didn't add up.

Now it was Andrew Douglas's turn. "There isn't any public safety risk anymore," he said, his deep voice echoing off the marble and glass walls. "The shooter is dead, and since he's dead we don't need to protect his right to a fair trial. What is behind your hesitance to provide details on what you know now? We understand that there are things you don't know, but what is your hesitance to provide details about what you do know now?"

Leather batted it back to Douglas. "So, for instance, the timeline. I would like nothing more than to provide the media and public with the timeline, but it is literally still a work-in-progress. And it would be unfair and inappropriate to give that out in its current state . . . We believe we have identified the locations and sites he attended and when he did, but there certainly are gaps that still need to be investigated."

"Why does it have to be wrapped up in a bow in order to give that information? Why can't you tell us what you know?" Douglas pressed.

"The concern is always that we give information that is not completely accurate," Leather said, looking a little more flushed than usual. "In a rush to provide the public and the media with that information we err."

"You received a firearms call at ten-thirty," Douglas continued. "By the time you issued your first tweet you had at least one homicide. I'm not clear how many you knew about, but you had at least one. You described that as a firearms complaint, which vastly undersold it, but then you sort of oversold it with 'Stay in your homes.' A very confusing message. Are you satisfied with the messaging that went out by the RCMP on Twitter?"

"I'm very satisfied with the messaging . . . Remember, until the following day we had some ideas where the suspect was located, some theories, but we had no idea," Leather said, stumbling a little. "The communications that were being provided were the best and clearest information that could be provided." Leather emphasized the heroic work of the Mounties on the ground, how they had done "door knocks," checking residences to make sure the occupants were safe and gathering other valuable information.

Douglas had tried his best to make an impact, but he couldn't budge Leather.

Thomas Daigle from CBC National News wanted Leather to explain this: "If you knew he had a police car, why wait two hours to warn the public about that detail?"

"It took some time to get that information," Leather said. "Once it was compiled, it was communicated."

"The picture came from a witness?"

"I can't speak to that," Leather replied. "We sent it out on Twitter."

"Clinton Ellison hid in the woods and didn't hear police coming for four hours," Daigle continued. "Can you explain to him and others what activity the police were doing that took them four hours not to see or hear him?"

"As I stated previously," Leather said, looking a little annoyed, "two perimeters were established. While that fellow may have thought there weren't police in the vicinity, there were a large number of police officers both in vehicles and on foot in Portapique."

There were a large number of officers? What were they all doing?

With no pack mentality among the reporters, no hunger for information and no following up each other's questions, the press conference deteriorated, and Clarke indicated she was cutting it off. Douglas shouted out that he had more questions. Clarke ignored him. Leather and Bergerman left the room.

◆

While the press conference was going on, the CBC's drive-home show, *Mainstreet*, called me to ask if I would come on the radio to talk about the Portapique situation in my capacity as "an RCMP expert." My first instinct was to say no.

Over the previous ten years, with rare exceptions, I had been reluctant to comment on the activities of the RCMP. The day after three Mounties—constables Dave Ross, Fabrice Georges Gévaudan and Douglas James Larche—were murdered in Moncton on June 4, 2014, I received a call from Global News. The manhunt for murder suspect

Justin Bourque was still on. It was pre-Zoom days. The producer wanted me to go to the nearest studio. I told them I was "on the road and couldn't get to a camera." In fact, Sharon and I were on our way to Prince Edward Island and about thirty-five minutes away from the crime scene. The media and much of its audience would want me to follow the ritual—say nice things about everyone, maybe shed a tear. There was no way I could do that because I was so angry that those three officers had died.

If I had gone on TV that day, based on my research, I would have said something like this: "The RCMP did not implement recommendations made after four underarmed, undertrained and undersupervised Mounties were murdered in 2005 in Mayerthorpe, Alberta . . . The RCMP is a danger to the community it serves and its own members." I didn't think anybody would want to hear that, so I just kept driving across the Confederation Bridge.

After Brenda Lucki was appointed commissioner, I was asked for my thoughts by another CBC radio show. The interviewer of the day clearly wanted me to praise the fact that a woman had finally been appointed commissioner and say that big changes were afoot. I refused to be a sound-bite whore. I said something on-air like: "One person can't fix the RCMP. In its present state, it is unfixable." I didn't get another call, which suited me fine.

By 2020, journalists in Nova Scotia and everywhere else had forgotten who I was and what I had written about the RCMP. I had aged out. But Sharon and I had built a great life for ourselves. I loved being a glass artist. Now this horrible event in Portapique had found me. It didn't happen in some distant locale, but right in my backyard. I could hear the story calling me, but I couldn't think of a good way to answer it. I hadn't written a story for twelve years.

Back when I was a newspaper editor, the Portapique story would have been one I could take apart, assigning reporters to investigate this or that, digging, writing, digging and writing some more until we got to the bottom of it all. Defending the public interest was in my blood. This radio thing, though, wasn't the easiest thing to do. There's no script. You never know what the questions are going to be. The answers have to come quickly and be delivered honestly. It's a high-wire act with no safety net.

The *Mainstreet* producer and I had a long chat, at the end of which she convinced me to go on the air. I was nervous but came up with a game plan. My goal was to highlight information that might help other reporters covering the story to find their way through the maze of information, misinformation and, likely, disinformation that the RCMP would hurl at them.

By the time the phone rang in my office, I was too shaky to sit. My mouth was dry. I took a long sip of water, glanced out the window and dove in as host Jeff Douglas (no relation to *Frank* magazine's Andrew) introduced me as an RCMP expert who had written three books about the force.

In those first few days after the killings, the broader issues were obvious to many. On so many levels the RCMP's performance was perplexing and concerning. "Questions are beginning to be asked now," Douglas said. "People are speaking out, including relatives of those killed and hurt, wondering why the RCMP didn't issue an emergency alert once they had determined that violence had broken out late Saturday night in Portapique and that a gunman was on the loose in an RCMP uniform and vehicle. What the RCMP did do instead of issuing an emergency alert that would come to each of our cellphones like an Amber Alert is to go with Twitter."

"I talked to my neighbours," I said. "They don't follow Twitter. I don't follow Twitter, but I got an alarm on Friday about COVID on my phone that woke me up. I think they didn't use it because they didn't want to draw attention. They thought they could resolve this in a short period of time and had no understanding of how complicated and how devious this guy was."

Douglas wanted to know what the RCMP was thinking, but I could only draw upon what I had read in the media and heard myself, some of which wasn't entirely accurate.

"No bars open. Not a lot of traffic. There's not a lot of people there," I said, describing the situation facing the police that night. "For a mad man to strike, it was the perfect location at the perfect time ... After the first constables arrived and saw the horror of the situation and that the shooter had disappeared, they did conduct a search," I continued, relying on what Chris Leather had described.

"They brought in helicopters and stuff," I added, based on newspaper reports. In fact, no helicopter was called out, but that bit of misinformation was still in circulation.

"But as the night dragged on and he was still active, the alert should have gone out then," I continued. "The question is, what stopped the alert going out? I think the very fact that he was using an RCMP replica car and an RCMP uniform caused them, the organization itself, to pause, because putting out an alert about an RCMP-looking vehicle with a fake RCMP cop going around shooting people everywhere would reflect badly on the RCMP, in their minds. Never mind that they should be sending a warning to citizens everywhere that something really dangerous was out there."

"It does put them in a difficult place of saying 'Beware of a man in an RCMP car and an RCMP uniform' when they may need the public to comply with them," Douglas said.

"In that kind of a situation, Jeff, no RCMP officer is going to come up knocking on your door. They have better things to do. I would rather be forewarned," I countered.

It was going relatively well, I thought. The topics were wide-ranging. I got hung up at one point on one of my long-time hobby horses—that the RCMP was operating too much like a business and not like a guardian organization. I stated at another point that perhaps the RCMP didn't immediately send enough officers to the scene because it was concerned about paying overtime. I could all but hear Douglas's eyebrows raise, and we talked about the RCMP's threadbare approach to policing.

"Rural communities don't really get twenty-four-hour policing," I said. "They operate in a minimalist way, one person to a car, reduced staffing, and they say that they are selling their services cheaper to the provinces and the cities where they are doing contract policing. In the long run, it's not cheaper. Man for man, they are probably the most expensive police force in Canada."

Chief Superintendent Chris Leather had indicated there was a significant response by the RCMP. Where were all those police officers
when Wortman was running around Nova Scotia killing people? The
absence of the Truro Police Service in the secondary response and subsequent manhunt was entirely unexplained, I pointed out to Douglas.
Did the RCMP call Truro for assistance? Every member of its thirty-
six-person force had tactical training. Did the RCMP call upon the
Amherst municipal force, 90 kilometres to the west? In both cases, if
not, why not?

Douglas shifted to the dangers of policing: "The RCMP have had
their share of fatal incidents involving members themselves over the
past decades."

I could hear the frustration rising in my voice. "It's the way the RCMP
police . . . minimalist . . . one person to a car," I reiterated. "It has nothing to do with the individual members . . . they are outstanding people.
They want to do the best possible job. But the system which they are in
defeats that purpose. If you look at any area . . . It's less dangerous to be
a policeman in downtown Toronto, Vancouver, Montreal, Calgary than
it is to be a policeman in the sticks. That's where the danger really lies."

We finally arrived at the circumstances surrounding the murder of
Heidi Stevenson. Nothing about what the RCMP did that night and
morning seemed right, I told him. One would think that the RCMP
would have blocked the roads and attacked toward Wortman instead
of either trying to catch him from behind or waiting for him at some
distant point.

"They were badly organized," I said, almost gasping for air between
sentences. "They didn't know what they were doing. And in the middle
of all of this you have a constable and a person from headquarters in
Shubenacadie who confront the shooter, and what happens there is
the constable gets killed and the other constable gets shot. Two other
people get killed in Shubenacadie."

I was now about to enter the most controversial territory for anyone commenting on the shooting of a police officer. I might not have
sounded calm and cool, but I was collected. I knew what I was going
to do.

"Why were those constables there?" I asked. "Those are not the people you want confronting this guy. You *don't* want those people there. Why were they there?" I repeated. "They knew he was coming south. Why didn't they send some of their army that were assembled around Enfield? Essentially, they put two constables at risk in Shubenacadie . . . They should never have been in that position. I know it's harsh to say. I'm not blaming her. I think she did what she had to do. She was being a brave police officer, but she was not in the position where she should have been." My voice quavered. "She should have had more backup or she should have had SWAT members there."

It was quite the rant, but I was glad to get it off my chest.

"It was not well organized, not well prepared, and I think heads should roll right up the line . . . There should be a giant inquiry," I said. As I listened to my own voice, I had reached the point where it sounded like I was about to explode. "Somebody has to wake up here. The government has to wake up. The citizens themselves who adore the RCMP have to look at this force objectively and see it for what it is," I said, my voice cracking. "It's not capable of doing the job it should be doing."

Douglas urged me to make it clear that I wasn't blaming all this on individual Mounties.

"The vast majority of the people working in the force are dedicated to serving the public and doing the best job they can, but they are working in a system that prevents them from doing their job properly and to the fullest effect," I concluded, but not before employing the ultimate Canadian phrase: "*I'm sorry* to be here in this situation, and I hope some good comes out of this."

When I hung up the phone, I thought I was about to have another heart attack. On the other hand, I suspected I wouldn't have to do another interview. I had gone a little—well, a lot—over the top. The CBC wasn't likely to call me back. And they never did.

◆

The pointed questions from Andrew Douglas and Thomas Daigle had had an immediate and profound effect on the RCMP's approach to press conferences about Portapique—there would be no more. The force instead concocted a list of questions and answers and distributed it to the media. In that Q and A, one portion, written in awkward English, caught my eye.

Q: What did the first call come in as?

A: The call RCMP first responded to was a firearms complaint.

Q: How much time passed between when the initial call came in and when Gabriel Wortman was apprehended?

A: The firearms call came in at approximately 10:30 p.m. on April 18 and Gabriel Wortman was shot at approximately noon on April 19.

Once again, the RCMP had changed the timeline. It had started out on Twitter as a firearms call at 11:32 p.m. The timing had since bounced to 10:15 p.m., then 10:26 p.m., and now 10:30 p.m. These are the police. Every word they speak on their radios is time-stamped. Every word they type into a computer is time-stamped. Four days after the first call came in, the RCMP still couldn't say exactly when it happened. People were beginning to ask questions.

Premier Stephen McNeil took a moment out of his COVID-19 update to talk about the growing public anger toward the RCMP. As the *Globe and Mail* reported, he urged citizens to withhold their criticism of the force. "There's a lot of people hurting in this province, there's no question, and I get the desire, why people want information . . . but we need to allow this process to happen. In due time, everyone will know exactly why [the Alert Ready] wasn't used."

The Smurf army was coming to the rescue of the force, and my CBC radio appearance hadn't gone unnoticed. The next morning, when I logged on to my computer, there was a Messenger notice. That was unusual. I wasn't a Messenger person. I wasn't even sure how to find it on the computer.

The message was from someone named Rachel Bailey. I googled her. She was the mayor of Lunenburg, the namesake town of the very county in which I resided. Lunenburg, a twenty-five-minute drive from my home, had disbanded its own municipal police force many years ago and hired the Mounties. I knew there was grumbling in the town about the quality of service from the RCMP, and talk about having the nearby Bridgewater municipal police take over the contract. Nevertheless, Bailey was all red serge this day: "I was appalled to hear your comments on CBC this morning . . . you throw mud at the people; not a system, not a machine, not an institution BUT fellow human beings who were and are working for the benefit of others and who are suffering right now while trying to do that work. Shame on you and shame on CBC for giving you airtime!"

I specifically didn't throw mud at individuals, but that's how it works. The wild-eyed Smurfs will say anything to discredit an RCMP critic.

10

THE FIRST MASSACRE

Over the three days following the massacres, the names of each of the twenty-two murdered people popped up in the news or on social media. Accompanying photos depicted so many normal people pursuing everyday lives before they were brutally snuffed out on an otherwise glorious spring weekend. It was mind-numbing and all but impossible to understand.

The same man, denturist Gabriel Wortman, had apparently committed all the shootings. From day one, the RCMP had declared with unusual certainty that he was the only suspect, although no one left alive had actually seen Wortman kill anyone—with or without an accomplice. There was no timeline detailing which victims were killed when. In fact, the RCMP had avoided putting names and specific times on anything.

The media had conflated it all into one grotesque murder spree— the Nova Scotia Massacre. It was a convenient headline, but it wasn't accurate. Lumping it all together blurred the lines of accountability and obscured what the RCMP had done and not done. In my mind, there were two separate massacres that were related by their known perpetrator, time and space, yet entirely distinct due to shifting circumstances, the RCMP's questionable responses and, perhaps, from Saturday night to Sunday morning, the desperate evolution of Wortman's motive, or motives, and tactics.

What I could patch together of the story at the time was murky and bewildering, so I have taken the liberty of incorporating a few details that I learned later, such as specific times and locations, information educed from some interviews, and my own analysis and that of knowledgeable others.

The first massacre took place at Portapique Beach. That sunny Saturday afternoon, some of the few permanent residents had been busy doing what they did every spring: running errands and cleaning up their properties.

At Wortman's properties, the work never stopped. Over the years he had managed to assemble a considerable chunk of land. He owned three properties under his own name—200 Portapique Beach Road, 136 Orchard Beach Drive and the twenty-acre plot at 287 Portapique Beach Road, which he had acquired on June 13, 2019. He also owned two building lots on Orchard Beach Drive, just south of the warehouse property, through one of his companies, Northumberland Investments. An adjoining third lot in that parcel had been sold off to his sister-in-law Maureen Banfield in March 2018. Wortman had big plans for the land, which he hoped to soon develop. He had cut trails through the properties, linking them through the woods. At 200 Portapique, he had built two stone breakwalls to prevent the sea from gobbling up his land.

That Saturday a neighbour was splitting wood for Wortman, repeating the age-old post-winter process of building up a stack of firewood for the next winter. Like many people, the COVID lockdown was making Wortman jittery, as he had told everyone willing to listen. He had plenty of cash on hand, lots of food and drink, and guns to get more food in the bush if he needed to do so.

Over on Orchard Beach Drive, Lisa McCully was laying out small stones to form a labyrinth on her large front lawn. As Andrew Vaughan of the Canadian Press later reported: "It's a pathway where people walk in circles to the centre and then back out again, reflecting on the patterns and concerns of their lives."

Next door to McCully, Greg and Jamie Blair were being a little more practical. Neighbour Leon Joudrey and friend Ron McGraw were helping them clear brush from their property so that the Blairs could expand their lawn. Joudrey was a forest technician for the Department of Natural Resources, while Ron was visiting for the weekend and staying in a camper on the beach. They loaded the brush onto Joudrey's trailer, and he made three trips hauling it all with his farm tractor down to a spot on the beach a little more than a kilometre away. It was another neighbourhood ritual. The brush pile would form a combustible mountain, and then sometime in the summer there would be a giant bonfire and a party to go with it.

After they were done for the day, Joudrey drove the half kilometre to his place on Portapique Crescent to clean up. He returned to the Blairs around 8 p.m. for dinner. A table was set up in the large red and white detached double garage to accommodate social distancing. Jamie cooked a steak dinner, which the four of them demolished in record time. Joudrey had been up since 4 a.m. Exhausted, he thanked the Blairs for the dinner and headed home with his two rough-and-tumble dogs, Yzerman and Basil, beside him on the front seat of his pickup. Joudrey was in bed by nine and fast asleep not long after.

What was going on elsewhere that night, we don't really know. Early reports mentioned a party and a fight, but only rumours and vague accounts seem to have survived. Then came the fires. Wortman's cottage went up in flames, as did his warehouse, 400 metres away through the woods. Then came all the dead, a microcosm of the greying population of Nova Scotia.

John Zahl, seventy, and Elizabeth Joanne (Jo) Thomas, fifty-nine, lived the closest to Wortman's cottage, about 500 metres south at 293 Portapique Beach Road. The three-quarter-acre property had sat on the market on and off for years, its price slowly dropping. The house was a modified A-frame with a log exterior and main-floor stone facade. The second floor had a typical chalet look: two floor-to-ceiling banks of angled windows and a balcony running the width of the second floor from which the occupants could lap up the view to the west over Cobequid Bay, equal to the one Wortman enjoyed up the road. Zahl and Thomas had purchased the property in 2017 for $240,000. They thought it was a steal, even though the price was high for the neighbourhood.

The Zahl-Thomas property also sat at the southern edge of Wortman's twenty-acre forested plot at 287 Portapique Beach Road. The only neighbours living close to Zahl and Thomas were another retired couple, Alan and Joanne Griffon, whose modest prefabricated cottage was on the other side of Faris Lane, just north of where the parking lot to the old dance hall used to be.

John Zahl was the only US citizen who died that weekend. He was born in 1950 in Morris, Minnesota, and had served in the United States Navy as a Russian linguist. During the Second World War he had a high-level security clearance and was stationed in Morocco and Scotland. He was the father of four children from his first marriage. Zahl had worked for Federal Express for more than thirty years.

Jo Thomas was from Winnipeg but crossed the border to attend the University of North Dakota in Grand Forks, where Zahl had started working in 1981. Married in 1985, they moved to Albuquerque, New Mexico, in 1987 and spent three decades there. Both Zahl and Thomas upgraded their educations. Before she retired, Thomas was working as an administrator for a large health corporation. After his retirement, Zahl worked part-time with troubled youth in the Albuquerque Public School system. He was also an elder at a local Presbyterian church in Albuquerque.

Although their lives looked innocuous, as in so many families there was drama hidden behind the front door. Zahl and Thomas had adopted and raised their grandchildren, Justin and Riley.

Shortly after the murders, Jo's sister, Lori Thomas of Brandon, Manitoba, told CTV reporter Josh Crabb that Zahl and her sister had decided in 2017 to make a change in their lives. Jo loved Nova Scotia and wanted to live by the sea. "They chose to leave Albuquerque and they moved to a quiet, idyllic setting of Portapique Beach . . . because it was beautiful. It was very different," she said. "I think they liked to try and explore new places."

At the time of Crabb's report, no one knew precisely what had happened to Zahl and Thomas. Lori told CTV she had exchanged text messages with Jo on April 18 and Jo mentioned that she and Zahl had driven up to Highway 2 in Zahl's convertible earlier that day. To get to and from the highway, they would have needed to drive past Wortman's cottage. Their house was burned to the ground with them in it. Had they seen something they shouldn't have?

As you may recall, Clinton Ellison and his brother, Corrie, had heard a single gunshot at around 10 p.m. Neither of them had checked the exact time. Then they noticed the glow of flames high in the sky immediately to the north. Corrie went to check it out and was killed. Clinton found his body just south of the steel gate to Wortman's warehouse at 136 Orchard Beach Drive, then ran south along the road and hid in the woods to the east of the road.

Directly across the road from where Corrie Ellison was murdered lived Lisa McCully. Almost five years earlier, the forty-nine-year-old divorced elementary school teacher had made the community a permanent home for herself and her two children, ages twelve and ten. Their pavilion-style house had about 2,500 square feet of living space over two floors. It featured a pitched roof that overhung the front porch like a nun's habit. The entire front of the house was a bank of five windows, each decorated with eighteen muntins flanked by French doors. Reaching to the top of the raised interior ceiling were five additional geometric transom windows. More windows surrounded the house, and even the basement had wrap-around windows. The house cost McCully $185,000—a bargain, it would have seemed at the time.

Between 2007 and 2010 that house had repeatedly been on the market. It was not prime real estate. The price kept dropping until it was low enough for Wortman's uncle, Glynn, who had been paroled from prison and was looking to move back to the East Coast. He had his condo up for sale in Edmonton when he bought the Portapique house in November 2010 for $169,900, thanks to Gabriel's negotiations. Glynn needed bridge financing from Gabriel to make the deal work, and Gabriel gave it to him after extracting a promise from Glynn that he would repay the money as soon as the condo sold. Gabriel lent

Glynn $160,000 and secured the loan by having his name added to the deed as a joint tenant.

Gabriel might have been family, but Glynn was naive about the man he was dealing with. Gabriel and his father, Paul, had long been real estate sharks, always on the lookout for prey in distress. They liked getting their names on deeds by hook or by crook and then squeezing their victims hard to gain full ownership.

In 2004, Steven Zinck, who ran an auto body shop near Wortman's denturist clinic, fell upon hard times. He was going to lose the house his father had built in Mineville, an eastern suburb of Halifax, because he couldn't qualify for a $38,000 mortgage. Someone introduced him to Wortman, who lent him the money with the proviso that Zinck pay him back an extra $10,000. Before he knew it, Zinck was locked out of his own house after Wortman got a judgment against him in small claims court. Zinck didn't have the money or know-how to fight back.

"Somehow in the paperwork he got it that he owned the house," Zinck told Stewart Bell and Andrew Russell of Global News two days after the massacres. "I couldn't believe it, but I also knew what he'd done to me . . . I was down and out, and he stepped right in."

The most chilling image from Bell and Russell's report was Zinck's description of Wortman's demeanour when he was clearing Zinck's possessions out of the house into dumpsters before selling the property for a tiny profit. "He was smiling while doing all that; he thought it was funny," Zinck said. "How could somebody do that to somebody and basically smile while they're doing it?"

In Glynn Wortman's case, he repaid the loan in full and then some the next year, after the Edmonton condo sold, but Gabriel refused to take his name off the title. He fought off his uncle for years.

The family battle was similar to one Gabriel had had with his father over the property at 200 Portapique Beach Road. Paul Wortman's name was on the title for tax purposes, and he wouldn't step aside when Gabriel wanted him to do so. At one point Gabriel threatened to drive to Moncton and shoot Paul and his wife, Evelyn, but didn't. The dispute blew into the open during a family vacation to the Caribbean when Gabriel beat his father to a pulp at poolside one day.

An acrimonious relationship with Gabriel proved too much for his uncle, and Glynn sought to sever ties. He put his house up for sale but found himself with two problems: real estate wasn't moving around Portapique Beach, and Gabriel refused to budge. He threw a slew of excuses at Glynn. He said he needed to consult a lawyer but was too busy. Further, he argued, Glynn still owed him money for "goods and services" and also for negotiating such a good price on the purchase of the house. And he believed the house should eventually be gifted to him. Glynn hired Truro lawyer Alain Bégin to file suit and force Gabriel off the deed. Confronted with having to testify under oath and spend money on a lawyer, Gabriel finally let the house go.

Like so many of those killed that weekend, Lisa McCully saw Portapique Beach as a tranquil and safe place. Glynn's roomy house was perfect for her needs and budget. She proved to be a shrewd negotiator. Glynn was asking $208,500 for the house, but McCully got him to knock off $23,500, and she and her children moved in.

If the RCMP was trying to make Heidi Stevenson the face of the tragedy, the cheerful, blond-haired McCully was her early competitor. McCully was born and raised in Quispamsis, on the other side of the Bay of Fundy, near Saint John, New Brunswick, and most recently had taught at the Debert Elementary School, a twenty- to twenty-five-minute drive east toward Truro.

"She was vivacious, creative, always smiling," a family friend named Bonnie Williams told CBC News. "She just always had a positive energy. She was always smiling."

Descriptions and images of McCully were published and broadcast everywhere. She had been a high school student council president. She was trilingual. Like many in her cohort, she had her children in her late thirties. She was a down-on-the-floor mom with her two children, Alex, twelve, and Marcus, ten. There she was, hugging her big black dog. Her colleagues and students loved her. She was the kind of person who did the little things, like arranging a flurry of get-well cards and messages for her brother, Jonathan, when he was sick and dying in the hospital. She was loquacious and daring and the life of the party. A lasting image depicted her doing a joint head-to-head yoga pose with her sister, Jenny Kierstead, on a patch of grass next to a small lake. Lisa was in downward dog pose while Jenny performed a forearm-stand scorpion pose with her feet resting on Lisa's butt.

In the Nova Scotia tradition, McCully also loved music. She had posted a YouTube video on March 23, almost four weeks before she was murdered, in which she was sitting on a chair, her back toward the kitchen. Her son, Marcus, was on her right and her daughter, Alex, was on her left. In blue jeans and a green turtleneck, Lisa looked entirely casual, comfortable and happy. The three of them were getting ready to sing a good-night song to their family and friends, whom they hadn't seen for awhile because of the COVID lockdown. The song she chose to play was one the great ukulele standards: "Patience and Prudence: Tonight You Belong to Me," written in 1926 by Billy Rose and composer Lee David. It was featured in the 1979 Steve Martin movie *The Jerk* and has been covered by many musicians, including a popular duet by Eddie Vedder and Cat Power on Vedder's *Ukulele Songs* album. Lisa strummed the opening chords and then harmonized with her children as she played along: "I know (I know), you belong to somebody new, but tonight you belong to me . . ."

The video is sweet and moving, and the single mother comes across as the kind of person who would be impossible not to like.

Next door to McCully, at 123 Orchard Beach Drive, lived the Blairs. There was a pathway through a stand of trees that connected the two properties so that the two young Blair boys, Alexander and Jack, ages twelve and ten, could take the shortcut over to the McCully house and vice versa. Forty-five-year-old Greg Blair also had two older sons, Tyler and Craig, from an earlier relationship.

The Blairs and their elder sons operated GB Gas and Energy on Old Tatamagouche Road in Onslow Mountain, just outside Truro. They sold and serviced natural gas and propane furnaces, residential and commercial appliances and fireplaces, among other things.

Greg Blair had come from Hiram Lynds Road in Central North River, north of Truro. The road had once been home for Blair's current neighbour Leon Joudrey, as well, and also the former top Hells Angel in Nova Scotia, the late Jeffery Lynds. In 1999 Lynds, an elite Hells Angels Nomad, turned on his confederates as he was dying in prison. His nephew, Curtis, was charged and convicted of murder in a Hells Angels–related case the next year. Sources say the Blairs and Joudrey were not outlaw bikers.

Greg and Jamie Blair had vacationed for years in Portapique, usually renting a trailer down at Orchard Beach—$1,500 for the year. Greg's father had a place on Orchard Beach Road, just up from the water-front. The beach was the focal point of social activity in the neighbour-hood. Weekends in the summer tended to be one big party of drinking, carousing and arguing around the giant bonfire for the twenty or so permanent residents of the neighbourhood and the almost-permanent ones like Wortman and his common-law wife.

Greg and forty-year-old Jamie were typical Nova Scotians for their age and locale. Rough around the edges, they were both quick-witted and, some would say, familiar with the odd raunchy or risqué retort.

In 2016, Greg and Jamie had purchased the vacant lot next to Lisa McCully for $5,000 with a plan to build a new house on it so that he and his children could be closer to their grandparents. The house was finally completed in 2019.

At the entrance to the Blairs' driveway there was a small, charm-ing gatehouse-cum–storage shed on the right with a sign in the door window: "WARNING: This property is protected by a double-barrel shotgun 3 nights a week. You guess which ones." It was a joke. Another sign, beside the front door, shouted "WELCOME." Just about every-body was welcome at the Blairs.

Straight ahead up the driveway was the double garage, maybe 40 metres from the road, where the Blairs had dinner with Leon Joudrey and Ron McGraw. All the buildings were done up in red with white trim, like the Canadian flag.

Life was good. The Blairs had quickly paid off their mortgage and Greg found himself debt-free for the first time in his life. Greg and Jamie's first grandchild, Hayden, had been born recently, and they were the typical over-the-moon first-time grandparents.

Before that night, Wortman had asked Greg to come over to his warehouse, which was a short walk away, and give him an expert's opinion on the work he had done on a propane line to the heater he was using to warm the building. Greg told Wortman he didn't think the set-up was done properly and it likely would not work. Fancying himself a man of many talents, Wortman disagreed. As it turned out, Greg was right, which had angered Wortman—but no one thought his ire was on the level of a murderous grudge.

Greg and Jamie Blair were living their own version of a normal life when they were murdered. It had been a fine spring day, but as night came the temperature was plummeting to zero Celsius. They stoked the fireplace with a couple of logs. The wind was picking up as it normally did when the tide rushed into the bay. It would peak at 11:08 that night.

Greg was shot numerous times with a rifle and fell just outside the front door. His young sons later told other family members they had heard him say "What the fuck are you doing with a gun?" before shots rang out. Perhaps signs of a struggle, a bullet had punctured the soffit of the house and another had hit the garage door to the right. The Blairs' dog, Zoey, a nine-year-old miniature pinscher, was shot and wounded in the hind end.

When Wortman entered the house, Jamie had already put her children in a bedroom and closed the door, and was on the phone with 911 when Wortman found her. Had he heard her call to 911 on a police radio? He shot her repeatedly in her own bedroom and killed her. The RCMP has never released the 911 tapes, citing privacy issues.

Wortman then began firing through the closed bedroom door, eight shots in all, narrowly missing one of the boys. Two bullets pierced the wall and flew outside, as did another through a window.

A friend of the Blair family says Wortman yelled out, "She should have died the first time!" The older Blair sons declined to be interviewed.

One source says that on his way out the door, Wortman pulled some logs out of the fireplace and arranged them on the floor around Jamie in what appeared to be a half-hearted attempt to burn the place down. Neither the police nor the Blairs would confirm this.

Why were the Blairs targeted? There had to be a better reason than Wortman being offended by Greg's assessment of his pipefitting skills. Jamie Blair was not only shot multiple times but almost ritualistically prepared for immolation. It smelled of a personal vendetta, but about what?

After Wortman appeared to have left, Alexander and Jack Blair made their way out of the bedroom and past their mother's dead body. They gingerly placed the logs back into the fireplace. One of them reached into Greg's pants pocket and retrieved his cellphone, and then the two boys headed outside. They hid in a chicken shed at one point and then found their way across the path in the wood stand over to the McCully house.

During their escape, sources say, the boys noticed Wortman circling past the house twice, which suggests he had driven to the intersection of Portapique Crescent, turned onto it and followed it to where it met the southern end of Orchard Beach Drive, on which he then passed the Blair house the second time. The round trip would have taken him past Leon Joudrey's house. Joudrey was asleep. At least two other permanent residences were occupied that night. Why did Wortman not stop at them? He was clearly not in a state of panic. Was he looking for specific people who were up or who might have seen him or his car?

Lisa McCully put the frightened Blair children in her basement with her own children, and then went to investigate. She did not go north, toward the Blair house, but west across her lawn to the rail fence near the road, perhaps to talk to a police officer she saw sitting there in a cruiser. McCully was shot by the fence and killed.

North of the Blair and McCully homes, across the intersection with Portapique Crescent, Frank and Dawn Gulenchyn lived at 71 Orchard Beach Crescent. They had purchased the newly constructed house, which sat on four and a half acres of land, in 2011 for $128,696. This was the second marriage for each of them, and the little house was an irresistible opportunity.

Dawn, sixty-one, used her maiden name, Madsen, on social media. She was originally from Nova Scotia and had longed to return and live out her retirement in a peaceful and beautiful setting by the sea. It was a two-step move. Frank, sixty-two, had moved to Nova Scotia in 2011, while Dawn stayed behind in Oshawa, east of Toronto, until the late summer of 2019. Frank had left behind his job in Oshawa as a designer at Steelhawk Plate and Profile Ltd., a structural steel company. Among the notable projects to which he had contributed his talents were the new Terminal 1 at Toronto Pearson International Airport and the Toronto Blue Jays' pitching mound at Rogers Centre.

According to their son, Ryan Farrington, once Frank was settled in Nova Scotia, he took a job at Masstown Market, a popular produce, seafood and grocery emporium about twenty minutes down Highway 2 toward Truro. That lasted only a few months before he decided his time would be better spent fixing up the house. Frank spent $20,000 on a custom-made woodworking shop, which was located about five metres from the house, and spent eight years meticulously renovating their retirement nest, waiting for Dawn to join him. She would fly down east once a month and stay for a week. Frank didn't interact with many in the neighbourhood and liked to spend his downtime sitting on the front porch, coddling a drink or two and watching the world go by.

Dawn continued to work in the kitchen at Hillsdale Terraces, a long-term seniors' facility in Oshawa. As Dawn's former boss, Spatzie Dublin, told the CBC's Shanifa Nasser: "When she came into the building, her residents were her family. And she treated them exactly like they were her family and her best friends. She was like a beam of sunshine."

Dawn finally retired in August 2019 and made the big move east. By all accounts the Gulenchyns were harmless and kept to themselves.

In his circling of the neighbourhood, did Wortman see one of them looking out a window? Why was their house, including Frank's wood-working shop, burned down?

By the time the Gulenchyns lay shot dead in their burning house, Wortman had already killed at least five and perhaps as many as eight people: Greg and Jamie Blair, Lisa McCully, Frank and Dawn Gulenchyn and, likely, John Zahl, Jo Thomas and Corrie Ellison.

Houses and buildings were on fire. Bodies were strewn about. People were calling 911. One might think Wortman would be frantic to get away from the scene of his crimes, but he was just sitting in his replica police car at one end of the Gulenchyns' semicircular driveway, facing out to the road. It was dark. He had his headlights on.

Across the road and hidden in the bush was the house occupied by carpenter Bjorn Merzbach, his wife and his two children. Merzbach and Wortman were anything but friendly. Merzbach has refused to talk to the media but told friends afterwards that he suspected Wortman had lit the Gulenchyns' house on fire to attract his attention. It did, but not as Wortman would have intended. Merzbach stowed his wife and the children in a back bedroom, armed himself with a rifle and went outside, where he took up a defensive position and waited for Wortman to make a move toward his property. That didn't happen, because someone else stumbled onto the scene.

Andrew and Katie MacDonald owned a well-appointed log cabin at the junction of Portapique Beach Road and Orchard Beach Drive, about 300 metres from the Gulenchyns' house. MacDonald and his father, Edward MacDonald, owned Maritime Auto Parts and a few other scrap-related businesses. Their company sponsored the police hockey team in the local beer league.

The MacDonalds noticed the flames and drove over. As they passed the Gulenchyns' house, they saw the RCMP car in the driveway and then a flash inside the house behind the French doors. They drove south down the road and came across Wortman's burning ware-house. They turned their vehicle around and drove back toward the Gulenchyn property. As they approached the driveway, the RCMP vehicle pulled onto Orchard Beach Drive and met them door to door. Andrew recognized Wortman, saw him raise a handgun and then saw the red beam of a laser sight engage. He ducked and stepped on the gas, squealing away. A bullet grazed his head. As he came up to his house a few seconds later, he turned right toward Highway 2 and met Constable Stuart Beselt, the first police officer to arrive in the neigh-bourhood. The RCMP would later say they got to the scene at about

10:26 p.m., but they have never clarified exactly what happened upon their arrival or thereafter.

Andrew MacDonald knew Beselt, a player on the police hockey team. He told Beselt that his neighbour Gabriel Wortman was dressed as a Mountie and was in an RCMP car, information that Beselt reportedly told his dispatcher. Around then, another bullet fell out of Andrew's parka. He and Katie were lucky to be alive.

After failing to kill the MacDonalds, Wortman needed to find a way out of the area. The route to the south on Orchard Beach Drive was clear, and police said a witness came forward days later and told them Wortman was seen leaving the neighbourhood at 10:35 p.m. via a little-known dirt path directly east of the subdivision, through a 250-acre wild blueberry field. That path connected to a dirt road known as Brown Loop, a 750-metre semicircle that touched Highway 2 at two points east of Portapique Beach Road. (The RCMP made it clear that the witness was not a force member.)

If that was indeed Wortman's escape route, it suggests that, after the run-in with the MacDonalds, he drove south on Orchard Beach Drive almost a kilometre until he came to the intersection of Cobequid Court. To his left were a couple of properties on a stretch that ran about the length of a short city block, at the end of which, between a row of trees, was the muddy entrance into the blueberry field.

Let's put ourselves in Wortman's head for a moment. Over the previous thirty-five minutes to an hour, he had killed several people and set fires that could be seen from kilometres away. He had to realize that police and fire departments had been called and might even already be on the scene. He had just shot at Andrew MacDonald, who had escaped and would surely have called 911. Wortman had to expect the RCMP to come roaring down Orchard Beach Drive at any moment. That's normally what would have happened. But Wortman coolly continued his mission. Was he a true psychopath whose heart rate dropped while he was perpetrating his horror? Or did he know where the police were—and that they weren't coming? Was he somehow tuned in? Did he have a scanner or a police radio?

We really don't know, and may never know, why the eight people we've already met were murdered. Only one thing appears to unite them: all eight lived close enough to Wortman's house or warehouse to either hear gunshots or see the flames from the fires he had set.

The people we'll meet next lived on Cobequid Court, surrounded by forest that would have obscured their view of the flames, and too far away to have heard any gunshots. Wortman didn't just happen upon them, without intention. From Orchard Beach Drive, he could have turned left at Cobequid Court into the blueberry field and made his escape.

He turned right.

◆

Heading west from Orchard Beach Drive, Cobequid Court runs the length of a Canadian football field. There are only three houses on it, and a fourth is tucked behind in the woods. No one was home in the cottage to the right or the house in behind. Straight ahead of Wortman was the neatly appointed home of Peter and Joy Bond. They were ready for bed, watching television.

To Wortman's left, hidden in the trees, was the ramshackle Tuck residence. It looked like two poorly conceived and entirely different structures that had been haphazardly slammed together, one with a gambrel, or Dutch, roof and the other with a conventional shallow pitch. In the latter section was a built-in garage with a room above it. It was all wrapped in light-blue siding.

The place was a mess. There was a disconnected toilet resting on the stoop, where the more pretentious might have had a stone lion guarding the place. A clawfoot bathtub rested beside the driveway, filled with empty liquor bottles. The overwhelming favourites were Alberta Premium rye and Kahlúa. Boxes containing empty white wine bottles sat on the ground nearby. Discarded beer cans were scattered through the bushes.

"They were working to fix it up," said Tammy Oliver-McCurdie, Jolene Oliver's sister. "It was ten times better than it was when they took it over."

Jolene's husband, Aaron Tuck, had spent time in the house when he was younger. He had been adopted by Bruce Tuck, a retired military man, and his wife, Gloria Mae. Bruce went by the nickname Friar Tuck, a nod to Robin Hood's legendary band of merry outlaws. Bruce was not an easy man to live with. He was a hoarder. The house had begun to fall apart, and he was not very good with money. His marriage to Gloria Mae ended.

Aaron had a rough upbringing and drifted onto the wrong side of the law. He landed in jail for a time. Afterwards, Aaron grew closer to Gloria Mae and her second husband, Angus Rogers, who lived in Sydney.

Tara Long says she is Aaron Tuck's sister by his Nova Scotian birth mother, though there is no birth certificate to prove the relationship. Long and Tuck reconnected in the 1990s and spent time together in London, Ontario, where their mother was living.

"When we were teenagers, he always had access to money. He always had weed," Long recalled. "In 1995, we were in London. Aaron took me and my underage friend out to a bar called the Ramp. It was like a biker bar. I was sixteen and Aaron was nineteen. He walked up to the bouncer and said: 'This is my sister, we're going in' . . . and we got in. We were clearly underage, but it was no problem. He was very protective of me."

Long said Tuck's introduction to the biker underworld came in London: "Aaron met a guy from Truro there who already knew him from Nova Scotia. That began his connection to the Outlaws."

Over the years Tuck developed many talents. He made things out of leather, including a purse that Jolene cherished. He was a backyard mechanic who could fix just about anything. He liked to drink. Like so many Nova Scotian men and women of his age group, he ended up chasing the big money in oil-rich Alberta. Back then there were regular flights connecting a number of East Coast cities and Fort McMurray, in the heart of the oil patch.

Jolene Oliver grew up in Calgary and was working as a "career waitress" there when she met Tuck. They fell in love and their only child, Emily, was born there. Tammy Oliver-McCurdie described her sister Jolene as a resilient person with a soft side. She was an avid bird-watcher and dabbled in poetry. "She was a good listener" and "she really loved people."

Jolene's life with Aaron certainly wasn't an easy one. Many of the empty white wine and Kahlúa bottles in the bathtub out front were drained by her. The couple appear to have maintained a "yours" and "mine" approach to family finances and expenses. Nevertheless, Jolene followed wherever Aaron led. In March 2013 they moved to Sydney to help take care of Aaron's widowed adoptive mother, whose health was fading.

In 2016 Bruce Tuck passed away and left 41 Cobequid Court to Aaron, along with the nickname, Friar, which Aaron soon adopted. Inheriting a house might seem like a stroke of luck, but for the Tucks it was more like the lyric in the Temptations song "Papa Was a Rollin' Stone": "all he left us was a loan." There were debts to pay. The house had no electricity or running water. The property was overrun with Bruce Tuck's hoarding. The only upside was that the house backed right onto the wide sands of Orchard Beach.

"They were living off the grid, and Jolene was a real trooper. She went along with it all," said Oliver-McCurdie. "Aaron rigged up a bucket shower for them to use. They had a greenhouse where they grew some of their food. They had a propane fridge. When Jolene said she wanted a washer and dryer, Aaron made them for her. He hooked them up to an electric motor that was powered by solar energy. Jolene was so excited: 'Aaron made me a washer and dryer!'"

All this wasn't easy on Emily, either. But she grew up by her father's side and was wielding wrenches with him by the age of three. Father and daughter spent more than a decade restoring a 1977 Ford Pinto that would be hers on her eighteenth birthday, which was coming soon. She liked working on cars so much that she planned to get her welder's ticket someday. In school, Emily had some troubles. Jolene thought learning to play the fiddle would help her daughter. Emily took some lessons and began to blossom.

Emily's interest in the fiddle helped grow her appreciation for her father's vast music collection. Their house was anything but palatial, but they loved sitting around drinking, smoking and spinning a record or ten. A delightful photo captures the Tucks' life and spirit: a bespectacled Emily, wearing a black dress and running shoes, is dancing with Aaron in what appears to be the living room. There is no flooring, just a plywood subfloor. Belongings on the floor are pushed up against the wall. Aaron and his teenaged daughter are facing each other in mid-groove and making their own fun. He is wearing a T-shirt, knee-length baggy cream shorts and worn moccasins—with socks. In his right hand is a can of Coors; a cigarette fat with ashes is in his left.

In Portapique Tuck had been slowly turning his life around, but he still hadn't completely abandoned the biker world. At one point he had borrowed around $10,000 from bikers. He was slow to repay the loan, and they occasionally paid him visits. Tara Long described a number of situations where Tuck had confrontations with men she believed were associated with the Hells Angels. They had come to collect. "He'd face them down and they'd go away," she said. "Every so often, they would come back, park out front and just stare at the house. He'd go out and meet them. He wasn't afraid."

On his Facebook page on November 17, 2018, Tuck posted a photo and caption: "Support Your Local Devil's Diciples MC" (a US-based motorcycle club known for its accidentally misspelled name—which it never changed). He also posted photos of himself cuddling some fresh marijuana plants.

Many described Tuck as being "rough around the edges," but Tara Long was a little more indelicate: "My brother was an asshole, but he was a really good guy. He loved his family. He would do anything to protect those girls. He would do anything for anyone . . . and usually wouldn't charge them a dime for doing it."

Long's comments might seem like the typical hagiography that comes with death—just about everyone who dies becomes a sinless angel. But there does seem to have been more to Tuck than met the eye. One of his mother's friends, Doreen Coady, had published a book, *100 Moms, 1000 Tips, 1 Million Reasons*. She was following it up with a companion book about dads and asked Tuck to contribute to it. Here is what he wrote about his late stepfather:

When I got "out" [of prison], Angus put a wrench in my hand. That changed everything. Together we worked on a Mustang. He gave me what I needed; he rearranged my world. Angus was the Father I always wanted. He taught me what a man should be. He taught me to cut the grass and fix the mower. He later put me in a small engine repair course. He was the biggest influence in my life.

The "good guy" in Tuck was evident in his own approach to parenting, as described by Coady. He wrote about independence and instilling resilience in a child. He was proud that Emily could build a cabin or a composting toilet, chop wood or run a chainsaw. He said he "put Jolene on a pedestal, and I want the same for my 'little girl.'" Tuck's creed included exposing his daughter to music and teaching her to be truthful and to show and talk about affection. "Start each day with 'I love you' . . . I always hug her . . . Don't take life seriously. Have fun . . ."

By the late fall of 2019, however, Tuck was struggling both physically and emotionally. He had hurt his back while trying to lift a car engine and couldn't work.

"The last time I saw him was October," Tara Long said. "He told me he got rid of all his guns. He was going through hard times. He was suffering from depression. It was better to get rid of them. He told me privately that he thought he was going to die soon and then he went and had a will made. He had this feeling."

That October 25, Long said, Tuck had a confrontation with Wortman at his warehouse. The conflict between them had been brewing for about a year. In November 2018 Tuck was invited into Wortman's warehouse and took the opportunity to take photographs of himself leaning on the Captain America bike. He took other shots of Wortman's collection of motorbikes mounted on the wall and posted them on his Facebook page. The next day, Long said, Tuck's Facebook page was hacked, and he couldn't get into it anymore.

At another point in their relationship, Wortman offered to fix the gaping holes in Tuck's smile by making him a set of dentures for free.

Eventually, he did get a set of dentures, but it's not known if Wortman provided them. However, Tuck soon came to realize that Wortman did little out of the goodness of his heart. Just about everything with him was transactional. Wortman really wanted to add a place on the beach to his land holdings. "I'll give you $18,000 for it," Wortman offered Tuck for his property. The offer was an insult—well below the normal asking price for a tract of land right on the water.

On October 25, Long said, Tuck was invited over to Wortman's warehouse for what was known as "the Friday afternoon drinking club." Wortman and a few of the neighbours would gather at the Black Bear Lodge and pound back more than a few. Everyone who knew Wortman says approximately the same thing: he was a cheap drunk. Three beers and he turned from Dr. Jekyll to Mr. Hyde. That day, the typically belligerent Wortman tried to pick a fight with Tuck, who declined the offer.

"Aaron studied martial arts," said Long. "He was as wiry and skinny as you can imagine, but he was super strong. He told Wortman that he wasn't afraid of him. He could kick the shit out of him if he wanted to, but he just sat down and finished his beer and then left."

Whether it had been the insulting offer from Wortman or the building drama in the neighbourhood, Aaron and Jolene began to think about fixing up the property and selling. To that end they had the power company hook them up to the grid.

In mid-February 2020, Jolene rolled their pickup truck into a ditch, but was not seriously injured. She was, however, broke and borrowing money from her sister Tammy to get by. In February, Aaron inherited some money from his adoptive mother, Gloria Mae. He bought thousands of dollars' worth of tools and equipment so he could get to work on the house. As COVID-19 began rolling into Nova Scotia, more money was on the way through government relief programs. Each adult would be getting $2,000 a month. That was big money. The house became a priority.

"He really wanted to move back to Cape Breton," Tammy Oliver-McCurdie said.

Tuck was one of many who knew about the replica police car in Wortman's warehouse. He had seen it and had told others about it. When Jolene's nephew, Ricky, had come for a visit from Alberta in February, Oliver-McCurdie said, Tuck had warned him not to go near Wortman and that he was crazy. Oliver-McCurdie was certain that Tuck or someone close to him had called the RCMP about the fake cruiser, but the RCMP later told her that it had no record of such a complaint.

Now the family was dead. Coldly executed.

"Emily had stopped texting at 10:07," Oliver-McCurdie said. "Their three cellphones were near the couch like they had been watching a movie or listening to music. Aaron had just cracked open a beer. It looked like there had been a fight at the door. I can't believe that Wortman did this alone. Aaron knew how to fight, and his injuries suggest he was in a fight." Aaron Tuck was shot at close range in the roof of the mouth and elsewhere. "Jolene was right there in the hallway behind him. She could have ducked into the bathroom there, but it looked like she was turning to go protect Emily." She was shot twice where she fell. "Her body was three feet in front of the sliding door in the living room."

We don't know if Wortman acted alone at the Tucks' house. The RCMP report said there wasn't a fight at the door.

When he left the Tucks', Wortman drove down the semicircular driveway and back onto Cobequid Court. To his left was the home of Peter and Joy Bond.

◆

Peter Bond, seventy-five, and Joy, seventy-one, hailed from Chester, on the other side of Nova Scotia, on the South Shore. Peter had been a truck driver, while Joy was a former cook and stay-at-home mother. A beautiful place, the Chester area is home to the most expensive real estate in the province. It has been said that during the summer the seasonal residents of Chester have the highest per capita income in Canada. It's not the kind of place where a former truck driver and his wife could possibly find a reasonably priced place by the water. So thirteen years earlier they had bought the modest 1,075-square-foot two-bedroom, one-bathroom house on Cobequid Court for around $100,000. It came with a double lot, the other one touching on the southeastern edge of Wortman's twenty acres of scrub forest known as 287 Portapique Beach Road.

"They were getting ready for bed," Harry Bond, one of their two sons, said in an interview, after hearing the details second-hand from acquaintances with connections in the force. "They were in their pyjamas. My mother was shot at the front door and my father was right behind her."

What provoked Wortman to kill them? Two theories were making the rounds. One was that he wanted to buy a right of way through their property so he could access the beach from 287 Portapique Beach Road; maybe they'd refused and he killed them out of spite. Another was that Wortman didn't like the Bonds because he believed Peter had not paid for a load of firewood from another neighbour. True or not, why would he care to the point of killing them? Neither theory made much sense.

That Sunday morning, when they heard what was going on in Portapique, Harry and his brother, Cory, desperately tried to contact their parents.

"My mom's cellphone was on," Harry said. "It was ringing, and no one was answering. Your mind runs a million miles a minute."

As far as anyone knew the week after the killings, by the time Wortman got to the Bonds' house, he had lit fire to four properties: his cottage, his warehouse, the Zahl-Thomas house on Portapique Beach Road and the Gulenchyns' house on Orchard Beach Drive. He hadn't burned down the Blairs' house, Lisa McCully's or the Tucks'. After he killed the Bonds, he didn't burn their house down, either. Was there some unfathomable criteria in his head dictating which houses needed to be destroyed?

Months later, when the house was sold, the new buyers told Harry Bond they had heard that Wortman had seen Joy looking out the window when he left the Tucks' and killed her and Peter for that reason alone. It was a solid theory, except for one important thing: Who would know that information? Wortman and the Bonds were dead. Was there someone with Wortman who had talked to the police?

With unanswered questions like that floating around, Harry Bond and the rest of the family have grown increasingly angry at the RCMP and its secretive ways.

"If you're telling the truth your story doesn't change," Harry said. "Their story keeps changing."

11

THE COMMISSIONAIRE'S ERROR AND A MOUNTIE'S TWITCH

By the Friday after the shootings, the RCMP was still struggling to get its story straight. It was equally remarkable and disturbing to watch it play out.

In April 2018, after a crazed man in Toronto drove a van down Yonge Street, killing ten people and injuring sixteen, Toronto Police constable Ken Lam made a dramatic non-violent arrest of the suspect. By the next day everyone knew Lam's name, and he was being proclaimed a hero around the world. In disaster after disaster, in Canada, the United States and many other countries, the public is kept informed about developments in major crimes and threats to public safety. The exceptions typically involve cases in which the Mounties are the police.

If one was to believe the RCMP's story, an alert Mountie at the Irving Big Stop had recognized Wortman, confronted him and killed him. The RCMP was hiding the member's name. There was no video evidence. Nothing.

After failing to reassure the media and public with its Q and A handouts, the Mounties shifted gears. If it had to face the media, it would decide who could participate. The RCMP announced that another press briefing was being held that Friday, April 24, but it didn't tell everyone the full details. One of those left out of the loop was Andrew Douglas, who heard about the event from other reporters and arrived at RCMP headquarters anyway.

Douglas brought along Bev Keddy (no relation to Kaitlyn Keddy from Chapter Six), who wrote for *Frank* about unsolved murders and missing persons cases in Nova Scotia. He was there to take photographs, freeing up Douglas to question the Mounties. They were met at the door by a commissionaire, a uniquely Canadian brand of security guard. Formed in 1925, the non-profit company was created to provide employment for retired military and RCMP members.

The commissionaire allowed the two men into the pavilion where the carved buffalo head had played its background role in the three previous briefings. There was no one there. The commissionaire then escorted them through a security door and into the inner sanctum. Down a corridor they arrived at a small conference room. Standing there were Corporal Lisa Croteau and Alex Vass, a civilian member in the RCMP's Strategic Communications unit.

"It was more like a broom closet," said Douglas. "They told me that it was a teleconference because of COVID restrictions and social distancing."

"We sent out an advisory to the media," one of the Mounties told the visitors.

Douglas couldn't remember seeing any such message. He smelled a rat. A brief, heated discussion ensued.

"Why are you having it in a place where there's no room?" Douglas asked. The spacious pavilion had worked fine previously. But the answer was obvious. The RCMP didn't want the public seeing aggressive local reporters on the six o'clock news challenging the narrative it was building.

As Douglas and Keddy retreated down the corridor to leave the building, they met another reporter the commissionaire had let in. It was Tim Bousquet from the online *Halifax Examiner*, who had also asked probing questions of the Mounties earlier in the week. Since then, the *Examiner* had done exemplary work in laying out elements of the evolving story. Bousquet hadn't been officially notified of the broom-closet press briefing, either.

After leaving 80 Garland Avenue, Douglas pestered the RCMP to tell him why he had been excluded. It was six weeks before he got an e-mail from Corporal Jennifer Clarke: "Hello Andrew. We will not be sending you registration information for the teleconference/presser today. Our rationale for that is that in past media events, you have been disrespectful, unprofessional and disruptive. The material we are presenting today will be available on our website following the presser. Thank you, Jen."

Douglas tried to smooth things over with a letter to Clarke pointing out that the notoriously secretive Nova Scotia government had tried in the past to ban him in a similar way, an injunction that was rescinded after he threatened legal action.

"Wouldn't it be easier to let cooler heads prevail and, at the very least, put us back on the mailing list?" Douglas wrote to Clarke, but to no avail. The RCMP refused to bend.

In typical *Frank* fashion, Douglas cheekily responded by reworking Clarke's comments into the magazine's motto for several issues: "Frank by Name, Disrespectful, Disruptive & Unprofessional by Nature."

Dejected as Douglas was about what had taken place, he didn't appreciate at the time that he had seen someone he possibly wasn't meant to see.

Alex Vass was a former radio and television reporter who had spent almost thirty years working in New Brunswick, the last sixteen of those years with CTV, the most popular network in the Maritime provinces and across the country. In April 2005 Vass joined the RCMP's Strategic Communications department. By 2020 he was a senior crisis and communications strategist. Vass brought added value to the RCMP because he had a pipeline back to his former comrades.

Part of Vass's backstory sheds light on why the RCMP had put its faith in social media during Wortman's rampage and why it was continuing to defend that mystifying decision. Days earlier Chief Superintendent Leather had called Twitter "a superior way to communicate this ongoing threat" and added, "I'm very satisfied with the messaging."

Vass was instrumental in convincing the force to use social media in a crisis and was working behind the scenes to manage the force's response to the growing criticism of the practice. A lengthy story about Vass and Twitter was written by Deidre Seiden and published on October 3, 2014, in the *RCMP Gazette*.

Vass's interest in social media had been sparked earlier that year by the murders of three Mounties and the wounding of two others in Moncton. The shootings had begun around 7:30 p.m. on June 4, 2014, and the manhunt for killer Justin Bourque went on until he was captured around 12:30 a.m. on June 6. The following excerpt from Seiden's article captures the RCMP's thinking about social media: "Almost immediately," described Seiden, "the public took to social media—Twitter and Facebook—describing what they were seeing, everything from police vehicles racing down their street to an image of a then-unknown suspect wearing fatigues and carrying two rifles to a video of a woman witnessing gunfire from her house." While police tracked the shooter through a residential area, Vass realized that social media could allow the force to notify the public of the danger directly, circumventing the usual rumour mills and gaps between nightly news broadcasts. "The idea of posting new messages was to reassure people that if they were sitting in their basement, and a lot of people were," Seiden explained, as if to reassure the police as much as the police were looking to reassure the public, "the RCMP was still there with them."

The RCMP team even got an industry Oscar for what it did in Moncton—the Connected Cops Social Media Event Management award. Vass dined out on this in the ensuing years, being invited to institutions such as the Ontario Police College to talk about his revelation in Moncton. He expounded on the efficiency of social media, and how it allowed the RCMP to reduce the number of conventional interviews it did with the media and target the audience it wanted to reach.

Prior to the Moncton shooting, Vass said, the RCMP Twitter and Facebook accounts respectively had 8,000 and 10,000 followers among the almost 800,000 residents of New Brunswick. In the days after the shooting, these numbers shot up to 56,000 for Twitter and 28,000 for Facebook. When the RCMP tweeted a video about a police dog employed in Moncton, viewership shot up to 100,000. The force took the dog video as proof that this new technology really worked. But no one in the force seemed to have a realistic view of the audience. As popular as the dog video might have been, it was a one-hit wonder. Without the dog for entertainment, the RCMP Twitter feed was a dog of another kind. The vast majority of Nova Scotians did not use Twitter, a variety of media outlets reported afterwards.

The RCMP became so enamoured with Twitter after the Moncton experience that before the dust had even settled it hired CBC reporter Angela Chang. She had covered the shootings and had actively encouraged the CBC's audience to tune into the RCMP Twitter feed at the time. Once inside the RCMP she became the force's director of Strategic Communications in Fredericton.

Vass likely wasn't supposed to be seen that day at 80 Garland Avenue. The commissionaire who let Douglas and Keddy in had surely made a mistake. The plan being executed by Vass, undoubtedly with the approval of his masters somewhere in the higher echelons of the force, was to eliminate interference from the press in the force's messaging to the public. That Vass was there and involved is beyond curious, in my opinion. The Nova Scotia RCMP is the largest detachment in the Maritimes. Vass was based out of "J" Division in New Brunswick. He appeared to be the point man calling the shots in Nova Scotia on this file. Why? Who was giving him his orders?

◆

As the disheartened Douglas and Keddy drove back over the bridge to Halifax, the conference call press briefing continued at headquarters. Bergerman and Leather had been cancelled. The force trotted out the next in line: its tank, Superintendent Darren Campbell—true believer, second-generation Mountie, designer of the generational insignia and chief dispenser of the Kool-Aid. He would be designated to handle the media from now on.

Press conferences are a strange beast. In the old days they were unruly affairs. Today, in general, they are carefully orchestrated. Those being asked the questions say only what they want to say. The journalists fielding the answers typically write about the question they asked while stealing some of the more colourful quotes generated by their colleagues. In other words, journalists tend to get caught up in their own trees and ignore the forest. What gets lost time and time again is the message gleaned from an entire event, especially from what is left unstated and hidden between the lines.

The setting for the presentation was anything but slick. A lectern had been set up in front of three flags: Nova Scotia's, Canada's and the RCMP's. In lieu of the buffalo, a flat-screen TV showed a static image of the RCMP insignia. The grey curtains used as a backdrop were far too long for the purpose and bunched on the floor. The tight quarters made the officers look backed into a corner.

Campbell's task that day was to provide a firm timeline for the killings and police response. He didn't have a track record as a spokesperson for the force, but his first wife, Catherine Galliford, had been a prominent and respected Mountie in that position. Campbell's brother was a spokesperson for the federal Department of Oceans and Fisheries. The Mounties must have been hoping some of their skills had rubbed off on him.

After expressing his condolences to the families of the dead and calling some of those who died heroes, Campbell said: "The RCMP implements a Critical Incident Command structure when responding to complaints that may impact public safety. Highly skilled and trained officers come together as a team in order to direct emergency personnel and the multiple specialized policing units deployed when responding to a complaint. These two elements are important to be aware of as I go through the timeline of the incidents.

"The following details I will be sharing with you have been put together because of the benefit of hindsight, of knowing what happened. The police officers responding to the initial 911 call and the subsequent calls did not have the benefit of the knowledge I am about to share with you. The initial complaint was of a shooting . . . officers arrived at 10:26 p.m.

"In total there were over seven locations where people were found deceased. Many of the deceased were discovered while responding members were checking homes for victims and/or suspects. At this time, police began looking at a number of possible suspects as a result of the information they were receiving.

"While the situation was unfolding the Critical Incident program was engaged and staging to take control of the critical incident. During this point perimeters were established. Specialized units responded, including Police Dog Services, Emergency Response Teams and a DNR helicopter. We also had the Explosives Disposal Unit, crisis negotiators and the Emergency Medical Response Team on standby. Within a very short time, we also engaged specialized units and resources from 'J' Division in New Brunswick.

"Over a lengthy period of time, first responders engaged in clearing residences, searching for suspects, providing life-saving measures. Telecommunicators remained on the line with witnesses in the immediate area."

The RCMP and Alex Vass had had six days to think about how it would describe its actions, and this was its considered response. At face value it sounded like a workmanlike description of the police actions that night, but those paying close attention were rightfully dubious. Every word might well have been true, but I have learned over the years to be especially alert when the Mounties provide no context or firm timelines. When it comes to this shading of the truth, the RCMP way is to either omit facts or hide them in plain sight in a blizzard of sexier information.

Campbell referred to a Department of Natural Resources helicopter being employed. When? What was its mission? If there was a helicopter in the air, it would have been easy to track Wortman. He was active for five hours of daylight in a marked police car that was unique—it had a ram package.

Another intriguing comment Campbell slid in was about the call for help from New Brunswick. The RCMP could have engaged nearby municipal police forces in Truro, Amherst and Halifax, as most of their officers have superior tactical training to regular RCMP members. Why didn't they?

The Mounties had settled on a time—10:26 p.m.—when its first officer had arrived on the scene, but Campbell still didn't say when the first call had been made to 911, or by whom. The evolving police narrative was providing a timeline minus many of the times. He said several units responded to the area and "upon arriving located several people who were deceased lying in the roadway. There were several structures already on fire."

Campbell said the Mounties found the bodies "while checking homes for victims and/or suspects." We already know that whatever checking of homes police did was far from thorough, as the Mounties didn't find the murdered Tuck family until Sunday night, just as Bergerman and Leather began their disastrous first press conference.

Campbell briefly addressed public concerns about the force's short-comings, especially that its command structure seemed to have failed. He suggested that the RCMP's Critical Incident Command structure had worked as intended, but he steered clear of the obvious lapses—specifically that Wortman had slaughtered numerous people over a period of more than thirteen hours and a range of nearly 200 kilometres, almost all of it occurring well after 10:26 p.m. Saturday night.

He said the RCMP got residents to safety, implying that there was much heroism involved, without providing names or details. But it was the last line of his prepared text that caught my ear. In the middle of all that chaos, why was the RCMP "on the line with witnesses"? Which witnesses? Why were the witnesses on the phone when police were in the neighbourhood? What did that all mean? It was a perfect example of speaking in shades of truth. There was something important in that sentence, but what it was, Campbell wasn't saying.

Campbell then introduced some "new" information that everyone on social media and the street had been talking about for six days, since Sunday morning. "Before the first call came in there was an assault between the gunman and a person known to him in Portapique," Campbell said. "The victim managed to escape from the gunman and hid overnight in the woods."

He wouldn't name this victim, but Campbell said she had emerged from hiding in the woods at daybreak—6:30 a.m. "She called 911. Our officers responded and it was at that time that, through a signifi-cant key witness, we confirmed more details about Gabriel Wortman.

This included the fact that he was in possession of a fully marked and equipped replica vehicle and was wearing a police uniform. He was in possession of several firearms that included pistols and long guns."

Fully equipped? Did Wortman's car have a police radio, too?

Campbell added that there was also another victim, "a man leaving the area with an apparent gunshot wound. They [the RCMP] learned that this man was shot while driving his vehicle. The victim indicated a vehicle drove by him while he was driving, and the shot came from the passing vehicle."

Two compelling cases, the woman and the survivor who'd been shot, colourful stories that the media could readily digest. But no details, once again—the outlines of a story but not the story itself.

At one point, Campbell turned to the map on his right to illustrate the deadly path that Wortman had travelled. By then Campbell had been a resident of Nova Scotia for about seven months. His father, Lionel, might have been a dyed-in-the-wool Cape Bretoner, but Darren came across as a dreaded Come from Away. He'd had almost a week to study Wortman's route, but grew flustered trying to locate places on the map. He got directions wrong, stating that Wortman went south on Highway 4 to Wentworth when he had gone north. He nervously guessed that Glenholme was west of Wentworth, when in fact it was south, not far from Portapique.

Campbell said that a second series of calls came in "more than twelve hours after our initial arrival in Portapique." Not true. It was about eleven hours or less, sometime around 9 a.m.

He said that Wortman drove down Highway 224 to the Irving Big Stop, where he was killed, but that's not what happened. A few days later the RCMP would begin to rely on a blurry photo of a vehicle exiting Highway 102 at Enfield near a government weigh station. The RCMP said that Wortman was driving the vehicle, but it was impossible to discern the make and model of the car. The RCMP said the Enfield photo was taken at 11:23 a.m., but the official Nova Scotia government weigh-station camera was stamped 10:23 a.m. It seemed improbable that an official weigh-station camera was an hour off. The photos would be useless as documentary evidence in any court case.

Campbell stated that the police responding that night knew Wortman had a pistol and long-barrelled weapons, but that was before the female victim came out of the woods and spoke to police. However, the details about the weaponry were in the RCMP messages overnight, hours before she came out of the woods. Obviously someone else had told the RCMP about the weapons, but who?

As he read from a script, it was as if Campbell was telling someone else's story. And like Leather before him, he didn't know it inside and out. That's not how the police typically operate. This press conference was unusual to the core.

After the Mounties opened up the phone lines to the press, Campbell revealed a little more. Asked if Wortman managed to get away before the "initial response" by the RCMP, Campbell said: "I've been a police officer for almost thirty years now and I can't imagine any more horrific set of circumstances [than] when you are trying to search for someone that looks like you." He looked into the camera and continued: "The dangers that causes, the complications that causes . . . That obviously was an advantage that the suspect had on the police, that he had on the public, that he had on every person he encountered through the course of his rampage."

The Mounties were auditioning for the victim role in their own play.

Wortman did get away and had hidden somewhere undetected. Almost a week later, the RCMP had no idea where that might have been. Campbell said the force had received more recent reports that Wortman may have driven across a field and escaped to the west of Portapique, but they were still unsure. "What the suspect did during that period of time before the second cluster of incidents we do not know at this point," Campbell said. "That's why we are appealing to the public because somebody may know something, somebody may have seen something. We are collecting all the evidence and video along the way in order to retrace his steps."

Campbell was asked by Steve Scherer of Reuters about the unidentified woman who had escaped from Wortman. "I can confirm that that individual is a female, and that female was in a relationship over the course of a period of time with the gunman," the Mountie said. "That female did escape, and that female, as I indicated, had hid in the woods and was the same individual that had key information for us that was necessary for us to understand more about Mr. Wortman and what he was currently in possession of at that time."

"I don't want you to speculate, but is there a sense that this assault and the escape of his girlfriend was the trigger that set off this terrible series of events?" Scherer asked.

"Obviously, as part of the investigation, that is a consideration that we have. It could have been a catalyst to this," Campbell said. "It was a significant incident. It was a significant assault. This individual female did manage to escape, and that very well could have been the catalyst to start the chain of events. However, we are not going to discount any possibility of any preplanning at this time."

Who was this mystery woman? Was she in the hospital? Campbell clearly emphasized that she had suffered a "significant assault."

Then came a natural question from Christopher Nardi of the *National Post*, provoked by what Campbell had stated in his opening. "I wanted to ask about the use of the police cruiser," Nardi said. "Did the killer have access to a cop radio or radio frequencies? Was he aware of where your operations were headed and where you were possibly looking for him?"

The question seemed to throw Campbell off. As he considered it, his bottom lip twitched for an almost imperceptible blip. It was a dramatic microexpression of apparent discomfort, distress or even sharp pain. It was one of those things that often goes unnoticed, but once I saw it, I couldn't unsee it.

"To the best of my knowledge the suspect did not. Obviously, that was a concern after the incident with Constable Stevenson," he said, hesitating, as if he had caught himself treading into dangerous territory. "But I know that our radio channels are encrypted here in Nova Scotia. His ability to actually have some form of radio and monitor our communications, I don't believe that was an advantage that he would be given."

Looking down and seeming to close his eyes for seconds at a time, the RCMP spokesperson didn't sell the answer very well. And the segue to Heidi Stevenson suggested a possibility that Wortman knew where she was when he attacked her.

Emily Baron Cadloff, a prolific freelance reporter on assignment from *Maclean's* magazine, also had a good question: "You have mentioned the benefit of hindsight. Looking back now, is there a feeling that it was a mistake not to utilize an EMO [Emergency Management Office] message earlier in the night or morning?"

Campbell's answer was, essentially, no. But he said so much more in his reply. He had commented earlier that he "didn't like to make assumptions" and that police do not rely on assumptions, but he now revealed that they seemed to have made a crucial one: "I have had conversations with the Critical Incident Command team that was on the ground at that time and you know, you have to appreciate that they believed that they had that area contained. They believed [there were] a few possibilities: the suspect was still in the area; the suspect had escaped; or the suspect was in one of his burning residences and had actually committed suicide." The belief that Wortman hadn't escaped seemed to be rooted in a key assumption: that they had a reliable understanding of Wortman's fleet of fake police cars. "As I had mentioned earlier, we had believed that he had access to three police vehicles and there were two police-style vehicles burning on his property and there was a third police vehicle that was located at his residence in the Halifax regional municipality . . . It's fluid. It's dynamic. It's a situation that's evolving. The Critical Incident commanders consider all opportunities available to them at that time. We have a localized incident, as I mentioned earlier. It's essentially two kilometres by two kilometres, a four-kilometre square radius that was heavily locked down with a significant number of resources, so at that particular time, I can't speak for the Critical Incident commander, but [the EMO message] was not a consideration, I understand, at that particular time."

If the RCMP didn't rely on assumptions in conducting investigations, why did it assume Wortman hadn't left the area, and that the destruction of two of his police-style cars meant he'd probably committed suicide?

Another key issue was raised by the venerable Maurice Rees of the *Shoreline Journal*. The *Globe and Mail* had printed a story quoting a Glenholme resident, Nathan Staples, who said he had been told by the RCMP that he was on Wortman's hit list. An ERT member had visited his residence, about ten kilometres east of Portapique, at 12:35 a.m. on April 19, only a few hours after Wortman had begun his spree. It was a sensational, blood-curdling story that spoke to the preplanning Wortman must have undertaken.

"I understand that there was a media report published this morning that the assailant had a hit list and the person that was in the media report said that he was told by the RCMP that he was seventh or eighth on the list," Rees stated. "Can you confirm?"

Campbell said there was no such list, but what he added to his answer provided an insight into the RCMP operation that night— where it was getting its information and what it was doing with it. "While the situation in Portapique continued to unfold, there was a lot of investigative work that was going on behind the scenes. Not just those who were at the Portapique area. While we were trying to confirm the location of that third police vehicle . . . it was at that time when a critical witness [the unnamed female] came forward with critical information for us. We identified other family members who could be potentially at risk, so we were contacting individuals who we believed could have been on a list or were potentially at risk. We were contacting them. We were bringing them to safety, and we were interviewing them at that time."

Although Campbell denied the hit-list story, the image it created in the imagination of the public was indelible. The notion was set aside for the rest of the press conference, but it flourished unabated in the minds of many.

Ross Lord of Global News asked if the unnamed female was helping the RCMP.

"That former partner is a critical witness," Campbell said, upgrading her relationship status to a likely girlfriend or common-law wife. "She is being co-operative with us. She is currently recovering and with that it limits the amount of time that we can spend with her. But, of course, she is assisting us, and she is identifying other avenues of investigation that we need to pursue."

Paul Withers of CBC asked a pointed question about what guns Wortman might have used and "did he use any explosives to burn down the houses?"

Campbell replied that Wortman had used a handgun and a long gun, and that the force had tracked down the Canadian origin of one of the guns. He totally ignored the second part of the question, about explosives.

The CBC's Thomas Daigle, who had joined Andrew Douglas at the previous live press conference and had asked incisive, uncomfortable questions, got the last seat on the teleconference train. He picked up on news reports that the man Wortman had shot at and missed had told the Mounties only moments later that Wortman was driving what appeared to be a fully-decked-out police car. The time of that shooting was somewhere around 10:25 p.m. on Saturday night, but police didn't share with the public that the shooter was in such a vehicle until Sunday morning.

"Why wait twelve hours?" Daigle wanted to know.

Campbell replied that the RCMP really didn't know details about Wortman's "police car" until "the critical witness emerged from the woods" the next morning.

Daigle was right—there was a gaping discrepancy in the RCMP narrative—but the CBC reporter's challenge would be left unexplored. The teleconference was over. It hadn't been pretty, but it had achieved its purpose for the RCMP. The key narrative was set for the media. This was likely a case of domestic violence that had escalated to an unfathomable scale. A madman had beaten his partner and then set out to kill his neighbours and others, for whatever reason. The murderer's rampage was an unprecedented and near-impossible situation for the police to deal with.

But in those seventy minutes that Campbell spoke, he had given glimpses of so much hidden between the lines:

1. Campbell had called it a localized incident that the RCMP was confident it had locked down. The notion was crazy. The RCMP's own timelines were all over the place. The incident seemed to have started around 10 p.m., and the first RCMP car didn't get there until 10:26 p.m. Backups didn't get there until later, presumably much later. Campbell said the neighbourhood was a four-square-kilometre area. Wortman had plenty of time to roam around and continue killing before he left. Why did the RCMP continue to assume it was a localized incident?

2. Campbell said the police didn't like to make assumptions, but then went on to say the RCMP had speculated that Wortman was dead because officers had found three decommissioned police cars registered to him and somehow concluded that he had committed suicide because the two he kept in Portapique were on fire. At that point I wished I could have asked a question through the television screen, because it seemed to me there was a glaring flaw in that version of events. The RCMP said it knew about his decommissioned cars during the overnight hours, but never explained how it knew for a fact that Wortman was driving one. After all, he owned a number of other vehicles that were not decommissioned police vehicles—a pickup truck, an SUV, motorcycles and a Mercedes. By its own actions and statements, the RCMP was admitting that it knew Wortman was using a look-alike police car. The Mounties either had not properly digested that information or were hiding it for some unknown reason.

3. Campbell said the list of at-risk people came from Wortman's girlfriend after she emerged from the woods that morning, but the *Globe and Mail*'s report had said that Nathan Staples was visited at 12:35 a.m., while she was purportedly still hidden in the woods. Staples told the *Globe* the RCMP had told him that Wortman's girlfriend had pointed him out. If she hadn't directed police to Staples, then who had? Why did the RCMP visit Staples?

4. Campbell said that, based on what Wortman's partner told them that morning, the force evacuated certain individuals, yet it inexplicably never put out a public warning. Why were those individuals more important than the people who were eventually murdered? The natural conclusion was that the RCMP was trying to keep something hidden and hoping to find a quiet resolution.

5. Campbell said twenty-five or more resources were dispatched to Portapique. Who? When? From where? No timelines were given.

6. Campbell said he didn't know of Wortman having a police radio—which is not the same as saying Wortman did not have a police radio. I couldn't get Campbell's pained microexpression out of my head.

◆

It was easy to see why the RCMP preferred a teleconference over a live press briefing. Each reporter got to ask a question and perhaps a follow-up before the moderator moved on to the next. It was the illusion of an interview being conducted in public—the verisimilitude of accountability. There was no room for any reporter to pursue the discrepancies and gaps evident in Campbell's narrative. In such circumstances, even the most intrepid reporters are reduced to Conradian stenographers.

As I watched Darren Campbell, I wished I could be a reporter again, just for this story. I sensed there was so much that needed to be done, but even if I did it, who could I write for? I had disappeared myself. I was a nobody. Few knew or remembered me, and those who did likely thought I'd gone soft, fiddling with all that glass. I tossed the notion aside and decided I would leave it up to the ones who were getting paid to do it. Maybe I could help them out a little with a news tidbit here and an insight there.

12

THE INTERLUDE BETWEEN THE MASSACRES

It had been twelve years and two months since Lindsay Jones had worked in the daily media, after, along with everyone else, being unceremoniously thrown out on the streets when the doors of the Halifax *Daily News* were shuttered in 2008. Things had worked out for her, though. She was married to a lawyer, had a few children and was living in Halifax's south end—the posh side of "the Peninsula." Her husband's family owned a farmhouse up north in Wentworth, an idyllic weekend retreat for the family. Nowadays, she dabbled in journalism as a freelancer, trying to find space for her long, detailed pieces in the dwindling number of publications across Canada. The coalescence of the COVID-19 lockdown and Gabriel Wortman's murderous rampage meant reporters from outside the Maritimes wouldn't be flocking east. One of Jones's regular clients was the *Globe and Mail*, Canada's self-proclaimed national newspaper. She was in the right spot at the right time. It would prove to be a busy month for Jones.

Trying to make sense out of Wortman's killing spree and the police response to it was all but impossible, because so much of it didn't make any sense. Anyone looking at a map of Nova Scotia could readily see there was just about no way that Gabriel Wortman should have been able to escape Portapique that night. A week later, no one had any idea where he had been during those freezing overnight hours. Had someone taken him in? Did he have an accomplice? Would the police find more dead bodies somewhere?

The gritty and enterprising Jones used the family farmhouse, which was close to Portapique, as a base of operations and began to try to learn all she could. Roadside memorials were popping up at the places where people had been murdered. There was a large one at the Portapique community hall. There were two on Plains Road in Debert, one for nurse Kristen Beaton and the other for her colleague Heather O'Brien. It was at one of those memorials that Jones stumbled onto her first clues to what the RCMP might have done at Portapique Beach.

RCMP sergeant David Lilly was a twenty-three-year veteran of the force. As Jones described it, Lilly and his wife had driven to the various memorials to pay their respects ahead of an online vigil scheduled for that Friday night. When Lilly, in full ceremonial dress, spoke to Jones, his voice cracked with emotion, she wrote. Her story was published two days later in the *Globe and Mail*. In it, Jones captured both valuable new information and the fudgy essence of the original RCMP narrative in just five short paragraphs.

"We feel guilty. We wish we could've done more," he said, dressed in his formal uniform of red serge tunic and Stetson. "Any of us would've taken a bullet for any of these victims."

. . . When RCMP arrived at 10:26 p.m. on April 18, they found people dead on the road and several homes engulfed in flames. Inside some of the homes, they found more victims.

Sgt. Lilly drove the children of Lisa McCully, one of the victims in Portapique, to a nearby hospital. When he returned, a perimeter had been set up in the beachfront community to contain the area.

At that point, RCMP say they knew who they were looking for. They knew the gunman had a pistol and long-barrelled guns. His home and garages were ablaze as were two of his replica police cars and another vehicle. They thought they had the scene contained, Sgt. Lilly said. So he and some of his colleagues headed for home, at around 6:30 or 7 a.m. on April 19.

"A lot of us broke off and went home after an exhausting night," he said. "I went to bed thinking he was gone and finished and contained. And if I would have known [the shooter was still at large], I would've stayed out and continued looking, but we didn't know. We tried our best and we're feeling guilty that we sort of failed in that regard."

Police are generally not big on contrition, so Sergeant Lilly's statement "We feel guilty" was a highly unusual admission that some Mounties knew they had fumbled the ball. Coming from someone like Lilly, it was even more noteworthy. He was seen as a no-nonsense, true-blue member of the police brotherhood, the kind of guy who didn't take outside criticism of the force lightly.

Jones reiterated the original RCMP narrative that the rampage began after Wortman had assaulted his unnamed partner, and when the Mounties first arrived at the scene they had found bodies on the road and several homes in flames. I was beginning to wonder if things really had played out that way. From all I had read or seen, someone in Wortman's situation usually kills the object of their affection first and then goes on a rampage. They don't save that person for the end. Then again, maybe this was a new twist on an old crime. Time and investigation would tell.

Lilly told Jones he had driven Lisa McCully's children to the hospital. That seemed reasonable. The children were home when McCully was killed; someone had to take them out. However, following the vague timelines begrudgingly doled out by the RCMP, the children would presumably have been removed from the house around or shortly after 10:35 p.m., when the RCMP cavalry began to arrive in Portapique. Jones also reported Lilly as saying that when he returned to Portapique from the hospital—about a forty-five-minute round trip without any lingering—"a perimeter had been set up." Once again, there was no set time given by police for when this all happened.

Jones wrote that "at that point"—sometime after midnight—the Mounties knew who they were looking for and that he was armed with various weapons. This was confirmed later elsewhere. If the RCMP knew all this around midnight, why did it not put out a broader alert? Instead, Campbell had promoted the scenario that police didn't know the full details about Wortman until his unnamed partner came out of the woods at 6:30 a.m.

Finally, deep into the story came the biggest news in Jones's report— the prototypical buried lede: that most of the Mounties had called it a night and gone home at 6:30 a.m. It was an astonishing revelation, something the apologetic Sergeant Lilly was unlikely authorized to divulge and had let slip inadvertently. Over the previous week RCMP leaders Lee Bergerman, Chris Leather and Darren Campbell had only vaguely described what the Mounties had done that night. They each had suggested that members performed heroically, sealed off the area and evacuated those in harm's way—the very things police are supposed to do.

If Lilly's description was accurate, the RCMP had assumed Wortman had killed himself and let its collective guard down. With all the chaos and destruction in Portapique, it seems counterintuitive that the RCMP would call it a night just because there were no more bullets flying. No police force in this day and age, not even the dysfunctional RCMP, could be that incompetent. What was really going on?

In a normally functioning, competitive journalistic milieu, the collective media would have jumped on what Jones had reported and shared it with everyone who read newspapers, watched television, listened to the radio or got their information from the Internet. But that world barely exists today. During the first week after the massacres, the *Globe and Mail* team led by reporter Greg Mercer had consistently brought out new information, most of it good, some of it not. In the grand scheme of things, though, their work didn't mean much to Nova Scotians. The *Globe* may well aspire to be a national newspaper, but its reach in the Maritimes is limited. As for its "competition," the CBC, CTV, Global News and the *Halifax Examiner*, to name some, occasionally broke new ground, but most in the media were too often parroting every word generated by the RCMP.

The net result was that parts of the whole story were being reported, but the vast majority of the public were only getting fragments of it— and the RCMP and its enablers weren't going to help make it any more easily understood than what they deemed necessary.

◆

It was now Friday night, six days after Wortman had begun his spree and five days since it had ended. While the Mounties were asking the public for clues, the public was at a vigil online—Nova Scotia Remembers. It took the form of an online kitchen party, where people were expected to imagine themselves jammed into close quarters in a noisy, smoky kitchen, listening to beer glasses clinking, rum bottles draining and politicians spewing. And then there was all that Nova Scotian music.

The vigil was hosted by Nova Scotian actor Jonathan Torrens, who made his name in the cult hit *Trailer Park Boys* and later, among other things, in the internationally renowned Canadian comedy series *Letterkenny*. The governor general read a statement, as did the prime minister, standing in front of his Ottawa home. Every available Nova Scotian celebrity made an appearance. During the week, Premier Stephen McNeil had worn a blue-and-green Nova Scotia tartan pocket square and had urged everyone to wear the tartan or at least something blue to show their solidarity. In his brief comments at the kitchen party, the often-sullen premier continued the theme, stating that he would be wearing tartan at home in remembrance of the victims. A few other local politicians got bromides in as well. Hockey star Sidney Crosby called in from Pittsburgh. Actor and director Cory Bowles, also of *Trailer Park Boys* fame, shared the spotlight with a priest, a rabbi and preachers from every major denomination.

While the universal message imparted by all was about grieving and healing, Torrens, who had lived in Colchester County for twelve years, captured the larger ethos. "As you can imagine, over the last several days, the people here have been reeling, trying to make sense of something that just doesn't make sense," he said. "It feels like there are millions of questions and no answers, so much pain, so much sadness."

A dozen Nova Scotian musicians made an appearance, including Heather Rankin, George Canyon, Jenn Grant, Matt Minglewood, Reeny Smith, J.P. Cormier, the Stanfields, Rose Cousins, Dave Gunning, Chad Peck, Charlie A'Court and rapper Classified. But two musicians stole the show with an indelible performance. A month earlier, the first Ultimate Online Nova Scotia Kitchen Party had been held in response to the COVID lockdown. It featured music, of course, and one of the performers that night, broadcasting from her living room in Portapique, was seventeen-year-old Emily Tuck.

Aaron Tuck introduced his daughter. His voice was a bit raspy and gruff. You could hear all those cigarettes and beer when he spoke. He had a noticeable down-home accent, but in those few words you could hear how much he loved his girl. Wearing plaid pyjama bottoms tied at her ankles and a crop top exposing her midriff, the bespectacled teenager played the first tune she had ever learned, the waltz "In Memory of Herbie MacLeod."

Stephen Maher, a journalist who grew up in Truro and who at the time of the shootings was working in Ottawa for *Maclean's*, described the video this way in the magazine:

> "OK," says her dad. "Your contribution to the COVID kitchen party."
>
> "Herbie MacLeod," she says, and smiles shyly, and then bends to her fiddle and lifts her bow.
>
> "Wicked," he says, right proud of her.
>
> The song is *In Memory of Herbie MacLeod*, a sad but sweet air, written by late Cape Breton fiddler Jerry Holland in honour of a friend in Massachusetts who often hosted travelling Capers. It is a slow waltz, wistful and lilting, with a bittersweet Celtic sadness, and in the video Emily plays it well, head bent, intent.
>
> Then, when she finishes, she grins at her dad, her chin stuck out with pride. "There's some fiddle for ya."

After Emily's murder, Cape Breton fiddle virtuoso Natalie MacMaster saw her performance on YouTube and decided to perform a tribute to Emily during the online vigil. "She was a fiddler, so I thought I would unite myself to her performance and play this tune for all the souls who lost their lives," MacMaster said from her home in Toronto.

Now Emily's video was being replayed on a split screen. She was in the middle, with MacMaster on one side of her and an unidentified female pianist tickling the ivories on the other. It was a heart-rending dirge made even sadder by the situation—a young, obviously energetic spirit so cruelly snuffed out.

Emily's last line and the way she delivered it said so much about the Tucks. "There's some fiddle for ya."

Yes, it was.

♦

One week after Gabriel Wortman was brought down and two days after Superintendent Campbell's appeal for help from the public, Brian MacDonald said had a feeling that Gabriel Wortman might have been around his welding shop in Debert, 26 kilometres from Portapique.

For those keeping count, Brian is the fifth MacDonald in this story. He is not related to the other four. The name and its variations, such as McDonald, are more popular in this province than Smith, which comes second. One of every fifty-seven Nova Scotians is a McDonald or MacDonald. In the spirit of full disclosure, I, too, have distant Nova Scotia relatives named MacDonald who are also unrelated and were not involved in these events, as far as I know.

Brian MacDonald knew Wortman and had worked on his dozens of motorbikes and a backhoe over the years. MacDonald hadn't seen Wortman since the previous summer, when he had visited Wortman's Portapique warehouse. He didn't see a replica police car there at that time.

He didn't see Wortman at his welding shop the night of the Portapique murders, either, but he didn't need to. "I knew that he was around somewhere, and I didn't know where," MacDonald told the CBC's Haley Ryan. "I just had a feeling that he was here."

MacDonald's shop is located at 123 Ventura Drive in an industrial park on the site of what was once a Royal Canadian Air Force station and munitions dump. The welding shop is built into the thick earthen and concrete walls of one of the now abandoned ammunition bunkers, which are spread out over several acres.

Today the industrial park houses a number of businesses, including the Farmhouse Bakery, a paintball facility and a relic of the Cold War, the Debert Diefenbunker, which is next to MacDonald's welding shop. The underground facility—now a tourist attraction—was one of two named after former prime minister John Diefenbaker and was part of Canada's nuclear war defence strategy, a vestige of the late 1950s and early 1960s. The other, larger Diefenbunker is near Ottawa. Wortman was fascinated by the Debert Diefenbunker and had visited it on a number of occasions.

That Sunday morning, MacDonald and his daughter, Leah MacDonald-White, decided to check out the wooded area behind the welding shop. There used to be a structure there that someone might be able to hide a car under, but it had been demolished. There is access to the area from Messina Drive, an empty dead-end road that had long been awaiting development. A path ran off it behind MacDonald's business. Alongside that path MacDonald and his daughter found an empty gun holster, leather RCMP dress boots and an empty box of shells and cartridges.

"I knew right then it was him. He put them there," MacDonald told me in an interview.

He called the RCMP, and officers arrived within an hour and searched the area. They collected a number of items and marked the locations with ribbons tied to branches, bushes and plants. The Mounties didn't tell MacDonald what else they found: a pair of Canadian-made Nuknuuk slippers.

Now that the Mounties knew where Wortman had been after leaving Portapique, they scoured the area. High up on the wall of the Farmhouse Bakery building was a surveillance camera, which covered part of Ventura Drive. The Mounties looked at the video. In a future press briefing that June, they would say they found two important images. One showed what appeared to be an RCMP cruiser entering Ventura Drive at about 11:12 p.m. on April 18. The Mounties were on record saying they believed Wortman had left Portapique at 10:35 p.m. It was only a twenty- to twenty-five-minute drive between the two points. What was Wortman doing for those extra twelve to seventeen minutes?

The second image showed what appeared to be an RCMP cruiser creeping through the darkness and leaving Ventura Drive at 5:43 a.m., about forty-seven minutes before sunrise.

Both images were hazy and unconvincing. The car's ID number couldn't be seen, nor whether it had a push bar, but the Mounties stood by their story that the person in the videos was Wortman, driving his replica police car. How could they possibly have known for certain?

13

THE SECOND MASSACRE,
PART 1: HUNTER ROAD

Alanna Jenkins was up early that Sunday morning, as she and her partner, Sean McLeod, usually were. The sun had just begun to rise. At 6:26 a.m. Jenkins texted Angie Brown, a Facebook friend who was searching for the necessities that any grandmother might need to make her house suitable for a new grandchild. Jenkins had a stockpile of kids' clothes and other useful things from her own grandmotherly years, although Jenkins technically wasn't a grandmother. The object of her affection, Ellie, was the child of Sean's daughter from his first marriage.

In the darkness shortly before dawn, Gabriel Wortman left the Debert industrial park and made his way up Plains Road to where it ended at Highway 4, the old two-lane Trans-Canada Highway route that crosses Nova Scotia. The narrow highway had claimed many lives before the four-lane was built to the south through the Cobequid Pass.

Wortman turned right on the highway and headed north up Folly Mountain, past Folly Lake and through the Wentworth Valley into Cumberland County. To his right was Ski Wentworth, the largest ski resort in Nova Scotia, with just one chairlift, three ground lifts and a maximum drop of about 250 metres. After about twenty minutes Wortman turned his replica RCMP cruiser into the lot of Wentworth Market, a one-pump rural gas station, grocery and mini-liquor outlet. Nothing was open until 7 a.m.

Depending on one's point of view, the property could be viewed as either a tribute to lax zoning standards or an architect's nightmare. The main market was a typical one-storey country store with a shingled facade. Jammed into its northern wall was a long, galvanized steel Quonset hut, looking very much like a caterpillar burrowing into the wall. The liquor store was in the Quonset hut. Wortman drove across the dirt parking lot and turned in behind the Quonset hut, where he parked. We don't know what he did there. The RCMP insisted that he didn't have a police radio, and in future documents they would add that he didn't have a cellphone.

As the sun came up, Wortman left Wentworth Market and continued up Highway 4. It was a short drive to cross the bridge over the Wallace River into West Wentworth, and then after a few more kilometres he turned right onto Hunter Road. As Alanna Jenkins was texting Angie Brown about a baby swing at 6:26 a.m., Wortman was already on Hunter Road. The water table is high here, and Mother Nature need work up only a bit of a sweat to turn parts of the dirt and gravel roads spongy and almost impassable. It was a five-kilometre drive for Wortman from Highway 4 to 2328 Hunter Road. At 6:29 a.m. a surveillance camera on the house of Lisa Owen and Darrol Thurier, at 2205 Hunter Road, caught the fake police car passing by. The mass murderer was closing in on McLeod and Jenkins.

McLeod, forty-four, and Jenkins, thirty-seven, were federal corrections officers. They were both keepers, the old-fashioned name by which current managers are known inside Correctional Service Canada. McLeod was a unit keeper at Springhill Institution, a medium-security men's facility that was a thirty-minute drive to the west, just inside the border with New Brunswick. He ran Unit 57. It was a day job. He was known as a solid, respected officer who enjoyed an especially good rapport with Indigenous co-workers and inmates. Recently, he had been studying Native healing practices and had become fascinated with cleansing. When he'd left work on Friday, the only thing left on his desk was a smudge kit that he intended to give to a friend.

Jenkins was a desk keeper at the Nova Institution for Women in Truro. The twenty-five-year-old facility is a smaller operation that houses about seventy prisoners. It has a maximum-security component. Her job was to brief and deploy staff and implement orders from the warden. When the warden is away, a desk keeper runs the institution.

McLeod and Jenkins had been living together for five years on Hunter Road with their two black Labrador retrievers, Bama and Remi. McLeod had bought the house in 2009 during his second marriage, which lasted three years. The nine-acre park-like setting was the epitome of serenity. The chalet-style 1,542-square-foot house sat on the edge of a 10-metre bank, looking down to the meandering Wallace River.

There were about a dozen permanent residents on Hunter Road. Many of the rest had cottages, or camps, as the locals call them. The phrase "close-knit community" is often bandied about when it comes to small towns and hamlets, but Hunter Road was the very definition of it. After work that Friday, Sean and his brother Scott, also a corrections officer at Springhill, had run some errands together. One was picking up a couple of cases of beer for Sean's neighbour Tom Bagley. When the brothers parted ways, Sean headed to Hunter Road, while Scott made his way over the New Brunswick border to Moncton.

On Hunter Road, the residents liked to party together, be it on land or on the water. In the summer there might be rafting and kayaking along the fast-moving Wallace as it made its way north. At other times there would be "camp hopping" from one property to another. During the winter there would be a monthly get-together—lotto night. Everyone would throw in $20, eat, drink and listen to music. At the end of the night, there might be as much as $450 in the kitty and the winner would get $300 of it. Second prize was the remainder. The deal was that everyone else had to be told what the winners purchased with their windfall. The McLeod house, with its vaulted living room ceiling and stacked windows, was long the favourite venue. McLeod had even built himself an outdoor "man cave" where he could store his fishing gear, smoke, drink and listen to music.

Both McLeod and Jenkins had a past with Wortman. After his first marriage broke up, McLeod had moved in with a friend who owned a place in Great Village. His friend eventually bought another house on Portapique Beach Road, north of Wortman's cottage at number 200. McLeod had two daughters from his first marriage: Amielia, who was his biological daughter, and Taylor, who was fathered by another man. He had raised Taylor as his own and acted as her official guardian.

In the confines of the tiny Portapique community, it didn't take long for Wortman and McLeod to meet. They were both into fishing and hunting, and especially the guns that come with the latter. McLeod was in law enforcement and Wortman was fascinated by anyone in the vocation. McLeod became part of the Portapique Beach drinking club circle. It was a curious relationship. Over the previous twenty years Wortman had barely concealed the fact that he had made loads of money smuggling and selling illegal cigarettes and prescription drugs as well as other illegal contraband across the border from Maine into New Brunswick. For whatever reason, McLeod gave some law enforcement paraphernalia to his new friend, who was an avid collector. One of the items was a set of real handcuffs.

After McLeod met and married his second wife, they purchased the house on Hunter Road. McLeod and Wortman remained friends throughout the intervening years, although McLeod's father, Dale, and his brothers, Scott and Chris, said in interviews that Sean had not brought up Wortman's name until recently.

"He had offered to make some dentures for my father," Scott said in an interview. "He promised him a better price, but at the end of the day, he got them from someone else."

Alanna Jenkins brought an unlikely credential to her relationship with McLeod: she had experience as a third wife. In her first marriage, she was the third and much younger wife of former Springhill warden Alfred Legere. The marriage didn't last long, and by the time Jenkins left, Legere was a broken man and virtually penniless. They never divorced.

In 2013, after leaving Legere, Jenkins appears to have met Wortman, who was already in a long-term relationship. There are two distinct views about whether they started a relationship of their own. Some say it happened; others say it didn't. Jenkins's family members, including her father, Dan, her brother, Josh, and McLeod's daughter, Taylor, are adamant that she never had a relationship with Wortman.

"Alanna would have had nothing to do with someone like him," said Dan Jenkins. "She was an absolutely beautiful person. We know everything she did. She never did anything without us. To say anything like that about her is pure innuendo. If you say that, I will hire a lawyer and sue you." Josh Jenkins's remarks were somewhat more colourful.

There is no question that many people liked Alanna Jenkins. She was always organizing events, and ever mindful of birthdays and special occasions. She spent wads of money on McLeod's daughters and was more their friend and drinking buddy than a parental figure. On April 18, she and McLeod had ridden down the road on their four-wheeler to deliver a birthday present to neighbour April Dares. "They gave me two tallboys of beer," Dares said. "She was really sweet that way."

But others—members of the McLeod family, friends and acquaintances of Jenkins and confidential sources inside policing—say Jenkins had an undeniable wild side and was a bit of a risk-taker. Many of them believe Jenkins did have a previous, hidden relationship with Wortman. In 2013, for example, police officers from Amherst, Nova Scotia, who were on vacation in Cuba found themselves staying at the same resort as Jenkins. They knew her from work and noticed that she was with a man wearing an RCMP T-shirt. That man was Wortman, they say. Naturally, they approached Wortman and tried to chat him up. He was reticent about talking to real police officers and left without speaking to them. He then made himself virtually invisible for the rest of the week.

While McLeod and Jenkins's partnership looked solid to some family and friends, there were growing cracks. One relative, who asked not to be named, told me that there were suspicions about the source of "all the money they had and were spending. They seemed to have more money than they should have had, or they were deeply in debt."

Prior to his relationship with Jenkins, McLeod would regularly visit his parents in Truro, but that had become a rare occasion. "After he was with Alanna, he'd drop in for a few minutes and never even take his coat off," Scott McLeod said. "They spent most of their time with Alanna's family." But a few days before April 19, Sean visited his parents alone. He sat down and had a coffee, which was a pleasant surprise. He'd recently taken his mother, Audrey, to a doctor's appointment in Halifax. She was largely bedridden, suffering from advanced cancer in multiple organs. "He told her that he wasn't happy with himself," Scott said. "He was tired of all the parties and the drinking. Things were getting out of hand. At their last St. Patrick's Day party, one of the neighbours was dropping the 'N' bomb in front of one of Sean's Black friends. The neighbour wouldn't relent and said to him, 'This is me and this is how I talk.' One thing led to another and they took it outside and got into a scrap over it. Sean wanted to take a break but said that Alanna didn't want to. She kept bringing people over."

In the days and weeks leading up to April 19, McLeod and Jenkins were in contact with Wortman, as they had long been occasional visitors to 200 Portapique Beach Road. Jenkins had lost a tooth and Wortman had offered to build a replacement for her. McLeod eventually became angry with what he believed was Wortman's open flirting with Jenkins. "Sean thought that Wortman was trying to hook up with Alanna, so he confronted him and told him to piss off and stay away from us," Scott McLeod says.

At around 6:31 a.m. that morning Gabriel Wortman pulled into the long driveway and approached the house. We don't know if Jenkins had caught wind of the trouble in Portapique. We don't know if Wortman had contacted her from the parking lot of Wentworth Market. If he did, perhaps he wanted to see if she knew anything about what he had been up to. He certainly didn't want to show up incautiously at a house with as much weaponry as McLeod and Jenkins had on site, along with the requisite professional training and experience to use it. To Wortman's advantage, however, McLeod's gun cabinet was in the basement.

We don't know and will likely never know what happened inside 2328 Hunter Road that morning. Scott McLeod said he was told by a person close to the investigation that Jenkins may have tried to place a 911 call but there was a problem identifying her location, which is common with some cellphone calls and land lines that use Voice over Internet Protocol (VoIP). The police refused to release 911 tapes, and it could not be confirmed whether such a call was made.

What we do know is that between 6:40 and 7:00 a.m. neighbours heard three shots. Two of the witnesses were Cindy and Carlyle Brown (no relation to Angie—Brown is the third most common surname in Nova Scotia). Like McLeod, Jenkins and three or four others on the road, Carlyle had been a corrections officer. He had retired eleven years earlier. Cindy was a retired nurse, but was still putting in shifts at the hospital in Springhill. They lived in Springhill but had come to their camp that weekend to turn on the water. The evening before, McLeod and Jenkins had shared some drinks and talk with the Browns before going home at around 7 p.m. "Sean said he was going to put some steaks on the barbecue and have a quiet night," Cindy Brown said.

The next morning, Cindy said, "It was sometime before 7 a.m. We heard three shots and a dog yelp each time and then it went silent. We didn't think anything of it because you always hear gunshots around here."

Others heard those first shots, too, but had a more specific time. "It was between 6:25 and 6:30 a.m. when I heard a vehicle go by," said April Dares. "There aren't many cars passing by here and you pretty well know the sound of everyone's vehicle. I always look out. It was around 6:40 a.m. that I heard the dog yelping. I heard three yelps and then nothing. I said to myself: 'What the fuck was that.' I sat there for awhile and the feeling wouldn't leave me. At 7:30 a.m. I went down the road to check and see if there was a dead dog, but I didn't go right to Sean and Alanna's house. Thankfully, a little voice told me I'd gone far enough, and I turned around and went home."

Neighbours also heard muffled shots, likely from inside the house. Wortman lingered at 2328 Hunter Road for about two hours and forty-five minutes. Scott McLeod said his brother talked about having secret hiding places built into the house but didn't know what was in them. What was Wortman doing all that time? Was he searching for something, perhaps guns or ammunition? Sean McLeod's body was found in charred wreckage where the bedroom would have been. Jenkins's remains were found near his. One of the dogs, Bama, was found dead out back over the bank to the river. Remi's body was in the house.

Having worked in a funeral home for a time, Wortman wasn't uncomfortable around dead people. In fact, he saw so many cadavers with dentures or holes in their smiles that they were what led him to become a denturist. Sometime after 9 a.m. Wortman began to burn the house down. He hadn't burned down the Tucks' house or the Bonds' or Lisa McCully's. He had made a half-hearted attempt to set the Blairs' house on fire by pulling logs out of the fireplace and setting them on the floor. Why burn down McLeod's house? Was there evidence there that might be embarrassing?

Neighbours noticed the smoke. "The night before Sean said he was going to burn some brush in the morning, and I thought that's what he was doing," said Cindy Brown. "Then he said that Alanna's parents were coming over for the day. When we smelled the smoke, we didn't think much of it."

For seventy-year-old Tom Bagley, it was a beautiful Sunday morning in his favourite place on earth. He and his wife, Patsy Aucoin, had a house in Elmsdale, but had bought an old hunting cabin on Hunter Road from a friend. Over the years in their retirement, they had fixed it up and were now spending more and more time at their camp. It was located on the other side of the road from McLeod and Jenkins's, and a couple of properties to the north.

Bagley was a former leading seaman in the Canadian Navy, and he had spent thirty-one years as a professional firefighter at Halifax's international airport and twenty years as a volunteer firefighter in Elmsdale and Enfield. He had paramedic training. He was president of his local union for a time, and he loved Harley-Davidson motorcycles.

That morning, as always, Patsy talked to their daughter, Charlene, on speakerphone. Tom was in the background, weighing in here and there. The conversation ended around 8:30 a.m. Tom and Patsy were totally unaware of what was going on in the world beyond Hunter Road. At around 8:50 a.m., Tom went for his regular morning walk, complete with walking stick.

"He had ear cancer a couple of times and was nearly deaf," Charlene Bagley says. "I don't believe he brought his hearing aids with him."

Bagley was the social type. Any walk might be a short stroll or a long one. Neighbours got used to hearing the tap-tap of his walking stick on a windowpane announcing that he was stopping by for a chat.

On his way down the road, Bagley would have passed 2328 Hunter Road on his left. He likely went down to the one-lane rickety bridge a few hundred metres down the road, or maybe even crossed it.

"I think he was on his way home and something caught his attention at Sean's house and he decided to investigate," said Charlene. She said her father wasn't shy about dealing with the injured or dying. He'd seen plenty of catastrophe over his years in the navy and fire departments.

We don't know if Wortman had yet started the fire, but Bagley ventured down the long driveway, likely curious about the police car parked there. He dropped his walking stick, probably thinking he would collect it later.

"If there was smoke, he likely thought the police were already there," Charlene says, "and he would go down and offer to help."

As Bagley got closer to the house, he probably saw one of the dead dogs near the deck on the south side of the house. We don't know if he went into the house, but some observers have speculated that he might well have because it was in his nature. He might also have taken off his boots when he did.

Whatever happened, Wortman confronted Bagley and shot him three times. One of the shots was at extremely close range. Bagley fell face first to the ground, his head toward the river.

Everything on the property, even McLeod and Jenkins's vehicles, was soon on fire. Wortman got into his car, pulled onto the road and started the five-kilometre drive back down to Highway 4. He was recorded at 9:23 a.m. by the same security camera that caught him going up the road at 6:29 a.m.

"I saw him go by," said April Dares. "He was in no hurry."

Neighbours were calling 911 and began to congregate as the fire took hold. Ammunition inside the house and propane tanks were exploding. A volunteer firefighter showed up but left when told there had been gunfire. Darrol Thurier found Tom Bagley's body lying a few feet from the deck. The intense flames had singed his clothes and severely burned part of his upper body.

During her call to 911, Lisa Owen was asked to check Bagley for vital signs. "So I had to go over and look at him and tell them, and verify that, you know, there were no signs of life," Owen told the CBC's Haley Ryan. "It's your friend, you know. It's hard."

Cindy and Carlyle Brown loaded their dog into their car and decided that they would drive to their home in Springhill. They were in such a hurry that they forgot their cat. Cindy's phone was recording as it rested on the console, shooting up at the mirror and through the windshield. First there was blue sky and a few clouds, and then smoke from the fire billowed over the car. They were beyond frantic. "I think she knows," Cindy said, referring to the dog. "Oh my gosh. Oh my gosh," she said as Carlyle slammed on the brakes and warned people to "Go back, go back, because there's gunshots and Sean's house is on fire."

Carlyle then called 911: "I'd like to report a fire," he said. "There's gunfire."

A few minutes later the Browns followed in Wortman's tracks. They didn't see a police car during the six minutes or so it took them to reach Highway 4. They turned right and headed to Springhill. Along the way they came across four RCMP cruisers, likely coming from Oxford, Springhill or even Pugwash to the west, heading in the direction of Hunter Road.

"They didn't look like they were in much of a hurry," Carlyle Brown said. "They didn't have on their flashing lights or sirens."

Meanwhile, back on Hunter Road, Patsy Aucoin called her daughter, Charlene, at 9:43 a.m. and told her that "Sean's man cave was on fire." That was all Patsy could see from her vantage point. She wasn't too worried about her husband because she was used to him going to someone's rescue.

"Where's Dad?" Charlene asked.

"He hasn't come back from his walk yet," Patsy said.

"Yeah, he's probably there," Charlene said.

"Yeah."

Later they learned the devastating news, some of it very strange and disturbing. Tom had been burned when the house he lay outside was torched. His boots were missing. Maybe they had burned up inside the house. Charlene Bagley wanted answers. "My father's boots were missing," she said. "I think Wortman took his boots. And I wanted his phone back. It would have been in the left inside pocket of his coat, but the police said it was destroyed in the fire. I don't believe them."

The answers never came.

14

THE SECOND MASSACRE, PART 2: NO ROADBLOCKS

Approaching her sixty-fifth birthday, Lillian Campbell Hyslop and her husband, Michael, were enjoying their retirement in the scenic Wentworth Valley. They had moved there in 2014, after Michael had inherited a property that sat near the corner of highways 4 and 246, known locally as the 4 and the New Annan Road.

It was a good fit genealogically for her, a return to her roots, as it were. Lillian Campbell (no relation to RCMP superintendent Darren Campbell) was raised in the Scottish settlements of Glengarry County in Eastern Ontario, which were founded in 1784 by United Empire Loyalists who fled across the border from New York State. The area had long clung to the Gaelic language, just as Gaelic traditions continued to thrive in northern Nova Scotia and Cape Breton Island. There was even a Gaelic college not terribly far from Lillian's new home—Colaisde na Gàidhlig, just south of Englishtown, of all places, on Cape Breton.

Between Lillian's Ontario childhood and Nova Scotia retirement, she and Michael had spent thirty years in Yukon, which was about as far from Nova Scotia as they could reside in Canada. Lillian worked as a nurse at Whitehorse General Hospital and later for the Yukon government in its health services branch. She sang alto in a choir. As Gabrielle Plonka described it in the Whitehorse *Daily Star*, Lillian and Michael were active in the "mushing community." They raised sled dogs when they lived in the Grizzly Valley. Michael had once managed the Yukon Quest, a 1,000-mile international sled dog race that runs every February from Fairbanks, Alaska, to Whitehorse. In later years, both he and Lillian volunteered during the race, which could take ten to sixteen days to complete over exceptionally rugged terrain.

"Her nature, her compassion, her gentleness, her spirits were just so good," Lisa Triggs, an old friend of Lillian's, told Plonka. "She would walk into a room and literally, Lillian would scan the room and right away from across the room she'll smile at you and make you feel like you're the only person in that room. I think her nature is just what made her an exceptional soul. There was nothing violent about her nature; she was always kind. She could deal with any situation."

After breakfast on the morning of April 19, Lillian put on her safety vest and got ready for her regular morning walk down to Old Station Road—almost 10 kilometres there and back. Neither she nor Michael had any idea about the horror going on all around them. There had been no alerts. Even those who had access to and could decipher the RCMP's tweets could be forgiven for not recognizing the extreme danger. No one knew where Wortman was.

Shortly after Lillian went out the door, around 9:30 a.m., Michael began to hear from friends about the murders. The RCMP was in the midst of responding to the first 911 calls from Hunter Road, about 13 kilometres to the north. By that time Lillian had already turned the corner and was heading south on the 4.

As Wortman sped along the smooth, recently paved highway, the RCMP was nowhere in sight. Cindy and Carlyle Brown had seen four RCMP cars coming from Oxford or Springhill, but they were well behind Wortman in Cumberland County. He was headed back to Colchester County. Same police force. Different jurisdictions. Under normal circumstances, they aren't tuned in to the same assistance channel.

The RCMP said it knew from Wortman's partner that he might be targeting other people. Even though a public warning hadn't been put out, the RCMP on its own or with the assistance of Halifax Regional Police had evacuated or offered protection to a number of people, including former lawyer and now judge Alain Bégin. With the flood of 911 calls coming in from Hunter Road around 9:15 a.m., the RCMP had to know where Wortman was and that he was continuing to kill.

Wortman drove for about six minutes from Hunter Road and was approaching the New Annan Road intersection. He could likely see Lillian Hyslop turning the corner and walking away from him on the other side of the road. She got a little more than 100 metres down the road, just past the big, green rectangular road sign alerting drivers to turn right for West New Annan and Tatamagouche.

It was around 9:34 a.m. when Wortman either drove across the highway or made a U-turn, stopped near Hyslop, took aim at her head with his laser sight and shot her, killing her instantly. She was his seventeenth victim in about eleven and a half hours. A witness called 911 immediately and said they had "heard a bang" and seen an RCMP car leaving the area.

At 9:43 a.m. the RCMP alerted the Truro Police Service that a woman was lying by the side of the road and may have been hit by a police car. The RCMP cars responding to the call would have been coming from Oxford, Springhill or even Pugwash, a little farther away but still closer than Truro.

Wortman continued on his way south. By now, even he had to be amazed by the lack of police presence. He was driving down a main highway, heading back to the very area where he'd started killing, and there wasn't a roadblock to be found. A few kilometres down the road he reached Folly Lake and was back in Colchester County. A few minutes after that he crested Folly Mountain and began his downhill descent to near sea level. In the middle distance he could see the sun glistening off his beloved Cobequid Bay. Did he wonder if he would ever witness those glorious tides again? Or did he have a plan to somehow escape with his life?

Soon he was back at the intersection with Plains Road, from which he had come earlier that morning. He didn't turn, and continued south. About 400 metres down the road on his right was the Hidden Hilltop Family Campground. He had driven about 41 kilometres in twenty-five minutes and had killed Lillian Hyslop along the way. He had so far gone undetected, but now there was a Mountie approaching him from the other direction.

The Mountie passed him and recognized Wortman's vehicle. The RCMP says the time was 9:47 a.m. The location they provided was not specific. The Mountie radioed his dispatcher and then made a U-turn to go after Wortman, but the killer had disappeared.

Wortman had continued on for another 1,500 metres to a driveway on his right with a sign by the road—"Ditch Doctor Atlantic Limited." If he had driven past it, Wortman would have been only a few minutes from Highway 104, the road leading to his Portapique neighbourhood. Instead, he turned into the long driveway, drove up the hill and parked in front of the house. He knew the people who lived there, Adam and Carole Fisher. The Fishers had been visitors to Wortman's cottage at 200 Portapique Beach Road in the past and reportedly liked him. However, Adam had done excavating work for him, which had ended in some kind of dispute. When they woke up that Sunday morning, the Fishers were plugged into the social media news loop and aware of what was going on. They have never talked publicly about what happened, but information gleaned from court documents and their friends and acquaintances, who have asked for anonymity, paints the following picture.

The Fishers had known Wortman for eight years. They knew about the replica police car. One of Carole's best friends was a female RCMP corporal. Based on their social media relationship and observations by those close to the two women, it seems very possible that Carole would have mentioned the car to the corporal.

Carole held Wortman in high regard, it appeared. In partially unredacted documents, she told the RCMP "that Gabriel Wortman was a person that people enjoyed talking to." As the Fishers were trying to piece together what was going on that Sunday morning, one of them commented: "Jeez, hope it wasn't Gabriel that lost it . . . it would be a disaster if he was in a police car."

The couple decided to call 911 about their concerns. Fifteen minutes after making the call they noticed a fully marked RCMP car turning into their driveway. When the "Mountie" got out of the car, they recognized Wortman, who was carrying a long gun. Adam Fisher got out his shotgun, loaded it and took cover. Carole hid upstairs in their bedroom.

Carole heard the doorbell ring and her dog bark, then her dog stopped barking. She thought Gabriel had entered the house, because the dog usually did not stop barking. Carole then heard banging on the glass.

The Fishers could hear a helicopter flying nearby. Carole was back on the phone with 911. The call was logged at 9:48 a.m. According to the RCMP's official logs, only a minute or so had passed between Wortman being seen by a constable on Highway 4 and Carole's call, which seems somewhat unlikely, given the distance Wortman would have had to travel. It would have taken him almost a minute just to get up the Fishers' driveway.

Outside their house, Wortman did another strange thing: he pretended he was a police officer there to arrest himself. "Come out with your hands up, Gabriel. Come out with your hands up," the Fishers heard Wortman shouting.

A close friend of the Fishers says Carole told them she had heard the details of her call to 911 being broadcast from a radio in Wortman's car. Later, a spokesperson for Carole denied that, saying, "Wortman looked back at his car as if he had heard something, suddenly turned, got into the car and drove away."

The Fisher episode suggests once again that Wortman had the ability to at least monitor RCMP communications. If he had wanted to kill the Fishers, why didn't he do so earlier in the day, as his first priority, before heading to the more distant Hunter Road? Perhaps it was just a coincidence, but Carole's first call to 911 would have occurred just before Wortman came upon Lillian Hyslop. Did he hear enough details and recognize who was making the call? He was in striking distance of their house. Did he then make a beeline to the Fisher residence? Did Wortman, as he pounded on the Fishers' door, hear Carole's second 911 call, which alerted him to flee?

When he got to the end of the Fishers' driveway, Wortman could have turned right onto Highway 4 and headed into Masstown, but that's where the RCMP cavalry, such as it was, would likely be assembled. Instead, Wortman turned north and, daringly, retraced his route up Highway 4 for about two kilometres. It would take him about four minutes to get to the intersection with Plains Road, turn right and head back toward the Diefenbunker, where he had spent the night. Where were the Mounties?

At 10:03 a.m. a call came in about a dead woman in a car at the campground. One minute later, as you may recall from Chapter Two, the RCMP sent out a tweet warning about Wortman.

#RCMPNS is advising people to avoid Hwy 4 near Hidden Hilltop Campground in #Glenholme. Gabriel Wortman is in the area. Please stay inside your homes and lock your doors. #Portapique

Even though he'd just been spotted by an officer and then identified to 911 dispatch by Carole Fisher, the RCMP had no clue where Wortman was. As for the report about the dead woman in the car, it came and went. Some said, months later, that a woman had suffered a heart attack or stroke and had died there. But no names were ever given and there was no published obituary, all of which raises some reasonable questions: Did Wortman have a radio, and did he call in a tantalizing report that the RCMP couldn't possibly resist? The RCMP has never clarified what actually happened.

◆

Kristen Beaton, thirty-three, was a born-and-bred Colchester County woman. She lived with her husband, Nick, on Onslow Mountain in Belmont, just to the west of Debert. It isn't much of a mountain, more like rolling hills, but it's picturesque all the same.

By all accounts Kristen was a doting mother to her young son, Daxton, and she was pregnant with a second child. She worked as a continuing care nurse for the Victorian Order of Nurses, a non-profit

Canadian institution dating back to the late 1890s. Like the Mounties, the VON was a fixture in rural Canada.

With the COVID lockdown, pregnancy and a young child at home, going to work every day was a source of increasing stress for Kristen, aggravated by the fact that in the early weeks and months of the lockdown there was a serious shortage of personal protective equipment. Nurses had to wash and rewash masks, then hope and pray that the virus didn't float their way.

"She cried every day before and every day after work, scared to bring this COVID home to her son," Nick Beaton told CTV News. He described his wife as "stressed to the max doing a job she truly loved."

The Beatons had been on social media monitoring the situation in Portapique from the night before. They had taken the word of the RCMP Twitter feed that police had everything under control. The couple didn't know that Wortman was dressed as a police officer and driving what looked like a police cruiser. "If I had known he was on the loose, I would not have let my wife leave the house that day," Nick told CTV News.

By the time he learned about Wortman, it was already too late. Kristen had left home and driven west, where she connected with Plains Road and headed north toward Debert. As she neared Ventura Drive, there was a cleared area on the other side of the road where drivers could park and sit for awhile. There was also a driveable dirt path that dead-ended in the brush. Kristen crossed the centre line and parked the car, likely to review her work notes and prepare for her next home visit.

At 9:57 a.m., the RCMP said, Wortman was videotaped driving south on Plains Road, not far from where Kristen was stopped. Why did he go back to that area? Was he planning to hide behind the welding shop again? Did he want to retrieve something he had thrown away? Whatever his reasoning, it was getting later in the morning. Even though it was a Sunday, people were moving around. If he went into the industrial park, he could easily be trapped. He passed Ventura Drive and within seconds came across Kristen parked to his right, facing north. He pulled in, stopped the car and got out. Now he was playing Mountie, it seemed.

Wortman told Kristen to get out of her car. It was around this time that her husband was trying to call her. Wortman clearly was not shooting everyone he saw, but he did seem to be targeting random victims, like Lillian Hyslop, to create chaos for an already flummoxed police force. He pulled out his handgun and shot Kristen Beaton dead. She fell to the dirt near the rear of her car, his eighteenth victim. Her unborn child lost its life, too.

The shots did not go unheard. Coincidentally, another VON nurse, Heather O'Brien, was driving south on Plains Road, coming from a home visit in Debert. A licensed practical nurse—a job she loved—O'Brien had been with the VON for seventeen years. The fifty-five-year-old was the mother of five children, grandmother of twelve, and claimed three more children under her care. She was active for a time on a dating site, Plenty of Fish, where a flattering photo made her look younger than her years. To most people who knew her, the lifelong resident of Masstown was unforgettable, with her sparkling eyes, her determination and the distinctive gap between her top two front teeth. Many considered her to be a natural healer and enjoyed her daily Facebook posts flipping tarot cards.

If true to her habits, O'Brien was heading for the Tim Hortons a few hundred metres ahead on MacElmon Road, where she would grab a coffee before continuing on in her new Sunday routine, which was described by Stephen Maher of *Maclean's* magazine:

"She was on her way in the circle to see her grandbabies, that she went every Sunday since this COVID thing started," said her daughter, Darcy Dobson, a 30-year-old bartender. "She would talk to the kids through the windows. That's what she did on Sunday, because we have all the babies."

O'Brien's six children all live within five minutes of their parents' home in small communities outside Truro, 110 kilometres from Halifax.

As she drove down Plains Road, likely headed to Dobson's place, O'Brien was talking on the phone to a friend and colleague, who we will call Mary, because she doesn't want her name published.

While Dobson was waiting for her mom, Mary called with terrible news.

"Mary called and said she was on the phone with Mom. And her words to me were that Mom was coming down Plains Road when she was talking to her on the phone and she said to her, 'I hear gunshots, Mary.' And Mom said, 'I'm almost to Lancaster (Crescent).' Mom had said to her, 'It's OK, Mary, the RCMP are here.' And the next thing Mary heard was Mom scream."

O'Brien had slowed down to see what was happening when Wortman fired at and hit her. Wounded, she attempted to drive away, but soon rolled off the road and into a clump of bushes. It's not clear if she died from the initial salvo or if Wortman followed her, got out of his car, walked close and then fired his kill shots. Spent cartridges would later be found inside O'Brien's vehicle.

It was Wortman's nineteenth murder in a little more than twelve hours. The RCMP said it happened at 10:08 a.m., but for reasons I'll explain below, it was likely closer to 10 a.m.

While passersby called in the shootings as an apparent two-vehicle car crash with people trapped, Wortman headed south, likely staying on Plains Road until he got to Belmont Road, where he turned right and drove down to Highway 2, west of Masstown. He turned left and went toward Truro on the two-lane. Why didn't he take the expressway? Was he just plain lucky, or did he somehow know that the Mounties now had a single officer stopping traffic near Truro?

◆

Wortman drove through Lower Onslow, a farming community that was once home to Fort Belcher, a long-gone British military encampment on the Salmon River. There are houses and some businesses on either side of the highway and a couple of side roads running off it. Wortman passed by the Onslow Belmont fire hall on his left. It was being used as an evacuation centre, run by Fire Chief Greg Muise and Deputy Chief Darrell Currie.

Only a handful of people had been evacuated from Portapique, 28 kilometres away. Richard Ellison—the father of Clinton, who had hidden in the woods for four hours, and Corrie, who had been shot on Orchard Beach Drive—had been at the fire hall for a couple of hours. A couple from Portapique who were taking shelter had just stepped out to get a bite at a restaurant down the road, almost encountering Wortman for a second time.

In the parking lot out front, an actual RCMP cruiser was backed into a spot between neatly spaced safety cones. The Mountie assigned to the car was from the Pictou detachment, about 80 kilometres away from Lower Onslow. A compact car was parked in front of the police cruiser. The Mountie and an employee of Colchester County who was acting as an Emergency Management Office (EMO) official were talking to the driver of the car.

While they were in conversation, one of four surveillance cameras mounted on the fire hall captured Wortman driving past. In the background of the video was Tim McLellan's machine shop. The time stamp on the shot said 10:17:04 a.m., but the clock was running ten minutes fast. It was actually 10:07 a.m. It is not known if the Mountie with the blocked-in cruiser even noticed Wortman.

Although it was a sunny Sunday morning, fifty-six-year-old Tim McLellan was already at work. He had lived on the property his entire life. His wife, Sharon, had been with him there for ten years. She had stayed in bed until awakened by a phone call from her sister, Mary Brown (no relation to the Browns on Hunter Road). Neither Sharon nor Tim saw Wortman drive by. Mary wanted to alert Sharon to the latest developments. There was something going on up in Wentworth. More murders. More fire. And the RCMP had just tweeted something important.

At 10:17 a.m., ten minutes after Wortman had passed the fire hall, the Mounties finally admitted to the public that Wortman was dressed as a police officer and driving what looked like a real police car.

#Colchester: Gabriel Wortman may be driving what appears to be an RCMP vehicle & may be wearing an RCMP uniform. There's 1 difference btwn his car and our RCMP vehicles: the car #. The suspect's car is 28B11, behind rear passenger window. If you see 28B11 call 911 immediately.

The news about the murders of Kristen Beaton and Heather O'Brien on Plains Road hadn't gotten out. Those crime scenes were a seven-minute drive away from the fire hall. As the two sisters chatted, Sharon paced back and forth between her kitchen and living room, which both faced Highway 2 and the fire hall directly across the road. By now the compact car had left the lot.

"There was a police car parked there, backed right up to the fire hall, and there were safety cones on both sides," said Sharon. "I thought that was odd. I had never seen that before . . . The EMO was wearing a lime-green safety vest, and he was talking to the Mountie, who was sitting in his car. Everything seemed fine."

As she was peering out the kitchen window, she saw what she thought was a grey Hyundai sedan (actually a Nissan Altima) appear to her left. The car pulled over near some trees on her side of the highway. It was short of the property line of the fire hall, about 80 metres away from the Mountie's car. The doors of the grey car swung open and two men carrying long guns sprung out. One crossed the road and went down into a ditch. The other ran behind the corner of the fire hall.

It was precisely 10:21 a.m. Two things were happening at the same time.

First, the RCMP had tweeted an update:

Gabriel Wortman is currently in the #CentralOnslow #Debert area in a vehicle that may resemble what appears to be an RCMP vehicle & may be wearing what appears to be an RCMP uniform. Please stay inside and avoid the area. #RCMPNS

While this tweet was going out, the two Mounties at Onslow opened fire, having made no attempt to arrest their target and apparently without following basic procedures for identifying the person they were shooting at.

"They started shooting at the EMO," Sharon said. "The EMO dropped his radio near the door. That's his lifeline. He stopped, picked it up and ran into the fire hall and disappeared. The cop got out of his car and was standing near the driver's door looking over the rooftop toward the shooters. I couldn't hear him, but he had his hands up and was waving his hands and saying, 'Don't shoot. Don't shoot.'"

"I heard three shots," Sharon said. "I called out the back door to Tim. He was standing in the doorway of the workshop."

"I could hear three gunshots," Tim said, "and I didn't want to move. And one of our neighbours out back heard just the three shots, too."

Apparently realizing the error of their ways, the pair of Mounties stopped firing and approached the fire hall.

"It was only then that I could see the word 'police' on the back of their jackets," Sharon said.

One of the Mounties doing the shooting, later identified as Constable Terry Brown (no relation to all the other Browns), went around the building. The other officer stepped into the building and asked if everyone was okay. When Deputy Chief Currie said yes, the Mountie turned and retreated to his car, along with Constable Brown. They drove away. The whole episode lasted about three minutes.

There were bullet and fragment holes in the walls of the fire hall. Shots went through a bay door and punctured a fire truck's windshield, fender and engine. Some just missed the people inside. Later the fire hall would claim that its electronic billboard outside was damaged, although it didn't appear to be in the line of fire. The RCMP would pay about $40,000 to replace the sign and even more to fix the damage to the building and equipment.

"I don't know why they thought he was Wortman," said Sharon. "Wortman was over six feet tall. The Mountie at the fire hall might have been five foot seven. Look at the photos; he could barely see over the roof of his car. Didn't they notice the safety cones around the car? Did they think that Wortman would have backed his car up to the fire hall and placed safety cones around it? What killer on the run would take the time to do that?"

A few hours later, in the old-fashioned tradition of good country neighbours, Sharon and Tim walked over to the fire hall and asked if they could get anyone a coffee or food. Sharon ended up having a short conversation with the Mountie from Pictou.

"Can I ask you a question?" Sharon inquired.

"What's that?"

"Why were they shooting at the fire hall?"

"You saw that?"

"Yeah, I seen it all," Sharon said.

"Well, that changes everything," the Mountie said. "I'll need your name and number."

Sharon gave him her information and thought she was doing the right thing. It never occurred to her that something nefarious might be happening.

Tim was a little more skeptical. "I think they were trying to hide it."

Both McLellans soon came to believe that after the wild shoot-up, the Mounties concocted a plan to cover it up.

"Were they going to try to blame Wortman for all that?" Sharon asked.

"I think so," Tim said.

Pinning the fire hall shoot-up on Wortman would have been difficult. The 10:07 a.m. video showed that the driver's side window of his car was rolled up.

The incident was referred to the SIRT for investigation. It would have three months to report back on their findings. The question remained: What made the two Mounties believe that the officer in the car at the fire hall was Wortman?

As Sharon McLellan put it: "The RCMP was told that Wortman was wearing an orange safety vest. The EMO was wearing a lime-green one. They just came up shooting at the wrong guy. There was no warning. That's what I saw."

Once again, did Wortman have a radio? Did he sic the RCMP on its own member to throw them off his scent? Why didn't the Mounties try to arrest the EMO they thought was Wortman instead of immediately trying to kill him?

Meanwhile, Wortman was now entering the final leg of his murderous mission.

15

THE SECOND MASSACRE, PART 3:
A FAILURE TO COMMUNICATE

By mid-morning Sunday, even the most news averse in Nova Scotia couldn't help but become aware of and alarmed by Wortman's ongoing horrific escapade. The Mounties, meanwhile, seemed to be trying to play hide the pea, even stymying the Government of Nova Scotia's Emergency Management Office (EMO) in its efforts to raise the alarm.

Shortly after 8 a.m., when the RCMP knew that Wortman was armed to the teeth and roving somewhere in the province, the EMO was discussing the possibility of issuing an alert. The problem was that it could not break through the RCMP's wall of silence, as reported by the CBC's Elizabeth McMillan:

> The first recorded mention of an alert came at 8:19 a.m., when Paul Mason, the EMO executive director, asked Jason Mew, the director of the office's incident management division, to bring in extra staff to the Provincial Coordination Centre, which is the hub of emergency decision-making in Nova Scotia during situations like natural disasters and was already being used due to the COVID-19 response.

According to McMillan's report, by shortly after 8:30 a.m. Mew said his team was ready to post an alert "at the request of the RCMP." But two hours later, wondering if that request would ever come, Mew's EMO colleague, planning officer Dominic Fewer, called the RCMP three times, receiving nothing in return but a text from Glenn Mason of the RCMP saying they "would like to have a discussion on alert ready message." McMillan continued:

> Fewer asked his colleagues to get in touch with Glenn Mason of the RCMP at 11:12 a.m., and Michael Bennett, listed as being the incident commander at the provincial centre, called two minutes later "advising we were prepared to use Alert Ready."
>
> At 11:21 a.m., Glenn Mason called "indicating it would be used" and asked Bennett to reach out to Insp. Dustine Rodier. After Bennett failed to get through to Rodier twice . . .

Wortman was shot by the RCMP before Rodier could be found.

Dustine Rodier and her husband, Pascal, had begun their careers in Richmond, BC. She joined the force in 2000 as a general assignment officer and quickly worked her way up the ranks. By 2010, after having volunteered to be a tactical officer and having represented Canada at a ceremonial event in Japan, Rodier helped create and lead the Serious Victims team, "working with serious sexual assault offences, child abuse, domestic violence and offences by persons in authority."

Pascal Rodier wasn't a Mountie, but tailored his career to following his wife around the country. In 1988, Pascal began working as a paramedic in the BC ambulance service and over the next fourteen years rose to become a highly regarded superintendent of the agency. He received numerous accolades and awards for his knowledge and leadership in the area of emergency response and public safety. One of his specialities is "responder interoperability," which in the simplest of terms means agencies working together in a crisis.

In 2013, Brookfield, the RCMP's movers, got the call to move the Rodiers and their three children to New Brunswick. Now a corporal, Rodier was made a team leader in federal policing operations, "with a mandate of large-scale operations including Organized Crime, Drugs and Proceeds of Crime and Money Laundering," as her LinkedIn profile puts it. By 2015, she was also lending a hand as a media relations officer for "J" Division, "but her focus on vulnerable victims has continued as she donates her time and represents the RCMP on many committees . . . Since 2014, Sgt. Rodier has represented the RCMP on the Board of Directors for the Dr. David Stephen Foundation, a non-profit organization whose mandate is on child sexual abuse prevention and awareness. She also represents the RCMP on the Paediatric Sexual Abuse multi-disciplinary committee and is working toward the goal to develop a Child Advocacy Center in the Saint John region that would serve child victims in Southern New Brunswick."

Now in the fast lane for promotion, Rodier was made a sergeant in 2016 and put in charge of the RCMP's Hampton detachment, which is located northeast of Saint John. It might sound like a remote rural area, but, among other things, many high-level anti-biker operations across the province were being run out of the detachment. In 2018 she was named Officer of the Year.

Pascal Rodier had a career change, too. In New Brunswick, he became the director of the Emergency Management Office in Quispamsis, where victim Lisa McCully had once resided. It is located between Saint John and the Hampton detachment. Pascal oversaw the response to the 2018 freshet floods, a yearly event on the mighty Saint John River. In his online LinkedIn bio, Rodier is described as a certified emergency manager and a situation awareness specialist.

In June 2018 the Rodiers were on the move again, this time to the RCMP's "H" Division in Nova Scotia. Dustine got bumped up to inspector and put in charge of Operational Support and the Operational Communications Centre. Her priority was to consolidate the RCMP's two communications centres into one operation at the Dartmouth headquarters.

Pascal landed a job in Nova Scotia, too, as the emergency preparedness manager for the Nova Scotia Health Authority. In that position he was the go-to guy for large-scale incidents and events.

The Rodiers, therefore, should have been at the centre of what was going on that weekend. Since she had spent her entire married life with an expert in emergency response, one would think Dustine Rodier would easily recognize a crisis situation and know to alert and protect the public. But she and the rest of the force weren't even returning phone calls about issuing an Alert Ready. What was holding things up?

Dustine Rodier had strong ties to the leadership in New Brunswick and recent operational experience there. Was she the one who called in the ERT teams and others from New Brunswick instead of from more local forces?

◆

If Wortman had a so-called hit list and was intent on exacting revenge on a host of individuals, as his partner apparently told police he was, he was passing up a surprising number of opportunities to do so. He passed nearby purported hit-list target Judge Alain Bégin's house, as well as the homes and businesses of a number of individuals with whom he had had personal and commercial contact over the years, some favourable and some not. He didn't stop at those places. Like a shark, he just kept moving, heading south toward Halifax for some unknown reason.

After murdering Beaton and O'Brien, Wortman had driven for about seven minutes to the Onslow Belmont fire hall and another five minutes to the entrance to the controlled-access Highway 102 express-way, but then didn't turn onto the expressway. Did he sense a trap?

To go south, he had to first continue driving east. There are few roads in the area, mainly because of all the water—ocean, lakes and winding rivers. Wortman was driving through a natural choke point between the tidal Salmon River on his right, which ran roughly parallel to the combined highways 2 and 4—called Onslow Road on that stretch—and the Highway 104 expressway on his left. There were not many other options left for him. It might serve you well to take a moment here and call up a map of Truro to see it for yourself.

Wortman could have crossed the Salmon River over the train tracks at Park Street or continued to Main Street, a route known as the sub-way, to the Bible Hill bridge to get over the river. The bridge was about three kilometres south of and perilously close to the RCMP detachment and communications centre on Dr. Bernie MacDonald Drive (no apparent relation to all the other MacDonalds). Another alternative for Wortman would have been to drive farther east to Valley Station, but that route would have taken him right past the RCMP detachment.

By now, the RCMP knew he was killing innocent bystanders, like Lillian Hyslop, Kristen Beaton and Heather O'Brien. Even if the RCMP didn't know where he was, any competent police tactician would recognize that roads in the Truro area—the hub of Nova Scotia, as it calls itself—should have been locked down. It would not have been difficult. All the RCMP had to do was engage the ready and willing Truro Police Service and call in some more of its own almost 1,000 members in Nova Scotia to throw up a few roadblocks and put an end to Wortman's terror. That never happened.

The Truro police communications room was feeling helpless and frustrated. More than an hour before, the RCMP had let Truro in on the fact Wortman was driving a marked police car and still killing. Now he was about to knock on the town's door and come crashing in.

At 8:45 a.m. the following exchange was one of a number going on between the Truro communications room and its officers:

DISPATCH: Truro Police Dispatch.

DAN TAYLOR: Hey, it's Dan.

DISPATCH: Just to let you know, he is in a fully marked police cruiser right now. Ford Taurus.

TAYLOR: What?

DISPATCH: Potentially using fully marked Ford Taurus, car number 28 Bravo 11.

TAYLOR: 28 Bravo 11.

DISPATCH: And he was last . . . the last information given was that he was loading firearms into the vehicle.

TAYLOR: Where?

DISPATCH: It doesn't say where exactly that it was. It just says he could be anywhere in the province.

TAYLOR: RCMP vehicle.

DISPATCH: That's what it's looking like. The [RCMP] risk manager is now on the phone with Ed, so he should have a bit more.

TAYLOR: Ok, thanks.

DISPATCH: Oh, wow. I just got a text from [redacted] that says that [name unclear] messaged Rob and said there's eight dead and he shot at a cruiser. Jesus.

Truro Police Chief David MacNeil followed protocol and immediately e-mailed the RCMP CROPs officer, Chief Superintendent Chris Leather. It was 8:50 a.m.

"If Colchester needs any support from Truro Police Service today let me know. Take care. —Dave," the chief wrote.

Logs of communications between the two police forces that morning reveal no immediate response from Leather.

For more than an hour, the Truro police were picking up information second-hand, from Mounties stationed at the hospital in town, through social media reports on Facebook and Twitter, and from the grapevine. That's not the normal way for police forces to communicate in an evolving disaster. Take this exchange, which was reported by the CBC's Elizabeth McMillan and Karissa Donkin. It began at 9:43 a.m., almost an hour after MacNeil tried to contact Leather, and is condensed from pages of similar transcript:

TRURO DISPATCH: I heard that somebody was found dead on the side of the road, but I thought that was last night.

RCMP: Yes, that was a different one, but we think they are in relation.

TRURO DISPATCH: So he might be in the Wentworth area?

RCMP: . . . I'm calling because [the suspect vehicle] did leave heading toward Truro.

TRURO DISPATCH: Oh, goody.

At 9:43 a.m. Wortman was still nowhere near Truro. He was about to drive by a Mountie and arrive at the Fisher house in Glenholme, having already murdered Sean McLeod, Alanna Jenkins, Tom Bagley and Lillian Hyslop. He had driven down Highway 4 and back up it a few kilometres, entirely unobstructed. At that point, he hadn't yet killed Kristen Beaton and Heather O'Brien.

Finally, at 10 a.m., seventy minutes after MacNeil e-mailed Leather, the RCMP CROPs officer replied: "Thanks Dave. It sounds like we may have the suspect pinned down in Wentworth. Will be in touch. —Chris."

Even though the Truro police had been told by an unofficial source at 9:43 a.m. that Wortman might be headed their way, the RCMP effectively told them to stand down. It was contrary to every police instinct, procedure and all training.

Wortman drove past "the subway" and eventually veered left to go over the Bible Hill bridge. As he entered Truro, he didn't come across any Mounties. He quickly made his way through town, starting on Walker Street. On Esplanade Street, a camera caught him near Murphy's Fish and Chips at 10:17 a.m. A couple was walking on the sidewalk as Wortman came up behind them. They had no idea that a man who had just killed nineteen people was approaching. He didn't slow down, and he didn't shoot them. Esplanade continues onto Arthur Street and ends at Willow Street, next to Nova Scotia Community College's Truro

Campus. He didn't bother with the college, either. He turned left onto Willow Street, which put him back on Highway 2 South. Police Chief MacNeil had no idea Wortman had been in the town until days later, when video surfaced.

Wortman's three-minute ride through Truro was entirely uneventful. He even passed near the hospital where his still-unnamed partner had been taken. He was back on Highway 2, driving toward Halifax. It was around 10:19 a.m.

With Truro a few minutes behind him, Wortman pulled over at the Mi'kmag'ki trading post, a cigar shack in Millbrook First Nation. An instantly famous surveillance video reveals that the car was not a perfect replica of an RCMP cruiser. The back bumper of an actual RCMP cruiser is decorated with two groups of four slightly diagonal dashes on each side of the centre line, leaning toward the middle. Wortman's car had six dashes on each side. Was that sloppiness or was it a code to identify him to somebody?

It was the first time he could be seen in action, as it were. Wortman, looking somewhat paunchy, with slouched shoulders, got out of the car, peeled off a blue RCMP jacket and put on a yellow safety vest. He got back in the car and resumed the trip south toward Halifax. The video's time stamp showed it was seconds short of 10:56 a.m., but like the one at the Onslow Belmont fire hall, it was wrong. The RCMP said it was a half hour fast. The actual time was 10:26 a.m. Wortman had been at this for twelve and a half hours, including his overnight break near the Diefenbunker.

Wortman drove for another eight minutes to the village of Brookfield, population 500. At the intersection of Highway 289, he had a choice. He could go straight, taking the old highway down to Enfield, north of Halifax Stanfield International Airport, or he could turn right and head to the expressway, a minute or so to the west. A surveillance camera at Roop's Esso station caught him turning right at 10:35 a.m.

The area was not unfamiliar to him. If Wortman had chosen not to go on the 102, he could have driven straight ahead for about ten minutes down Pleasant Valley Road and gone to his friend Dana Geddes's home and garage in Green Creek. Wortman chose the expressway.

At 10:37 a.m., eighteen minutes after Wortman had left Truro, the RCMP alerted the Truro police to lock down the town. "Unsure if still in police car," a dispatcher said. "Advises of [Ford] F-150 seen in the area and links that to possibly the shooter." No, this is not a farce, but the RCMP seemed determined to make it one.

Someone reported seeing Wortman on the controlled-access Highway 102. He had gotten on the highway around 10:37 a.m., the same time the RCMP was asking Truro police to lock down the town already well behind him. If there were Mounties stationed on the highway, it would have been a cinch to stop Wortman. There weren't.

Who saw him on the highway? Whoever it was, they didn't seem to trigger any alarms for Wortman. Was it an off-duty police officer in a private car, or a regular citizen who'd been following the events online? Or, once again, was Wortman monitoring the situation on a radio and calling in a plausible but entirely wrong position? He went down Highway 102 and exited at the first opportunity, at Stewiacke, and headed back to the old two-lane highway. He continued south across the Stewiacke River Bridge.

A few minutes ahead, as I described in Chapter Six, Constable Chad Morrison was positioned on Highway 224, east of the intersection with Highway 2 and south of the entrance to the Shubenacadie Wildlife Park. Wortman either saw him or knew he was there. He turned left, pulled up door to door and fired a couple of shots at the Mountie, wounding him. Morrison took off, turning left onto Highway 2, grazing the guardrail on the other side of the road. He then raced across the Shubenacadie River Bridge. A few seconds later he was approaching Cloverleaf Circle. If he had taken the ramp to his right, Morrison would have continued onto Highway 2 and likely would have encountered Constable Heidi Stevenson coming the other way. She was about to pass under the highway and would be circling around Rex McCoul Park to get back onto the northbound Highway 2.

Instead, Morrison drove straight ahead. On the other side of Cloverleaf Circle, the fairly straight Highway 2 crosses the meandering Highway 224, which after about six kilometres intersects with Highway 2 again at Milford Station. Morrison went that way and stopped at the ambulance station just south of the intersection, parking his cruiser, with its rear driver's side window blown out, around the side of the building. There was no one in the station, so Morrison ran into the woods.

When Stevenson came up the ramp, Wortman veered his car across the highway and crashed into her. As previously described, he shot and killed her as she sat behind the wheel. Stevenson was Wortman's twentieth victim. It was around 10:48 a.m.

The twenty-first victim was another Good Samaritan who, like Heather O'Brien, Tom Bagley, Corrie Ellison and maybe even Lisa McCully and a couple of others, just wanted to help. His name was Joseph Gordon Eric Webber. Some people called him Joe, while others called him Joey. He was thirty-six years old. Although he'd been born in Halifax, he was a down-to-earth country boy who lived back in the woods on Old Guysborough Road in a hamlet called Wyses Corner, northeast of the airport. Webber was the father of three girls, Emily from a previous relationship and Rory and Shirley with his current partner, Shanda MacLeod.

The tall, affable, bearded Webber was a woodsman who grew up the son of another woodsman. His father, Tom, used to run a business in the community, hauling logs with horses and machinery. In recent years, Webber had worked at the Northern Pulp mill in Pictou County but had been out of work since the mill closed in early 2020. He had just found a new job. Those who knew him described him as someone who did what needed to be done without expecting something in return. There was nothing transactional about him.

In situations like this, it is sometimes incumbent upon a writer to vacuum up every piece of information to build a profile of an individual. Perhaps the most wonderful service provided by the Halifax *Chronicle Herald* is its colourful obituaries, in which there are often all kinds of nuggets. Webber's obituary succinctly told his story:

> Joe was a loving father, partner, son, brother, uncle and a friend to many. Though family was at the top of the list, he had other passions in life. Bow hunting was one pursuit he enjoyed over the

past ten years and he was continually honing his skills. He was a gifted horseman, he had an innate ability to work with draft horses; recently he was able to "break" a very headstrong horse. In his younger days, Joe loved racing at Scotia Speedworld. He had worked his way up from Thunder and Lightning Class to Hobby Class while always carrying the #75 on his car. He enjoyed the competition and the comradery. A true country boy, Joe genuinely liked working in the woods and couldn't imagine living in town. He loved his family immensely.

That morning, Webber knew Wortman was out there somewhere in Nova Scotia, thanks to the vague RCMP alerts, but he needed to get some errands out of the way. Darren Bezanson, a neighbour and long-time family friend told the CBC's Haley Ryan what Webber was thinking. In rural Nova Scotia, wood stoves are the standard, with oil, propane or electric as a backup. Webber needed some furnace oil. Buying the oil a couple of jugs at a time is a rural Nova Scotia tradition. No one wants to tie up all their money in a 1,000-litre tank in the basement.

Webber drove his silver Ford Escape along the winding country roads to Milford Station to get the oil. As Bezanson told Ryan, he wanted to do it "before that crazy guy" came closer.

On his return trip home, Webber came upon a confounding scene at Cloverleaf Circle. Two RCMP cruisers were crashed together up against the guardrail at the top of the ramp. One Mountie was outside his car. Webber, wearing a hoodie, pulled up next to the cruisers, stopped and got out of his vehicle. He walked over to the side of Constable Stevenson's car, which had its nose in the guardrail.

One cannot possibly imagine the confusion going through Webber's brain when Wortman ordered him at gunpoint to get into the back seat of his fake police car. Once Webber was inside, Wortman shot him dead. Wortman then calmly went about his business as onlookers gathered at various points around Cloverleaf Circle. He didn't try to address or shoot any of them. He casually collected what he wanted from Stevenson: her gun, her ammunition and, perhaps, her radio. He moved clothing, guns and some other items from the fake cruiser into Webber's vehicle, started a fire in the fake cruiser's trunk and drove off south down Highway 224, the same route Constable Morrison had taken to make his escape. It was around 11:05 a.m. Craig Vanderkooi said, "He was at the traffic circle for twelve to fifteen minutes. He was in absolutely no rush."

As the first ERT members pulled up to the scene around 11:06 a.m., Vanderkooi told them that Wortman had driven off in a silver Chevy Tracker, which it wasn't. It was a Ford Escape. Just south of Cloverleaf Circle, Wortman passed by the driveway leading to his accountant's house up on a hill. The accountant had seen everything unfold below and was shocked at what he had witnessed. Until then he had thought of Wortman as kind and health-conscious, someone who dropped by to chat every Wednesday on his way up to Portapique, even leaving behind a box of PPE masks, part of a stash he had assembled and was selling on the Internet.

If you thought the RCMP was lost at the end of its leash prior to this moment, unbelievably, their grip on the situation was even worse than it seemed. At 11:04 a.m., around the time Wortman left the traffic circle and headed south on Highway 224, with Stevenson and Webber dead in his wake, the RCMP tweeted:

> Gabriel Wortman, suspect in active shooter investigation, last seen travelling southbound on Hwy #102 from #Brookfield area in what appears to be RCMP vehicle & may be wearing RCMP uniform. Suspect's car is 28B11, behind rear passenger window. If you see 28B11 call 911.

The tweet came twenty-nine minutes after Wortman had been seen passing through Brookfield. It was followed up two minutes later, at 11:06 a.m., with:

> Gabriel Wortman, suspect in active shooter investigation, now believed to be driving small silver Chevrolet SUV. Travelling southbound on Highway #102 from #Brookfield area. If seen, call 911.

Who was putting out these messages? With Mounties now flooding the area from everywhere, many were obviously unfamiliar with the local geography. The tweet had married the new information to the old. Brookfield is 22 kilometres to the north of Shubenacadie. Wortman was heading south on Highway 224 away from Shubenacadie. One police officer was lying dead on the pavement at Cloverleaf Circle in Shubenacadie. Another was injured and hiding in the woods by the ambulance station 7 kilometres to the south at Milford Station.

Twenty-one people were now dead and the RCMP would later state that at this point the force was still considering what it might say in a public alert. There appeared to be no consideration given to doing the simplest thing: throwing up roadblocks. As the RCMP spewed errant information, Wortman sought refuge at 198 Highway 224, a seventy-five-second drive south of Cloverleaf Circle.

Gina Yvonne Marie Goulet, fifty-four and a fellow denturist, lived in the house with her two dogs, Ginger, a big German shepherd, and Ellie, a ten-year-old chihuahua. Goulet had purchased the forty-year-old ramshackle bungalow on almost two acres of land in 2014. The house sat alone on a rise in the terrain, overlooking the rolling farmland and backing onto the Shubenacadie River. She finally had a perfect property for her horse. She also loved fishing for bass and travelling. One of her favourite destinations was Cuba, to which she returned a number of times. Her only daughter, Amelia Butler, described her this way to Global News: "She was so passionate about just helping her clients and she always just kind of joked that she literally got to put smiles on peoples' faces, which is exactly her personality."

An unusual feature of Goulet's property was that Highway 224 ran on roughly parallel tracks at the front and back of it. At the back it was known as Gays River Road, running from Middle Musquodoboit through Chaswood and Cooks Brook up to the intersection with Highway 2 where Wortman had shot Morrison. Then the highway looped back past Goulet's house down to Milford Station, where Morrison had gone for medical assistance after being shot.

As Wortman continued to drift southward toward them, Goulet and Butler were texting each other. They both knew Wortman's name.

"She was nervous when she found out who it was," Butler told Global News.

Goulet had gone back to school in her mid-twenties and studied to become a dental technician. She earned a designation as a denturist in 1993, at about the same time as Wortman. She was one of his many competitors in the province, eventually moving her operation to Shubenacadie in the late 1990s. Her business, Enfield Denture Clinic, was located on Main Street, right at Cloverleaf Circle. After she bought her house on Highway 224 in 2014, Goulet planned to move her business into it that summer. But the move didn't happen until the next September, by which time she had changed its name to Corridor Denture Clinic Inc.

In 2016 Goulet was stricken with brain cancer, but appeared to defeat it with surgery and follow-up therapy. However, the cancer returned in 2019 and Goulet underwent another surgery.

"She just had such a zest for life," her long-time friend Jodi McMullen told Graeme Benjamin of Global News. "She would go into a room . . . and come out of that with friends." McMullen told Benjamin about a vacation in Cuba. "When we came home from that trip, she actually joined a class. She began taking Spanish lessons and has ever since. Then she joined salsa dancing. I remember last summer, she would go in to the waterfront in Halifax, and they would have these big salsa dances right on the water, and she would go. She would take part in it. She just loved it."

Another friend, who asked for anonymity, said that after Goulet's cancer diagnosis her attitude about life changed somewhat. She largely threw fate to the wind. "She was determined to live life to the fullest after her health issues. She took some risks and became a little wild. She really didn't care what other people thought. It was her life, and she was going to live it her way." Like Heather O'Brien, Goulet was active on the Plenty of Fish dating site.

We don't know how the two met, but those who knew Goulet say she was nervous about Wortman, though nobody knew why. There were twenty-five denture clinics in Nova Scotia. Wortman clearly wasn't targeting all of them, but he did have an interest in Goulet's practice. According to friends of hers, he was thinking of retiring soon and had asked her to work for him. She had turned him down. Friends also noticed that in the two weeks leading up to that Sunday morning, Goulet hadn't been herself, bothered by something, perhaps the fact that she had been intimate with Wortman for a time.

Having just murdered Constable Heidi Stevenson and Joey Webber, and having wounded Constable Chad Morrison, Wortman must have felt the walls finally closing in on him. He turned left into Goulet's gravel driveway, climbed to the top of it, passed the porch and entrance to the house, and slipped between a shed and the house to the back-yard, where he came to a stop. Nobody could see him. The house sat alone on the road. There was farmland all the way back to the traffic circle and across the highway.

Goulet was now on the phone with Butler talking about what was going on. She told Butler she was afraid Wortman might come after her. Instead of getting in her car and fleeing the area, Goulet chose to lock her doors and hide in the house. If she was expecting Wortman to be driving a police car, the arrival of Joey Webber's stolen Ford Escape must have been perplexing. She called Butler, but when Butler answered the phone, no one was there. Butler tried calling her mother back on both her cellphone and her land line. No answer.

Wortman was in commando mode. He broke the glass window in Goulet's door, cutting his arm. He shot Ginger, Goulet's protective German shepherd, twice—once in the face, shattering teeth and her jaw, and another time in the back. Ginger would survive the gruesome injuries after surgery. Goulet was hiding in her ensuite bathroom. Wortman kicked down the door and shot her in the head, just as he had everyone else. Goulet was the third of his suspected ex-lovers to be killed by him.

Wortman needed to change his appearance. He had already burned one of his safety vests in the trunk of his fake cruiser. He got out of his RCMP pants with the yellow stripe down each leg and dressed in pants that were more casual. Where did they come from? He went outside and shuffled the last vestiges of his worldly possessions out of the Ford Escape and into Goulet's red Mazda 3. Wortman left behind

Sean McLeod's correctional services jacket, the Mountie pants, a grey RCMP shirt, a yellow reflective vest and a black one, other clothing and a red gas can. Was any gas left in that can? If so, Wortman could have used it. Goulet was notorious for running her car on fumes. "If you were going with Gina in her car somewhere, she always had to stop for gas," said fellow Shubenacadie resident Craig Vanderkooi. His comments were confirmed by others.

In all, Wortman had spent about seven minutes at Goulet's house. At around 11:12 a.m. he got into her car. She had two red tennis balls impaled on the antenna, ostensibly to improve radio signals or prevent the antenna from scratching the paint at high speeds. Wortman headed down the driveway to the 224, turned left and drove toward Milford Station.

At that exact time, there was a flurry of activity going on back up the road in Truro. The Mounties told the municipal police they had a report that Wortman was in the parking lot of the Sobeys supermarket on Robie Street in Lower Truro, right near the exit of the Highway 102 expressway. The RCMP warned them that Wortman was heavily armed. Truro police officers raced out to the scene, arriving at 11:16 a.m., only to find a lone RCMP ERT vehicle and a squad of Mounties twiddling their thumbs. The call to the Mounties was another in the growing list of convenient distractions that worked to Wortman's benefit. Who had made that call?

After leaving Goulet's house, Wortman apparently drove down Highway 224 to its southern intersection with Highway 2 at Milford Station. Just south of this junction, off in the woods behind the EMS station, wounded constable Chad Morrison was hiding with his rifle. It's not clear what Wortman did next. From that intersection there are only two direct ways to get to the nearest Irving Big Stop. He could have turned left on Highway 2 and driven south for about fifteen minutes through Elmsdale to Enfield, about an eight-minute drive. But that would have taken him right past the Enfield RCMP detachment, just 400 metres from the Enfield Big Stop at 6757 Highway 2. That's where Heidi Stevenson, now dead for about thirty minutes, had started her day a few hours earlier. Wortman could also have turned right at

Elmsdale, headed to the expressway and driven south from Exit 8 to Exit 7 at Enfield. There are shopping areas on either side of Highway 102. If he had tried to stop at the Sobeys on the east side of the expressway, as some suggested he might have done, the store was in lockdown and the pumps were closed. The same was about to happen at the Atlantic Superstore and the Petro-Canada gas station on the west side of the highway.

The RCMP has its own version of Wortman's flight path. It said in its first reports afterwards that Wortman went straight at the intersection and took Highway 224 to the Big Stop. That's not possible. Highway 224 ends at the expressway and becomes Highway 14 on the other side, heading into the Annapolis Valley and away from Halifax. There's a long, roundabout route back to Enfield, through what are known as the Hardwood Lands and past the source waters of the Shubenacadie River, but Wortman didn't have the time to do that.

If Wortman took the 224 and entered Highway 102 at Exit 9, that would present a rather unflattering truth about the police pursuit of Wortman. In this scenario, Wortman would have driven on the expressway for about ten minutes without running into any Mounties. They didn't know he was in Gina Goulet's red Mazda 3.

◆

Tim Krochak had been a photographer and visual journalist since 1992. He started out at the *Winnipeg Sun* before moving to the Halifax *Chronicle Herald* in 1997. He was now fifty-eight and laid off, a victim of the COVID-19 lockdown, and was working as a freelancer for the Canadian Press news service. Krochak called himself "a smug Canadian. I'm very strident about guns and America. I've never worked in a major market, and I never thought I'd cover a mass shooting."

That Saturday night, before going to bed at his home in Dartmouth, he had checked the RCMP Twitter feed and seen that a situation was developing in Portapique. "I said to my wife, 'If this is still an issue in the morning, maybe I'll drive up there and check it out,'" he said in an interview. "When I got up it was still going on, but the RCMP was being kind of vague. I called up my friend, Andrew Vaughan, from Canadian Press and he told me that a couple of people had been killed. Then there were some women shot on the road in Debert. I told him that maybe I'd come up and give him a hand."

Krochak left Dartmouth and took Highway 118, which connects with Highway 102 at Miller Lake, south of the airport. As he made his way up the 102, Krochak noticed something odd: "At two or three of the turnaround areas between the lanes, there were a bunch of RCMP and Halifax police," Krochak said. "Their cars were parked, and they were standing around with carbines in their hands."

Other witnesses independently confirmed what Krochak had seen. Marked and unmarked police vehicles were stationed along entrance ramps all the way up the highway as if they were poised to strike at something, but were not impeding traffic.

Shortly after Krochak had passed Miller Lake, the RCMP and Halifax police set up a roadblock at Exit 5A, south of the airport— but in the northbound lanes. This would not stop Wortman, moving toward the city, but people coming from Halifax were being prevented from getting to the airport. It didn't make sense to Krochak.

A story by Tim Bousquet in the *Halifax Examiner* later revealed that Halifax Regional Police had issued an order that Wortman was not to be shot but captured alive. What was that all about?

Krochak continued north, staying in communication with fellow photographer Andrew Vaughan. Krochak was then contacted by a friend in Winnipeg who was monitoring fire calls on a police scanner app. "He told me that all the fire and ambulance were on lockdown and can only go out with a police escort," Krochak recalled. "By now I was near Stewiacke and I hear on the radio that Wortman was last seen in the Brookfield area. That's, like, the next exit. Right then, over in the southbound lane, I can see a convoy of eight RCMP cars and an armoured car heading south toward Halifax. I turned around and started following them as fast as I could."

At around the same time, *Toronto Star* reporter Steve McKinley was driving in the area in his new SUV when he was pulled over by the Mounties. McKinley said in an interview for this book: "It was the one time in my life I was happy to be driving while Black. They took one look at me and let me go."

Meanwhile, Krochak got another call from his Winnipeg friend: "Dude, it's going down in Shubenacadie."

Krochak heard the fire call and could see the smoke from the two burning cars to the east of the expressway. He expected the convoy to head in that direction but it kept going south, so he followed. The police vehicles got off at Exit 8 and pulled into the Superstore lot where the Petro Canada station was located. He couldn't see what was going on, and after a time the police ran back to their vehicles and then sped to the southbound Highway 102 toward Halifax. "I got the sense they thought they had gone to the wrong place," Krochak said.

The Irving Big Stop at Enfield was 7.7 kilometres away, about a four-and-a-half-minute drive at normal speeds.

The RCMP would later say that a photograph from a provincial weigh station showed Wortman coming up the off-ramp on the other side of Highway 102, across from the Irving Big Stop. There were a couple of issues with the photo. The first was the official time stamp, which read 10:31 a.m. The RCMP said the clock was off by fifty-two minutes and the actual time was 11:23 a.m. As you may have noticed, clocks in Nova Scotia seem not to be precision instruments.

At the top of the photo, a white, unmarked pickup truck with a box at the back was coming up the ramp from Halifax. It appeared to be the forensic identification unit later seen in other photos and videos. Nearby, at the on-ramp, was what was later confirmed to be an unmarked police vehicle that may have been blocking anyone from getting back onto Highway 102. But otherwise the photo was so out of focus that it was not possible to tell if the vehicle said to be Wortman's was actually a Mazda 3 with two red tennis balls on the rooftop antenna. Even if it was a red Mazda 3, there was no way to discern if it was Gina Goulet's.

Assuming the RCMP timeline was correct and Wortman did pass by the weigh-station camera at 11:23 a.m., that meant he had no more than three minutes left in his life. But it would have taken him only a minute to get to the Big Stop and pull up to the pumps. Did Wortman linger somewhere, or are the RCMP times not accurate?

As the RCMP convoy, with Krochak in tow, was about to reach Exit 7 and Wortman was seconds away from the Irving Big Stop, the RCMP put out another tweet at 11:24 a.m. Adding to the public confusion, it read:

> Confirmed suspect vehicle is silver Chevy Tracker. Last seen #Milford. If seen, call 911.

Wortman was never in a Chevy Tracker, but rather a Ford Escape, which he had ditched behind Gina Goulet's house. Where did this information come from?

He pulled into the Big Stop with its bank of filling stations to the right. He wheeled into one of the stalls. Was he really intending to get gas, or was he hiding from the growing police presence all around him? Alternatively, was he eyeing Oldham Road, which began just across Highway 2 from the pumps? Oldham Road would take him through the countryside toward Musquodoboit and through the back door of Dartmouth. He would certainly need gas to go that far. Or, as some have suggested, did Wortman choose the gas station in order to surrender in a public place?

Krochak kept pace as the Mounties roared up the off-ramp at Exit 7, turned left, crossed over the highway and screamed into the Big Stop. They seemed to know where they were headed. "I literally followed them right to the pumps," Krochak said. "They got out and ran up to a van and used it as cover. It was really windy. They have this giant flag that was flapping, and there was a helicopter somewhere. It looked like they were yelling instructions to someone, but I couldn't hear anything. It was a bad place to be for a photographer. I had a bad angle. I took some pictures anyway and some video. I thought I heard shots, but I couldn't really tell from all the noise."

Krochak wasn't the only one there who saw something different from what the RCMP would later say happened. Glen Hines was driving past the Big Stop with his wife and was one of the first witnesses to go before television cameras. "I just happened to drive by the Irving and I seen this SWAT team come in and park beside the pumps and the fellow got out of the passenger side and he just went right out in front of the car with his gun and just opened up right through the windshield of the car. All I could hear was gunshots," Hines told CTV News.

Halifax resident Alex Fox was there, too. He posted this on his Facebook page:

> I woke up Sunday morning and had breakfast without check-
> ing the news. It's been Covid-19 exclusively for a while so I have
> been checking less and less. I had plans to go to a friend's house
> in Enfield to have mechanical work done on my motorcycle that's
> necessary to keep the old thing running. I drove out the Waverley
> Road from Halifax as it was still quite chilly out and wind on the
> highway is bad without a windscreen and cold weather gear. By
> the time I got to the Big Stop in Enfield I was still pretty cold. I
> decided to stop there and use the ATM to get cash out in order to
> pay for the work I was having done. After I used the ATM I stopped
> near the front doors to warm my hands up for a minute and put
> away my wallet. When I walked out the front door the parking lot
> and pumps were mostly deserted. There was only a small silver car
> at the pumps across from my motorcycle. As I'm walking along
> the sidewalk to my bike, a white truck pulls up at high speed to
> the opposite side of the gas pump from the car and two men in
> green tactical gear (thought they were soldiers at the time) got out
> and aim assault rifles at the car. They shout something like "Show
> us your hands!" There's a brief pause before they both open fire
> on the vehicle from close range. (I later read they shot ten times
> which I would believe). I am roughly parallel to this entire event
> and about 60' away according to Google Earth.

Perhaps the best corroboration of what Krochak witnessed came from two unidentified men in a car who streamed a short, hectic video on the Internet. They are obviously frantic about being in the middle of the situation, for safety and other reasons that will become apparent. Some might consider them imperfect witnesses.

"They got the killer right here," said the driver. "They got him on lockdown. They're going for him right now. They got the killer right here. Oh, they got him, Bud, they shot him. I heard the four shots."

A white pickup truck, similar to the one seen in the weigh-station camera shot, was parked at the gas station, to the right. Halifax police officers emerged from it and ran to join RCMP ERT members and a few regular members in uniform at the scene.

"They're letting the dogs out. Oh, brother, I got to watch this shit," the driver said, as he was backing his car away.

"I don't want to be here with all this money on me," said his passenger. "No way to explain it."

"Give it to me," the driver said with a little chuckle.

"No, just fucking get out of here before we get shot."

"More shots," said the driver. "You can hear them."

"Yeah," said the passenger in a pleading tone of voice. "I don't want to get shot."

As the driver backed up and panned the area with his camera, on his left he captured Krochak leaning over his car, closer to the scene, right where he said he was.

The entire event was filmed by surveillance cameras aimed at the gas pumps. Those recordings were never released to the public. Once again, the RCMP hid behind "privacy issues," which was kind of odd because all the victims' families wanted to see Wortman be killed, for closure.

The first official story from the RCMP was that Wortman had been shot by a lone Mountie. Wortman was no longer dressed as a Mountie, as last reported, and was driving an unfamiliar car that was not subject to a bulletin, but the RCMP said the Mountie became focused on Wortman after he noticed his "thousand-mile stare" and an abrasion on his forehead, presumably from the impact with Constable Stevenson or the guardrail back at Cloverleaf Circle. Was Wortman sitting in the car or was he pumping gas?

In the days ahead, the RCMP would stick to its story that one officer had shot Wortman. That's what the force would tell Prime Minister Trudeau, who retold the tale to the rest of the world.

We didn't know if Wortman had a gun in his hand. We didn't know if he fired a gun at the Mounties. We did know that the Mounties fired at and hit Wortman. How many times did they shoot him? Witnesses who saw Gina Goulet's car afterwards said there were about fifteen bullet holes in the vehicle, which was subsequently destroyed at Andrew MacDonald's scrapyard. Remember him? He was the Portapique neighbour whom Wortman shot but missed near the Gulenchyns' house on Orchard Beach Drive.

The time was 11:26 a.m. A lot had taken place at the Big Stop in a matter of seconds. The Mounties quickly sent out a message that Wortman was "in custody." Five minutes later, at 11:31 a.m., the Emergency Management Office got the go-ahead from the RCMP to send out a public alert. There was now no need to issue it, and they didn't.

For Krochak and other photographers at the scene, the RCMP messaging was as confusing as ever. "I had shots of the dead guy beside the Mazda," Krochak said. "I think they shot him dead in the car and then the next wave came and ordered him out of the car. He didn't answer, so they [shot] him again. The CBC camera was shooting the scene and I pointed out to him that the guy was dead. He said: 'Oh, shit,' and they put him on live."

All these photos of Wortman lying dead, and the RCMP continued to insist for almost four hours that he was "in custody."

Of the twenty-two people Wortman had killed, ironically, it was a fellow denturist who inadvertently exacted revenge. If her gas tank was near empty, as usual, Gina Goulet's quirk of not tying up her money in fuel had led Wortman into the kill zone.

One of Krochak's photos, distributed around the world, captured Wortman's final moment in the sun, literally and figuratively. It was beating down on him. His hands were bound behind his back. His chin was resting on the pavement. He looked uncomfortable, even unreal— like a mannequin. There was a splotch of blood on his forehead and more had pooled around him. He had been shot in the head and the torso. It had taken thirteen and a half hours, but the killings were done.

Now it was time to figure out what had really happened, because a whole lot of what I've just told you was never revealed to the public.

16

A BATTLESHIP
TRAPPED ON A SANDBAR

The official story about Portapique was shaping up to be a perfect modern fairy tale—the Monster and the Maiden. It was a macabre morality play and just about everyone in the media was eager to put it to music. The RCMP's excuses for its failures were treated with less than an ounce of skepticism. The belief that the media have a duty and responsibility to hold institutions accountable seemed to be over-ridden by the undeniable and unhealthy deference to authority that permeates much of the Canadian psyche.

Both the federal and provincial governments were oddly nonchalant about it all. Obituaries for the dead were still running in the *Chronicle Herald* and Premier Stephen McNeil and Attorney General/Justice Minister Mark Furey were already downplaying any concerns they might have about what the RCMP had done and not done that weekend.

"Restorative justice" and "a judicial review" were two concepts being openly floated by the government, eagerly supported by federal Solicitor General Bill Blair. Another notion gaining prominence was that domestic violence was somehow obviously at the root of

Wortman's murder binge, so any investigation should be conducted "through a feminist lens." The goal was to prevent the families of the victims being further "traumatized."

Like most journalists, I usually arrived at a cover-up long after it had been executed and would then have to spend an inordinate amount of time doing the near impossible—unravelling all the threads and misdirection—to get to the truth. This was happening in real time. The clues were there for anyone who cared to look.

The first clue had to do with calls to include restorative justice, an Indigenous concept promoted as an alternative to the court process, as a key element of an inquiry into police handling of Wortman's killing spree. Here's an excerpt from Nova Scotia's restorative justice template: "Restorative justice . . . ensures that those affected [by crime] can have a voice and role in the [judicial] process. This results in more meaningful and effective outcomes for both those affected and those responsible for harms."

In this case, the person responsible for so much harm was dead. Further, even advocates of the concept objected to its use in a murder case with an astonishing twenty-two victims. A group letter was sent to Furey, Blair and federal minister of justice David Lametti from the directors and leaders of Canadian organizations that work to eliminate or reduce domestic violence, sexualized violence and other gender-based violence. It read, in part:

> We were shocked to see media reports that the launch of an inquiry into the April 2020 massacre in Nova Scotia was being held up by an attempt to graft a "restorative approach" onto the traditional federal-provincial public inquiry. We wish to express our grave concern about, and opposition to, the use of any process for the federal-provincial response to the Nova Scotia mass shooting which is not fully open and public, or which does not mandatorily compel the pertinent institutions and state actors to provide relevant information.
>
> In Nova Scotia, there is a moratorium on the use of restorative justice processes for offences involving domestic or sexual violence.

It is clear that an examination of the Nova Scotia massacre and the social context in which it arose will require inquiry into institutional and individual responses to allegations of domestic violence. We question whether the use of a "restorative approach" in this instance is a breach of this moratorium.

Adoption of a restorative approach would likely be contrary to the public calls and need for an open, fully transparent, inquiry. A restorative process would most likely involve bringing select people together in circles, meeting with different cohorts privately.

The real story, therefore, would be hidden behind privacy laws and good intentions. It was the opposite of transparency. McNeil and Furey knew that.

The next signal that someone might have something to hide was the notion of a judicial review. There are two important details about a judicial review that might not be clear to a concerned public. First, a judge sitting on such a review cannot issue subpoenas and compel testimony. The second thing falls from the first—there are no witnesses or public testimony. All the judge can do is review the papers made available, review the policy and make recommendations that are not binding. It's the verisimilitude of an investigation, perfect for hiding the facts.

The last hint of a cover-up might have been the most unconscionable. I fully appreciate how women get trapped in situations with abusive partners and how difficult it is for them to get out. I've seen it up close many times in my life. I have in the past helped anyone in that situation and will continue to do so in the future. In this matter, however, there were mere whispers of abuse in those first few weeks and nothing conclusive. The narrative began with one prominent allegation against Wortman made by a former neighbour seven years before, and she had heard it second-hand and reported it to the RCMP, who did not lay charges. In fact, Wortman's unnamed partner never pressed charges. That's not unusual in such circumstances. Nonetheless, the RCMP said that a fight the night of April 18 had initiated Wortman's rampage. No proof of this fight has ever surfaced. The RCMP has said only that Wortman's partner had given a statement and that she was "a victim."

For all I knew, it might have been true, but the narrative didn't smell right to me. The RCMP story was that the unnamed partner had been beaten, terrorized and handcuffed in the back of a decommissioned police car, but managed to escape and hide all night in the woods. It was a terrific story, but that's not how these tragedies usually work out. Typically, the abuser kills the object of their affection or anger and then moves on to kill others and maybe themself. The abuser doesn't save the person who was the initial focus of their rage until the end—or leave them for the police to find.

For the government to suggest that the entire case be viewed "through a feminist lens" made me even more suspicious. Twenty-two people had been murdered. Several were men, and none were the allegedly abused partner of the killer. For thirteen and a half hours, the RCMP had failed in its duty and the entire province of Nova Scotia had been terrorized. Yes, the families of the victims were traumatized, but it wasn't made remotely clear how any of the proposed notions would make that better.

"Having my father brutally murdered traumatized me," said Charlene Bagley, daughter of Tom Bagley, who was murdered when he went to check on Sean McLeod and Alanna Jenkins on Hunter Road. "I want to know what really happened. I can't possibly be more traumatized by that than I already have been. All I want is the truth."

Since I was retired from journalism, all I thought I might do was monitor the situation, perhaps dig up a tidbit or two and serve as an unpaid resource for other journalists. My experience might help them and their audiences better understand a complicated and difficult subject. So I started with the fact that Wortman had a push bar on his car. The province of Nova Scotia had opted not to install them on its RCMP cars. The province argued that it was saving money, but there was also a rising sentiment in some vocal quarters about police vehicles looking too aggressive and militaristic. Nova Scotia chose the softer, gentler look to policing. Scott Anderson, Thomas Daigle and Madeline McNair of the CBC published a very good story on the subject, with a photo showing two municipal Truro police cars with push bars.

I raised questions about why the RCMP had eschewed the opportunity to call in the Truro and Amherst municipal police forces for help. The CBC's Haley Ryan investigated and published that story, although the police chiefs of each force declined the opportunity to be critical of the RCMP. They couldn't, because the RCMP controls the purse strings for major provincial operations and access to provincial crime labs, among other things.

As the days after the massacres turned into weeks, I could sense the interest in the killings already beginning to wane. In the early days almost every media outlet had done the usual bang-up job of collecting emotional stories and some useful information and throwing it at their respective audiences. But it didn't take long for editors, more so than reporters, to begin to lose their focus on Portapique. There were always new stories to cover. It would soon be time to do a feature piece or two and move on.

The collective media herd might have been heading to the next pasture, but something I came across the weekend after the massacres stuck in my head. It struck me as being a key to what was really going on inside the RCMP that Saturday night. I searched the media every day for a story about it, but nobody had covered it.

Since moving from Ontario to Nova Scotia in 2000, I had become all but addicted to the obituaries published in the Halifax *Chronicle Herald*. One that had caught my eye was that of schoolteacher Lisa McCully. She was one of the first killed in Portapique. As you will recall, her house at 135 Orchard Beach Drive was located directly across the road from Wortman's warehouse. She was found dead on her front lawn. The obituary was written by McCully's sister, Jenny Kierstead. The fifth paragraph read: "Lisa's family expresses their profound appreciation to the members of the R.C.M.P. who responded to the horrific situation, for gently protecting the children and also to the anonymous 911 person who stayed on the phone with them for two hours."

Two children were trapped for two hours while their mother lay dead on the front lawn? How could that have been? After its multiple revisions, the RCMP had settled on the following timeline: the first call to 911 came in at 10:01 p.m. and the first RCMP cruiser arrived at 10:26 p.m., followed within ten minutes or so by four or five other Mounties. If this timeline was true, and I had no reason to believe it wasn't, and the kids had remained in the house for two hours, then the RCMP response to Portapique was even more unusual than it already seemed.

The other aspect that caught my attention was that the RCMP hadn't said a word about rescuing the children. In the pantheon of heroic RCMP deeds, rescuing children and small animals is normally high on the list of achievements. When something like that happens, the RCMP unleashes its public relations minions and floods the media with feel-good stories, followed by medals and awards. That the RCMP was silent about the compassionate 911 operator and its own members who had rescued the children strongly suggested to me that the force didn't want to draw attention to what had really gone down.

I know the Mounties. Weighing all the visible evidence—the shifting timelines, the uneven response, the refusal to put out a public alert or set up roadblocks, and the unprecedented carnage—it seemed entirely possible that the RCMP was clumsily trying to hide something. Trapped like a battleship stuck on a sandbar, the Mounties were dangerous but completely vulnerable. I didn't have a clue what that *something* might be, but some eager journalist needed to investigate it.

It couldn't be me. I had way too much on my plate. Sharon had been scheduled for surgery around the time of the shootings. That had been postponed because of the COVID-19 lockdown. Like most other small businesses, our retail and wholesale fused-glass business had all but dried up. My own health was in flux. I'd had three heart attacks over the previous twenty-two years. I had three stents. I had some other issues, and now I had been diagnosed with prostate cancer. I was about to begin hormone therapy and eventually would have to undergo daily radiation for a month at a Halifax hospital. No, it really couldn't be me.

On the morning of Monday, May 4, I told Sharon I would be a little late going to work at our studio. It had been fifteen days since Gabriel Wortman was shot and killed, and the media seemed interested in only the killer and his sordid history.

It was all swirling around inside my head, the evidence that he was a cold-blooded psychopathic killer, all his innocent victims and the fact that the RCMP did little if anything to stop him during those thirteen and a half hours. I had to get it all out of my head, so I sat down at my computer and began typing. It took me a little more than an hour. It wasn't polished. I just wanted to capture the attention of those in the media and maybe get them to refocus their efforts a little.

I sent the 1,606-word opinion piece off to the *Globe and Mail*, the *National Post*, the Halifax *Chronicle Herald* and even the *Ottawa Citizen*, and went to our studio to make some glass. I had long come to understand that the Canadian media didn't welcome unsolicited opinions. If it did accept one, that opinion had to be succinct and pithy— maybe half the length of what I'd just sent—and there was little room in the heavily formatted news outlets for spontaneity. I didn't expect to hear back.

◆

Enter Stephen Maher. I first became acquainted with Maher as a reader of the Halifax *Chronicle Herald*. He was the Ottawa correspondent at the time. He had called me once or twice about the RCMP to draw on my knowledge as the author of three books. Born and raised in the rural community of Valley, near Truro, he had been a journalist for thirty years. In 2011, he joined Postmedia News, where he earned a number of major awards, including a National Newspaper Award and a Michener Citation for an investigation involving political shenanigans during the 2011 federal election. In 2016, while working at Postmedia, he was chosen for a coveted Nieman Fellowship at Harvard University. He returned only to fall victim to budget cuts, but landed at *Maclean's* magazine as a contributing editor and columnist. That magazine was also struggling. First published in 1905, it had long been Canada's weekly newsmagazine, a staple of every doctor's and dentist's office across the land. In recent years it was published by St. Joseph Communications, owned and operated by the Gaglianos, a politically connected Montreal family that had made millions from government printing contracts.

Maher called to ask my thoughts about the Portapique story and the RCMP. He said he was doing a one-month-later follow-up feature and wondered if I could help him.

I told him that if I were going to do a story right then, I would be looking at why the RCMP left Lisa McCully's children trapped in the basement of their house for two hours.

I sensed Maher had not heard about that.

"It's near the bottom of her obituary," I said.

As we chatted, Maher wondered if I was going to write anything myself. I told him that was unlikely. I had whipped off my piece to the usual suspects in the media the previous week but hadn't heard back from anyone.

"Send it to me," Maher said.

So I did. Maybe, I thought, he would be the one I could help.

Maher investigated the story in the obituary. McCully's children weren't the only ones trapped in the basement at 135 Orchard Beach Drive. The two young sons of next-door neighbours Greg and Jamie Blair had been there, too. He used all that in his story "The Nova Scotia Shooting and the Mistakes the RCMP May Have Made," published May 13, 2020, in *Maclean's*.

It was a decent roundup, and Maher even quoted me about the lack of push bars on RCMP cruisers, but there was something about his story that bothered me. Using confidential sources, he reconstructed the police rescue of the children. He wrote:

In McCully's obituary, her family thanks the RCMP and "the anonymous 911 person who stayed on the phone with [her children] for two hours."

If that is accurate, police did not get to the children until an hour after the first officers arrived in Portapique. A source with knowledge of the events says the children stayed on the phone with the dispatcher during the 40-kilometre ambulance ride to the Colchester East Hants Health Centre, the regional hospital in Truro, which would have taken at least 30 minutes. . . .

"There was communication between the members on scene, the telecommunications operator and the kids for them to stay fast, stay hidden, stay on the phone and that the police would come to them, and that they would be rescued, because that was the only living people that the police had any contact with at that point."

When police eventually moved in, they did so cautiously, with their flashlights off so that they wouldn't present easy targets to the killer. "It would almost be described as a war zone," said a law enforcement source. "Fires. Gunshots everywhere. Miniature explosions, propane tanks in garages and in houses. It's dark. The only light you're going to get is whatever's from the police cars and whatever's from the burning houses."

As dramatic as Maher's description was, I didn't entirely buy into his account of events. My reading of the obituary was that the children had spent two hours in the basement. Maher said it was about one and a half hours and another thirty minutes or so in the ambulance. The latter part might have happened, and I didn't have any proof to the contrary, but it seemed unlikely to me that during such mayhem the 911 operator would have stayed on the phone during the ambulance ride.

The next day, May 14, *Maclean's* added my piece as a sidebar to Maher's story in its online edition, under the title "The Nova Scotia Shooting Encapsulates All That's Wrong with the RCMP."

When I awoke that Sunday, my wife, Sharon, was already having a coffee. She told me that she had just seen a Facebook posting that a gunman was on the loose near Truro, N.S.

"Since when?"

"Last night."

"Any details?"

"No. It says the guy may be driving a RCMP vehicle."

I made myself a coffee and then started scouting around for details. There were hardly any. Scraps of information really. There had been no warning put out to the public. From my experience in dealing with the Royal Canadian Mounted Police over the past 27 years or so, I got that sick feeling that comes from having seen this all before.

"This is bad," I told her. "Worse than you might think. The RCMP has gone into its shell trying to protect itself and its image. This is probably going to be really bad."

When the news finally dribbled out, we learned that 22 people were dead, including Mountie Heidi Stevenson. The gunman was also shot dead in a gas station by a Mountie. A messy story resolved. The mourning began for the Mountie . . . and the others. Tributes went out to the first responders. Flags were ready to be lowered. Funerals, such as they were in this age of COVID-19, were ready to be held.

I talked to a few people and quickly learned some unpublished details. The shooter had tied up his ex-girlfriend or wife to a tree, I was told at the time (though that turned out to be not quite accurate).

There were many dead. When the shooter was taken down at the Irving gas station north of Halifax International Airport, a source told me, the RCMP and Halifax police were in a state of chaos. No one knew who was in charge or what they were supposed to do. "It was a shit show." One police officer figured out that someone who looked like the shooter was at a gas pump and was acting "hinky." The shooter knew he had been identified, reached for a weapon and had been shot by the curious and alert officer. Story over, right?

I described how I'd been a commentator on previous RCMP debacles—Spiritwood, Mayerthorpe, the Dziekanski death—and had so often been told, in response to my efforts to point out the shortcomings of the force, "This is not the time for recriminations or criticism." In the wake of Portapique, I explained, CBC Radio in Halifax called.

. . . I got a little emotional about what had happened. I was extremely critical about the force and asked out loud why Stevenson, a 48-year-old mother of two, was alone in a car in the situation that got her killed. It had been at least 13 hours since the events had begun in Portapique, spread the next morning to Wentworth and elsewhere.

"Where was the cavalry?" I asked. "Getting gas at Enfield?" . . .

But my experience, if it has taught me anything, is the RCMP is adept at pulling at heartstrings during and immediately after an event, like they have over the past two weeks. We are told that there will be a time and place to discuss these issues, but that time never really comes. By then, it's all old news and time to move on, they will say.

Even now, without all the details in, it has become clear to me that the Nova Scotia massacre encapsulated all that has been and continues to be wrong with the current structure, ethos and performance of the RCMP. . . .

In my CBC interview, I was asked about how long it would take the RCMP to respond to the scene in Portapique on a Saturday night. I said that it took them, based upon what I knew, 30 to 35 minutes.

In its first timeline, the RCMP said it took 12 minutes. The next day it changed the timeline and fudged the response time even more. Finally, it came out with another timeline which said it took 26 minutes. What is the real story? . . .

The fatal conceit of the Mounties is that every Mountie can do any job, policing is policing. There is no magic.

Here's how that worked out in the Nova Scotia massacre. Nova Scotia, like other provinces that hire the Mounties to do their provincial or municipal policing, have no say who the RCMP puts in charge or hires in the province.

Bergerman, the officer in charge, spent almost her entire career in federal policing in British Columbia and Ontario. She didn't do much on the ground in-your-face policing.

However, working on organized crime and counter terrorism is akin to the difference between cricket and baseball. Both have bats and balls, but they are fundamentally different games.

Next, I talked about the RCMP's problem of "carpet cops" who ascend the corporate-style hierarchy without accruing much in the way of street-level policing experience.

Instead of tackling the issue head on, they planned and planned, so that no one could be accused of breaching "best practice" protocols.

"This incident was dynamic and fluid," said Leather in a statement on April 22. "The RCMP have highly trained and capable Critical Incident Command staff who were on site in Portapique. Operational Communications Centre operators assisting the response and police presence was significant. The members who responded used their training and made tough decisions while encountering the unimaginable."

But as they planned, they failed to put out proper alerts, failed to draw on other forces for help, like Truro and Amherst, failed to set up a secondary perimeter and failed to shut down the very few roads in Central Nova Scotia where the killer was wandering on his deadly mission.

For the RCMP this was an example of a cascading failure that began on Portapique Beach Road. . . . From the outset the Mounties appear to have become fixated on their own manpower problems and poor decisions at the original crime scene. They then evolved into magical thinking—the gunman probably killed himself because that's what these guys do.

Finally, I addressed the sad case of Constable Stevenson, with her thirteen years spent with the Musical Ride and her experience as a press liaison, community support officer and traffic cop.

Yes, she died a hero, but did she have to die? How did she die? Was she sent to her death by incompetent overseers? The Mountie union says she crashed her car into the killer's fake police car, or was it the other way around? Look at the photos. The only car equipped to survive such a crash was the one driven by the bad guy. His vehicle was fitted with a push bar or ram package, as it's called. The RCMP has resisted for years improving the safety of its vehicles after it became an issue in Spiritwood, Sask., in 2006. Back then two Mounties rammed a vehicle not equipped with a push bar. Their airbags went off and like sitting ducks they were each shot in the head by the person they were trying to apprehend. Did that happen to Stevenson, too?

Why was she alone there, 13 hours after the rampage had begun? Why were the heavily armed specialists still gassing up almost half an hour after she and another Mountie had been shot in Shubenacadie 20 minutes away? And the Mounties only got their man after one alert officer's instincts—his Spidey sense—told him something wasn't right about the guy sitting in a Mazda at a gas pump.

There are a thousand horrible questions for which answers are needed.

But Nova Scotians and Canadians must get over suspending their disbelief and their fond memories of the Musical Ride to do the hard work of addressing this very important issue.

The time has come for recriminations.

There it was. I was in print again. I wondered who even read *Maclean's* these days. Maybe a few journalists would see it and get inspired. I had no plans to start churning out copy again. I had personal issues to deal with and didn't think I could spare the time or energy to do much more. I'd just be there for anyone who needed me.

But you know the old saw about the best-laid plans of mice and men.

PART TWO

THE SEARCH FOR THE TRUTH

17

A LITTLE BIRDIE DROPS A DIME

A month or so after the massacres, just about every major news outlet had taken the same "ethical" position that it was not going to name Gabriel Wortman. He would only be known by his initials or some euphemism—the shooter, the madman or the denturist. His was a name not to be spoken. The Halifax *Chronicle Herald* described the policy on its front page:

> The SaltWire Network is now focusing its coverage on the victims of the weekend's shootings and helping communities heal and understand. From here on, we will only publish the murderer's name and photo responsibly, when it serves the public good. We're taking the same approach with photos of the crime scenes. In instances where we choose to publish any of these items, we'll explain to readers why and be as transparent about our decisions as possible.

The rationale for this proud self-censorship was that naming Wortman would only glorify his actions and provide a model for others like him. Despite their employers' high-minded proclamations, reporters were feverishly beating the bushes to find out every piece of dirt they could about Wortman. Other than his name and the details of his prodigious sex life, almost everything was considered fair game.

The RCMP, the government and most of the media had decided not to name the shooter's partner, either, because she had been unilaterally declared a victim, though no hard evidence supported the claim. It naturally pushed my brain into Karla Homolka territory.

Between 1986 and 1990, the so-called Scarborough Rapist terrorized women in the east end of Toronto and, unknown at the time, across the border in the Buffalo suburb of Amherst, New York. After at least twenty women were raped over that period, the attacks suddenly stopped. On June 15, 1991, Leslie Mahaffy went missing in Burlington, Ontario, about a thirty-five-minute drive west of Toronto. Her dismembered remains were found in a lake near St. Catharines, not far from Niagara Falls. On April 16, 1992, fifteen-year-old Kristen French was abducted off a street in St. Catharines and then was raped, tortured and murdered. Her body was dumped in Burlington, not far from Mahaffy's gravesite.

Almost a year later, in early 1993, a petite blond woman, Homolka, showed up at a Niagara Regional Police station in St. Catharines. She had a spectacular black eye. She told the police about being terribly abused but made no mention of what she knew about her husband—Paul Bernardo, the Scarborough Rapist—or the murders they had committed, including that of her own sister, thirteen-year-old Tammy, in 1990. Police had declared Tammy's death an accident. The police heard Karla's story about abuse and granted her immunity. She was a victim, not a suspect. Then they searched the couple's house in Port Dalhousie, near the Lake Ontario waterfront, and found that Karla knew a lot more than she was letting on about her husband and their partnership in kidnapping, rape and murder.

This is not to suggest that Wortman's partner was guilty of anything. We knew almost nothing about her. But she was being protected by police, government and the media, and it appalled me. Giving her a pass was the antithesis of the concept of blind justice—that justice must be seen to be objective and impartial. Like Karla Homolka, she was the last person to see her husband. She was there. What did she know, and what else had she witnessed, not only that night but during the days, months and nineteen years beforehand?

Not naming her also violated principles that are the bedrock of quality journalism: truth, transparency and accountability. To reiterate what Joseph Pulitzer said long ago, "Newspapers should have no friends." So were the media—and the police—allowing an exception for Wortman's partner? Nobody seemed to recognize the unintended ramifications of this overriding hunger for privacy and secrecy. Without transparency, the RCMP, the Crown and the government in general would be able to manage the narrative and keep a lid on any secrets, if there were any— and everyone was certainly acting like there were some.

Any attempt to hide the real story would begin with Information to Obtain documents (ITOs), in which the police use gathered statements and data to make the case for a search warrant. ITOs are supposed to be public information, but Sergeant Angela Hawryluk, the RCMP's chosen affiant, asked that the information in the Wortman ITOs be sealed to protect the ongoing investigation.

My police sources were suspicious from the moment Hawryluk was publicly identified as the affiant for the ITOs. A twenty-eight-year member of the force, she was transferred to the Legal Applications Support Team (LAST) in June 2019. But it was what she did prior to that posting that raised eyebrows. For the previous four years she had been a member of the anti-outlaw-biker squad in the Combined Forces Special Enforcement Unit (CFSEU). She had also spent a significant amount of her career in federal drug enforcement. Inside the force she was considered to be a solid team player and was well practised in the process for search warrants. In fact, inside police circles she was known to have a favourite justice of the peace, Kelly Shannon, with whom she liked to work.

Shannon gave Hawryluk sealing orders for all of the ITOs.

For the media, gaining access to the documents, and perhaps valuable information about Wortman and the RCMP, meant a court battle in Truro, the local jurisdiction. The media banded together and hired lawyer David Coles, and the fight began, word by word and sentence by sentence, to remove the black ink covering just about everything in Hawryluk's ITOs.

The judge who should have heard the media's arguments was Alain Bégin, but because he had been "a possible target" on Wortman's make-believe hit list, he stood aside. In came Judge Laurel J. Halfpenny MacQuarrie, who had a reputation in Nova Scotia for being pro-police, pro-prosecutor and close to Premier Stephen McNeil. Nova Scotia is renowned for its backroom dealings in politically sensitive cases, and Halfpenny MacQuarrie did little to disabuse observers of that notion. The media had to fight hard for every uncovered word. Take this exchange between Coles and Hawryluk from one of the hearings, as reported by Michael MacDonald of the Canadian Press, in which lawyer Coles asked Hawryluk a number of times why large sections of the documents were blacked out:

"I had no intention of any of the ITOs being revealed to the public," Hawryluk told the court.

Coles suggested that was an extreme position.

"Your position is that any information in the ITOs could compromise the investigation, even though the Crown has released some information?" he asked.

Hawryluk agreed.

Coles challenged Hawryluk's assertion that the information in every document should remain beyond public scrutiny to ensure the RCMP's ongoing investigation is not compromised.

The lawyer pointed to previously redacted content, saying its release would have no impact on the investigation, now in its third month.

In particular, he noted that Hawryluk's resumé was originally deemed off limits, as was the name of an anthropologist who was called in to help Nova Scotia's medical examiner on the case.

"If the anthropologist's name was released today, would that affect the investigation?" Coles asked Hawryluk.

"No, it would not," she replied.

The media wasn't going to see anything that the Mounties, legal system and government weren't ordered to surrender. The notion of indepen dence between the three institutions seemed to have evaporated, and with it the public interest. Meanwhile, Nova Scotians had little to no idea about the RCMP's dealings with Wortman prior to that weekend, nor even during it. Other than Sergeant Dave Lilly, who was described by reporter Lindsay Jones as having rescued Lisa McCully's and the Blairs' children, we had no clue about which individual Mounties had attended the scene. Knowing the names might seem like small pota- toes, but if we didn't know who did or knew what and when, then government and police could potentially massage witnesses, testimony and the evidence to their liking. The RCMP and its enablers were pre- pared to put up a vigorous defence.

I was keeping an eye open for the emergence of Chief Superinten- dent John Robin from his position as director of Covert Operations, an event, as you may recall from Chapter Four, that some of my sources had predicted would happen at some point.

I also had to wonder which, if any, journalists would take on the story that was simmering outside the courtroom.

◆

Frank's offices are on the fourth floor of an old building at the cor- ner of Lower Water Street and Sackville Street in downtown Halifax. There are five desks in the 1,500-square-foot unit, which is located at the back end of the building. "The only view we have is of the hotel rooms across the street. Sometimes the guests there put on a show for us," Andrew Douglas told me with a chuckle.

From their modest digs, Douglas and his colleague Cliff Boutilier were taking aim at the narrative about the massacres. Eight days after Wortman was killed, *Frank* came out, first online and then in print, with stories from every possible angle. There were photos of the victims and the perpetrator. There was even a photo of Wortman's former wife, Corinna Kincaid-Lowe, whom he'd met at the University of New Brunswick. She had started out writing papers for him and ended up marrying him. They divorced five years later, in 2001. To my eye, she looked similar to three of Wortman's victims: Lisa McCully, Alanna Jenkins and Gina Goulet. That got me thinking.

One *Frank* piece focused on the RCMP's ignoble attempts to garner sympathy for itself over the murder of Constable Heidi Stevenson. A pseudo-column—"Ponderings of a Pariah"—took the form of a letter addressed to RCMP commissioner Brenda Lucki. A cartoonish pirate sporting a tricorne, wearing sunglasses and smoking a rather long cigarette animated the piece. Here is a taste of what they wrote in typical *Frank* style:

> NOVA SCOTIANS HAVE A RIGHT TO BE ANGRY.
> VERY, VERY ANGRY . . .
>
> Commissioner Lucki,
>
> Sorry for your loss.
>
> Now that we have dispensed with the all-important "thoughts & prayers" portion of our program, let's get down to the meat & potatoes portion of our program, shall we?
>
> For instance, Commissioner Lucki, just what kind of shitshow is the Royal Canadian Mounted Police running in Nova Scotia?
>
> And my apologies for not coming up with a more flattering term in which to cloak your RCMP policing & communications efforts here in Canada's Ocean Playground. Flattering terms do not drip easily from the tongue these days . . .

Deeper in the magazine Douglas and Boutilier opted to defy the new journalistic convention that was stifling developments in the story. It had begun with a tip from a reader that they decided to pursue.

In the hurly-burly world of *Frank*, Douglas and Boutilier had briefly forgotten that they themselves had had a recent run-in with Wortman and his partner. On February 12, 2020, the partner had called them about a strange incident at Wortman's denture clinic at 193 Portland

Street on the somewhat seedy eastern flank of downtown Dartmouth. There had been a confrontation between Wortman and Halifax Regional Police officers who had parked their unmarked car in his lot while they went to the nearby Tim Hortons. Wortman had padlocked the lot and wouldn't let the police out. He was demanding that *Frank* run a story about it. *Frank* complied, and Wortman's partner provided a number of photos to illustrate the issue. Later that same day, Wortman was caught speeding on Portapique Beach Road by the RCMP.

Now, more than a week after the massacres, *Frank* was homing in on Wortman's unnamed partner. It seemed incomprehensible to them that the police and the media were not naming her after all she had supposedly done to survive. *Frank* published a photograph of her on the cover of the magazine with the headline: "Lisa Banfield, hero." The sub-headline read: "How many lives did the killer's girlfriend save?"

Frank did something it doesn't normally do: it gushed. The fifty-one-year-old Banfield was described as being a "vivacious brunette . . . our heroine who is still recovering from injuries." She came from a large family of eight children who were raised in suburban Beaver Bank. She had three sisters around the same age as her. She had graduated from Sackville High in 1986. She had once owned a house on Saluki Drive in Beaver Bank for six years with her unnamed husband, with whom she split in 2001, the same year that Wortman's first marriage had dissolved. She had worked as a clerk at a downtown store before joining Wortman in the denture clinic. Douglas wrote:

> Lisa Banfield, 50ish, is a hero. You knew that when you first read the stories, first from Global News, and then everyone else. You just didn't know her name. Handcuffed and assaulted by her common-law husband Gabriel Wortman at the very beginning of his murderous 13-hour rampage, she escaped her captor and hid in the woods until emerging at 6:30 a.m.—with a gift for police. Namely, information that not only was he driving a fully outfitted RCMP squad car, he was dressed like an RCMP officer. . . .
>
> If Lisa hadn't managed her escape, the already unimaginable body count might well have risen further. And if Frank Magazine

didn't have something of a history with Gabe Wortman and his denture clinic, her identity might have remained unknown. . . .

"They seemed like a great couple, full of fun," [a female reader] remembers.

"Always teasing back and forth."

During one of her visits, Lisa—she never knew her last name—showed her photographs of the interior of their cabin in Portapique.

"Like pictures out of a magazine," she says.

Frank had broken the ice.

"We decided to call her a hero," Douglas recalled. "Who was going to complain about that?"

Lisa Banfield's name and image were out, but the news was roundly ignored by mainstream and alternative media. They would remain steadfast in treating her as a victim and not publicly associating her with the massacres, no matter how tattered the RCMP narrative would become.

◆

For all its convictions about naming the killer and his partner, the media continued to scrounge for more details about Wortman. The Mounties obliged, chumming the waters with the promise of something vague and sexy: a psychological autopsy of the killer. The RCMP even posited that Wortman was an "injustice collector," a catchy concept intended to mean that he warehoused slights and insults against him over the years until he exploded in a rage.

From the breathless reporting of that announcement, one would have thought the RCMP had reinvented Sigmund Freud. Wortman had killed twenty-two people in cold blood. It was obvious he was a psychopath. But my sense remained that there was more going on here than met the eye.

One sunny afternoon, Sharon's cellphone rang.

"Just a moment, he's right here," she said with a quizzical look on her face, then handed me her phone. "It's for you."

I am not saying whether the caller was male or female but have referred to that person as male elsewhere and will continue to do so here. The very fact that he had called Sharon's number told me it was someone with access to internal police or emergency service systems, such as Nova Scotia's Justice Enterprise Information System (JEIN), which captures and records information from across the justice system from anyone who has had contact with it. I had used Sharon's telephone a few times to call the police. Once was about a drunk driver; another time was about a group of crazy motorcyclists driving in a pack at more than 160 kilometres an hour; and a third time was when we came across a man squatting by the side of the road on a bitter-cold night.

When the call was over, I was a little stunned. My piece in *Maclean's* had generated both positive and negative feedback from the public, which I'd expected, but now someone deep inside the power structure that commanded the RCMP had felt compelled to reach out to me. My Deep Throat had painted a picture for me of what was actually going on inside the walls of the force. I asked questions. He had answers. He told me records were being altered and destroyed. I kept that to myself. It was something to pursue as I developed more contacts.

I talked to Stephen Maher about the call. A single call is not enough to hang an entire story on, but I couldn't see how, short of spending a couple of years on likely fruitless research, I could develop the leads I'd need to confirm what I'd just been told.

The caller said I should focus on access-to-information requests. Deep Throat was seriously naive. The Freedom of Information and Protection of Privacy Act (FOIPOP) was largely seen by journalists as a joke. The RCMP, and the Nova Scotia and Canadian governments, had long done everything they could to stall and stymie anyone trying to find out sensitive information.

And there was zero chance of getting anyone to go on the record to confirm anything he had told me. I had been pointed in a certain direction, and I needed to do something quickly to move things forward. I wrote a column. To get it published I needed to torque it a bit— be a little provocative and controversial. I didn't know who I could sell it to, but *Maclean's* had just published a piece. I sent it to them.

A few days later, I'd gotten no response. When I pressed for an answer, I was told "It's more of a local piece." I could appreciate their reluctance, but when the protagonist in the story is the Royal Canadian Mounted Police, it's never a local story.

Stephen Maher suggested that I send the story off to Tim Bousquet and the online *Halifax Examiner*. I had yet to hear of the paper or Bousquet, so I checked him out to see if he and I would be a good fit. As it turned out, Bousquet and his growing team had been doing a remarkably good job covering the shootings.

Bousquet had grown up in Norfolk, Virginia, and attended California State University at Chico. In 1990 he was elected president of the Progressive Student Union. He was quite the student activist, promoting voter turnout and protesting the Iraq War and the War on Terror while engaging in his own war, as it were—Activists Against Apathy. For more than a decade Bousquet inserted himself into the community of Chico, opening a newsstand and then working as a columnist at the *Chico News and Review*. Later he set up the *Chico Examiner*, where he was publisher, editor and writer, and founded the ChicoLeft electronic mailing list.

In 2002, his wife got a job in Halifax, so he followed her to Canada's East Coast. Landing in the Nova Scotia capital, Bousquet didn't have a distinguished enough resumé to get hired at the *Chronicle Herald* or the *Daily News*, so he went to work for *The Coast*, the free weekly street paper. There he worked his way up to news editor before setting out on his own. In 2014 he recreated the *Chico Examiner* and named it the *Halifax Examiner*. It was a one-man blog, but Bousquet had latched onto an intriguing story about a Halifax man, Glenn Assoun, who had been contending that he was wrongly convicted in 1995 of murdering his girlfriend Brenda Way and should not have been incarcerated for sixteen years. Bousquet's investigations led to Assoun being exonerated in 2019 and receiving a settlement from the federal government in 2021. Bousquet was nominated for a coveted Michener Award.

A key element of the Assoun case was that the RCMP was caught destroying evidence that would have exonerated Assoun while likely implicating convicted serial killer Michael Wayne McGray. It wasn't the first time I had heard about the RCMP destroying evidence in a case, and it wouldn't be the last.

I sent him my column. I just wanted to get it published. I had no idea who read online newspapers, but it was worth a try. Bousquet ran the column soon after it was in his hands. The date was May 21, 2020, and these were its key segments:

CRACKS ARE FORMING IN
THE RCMP CONE OF SILENCE

It has been about five weeks since the Nova Scotia massacre, five long weeks during which the Royal Canadian Mounted Police have cowered inside a cone of silence.

Compare its approach to how police forces around the world have typically handled similar events. From Paris to Toronto to just about Anywhere USA, the police are quick to inform the public about what has transpired and about key information about the perpetrator or perpetrators. Little, if anything, is hidden.

So what's the problem here?

From the outset the RCMP right up to Commissioner Brenda Lucki seems determined to stall for time and control the narrative of this story. They have forced the media to go to court to find out what was in the applications for search warrants executed after the shootings. The law states that such information should be readily available to the public.

The Mounties have also taken refuge behind its claim that it has commissioned a psychological profile of the gunman and can't say anything at this time. It kind of sounds like then candidate Donald Trump's claim in 2016 that he couldn't reveal his tax filings because they were under audit. . . .

Since publishing an opinion piece last week on Macleans.ca, I've witnessed the typical gamut of comment. Among them, Philip Black wrote:

The RCMP are not perfect but does that justify the rampant jumping to conclusions and the widespread RCMP bashing.

And Brenda Carr, a 911 dispatcher had this to say:

> . . . They did their best. And you do not know nor will you ever know what these men and women did to stop this monster. This is a time for healing. This article is not helping, it is only hurting.

But to my surprise, many others have contacted me who don't fit the normal profile in that a number of them were current or retired RCMP and other law enforcement officials.

"I've read everything you've written over the years and while I agreed with some of it, a lot of it just made me mad," said one former high-ranking RCMP executive. "But now, I have to admit that I agree with you. The RCMP is broken. It's not ready. It's a danger to the public and its own members."

That Mountie's sentiments were echoed by another former Mountie, Calvin Lawrence, who first served in the Halifax police department before joining the RCMP, where he had a long career. He is the author of a book, *Black Cop*. He amplified the comment about readiness.

After the murder of three Mounties in Moncton in 2014, the RCMP changed its policies and all police officers were given long guns.

Lawrence says that while the Mounties carry the guns, they don't likely know how to use them in a desperate situation. He says that while the RCMP talks a good game about its training, in reality a lot is left to be desired.

I suggested to him that the first Mounties to respond to the scene, particularly the supervisor, a corporal, may have been frozen in place, not knowing what action to take.

"That doesn't surprise me at all," Lawrence said. "You would think they had something in place to respond to crazies," Lawrence said. "They probably put something in writing but didn't practice it. . . . Tactical training costs money. The officers had the guns but didn't know how to use them."

But the most interesting call of all arrived with a cryptic description on the cell phone call display that I had never seen before.

The caller, who could best be described as a Deep Throat whistleblower, was obviously nervous. I will call him "he" from now on because there are more hes than shes in the law enforcement world.

"This is the first time I've ever done something like this," he said. "But I felt I have to do something."

He said he was calling me to encourage the media to keep asking questions: "Don't give up."

In the column, I described running my most pressing questions by the caller, about the premier and Attorney General's hesitation in calling a public inquiry ("It's about the money"), and why Heidi Stevenson was alone in her car while attempting to intercept an armed killer ("It was just bad luck. . . . she shouldn't have been there").

The real issue, he said, was what the police are hiding about their previous knowledge about the gunman.

"Make requests about Wortman and what the police knew about him."

"RCMP or Halifax?"

"Just keep asking questions and filing access requests." . . .

"It seemed to me from the outset that he may have killed other people in the past," I said.

The whistleblower just hmmmed.

"There's something they are hiding that will blow the lid right off this thing," the whistleblower reiterated. "I can't tell you what it is. I shouldn't even be telling you this. Just keep pushing."

When I ran all this by *Maclean's* writer Stephen Maher, he immediately added another possibility. "Maybe he was a CI."

A confidential informant? With a licence to kill?

It's a crazy idea but in the absence of facts from the RCMP people will talk.

That's the situation we are in.

This week the RCMP and its government lawyers have continued to obstruct the information process, insisting upon redacting information contained in the applications for its search warrants.

And then there is the psychological assessment or "autopsy" of the gunman. Well, here's my independent analysis.

He likely wet the bed when he was young. He had a fascination with fire. He tortured little animals. He likely had an accident and sustained a seemingly minor head injury in his youth. He suffered from undetected frontal lobe brain damage. He had low self-esteem but masked that with a superficial outward face. He grew into a malignant narcissist. Like many serial killers and mass murderers, he had a fascination with policing but becoming a security guard was beneath his station. He was a misogynist, largely because he had sexual orientation issues. He had no empathy for anyone and was controlling. I could go on, but . . .

That's it. Send the cheque to a charity of your choice.

That being done, Commissioner Lucki, what's the BIG SECRET?

The response was immediate. People contacted me from far and wide across Canada, and even from the United States. Some liked it and some didn't.

One person complained about my reference to wetting the bed, writing: "It's not really cool to link that to someone's definition of a psychopath or sociopath." What could I say? It's basic criminal profiling.

One person who did like it was a senior police officer close to the RCMP investigation. He reached out to me through an intermediary. Through him, the officer even forwarded to me his cellphone number, but I was only to call in the gravest of situations. He didn't want any text messages. He told me this: "You are on the money. If the public ever finds out what really happened, that would be the end of the RCMP in Nova Scotia." He wouldn't elaborate on that, but promised to keep me informed about what was going on inside the walls of the RCMP and government, which he did.

Another comment came from Michael Marshall, who I soon learned was a former Dartmouth New Democratic Party politico. He was putting out a blog with an unusual title: *40 Gallons and a Mule*. He had been digging into Wortman's life and history and only used Wortman's initials, to comply with the *Examiner*'s policy.

> If GW did anything weird in his childhood or high school years he concealed it exceedingly well. But a good place to start would be at UNB, where he was voted weirdo of the year. . . . Even though he was an adult, he had gathered a pile of false IDs and false names and used them when he would mysteriously disappear for days, never explaining to his roommate where he had gone. People found him kinky, an exhibitionist, quick to take offence, always making mountains out of molehills, strange, odd.

Some of those who reached out to me would become allies and contacts. Then there were the Smurfs, like the person who identified himself as R.G. Bryce, a member of the RCMP. I had no idea who was, but his comments were not all that surprising.

> I'd like to reply to a few comments raised on this issue. First to the obviously esteemed former member of the RCMP, Calvin Lawrence, who would have, by my estimates, retired in approximately 2003. I can assure you, Calvin, as a member who served when you were in the force and still serves today, that the training related to active shooters is 200% greater than it was in your day. For you to sit there in your rocking chair and cast judgement on the members who responded to this tragedy, which is unprecedented

in virtually North America, let alone Canada, is incredible to me. As a former member, you should be supportive to your fellow members, instead, you for some unknown reason, feel the need to say that "although members carry guns, they likely don't know how to use them in a desperate situation." What factuality is this statement based on? Nothing of course. You continue to babble your bs, by saying that we should "have a way to deal with crazies." Well, we do now have yearly active shooter training, unlike in your day, when that was unheard of. You wouldn't have had a clue how to deal with a lunatic like this, because, quite clearly, when you were a member, this training didn't exist. I know, because I was there back then. So, to make myself clear, shut your mouth, because you don't have a clue what you're talking about.

I had clearly touched a nerve or two. As I stated earlier, the RCMP battleship was trapped and in a totally defensive posture. Its options were somewhat limited, but it was still dangerous. I recognized that the road leading to the truth was going to be a long, twisted and possibly treacherous one.

Going public with my suspicions, intel and questions seemed to be an effective way to draw out others who had something to say about the RCMP, but I knew with every positive outcome there would be hundreds of negative ones. I had to be prepared to be called every name in the book: out of touch, insensitive and the dreaded "conspiracy theorist." That one always made me laugh, especially when it came from incurious reporters whose stories relied almost entirely on handouts from the police.

My original plan was to focus on the story nobody was reporting—the activities and failures of the RCMP. But now I realized that I needed to understand the killer himself if I was to understand the police response. I believed my Deep Throat. What he told me fit with the meagre available evidence and the RCMP's shenanigans. After all, the killer was dead, so why was the RCMP playing games?

I had long joked with my former colleagues that I was Canada's only investigative glass artist, knowing full well that I hadn't done much investigating in the past decade. But with the COVID-19 lockdown, I had time on my hands. It was time to invest in some new pens and a notebook or two. I needed to do something I had not planned to do: find out more about Gabriel Wortman and why he murdered those twenty-two people.

18

GABRIEL WORTMAN: THE FORMATIVE YEARS

To appreciate the Nova Scotia in which Gabriel Wortman existed, allow me to begin with my father, Arnold, who was the sixth born in his family. He was conceived in Sydney Mines, on Cape Breton Island, and born in Hamilton, Ontario. It always struck me as funny that although he didn't grow up in Nova Scotia, he had sucked up a lot of its mentality. He was kind-hearted but frugal. He gave good advice. "Don't be a quitter," he'd say. "If you start something, finish it." He was an original social justice warrior. Even when he was at his poorest, he despised those who stiffed a waitress after a meal, especially the well-heeled ones. "He threw nickels around like they were manhole covers," he would say to describe one miser or another.

Nova Scotians are often funny and talented—especially when it comes to storytelling and music. Good with their tongues and their hands, they say. It's the kind of place where you might stop by the side of the road to get your bearings and someone will pull up in a car and ask you if you're lost. I've had that happen, and I'm not alone. Wortman was that kind of guy at times—helpful, caring and compassionate.

But there is an old saying of uncertain origin about Nova Scotia that goes something like this: "Nova Scotia was home to pirates, killers, bank robbers, smugglers, swindlers, conmen, rogues, scoundrels and scroungers. Nowadays, the pirates are gone." The province has its dark side.

Wortman wasn't a bank robber or a pirate, but he was as close to being one as you could get these days. He bragged about how he put himself through university by smuggling cigarettes from Maine. If you've ever wondered how big the cigarette smuggling business is in Nova Scotia, the COVID-19 lockdown provided real evidence. With the province's borders closed throughout most of 2020, and contraband almost entirely unavailable, legal retail sales of cigarettes in Nova Scotia, the most expensive in the country, went up by 21 percent from the previous year, according to a report by Ernst & Young.

Larceny runs deep in the heart of more than a few Nova Scotians. Our long-time employee Melissa Bond (a distant relative of the murdered Peter and Joy Bond) says this when warning us to be careful about someone she doesn't trust: "Lock everything down. They'll steal the eyeballs right out of your head."

A streak of frugalness is entrenched into much of the Maritime psyche. People tend to see themselves as poor even when they are not. A noted Halifax physician, worth a couple of million in real estate alone, once told me that on his annual retreat to Florida his preferred pastime was "going to my favourite dollar store."

Scrounging is like a religion in Nova Scotia and has all but been institutionalized. In 1971, Edwin Theriault, who was raised in an Irish-Italian neighbourhood in Boston, brought a 1,000-pound load of used clothing to Meteghan, in western Nova Scotia, where his Acadian mother's family still lived. The locals went wild over the clothing and soon Theriault started a business, Frenchy's (which has an optional apostrophe depending on who is making the sign). The politically incorrect nickname was bestowed upon him by his friends in Boston. As Theriault told author Chris Benjamin: "Our motto was, 'When you shop at Frenchy's you save enough money to go shopping again.'"

Wortman didn't scrounge because he couldn't afford things—he was a millionaire a couple of times over—but because he genuinely liked to get things for nothing or as cheaply as possible. Hell, as one of his friends said: "Gabe was in his fifties and still sharing his Costco membership with his dad!" Wortman once repaired his parents' house with siding that had fallen off a truck. He was always on the hunt for motorcycle and car parts. In Portapique, the field south of his warehouse was littered with truckloads of reclaimed building materials that he planned to use to construct something or other someday. He even bought a used red shipping container that he wanted to bury somewhere on the property. He sought out two people with excavators in the Portapique area to do the job. No one knows why he wanted to bury it or if he ever did. One day the shipping container was gone. He was a perpetual motion machine, always on the move but never accomplishing much of lasting importance.

◆

When Gabriel Wortman's name first blasted into infamy that Sunday in April, it seemed an entirely novel proposition that a denturist, of all people, could transform into a mass murderer. What could possibly make a man of such a delicate and benevolent profession snap so violently?

As is so often the case when a serial killer or mass shooter is named, the first published comments about him were of disbelief. Consider this tweet from Lisa Brush a little more than an hour after Wortman's death had been confirmed: "Wortman was a great friend and amazing person in High School. Always smiling. Always kind. This is nothing but shocking!"

The *Chronicle Herald*'s Stephen Cooke tapped into those sentiments in a piece that was first published on April 19. Cooke captured the dichotomous nature of Wortman's personality, but in a sign of the times, even straightforward and basic reporting made Cooke's editors queasy. They felt compelled to put this preamble before the story, an earlier version of the one noted in the previous chapter: "Some readers have expressed opposition to this story, not wishing to read about a mass murderer's background. . . . We don't ever want to glorify, but we must contextualize to begin to find the answers we all desperately want . . ." This is what made Cooke's editors jittery:

Former high school friend Scott Balser posted on Facebook that Wortman was a very nice guy who liked to help others.

"We never know what others go through in life that makes them make certain decisions," Balser wrote. "I am by no means defending his actions this weekend.

"It's a very sad and tragic situation and my heart goes out to all the families involved. I've tried to live my life by this principle, 'but for the grace of God, go I.' We never know how we are going to react to a situation until we are in it."

Going even further back, junior high school friend Pierre Little on Twitter recalled an early fascination with air-powered guns and target practice.

"We used to shoot his machine gun air pellet or BB gun, I can't remember which, behind his house in Bridgedale," Little said. "Quite a rare airgun for the eighties. He also was into bottlecaps with saltpeter stinkbombs."

New Brunswick comedian and TV host Candy Palmater considered Wortman one of her best friends when they attended the University of New Brunswick in Fredericton together in the late 1980s.

The pair met up while they were residents at UNB's co-ed McLeod House, where they bonded over shared tastes in music— Pink Floyd's The Delicate Sound of Thunder was a favourite album at the time—and motorcycles, since Palmater's family ran a Harley-Davidson dealership in northern New Brunswick.

"I knew right from the beginning that this guy needed a friend, so I befriended him," Palmater said. "Most of my friends didn't like him, but I didn't care. He met my parents and members of my family, and we were inseparable for that whole year.

"I always felt like he wasn't quite comfortable in his own skin, but I thought as he matured, he would grow into himself." . . .

She said she wasn't surprised by a CTV News story she saw in 2014 describing how he'd provided free dentures to a cancer survivor who couldn't afford them on her medical plan, but noted that watching the story she sensed the spark she remembered from their university days seemed to be missing.

"Gabriel always had a sadness about him, but I was so shocked to hear that he'd hurt other people," she said. "I don't know what his later adult life was like, but I can tell you that at university, people weren't nice to him.

"He was a little bit different, like I'm a little bit different, but he was beautiful and he had a really deep heart, but he was the brunt of everybody's jokes."

A former client at his clinic, who asked that her name not be used, recalled that Wortman and his common-law partner who worked with him were jovial and easy-going together when she received new dentures from him in September.

"He was nuts; I mean that in a good way," she said. "We were carrying on back and forth like we knew each other our whole lives.

"They seemed to get along fine, bantering with each other like you would with your good friends. They seemed like very nice people together, very happy people."

In those formative days of the story, stories like that one in the *Chronicle Herald* helped to provide some insight into Wortman's psyche, but none of the accounts jibed with his final, terrible actions. Mothers and fathers. Grandmothers and grandfathers. Husbands and wives. A pregnant woman. A teenage girl. Was he a good guy gone bad or just a bad guy who had reached his limits?

◆

As Andrew Douglas and Cliff Boutilier were putting the final touches on the Portapique issue of *Frank*, the phone rang. Boutilier took the call.

"I'm the fellow's father who did this horrible mess," Paul Wortman said, introducing himself to the sixty-two-year-old Boutilier, who was both surprised by who was calling and unprepared for the onslaught headed his way. He didn't switch on his recording equipment.

The senior Wortman, seventy-four, was calling from Moncton, New Brunswick, where he lived with his wife, Evelyn. He told Boutilier that he had tried other media, including the CBC, but no one would talk to him. There was no way of proving that. *Frank* was fresh in his mind because he had read the story in a previous edition about his son's kerfuffle with the Halifax police on February 12, after Gabriel had locked an unmarked car in his lot on Portland Street.

"My blood pressure, it's so high . . . that my eyes start doing something and I can start counting, and I'm right on the beat," Paul Wortman said, describing his heart disease issues and his pulse in the interview. "That's high blood pressure."

Wortman laid out a mini biography of his family and their trials and tribulations. Married on December 16, 1967, Paul and Evelyn Wortman took a long while to settle. Paul was an industrial salesman, among other things, which naturally led him to find work in Hamilton, Ontario, Canada's steel centre and industrial capital. Gabriel Wortman was born on July 5, 1968, less than seven months after his parent's marriage.

Over the next few years, the couple left Gabriel behind in Canada with grandparents while they embarked on an odyssey that first took them to Fitchburg, a paper-making centre in northern Massachusetts, near the New Hampshire border. There, in 1970, Evelyn Wortman had a second child, a son, whom they quietly put up for adoption, something Gabriel didn't learn about until he was forty.

Next Gabriel and his parents moved to Cleveland and then spent some time in the southwest, around Phoenix and Las Vegas. Eventually they all returned to Moncton before finally settling along the banks of the Petitcodiac River in the Bridgedale neighbourhood of suburban Riverview.

Boutilier found it almost painful to listen to Paul Wortman's flat tone of voice, his sadness and weariness evident as Boutilier gently prodded him along. Paul went on for four hours before Boutilier had to call for a break, gather his thoughts, turn on a recorder and resume the conversation—for another four hours.

Boutilier tried to lead Paul back over the well-travelled ground from that morning, hoping to capture an audio version of his recollections. Paul said he had two brothers and a nephew who were or had been Mounties. When Gabriel was fourteen, Paul took him to Regina to witness an uncle's graduation ceremony. Paul was also a motorcycle enthusiast who rode his chopper with a group of retired RCMP officers.

"As a kid, the gunman didn't make friends easily and sports wasn't his bag," Boutilier quoted Paul Wortman in the next edition of the magazine. "The parents tried him in Little League. He just stood motionless on the field with his baseball glove down by his side."

Contrary to what Gabriel's high school friend Pierre Little said about his "machine gun" toy, Paul Wortman never saw his son play with pellet or BB guns. "He was more interested in repairing gears on, say, an eighteen-speed bicycle." Gabriel loved anything with two wheels. He liked to repair and tune up his friends' bicycles and charge them for it. Then he graduated to a moped.

His father remembered how Gabriel and some friends would taunt the campus police at the Université de Moncton. They would initiate a chase, then try to escape the security patrols. Gabriel called it "tantalizing" the police. It was an unusual word for a teenager to use, derived from Greek mythology, something he was likely studying in high school. The word, which originally meant to torment or tease someone with the promise of something unobtainable, comes from the legend of Tantalus. He tried to serve his son at a feast with the gods. Zeus punished him by forcing him to stand in a pool of water below a fruit tree that was just out of reach. He would go hungry and thirsty for eternity.

Gabriel's tantalizing of the police once ended with him being chased home. He came roaring down the street, yelling to his mother, Evelyn, to open the garage door, which she did. He drove in, screeched to a stop and closed the door. "The cops are after me!" he told his mother.

"He was so happy that he got away," Evelyn recalled.

Before we get to what Paul Wortman had to say about Gabriel as he got older, we have to stop him right there. It sounded to me like he was intent on sugar-coating the family's past. Stories were emerging from every nook and cranny that Gabriel Wortman grew up in a largely mad and violent family. His grandfather, Stanley, was such a mean and nasty brute that Gabriel's uncle, Glynn, put a knife in his chest when he saw an opportunity to get back at him, which earned Glynn a stint in prison.

Glynn and Paul had two brothers who became Mounties, Neil and Alan. Now retired, Neil told Global News a series of stories about his father and his abusive ways. "I soiled my shorts. He made me put the soiled shorts on my head, inside out, and told me to start knocking on doors of neighbours to show them what I had done. Because I refused to go, he beat me instead."

"Wortman's family is beginning to remind me of one of those Hollywood movies set in South Boston," said blogger Michael Marshall on *40 Gallons and a Mule*. "You know the ones: where one Irish brother becomes a federal cop and the other an organized criminal; then years later they meet up with separate orders to 'take down' each other."

Gabriel was described as being a troubled and odd child, wrote Marshall:

> A close cousin . . . who basically grew up with Gabriel, a cousin who later became a career Mountie . . . said Gabe was paranoid, violent, obsessed with money and that his parents were, quote, "bizarre." . . .
>
> Maybe he meant because Gabriel's father was once accused by Moncton police of being a dog kidnapper—or because he used to "ride the rails" all over North America while his young teenage bride struggled, with no money, to raise Gabe on her own. . . .
>
> There is no way this family saga could ever be massaged into a feel-good Hollywood thriller.

The more journalists dug, the darker the family portrait became. Andrew Rankin of the *Chronicle Herald* sat down on a number of occasions with Glynn, who was suffering from dementia. Rankin produced a riveting story about Gabriel's early years, when relatives claimed that he had been severely abused by his father, citing violent incidents of beatings and choking.

"I wanted to get him away from them because I loved him," Glynn Wortman said, describing his brother Paul as "manipulative, possessive and [having] violent ways."

One anonymous source cited by Rankin recalled Paul Wortman "boasting to her about making his nine-year-old son shoot his pet dog because he'd not cleaned up its poop. On another occasion, he was angry that his son, five years old at the time, was still attached to his baby blanket. So, he sat him on a table and burned the blanket in front of him. Paul was telling [her] this like he was this great dad teaching his son important life lessons."

Although Evelyn Wortman never said much publicly about her son, a customer of Wortman's remembered an incident that was somewhat telling. The customer said she and Wortman were getting along well until she made a comment about how handsome he was and suggested that his mother must have been a pretty woman. "After I said that, the whole atmosphere in the room changed," the woman said. "He wasn't the same person anymore. I could tell that something was bothering him."

Evelyn Wortman subsequently told private investigator Todd McSorley that she had never seen Gabriel smile as a child. McSorley had served on the Shediac and Moncton police forces, and then with the RCMP for almost eight years after it took over municipal policing in Moncton. A summary of McSorley's interview with the Wortmans was slipped to me.

Evelyn recounted to McSorley a macabre story about Gabriel from when he was around ten years old. Gabriel told his mother that he had caught a bat and ripped it up. She hadn't seen the incident "but found it disturbing." No kidding. The notion of a connection between animal cruelty and a proclivity for domestic violence and murder has been kicking around since it was first described about 800 years ago. Here is an excerpt from the *International Journal of Environmental Research and Public Health* published in May 2020:

The connection between the treatment of animals being closely associated with the treatment of fellow human beings was first documented in the 13th century. . . . Writing in 1964, [Margaret] Mead found that across a range of cultures, extraordinary abuse of animals [e.g., torture, killing] by children may precede more violent acts by that individual as an adult. She argued that an act of cruelty towards an animal by a child could "prove a diagnostic sign, and that such children, diagnosed early, could be helped instead of being allowed to embark on a long career of episodic violence and murder."

Around the same time that he tore apart the bat, Wortman began experimenting with "smoke bombs" made with saltpetre and sugar. In one incident he set off an explosive device that cracked a windshield. His cousin Chris called him "a weird little guy"—for good reason, it seems.

In his 1986 graduation photo from Riverview High School, Wortman looked like a typical gawky product of the times. The caption wrapped up with: "Gabe's future may include being an RCMP officer. Best of Luck from all the grads of '86."

Wortman didn't venture far to attend university, going to the University of New Brunswick in Fredericton. He made his mark at Bridges House, the 100-male residence in which he resided, but not in the most positive of fashions. Away from his parents, he went wild.

Michael Marshall was the first to pick up this part of the story, in his *40 Gallons and a Mule* blog. Shortly after Wortman's killing spree had ended, Marshall noticed an online comment on a soccer forum located in Sunderland, England. The poster had lived in the residence at the same time as Wortman. One of the incidents Wortman was remembered for involved him having sex with a girl in the shower of the residence. In the late sixties, that might not have been an unusual sight in a university residence, but in this case some of the UNB students found it disturbing. Marshall continued:

He remembers vaguely Gabe having silver dyed hair and wearing a cock ring or nipple ring but what he found oddest was that Gabe never made any friendships, of even the most superficial nature, among the 100 boys, their friends and girlfriends: say an informal community of about 300 people. No one. None.

Now on a private forum devoted to discussing Gabriel Wortman's spree killings, a woman I will call "L", now living in Charlotte County, recalled first hearing about Gabe from her husband-to-be Rob back around 1989–1990. . . .

Rob merely lived in the same (100 person) dorm as Gabe, but Rob's best friend Greg actually roomed with Gabe and he filled "L" and Rob's ears with the inside dope on this seriously weird and mysterious dude.

("L" and Rob also noticed that Gabe never made friends, never tried to, and never ever talked at all about his family. A prickly guy who had to make a major issue about everything: widely disliked and the winner of the annual Chuck Cosby award. . . .)

Ah, the Chuck Cosby Award, otherwise known as the "Asshole of the Year Award." It was a public recognition handed out every April to the biggest loser in Bridges House. The day the award was handed out—Chuck Cosby Day—was a giant party with drugs, alcohol and, perhaps, youthful fornication. According to the *Brunswickan*, the campus paper, which bills itself as the oldest such entity in Canada, "residents looked forward to it for the entire year."

In light of contemporary notions about such things, it was an odious award. Its defenders argued that there was a well-intentioned logic to the Chuck Cosby. It "gave certain order to the house. People didn't want to get it, so they behaved better," said a student interviewed about it in 1991.

Wortman was chosen by a secret committee as the winner. His sex-in-the-shower episode, hair and body ornamentation aside, Wortman was an enigma to the students. He made no friends. He was considered arrogant, argumentative and obnoxious. He would disappear for days at a time, presumably on his cigarette smuggling runs. When he was seen around campus, he was often in the company of an older man, who some thought was a professor at the university. His name was Tom Evans. We'll get to him soon.

Choosing Wortman for the Chuck Cosby was not a wise move. Wortman lobbied the university to put an end to his public humilia tion. The university terminated the award, and students exploded in anger. They smashed windows in Bridges House, shower stalls and bathrooms were destroyed, and valuable items were ripped off walls as 400 students rampaged through the campus protesting the cancel- lation. The "riot" story made the news wires and was published across Canada. I now defer to Michael Marshall, who uncovered the story, for an excerpt from his blog:

> It is easy to feel sympathy for both those awarded the notorious mark of ignominy and those who had to suffer at their antics all year.
>
> Who doesn't fear having 'the roommate from hell'?
>
> Who doesn't want to be avoid being publicly bullied and ostra- cized by an entire, quasi-gated community of 15,000? . . .
>
> . . . It suggests a pattern we are familiar with from many school shootings: people who, for whatever reason are odd or judged odd, get a bad reaction back from the majority, and this cycles ever upward in a ratchet pattern of dislike and distrust, until for some, it all explodes in a murderous 'revenge on my oppressors' fantasy. . . .
>
> Clearly, one response we gather from people who knew him was that Wortman, from being a little odd and being seen as a little odd, developed a thick skin or mask of being the guy who was always smiling and who was always joking about.
>
> But sometimes the mask slipped and people saw flashes of extremely over the top anger.
>
> But more often the perceptive saw that beneath the mask were the signs of the inner sadness and depression that drove him to be a heavy drinker and eventually a mass killer seeking revenge and a final sort of fame.

It seemed like so much flailing about, journalists trying to impose a social justice explanation on the problem of determining what made Wortman snap. On the one hand, they would quote scientists who said that child victims of domestic violence and abuse were more likely to become criminals, but then they would find someone willing to say there was no proof either way. Myriad studies and anecdotal observations have shown that the majority of children raised by brutal, abusive or criminal parents eventually right themselves. Conversely, some children of supposedly normal and well-adjusted parents end up as violent criminals. Suffice it to say, in Wortman's case other factors might have been at play.

There were unconfirmed rumours that he had suffered a head injury when he was younger. A serious bump on the head or concussion without the skull fracturing can cause imperceptible brain damage in the frontal lobe. These are the kind of injuries that back then were ignored, underdiagnosed or undertreated and quickly forgotten. It's an obscure subject that I knew something about. Back in my days at the *Globe and Mail* I began looking into head and neck injuries suffered by young athletes. This led me to the University of Virginia in Charlottesville, where original research was being done on the long-term effects of seemingly minor head injuries.

Beginning around 1980, Jeffrey T. Barth, Rebecca Rimel and others at the University of Virginia Medical Center began to notice something unusual in patients being treated at the hospital. Many victims who had suffered seemingly minor head injuries, mostly in car accidents, were slow to recover. Thirty-four percent of them hadn't returned to work within three months.

Barth and Rimel dug deeper into the subject with an initial research project, published in 1981, and subsequent studies over the years. At the time doctors were writing off these seemingly minor head injuries as something that could be cured with "Take two Aspirins and call me in the morning." Barth and Rimel's revelation was that a fractured skull can actually protect the brain from more serious damage by absorbing the energy from an impact before it gets to the interior of the skull. When the skull doesn't fracture, however, the energy from a blow sloshes the brain around inside the skull cavity and can injure it on the craggy interior edges.

The damage is often subtle and reveals itself over time. As Rimel explained it to me: "Imagine an airplane taking off to a far-away destination. When it leaves the airport its course is a degree or two off. Nobody notices it at the time. But the longer the plane flies the farther it gets off course. That's what happens to these victims. Nobody realizes how much damage there was until sometime in the future."

One of the first signs of impairment is what appears to be a subtle change in personality. Close friends are forgotten and replaced by acquaintances, and those acquaintances are usually dropped for new ones farther down the social scale in an ever-increasing descent to the bottom. Sufferers tend to self-medicate with cigarettes, drugs or alcohol, chemicals that speed up the brain and make them feel normal. Typically, they are disinhibited, meaning they know no boundaries and have no signs of a conscience; they will say, do and wear whatever they want—with nothing being an option—unafraid to reveal themselves in every way. There is little sense of personal space or others' ownership of possessions. They tend strongly toward narcissism and promiscuity. The statistics for criminal behaviour and incarceration in the cohort is astronomically high—up to 80 percent of affected individuals. Further mental deterioration is common with age, and suicide and early death are pronounced. You get the picture.

The groundbreaking work of Barth, who retired in 2020, and Rimel, who now heads the Pew Charitable Trusts, eventually led the world to re-evaluate brain damage from seemingly minor head injuries. Contact sports such as football and hockey have had to change their rules, and young soccer players are now being coached on the dangers of heading a ball.

Can we ever substantiate the rumours that Wortman may have suffered undetected brain damage from a head injury? Probably not. His remains were quickly cremated, and we have no idea what an autopsy might have found, or further examination if his brain had been saved.

◆

Tina Kennedy (a pseudonym) read my column in the *Halifax Examiner* and contacted me. I had no idea who she was. Kennedy used to live in Nova Scotia. She had gone to the agricultural college in

Truro in the early to mid-1990s, where she earned the first of her two post-secondary degrees. While she was attending the college, a friend named Melissa (also a pseudonym) introduced her to Wortman, who was then in his mid-twenties and just getting out of the mortician business and into being a denturist.

"We went to his house one day," Kennedy told me over the course of several interviews. "The house was really beautiful, really nice," she said of his residence at Portapique Beach. "I just walked through and remember the antiques, and I was complimenting him. We were all just starting out on our careers then, including him, but the guy obviously had some coin. We couldn't figure out where it came from. Some of our parents helped us out and were supportive, but none of us were on that scale."

Many women found Wortman attractive, if somewhat effeminate. At six foot two, he was tall and relatively fit, and even as he grew bald, it came at a time when shaved heads were trendy. And then there were his eyes, which some described as green, while others said blue or a mix of the two colours; regardless, people never forgot how he looked at them.

Kennedy described her interactions with the killer-to-be as awkward. "I said nice things about his house, and I think he thought I was flirting with him, but I wasn't," she said. "He had no concept of personal space, but not in an aggressive or hostile way. He was eager, leaning in close, looking you right in the eye. He had so much energy it was like he was shaking from the inside out. I thought he was a cokehead. He'd look right in your eyes with real intensity. When you looked into his eyes, it was like there was a light behind them, like a laser looking at you from the back of his brain deep into your eye. You don't look so deep inside someone's eyes. That's a level of intimacy that normal people don't violate."

After Kennedy and Melissa left Wortman's, they went to Melissa's mother's house. "We were having a coffee and talking about him. I was joking about him liking me. Melissa and her mom just laughed at me. 'You could be his beard,' her mom said. They joked about how good I would have it. He had lots of money. 'You could have everything you ever wanted. He will never touch you sexually.'

"That's why I called you," Kennedy said. "I laughed when I read the profile. I said: 'Oh, my God, he's so right.' You must have talked to someone else about him."

"No," I replied. "The RCMP said it was doing a psychological autopsy on Wortman, so I just drew from the history of other killers. It was a flare sent up to see who would respond, and here you are."

Although she had moved out of Nova Scotia, Kennedy kept in touch with people here. Shortly after Wortman's murder spree she was on Facebook, surfing through various Colchester Community area pages when she saw something that caused her to stop in her tracks. Someone had posted on his wall about, as "Truro Woman" described it, "an off-duty RC at the party or the RC holding the party."

RC is the local terminology for the Mounties.

"I started flipping through the pages," she said. "Another guy said: 'Shut the fuck up.' When I tried to go back to the first page, it was gone, and the person whose page it was had taken it private. It was a mistake. It wasn't meant to be seen."

That was a twist I wasn't expecting.

And from the earliest moments of Wortman's rampage, there had been rumours of a party at Portapique and that something had happened at it. The first reports were that Wortman had gone back to the party and killed people there. But as time passed, the party in the stories got smaller and smaller until it was just Wortman and Lisa Banfield having a "virtual party" in Wortman's warehouse with a couple from Maine—and even that was just a rumour.

I tried checking out what Kennedy said she had come across, but no one was admitting to having seen anything. I would later hear from others in the community that they had received similar warnings to the one Kennedy had glimpsed. What was going on? Why were people being told to "shut the fuck up" if this was just a spectacular domestic violence blow-up?

It was an intriguing notion. An off-duty Mountie? Or was it an undercover Mountie pretending to be off duty? Was there something going on that might corroborate what my Deep Throat was trying to point me toward?

19

BATTLING THE SMURFS AND INVOKING MY GRANDMOTHER

Portapique Beach is on the other side of the province, a two-hour drive from where I live. I didn't jump in a car and head there for two reasons. I didn't yet know what I was looking to find out, and even I had, that cancer thing and the treatments were making me feel like death warmed over. I was easily tired and tended to fall asleep in the afternoon. I also had to keep an eye on Sharon and her situation.

In April 2020, I was virtually unknown as a journalist in the province. With the article in *Maclean's* and a couple in the *Halifax Examiner*, my profile was rising, but not enough. The more that people knew about me, the easier it would be to find leads. A higher profile would also provide me with more security, which was absolutely necessary, because I knew from experience that I would be dealing with some people on all sides of the story who would look for any excuse to cause damage to me.

My options were limited. The *Halifax Examiner* had a progressive vibe that I didn't think would support my work much longer, given where the story was headed, especially around Lisa Banfield. And I appeared to have been struck off the CBC's massive list of shows after having questioned why Constable Heidi Stevenson was all alone when she ran into Wortman.

There was a talk radio station in Halifax, News 95.7, to which I rarely tuned in. The locals called it "right-wing radio," which wasn't entirely fair, although its toe-the-line ethos sometimes made it feel like it was being run by the Masonic Lodge. There were two talk show hosts. With his booming voice and background in news reporting at various stations around the Maritimes, Rick Howe was holding down the morning seat. I had done his show a couple of times years earlier and found him to be reasonably fair, interested and professional. In the afternoon, Sheldon MacLeod eschewed almost anything controversial—that likely ruled me out.

Howe was interested in the reporting I was doing and gave me a few spots. I needed to find a way to make this work, for me and other reporters. So I used my most recent piece in the *Examiner* as a springboard to discuss a variety of topics around the Portapique killings. I made a point of focusing on or highlighting stories by other reporters. I usually concluded my spots with an appeal to the audience urging anyone who had any kind of information to call "me or their favourite reporter."

The Smurfs did most of the calling. Some called the station to complain. They e-mailed me, messaged me and called me at home. One afternoon, Sheldon MacLeod called to do a "pre-interview" with me. I played along but sensed that I was being set up. The previous evening, I had been bombarded by former RCMP staff sergeants attacking me on all fronts. One spent a long time on the phone with me.

"Show me your credentials," MacLeod said, arguing that I should not be commenting on policing and police procedures unless I had been trained and certified in any area about which I was making comments.

"So, by that logic, only hockey players can write about hockey, politicians about government and aliens about UFOs," I replied. "Is that your argument in a nutshell?"

He blustered on.

That night, another former staff sergeant went after me with words that were eerily reminiscent of what MacLeod had said earlier in the day. When I went on MacLeod's show the next afternoon, I was ready.

It all fit perfectly into my next column in the *Examiner*, in which
I continued to update events and tried to move the story forward.

MARK FUREY AND THE RCMP'S
SECRET ARMY OF SMURFS

It has been six weeks since the Nova Scotia massacre and as the
RCMP dribbles out the official facts of the investigation, many have
wondered why the Nova Scotia government has been reluctant to
call for a public inquiry. . . .

And then there are questions about Justice Minister Mark Furey.
He was a Mountie for 36 years before he became a politician. And
now he's in charge of all matters of legal and policing issues from
soup to nuts. . . .

Furey collects a healthy pension from his Mountie days and is
revered in Mountie circles as one who made a life for himself in
the outside world. He says he does not have a conflict. But does he?
He says he can deal dispassionately with the enormous task before
him. But can he? . . .

In my 2008 book I devoted a chapter to the Secret Armies of the
RCMP. It told how the force directs dialogue and policy from behind
the scenes, mostly covertly, sometimes overtly. This so-called army
consists of current and retired Mounties, their families, friends, and
a general coterie of typical right-wing zealots. In the United States,
there is a two-word phrase to describe these sorts: Trump supporters. In Canada, they advocate against change, reform or investigation of the RCMP. . . .

Over the past couple of decades, many in the RCMP, municipal
and provincial police forces have told me about how they've been
bullied and intimidated or afraid of the force. Most are so fearful
that they refuse to go on the record about it.

"The Mounties play dirty," Edgar McLeod told me for *Dispersing
the Fog*. He is the founding police chief of the Cape Breton Regional
Police department and the head of the Atlantic Police Academy at
Holland College in Prince Edward Island. Friday, in an interview

from his Summerside, PEI home, he elaborated: "Governments at both the federal and provincial level have failed in their duty to hold them accountable."

Another person extremely familiar with RCMP thinking said this: "The biggest fear the RCMP has is to be held accountable. It believes that no one can tell the force what to do." . . .

The stakes are high and the Smurfs are coming out of the woodwork trying to affect, narrow, and even shut down public discourse. . . .

After I did a radio interview in Halifax, the Smurfs started calling in, suggesting that because I wasn't physically at Portapique Road, I had no right to be commenting on what happened.

That evening, just after midnight, a person identifying himself as a retired Mountie named Staff-Sgt. Eric Howard contacted me. In a shirty rant, Howard demanded that I provide a resumé showing my expertise before I be allowed to comment on matters regarding Mountie tactics, operations, and human resources. "Should you continue to make statements without the expertise to back it up, you are just prostituting yourself for money or attention," Howard wrote. "Think about this before commenting on any situation. I await your reply and resumé."

He's still waiting.

Later that day I had a pre-interview with another radio show host. I could smell the Smurf on him. We booked a time for the next day. . . .

When I appeared on the radio the next day . . . [t]he first question [about my credentials to write about policing] could have come right out of Staff-Sgt. Eric Howard's mouth. I batted it down by reading the exact response I had sent to Howard, which began: "Sir: Many of your retired superiors say I'm 100 percent right. . . . The deep-seated problems afflicting the RCMP are obvious and a matter of public interest." . . .

. . . As I popped my head up in this story, I got a notice from LinkedIn that a number of top Mounties in Ottawa were interested in me, including Ted Broadhurst, an Ottawa-based cyber special projects officer in federal policing criminal investigations. What? Was he looking to hire me or work for me? Not likely.

Paranoid? No, the curious thing was that Broadhurst is an expert on doing sneaky things. His public resumé shows he was in the special services covert operations branch, tactical Internet open source and other creepy things. He's a guy who should know how to cover his tracks, but he didn't. Why? Maybe he was trying to spook me. That's what the Mounties tend to do. . . .

Now Mark Furey is the minister of all things touching on the law in Nova Scotia. He is the point man when it comes to holding the RCMP accountable. It's obvious that there are a thousand horrible questions for which we need answers. At the same time, the Mounties and their fervent Trump-like supporters are literally saying: "Move along. Nothing to see here."

But there is plenty to see and to suggest otherwise is pure negligence. If anyone who is a threat to the Mounties and doesn't say the right thing is attacked, how is Furey resisting this? Does he have some sort of immunity from overt and covert RCMP pressure? . . .

At this particularly delicate time in its history, when its very structure across the country is at stake, the RCMP will fight tooth and nail to maintain the status quo.

That means it will resist a public inquiry. Even its house union has taken that position, which should tell you something.

Can Mark Furey rise above all this, be the bigger man and be totally objective?

Or is he just another dyed-in-the-wool Mountie Smurf who, given the choice between defending the public interest or those of the Mounties, slyly tilts to the side of the red coats?

Furey says he doesn't have a conflict, but the smart thing would be for him to recuse himself and let Caesar's wife, someone above suspicion, take over the file.

◆

I needed to develop new sources, and my contrarian point of view and in-your-face provocation was attracting the right kind of attention. My list of people in the know was growing, especially inside the justice system, where I needed them most. It was getting to be just like my old days in journalism, with a major twist. I had never seen a podcast or watched much on YouTube. Now people were telling me that someone had recorded my spots on *The Rick Howe Show* and were rebroadcasting it all on the video-sharing platform. This person, whom I didn't know, had married the audio to a video of a car driving through pertinent places in Nova Scotia, as if my comments were being played on the car's radio. This was getting crazy.

The RCMP's last press briefing had been a month earlier. If dark and mysterious things were going on behind the scenes, the darkest was the black ink on the ITOs for search warrants. The RCMP and the government were making it difficult for the media to find out anything. For example:

RCMP FILE: 2020-493913
Base Court: Truro

PROVINCE OF NOVA SCOTIA

INFORMATION TO OBTAIN A SEARCH WARRANT
(Pursuant to Section 487.1 of the Criminal Code)
and a related
Assistance Order
(Pursuant to Section 487.02 of the Criminal Code)
and a related
Sealing Order
(Pursuant to Section 487.3 of the Criminal Code)

This is the information of Sgt. Angela HAWRYLJK of Dartmouth, in the said Province of Nova Scotia, a Peace Officer and member of the Royal Canadian Mounted Police, hereinafter called the informant, taken before me. The informant says that she has reasonable grounds to believe and does believe that there is in

The property of Gabriel WORTMAN located at 136 Orchard Beach Drive, Portapique, Nova Scotia including the structure, outbuildings, and vehicles on the property;

AND the property of Gabriel WORTMAN located at 200 Portapique Beach Road, Portapique, Nova Scotia including any structure, outbuildings, and vehicles on the property.

The following items (things, or some part of them):

a) Firearms, ammunition, explosives, chemicals, ███
b) Surveillance system;
c) Computers or any other electronic devices capable of storing data;
d) Police related clothing, identification, and equipment;
e) Police related decals for cars;
f) Documents related to planning mass murder events;
g) Documents related to acquisition of firearms, ammunition, explosives, ███ and chemicals;
h) Human remains.

One of my new sources was deeply ensconced in the policing hierarchy. I'll call him Top Cop. He set up a system whereby he would pass information to me through a trusted former law enforcement cut-out. He gave me his number but said I could text him only in an emergency. I always went through the cut-out. You never know who is watching and listening.

One of the first things Top Cop told me was what was hidden under the black ink in the list above. It was only a few days after the pages were released in May 2020.

"Grenades," the cut-out man said. "Possibly phosphorous grenades. They didn't start covering everything up until about two days afterwards. Now they're slamming down the lid on all information."

"Why would Wortman have grenades?"

"Bikers," he said. "It's a big thing with the bikers. The combined forces know they are out there, and they've been looking everywhere for them."

The next couple of times I was a guest on *The Rick Howe Show* I made a point of mentioning the grenades. I thought they might be an important part of the real story. My distant cousins in the media thought otherwise. Instead of following up on the lead, they dismissed me as "a conspiracy theorist."

Top Cop also told me that the discussions inside government and the RCMP were focused on making sure there would be no public inquiry. "They are going to announce a [judicial] review and then bury the thing," he said through his cut-out man. "There aren't going to be any witnesses, just a paper review to determine whether policies and procedures were properly followed. They are covering it up big time."

I had to figure out what to do next. Premier Stephen McNeil was riding high on his iron-fisted and laudable approach to COVID-19 and his now famous imperative: "Stay the blazes home." Add his current popularity to his having five brothers in policing, and he wasn't going to rock the boat. The collective media wasn't, either. While media lawyer David Coles argued in court every couple of weeks or so to remove more of the black ink from the redacted documents, a pattern was emerging. With every new unveiling, the media would take the uncorroborated, incomplete and sometimes erroneous information and breathlessly report it. It didn't really matter if the "new" information was actually old or self-serving to the RCMP, the media had paid good money for it and they were going to proudly report it—often under the most sensational of headlines. But the real story was what the RCMP had done and not done, and the media didn't have the money or personnel left for an investigation. They were content to leave that work to a review or an inquiry.

"There's not going to be an inquiry, just a review," Top Cop reiterated, after reporting back on another conversation. Another insider confirmed that.

A mere review would be both an outrage and disastrous. I had to find stories and put things on the record to make it difficult for the government to sweep it all under the rug. I didn't want the RCMP or government to say afterwards: "Oh, we didn't know about any of that." I planned to lay it all out for them and the public.

"Are you writing a book?" Lindsay Jones asked me at one point. She wasn't the only one.

"I have no plans to write a book," I told her. "I'm just trying to document what I see as soon as I see it and what I was thinking. I'm too old to write a book. I don't want to have another heart attack."

The problem I faced was that the government, the RCMP, some journalists and the public were treating me like an alien who had just landed in a Tic Tac from outer space. I remembered how aggressive, professional reporters like Andrew McIntosh once pushed a difficult story forward one new fact at a time to get to the truth. That's what he did with the investigation into shady links between Airbus industries and the government of then prime minister Brian Mulroney. I remembered moments like one at the *Globe and Mail* when editor-in-chief Norman Webster got down on the floor on his hands and knees to do a final edit on a 10-foot-long investigative piece that had just been pumped out of a dot-matrix printer. He was not taking things out, but trying to word the story in a way to get everything in. Then he sent his reporters back out to get even more.

The reporters now were like hamsters on a treadmill, gathering information, filing stories to their editors, then pumping their views via Facebook, Twitter and maybe even a podcast or two. They were doing their best, but all their efforts didn't get them under the surface of the story. From what I could see, the big problem was the editors—the Toadocracy, I came to call them. Instead of chasing leads and following their instincts, they were content to sit back and catch whatever story landed on their sticky tongues. They'd digest it and then wait for the next one to get stuck in their craw. It was a safe and predictable approach; so long as the RCMP threw them the occasional dead fly, the Toads would never have to go looking for a real meal.

Another issue was that I had come to Nova Scotia only after my retirement from journalism. Why should anyone in the province believe what I wrote or said? I felt I had to address these notions and let people know a little bit more about me. I wrote another provocative column for the *Examiner*.

PREMIER MCNEIL: A MESSAGE FROM MY GRANDMOTHER ABOUT THE RCMP

That horrible weekend last month, all Canadians witnessed what was likely the most catastrophic collapse of policing in Canadian history. Little, if anything, went right.

Twenty-two people were murdered. The gunman marauded around the province of Nova Scotia with seeming impunity, only being killed and captured because the last person he murdered had left her gas tank empty.

We all know that we can't let that happen again. Yet, in Nova Scotia, the premier and his ex-Mountie justice minister have been virtually silent, caught up in the COVID-19 disaster.

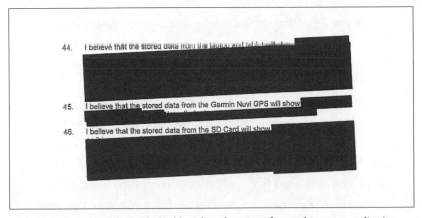

44. I believe that the stored data from the laptop and [redacted]

45. I believe that the stored data from the Garmin Nuvi GPS will show

46. I believe that the stored data from the SD Card will show

The Halifax Examiner obtained a highly redacted version of a search warrant application made by the RCMP.

People, even many Mountie supporters, want a public inquiry to hopefully clear the air, but the Crown and the RCMP seem tone deaf. Even if they are not in cover-up mode, it smells like that. They seem bent upon using up the provincial supply of permanent ink, blacking out large chunks of the various Information to Obtain documents for a search warrant.

Little seems to make sense about it.

The position taken by the censors is that the blocked information is key to an ongoing criminal investigation. Their focus is on the shooter. Just as much, if not more, attention must be paid to the Mounties.

What investigation arising out of the circumstances is going to change the fact that the RCMP embarrassed itself with its performance that weekend? There are supposedly more than 900 Mounties in Nova Scotia in contract and federal policing. Where were they all?

Logic dictates that since the shooter, who the *Examiner* is calling GW, was absolutely linked to the shootings and fires, any new criminal investigation should have little, if anything, to do with him. RCMP Chief Supt. Chris Leather said as much at a press conference three days after the rampage: that GW "acted alone."

Has the RCMP stumbled onto some new, sensitive, and dramatic case or are they and the government just slowing everything down to a crawl, to control the narrative and buy some time?

My gut tells me the latter. Prove me wrong.

There is a well-known public market in RCMP uniforms, badges, and patches and nothing has ever been done about it. That suggests there is not much room for a criminal investigation there. That is, unless Mounties were actually hawking their stuff to make a buck, and even then that's only a tiny sliver of the larger story.

Donald Walker told the *Toronto Star*, a week after the shootings, that GW "didn't hide this vehicle. This car was not like in a garage where he was secretly making it. . . . He was very proud of that vehicle. He told me he wanted to go to car shows, take it there, show off."

The Mounties apparently knew this, too, and it was widely reported that GW was told he could take the decked-out fake police car to shows, but not drive it on the road. . . .

To date, various media entities have reported on everything from the gunman's quirks, threats to others, illegal guns, replica Mountie cars, possible cigarette smuggling, and even the murder of someone in the United States, among other things.

Even if any of those allegations are worth pursuing, as I said, the perpetrator is dead. There do not appear to be reasons enough to run through Sharpies by the caseload.

The public has a right to know what was in those documents, and disclosure should not be unreasonably withheld.

Last week, I reported that a Deep Throat Whistleblower told me that the media must continue to push for information on the relationship between GW and the police, either the Mounties or Halifax.

There was a Big Secret there, the source said, big enough to blow the entire story into another dimension.

Which brings me, briefly, to my qualifications to write about these matters.

I am a citizen.

Reporters across the country tell me that the mention of my name draws immediate ire from the Mounties. "He hates the RCMP," more than one has been told.

For the record, here's what I think, based upon my considerable research over the years. The RCMP is a secretive, stubborn, archaic, and dysfunctional organization that is foremost a danger to its own hardworking and mostly loyal employees. All too often, young Mounties become quickly disillusioned when they begin to realize that they are mere faceless pawns in the force's over-arching ambition to protect its multitude of franchises. Because that's what they are: business-like franchises. Profit centres.

The issue of my competence and insights is politically heated among RCMP and other police supporters on talk shows and in Internet forums.

So here we go, wading into the past.

As a journalist since 1974, I've covered policing from a variety of perspectives.

In 1976, fellow reporter Steve Jarrett and I responded to a gun call one Saturday night where the then Hamilton-Wentworth Regional Police were using their SWAT team for the first time. As we approached the scene, one of the SWAT members was heard to say that they had hoped "Palango would show up." He jokingly implied he was going to take me out. I got so close to the scene that I had to push down the barrel of a tear gas gun a sweaty officer was about to fire into a room filled with his fellow officers. It was a pretty funny story. The police hated it.

Over the years, I learned a lot being close up and had not a few harrowing moments here and there facing down an enormous range of physical and legal threats.

In my thirties, as the City and later National Editor at the *Globe and Mail*, I was in charge of investigative reporting. As I look over at the wall in my office, there is a photo of me accepting the Michener Award from then Governor General Jeanne Sauvé, the highest award for journalism in the country, on behalf of the *Globe and Mail*. It is for disinterested public service journalism. Disinterested?

It means we didn't have a dog in the race. Why me? I was directly involved in the conception, reporting and editing of three different series of stories and had input on a fourth, all of which were co-winners of the award. One of the stories, the so-called Patti Starr Affair, resulted in nine Ontario Cabinet Ministers losing their jobs in one day.

After I left the *Globe*, I wrote three increasingly more critical books about the RCMP and its operations, as well as newspaper and magazine articles. I met hundreds of Mounties and policing experts. I rode around in police cars around the country and saw what the Mounties go through firsthand. I fielded hundreds of calls over the years from distressed Mounties. They all told the same stories about how the force has and continued to let them down. "I would go to a city police force in a moment," one Mountie told me when we met over an incident. "But I can't transfer my pension."

In fact, as I look around my office, I can also see another way the world has changed.

I'm looking at a large framed print of the Musical Ride charge by Bill McMillan from 1997. It was given to me as a gift by a detachment in British Columbia who invited me to speak at and attend their annual ball. Why me? The Mounties there believed back then that I was speaking for the rank and file, the ordinary members, trying to protect them from the scourge created by the incompetence of their masters. Not much has changed. In fact, almost all tell me, things have deteriorated even more.

But what has changed is the echo chamber mentality created in the closed, invitation only chat rooms on the Internet. I have had a peek into some of them recently and it's what you'd expect. It's like the Taliban in there. Anything perceived to be liberal or Liberal is the subject of scorn. Anyone who speaks out of turn is either castigated or threatened with banishment. People like me are accused of being libs, gay (not that there is anything wrong with that), stupid, greedy, or corrupt. In those rooms, as Donald Trump might put it, a Mountie could mow down everyone on 5th Avenue, and no one would hold it against him.

The final taunt, and you hear this one on the radio talk shows all the time. Neither I, nor anyone like me, can talk about policing unless you are a police officer.

No, I'm not one and never have been. I couldn't be. I'm partially colour blind, which in the context of what I've been doing for the past 20 years or so, glass art, should give anyone pause.

But when I argue that Constable Heidi Stevenson should not have been where she was, I say that because I understand the deep flaws in the system and I care about what happened to her.

Why do I care? Because it's the right thing to do. It's in the public interest. Caring about how she died might prevent it happening to some other police officer. And, secondly, contrary to what the mad-dog police defenders seem to assume, I am not some wimpy, money-grubbing theorist with no clue about policing and law enforcement.

I have a long family history of peace officers, people who have been on the line and are still on the line.

My father was military police watching over Nazi prisoners at Camp Barriefield, just outside Kingston, Ontario.

My brother, Dave, was a corrections officer in one of the most difficult jails in the country, until he retired.

Six weeks after she became a peace officer, my daughter had to use a weapon to protect a fellow officer during a near riot situation. When another one happened, subsequently, it was on her day off. She told me that when she asked [a] prisoner the next day about what had happened, the prisoner told her: "We did it when you were off, ma'am, because we know you shoot." She is now a crisis negotiator.

Her husband is also a corrections officer in a federal institution and an avid hunter, which brings me to my final qualification, which I self-admittedly dismally fail.

My son-in-law along with his buddies took their children on a weekend hunting trip to a camp. When they got back, I asked my grandson what he thought. He said: "It was boring."

When he gets older, I'll tell him what I really think: "Hunting isn't much of a sport, since the animals don't know the rules. It would be a real sport if the deer could put out donuts and jerky, perch in trees with long guns and shoot at the hunters. That would be a sport worth watching."

The long and short of it is that I am confident that I know what I am talking about.

The 30 law professors at Dalhousie who have been joined by others like former coroner, Dr. John Butt, are right in calling for a public inquiry. The sooner, the better.

And then there is that final thing, my last name. Palango.

Although I've lived here 20 years, I'm still considered to be a CFA, a come from away.

Well, these days, you never know who you're dealing with. My father was conceived in Nova Scotia and was born in Ontario, four months after the family arrived there. Here are my other Nova Scotia credentials. My great-grandfather was Big Allan MacLellan from the Inverness area on Cape Breton. My great-grandmother was Mary Kennedy from nearby Broad Cove. She was born on Campbellton Road. So was her daughter, my beloved grandmother, Mary Sarah MacLellan.

And, right now, I am calling on her to send a message to Premier McNeil. As she would have put it: "Jeezus snow-shovellin' Christ, Stephen, get the blazes off your arse and call an inquiry."

◆

A few days later Tim Bousquet gave me more space in the *Examiner*, and I used it for a news story, backed up by a column two days later.

The story was about the inadequacy of the RCMP system of policing rural communities. The RCMP won contracts because it promised a better price for policing, but it was no deal. There was no policing between 2 and 6 a.m. During those hours the Mounties were on call, but it wasn't like they were living in the community. Young Mounties wanted to live near urban areas. Community policing had become commuter policing.

Local governments had no control of the Mounties, even though they were paying for their services. The RCMP was accountable only to the federal government. For example, when the local police advisory board heard that the RCMP's Bible Hill detachment was short five or six of the members being paid for by the community, it tried to raise the matter with the RCMP.

"We couldn't get the real numbers," said Wade Parker, a former corrections supervisor who was now a councillor for the Municipality of the County of Colchester, which includes Portapique. "We tried our best, but the RCMP won't answer to anything. I know for a fact that we are not getting the proper policing that we're paying for and this in turn has left the community vulnerable," said Parker.

Another councillor who talked to me was Michael Gregory, who spent twenty-five and a half years in the RCMP and was also a member of the police advisory board. "Over the past several years, the RCMP policing has gone completely downhill," Gregory said. "It's pretty sad. To me we need twenty-four-hour policing. The world is changing all the time. In today's society most things don't happen between the hours of nine to five. There is a four-hour time frame when there are not police. That's when things are happening."

Edgar MacLeod, the former chief of the Cape Breton Regional Police and a long-time RCMP critic, concurred: "At 4 a.m. in the morning in many of these rural communities policed by the RCMP it's like the wild, wild west out there."

"The police are the public and the public are the police," said Gregory, quoting Sir Robert Peel, the founder of modern policing. "When I lived in the community, I prided myself that I knew everyone in the community. It paid off for me. Now, that's all gone."

Councillor Parker added: "The RCMP got away from community policing and instead of having officers rooted in the community, they are everywhere. I don't know where the police live or where they have to come from to get here. And when they do get here to do their job, they don't know the people in the area very well. The people don't know them. They don't know who's a criminal and who isn't."

Before the shootings, people in Colchester County were already complaining about the Mounties and searching for alternatives. I learned that the previous January, the Truro Police Service was asked to put in a proposal to take over the policing in Colchester County. Truro made a pitch showing how it could provide twenty-four-hour policing.

In the follow-up column, I focused on the RCMP's practice of getting by with fewer officers than might be considered safe—a practice known as "risking it out." One of those I interviewed was former Mountie Cathy Mansley. "The RCMP is always trying to do the most with the least amount of staff. That's their model," Mansley said. "The supervisors get bonuses for coming in under budget. So, when you show up for a shift and there are not enough bodies to cover the shift, the supervisors used to say: 'We are not calling anyone in on overtime, we are just going to risk it out.'"

Mansley said the stress of working alone without proper backup was mentally and physically draining. One of her commanders back then was Mark Furey, now the justice minister. Mansley said that under Furey the "risk it out" approach continued. "They say 'Risk it out,' but they weren't risking their lives," Mansley said. "What they do is risk us out. We are the ones out there in dangerous situations. They are risking each Mountie's life, and I can't believe they get bonuses when they do."

I pointed out in the column that the latest in a long list of federal reports on the RCMP had found that the force was unsustainable in its current form. The federal government threw more money at the problem. I ended the column this way:

Now here we are left in a situation that is right out of a Monty Python skit. Even though the RCMP clearly abrogated its responsibilities and duties that weekend, the governments of Canada and Nova Scotia are reluctant to call for a public inquiry because they say there is no money.

No money? Didn't the federal government just give $508 million to the desperate Mounties to fix a system that clearly cannot be sustained?

Instead, the premier of Nova Scotia, Stephen McNeil, leaves it up to his legal handyman, Mark Furey . . . to sort things out.

Their intention it seems is to have the RCMP investigate the RCMP for the failings of the RCMP and report back to Furey, the ex-Mountie who, nonetheless, proclaims he can be objective.

Why not call in an objective, competent outside police force such as the Ontario Provincial Police or the Sûreté du Québec, whose operations are not dissimilar to those of the RCMP?

Why not set up a public inquiry, which seems to make even more sense every day?

If nothing is done, there is likely another huge dollar problem on the horizon. Now that it's widely reported that the RCMP has likely been negligent in its operations and that there are severe flaws in the organization, what would happen, god forbid, if something else horrible takes place? There seems to be a ton of potential legal liability for governments and the police unless something is addressed quickly.

Or, Mr. Prime Minister and Mr. Premier, do you just want to risk it out?

The RCMP was a mess at the federal, provincial and local levels. Were they so out of touch in Portapique that they didn't have a clue who and what they were dealing with in Gabriel Wortman? Or was something more complicated going on?

20
NOT A WHITE PICKET FENCE LIFE

Gabriel Wortman had clearly made some people happy in his lifetime, and then he killed twenty-two others. There was one person who could fill in the enormous gap between the two sides of the enigmatic denturist. Since the massacres, his common-law wife, Lisa Banfield, had talked a couple of times to the RCMP, but to no one else. While Wortman's chin was still holding up his head in the parking lot at the Irving Big Stop, she had scoured Halifax, hunting for a lawyer. She then went to ground and wouldn't talk to anyone.

On May 23, blogger Michael Marshall joined *Frank* in naming Banfield and providing a little more context:

> Twenty years ago, Gabe & Lisa met, fell in love and stayed together till the day he died. . . .
>
> For six years, from 1996 till 2001, Gabe Wortman had a lovely house at the bottom of Pine Street in Dartmouth next to the park, which he shared with his wife Corinna Kincaid.
>
> For six years, from 1996 till 2001, Lisa Banfield had a very nice home on Saluki Drive in Beaver Bank which she shared with her husband.

Then sometime twenty years ago, these ill-starred married people met.

It could have been just a brief secret fling.

But instead, the pair fell in love, divorced their spouses, moved out of their lovely homes to the rooms above the shop—and stayed together for 20 years, until the day he died.

That little bit of detail was helpful. It gave me a starting point to piece together the highs and lows of their relationship. One early hurdle was that few people were truly close to the couple. For example, we don't know how or when Wortman and Banfield first met. We do know that he gave her two dozen roses on their first date. Banfield was overwhelmed with what she thought was a spectacular romantic display. Others might call it "love bombing"—a controlling personality buying their way into the heart of their prey.

The timing suggested that they may well have been still married to their respective first spouses, as Michael Marshall speculated. Did they have a secret love nest? Having an apartment on the side, like he'd later build in his warehouse in Portapique Beach, had long been part of Wortman's modus operandi. Did they meet at some kind of sex club? It's a fair question. There was a lot of formalized casual sex going on in Nova Scotia.

Prying into Wortman's world looked like it might be a difficult proposition. There were essentially two distinct groups: the outsiders and the insiders.

On the outside were the grieving families and friends of the twenty-two victims. A few of them might have third-hand knowledge, at best, about Wortman. And some of the families were, understandably, determined to protect the reputations of their murdered loved ones, some of whom were rumoured to have had sexual relationships with Wortman.

On the inside were Wortman's acquaintances, clients and neighbours and Banfield's family and friends. Those who talked could provide salacious bits, but few were close enough to know what was going on inside Wortman's head. The Banfields weren't talking.

Finally, deep inside Wortman's life was a coterie of rounders, ne'er-do-wells, grifters and serious criminals. By definition they were not the talkative type.

◆

Before it was amalgamated into the Halifax Regional Municipality in 1996, Dartmouth, population 62,000, was known as the City of Lakes. It had twenty-three of them inside its boundaries. Despite its many beautiful neighbourhoods with views of those many lakes, the harbour or the Atlantic Ocean, Dartmouth (which alternatively offered views of the three iconic red-and-white-striped smokestacks at the Tufts Cove electrical generating station) had a seedy reputation. The infamous television series *Trailer Park Boys*, with its wacky cast of criminally inclined characters, was set on the city's margins.

Wortman had already lived in Dartmouth for a number of years in a house at 26 Pine Street with his first wife when he bought 193 Portland Street, only four short blocks from home, in May 1998. He subsequently opened the Atlantic Denture Clinic at the new location.

Portland Street is a main thoroughfare in the old Dartmouth downtown. Wortman's building was just outside the core, past the Five Points, as the locals call the nearby intersection. St. James United Church anchored the corner, and Wortman's office was three doors away. That portion of Portland Street was anything but posh. Across the street and down two blocks stood a building that had long been home to a line of "motorcycle enthusiasts."

In 1981, the rollicking, shoot-'em-up 13th Tribe became the two-wheel kings of Portland Street. After getting caught by the police for firing a few too many bullets, in 1984 the 13th Tribe was absorbed by the world's dominant outlaw motorcycle club, the Hells Angels. A massive police operation put the Angels out of business in Nova Scotia in 2001, leaving the Darksiders, a Hells Angels puppet club, to fill the vacuum in Dartmouth. The club moved into 118 Portland Street, which is still their base at the time of this writing.

If the municipal government was intent on gentrifying that stretch of the dingy neighbourhood, Wortman had other ideas. He wanted his business to stand out, and its three-dimensional signage caught the planning department's attention. A giant 3-D set of dentures— bright white teeth and very pink gums—jutted from the corner of the building over the driveway and sidewalk. Beside it hung a giant, toothy smile in the same colour combination under a sign: "Dentures." The local council was not happy. The planning department fought to have it removed. Wortman resisted and eventually got his way.

He might have had a giant smile adorning his place of business, but the new denturist in the neighbourhood had a reputation as a volatile personality. While residing at 26 Pine Street, Wortman "was well known to neighbours as a guy who was consistently mean to children walking past his home, assaulting several physically," Michael Marshall wrote, quoting a female source. "One assault, at least, she knew was serious. His front steps have zero setback to the sidewalk, meaning I or you would find it very hard to walk along that public sidewalk, which I have done many times, without being 'too close' to GW's front door," Marshall added.

With the breakup of his marriage, the house on Pine Street was sold and Wortman moved into an apartment above the denture clinic. By now, he was making money hand over fist from his legal and illegal enterprises, but in 2000 he suddenly needed a whack of cash from his parents. We don't know if it was to buy out Corinna or to invest in something licit or otherwise.

Paul Wortman said he lent his son $250,000 plus interest around this time. He said his son repaid him promptly in $10,000 instalments, which is a solid indicator of Gabriel's cash flow.

Wortman was always dreaming up schemes to make money, and next on his agenda was real estate development. He wanted to build an apartment building on the site of 193 Portland Street, with commercial space at ground level that would include his denture clinic. The idea was well ahead of its time for the area, but he needed land for it, and he coveted the buildings between his clinic and St. James United Church.

That's when the fires started happening. In October 2000, the building at 191 Portland, next door to his clinic, mysteriously caught fire. Firefighters extinguished the blaze before the building could be entirely destroyed. Arson was suspected.

"It was in the bottom apartment and yeah, there was lighters all over the place in the living room," fire investigator Scott Wheeler told Tim Bousquet of the *Halifax Examiner*. "You could see where they were doing some illegal drugs back then like marijuana. . . . We found the gas can in [a] bedroom on the floor. It looked like somebody just poured some gas in [the window] and then threw the can in and lit it on fire."

As Banfield moved into Wortman's life in 2001, they shared the apartment above the business. The location was a perfect set-up for Wortman. At the back of the clinic was a series of garages where he could store some of his motorcycles. Meanwhile, Banfield became not only his live-in girlfriend but eventually his full-time personal assistant. Most Wednesday nights, and sometime Tuesdays, he would head out to Portapique for a long weekend, while she remained in Dartmouth running the clinic, serving customers and polishing and tinkering with dentures. Much of the business was conducted in cash.

Before long all telephone calls to Wortman went through Banfield. He told people that he valued his private time away from work and didn't want to be bothered. That's one way of looking at it. By then it was already known in the criminal world that cellphones and vehicles with GPS systems were trackable by the police. That was why career criminals didn't use phones that could be linked to them and why they disconnected GPS systems in their new vehicles. General Motors' OnStar roadside service and similar systems from other companies functioned as both cellphone and GPS—a fink to be avoided.

Taking his calls, Banfield got to know everyone who was in contact with Wortman. With her permanently installed in his life and business, the neighbourhood fires continued, and crazier and crazier situations continued to pop up around the couple. On September 14, 2001, flames erupted at 189 Portland Street, two doors down from the denture clinic.

Three weeks later, another fire was set in the same building. It makes one wonder if Banfield was oblivious to all this or whether she was getting a little nervous going to bed at night.

The latest fire came at a time when the police were ramping up their efforts against the Hells Angels down the street. There was always a surreptitious force lurking around the neighbourhood, but the RCMP's Operation Hammer was closing in on the Angels leaders. It was the kind of thing that someone like Wortman, always on the alert, might well see coming. On October 29, 2001, Wortman, then thirty-three, bought the two burned properties at a reduced price.

If he was pleased with his success, he didn't show it. That same day he roared out of his denture clinic and attacked fifteen-year-old Matthew Meagher, who was standing at the bus stop out front. Wortman yelled, "You're too close to my building," before laying into him with fists and boots.

"He came out, I guess in a drunken rage and ended up punching me as many times in the head as he could," Meagher told Andrew Russell of Global News. "Then he had a friend who came over from around the corner and hit me with a crowbar. Then the two men stomped on my head and all over my body."

"Stop, he's only a kid," a passerby yelled out at Wortman, and he and the other man fled.

No one knows who the other man was. Wortman was charged with assault. He had no other record at the time, other than a 1997 speeding ticket in Truro. The unprovoked assault was severe, and it looked like Wortman was a good fit for a five-year prison sentence.

First Wortman tried to bribe Meagher with cash to drop the charges. When that didn't work, Wortman hired Joel Pink, the doyen of the criminal defence bar in Halifax, to represent him. A preliminary trial date was set for January 10, 2002, and a Crown attorney was appointed.

Typically, not much happens at such an early point in the process, but as so often happens in Nova Scotia, a propitious backroom deal was easily worked out. A new Crown attorney suddenly emerged out of thin air and was appointed to the case. His name was David G. Barrett, and he had been practising as a defence lawyer for about thirteen years. A former Mountie in both Alberta and British Columbia, he'd also worked for four years with the Canadian Security Intelligence Service (CSIS), Canada's spy agency. In 1998, Barrett was appointed as an acting Crown attorney in both Halifax and Dartmouth provincial courts, and served as legal counsel to the RCMP Veterans' Association in Nova Scotia.

Wortman pled guilty to a minor assault, and the judge approved the plea bargain and gave him a conditional discharge and placed him on probation for nine months. He was fined a meagre $50.

"I think there should have been a little more justice there," Meagher told Global News.

In December 2003, there was another damaging fire at 191 Portland Street. This time the building was finally rendered uninhabitable. Wortman wanted the city to pay to tear it down. He put up a weak fight for awhile until the city ordered him to demolish the structure, which he did in April 2004.

Wortman had his land. He had a vision for a lucrative development that would include his dental clinic. But he had overlooked one important factor. In summing up Wortman's boondoggle, Tim Bousquet quoted Dartmouth historian David Jones: "Given the lengthy record of the discovery of human remains on the St. James Church hill (from 1844 and potentially earlier to 1954) and the 1894 discovery of a stone hammer at the site of the Church Manse, it is highly recommended that the Nova Scotia Museum, Special Places and the Mi'kmaq be contacted ahead of any potential further ground disturbances in the area of the hill," Jones wrote. "GW never applied for a development permit for the site."

All of this happened during the first three years of Wortman's relationship with Banfield. They struck me as an unlikely couple. What was the glue that kept them stuck together? Were they like-minded soulmates? Was she camouflage for a man who didn't want anyone speculating about his complicated sexuality? Or, as the RCMP and the news stories suggested, was she cowering in fear, terrified of stepping out of line? After all, Banfield had told various people over the years that Wortman was demanding, controlling and difficult to live with.

By the time of his death, Paul and Evelyn Wortman had been estranged from their son for about four years, but they had spent fifteen years before that getting to know Banfield. With Paul's sleazy history and Evelyn being a doting mother, they might not be considered perfect witnesses, but who was? Cautiously using the senior Wortmans as a guide, let's slip through the gate in the imaginary white picket fence, duck inside the back door of Gabriel and Lisa's nineteen years together and become a fly on their wall.

◆

Following their son's criminal rampage, Gabriel Wortman's parents recognized the failings in him and were immediately apologetic for all the pain, suffering, death and destruction he had caused. In Paul's eight-hour interview with Cliff Boutilier, however, he was reluctant to say anything about Banfield, critical or otherwise. In a later interview with private investigator Todd McSorley, Paul and Evelyn were more forthcoming.

Drinking was a big part of Wortman's and Banfield's life. His parents remember going to the cottage early on and finding seventy-two bottles of beer in the fridge and no food. The Wortmans agreed that Gabriel had begun drinking early in life and drank far too much. He may have been diagnosed with liver problems around 2005, but had continued to drink, they said.

The elder Wortmans and Banfield didn't see eye to eye on a lot of things. "The money was coming in like water," Evelyn told McSorley, adding that Banfield would sometimes get excited when talking about how much Gabriel was pulling in. "'This is like a money bank,'" Evelyn quoted Banfield as saying at one point.

Though Banfield came from a large rough-and-tumble family with its own issues, in their conversation with McSorley the Wortmans were—by their own admission—hardly likeable. They were corroborating stories about their own abusive and potentially damaging parenting style. Take their comments to Boutilier about Banfield for what they're worth, but they did spend well over a decade in regular contact with their son's common-law wife:

Evelyn answers that Lisa told her that she was "very insecure." Evelyn continues to describe how "out of the blue, she insults me." After her and Gabriel had had a fight. Lisa later apologised to Evelyn.

Evelyn stated that she found Lisa to be immature, extremely critical, jealous and a gossip. Evelyn once suggested to Lisa that she should seek a "counsellor" out of concern, to which she stated that she had. Evelyn describes Lisa's behaviour similar to that of a "sixteen-year-old" adult with a "security blanket." To elaborate on Lisa's jealousy, Evelyn recalled a Mother's Day when Gabriel had bought her a bike as a present. Lisa took offense to this present, which was later stated to Evelyn by Gabriel.

Paul stated that when Gabriel and Lisa travelled, which was always first class "because he could afford it" and stayed at five-star resorts that Lisa would get upset when Gabriel would give the staff at resorts expensive gifts in return for good service. He also commented on how Lisa would brag to other guests on how many times they had visited a particular resort. Evelyn states how one of Gabriel's neighbors in Portapique stated to her that "nobody goes to see Gabriel when she is there . . ."

Paul describes how Lisa became the "wedge" between their relationship with their son. Lisa also had Gabriel's body cremated before his parents had an opportunity to view him.

Paul continued to describe Lisa's immature behaviour by giving an example of her storming off a beach in Mexico. Gabriel was in the water with Paul when he removed his shorts, Paul states that the water was deep enough that Gabriel was not exposing himself, waved them in the air while calling out to Lisa who was sitting on the sand. This infuriated Lisa to the point that she packed up her towel and left the beach.

Evelyn recalls an occasion when Gabriel described an incident
that occurred at the Portland St property where Gabriel was hav
ing a beer with some friends in the Garage. Gabriel stated that this
made Lisa "furious" and she did/would not join in with his friends.
Lisa remained in the house.

Paul states that there was a couple "George and Bo" who resided
"down the road" in Portapique from Gabriel and recalls a conversation that he had with the couple where Lisa was present and was
quite rude towards George and Bo without any cause.

Paul and Evelyn both give more examples of incidents describing Lisa's jealousy towards other women, that were also strangers
in public settings.

Banfield's friends and acquaintances interviewed for this book
described her as anything but a shrinking violet. "If anything, I believe
she was the boss," said one old friend.

The Wortmans put some of the blame for their son's state of mind
on Banfield, which may or may not be fair. Who knows what goes on
inside a relationship? We do know that after Banfield entered his life,
Wortman didn't put the brakes on his criminal behaviour.

By 2004, Wortman was well involved in grifting. As I described in
Chapter Ten, he cruelly flim-flammed auto-body man Steven Zinck
out of his family's house by helping him with his $38,000 mortgage,
then sneaking his own name onto the deed and changing the locks.

In the summer of 2004, Wortman threatened to shoot a neighbour,
John Hudson, if he stepped onto the Portland Street property to help
Banfield with her luggage. Later, the incident would be described as an
example of Gabriel's extreme jealousy. But his cartoonish defence of
his possessions and property was starting to look like something more
prosaic than jealousy. He was acting like a prototypical criminal who
was leery of and unnerved by other criminals—or the police—getting
too close to his stash. He mounted surveillance cameras around his
business in Dartmouth and his properties in Portapique.

In 2008, Wortman called the police to investigate a break and enter
at the Portland Street clinic. Paul Wortman recounted that Gabriel

had caught someone in the act of trying to steal a fax machine. Gabriel said he had confronted the man with a shotgun and the thief fled. "Gabriel got a lot of shit from the police officer," Paul recalled, adding that, as far as he knew, the police did not seize the shotgun or do anything further. Paul confronted his son about the incident and wondered why he would get so upset about someone trying to steal a fax machine, especially after he had thwarted the theft. Gabriel's anger didn't make complete sense to his parents. It doesn't to me, either. Whatever happened that day incensed and consumed Gabriel for years. In his view, the police had done nothing to help him.

If Banfield was unaware of all the activity swirling around her, there was someone hanging around from Wortman's past life whom she couldn't help but notice.

◆

At the University of New Brunswick in the late eighties, many assumed the older man often seen with Wortman on campus was a professor. But he wasn't faculty. He was a lawyer and a long-time family friend of the Wortmans. His name was Tom Evans.

In the wake of Wortman's killing spree, Tom Evans was pursued by various reporters. Once they finally learned his story, some of them were like the joke about the dog chasing the car: they didn't know what to do with what they'd bit into.

First up was *Frank*. It had the early advantage of insider information gleaned from Cliff Boutilier's interview with Paul Wortman. During that eight-hour call, Paul had described, among many other things, how his son was introduced to guns by a mystery man from Michigan. "He ordered [a gun] in the States somewhere," Paul said. "It was sent from wherever he ordered it to Houlton, Maine. His friend gave him the information, or probably made the arrangements or told him who to contact."

Paul claimed to know little about Evans. "Can't even remember his name. He was a well-educated man, knew my brothers and my mother, Gabriel's grandmother, but I wasn't close to him at all. I had little to do with him." This struck both Douglas and Boutilier as odd. Paul was "acting the way a father of a certain age might act when trying to cover up his son's relationship with a gay man," the *Frank* writers added in their story.

In typically coded *Frank* language, the article described Evans as "a confirmed bachelor" who had lived in an apartment complex on Northumberland Street in Fredericton. Photos of Evans with Gabriel's uncle, Glynn, soon surfaced, appearing to show that they were close friends. The *Frank* piece depicted Evans as "a brash Fredericton lawyer in the 1980s," saying "his King Street practice was the type that advertised flat-rate services (Wills prepared for $30 a crack! Drunk driving charges, $300!), and the UNB/University of Detroit grad often ruffled judges with his habit of going to trial without even a hint of an arguable case."

In 1986, Evans filed a complaint with the Fredericton Police that a nineteen-year-old male prostitute, whom he regularly hired for sex, had assaulted him. The young man was acquitted by a jury.

"While the mid-1980s saw the cocky lawyer featured in flattering newspaper profile puff pieces, by 1988 everything started to fall apart," *Frank* continued. That year the Law Society of New Brunswick suspended him for a year for conduct unbecoming a lawyer. The outdoors enthusiast and gun aficionado had just been convicted of careless use of a firearm for shooting at skeet targets near a children's Bible camp—never mind the convictions for tax evasion and selling liquor to a minor.

"It wasn't long before the bottom fell out of his law career completely when, at the age of 41 in 1990, he was convicted of plying a 17-year-old boy with alcohol and 'seducing him against his will,' as the Irving-owned fishwrapper [the Fredericton *Times & Transcript*] put it at the time. He spent three years in jail and never practised law again."

There was much more to the Evans-Wortman relationship than sex. *Frank* wrote:

During the final months of Tom's legal career in 1989, the New Brunswick papers were full of stories regarding the arrest of five South Americans on a conspiracy to break a pair of Colombians out of jail.

The two men had the unfortunate luck of crash-landing their plane, packed with 500 kilos of cocaine at an airport just outside Fredericton. The Colombian cartel that owned the cocaine had sent the five men to Canada to either spring 'em or kill 'em, as Colombian drug cartels are wont to do.

Two of the five men were represented by a deliciously shady, Better Call Saul type by the name of Tom R. Evans.

The Colombians had approximately $250 million in drugs on the plane. Their five "rescuers" on the way to the prison in which they were incarcerated were found with an AK-47, an Uzi submachine gun and nearly 2,000 rounds of ammunition.

Evans's relationship with heavy-duty drug dealers meant there was a one-degree separation between Wortman and the cartel members. That might be one reason for the friction between him and Banfield. According to Paul and Evelyn Wortman, Banfield was not happy about Wortman's relationship with Evans, or with other men, at least one of whom she once shooed off the Portapique property. If she didn't know that Wortman was continuing to have sex with men, she was one of the few in Nova Scotia.

"Gabriel did have a bad temper," Evelyn told investigator McSorley, who added in his report: "She remembers one incident that Gabriel spoke to her about how a visit from Evans had upset Lisa, which in turn upset Gabriel and he said, 'I punched her.'"

Stephen Maher then took a run at the Evans story in *Maclean's*. He tried to explain how Wortman had come into possession of two rental properties that had been owned by Evans. It was difficult to pierce the veil of any financial or business relationship between Wortman and Evans because New Brunswick law does not require that wills be probated. Wortman had claimed to have inherited the properties. Maher went on to write:

Corporate records show that in 1996 Wortman became the president of Northumberland Investments, the holding company that Evans established in 1984 to handle his two rental properties in downtown Fredericton, including one on Northumberland Street. In 1997, Wortman's signature appears on a $100,000 mortgage with a private lender on one of the properties.

[Gabriel] El Zayat, who bought the properties from Wortman after Evans' death, said he was told Evans lived off rental income from those properties, and he lived in one of the buildings himself.

El Zayat said Wortman's acquisition of the properties, which he believed was an inheritance, seemed odd to him. "I found it really odd that somebody would leave a bunch of properties to a guy. I just found it odd. I remember telling my real estate agent, this is weird."

Corporate records show that in 2008 Wortman was removed from the company. (Public records do not outline why this change was made.) A friend of Evans who was the lone director of the company at the time says Evans was upset with how Wortman was spending money.

The former company director was surprised to learn that Wortman had managed to sell the properties belonging to Evans. "Tom didn't want Gabe to inherit anything because he felt he was being foolish with his money, so he asked me to sign [corporate documents to remove Wortman]," she said.

On Jan. 8, 2010, two months after Evans' death, Wortman was reinstated as president of Northumberland Investments, corporate records show. The director believes Wortman tricked her into signing the document that made that possible. "When Tom died Gabe asked me to sign off or I would become responsible for the debt. So I did."

She never saw Wortman again.

After selling the buildings in February 2010, three months after Evans died, Wortman made "atypical cash deposits" worth $200,000 and a term deposit worth $46,600, according to a Suspicious Transaction Report filed by Toronto-Dominion Bank later in 2010 to the Financial Transactions and Reports Analysis Centre of Canada, documents released in court show.

Property records show that one day before the deed of the Fredericton properties were transferred, Wortman became the director of Berkshire Broman Corporation, another New Brunswick company. The previous owner was Kipling Scott MacKenzie, a Nova Scotian who was convicted of arson in 1996 and is currently facing several charges in provincial court. Wortman later used that company to buy the RCMP cruiser he used in his rampage.

Kipling Scott MacKenzie brought a tool chest worth of criminal thinking and technique to Wortman. It is not known whether Wortman and MacKenzie knew each other in the past, but they were from the same area of New Brunswick. MacKenzie was a career criminal who had frequent run-ins with the authorities. The mysterious company he sold to Wortman, Berkshire Broman Corporation, was described in corporate filings as a tree maintenance business. Nobody knows what the company actually did, because it seemed to have few visible sources of revenue.

MacKenzie hung around in the background of Wortman's life. He was not only your garden-variety arsonist, he had friends and connections across the breadth of the Maritimes underworld. We know this from confidential police sources and social media.

"Tell old jimmy to call his old buddy kippy 506 . . . - . . . ." MacKenzie posted on his Facebook page on December 16, 2011, along with references to a website 123people.ca, where he was also looking to find "Jimmy Melvin."

Old Jimmy was convicted drug dealer and purported crime boss Jimmy Melvin Sr. of Fall River, a Halifax suburb. In 1991 he was caught trying to import three and a half tons of hashish from the Middle East to Nova Scotia. While serving his prison sentence, he was implicated in an attempt to bring $20 million worth of cocaine into the country.

His son, Jimmy Melvin Jr., terrorized the Halifax area between 1999 and 2010 or so as his family and the Marriotts, another crime family, battled for control of the drug trade. Melvin Jr. was convicted of many violent crimes, including attempting to murder and conspiring to murder Terry Marriott Jr. in 2008. Marriott survived that attack but was murdered a few months later. Melvin was declared a dangerous offender in January 2021.

The colourful battles between the Melvins and the Marriotts is the stuff of Maritime legend. As Nathaniel Janowitz described it on Vice. com., it was "a crime saga like 'Goodfellas,' but with bizarre, violent characters out of the 'Trailer Park Boys.'"

> Melvin Jr., 35, made national news numerous times during his decades of crime, but perhaps nothing is more memorable than the website, Real Live Street Shit (the url is now dead), which he launched four months after the February 2009 murder of Marriott Jr.
>
> The short-lived website featured videos of him wearing only his underwear, proudly showing off his bullet wounds and colostomy bag while waving around multi-colored Canadian bills. It also featured local TV news clips about his various criminal activities set to hip-hop beats.
>
> Although the website was quickly removed, highlights from the various videos can be seen in [an] old CBC News clip, including him shouting his most famous quote, "There is no rats in the Melvin family!" after an attempt on his father's life.
>
> After the Marriott Jr. murder, Melvin Jr. appeared to feel invincible; nearly all his enemies were dead or imprisoned after a years-long feud. He felt so confident that in one video he referred to himself as "the cock of the walk, king of the talk."
>
> The Melvins and the Marriotts have become synonymous with crime in Nova Scotia . . .

With Evans and now MacKenzie by his side, Wortman was within hailing distance of serious, top-shelf drug traffickers.

The next episode of the saga of Gabriel Wortman and Tom Evans came much later, when a team of Global News reporters and researchers, led by Sarah Ritchie, Alex Kress and Brian Hill, weighed in with a thoroughly researched story for episode 7 of the podcast series *13 Hours*, which they had mounted for Global TV.

The new information they uncovered showed conclusively that it was Evans who introduced Wortman to many of the tricks of the underworld. The sleazy lawyer had secret compartments at his residence and his business. He had guns. He had a sailboat, and he taught Wortman how to use it to make money by sailing across to Maine and bringing back illegal cigarettes and alcohol, among other things.

Global News also found a man who said the fiftyish Evans had taken him in when he was a fifteen-year-old who had left foster care. His name was Joe Cartwright, and Evans had set him up with an apartment. Cartwright and Evans became good friends over the years. Cartwright would help Evans with carpentry, and Evans would take him hunting—and drinking. Along the way, Cartwright met Wortman, whom he described as "a violent and scary man." He claimed to have seen Wortman physically assault his common-law wife and punch a contractor for walking across his lawn.

Evans had a calming effect on Wortman, Cartwright said. "Tom was like a father to Gabriel. Gabriel wouldn't have been Gabriel without Tom. He moulded him into the professional person that he would become, I think. But he also moulded him in other ways."

The relationship with Evans provided a springboard for Wortman's financial situation. Evans died in 2009, leaving everything to Wortman, including cash, real estate and a Ruger Mini-14 semi-automatic rifle. That gun was one Wortman used during his rampage. "I give, devise and bequeath the residue of my estate to my dear friend Gabriel Wortman," reads a notarized copy of Evans's will.

"Tom R. Evans and I have been friends since childhood," Wortman said in an affidavit submitted to a New Brunswick court in 2010.

There were some colourful twists in Evans's last will and testament that were typical of the man. He asked that his cremated remains be buried at sea in the Old Sow whirlpool in the Bay of Fundy, with a dram of Irish whiskey. He told Wortman to spend $500 from the estate on "eats and strong drink" at a wake for him. Evans also wrote his own obituary, under the name Thomas Robert Evans-Kennedy, the name he had adopted after his convictions. Wortman had it published in a Sunday edition of the *New York Times*.

The death of Tom Evans seemed to affect Wortman deeply for the next few years, as he descended into an enhanced manic period.

◆

Flush with cash from the money he had inherited from the Evans estate, the first thing Wortman did was to buy Banfield three rings for her fortieth birthday. One was a solitaire diamond being advertised by a private seller online. It came with a fresh appraisal from a company in Belgium valuing the stone at $10,500. Wortman paid $9,000 for that ring.

The solitaire may have looked like "a rock" to the uninformed, but it was less than that in the eye of an expert. It came with an S12–S13 rating, which meant the diamond had flaws and was not "eye clean." The higher the number, the lower the grade. Gemologists debate whether S13 is even a true grade of a quality diamond; many consider it to be merely a marketing gimmick to sell lower-quality diamonds that are not as shiny as the pricier pieces of carbon.

Soon after receiving the gifts, Banfield had a bright idea to make the rings shine. She put them in an ultrasonic cleaner that dentists and denturists use, along with a denture cleaning solution. Rather than making the rings dazzle, the solution corroded the gold on all three pieces. Banfield tried to fix her mistake by taking the rings to a jeweller in Dartmouth. When she got the rings back she wasn't happy with the work. She took the jeweller to small claims court, stating that "she noticed that there were dark grey spots or flaws noticeable to the naked eye." She contended that he had "damaged her stone, somehow causing the enhancement to leak out or otherwise become defective." An adjudicator noted the flaws in the stone: "While subtle at first glance, they are noticeable and arguably detract from the beauty of the diamond." But he also determined that the Belgian appraisal carried no weight and ultimately dismissed the claim.

As the ring debacle was unfolding, Wortman appeared to be spinning out of control. He had put his Portapique cottage in his father's name to hide it from the Canada Revenue Agency, but now he wanted Paul's name off the deed. Paul resisted. Gabriel threatened to go to Moncton and shoot him. Greg Mercer of the *Globe and Mail* recounted what happened:

> In June of 2010, an extraordinary reunion was organized in the tiny beachside community of Portapique, N.S., where two brothers who had spent 40 years as strangers would finally meet.
>
> Gabriel Wortman, a denturist from Dartmouth, had invited Jeff Samuelson, his younger brother who had been given up for adoption as an infant in 1970, to his Nova Scotia cottage to get to know his biological family.
>
> The occasion was a birthday party for their father, Paul Wortman, a man Mr. Samuelson had met only a few months earlier after spending years trying to track down his birth parents.
>
> But instead of a feel-good gathering, and the beginning of a new relationship, the Portapique reunion quickly dissolved into an ugly fight between Mr. Wortman and his elderly father over title to a property, according to a number of people at the party. Police were called after the denturist threatened to kill his parents.

Halifax police investigated Wortman for uttering death threats and being in possession of illegal weapons, but did not press charges. Wishing to avoid any further problems with his son, Paul Wortman relented and took his name off the deed for 200 Portapique Beach Road, but even that was not enough to dampen his son's paranoia. He didn't want people building close to his property.

Still stewing three years after the 2008 break and enter allegation that he believed the police had not properly investigated, Wortman started babbling about the incident and saying he was going to kill a cop to exact his revenge. Someone passed that news on to the police, who mounted another investigation in May 2011. On May 3, Truro police corporal Greg Densmore issued an officer safety memo to the force's uniformed members about Wortman's alleged threat:

Source [unknown identity] advised that Mr. Wortman is in possession of at least one handgun, make and model unknown, and may be transporting this firearm back and forth between (Halifax-Dartmouth) and (Portapique). Mr. Wortman may also be in possession of several long rifles located at his cottage. . . . These firearms are stored in a compartment behind the flue.

Source advised that Mr. Wortman is under a lot of stress lately and is starting to have some mental issues ('is becoming a little squirrelly'). Source advised that they had seen the firearms and stated that Wortman stores the handgun in his nightstand beside the bed. . . . Wortman has six vehicles registered in his name (plated) and 1 vehicle unplated.

The police investigated and found no probable grounds to lay charges.

Enter Portapique neighbour Brenda Forbes, known as Bo, and her husband, George. Bo came from a military family and had graduated from high school in Germany in 1993. In the armed forces, she was involved in, among other things, intelligence gathering and security.

After the murders, Forbes told reporters she had called the RCMP in 2013 after she had learned from three unnamed men that Wortman had beaten Banfield up. Forbes's version of events was well captured by Carol Off on the CBC radio show *As It Happens*. Off asked Forbes to describe Wortman in a word. Her answer? "Psychopath."

OFF: Is that how you would have described him before you knew what he did?

FORBES: Oh yeah. Both me and my husband knew what he was like. And I let other people in the community know the same thing and what he had been doing with [Banfield]. A lot of them just said to me, "Oh no, he's not like that."

OFF: How did he treat her?

FORBES: Like his possession. He drank quite a bit, and when he drank, he got violent. And he had her totally under his control.

OFF: You witnessed that he was physically abusing her as well. What can you tell us about that?

FORBES: The first time . . . she ran over to my house, actually, and she said that he'd been beating her and he had blocked her car in so she couldn't get away. I said, "You need to get help." And she said, "No, I can't, because he will hurt me again."

OFF: There was a second time, another incident, I understand, where you wanted to get the RCMP involved. Can you tell us about that?

FORBES: He got into drinking. She was there. And there were three other people that were there, three other guys. One of the guys told me he had her on the ground, was strangling her and screaming at her. And she actually said, "Don't get involved or you're only going to make it worse."

Forbes told Off it was at that point that she called the RCMP and shared what one of Wortman's friends had told her. But when Forbes asked him if he'd tell the police what he'd seen Wortman do, he had refused, saying, in Forbes's words, "No way. . . . He'll kill me." Forbes also told Off that she and her husband knew about the illegal firearms because "he showed them to us."

The RCMP had investigated Forbes's allegations and, once again, found nothing. This was not surprising. Forbes wasn't an eyewitness, and no one else, not even Banfield, would corroborate her story. Forbes said after she called the police on him, Wortman would terrorize her by standing outside her house at 293 Portapique Beach Road and staring through the windows. She sold the house three years later, in 2016, to John Zahl and Jo Thomas and moved to Alberta, where she set up a private safety and security company in Camrose. By 2021, she was back in Nova Scotia.

Forbes's story was seized upon by domestic abuse activists in the government and the public. Jason Buxton, a Nova Scotia film director, told me he was commissioned by the National Film Board to produce a film on the massacres. We had a meeting at which he revealed that his film would be centred on domestic violence and its outcomes.

"Don't rent a camera," I told him. "At the end of the day, I don't think that's going to be the story."

"The NFB only wants that story," Buxton said.

"Good luck," I told him.

Not one reporter dug beneath the surface to check Forbes's backstory and motivations, which ought to be standard-issue legwork on a story from such a small and close-knit community.

Neighbour Dana Geddes thought Wortman might have been infatuated with Forbes, and said he was a regular at the "wild parties" she hosted back in the day. Another neighbour said the opposite was true—that Wortman had no interest in her at all, which might have angered her.

Even some of Banfield's close friends didn't buy into the domestic abuse story. As one put it to me: "I loved the girl, I really did. . . . No way in hell was she abused. I don't believe it for a second. Like I said before, I saw her often alone or with her sisters. She was happy as a pig in shit. I know those girls like they were my own three sisters. No way in hell would she live or have to live in an abused situation."

In Forbes's story, Wortman's inflated ego was on full display. He was manic, dangerous and yet weirdly open and trusting. He had shown them some of his illegal guns. He had the Ruger Mini-14 from Tom Evans's estate, a semi-automatic rifle similar to the one used by mass murderer Marc Lépine in 1989 at Montréal's École Polytechnique. He had a Colt C8 rifle, the AR-15 equivalent that the Mounties used. His handguns were a Glock 23 pistol and a Ruger P89 pistol. He had a special ammunition box designed to carry extra bullets. All of his guns were illegally obtained, and three were restricted. Why would he show people those weapons? In Canada most people are leery of guns, especially illegal ones. Finally, why would he believe he could so flagrantly physically abuse his partner in front of people, if he really did? Did he think he was so invincible that no one would ever say a word?

It all made me wonder about the social dynamics of the neighbourhood. It was like everyone was in everyone else's kitchen . . . until they weren't. And then there was lots of drama. It was all something to look at as I plodded along.

◆

With all the heat he was drawing from people complaining about him to police, Wortman was perilously close to being charged with a criminal offence. That would have been disastrous for his business. He ripped a page out of the RCMP's crisis management handbook: he buffed his reputation with some instant positive headlines.

Sheri Hendsbee, a single mother who claimed to have lost all her teeth due to a reaction to a medication, was featured on a CTV News broadcast on July 23, 2014. She could not afford to buy dentures. Wortman saw the broadcast and offered her a free set of dentures. "If my mom were here today, she always used to tell me that there's angels among us that walk on the face of the earth, and to me, that's what those people are," the ecstatic Hendsbee told CTV News.

Wortman was suddenly a local hero. "My heart went out to her," he said in an interview. "There's so many ways for people to get dentures, but it seems like the people who really need them are the people who are getting left behind."

Wortman was looking more and more like a modern-day Dr. Jekyll and Mr. Hyde. He even let another denturist use his shop on Saturdays for her own practice and didn't charge her rent for years.

In his private life, however, Wortman was making regular excursions to Maine, where he was picking up his motorcycle parts and smuggling into Canada everything from cigarettes and alcohol to guns and explosives. The trips were a real-life version of *Easy Rider*, and in the two years before the massacres, he made the journey fifteen times, sometimes accompanied by Banfield, who friends described as being in love with all things American. Wortman had been pre-screened for a NEXUS card as a "trustworthy traveller," which usually allowed him to breeze through customs. During one week in April and May 2019, authorities said, Wortman crossed back and forth five times, once returning to the United States just thirteen minutes after he had left. On at least one occasion (date and reason unknown), Canadian customs officials flagged him down and searched him and his vehicle.

Banfield later said Wortman was outraged by the search and called it harassment. She said he complained vociferously to the Canada Border Services Agency, which fit with his character, and that the CBSA eventually sent him a letter of apology. No one has ever seen the letter, and law enforcement sources are skeptical that it exists. There might be a rare exception deep in the bowels of CBSA headquarters, but customs and immigration officers are not known to be apologetic types.

Banfield told the RCMP in her post-massacres interviews that Wortman hadn't smuggled anything in from Maine when she was with him in the vehicle.

I tucked all that information into a special compartment deep inside my memory banks.

◆

In 2016, Wortman took his parents to a resort in Cuba. He told them he had won the trip, but after they arrived admitted that he had paid for it himself. The trip was Gabriel's attempt to make amends. But if Paul Wortman thought that removing his name on the deed for 200 Portapique Beach Road was all he had to do to make peace with his son, he was wrong. Once they were soaked in poolside sun and alcohol, a lifetime's worth of Gabriel's internalized scabs burst open.

"You weren't much of a father to me," he told his father in a rage.

Paul told Todd McSorley he thought Gabriel was referring to his "lack of patience as Gabriel was growing up," as if he had forgotten the shoot-the-dog episode and other horrors, small and large, that he had inflicted upon his son. In Cuba, Paul said, he began to cry and apologized to Gabriel, admitting that he had failed him. Gabriel started throwing punches at his father, who refused to fight back. Gabriel kept pounding on him as Paul fell to the pool deck, unconscious. Gabriel's cousin Chris was also there and told both local authorities and other family members what happened.

"I was a bloody mess," Paul said, describing what he looked like when he regained consciousness.

A furious Gabriel stormed away and got into another scrap with, as Paul described him, "a coloured man."

Banfield told police that, later that same night in Cuba, Paul said to her: "I was a bastard to my wife. I was a bastard to my son, and you need to leave Gabriel now."

About two months after they got home, at Paul's suggestion, Evelyn invited Gabriel over to apologize to his father, which the parents say he did.

"It was never mentioned, again," Paul said.

Apologies are not typically in the playbook of psychopaths, sociopaths or malignant narcissists, whichever mantle best fit Wortman. Paul and Evelyn's other statement about that gathering perhaps provides a better measure of what happened: they never saw their son again.

◆

Wortman's chin was barely off the pavement at the Irving Big Stop when stories began circulating about the alarming things people knew about him, as if they were common knowledge. I have touched on most of them already, but think about it all again. People knew Wortman smuggled cigarettes, alcohol and guns across the border. How could they know that unless Wortman was, as they say in Nova Scotia, flapping his lips about it? And if people knew he was smuggling, why hadn't the police intervened? In my experience, cigarette and alcohol smuggling are ubiquitous in Nova Scotia, but one by one the police pick off everyone who is doing it. Why not Wortman?

An unnamed man known as "the Carpenter," who had a long criminal record and who had worked for Wortman, told the RCMP about some of Wortman's activities and behaviour. Here's what his statement looked like in the redacted, unredacted and later re-redacted documents released to the media:

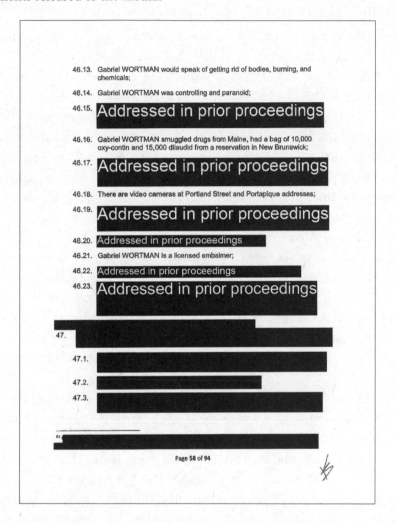

46.13. Gabriel WORTMAN would speak of getting rid of bodies, burning, and chemicals;

46.14. Gabriel WORTMAN was controlling and paranoid;

46.15. Addressed in prior proceedings

46.16. Gabriel WORTMAN smuggled drugs from Maine, had a bag of 10,000 oxy-contin and 15,000 dilaudid from a reservation in New Brunswick;

46.17. Addressed in prior proceedings

46.18. There are video cameras at Portland Street and Portapique addresses;

46.19. Addressed in prior proceedings

46.20. Addressed in prior proceedings

46.21. Gabriel WORTMAN is a licensed embalmer;

46.22. Addressed in prior proceedings

46.23. Addressed in prior proceedings

47.

47.1.

47.2.

47.3.

Page 58 of 94

Nova Scotia isn't a big place. Word about everything eventually gets around, yet Wortman was absolutely bold in his defiance of the authorities. They were about the only ones who appeared not to know what he was doing—or claiming to be doing.

After Wortman was killed, a promotional video for the Atlantic Denture Clinic was found on the Internet and rebroadcast. In it, Wortman was tending to a happy customer, a dark-haired young man who was entirely pleased with the denturist's work. Wortman looked every bit the kind, empathetic professional. Like most viewers, I focused my attention on Wortman, his voice, mannerisms and body language. I didn't think any more of it until one day a friend of a friend contacted me. She had seen something in the video that had been entirely overlooked: "The guy in the chair is Justin Sooley," she told me. "The last time I saw him, he had a gun in his hand. He's a scary dude."

Justin Wade Sooley was, in fact, Wortman's customer. Over the previous eleven years, Sooley had also been a one-man wrecking crew. In 2009, the then twenty-five-year-old Sooley had rammed an unmarked police car in Halifax after being caught driving a stolen car sporting a stolen licence plate. In 2017, he stabbed a man in downtown Halifax. And there were lots of crimes in between and afterwards. He was a scary dude, indeed.

Wanting to know more, I checked out Sooley's helpful Facebook page and found that his connections to the underworld filled in more of the circle of Wortman's criminal acquaintances. One of Sooley's friends was the notorious B.J. Marriott—or B.J. Bremner, as he is also known. The ultraviolent scion of the Marriott crime family was locked up almost as deep in the prison system as his arch-enemy Jimmy Melvin Jr.

There it was. Wortman was a seemingly respected businessman whose connections put him at the main intersection of the criminal underworld in Nova Scotia. Wortman had money and guns stashed all over the place. And then there were the grenades. Under the deck at Wortman's Portapique cottage, a witness told police, were two cases of grenades—likely phosphorus grenades. The same unnamed witness later told police he saw a grenade on a workbench at the warehouse on Orchard Beach Drive, the home of "Lisa's Bar."

Did Banfield notice the grenade on "her" bar? If she knew about the grenades, did she ever wonder what her common-law husband was doing with them? Did Wortman, at the very least, tell Banfield to be careful around all those explosives?

One key measure of how Banfield might have felt about her situation was the relationship between her family and Wortman. In recent years, Banfield's sisters and brothers and their families had been the only regular visitors to 200 Portapique Beach Road, at least when Banfield was there. She wouldn't suffer anyone else. Wortman's acceptance of this flies in the face of the typical profile of a controlling domestic abuser, who will usually isolate his prey from their family. Wortman did the opposite. In fact, it appears that he was rather cordial to the Banfield family. According to an acquaintance in her circle, in 2018 Banfield encouraged her sister Maureen to buy one of the lots on Orchard Beach Drive that Wortman owned through Northumberland Investments. There were big plans for a subdivision. The land was cheap. If Wortman could persuade the Bonds or the Tucks to sell him some or all of their properties, there would be direct access to the beach. Maureen Banfield bought the property.

Did any of the Banfields happen to notice signs of rampant criminality and domestic violence? Did they say or do anything to protect their sister? We don't know because they have remained silent since the murders.

Wortman and the Banfields looked like one big, happy and kind of weird family.

21

DANA, EDDIE AND A FORD TAURUS

In the aftermath of the killings, the RCMP said Wortman was unknown to them, which seemed an impossibility. Criminal acts had followed Wortman around from the time he was a teenager. This was Nova Scotia, which had fewer than a million people. From the articles I was writing and my now almost weekly radio appearances, it was beginning to feel like every second person in Nova Scotia knew something about him, good, bad or otherwise.

Among the many curious things they shared with me, it appeared that Wortman had a fascination with coffins. Apparently, he liked to carve miniature coffins for entertainment, but two of his denture-clinic clients told me that he ushered them into a back room there and showed them a full-sized coffin.

"It's for me," he said. "I have Stage-3 liver cancer," he told them.

Claiming that he was on the verge of dying had long been one of his favourite sympathy ploys.

An artist who lived just outside Brookfield had an eerie story about something he and his painting partner had seen one night. They had lost friends in the shootings and asked not to be identified by name. "It was one night in November at about 3 a.m. We took a break from painting and went for a ride," the artist said. "At that time of night, after 2 a.m., there usually are no Mounties around here until like 6 a.m." What the two artists saw was beyond bizarre. At the main intersection in Brookfield, where Roop's Esso is located on the northwest corner, a Mountie in a fully marked cruiser appeared to be playing a game, flashing his lights on and off and rushing back and forth across the road from one parking lot to another. He would stop, turn off his lights, turn them on again and then rush across the street. "It went on for a long time. It was something I couldn't forget," the artist said. "After what happened, I wondered if that was Wortman."

There is no way to know.

That ended up being the case with several intriguing leads shared with me during those weeks, drawn out of the backwoods by my talk radio appearances. A military source told me that on the morning of April 19, while Wortman was roaming around killing people, the RCMP had called Ottawa for help. "JTF 2 was in the air on its way to Nova Scotia when Wortman was shot," the source said. Joint Task Force 2 is an elite and secretive part of the Canadian military, the equivalent of the US Navy Seals. The RCMP wouldn't ask the nearby Truro or Amherst municipal police forces for help, but they had called in JTF 2? It seemed unlikely that the unit was ever on its way, and no one would confirm that the call had been placed.

I also heard that Wortman had picked up a hitchhiker while driving his replica police car in New Brunswick only a week before the massacres. That tip really appealed to me because other sources were telling me there was a good possibility that the events in Portapique had something to do with the RCMP in neighbouring New Brunswick. But the hitchhiker story struck me and one of my newly found citizen-investigator helpers as not being credible.

Another tip came my way about Wortman's relationships with female temporary workers from Jamaica who were brought to Nova Scotia to pick strawberries and blueberries in the fields of Colchester County. As the story went, Wortman had befriended many of the women, who were upset about being yelled at in the fields by one of the proprietors. "You can't do that to them," he apparently told the man, scaring him to the point that he worried he might have been on Wortman's so-called hit list. Alas, the story didn't appear to be true.

One of the most intriguing tips came from Stephen Maher of *Maclean's*. He had heard that Wortman had $1 million delivered to his business in a Brink's armoured truck days before the massacre. It was, as Wortman himself might have put it, a tantalizing lead. Maher tried to track it down, but to no avail.

I heard from an entirely unrelated source that the amount Wortman had received was $500,000. As in Maher's version of the tale, I was told it had been delivered to 193 Portland Street in a Brink's truck. My source, who operated a business on Portland Street near Wortman's denture clinic, then went silent. The Wortman stigma was driving people into the shadows.

Perhaps there were two different deliveries. But how did people know about any of this? Was Wortman spreading stories about himself?

Two different law enforcement sources told me there might be a link between Wortman and the New Brunswick RCMP, suggesting that he may have been operating as an undercover operative in that province. Part of the story apparently involved the suicide on October 25, 2019, of RCMP staff sergeant Bruce Reid. The veteran Mountie shot himself at a baseball field in Rothsay, a suburb of Saint John. "Reid was a highly experienced and respected guy," a source I'll call Jimmy McNulty said. "There was a UC [undercover agent] who was getting out of control. Reid thought the informant or agent was erratic, unstable and dangerous. He was really worried about what was going on. He wanted to stop the operation, but he was overruled. He didn't have any faith in the people running the operation. Eventually, two people were murdered, and he was sickened by it. He killed himself. The Mounties just plowed ahead."

In the world of the RCMP, such an undercover informant is known as a restricted-level source, according to documents obtained during my investigation. An informant is deemed to be "Restricted Level 1" when their actions "have or are adversely affecting or compromising the integrity of the RCMP, its programs, members or an investigation" or "could jeopardize his/her safety or that of an RCMP member or the public." A more difficult agent is identified as Restricted Level 2 "when the source exhibits or had exhibited manipulative and/or controlling behaviour that makes him/her difficult to manage and/or maintain an effective source/handler relationship. This source would only be considered for use under the condition that trained, experienced handlers be assigned."

I heard a similar story from another source who had no professional connection to McNulty. This source also said that two people were murdered, but added a twist: one of them might have been in New Brunswick and the other in Nova Scotia.

In an attempt to find out whether there was any substance to this rumour about a rogue agent who could have been Wortman, I spoke about Bruce Reid and his suicide on talk radio. My appearances on *The Rick Howe Show* were getting to be like investigative journalism performance art. I was openly interviewing the audience and fishing for sources in public.

Thankfully, not everything was a dead end. Verifiable stories kept finding me. Some were from our customers at Chez Glass Lass in Chester, where Sharon and I sold our glass sculptures.

Tammy Mercier went to the University of New Brunswick, a year behind Wortman. She had acquired from a friend a Halloween night photo, taken in 1988, at McLeod House, a co-op residence. In it, a group of about ten students were posing for a picture. Wortman was front and centre, wearing wire-rim glasses and dressed as a priest in a black cassock, with a cross dangling on a chain. His hair was tidied up from his high school graduation photo, in which the back was creeping down into a mullet near his shoulders. He hadn't yet dyed it silver or purple, as Michael Marshall had reported earlier.

Wortman had been raised a Catholic. I suspected he might have pilfered the cassock. People say he liked to dress up and role-play. During his later years, I saw a photo online of him dressed as a Mountie at a party. He appeared to be standing in the space between two rooms, as I recall. Then the photo disappeared, and I couldn't find it, again.

Another of our Chez Glass Lass customers, Angie Anjoul, had her own tale. She came from one of the large Christian Lebanese families in Halifax who had emigrated to Nova Scotia more than a century ago. The close-knit community has spawned some of the most successful real estate developers, restaurateurs and small-business owners in the province.

Anjoul and her husband had taken her mother-in-law to Wortman's office to be fitted for dentures about two years earlier. "He was very friendly but got a little too close in sort of a creepy way," Anjoul said. "He was all over my husband's BMW X6 and then he invited him back to the garage to look at the two motorcycles he had there," she said.

Two years later her mother was having some problems with her dentures and needed Wortman to do an adjustment. Wortman still had their $75,000 car on his mind. "When we brought her there, the first thing he mentioned was the X6. He wanted to know if we still had it. I couldn't believe that's what he remembered after all that time."

"Creepy" was an adjective that arose frequently from Wortman's clients. Some said, without giving details, that he was inappropriately suggestive in a sexual way. He was always on the hunt for new sex partners. Eventually, I found someone who would describe his modus operandi. "He was very proud of his endowment," she said. "He liked to measure the size of his patients' mouths to see if he could comfortably fit inside."

One night, I thought I was having another heart attack. Sharon called an ambulance, and I was rushed to South Shore Regional Hospital in Bridgewater. I could tell that the two nurses taking care of me were curious about me.

"Why is your name so familiar?" one asked.

"I don't know," I said. "I've been on the radio lately talking about what happened in Portapique."

"That's it," one nurse said. "My mother loves listening to you."

The doctor treating me was more circumspect. He determined that my ailment was due to me having lost a little weight with my cancer treatments and tightening my belt too much in an effort to hold up my pants. When discharging me the next morning, he had something to share. "I don't want you to use my name, but I ran into Wortman back when I was in medical school in Halifax," he said. "I didn't realize at the time that I was dating a girl that he liked. One night there was a knock on my front door. I answered it and he punched me in the nose."

I was also drawing in new sources within law enforcement. One—call him Bill Moreland—was another former officer who was tapped into the upper echelons of police and government. He said that inside those echelons my stories were viewed as on target. "You're rattling them," Moreland said. "They're watching every move you make. Be very careful. Maybe you should get yourself some security. You got a gun? You can't trust these guys."

Moreland also said Wortman was involved in some sort of drinking club in Portapique. "I hear that there's a mix of people. One of them might be a lawyer. There might be a cop or an ex-cop. Another guy is a heavy-duty criminal. I'll try to get his name for you."

It felt like progress. Almost every day, someone new was stepping up with a tidbit or two.

McNulty, meanwhile, had tentacles into policing operations and brought me up to speed on what he saw going on inside. "They are pasteurizing evidence," he said.

"What do you mean?"

"They are stalling for time and probably running all the electronic stuff, like any cellphones they found, through a lab and cleaning it up," McNulty said. "Why do you think there are no 911 tapes or anything? There's stuff on them that they don't want anyone to hear. They are doing whatever they can to make the bad stuff go away. It's really bad. They're creating a new script."

McNulty was echoing what my Deep Throat had told me a month earlier. But if I wrote that the RCMP was destroying evidence from the massacres, the force would just laugh it off as a "conspiracy theory." I needed to use the information on *The Rick Howe Show* and see what I could flush out.

The RCMP still had the word "grenades" blacked out in the court documents, but McNulty said I should continue pushing the topic. "The grenades are a big deal," he said. "What the fuck was he doing with them? That's a biker thing. There's something fishy going on, for sure."

The more people I met, the more I wondered how Wortman had seemingly evaded the attention of the Mounties, the Halifax Regional Police or any other police force.

McNulty then remembered something else, involving unknown activities or transactions taking place at the Glooscap Trading Post in the Millbrook First Nation, located off Highway 102 just south of Truro. There was a restaurant there, a couple of fast-food outlets, a gas station and a handful of other businesses. "A couple of years back we were doing a lot of surveillance on the [Hells] Angels and their affili- ated clubs," he said. "One of the strange things was that they would always stop at Glooscap for awhile. Something was going on, but we could never get close enough to see what it was. Another time we had a meeting and there was a guy there—a handler. We'd never seen him before. He sat at the same table as the boss. He was in charge of some new, high-value informant. That's all we were told. We were never given any details, but they were all pretty excited about what was going on."

Sources were dragging me in every direction. Maher suggested that I join the social media chat rooms where the victims' families were congregating. While I empathized with the survivors, I didn't see how they could help further my investigation. Based on my experiences over the years, getting too close to survivors is a potential road to disaster. I'd learned long ago that when you start digging for the truth, you never know what secret treasure you might find or whose feathers might be ruffled.

Meanwhile, another new source pointed me to a friend of Wortman's who apparently had stories to tell that had never been reported. The COVID-19 lockdown had been lifted, so I got into my car and set out on a day trip.

◆

A Nova Scotia country boy all grown up, Dana Geddes looks like a typical mechanic, which he is. On the side, he hauls things around with his tow truck. He fixes vehicles and sells them. In the spring—until the end of May—he's a fisherman, riding out the tide on the Bay of Fundy to catch shad and gaspereau, otherwise known as alewives or kiacks.

"Do you make a lot of money fishing?" I asked him.

"Let me put it this way," he said. "During the big recession, people in Ontario were falling off buildings because they weren't making sixty grand. That's a lot of money for us. 'We're rich!'" he said mockingly. "Lobster fishermen? They make $250,000 to $300,000 in six weeks. Poor buggers."

Geddes began holidaying at Portapique Beach in 1994. He and his wife, Brenda, would park a tiny three-metre-long camper trailer on the beach and cram themselves into it at night, along with an Irish setter. It was a peaceful and remote place. People would gather on the beach to drink, party and have fun.

Geddes remembered another time at Portapique, and another dog. "I had this big, old Newfoundland dog with a deformed tail. He must have weighed 180 to 200 pounds. At the clam festival one year, he'd walk along the bank there—just sauntering along—and people thought he was a bear. They called him the Portapique Bear. Back then, there weren't that many people here. You could go shotgun hunting in the woods. There were ducks on the beach. It was beautiful."

Eventually, Geddes built a cottage on Cobequid Court, directly across the road from where the Tuck family lived, and next to Harry and Joy Bond's place. In 2002, around the time Wortman bought 200 Portapique Beach Road and moved into the community, Geddes was elected president of the Portapique Beach residents' association, a position he held until 2019.

Today, he has a newer and improved cottage, kitty-corner from the old one, on the other side of Orchard Beach Drive, with a clear view of the bay from his back deck. He has a 12-metre flagpole, and this year he bought a new flag for it. The highlight of the interior is an oak floor milled from an old tree Geddes had to take down on his home property, a half hour to the south. The two-bedroom cottage is his pride and joy.

If Geddes's cottage is the picture of neatness and solitude, his property on Spring Valley Road is breathtakingly cluttered. Heading up the muddy driveway, his place of business—Green Creek Auto Body and Sales—is on the right, situated in a battered barn with a garage bay. To the left, almost entirely encircled by soon-to-be-repaired cars and pickups is the forty-five-year-old house he built. A vestige of mid-seventies design, the rectangular raised bungalow almost disappears into the sea of vehicles that extends into the one-acre field behind it and off into the distance. It looks like a final resting place for dead machines.

Geddes and I entered the house through the back door and into what likely was designed to be a boot room and now served as his office.

The Geddes were not in Portapique Beach that Saturday night when Wortman came to kill the Tucks and Bonds on Cobequid Court. "Brenda had to work," Geddes told me. "I guess we were lucky. He was always good to me. I would hope that he wouldn't have killed us. He didn't kill everyone, you know."

Geddes paused for a moment to reflect, and I could see the sadness in his eyes. "The worst thing about it is that thirteen of my friends and neighbours were murdered, and my friend is the one who killed them all."

"What was Wortman like?" I asked him.

"I knew him well, very well, for almost twenty years," he said. "He was a good guy, but he couldn't really hold his liquor. Two or three beers and he would get a little squirrelly sometimes."

Geddes recalled an incident two years or so earlier, down at the beach during one of the bonfire parties. Some people, including Wortman, would tear around the neighbourhood on their ATVs and side-by-sides. There would be arguing and taunting. The longer the party went on, the louder and uglier it got. "I wasn't there, but he got mad as hell after somebody said something about pulling a knife," Geddes said. "He said: 'Knife? I'll go home and get a gun and I'll fix you bastards . . . right quick.'"

As distraught as he was about Wortman's murder spree, Geddes remembered the things, big and small, that Wortman did. "I remember when he bought the log cabin beside the graveyard. He done a lot of work to it. He put a glass thing on the back of it. He never stopped working on it. He'd come up here for a weekend, Thursday till Sunday, and work and work and work and work. He'd bring materials up with him. He put a roof on it. He never really expanded the building itself. He put a garage out to the side of it. He really, really worked on it."

Wortman and Geddes got to know each other well and would visit back and forth. "My mother lived with us for three years," Geddes recalled. "Her teeth had broke and he said: 'I'll fix them up for you, and I'll do them both.' Gabe couldn't do enough for her. He made her a set for just $400. When COVID happened and people couldn't find masks anywhere, he dropped off a whole bag for me and Brenda. I know he brought some to other people, too. He was like that."

Brenda had two sets of dentures made for her, one by Wortman's victim Gina Goulet and the other by Wortman himself.

"All kinds of people say he was a nice guy," I said. "But almost everyone says he was a bit odd."

"Everyone has their ways," Geddes said. "He was always good to me, and he was always good to Lisa, too, when I was around him."

It wasn't all roses. When Geddes and his sister, Pam, took their mother to get her dentures from Wortman, the women were alone in the room with Banfield. Pam later told her brother that Banfield had said "Gabriel wasn't all he seemed to be. He was a hard person to work for and a hard person to live with."

"What was Lisa like?" I asked Geddes.

"She was nice," he said, and then, with a little giggle, added: "She liked to have a little rub on her back sometimes."

"A little rub?"

"She could be kind of a flirt," he said with a twinkle in his eye.

"I'd heard from someone else that she would be like that at social gatherings," I said. "One woman told me Lisa wanted to be seen as the life of the party. You saw that?"

"Yeah," he said. "She'd kind of smile and be kind of assertive and insinuating things a little bit. There's one time, I was going up to Gabriel's and I met Lisa and her sister on the road on their four-wheeler. They were going down the road. They both said, 'Hi, Hi, how are you doing?' Really, really friendly. I drove up there to Gabriel's, and we were talking about a boat I was buying from him. I said I seen Lisa and her sister down there. 'Oh yeah,'" he quoted Wortman, "'they're out slutting around today.' We laughed."

Geddes saw Wortman often. "He would stop in on Thursdays and talk."

After Wortman had bought a Ford F-150 truck and brought it to Geddes to show off, Geddes told him, "It's a nice-looking truck, but it's so plain." Wortman returned sometime later with the truck, excited to show Geddes pinstriping decals he'd added to liven it up.

Wortman felt comfortable around Geddes, who witnessed the fissures emerging in his friend's psyche during the last weeks he was alive. One moment stood out. Geddes can never forget the time Wortman came to visit him on March 1, seven weeks before the massacres. He wanted to have a trailer inspected, which was something Geddes did.

"He hadn't had a drink since September, he told me," Geddes recalled. "He says: 'I got alcohol in the truck with me, and I know I shouldn't be drinking, but what else can you do when you're over there [at home during lockdown] like that?' He came inside to pay me. We were talking, and I made a couple of jokes and stuff . . . I could see how he could be kind of moody sometimes or he had things bothering him, maybe stress with his business."

Wortman had one knee on an old, worn armchair in Geddes's office and was looking out the window. He let out a little laugh and said: "I'm so glad to stop in here once in awhile. I just came from the fuckin' city, you know. I like coming here. You brighten my fuckin' day up. You just always make me feel good . . . the way you live and your attitude toward things. You're wealthy as can be. You don't need money to be wealthy. Your culture is your wealth."

Around this point in my conversation with Geddes, there was a knock at the door and in came Eddie Creelman and his wife, Annie. A long-haul truck driver, Creelman is a large man with a full face, whitening hair, and a great down-home accent. He was recovering from a broken back after falling off his rig two months earlier while in Ontario. Geddes had flown in and driven Creelman's rig, loaded with 40,000 pounds of donair meat, back home for him, a 2,000-kilometre trip. "Donair meat is an essential in Nova Scotia," Geddes said with a chuckle.

Creelman and Geddes were childhood friends. In recent years, Creelman had suffered from gum disease and had lost most of his teeth. He first met Wortman during the fall of 2019. "My teeth were impacted. I was sick a lot. Poison was through my body. It was going to kill me," Creelman recalled. "They put me in the hospital a couple of times. How I met Gabe was through Dana, and Dana tricked me. I have a fear of needles and dentists. He asked me to go help him move a boat one time. All right, sure. We got out there and Dana says, 'I got to stop and see this guy.' I knew, right then, who it was. I never met the man. He comes out. He's a big man. He goes: 'You're scared of dentists and needles.'"

"Yeah," Creelman replied.

"Let me look at your teeth," Wortman said.

"I showed him. I opened my mouth. I only had two left, or three. It wasn't very many. I pulled them all myself," Creelman said.

I couldn't help but interject: "You *are* from Nova Scotia, aren't you?"

"They was a mess and they were getting impacted a lot."

"I'll be honest," Wortman told Creelman. "If you don't get them looked after, you'll die within a year. It's your choice. I don't care."

"I guess it sunk in," Creelman said. "All right, I told him, do whatever you got to to get it done."

Several weeks later, Creelman visited 193 Portland Street in Dartmouth for an assessment at Wortman's clinic. When he showed up, he was stunned by the first thing he saw. "There was my name—Creelman—and my telephone number written on the board in big letters. I asked Gabe why my name was there, and he said: 'I didn't want to forget about you.'"

Wortman offered to build Creelman's dentures for $1,500, "a heck of a deal," to which Creelman readily agreed. "He got the number one surgeon in Nova Scotia to take me on," Creelman said. "That only happened because of Gabe."

About a month later, Creelman went in for the surgery to prepare his mouth for the new dentures.

"Do you want what Gabe told me to do?" the surgeon asked Creelman.

22 MURDERS

"I said to the surgeon: whatever Gabe said, do, and I fell off to sleep."

After the surgery Creelman had to wait about a month for his mouth and jaw to heal before Wortman could prepare his dentures. Wortman offered him a $500 discount on the job if Creelman could do him a little favour, the curious nature of which we will get to later. Once the favour was completed, Wortman would make Creelman's new teeth. Wortman got himself killed before that could happen. Creelman had to find another denturist.

Some people who had dentures made for them by Wortman are now distressed that his work is in their mouths. But Eddie Creelman has no regrets. Expecting that I might ask him to say something negative about Wortman, Creelman said: "You won't get me to say a bad word about Gabe. If it wasn't for Gabe, I'd be dead. He saved my life."

Afterwards, as we were leaving, Dana Geddes had something to show me in his yard. Parked among all the vehicles outside his back door was a 2011 Ford Taurus in near-mint condition. The four-door sedan was painted in what Ford described as "gold leaf," a bronzy metallic finish that shouted Grandpa and Grandma. He patted the car and told me its story. "This was my mother's car," he said. "After she died a few years back, Gabriel was over here one night, and I showed him the car. We opened the door and these lights come on here and all the way down here and all inside. He commented about the lines and how smooth and sleek it was. He just loved it. He had to have one. He loved the colour. He was going to buy the identical car, but he didn't."

The car in Geddes's yard was the civilian version of the Police Interceptor, a specially built vehicle with bigger brakes, a reinforced body and roof, and a more powerful and more durable engine and transmission, among other features. But paying full price for a new Taurus was not in Wortman's character.

"Instead, he started going to police auctions and bought one and then another and another. He began collecting them. I know that's how he got started on them."

◆

Nathan Staples was also buying up decommissioned police cars. He lived off Highway 2, east of Great Village, about a fifteen-minute drive east of Portapique. As you may recall from Chapter Eleven, he was supposedly on Wortman's so-called hit list and had been visited by a combat-ready RCMP ERT member just after midnight on April 19, a little more than two hours after the first calls to 911 had been placed from Portapique.

Staples liked to park a decommissioned police car on the lawn by the highway "to slow down drivers speeding past here." He remembered Wortman dropping by one day and asking if he wanted to sell the car. "I didn't want to sell it and he left," Staples said in an interview. "We didn't even discuss a price. It was no big deal."

In October 2019, six months before the massacres, Staples found himself at a federal government surplus auction in Dartmouth, looking to buy something for a friend. He found himself competing against Wortman for another RCMP castoff: a Zodiac (a rigid-hulled inflatable boat). "He really wanted that boat," Staples said. "I decided to have a little fun." As the eager Wortman put in each bid, Staples would up the ante. "I think it went up to $11,000 or $13,000, something like that. I tried to find the records, but it's wiped off the website."

It was a lot of money for a used Zodiac.

"I think that sort of pissed him off," Staples said.

"How do you know he was pissed off?" I asked.

"Because that's what his wife had been saying, or he had been saying to his wife."

"From what I can see, they sort of telegraphed everything they were doing," I said.

"The police made it sound like they were really, you know, quiet. I don't think he could keep his mouth shut when he was drinking."

After the auction Staples got to take a good look at the boat Wortman had bought. "That boat was still sitting there," he said. "There was one pontoon that was flat on it. It was fairly beat up. I was like, 'Shit, I'm glad I didn't win that. Thing's a piece of junk.'"

So why exactly did Wortman want it?

◆

In rural Canada, as in the rural United States, the easiest way for an average student to make a good living or get out of town is to join the military or police or get a government job. That so many rural people follow those career paths is the foundation of public support for the RCMP. Everyone is related to or knows a Mountie if they live in the sticks, as Wortman did. He had even been to one of his uncle's graduation ceremonies. Country people rarely flinch in their support. If worse comes to worst, they just say: "They may be assholes, but they're our assholes."

Wortman was clearly fascinated with the force. His father, Paul, belonged to a motorcycle club and hung out with Mounties. Gabriel hobnobbed with Mounties whenever he got the chance.

Dave B., seventy-five, is a retired Halifax firefighter living in Bass River, just west of Portapique. He remembers an incident back in November 2004. It was hunting season, and one of his friends invited him up to his camp, the Stagger Inn, on nearby Economy Mountain. There were about ten to fifteen people partying there, mostly men. "It was a Saturday. I didn't go so much for the hunting but just to have a few drinks in the nighttime," Dave told me. "My friend, Gary, pulled me aside and told me: 'These guys are all Mounties. I thought I'd better tell you this in case you start telling some stories you shouldn't be telling. They're all Mounties, except for that fellow over there with the baseball hat. He's just a hanger-onner. He's a grouper.'"

Dave said the hanger-onner was Wortman. He was with a woman, whom Dave didn't meet or couldn't identify, but he remembered that she was spending a lot of time with Gary's son. "Later that night something happened, and Gary's son was in trouble," Dave said. "I think it had something to do with Wortman. There was a fight or something outside, and then Gary's son disappeared. We had to go find him."

In the intervening years, one of Wortman's closest acquaintances was supposedly a Halifax Regional Police officer, but after the massacres, any officer who might have associated with Wortman suddenly had no idea who he was. Over time, he'd collected uniforms from one of his uncles, and possibly other Mounties. Some of the pieces fit him and others, like a jacket, didn't. He swept up other trappings of Mountie life, too, including vests and equipment.

He was moving around so much and doing so many different things, it was hard to imagine how he kept his denture practice running, even with Banfield managing the office. He was spending half the week—from Thursday to Sunday night—in Portapique, often starting the weekend on Wednesday night. He was importing motorcycles and parts from the United States and selling rare, restored motorcycles.

In June 2017, Wortman advertised five Honda ATC 250SX three-wheeler sport utility bikes for sale. Jeff Crawford, who lived in the area, liked what he saw. "We met at his cottage," Crawford recalled. "It was a beautiful place. A log cabin. It was so impressive, something you'd build if you had a lot of money. I remember there was a spiral staircase up to his bedroom."

The awestruck Crawford said Wortman sketched out his motorcycle import business. "He said he had a house in Houlton, Maine, and he shipped everything there. He would then smuggle them across the border in a utility trailer."

Crawford, a seasoned businessman, had come prepared to haggle. "I had $10,000 cash in my pocket," he said. "I wanted all five bikes, but he wouldn't budge. He changed his mind and decided that he would only sell me two of them. He wanted $2,500 apiece, and that's what I ended up paying."

Something else lingered in Crawford's memory. "There was a long hall that we had to walk down to get to the garage where the bikes were. We were talking about bikes and his younger days, and all of a sudden he got really excited. He grabbed my collar with both hands and pulled me toward him, maybe two inches from his face. No man has ever done that to me. He said: 'Remember that, Jeff, remember that feeling, what it was like when you were young. You always had that kid in the neighbourhood who was riding a nice new Honda bike and you couldn't afford it, and you wanted it so bad. Remember that!'"

Once again, Wortman had shown how socially awkward he could be, hardly different from when he got in Kristine Kennedy's face back in the mid-1990s with his laser-like stare. "I would have liked to have been friends with him because he had so many of those nice bikes, but it was all so creepy," Jeff said. "He really creeped me out."

After the massacres, the RCMP and the media gave the impression that Wortman had assembled his mini fleet of decommissioned police cruisers obsessively over many years, which was not true. He bought all four vehicles over a six-month period, the first on March 21, 2019, from GC Surplus, the branch of a government agency, Public Services and Procurement Canada, that sells off used or unneeded inventory. Wortman paid $4,194.05 for the 2013 Ford Taurus Police Interceptor. The car was registered in the name of his New Brunswick company Berkshire Broman Corporation, but was plated in Nova Scotia. Its licence plate was GJX 365. It was one of the two incinerated cars found in Portapique after Wortman's rampage.

At the end of April 2019, Wortman and Banfield travelled to Houlton, Maine, to attend the Houlton Rifle & Pistol Club Gun Show at the John A. Millar Civic Center. The show was held on the weekend of April 27 and 28. Houlton is the northern terminus of I-95, the longest north-south highway in the US interstate system, which runs all the way to Miami, Florida.

Wortman and Banfield stayed in Houlton for almost a week. This was the week that Wortman drove back and forth across the border five times, including on the first day of the show, April 27, when he crossed back into Canada and then returned to the United States thirteen minutes later. Recall that Banfield said Wortman never smuggled anything when she was with him. (She later told the Mounties that on one occasion he had smuggled a gun while she was with him.) Wortman and Banfield returned to Canada on May 2, 2019.

On June 27, 2019, Wortman paid $10,990.55 for a 2017 Police Interceptor. It was also registered to Berkshire Broman Corporation. The sale was completed on July 3 and included other paraphernalia for a total price of $13,500. The car had been involved in a minor crash and written off by the RCMP. Wortman never registered or plated it.

One person who saw the vehicle in Wortman's warehouse said it was in near-mint condition. "They said it had front-end damage, but even the windshield washer container was in perfect condition."

On July 18, 2019, Public Services and Procurement alerted Wortman that he was the winner of a bid on another 2013 Police Interceptor. The ownership wasn't transferred from the RCMP to Berkshire Broman Corporation until October 2, and the car wasn't plated in Nova Scotia until November 6, 2019. This was the car located by police in the parking lot at 193 Portland Street, Dartmouth, bearing the Nova Scotia licence plate GMK 905.

On September 5, 2019, Wortman won another auction for a third 2013 Police Interceptor. This one cost him $2,607, plus 15 percent harmonized sales tax, for a total of $2,998.05. He put it on his Visa card.

Wortman's collection of police-related items in 2019 attracted the attention of the Financial Transactions and Reports Analysis Centre of Canada, the watchdog agency that tracks money laundering. The agency was also concerned that he might be involved in domestic terrorism. The question remains: Why did he buy all these vehicles? He already owned the 2017 Ford F-150 and a 2005 Jeep Wrangler. Banfield was driving a 2015 Mercedes C series. He had more motorcycles, dirt bikes, three-wheelers and side-by-sides than a tourist-haven rental shop.

After his murderous spree, the popular conjecture was that he had some unknown but nefarious purpose in mind. Was he creating a fleet of vehicles as part of a secret undercover project? Was he an agent for a criminal organization that would use the decommissioned cars as part of some subterfuge? It wouldn't have been the first time something like that had happened. About twelve years earlier, bikers in Ontario had been arrested for dressing up as police officers and robbing drug dealers.

All the theories ran to the dark side, yet were reasonable under the circumstances. But perhaps there was a simpler explanation for all those Police Interceptors. Wortman was a wheeler-dealer. He was smuggling motorcycles, parts and whatever else across the border. He was making money on motorcycles, dirt bikes and their mechanical spawn. What if he saw the police cars as a money-making hobby? They were cheap. He liked to tinker. There was a market for them. He could drive them for awhile, then fix them up a bit and sell them to the desperate owner of a taxi medallion.

After he bought them, Wortman and Banfield each drove the cars around. When asked why he liked them, Wortman said: "The power." Did he mean the horsepower? Or the fear it stoked in drivers when he came up hard behind them on the highway? We just don't know.

What we do know is that he hid the best of the lot, the writeoff he bought on June 27, and immediately began dressing it up to look like a real RCMP cruiser.

◆

On May 29, 2020, Elizabeth McMillan and Karissa Donkin cleverly obtained documents from the Truro police that shed some light on what the RCMP was hiding about Wortman. One was a copy of Truro corporal Greg Densmore's 2011 report about Wortman possessing guns and threatening to kill police. The reporters contacted RCMP spokesperson Jennifer Clarke for comment.

"We can't speak about specifics of the follow up to the 2011 bulletin because our database records have been purged as per our retention policies," Corporal Clarke wrote in an e-mail to them.

The story created a flap. The RCMP was operating like a business and forgetting its guardian role. As ever, the RCMP could be expected to respond to criticism with a sensational rejoinder, which it did the next week. The three RCMP leaders in Nova Scotia read statements into a camera as if they were members of the Politburo.

True to form, Assistant Commissioner Lee Bergerman opened her remarks with an appeal to Canadians' sympathies—for the force: "To begin, I must first acknowledge that today is June 4, a day many will never forget, as it was six years ago that we tragically lost three RCMP officers in Moncton. Those incidents continue to affect all of us—the families of our fallen, the force and the community." Bergerman spent a few more seconds consoling the families with vague sentiments: "To the families of the victims so deeply impacted by the incidents . . . your lives have changed in ways that most will never understand."

She quickly turned to extolling the virtue, heroism and hard work of the RCMP. "H-Strong is the operational name that represents teams of people who are invested, selfless, smart, dedicated and proud. . . . Hundreds of RCMP personnel have come to Nova Scotia from across Canada—to work on the front lines, to support the Operation H-Strong investigation and provide unit-to-unit assistance."

As Bergerman waxed eloquent about the Mounties, especially the "more than 100" who had responded on that weekend, she left out something important that reporter McMillan caught later. McMillan uncovered government records that showed seventy Mounties were taking the summer of 2020 off for alleged mental health reasons caused by stress from the massacres. More had taken early retirement. In fact, the entire Enfield detachment was told to beef up their tans for the next few months while replacement Mounties were brought in from Ontario and Quebec. Many of the substitutes kept getting lost in the community, and in the different laws and regulations in Nova Scotia. Former Mountie Mark Furey, the justice minister in charge of overseeing the RCMP, had approved all this, costing the provincial treasury millions.

Chief Superintendent Chris Leather spoke for less than two minutes, during which he tersely stated that the Nova Scotia Serious Incident Response Team (SIRT) was investigating the shooting of Wortman and the discharge of weapons at the Onslow Belmont fire hall.

The meat was left to Superintendent Darren Campbell. He made it clear that the RCMP was implicitly "mindful that when information is released publicly, it may cause distress for families and others closely associated to those who lost their lives or were injured." Was the RCMP defending its secretive approach as a humanitarian effort meant to avoid traumatizing survivors? Even the family members didn't buy that.

"There's something pretty major that they're fucking hiding, but I can't figure it out yet," Nick Beaton, the husband of pregnant murder victim Kristen Beaton, told me.

Campbell went on to summarize many of the questions that were being raised about the RCMP's performance in Portapique and its subsequent investigation. Read carefully what Campbell said:

The initial RCMP first responders arrived within minutes of each other. As previously described, the search area was spread out, contained several acreage properties, much of which are covered in wooded areas and several residences and outbuildings, some of which were already on fire. Aside from the fires, the search area was very dark.

As the incident was being treated as an active shooter incident, the initial RCMP first responders quickly formed an Immediate Action Rapid Deployment Team, otherwise known as an IARD Team. The IARD Team immediately entered the community in search of the threat. As dictated by their training, their objective was to locate and stop the threat. This is exactly what those RCMP first responders were working toward.

Within minutes of receiving the initial call, the on-duty RCMP risk manager, who is stationed within the RCMP Operational Communications Centre, notified North East Nova District on-call management, who immediately initiated the call-out of a full Critical Incident Package . . . [which] added more than thirty additional highly specialized resources to the response.

Questions have been raised with respect to survivors who stayed on the line with 911 operators for a significant period of time during the initial response. It is true that survivors remained on the line with 911 operators. . . . They were instructed to shelter in place and to hide while the IARD Team members continued their search for the threat. IARD members set up containment around the survivors' residence while other first responders set up containment around the community of Portapique.

As the Emergency Response Team members arrived, the gunman was still believed to be in the area, and if alive, was lying in wait, meaning that he would be hiding, ready to shoot or kill anyone. This contributed to a decision to instruct area residents to shelter in place as opposed to evacuate. The Emergency Response Team continued to carry out extensive tactical searches for the gunman while responding to numerous possible sightings in the area and effecting the rescue and eventual evacuation of

a number of survivors and witnesses, partly with the use of the
Tactical Armoured Vehicle.

I just summed up these aspects of the response in a few sentences, but it's important to understand that this was covered over
a period of hours.

If you believed Campbell, it appeared that the RCMP did precisely
what any competent police force would have done in that situation.
But as I've stated, I'm experienced in the RCMP's shades-of-truth communications style. And Campbell's story wasn't sitting right with me.

In other comments, Campbell walked back earlier statements
by the force and its union leader Brian Sauvé that Constable Heidi
Stevenson had rammed Wortman's vehicle at Cloverleaf Circle. He did
say "there was an exchange of gunfire between Constable Stevenson
and the gunman." Was there?

Campbell said three of the guns found on Wortman were illegally
imported from the United States, one came from the estate of his late
lawyer friend Tom Evans, and the other was the service weapon he had
taken from Stevenson.

Campbell also emphasized that RCMP investigators had interviewed 650 people in Nova Scotia, New Brunswick, Ontario, Alberta,
British Columbia and the United States. This sounded impressive.
But to those in the know, it was the RCMP way of doing business—a
massive, unfocused investigation replete with giant, impenetrable files
bursting with useless information.

Finally, Campbell addressed a point I had been making on my
almost regular spots on *The Rick Howe Show*. "As another point of
specific interest, the gunman was never associated to the RCMP as a
volunteer or auxiliary police officer, nor did the RCMP ever have any
special relationship with the gunman of any kind," Campbell said.

My distant cousins in the media couldn't resist taking that statement as an outright refutation of what I was trying to investigate. I
was now unofficially being crowned "a conspiracy theorist." That the
RCMP had a long and dubious record of making misleading statements, deflecting and distracting seemed to escape many of the new

reporters. History, however, had shown that the RCMP would do any-thing to protect a source. In a previous statement, the RCMP had said it had "searched" its records and could not find "evidence" of Wortman being on the payroll. Now Campbell was saying, in what appeared to be no uncertain terms, that Wortman had no relationship with the RCMP. While the media took this at face value, I sensed there might be another scenario.

Maybe what Campbell was saying was actually true in that sense. There was a clear possibility that Wortman might not have had a "spe-cial relationship" with the RCMP—in Nova Scotia. But what about New Brunswick, which was right next door? Or the Halifax Regional Police? Information about informants is tightly held within a police force. Quite often, only the informant's handler and a few others are in the know. I planned to turn my attention to New Brunswick in due course.

Campbell ended his short but meandering briefing with what would become the sensational headline everywhere. He said that in its attempts to understand the motivations of the gunman, "RCMP profilers and RCMP forensic psychologists from the RCMP National Headquarters Behavioural Analysis Unit have provided valuable assis-tance to the ongoing investigation." Then he trotted out what would become the Mounties' go-to phrase: "injustice collector." "Some recip-ients of his wrath of violence were targeted for perceived injustices of the past, others were reactive targets of his rage, and others were ran-dom targets. We may never uncover all of the details or fully under-stand why the gunman did what he did."

Six days later, McMillan and Donkin fired another rocket at the RCMP, doggedly uncovering information that seemed to put its narra-tive about its response to Portapique in a much different light. Through an access-to-information request, they had rooted out call logs from the Truro Police Service for the weekend of April 18 and 19. The logs depicted the RCMP's chaotic behaviour. This exchange took place between Dan Taylor, the constable we saw earlier in a call to Truro headquarters, and a colleague inside the Truro police communications centre around 9:46 a.m. on Sunday, April 19:

(CONSTABLE DAN) TAYLOR: . . . I was just talking to the Mounties.

(CORPORAL ED) CORMIER: Just one sec.

TAYLOR: They think they got him. They got a fully marked cruiser on Highway 4 by Wentworth, and a deceased driver. So, he might have shot himself?

CORMIER: No, they got a deceased lady . . .

TAYLOR: Well, the Mountie here just told me that they think they might have got him. They found a marked cruiser on Highway 4 near Wentworth and the driver was deceased, is what he told me. So, fuck, it could be a real Mountie, but I don't know.

DISPATCH: Oh no, oh no.

CORMIER: We'll treat it as [if] he is still on the loose.

A half hour later the Truro police were told that Wortman was heading toward the town, although he had already passed through it. "My god. This is nuts," a Truro police dispatcher said when given the news that Wortman was on his way.

The RCMP never said a word about the Truro tapes, although a well-placed source said it did what the force normally does: in private, it made its displeasure known to Truro police chief David MacNeil.

◆

My sources, meanwhile, were telling me that the unconvincing "injustice collector" assessment was intended to signal the announcement and planning of the intended "review." The system was determined to push ahead even though no one had a clue about what had really happened, which seemed to be as intended. The curtain was coming down. I believed I had to find a way to stop it from hitting the floor.

Over the next week to ten days, Maher and I kicked story ideas around. I wanted to go after the New Brunswick angle, suspecting that Wortman had no relationship to the Nova Scotia police but might well have had one with the RCMP in the next province over, and that was the kind of information police are rarely at liberty to share. Maher wasn't biting. A couple of my sources told me that all anti-biker investigations in the Maritimes were now being controlled by Assistant Commissioner Larry Tremblay and his underlings in New Brunswick. I began to try to piece together the fragments of information I could find. It was going to take awhile. We needed something easier in the meantime.

There were the supposed cash deliveries to Wortman by Brink's. Did he get $1 million or $500,000—or was it just a salacious rumour? I just couldn't let that one die in a notebook. It had to be proven or disproven. If it was true, it might open a few doors in the investigation. If it wasn't, it was best to know decisively and move on.

Another possible angle was the hardened criminal in Wortman's Friday afternoon drinking club. Since most of Wortman's closest neighbours were murdered by him, it wasn't easy to learn the man's identity, and the Mounties could be counted on not to tell us. Maher and I began to check property records of landowners in the Portapique Beach area. The name of one couple stood out. Alan and Joanne Griffon lived at the bottom of Portapique Beach Road, at the intersection of Faris Lane. Their neighbours across the road, John Zahl and Elizabeth Joanne Thomas, had been murdered and then incinerated. But the Griffons managed to escape the neighbourhood without being attacked or harmed. Their house was a well-kept modest place, facing the water, near where the northern edge of the huge parking lot for the old dance hall used to sit.

It wasn't the couple themselves that caught our eyes, but rather a name that kept coming up on search engines: Peter Alan Griffon.

The first RCMP notification that something was wrong in Portapique Beach went barely noticed by the public.

The view of the Minas Basin arm of the Bay of Fundy from the back porch of Dartmouth denturist Gabriel Wortman's Portapique Beach cottage. *(Palango)*

Wortman's cottage seen from the road.

The life-size "hillbilly" carving on Wortman's porch typified an unusual personality that made him many friends but left others uneasy.

Residence of Lisa McCully and her daughter and son, where the children were trapped along with the Blair children for three hours. *(Palango)*

Wortman and his common-law wife, Lisa Banfield, celebrated nineteen years together on the night of April 18, 2020, an event rumoured at one point to have gone wrong and touched off his killing spree.
(Facebook)

Wortman's denturist clinic in Dartmouth, Nova Scotia.
(Sean Dewitt)

Wortman sharing a snack with the animal that gave the "Black Bear Lodge" its name.
(Facebook)

The intersection of Portapique Beach Road and Orchard Beach Drive, a kilometre-long road where 11 people were murdered.
(Palango)

Neighbour Aaron Tuck on Wortman's Captain America Harley Davidson in the warehouse. *(Facebook)*

Neighbour Dana Geddes with the gas tank he'd arranged to collect for Wortman from Ontario and deliver to him the Tuesday after the massacres. *(Palango)*

Nova Scotia RCMP finally communicated to the public on the morning of April 19 that the killer's identity was known and he was driving a replica police cruiser.

← **Thread**

RCMP, Nova Scotia ✓ @RCMPNS · Apr 19   •••
#Colchester: Gabriel Wortman may be driving what appears to be an RCMP vehicle & may be wearing an RCMP uniform. There's 1 difference btwn his car and our RCMP vehicles: the car #. The suspect's car is 28B11, behind rear passenger window. If you see 28B11 call 911 immediately.

○ 246   ⟲ 2.6K   ♡ 1.6K   ↑

RCMP, Nova Scotia ✓ @RCMPNS · Apr 19   •••
Gabriel Wortman is currently in the #CentralOnslow #Debert area in a vehicle that may resemble what appears to be an RCMP vehicle & may be wearing what appears to be an RCMP uniform. Please stay inside and avoid the area. #RCMPNS

○ 34   ⟲ 550   ♡ 436   ↑

Security footage of Wortman passing the Onslow Belmont Fire Brigade Fire Hall minutes before two RCMP officers mistakenly shot at an emergency management office worker and a Mountie parked in front.

Wortman passing unnoticed through downtown Truro in the final hour of his troubled life after having already killed 19 people.

Wortman's fake cruiser (left) stopped where it had rammed the car of Constable Heidi Stevenson (right). The Ford Escape of Joey Webber is in behind. *(Craig Vanderkooi)*

The two cruisers, set alight by Wortman and left to burn. *(Craig Vanderkooi)*

The scene moments before erupting into flames, as witnessed by caregiver Kaitlyn Keddy, who wisely declined a 911 dispatcher's request that she get closer to the crime scene. *(Kaitlyn Keddy)*

Security footage captures ten bullet holes in the windshield of Gina Goulet's Mazda, signalling the end of Wortman's rampage.

The shooting was over, and the killer is left on the pavement of the Irving Big Stop gas station at Enfield, Nova Scotia. *(Tim Krochak)*

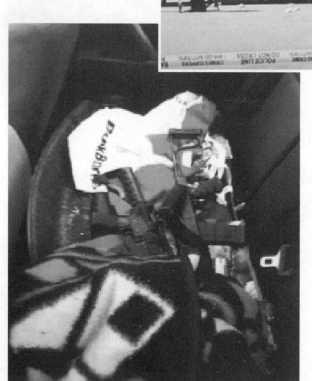

The back seat of Goulet's car, filled with the weaponry Wortman had hoped would get him through to whatever conclusion he had imagined to his thirteen hours of murder.

Nova Scotia RCMP assistant commissioner Lee Bergerman stands watch as chief superintendent Chris Leather addresses the media, more than six hours after Wortman's death. *(Sean Dewitt)*

CBC TV came under fire from viewers for its decision to broadcast its interview with an emotional Clinton Ellison, who had spent four hours hiding in the freezing cold after finding his brother, Corrie, dead outside Wortman's burning warehouse.

JOUDREY

Leon Joudrey never changed his story, for all the times he told it to media outlets who dismissed what he had to say. His consistent story changed our investigation.

The business card of chief superintendent John Robin, indicating an association with the Nova Scotia Mass Casualty Commission.

The author (centre) at the office of *Frank* magazine, with the rest of the investigative team: Andrew Douglas (left), Chad Jones (beard) and Jordan Bonaparte (right), doing the grim due diligence of listening to the children on the 911 tapes and viewing the security cam footage of Wortman's death.

It was three days before the RCMP finally released the identities of all twenty-two victims, which were quickly reported by media outlets across Canada and around the world.

22

PETER ALAN GRIFFON
AND THE HELLS ANGELS

When I first told someone twenty years ago that I was planning to move to Nova Scotia, that person, who was knowledgeable about the province, said this: "Don't go near the Truro area. It's filled with bikers and Bible pounders." I didn't think much about it at the time. But the more I got to know the East Coast, the more I realized that the warning severely understated the presence of bikers in the Maritimes. Nova Scotia, New Brunswick and Prince Edward Island are lousy with outlaw motorcycle clubs. The police thought they had it under control when they booted out the Hells Angels in 2001, but the clubs slowly began slinking back and setting up shop.

On March 2, 2021, the CBC's David Burke reported that there were fourteen active outlaw motorcycle gangs in Nova Scotia, from the Outlaws in Cape Breton to the Highlanders in Antigonish to the Red Devils in Halifax. The oddly named Katt Sass MC folded shortly afterwards, to be replaced by the Sea Titans in New Glasgow.

The twenty-year concentrated battle by the RCMP against bikers hadn't done much to curb popular interest in that calling. Some bikers went to jail, some Mounties got promoted, the bikers got out of jail, new Mounties arrested them and got promoted, and so on. In New Brunswick, the Bacchus MC reigned. Formed in 1948, it was located in the Moncton suburb of Riverview, where Wortman had grown up. A Bacchus support club, the Mountain Men Rednecks, operated in Londonderry, Nova Scotia, just north of Portapique, for a number of years until December 2019, when the club was forced to close its doors after its members were charged with the relatively minor provincial offence of illegally selling liquor at their clubhouse. That didn't kill the gang; it just moved underground, sources say.

In New Brunswick, there were also the Gate Keepers, a Hells Angels farm team in Fredericton, and the Black Pistons, an affiliate of the Outlaws MC. The big concern for the police was that an elite group of Hells Angels, known as Nomads, had also set up shop in the province. They were called Nomads because they had no formal clubhouse and wandered freely across a large territory.

Finally, in 2017, on tiny Prince Edward Island, population 159,000, the Hells Angels snuck into the capital, Charlottetown, and set up a clubhouse in a former skate-sharpening shop in a downtown residential neighbourhood, setting off alarm bells. The PEI charter, which is how the Hells Angels describes its "franchisees," had links to two of the most powerful and connected Hells Angels charters in Canada, in Sherbrooke, Quebec, and the suburb of Woodbridge, Ontario, north of Toronto.

"The PEI club has good bones" was how veteran crime reporter Peter Edwards put it in an interview. By "good bones," he meant criminal connections to traditional Italian organized crime, among other allies.

Which brings us to Peter Alan Griffon. Facebook revealed not only that Peter was the son of Alan and Joanne but also that his parents were evacuated from Portapique Beach by the RCMP at around 11:30 p.m. on that April Saturday night.

The reason Peter Griffon had caught our attention was that on December 11, 2014, he had been arrested by the Edmonton Police Service. The police were conducting an investigation into what is known as a security threat group. Members of two notorious international crime organizations were operating in concert in the city. One was La Familia, the Mexican drug cartel; the other was MS-13, the ultra-violent Salvadoran street gang also known as Mara Salvatrucha. Police identified Griffon as being linked to both groups. When they stopped his car, they found cash, cocaine, a score sheet, a portable hard drive, a camera and multiple cellphones. The warehouse where Griffon was living was later raided. There police found multiple firearms, including two .22-calibre rifles, one with a silencer, ammunition, four kilos of cocaine, $30,000 in cash, and equipment to package and traffic cocaine. Eleven days later, on December 22, the police announced three further arrests and linked Griffon and the others publicly to La Familia and MS-13.

"[La Familia's] presence in Alberta should be of concern to Albertans," Inspector Darcy Strang told CBC News on December 17. "Their connection to Mexican cartels and MS-13 creates a linkage to violence that is incomprehensible to most. I can tell you that Peter Alan Griffon was one of the targets of this investigation."

In his defence Griffon admitted to having a $1,000-a-day cocaine habit, and he downplayed his connections to La Familia and MS-13. As the parole board put it: "You report that you were living in the warehouse part time. In terms of the weapons, you state you held a party, and found the guns and ammunitions in the warehouse the next day, which you stored in a locker and forgot about."

When he was convicted in 2017 in an Alberta court, Griffon had received a global sentence of six years, four months and one day. He was immediately given credit for time served and other credits, which reduced it to two years, nine months and eight days. The then thirty-eight-year-old Griffon was paroled a year later in 2018 and sent back to Portapique Beach to live with his parents.

Three law enforcement officers who reviewed Griffon's file for me all came back with the same conclusion. Two words were missing, they each said: "Hells Angels."

"The Hells Angels control everything that moves in Alberta," said a senior investigator familiar with the drug trade. "There's no way someone could move in and push around that much weight without the Angels either knowing about it or approving it."

As much as Griffon had attempted to downplay his Alberta criminal connections, I couldn't help but wonder how he ended up with such a notorious group of people. Not many people who leave home seek comfort and fortune with organized-crime figures. An old proverb came immediately to mind. One of its first recorded uses was in 1545, by William Turner in *Rescuing of Romish Fox*. "Byrdes of on kynde and color flok and flye allwayes together," Turner wrote.

Griffon fit the profile of Wortman's drinking partners, but if he truly was a bird of a feather with cartel members and bikers, I had to wonder where he had been hatched.

It was around this time that I met someone who, in a roundabout fashion, would lead me not to Griffin's roots, but to the dark underside of this entire story. His was a tale that would be largely ignored by the public and most of the media because it came from a special, long-ignored well of knowledge known as History.

◆

Gilles Blinn was one of the many current and former RCMP staff sergeants whose attention I attracted with my recent articles and radio guest spots. Unlike most of the others, Blinn came off as reasonable and, for someone who had taken the RCMP oath, relatively open-minded. In our first conversations he mildly chided me for being "too negative" about the RCMP.

"Paul," Blinn messaged me, "I don't want to be an asshole, but it seems that you always trash the RCMP. You know, serving is not easy and split-second decisions are made all the time. Why don't you go out with the front line to get a perspective for yourself?"

I pointed out to him that I had been in many police cars across Canada, some of which I had detailed in previous books.

At another point, Blinn wrote: "I am very frustrated at the media for being biased and one-sided. I have written many emails to the CBC, CTV and didn't even get a response."

"You don't know everything that happened that weekend," Blinn told me more than once. "The RCMP does good things. Why don't you spend some time talking about that? Why doesn't Rick have someone on the show like me who can tell the other side of the story?"

"This was a world-class fuck-up," I'd reply, or words to that effect. "You say I don't know everything that happened, but that's the problem. Nobody does. It's clear the RCMP is hiding something."

"You don't know that," he'd respond.

The circle continued like that for many months.

From my long experience dealing with distressed former and current Mounties, I could sense that Blinn fit that troubled profile. I had done a little research on his background, as I do with just about everyone who contacts me, but I didn't want to push him on it too early. Eventually, the day came where we got into that area of his life and I revealed that I knew more about him than he might have suspected. "Like the Dany Kane thing," I said.

He seemed comforted that I knew something about his past. The floodgates opened. What Blinn had experienced foreshadowed what appeared to be going on in Nova Scotia: RCMP confidential informants, murders and a justice system that appeared to be a willing partner in all the intrigue.

In February 1997, Blinn was an RCMP constable who, along with auxiliary constable Dale Hutley, was on highway patrol near Mactaquac, west of Fredericton. The larger community, known as Kingsclear, has a special place in the pantheon of Canadian cover-ups. The Kingsclear Boys Training School was home to Canada's worst sex scandal, involving guards and reputedly politicians and police, including Mounties. The RCMP investigated itself for more than twelve years and cleared itself and its individual members of any wrongdoing, generating much controversy . . . but I digress.

Blinn was a highly trained highway interdiction officer. His job was not only to spit out traffic tickets but also to identify travelling criminals using the Trans-Canada Highway, which connects the Maritimes to Upper Canada. In one RCMP project that Blinn worked on, Operation Pipeline Convoy, the Mounties were stopping suspicious vehicles travelling through New Brunswick, looking for illegal drugs, contraband cigarettes and alcohol, and guns.

"I was always on the lookout for something that didn't look consistent with the honest motoring public," Blinn said. "I used my observational skills and advanced interviewing skills for things that piqued my interest. If it's a rental car, I might check the contract and the actual mileage. If the car was rented three days earlier and it has 10,000 new kilometres on it since then, I know these people have been doing a lot of driving."

One frigid February day, the temperature was hovering around −20 degrees Celsius. Blinn and Hutley were driving along the two-lane highway parallel to the winding Saint John River west of the Mactaquac Dam. Blinn noticed a new white Buick LeSabre in the other lane heading east. As he studied the car, Blinn ran through the checklist in his head. The vehicle had no front plate, which was required in New Brunswick, meaning it was from out of province. He caught a glimpse of the two men in the car. They were relatively young but were driving what Blinn described as "a grandpa car." Blinn made a U-turn and came up behind the LeSabre. He didn't turn on his roof lights but just followed the vehicle, observing.

"When I got behind them, I could see that the car had a Quebec licence plate. The car was likely a rental. In Quebec, rental and leased cars have the letter 'F' designating that fact," Blinn said. "We knew that drug smugglers and other criminals like to travel in rental cars. Quebec was also a known source province for illegal activity. As I followed them, they weren't speeding, but I could see that their behaviour was not normal. They were making a huge effort to look calm, calm, calm. They were talking to each other but never checking the rear-view mirror. If I am in my private vehicle and a police car comes up behind me, even I get nervous."

Blinn pulled the car over in a remote area about six kilometres west of the Mactaquac Dam. The driver was Aimé Simard. Blinn dealt with him, while Hutley engaged the passenger, Dany Kane, on the other side of the vehicle. "Simard was very polite with me, very honest," Blinn said. "I asked him if I could look in the trunk. He said no problem. He opened it for me. They had two-way radios, a scanner and a lot of luggage in there, which struck me as odd at the time. As we were talking, my ears were freezing. I asked him if he could come back and take a seat in my car just so I could get warm. Kane stayed in their vehicle. Hutley let Simard into the back seat so he and Blinn could chat in the cruiser.

"Simard told me that they were in the stripper business or dancing girl business—*danseuses nue* as they are affectionately known in Quebec—and were headed to Fredericton. I couldn't prove otherwise. I ran their names on CPIC [Canadian Police Information Centre] and they both had records, but they weren't wanted by the police. My experience, my sixth sense, told me that something wasn't right. I went to talk to Kane, but he wouldn't speak. He just stared me down. I had to let them go. Lucky I did, because I might be dead today."

A few days later Blinn noticed a story about the murder of a Halifax drug dealer named Robert MacFarlane. A former Hells Angel, MacFarlane had been the manager of the Spy Shop at the Halifax Shopping Centre. He had encroached on the Hells Angels territory in the illegal drug trade and was targeted for execution by the gang's bosses in Quebec. He had been shot and his body left behind a dumpster.

Halifax police were looking for two men in a new white car, described as a Chevrolet Lumina with a Nova Scotia licence plate. Blinn wondered if it was actually Kane and Simard, but didn't say anything to homicide investigators because their vehicle was a similar-looking but distinctive Buick LeSabre with a Quebec plate.

About three months later, Blinn was in St. Louis on vacation when he got a call from the Major Crimes division in Halifax.

"I knew right away what they were calling about," Blinn said.

Kane and Simard had been arrested for the murder of MacFarlane. Investigators wanted to know about the traffic stop Blinn and Hutley had made near the Mactaquac Dam in February. Simard had rolled over on his lover, Kane. Both were connected to the Hells Angels, Kane at times as a member of the Condors, the Rockers and the Demon Keepers, all Hells Angels puppet clubs. He and Simard had hidden from other bikers their romantic relationship, which began when Simard answered an ad that the colourful Kane had placed in a gay-sex magazine that he had started and was running. On their first date, the men consummated their relationship in Simard's mother's hot tub.

Blinn and Hutley were dragged into the MacFarlane murder investigation. In the pretrial manoeuvring, they were required to travel back and forth to Halifax for a number of conferences and hearings. Their evidence was critical. They could conclusively place Kane and Simard in a white car heading toward Halifax in the days before the MacFarlane murder.

That's when strange things began to happen. Suddenly, a new prosecutor, one from Quebec was appointed to the case. As Blinn and Hutley were getting ready for the trial, there was another twist. "Usually, before you go to trial, you meet with the Crown beforehand and go over your evidence," Blinn said. "In this case the Crown wouldn't do that. It was friggin' weird. We were told that no meeting with us was necessary. That's not the way it should be."

When the trial began in 1998, Nova Scotia Supreme Court judge Felix Cacchione was appointed to hear the case. A law graduate of Dalhousie University and a justice of the Nova Scotia Supreme Court since 1993, Cacchione was a minor celebrity in Halifax, known for his long locks and the tam he sometimes wore. "Felix and Barbara Beach were not really hippies, just nice moderately left winger NDPers" said blogger Michael Marshall.

During the lead-up to the trial, investigators had come from Halifax to New Brunswick to show Blinn and Hutley photo lineups. Hutley correctly picked both Kane and Simard from the photos; Blinn did not. "I didn't have much dealing with Kane," Blinn said. "Hutley looked after him. In the photos they had two guys who looked very much the same. It's not like a real lineup. It's all one-dimensional. I picked the wrong guy. I knew who Kane was. I'd have no trouble picking him out of a real lineup.

"In court I only testified for five or ten minutes. The defence went after me. They said I had no grounds for pulling over Kane and Simard. Under the law it is perfectly legal for me to pull someone over for any number of reasons. They said I didn't pick Kane out of the lineup. Dale Hutley was right there. We had an active auxiliary program [in which qualified people work part-time as police officers with limited powers], and he was one of the best in the bunch. He was the one who talked to

Kane. He got more information than I did. They said that I influenced Dale and told him to lie. There was nothing to lie about," the still frustrated Blinn said.

Cacchione tossed the case, strongly suggesting that Blinn was a liar, an allegation that had no problem making it into the headlines and the evening news. "Hells Angels hit man now a free man thanks to a New Brunswick RCMP officer who lied on the stand." That's how Blinn found out about the outcome of the case. The hurtful words from a television newscast still resonate in his head. "They blamed everything on me. I wanted to pick up my TV and throw it out the window. The RCMP didn't even have the balls to call me and tell me what happened earlier that day. After that, I couldn't win a speeding ticket case in New Brunswick because a Supreme Court judge had called me a liar."

As angry as Blinn was, today he is somewhat sanguine about it: "It was bad what happened to me, but I guess, in a way, it was good because it served the public interest." That's because the story wasn't over with the dismissal of Kane and Simard's case. Over the next couple of years, long after Blinn's name had disappeared from headlines, the real story about what had happened began to emerge.

In September 1999, a year after Justice Cacchione had dismissed the case against him, Kane was on his way back to Nova Scotia. His target this time was Randy Mersereau, a founding member of the original Hells Angels charter in Nova Scotia. Mersereau was believed to have put out a contract on three top bikers: David "Wolf" Carroll, a Dartmouth boy who had moved to Montreal and become the head of the Nomads; Maurice "Mom" Boucher, the Hells Angels president; and Mike McCrea, a former president of the Halifax Hells Angels charter. Carroll, who controlled much of the Angels' illegal business in Nova Scotia, ordered Kane to mount a pre-emptive strike.

On September 23, 1999, Mersereau's car dealership in Truro was bombed, injuring seven people. Mersereau escaped, but had only five more weeks to live.

Dany Kane's assignment to kill Mersereau meant police had a problem they could no longer ignore or effectively cover up. Kane had been the RCMP's top confidential informant—code number C-2994—inside the Hells Angels organization. He had signed a thirty-page contract with the Mounties that had promised him about $2 million—promised, but never entirely delivered. Even though he was working for the RCMP, he continued to be a prolific hit man, killing at least eleven people, including an eleven-year-old Montreal bystander.

After Cacchione dismissed the case against him in Nova Scotia, Kane sold his services to Quebec's provincial police, the Sûreté du Québec (SQ), as well. The SQ had set up an elite anti-biker unit, the Wolverine Bike Squad. A biker war was going on that would leave at least 160 people dead across Canada over the course of a few years, including several in Nova Scotia.

Kane and Carroll were driving from Montreal to Nova Scotia when they were pulled over near Rivière-du-Loup by the SQ. The officers found guns in the car and Kane and Carroll were arrested. Another hit team, however, found Mersereau. On Halloween day, October 31, 1999, he was lured to the basement of a house in Onslow Mountain and shot five times. His car was found abandoned on Highway 102 between Truro and Halifax. His skeleton was finally found in December 2010, buried in a shallow grave in North River, just outside Truro.

After Randy Mersereau disappeared in 1999, his brother Kirk took over the Nova Scotia criminal drug enterprise, continuing to defy the very territorial Hells Angels. It didn't take long for bullets to find him. On September 10, 2000, Kirk Mersereau, forty-eight, and his common-law wife, Nancy Christensen, forty-seven, were murdered in their home in Centre Burlington, near Windsor. Harry Sullivan of the *Truro Daily News* later described how the two were killed, and the RCMP response, through the testimony of Hells Angels Nomad Jeff Lynds, who was not charged in the case:

"Lynds says the Hells Angels ordered that hit and provided the guns and in a grisly description of cold-blooded murder he points the finger at his close friend Les Greenwood and an unnamed man," the CBC reported. "According to Lynds, Greenwood entered the couple's home and shot both Mersereau and Christensen in the stomach and then left the house. He says the second man then went inside and shot them in the head to be sure they were dead and then left the couple's (18-month-old) child inside with the bodies. He says his nephew Curtis Lynds helped organize the hit."

The CBC said police did not take Lynds at his word and subsequently set up "... wiretaps and launched an elaborate sting involving undercover police officers posing as outlaw bikers to work on the subjects."

Gilles Blinn didn't learn Dany Kane's real story until years afterwards, when the details began to leak out in court testimony. Three major books were subsequently written about the Hells Angels and Kane: *The Road to Hell: How the Biker Gangs are Conquering Canada* by Julian Sher and William Marsden, *The Biker Trials: Bringing Down the Hells Angels* by Paul Cherry, and *Hell's Witness* by Daniel Sanger.

Blinn is haunted to this day. When he stopped Kane and Simard near the Mactaquac Dam in New Brunswick, he had entered their names on CPIC. That set off a silent alarm inside the RCMP, who were monitoring Kane's movements as one of their paid informants.

Simard, who would subsequently be murdered in a Saskatchewan prison, had come clean with the police. He told them everything, including his side of Blinn's traffic stop. When Constable Hutley ushered Simard into the back of the cruiser, he didn't pat him down. Simard had a handgun tucked inside his waistband the entire time. Kane had one under the front passenger seat of the car.

As more of the story came out, Blinn learned that he wasn't the only one who thought what happened in Judge Cacchione's courtroom was screwy, to say the least. In his *Globe and Mail* review of Sanger's *Hell's Witness*, Toronto police officer and novelist K.G.E. (Chuck) Konkel had this to say:

Back in Montreal with the newly formed Provincial Wolverine Bike Squad hot on his tail, and with Simard arrested for an unrelated murder and festering in jail, Kane finds himself kidnapped without warrant by Nova Scotia RCMP and air taxied to Halifax for a show trial, in a tactical manoeuvre that is Machiavellian in its

sophistication and morality. After 18 months cooling his heels in
custody, and as the direct consequence of confused and contradic-
tory evidence by RCMP officers, Kane is freed.

Blinn had been made the fall guy and there was nothing he could
do about it. His personal situation was further aggravated by a near-
death experience soon afterwards. He was doing a "blood run" from
Fredericton to a patient in Saint John, driving at speed. There was a lot
of construction, as the highway was being widened into an expressway. There was dirt on the road from dump trucks. Blinn hit the dirt,
lost control of his cruiser and slammed sideways into an embankment.
His seat belt was ripped off and he suffered serious injuries, including
closed-head brain injuries that made it impossible for him to return to
regular policing. He did other jobs in the force and, despite Cacchione's
ruling unfairly labelling him a liar, rose through the ranks to become
a staff sergeant before he retired.

What really bothers him is how his beloved force let him wear the
stain of the Kane cover-up. "Some time afterward, I got a letter from
one of my superiors telling me that I had done a good job on the Kane
case. I was so mad I just ripped up the letter and threw it in the garbage."

Dany Kane died in a mysterious "suicide" by carbon monoxide poi-
soning in 2000 in the garage of his house in Montreal. But he wasn't the
only problem informant the Mounties were employing in Nova Scotia.
Another was biker and career criminal Paul Derry. He didn't commit
any murders but was aware of one being plotted against a biker named
Sean Simmons. Simmons was murdered in Dartmouth in 2000. Derry
went into the Witness Protection Program and changed his name three
times over the years. He later sued the force.

All of which brings us back to Portapique resident Peter Alan Griffon.

◆

Peter Griffon grew up in Trenton, Nova Scotia, in what appeared to be
a normal working-class Nova Scotia family. His father, Alan, worked
at a Michelin tire plant in Granton, about an hour's drive to the east,

near New Glasgow. For most of his life Alan was a volunteer firefighter. Peter's mother, Joanne, was very proud of her two sons, Fraser and Peter. She liked to dress them up and give them the best of everything.

Fraser became a solid citizen. He liked to play hockey, and one of his teammates was Peter MacKay, with whom he became lifelong friends. Peter MacKay was the son of Elmer MacKay, once the top federal politician in Nova Scotia. Elmer had surrendered his seat in Parliament in 1983 so that the Progressive Conservative Party's new leader, Quebec businessman Brian Mulroney, could run and get a seat in the House of Commons. Afterwards, Elmer was rewarded with high-ranking cabinet posts such as solicitor general, the chief legal adviser to the government. Peter MacKay became a political powerhouse in his own right as a leading figure in the renamed Conservative Party of Canada. He served as minister of justice, attorney general, minister of national defence and minister of foreign affairs under Prime Minister Stephen Harper.

Peter Alan Griffon went in the other direction.

"He was an odd little boy," said a family acquaintance in an interview. "When he went to school in Trenton, he used to get beat up regularly. Nobody liked him. Joanne would buy him a new jacket and the boys at school would just take it from him. He would never fight back or retaliate. When his mother asked him where the jacket went, he would just tell her that he gave it away." When he grew up, the family acquaintance said, Griffon was a loner. "He wasn't into girls. I don't remember him ever having a girlfriend. And he wasn't a leader. He was a gofer."

Over the years Griffon drifted into drugs and the underworld. He didn't have far to travel. There was a long history of outlaw bikers in his family, beginning with one of his grandmothers, Kathleen Ryan, and her husband, Ed Simons, who were both in the military. "She was really close to Randy Mersereau. They first met on Portland Street in Dartmouth. They all lived in that area," said a source. "The murders of Randy and Kirk hit close to home, especially Randy."

One of Peter Griffon's uncles was Mike Simons, a notorious outlaw biker who had spent ten years in prison for a series of violent crimes. All the criminality hovering around him was interesting, but when I dug into Griffon's background, another intriguing fact popped up in an obituary: Griffon's mother was the first cousin of the mother of slain corrections officer Sean McLeod, who had been murdered on Hunter Road that Sunday morning. They were first cousins, but they had been raised like sisters. Peter Griffon and Sean McLeod called themselves cousins.

Wortman, McLeod and Alanna Jenkins had all been buddies. Now Griffon was part of it, too, in some unknown way.

"He was Wortman's handyman and gardener," a source told me. "And probably his boy toy."

"Gardener?"

"For the grow-op Wortman had," the source said. "I seen it." But the source wouldn't tell me where, out of fear for their own safety.

The marijuana grow-op had long been rumoured. Some said Wortman had buried a container on his warehouse property and was using it as a lab of sorts—a page ripped right out of *Breaking Bad*. This was the closest I got to verifying that it existed. Wortman was no Walter White, but given reports that he was smuggling and trafficking prescription pills and other contraband, he was still a busy little criminal. All that activity would certainly bring him to the attention of the Hells Angels, who are always on the lookout for competitors—or new money-making ventures.

I wasn't the only one on Griffon's trail. I didn't know it at the time—which left me a little peeved—but *Maclean's* had sent reporter Shannon Gormley to Nova Scotia. She followed leads to a shop called Sid Sells Signs in Truro and learned that one of the workers at the shop had secretly used its equipment after-hours to apply the decals to Gabriel Wortman's fake police cars. The worker had learned how to do the job while serving time in prison. His name was Peter Alan Griffon.

The understory of the massacres was filling with more and more dark characters. But before we at *Maclean's* would break the story together about Griffon's connection to the replica police car, something else emerged after I, once again, went on *The Rick Howe Show* and did another segment in my investigative journalist performance art sessions.

23

THE BRINK'S JOB AND
MACLEAN'S MAGAZINE

Thursday morning at 10 a.m. was becoming a regular spot for me on *The Rick Howe Show*. Howe was a bit nervous that morning, June 11. I could hear it in his voice, and it was making me nervous, too. It was like he was waiting for me to explode into a ball of conspiracy theory nonsense that he would have to spray down with a hard dose of status quo. He had nothing to be afraid of. I had a firm and defensible basis for everything I was saying, even if people thought I was a little cuckoo for dragging the Hells Angels, phosphorous grenades, the New Brunswick RCMP and other factors into play.

I needed to know more about Peter Alan Griffon, so I introduced him to the public as one of Wortman's regular drinking buddies. I felt that Griffon, with his heavy-duty criminal background, might be a key to the real story. With the province in a COVID lockdown, I could use radio to speak directly to anyone stuck in quarantine who might know something useful.

Peter Griffon aside, what I really wanted to know was the Brink's story. In the days and weeks prior to the massacres, I told Howe, it appeared Wortman had been acting erratically. And then I dug into it.

"There are reports of him withdrawing large amounts of money—
$500,000 some say, $1 million others say. The money was said to be
delivered to his denturist operation on Portland Street in Dartmouth.
What was he doing? Did he owe money to the Hells Angels?" I asked.

"Heavy stuff," Michael Marshall wrote on *40 Gallons and a Mule*.
"Is Paul just dropping bad acid and spinning this stuff out of his butt—
or what?"

By the time I hung up the phone with Howe, I was kicking myself.
I had forgotten to mention Brink's. Seconds later, I got the shock of my
life. My appeal to the public had worked. Someone I didn't really know
but who was connected to our business in Chester contacted me. "I can
give you the scoop on the whole thing," they told me.

"I'm all ears," I said.

"The amount he got was $475,000."

"Delivered to his business by Brink's?"

"No, he picked it all up in Burnside."

"How can you prove this?"

"I have the videos."

"The videos?"

"Yeah," the person said. "The two videos I have are of him arriving
at Brink's in an unmarked car and driving into the garage. The other
one I have is him in the 'man trap' waiting for his bag of money, and
then he is seen putting the bag of 475K in hundreds into his trunk and
driving away."

"Is there any chance that there was a second delivery by Brink's?"

"No, that was the only one."

"How can I get these tapes?" I asked, admittedly a little surprised by
what might be a legitimate journalistic scoop.

The source wasn't just going to hand them to me. They didn't ask for
money, but they wanted an assurance of anonymity.

◆

Sharon and I were sitting in our car, backed into a spot beside a reek-
ing dumpster. We were in the Tim Hortons and Wendy's parking lot

at 106 Ilsley Avenue in the Burnside Industrial Park, not that far from the Dartmouth RCMP headquarters at 80 Garland Avenue. I didn't care about the odour, because from that vantage point I had a view of the entire lot and three sides of the doughnut shop. We got there early. The meeting was supposed to happen at 2:30 p.m.

I had been under strict instructions from *Maclean's* that I could not meet with my source alone. Shannon Gormley was going to meet me there. I looked her up and saw that she came from a politically connected family. Having reported from around the world, she had an impressive curriculum vitae. In 2016, she was the recipient of the Fellowship for International Development Reporting from the Canadian Association of Journalists and the Aga Khan Foundation Canada. She had been based in Istanbul and had reported for years from Syria. She had been a global affairs columnist for the *Ottawa Citizen*, writing every Saturday about "the state of democracy and liberalism around the world." She was now at *Maclean's*.

A well-used economy car backed in across and down a bit from the front door of the Tim Hortons. Eventually, a woman I recognized got out and started striding toward the doughnut shop.

"Shannon," I called as I got out. We introduced ourselves and she took me to meet her boyfriend, who was sitting behind the steering wheel.

"Paul, this is Andrew," she said.

"Nice to meet you, Andrew," I said to the bearded older man in the car.

That's where my prosopagnosia, otherwise known as face-blindness, rose up to bite me. I'm terrible with faces but good with voices. I can remember almost verbatim what people say, but faces stump me. His was a face I should have known. He was a fixture on Canadian television, an esteemed commentator on politics and a nationally published columnist—Andrew Coyne.

I had met Coyne a number of times before and every time he appeared to regard me as an upstart member of the hoi polloi, a social standing for which I had a binder full of qualifications. I remember one time telling him that I had a distant relative named Coyne. The look he shot me down his nose was hilarious. Coming across him in a Tim Hortons parking lot in the north end of Dartmouth, Nova Scotia, was so out of context that he just looked like someone's well-preserved grandfather. Coyne was an Ottawa insider if ever there was one. His father, James Coyne, used to be the governor of the Bank of Canada. James Coyne's name was on our money when I was much younger, at a time when we didn't have many of those bank notes floating around our house. Coyne's cousin Deborah was the mother of a daughter with the much older former prime minister Pierre Elliott Trudeau.

We waited and waited. Nothing was happening as 2:30 p.m. stretched into 3:15 p.m.

At one point two men pulled up and parked across from me. My phone rang. It was Gormley. She was concerned about the men. I said they were just parked having a coffee and a doughnut.

Then my phone rang again. It was *Maclean's* head office.

"What about that car?"

"They are just looking at my car."

"Why are they looking at your car?"

"It's a Kia Stinger. It's pretty fancy and pretty rare around here. I think they're just admiring it," I said. It was an even rarer thing in my long life to have a car that people admired, and that could reach speeds of 300 kilometres per hour.

Maclean's suggested that maybe we should call the whole thing off. They thought it was getting a little too hairy. I wasn't going to do that. Uncertainty was normal for this kind of work.

Finally there was a ding on my phone. I could hardly see the message in the bright sun—and then I did. My source had scoped out the situation and declined to attend in person. I got a text instead. It was a video, as promised, showing a white Ford Taurus pulling into the Brink's yard. And then there was another video of a man who looked like Wortman doing a transaction inside a building.

I hustled, such as I could at my advanced age, over to Gormley. We had to duck under the roof overhang at the Tim Hortons to see what we had. It was gold. My source added that the money had originally come from the CIBC bank and was routed through Intria,

which provides money for ATM machines and the like, before landing at Brink's.

Now we had to confirm that the Brink's yard was the same as in the
video. As it turned out, the office was just down Ilsley Avenue from
the Tim Hortons, at number 19. Gormley and I both got a little lost,
and I arrived first. The gate was closed, but I drove up the ramp and
parked in front of it. I took my camera out and started to take some
photos, hoping to lure out a guard to interview, which worked. I told
him who I was and what I was doing.

"We've been expecting you," the guard said, meaning reporters.
"You're the first one."

By the time Gormley pulled in, I'd already had a few minutes of
conversation with the affable guard, but now I had to slyly walk him
back through everything so that Gormley could hear what he had to
say for herself.

When we were done, we quickly reviewed what he had said. There
was one minor point that Gormley said we couldn't use because she
hadn't heard it spoken.

"Yeah, right," I said, or words to that effect.

◆

On June 17, 2020, two months after the massacres, *Maclean's* ran the
story about the video, with mine being the first of the three bylines,
although I wasn't allowed to write a word. The headline and subhead
pretty well told the story:

THE NOVA SCOTIA KILLER HAD TIES TO
CRIMINALS AND WITHDREW A HUGE SUM
OF CASH BEFORE THE SHOOTING

New evidence including a video of the killer raises questions
about his activities prior to the Portapique shooting
and RCMP transparency around the case

The story confirmed when Wortman had taken out the money. It was on March 30, nineteen days before his rampage. *Maclean's* released the videos online, creating a flurry around the world. The grainy and distorted black-and-white images of Wortman looked like they had been shot with an 8mm camera from the 1950s. We didn't reveal that we knew Wortman's money had routed from CIBC through Intria to Brink's and, finally, Wortman. That was left for another story.

As is often the case in journalism, one powerful story begets another. In this case, a partial copy of the RCMP's undercover manual fell into our hands. It was missing the section on how undercover informants and agents are paid. We published our second article two days later, under this headline: "The Nova Scotia shooter case has hallmarks of an undercover operation: Police sources say the killer's withdrawal of $475,000 was highly irregular, and how an RCMP 'agent' would get money." In the story we also revealed Peter Griffon's connections to Wortman, his role in putting the RCMP decals on the replica police car, and the CIBC Intria link. Although I again didn't write a word, "we" described how unusual the transfer of funds to Wortman was. It was a narrative-changing story that the RCMP and governments tried to bat down and smother.

Sources in both banking and the RCMP say the transaction is consistent with how the RCMP funnels money to its confidential informants and agents, and is not an option available to private banking customers.

The RCMP has repeatedly said that it had no "special relationship" with Wortman. RCMP Supt. Darren Campbell reiterated that statement during an interview with the *Toronto Star* published online, and in its print newspaper on Sunday, saying: "The gunman had no special relationship with the RCMP whatsoever." Campbell told the *Star*: "The investigation has not uncovered any relationship between the gunman and the RCMP outside of an estranged familial relationship and two retired RCMP members."

According to the *Star* story: "Campbell said the reason for Wortman's large cash withdrawal, which he confirmed was hundreds of thousands of dollars, was not fully known, 'however, there are indications that near the time of the withdrawal the gunman believed that due to the worldwide pandemic, that his financial assets were safer under his control.'"

Campbell declined to be interviewed by *Maclean's* on Friday, prior to this story's publication online, and again on Tuesday. . . .

The RCMP Operations Manual, a copy of which was obtained by *Maclean's*, authorizes the force to mislead all but the courts in order to conceal the identity of confidential informants and agent sources.

"The identity of a source must be protected at all times except when the administration of justice requires otherwise, i.e. a member cannot mislead a court in any proceeding in order to protect a source." . . .

The RCMP Operations Manual requires officers handling confidential informants and agents to send reports to the director of the Covert Operations Branch at National Headquarters.

Headquarters' media relations office said in an email Friday that Campbell's statement that the force never had a "special relationship" with Wortman "still stands."

The attorney general of Nova Scotia, former RCMP staff sergeant Mark Furey, has said the province is in talks with Ottawa about a joint federal-provincial inquiry or review of Wortman's murderous rampage.

Furey's office did not reply before deadline to a question about whether the terms of the inquiry would allow inquiry counsel to pierce the powerful legal privilege that attaches to confidential informants.

Family members of the victims have complained that the process is dragging out. As calls for an inquiry mount, so does speculation about what happened, among both the general public and the RCMP.

One former Mountie says he doesn't understand why Wortman would turn against the Mounties if they were paying him. "What seems inconsistent to me is why are you going to bite the hand that feeds you? If he's getting money, and that's a lot of money for an agent, or a CI, that part doesn't make sense to me."

The former investigator pointed out that if Wortman was acting for the RCMP, and receiving that amount of money, he would eventually be expected to testify.

"If he was an agent, he should show up on a witness docket."

But another Mountie says, "This guy always wanted to be a Mountie. He was acting like a Mountie. He was doing Mountie things. It's clear to me that something went wrong."

The RCMP Operational Manual contained much more that seemed to apply to details of this case that had not yet been reported. Most importantly, we learned that the RCMP can lie to everyone but a judge in a courtroom to protect an informant's identity. A little digging and anyone could have learned that an informant or agent's name is protected—even in death.

The RCMP's denials of a "special relationship" with Wortman were, therefore, to be viewed with skepticism. Typical of the force when under fire, it had not responded to questions from *Maclean's*, who had Gormley and me in Nova Scotia, actively pursuing this story, but turned instead to a reporter on the West Coast, the *Toronto Star*'s Douglas Quan. With so many senior members of the RCMP coming from British Columbia, this raised a red flag for me.

Regardless, the sensational back-to-back stories had the effect of putting a temporary dent in the RCMP's domestic violence narrative. Some people began to see that the story was much more complicated than police were letting on. The federal and provincial governments, ever so eager to set up a "review" and sweep everything under the rug, had a giant elephant in the room to deal with. Was Wortman some sort of police agent?

I sensed we were cutting close to the bone when Stephen Maher called: "We're getting some pushback." He told me he had received two calls. One was from a woman named Jessica Davis, who said she had worked at the Financial Transactions and Reports Analysis Centre of Canada (FINTRAC), the institution that tracks suspicious financial transactions. She told Maher that there was nothing abnormal about Wortman's transaction having gone through Brink's. I had no idea who she was.

"That's a Smurf," I said to Maher. "I can smell them a mile away. She's probably an ex-Mountie, and her job is to spread disinformation and doubt in the media."

Maher was skeptical, but he looked into her further. "I checked out her website," he said. She wasn't an ex-Mountie. "She's ex-CSIS."

Davis was no ordinary observer of the situation. She had been a senior strategic analyst with CSIS and a team leader at FINTRAC. Now she had her own company, and she was well connected. Her CV was both impressive and disturbing.

> Jessica Davis is the President and principal consultant at Insight Threat Intelligence. Jessica draws on her extensive experience in the security and intelligence world to bring her clients accurate, relevant and timely intelligence and help them deal with uncertainty and complexity. Jessica is an internationally recognized expert on terrorism indicators, women in terrorism, illicit financing, and intelligence analysis, and is also the President of the Canadian Association for Intelligence and Security Studies.
>
> Jessica spent the first 17 years of her career in the Canadian security and intelligence business, starting in the Canadian Forces, and then transitioning to roles at Global Affairs Canada, FINTRAC (Canada's financial intelligence unit), and the Canadian Security Intelligence Service (CSIS). Jessica left CSIS in 2018 in order to share her knowledge more broadly, enhance the Canadian dialogue on security issues, and bring new perspectives to efforts to counter illicit financing.

I had to wonder if Davis and Wortman's neighbour Brenda Forbes had known each other in the military. They both had security backgrounds. Forbes came forward early on with her story about Lisa Banfield being attacked in 2013 and the RCMP ignoring her vague and unsupported claim. Now here was Davis working behind the scenes to shift public interest away from covert activities. Maybe they were both right, but it just made me all the more suspicious. Davis didn't have any influence on the *Maclean's* story, but she dogged it for months, telling any journalist who would listen the same thing—and many of them reported what she had to say as "a banking expert."

The second call Maher got was from a mysterious man in the Toronto area who said he was a lawyer and a friend of Wortman's named Kevin Paul von Bargen. Maher told me this purported von Bargen fellow said he knew what was going on but wanted to be paid for the information. Maher had done some background on the lawyer and declined the offer. "He used to be general counsel for Brookfield Properties."

"Brookfield Properties?" I asked. "They're the federal government's relocation company. They move all the Mounties."

"It's a huge company," Maher said. "It's probably just a coincidence."

"Maybe it is, maybe it isn't," I said. "I just don't believe in such coincidences."

A quick check on the Internet showed that von Bargen was from Beamsville, in the Niagara Peninsula of Ontario. He had gone to Brock University in St. Catharines, near where he had grown up. He earned two overlapping law degrees, from Michigan State (1994–97) and York University's Osgoode Hall Law School in Toronto (1995–96). He had worked for a couple of top-shelf law firms in Toronto from 1997 to 2005 and had then gone on to be general counsel and corporate secretary at Brookfield Residential Property Services.

Despite the slight difference in name, that appeared to be the same arm of the company that moved government employees. I couldn't get anything out of Brookfield about von Bargen, and he was almost impossible to reach. I left a message for him at a phone number I had found, but he never returned my call.

Of all the people in the world who appeared to know Wortman, how did von Bargen get hooked up with him?

For all I knew, Davis and von Bargen were being forthright, but their obvious connections to the RCMP and CSIS were a hallmark of what the RCMP does when it's in its dirty-fighting mode: using proxies or Smurfs to flood the media with suggestions that our investigations were nothing more than a "conspiracy theory."

At 9:30 p.m. one night the phone rang. It was Elizabeth McMillan from the CBC. She told me she had just done an interview with Superintendent Darren Campbell and he'd called our stories "a fairy tale." If McMillan was expecting me to bite, she was sadly disappointed.

"Thank you, Elizabeth," I said, adding something like: "You're doing a great job. Keep up the good work."

I would deal with Campbell's "fairy tale" in due course. What surprised me and some of my CBC contacts in the meantime was how easily good reporters were being duped by an "official source." They were glossing over the fact pointed out in our story that the RCMP can and will lie about informants.

When McMillan's story appeared the next day, it captured some very important and likely unwitting statements by Campbell: "From what people tell us, [Wortman] was hardworking and had many holdings," he told McMillan. "He was able to amass what wealth he had based on opportunities he took. He was also a recipient of some inheritances. All of those things contributed to his wealth. . . . Recent media articles painting him as some underworld, organized crime figure, nothing has been uncovered whatsoever that would suggest that."

According to Campbell, Wortman was just an ordinary but highstrung guy who had a history of doing things to the extreme. Asked by McMillan about the replica police car, Campbell said: "Many people from the community knew about that police car he was constructing. Why he was doing that—the answer was it was to be representative of fallen officers, so people bought that story."

As for Peter Griffon, Campbell told McMillan that he hadn't committed a criminal act by helping to make a fake police car: "Campbell said police have spoken to Griffon and he has been co-operative. He said while there may have been copyright issues related to the RCMP logo, printing the decals isn't a criminal offence."

Oh? Twenty-two people were dead, partly because the RCMP didn't have the wherewithal to figure out how to stop a madman in a real-looking RCMP cruiser. Griffon, the man who had dressed up the police car, was now, my sources told me, considered to be just a drug addict and a criminal who made a little mistake. In the logic of the RCMP, Griffon's role was being reduced to small potatoes.

"The reason they are not charging Griffon is because they don't want to create any kind of record," a senior police officer told me. "They're trying to hide every little thing."

Many of our sources were convinced that, based on the evidence and the odd behaviour of the RCMP, it was a real possibility Wortman had been a confidential police informant. We said very carefully that the evidence fit the "hallmarks" of an undercover operation. We didn't know whether it was. But rather than doing their own digging, the CBC was finding it easier to write us all off as untrustworthy conspiracy theorists, which was exactly what the RCMP wanted.

Other media wrote off Wortman's visit to Brink's as a normal business transaction. There was nothing normal about it. I couldn't find anyone inside any security firm or bank who had seen anything like it before, despite the suggestions to the contrary by the ex-CSIS officer. If it was normal, the Hells Angels would be doing it, because there was virtually no way to track the transaction—it effectively skirted the money-laundering systems that were in place.

I watched the videos over and over before noticing that the gate to the Brink's yard was already open for Wortman as he turned off Ilsley Avenue. How did they know he was arriving? Lisa Banfield later told police she was also there, in a separate car providing backup, such as it was, although she doesn't appear on the video.

Eventually, a man claiming to be a former RCMP confidential informant called me. There was no way of checking his work record with the force, but what he had to say was on point. "When I saw that video, I knew right away that he was an informant. The RCMP always uses CIBC and Brink's. I made two cash pick ups at Brink's (at two different locations in Western Canada). The first one was in 1996. I got $150,000 once and, I think, $175,000 the next time. I had to sign all the paperwork in advance, and I got a chit for the money. I went to the

Brink's yard, rang the bell and was shown into a little room. I had to show them the chit and my driver's licence, and I got the money. It was exactly the same thing."

The story, with all its similarities to Wortman's cash collection at Brink's in Dartmouth, couldn't be proven one way or the other.

Meanwhile, as we moved forward on our investigation, excited as Maher seemed to be, he had some new ground rules for our pursuit of the story. "We have to be careful to be respectful of the families," he said. "We don't want to traumatize them any further."

Maher's approach to investigative reporting—creating a new narrative—was similar to mine in some ways but also different. He was thorough and had some good contacts. I was impressed by how professional he was. He would record everything and transcribe it all. I pictured large volumes of these transcripts at his desk.

Maher was a post-to-post guy who liked to get close to people he was interviewing and wheedle his way into their hearts, even go fishing with them. He developed controversial elements of a story by planting a tiny seed or two in the one he was writing—to test the waters, as it were, before gradually wading in to judge how deep he wanted to go. In my view he was an unwitting captive of the positive feedback machine that is social media.

It was here that my approach differed from his. Once a plausible target emerged, I would go after it, do the story and then disappear into the shadows. I didn't record many conversations, but I did when an issue might be contentious or if I was talking to someone who I suspected might hang up on me or never talk to me again. I interviewed people over and over until I had every nuance of their story firm in my mind. When I was writing the story, I did it from memory and refused to let my notes or transcripts write it for me. If I got stuck on something, I would call the appropriate source back and clarify exactly what they had said or done—and then type it right into the story. My style was to gather intelligence and facts and publish big, bruising stories— even if somewhat speculative—in an effort to jog people's memories, give witnesses courage and flush out more information. My articles were implicitly designed to move the overall story incrementally forward. I didn't get close to anyone. I hated fishing.

As we worked somewhat together, I could see that Maher had a caricature of me etched in his mind that was not much different than the one being touted by the RCMP. He thought I was a wily but dangerous and undisciplined fact gatherer. I didn't follow the new rules of journalism. I was also a little too brusque, the kind of person who couldn't be allowed to go door to door because I would likely be disrespectful to the families. The last part was not true, but it wasn't worth arguing about, either. Maher even had a description for me that I found both telling and amusing: "When people ask me what Palango is like, I say: 'He comes from the school they knocked down to build the old school.'"

"I see myself as the agent of the story," I'd reply when he said it. "I will not allow myself to be politicized."

Throughout all this, I could empathize with Maher's dilemma. He was a freelancer tethered by a tenuous contract to a once-great magazine now struggling to survive in the digital-media world. There were few other places for him to ply his trade in Canada. I was a freelancer who was anything but desperate. I didn't need to be doing this, and it didn't affect my financial future one way or the other. Maher's heart appeared to be in the right place, but we were both dealing with a system that had been so corporatized and politicized that it was all but impossible for truth tellers to find their bearings.

The day after the second article was published, Shannon Gormley bailed on the story, and never published another word about Portapique. Maybe it was the outlaw bikers and intrigue, although she had been a war correspondent in Syria and had surely seen worse. Instead, it seemed to me that the RCMP whispers and sly allegations had been doing their intended work. A messy story like this, in the company of an alleged conspiracy theorist like me, certainly didn't look like a good career move for anyone at the top of the media food chain in Canada.

As pleased as I was about getting those articles published, I wasn't all that hopeful that the *Maclean's* relationship was a marriage made in heaven. I was prepared to help Maher move the story forward, but

I sensed that the magazine would never let me publish my own work in its pages.

After the stories were published, I reached out to the source who had shared the Brink's videos and told them that I was not supposed to offer money.

"All I want is to help you get to the bottom of all this," they said. "I'm not in it for the money."

"Well, let me take you out to the fanciest restaurant in Halifax when this COVID thing settles down," I said.

"No, that's all right. You don't have to do that. Just send me $50 and we'll call it even."

I slipped a red bill into an envelope and fired it off in the mail.

24

THE CORPORAL IN THE BUSHES

After publication of the Brink's stories, attention picked up. Calls were coming in from documentary producers. One was from Ontario. Their specialty was reality shows about heavy tow trucks on Highway 401 and the like. A top podcaster had called from England wanting to do a deal. There were many other queries.

As riveting and twisted as the story might have sounded to outsiders, in my opinion it was still in its infant stages. I couldn't get out of my head what I had been told about Chief Superintendent John Robin, the director of Covert Operations, whom I introduced in Chapter Four. I was told by sources that I should be alert for him to get involved, but he still hadn't crossed any of my tripwires.

Meanwhile, I was stuck in a journalistic limbo. The mainstream media wouldn't touch my stories, citing their preference for their own work. Although they would never say as much, I sensed they were buying into attempts to discredit my work as "fairy tales."

On the other side were the podcasters. From what I had read, most of them were preoccupied with biblical revelations, false-flag operations, anti-vaxxing, the 'Oumuamua asteroid being an alien spacecraft, lizard people and endless speculation about the demises of Bruce Lee,

Tupac Shakur and Biggie Smalls. Since I was getting so many inquiries from them, I took it upon myself to learn a little more.

One podcaster was persistent about talking to me. Fronting the show was a woman named Laura-Lynn Tyler Thompson in Vancouver. She had been a former co-host of religious talk show *The 700 Club Canada*. As her website, Laura-Lynn TV, puts it: "God called her to the media miraculously one night in 1999." She also appeared to be extremely right-wing, which was not a good fit for me, but a show that attracted a lot of right wingers meant I'd be heard by police and former police—the audience I wanted to reach out to.

I was starting to get the hang of this Zoom thing. At one point, I looked directly into the camera and said something like this: "Bad policing makes for bad law. What happened in Nova Scotia was an epic failure of policing. Something has to be done. We need police to step up and help everyone get to the bottom of this case. That's the right thing to do."

It went better than I could have dreamed, except that I was drenched with sweat from the sun beating down on my office. I was embarrassed by how red-faced and soaked I was, but the feeling didn't last for long.

The next day A&E contacted me from New York and Los Angeles. Someone had seen me on Laura-Lynn TV and wanted to talk about a documentary. Other people I didn't know called, too. I was shocked. Laura-Lynn really did have reach. But I had to keep generating stories in print that would earn me more airtime.

The drumbeat about the federal and provincial governments calling a review was also pounding. The surviving families of the twenty-two dead were getting angrier and angrier about all the obfuscation, excuses and inaction. Even the former chief pathologist of the province, John Butt, was calling in from his new post in British Columbia to offer a similar opinion.

Nova Scotia justice minister Mark Furey was largely silent. He was helped by the fact that the Nova Scotia Legislature had been shut down by the COVID pandemic, which meant he didn't have to face daily questioning from the opposition parties. Mind you, that was a theoretical issue, at best. Neither the right-wing Progressive Conservative

Party or the left-wing New Democratic Party had shown much interest in pressing the government on the topic. When Furey did show up on radio, the media didn't challenge him.

"We are committed to finding the answers you need to help you heal, to allow you to begin to . . . to live your lives in spite of these very, very difficult circumstances," Furey told CBC radio's *Information Morning* on June 3. Even though the RCMP was employed under contract as Nova Scotia's provincial police force, he continued to make the case that the province really didn't have jurisdiction over it. The RCMP in Nova Scotia was subject to provincial laws and statutes, but Furey was prepared to demur to the federal government. It was a lesson in surfing the boundaries of the provincial and federal jurisdictions to avoid accountability.

Furey went on to say: "The broader that inquiry, given the circumstances, the more questions we would be able to ask, the more answers we would get, and the more recommendations we would get that would be applicable to both federal and provincial entities."

Furey referred to an "inquiry," but whether there would be a proper inquiry or merely a judicial review of the police performance on April 18 and 19 had not been determined. Dalhousie University law professor Richard Devlin made his preference between the two options very clear on June 3 to David Burke of the CBC: "The best mechanism to achieve the goals of independence and impartiality, transparency and comprehensiveness is a public inquiry. If you simply have a review that would focus on police conduct, that would be inadequate and not deal with the larger structural issues."

I needed to put more information on the public record before any review or inquiry was called—the more that was out in the open, the more likely we'd get at the truth. I'd heard from a number of reliable police insiders about a compelling story from that Saturday night at Portapique Beach Road that no reporter seemed prepared to pursue or publish. I investigated the leads and then framed the story as a new and revised timeline of the events of April 18 and 19.

One of my missions was to put names of the RCMP members involved in the response on the public record. By doing so, I hoped to provide more ammunition to the victims' families and the legal team, led by litigators Robert Pineo and Sandra McCulloch, that was being assembled to mount a class-action suit against the RCMP and governments. Once my story was completed, I thought it was an important one. I offered it to *Maclean's*.

"We would like you to work with Maher on this," editor Colin Campbell told me.

"But it's my story," I said. "I conceived, researched and wrote it on my own." I knew full well what was going on. *Maclean's* sat on it for more than a week before passing on it because, as Campbell put it: "It's more of a local story." He also suggested that, at 5,000 words, it was too long. Too long? *Maclean's* was now a print monthly with a regularly updating digital platform. Online, it could publish *War and Peace* if it wanted to.

My only other choice was the *Halifax Examiner*. To my shock and surprise, Tim Bousquet not only was excited about the story, but ran it on July 18, the three-month anniversary of the murder spree, excising the name of the offender, as is his outlet's wont. The story filled in some gaps in the RCMP timeline and gave the public some context for the events. For this book, it should serve to reacquaint the reader with the details and central issues of my investigation—what happened that night at Portapique and the practices and performance of the RCMP. For example, in Chapter Fourteen I related Adam and Carole Fisher saying they heard a helicopter flying nearby while Gabriel Wortman was pounding on the door of their home. Wortman left the scene and continued on to Debert, where he killed pregnant Kristen Beaton and Heather O'Brien. The impression the RCMP left through its own references to the helicopter was that Wortman narrowly avoided being caught in a wide dragnet. In this story, among other things, I first revealed what the helicopter was really doing. The story also shows the state of public knowledge twelve weeks after the massacres.

In the original story there were a few errors, a couple of which were persistent in the RCMP accounts and never corrected, like Joey Webber's "Chevy Tracker." In my haste in writing the story, I also made a couple of minor errors, which I have corrected here.

"AN EPIC FAILURE": THE FIRST DUTY OF POLICE IS TO PRESERVE LIFE; THROUGH THE NOVA SCOTIA MASSACRE, THE RCMP SAVED NO ONE

By Paul Palango

The RCMP has claimed it did its best in trying to deal with the Nova Scotia mass killer on the weekend of April 18 and 19, but a reconstruction of events by the *Halifax Examiner* strongly suggests that the police force made no attempt to save lives by confronting the gunman or stopping his spree at any point.

"Public safety and preservation of life are the primary duties of any peace officer," said a former high-ranking RCMP executive officer who asked for anonymity out of fear of retaliation by current and former law enforcement officials who are vigilant about any criticism of policing by those in the field. "As far as I can tell, the RCMP did nothing in Nova Scotia to save a life. They weren't ready. It is embarrassing to me. The entire thing was an epic failure."

Based upon interviews with other current and former police officers, witnesses, and law enforcement, and on emergency services transcripts, it seems clear that there was a collapse of the policing function on that weekend.

At no point in the two-day rampage did the RCMP get in front of the killer, who the *Examiner* identifies as GW. It also seems apparent that some Mounties, many of whom were called in from distant locales, were stunningly unaware of the geography and landmarks in the general area as the RCMP tried to keep up with GW.

Sources within the RCMP say a major problem was that communications between various RCMP units were never co-ordinated. "Everyone was on their own channels," the source said. "Nothing was synchronized. They could have gone to a single channel and brought in the municipal cops as well, but for some reason they didn't. It was like no one was in charge."

RCMP Chief Supt. Chris Leather said in the days after the incident that the RCMP was responding to a "dynamic and fluid" situation. "The fact that this individual had a uniform and a police car at his disposal certainly speaks to it not being a random act," he said.

In the days and weeks after the shootings, RCMP spokespersons repeatedly portrayed the gunman as a clever, psychotic criminal who had conceived what was essentially a brilliant plan to dupe police and evade capture. This subtly changed in an interview with the CBC earlier this month when Supt. Darren Campbell said: "There's been no evidence that he was pre-planning [the mass shooting]."

As chaotic as the situation might have been for the RCMP, it is evident that the force failed to contain the shooter on the evening of April 18 at the initial multiple crime scenes in the Portapique Beach area of Central Nova Scotia. Thirteen people were murdered that night in what might well be called the first massacre. As has already been acknowledged, the RCMP did not set up roadblocks and perimeters around the area, even though it knew within minutes of arriving at the scene that the shooter was armed and likely on the loose in a replica Mountie police vehicle.

On April 19, the second massacre took place. Unlike the night before, the RCMP knew beforehand who the suspect was, how he was dressed, and what kind of vehicle he was driving, a replica RCMP vehicle. The RCMP had sightings of the killer that morning, but again inexplicably did not seal off roads and highways and try to contain him after numerous 911 calls about sightings. Nine more people, including RCMP constable Heidi Stevenson, were murdered that day.

Preservation of human life is generally accepted to be the ultimate duty of all law enforcement officers in critical incident management. In basic training all Canadian police officers are taught to understand that when confronted with a life-threatening situation, the "priority of life" is demonstrated in this order: hostages, innocent by-standers, police/first responders, and suspects.

The RCMP has said that officers who responded to the original incident employed a tactic known as Immediate Action Rapid Deployment (IARD). With such training, as well-described on-line, the first responding officers are authorized to be proactive and disrupt a crime before criminals become "active shooters."

"We are taught to move past injured victims and attack the situation," said one current RCMP member. "If the suspect is in a building, we use a T formation. If he's outdoors, it's a diamond. You typically need four officers, but, if need be, you can do it with fewer. The point is to neutralize the suspect as quickly as possible and prevent further injuries or deaths."

In spite of what the RCMP has publicly stated, law enforcement sources and others have told the *Examiner* that the first RCMP responders did not actively intervene after arriving at the scene. After discovering a considerable number of slain victims around a property and on or near the road, the officers retreated to a point near the top of Portapique Beach Road, where they congregated to wait for reinforcements.

Several RCMP and law enforcement sources say that a corporal from a nearby detachment who was the initial supervisor on the scene froze in place, to the distress of other Mounties. The corporal later ran into nearby woods and turned off their flashlight and hid. That officer continues to be off work on stress leave.

Some veteran Mounties say that there were likely a number of factors that caused the first Mounties on the scene to hesitate.

"It could have been inexperience. Maybe there was no backup. And then there's always that Canada Labour Code thing," said one long-time Mountie.

He was referring to a $550,000 fine imposed on the RCMP in January 2018 for failing to properly arm and train its members after three Mounties were murdered and two injured in a shooting rampage in Moncton on June 4, 2014. Since the Labour Code decision, all RCMP members on patrol are trained in the use of assault weapons. Every Mountie carries a Colt C8 rifle with a 30-shot magazine in their patrol cars. The high-powered gun is considered to be an upgrade to the American-made AR-15.

"They were in a bad situation," said the Mountie. "Their duty is to save lives, but whoever the supervisor was, he or she might have been thinking that they could be criminally sanctioned and go to jail if they send officers into a life-threatening situation. At the very least, it could be the end of their career. That's how the Labour Code fine is interpreted, even if the police are supposed to be exempt from it in the performance of their duties."

Others have suggested that the RCMP called what has come to be known in policing circles as a FIDO—Fuck it, drive on. What that means is that police deliberately avoid dangerous situations and delay or wait until everything has calmed down before making a move.

Within an hour or so after the first call came in, Staff Sergeant Allan Carroll took over as the officer-in-charge at a command centre set up in the RCMP detachment at Bible Hill. Sources say that Carroll did not attend the scene and it is not known precisely what he did or didn't do.

It is noteworthy that his son, Jordan, an RCMP constable, was the second officer to arrive at the scene in Portapique. A knowledgeable source told the *Examiner* that Staff Sergeant Carroll retired from the force three weeks ago. A party was held on June 27.

As the Mounties maintained their static position at Portapique Beach Road, tensions were rising. "It was a shit show," one Mountie said.

Some of the frustrated Mounties wanted to follow their training, move forward and attack the situation. A RCMP tactical officer from Cole Harbour who was called to the scene became frustrated with the fact the Mounties were not attempting to move from their fixed position, save lives and possibly confront the killer. When that Mountie and another said they were going to do it on their own, an unknown supervisor told them: "If you go down there this will be your last shift in the RCMP." The Mounties held their position.

The RCMP has refused to release its own communications from that night or transcripts of them, but interviews with and transcripts of communications from the nearby Truro Police and Emergency Medical Services along with other already noted sources helps fill in some of the gaps and paint a picture of the chaos inside the RCMP.

In the days after the shootings, the RCMP gave three different versions of how long it took the force to respond to the first 911 call, which was at 10:01 p.m. First it said officers were on the scene in 12 minutes. On April 21, the RCMP said the first call came in at 10:30 p.m. The next day this was corrected to the call coming in at 10:01 p.m. with the first Mounties arriving on the scene at 10:36 p.m.

A local man was driving out of Portapique Beach Road when the killer in his replica cruiser approached him from the other direction and shot at him in his vehicle, wounding him in the arm. According to search warrant documents obtained by the *Examiner*, that man told investigators he drove up the road and met the cordon of Mounties waiting there. Police sources tell us that the man told Mounties that a man he believed was GW was in a marked police car and had shot at him. This occurred sometime after 10:26 p.m. and before 10:35 p.m., when the vehicle was seen leaving the area driving across a field to Brown Loop, which is about 200 metres to the east of where the police were positioned.

That man's report is the first time, as far as we know, that the RCMP were aware that GW was in a recognizable police vehicle.

At or around 10:45 p.m., the killer and his vehicle later were identified as passing by a residence on his way to Debert, where he arrived at 11:12 p.m. He parked his car behind a welding shop. He stayed there for six hours.

Until midnight, the fires raged but the RCMP held back the fire department. At least two people were hiding in the woods. One was Clinton Ellison, who had found his brother, Corrie, dead on the road and was stalked by the killer, who was using a flashlight to try to find Ellison. The other was GW's girlfriend, who later said she escaped being handcuffed in the back of another former police vehicle and ran into the woods, where she reportedly stayed until 6:30 a.m.

The RCMP put out its first alert to the public on Twitter at 11:32 p.m. It read: "#RCMPNS remains on scene in #Portapique. This is an active shooter situation. Residents in the area, stay inside your homes & lock your doors. Call 911 if there is anyone on your property. You may not see the police but we are there with you #Portapique."

The RCMP did not alert the two municipal police forces on either side of Portapique, in Truro, 20 minutes away, and Amherst, 45 minutes away. This is significant because in both police forces most of the members have tactical training, a necessity in small departments where any officer could find themselves in a difficult incident without much or any notice. Both police forces had considerable numbers of officers primed and ready to go.

On the Truro Police communications log, at midnight the department received a call from someone at Colchester Regional Hospital reporting that they have a gunshot victim from Portapique and advised that the hospital is in lockdown.

Truro Police Sgt. Rick Hickox called the RCMP six minutes later at 12:06 a.m. looking for an update.

The RCMP returned his call 49 minutes later at 12:55 a.m. to inform the Truro police of an active shooter in Portapique, although GW was long gone from that area.

Three minutes later at 12:58 a.m.: "RCMP dispatch calls advises shooter is associated to a former police car possibly with a decal on it."

Nine minutes later at 1:07 a.m. the RCMP issued a BOLO (Be on the lookout) for GW as an active shooter and suspect. The RCMP "ID's some vehicles and girlfriend who is unaccounted for."

At 1:07 a.m., therefore, the RCMP clearly knew the identity of the suspect and that he had killed many people. The RCMP was not sure about how many because the fires were still raging. Yet the RCMP advised police departments outside the scene to look for this incredibly dangerous person but did not themselves or ask anyone to put up roadblocks and lock down the area. Most importantly, in its tweets the RCMP fudged the markings on the car. The local man who was shot by GW told them it was a police car. The RCMP described it as a former police car with a Canada decal on it. Why the obfuscation?

Informed sources close to the investigation say it was around this time that an Amherst Police officer was told that the RCMP did not need that force's assistance because the Mounties had deemed the situation to be a murder-suicide and that the shooter was dead. Amherst Police Chief Dwayne Pike denied in an interview that such a conversation took place. When told about the chief's denial, the original source persisted in his claim. "Municipal forces like Amherst depend upon the RCMP for lab services," the source said. "They don't want to say anything to piss off the Mounties because they will cut them off from the labs. That would cost the locals a lot of money. The RCMP plays rough and the local forces know it, so they keep their mouths shut."

Chief Pike said recently in an e-mail response to the *Examiner* that his force was still putting together a timeline of the force's involvement that weekend.

Back at Portapique Beach, the RCMP continued its investigations at the multiple crime sites. It obtained a search warrant for the killer's properties at 200 and 287 Portapique Beach Road and 136 Orchard Beach Drive. In the search warrants it cited human remains as one of the things they were looking for.

The RCMP remained silent until 4:12 a.m., when it told Truro police about a Ford F150 truck associated with the suspect. Two minutes later at 4:14 a.m. it updated Truro about another vehicle. Ten minutes later at 4:24 a.m., the RCMP provided a list of vehicles the killer may be driving and noted: ". . . he is still not in custody." The RCMP didn't know where the killer was. They knew he had killed about a dozen people by that time (some victims had not yet been located). But the force did not send out a provincial alert or set up roadblocks around the greater area.

In its communications the RCMP seemed to be suggesting that it was searching for GW, dead or alive, but it still had not done anything proactive to preserve life by obstructing his possible paths, if he were still alive.

In the overnight hours the RCMP says it was busy clearing the various crime scenes in the Portapique Beach area. It is not clear how many Mounties were at the scene or where they came from, although some eventually were called in from New Brunswick. The RCMP has not been clear about any of this, stating that at times there were 30 members there and eventually "100 resources," whatever that entails. Transfixed as it seemed to be with the nightmarish crime scenes, the force seemed to have put the notion that the killer was alive out of its collective thoughts. No one seems to know what he was doing in Debert.

Some police sources have suggested that GW was perhaps in touch with the RCMP during this period. It is known that an RCMP crisis negotiator was on the scene in Portapique, but Supt. Campbell denied to the CBC in an unpublished interview that the force had any contact with the killer during the overnight period.

While the RCMP was putting out BOLOs as perhaps a hedge, by its actions over the next few hours, the force seemed to be convinced the shooter was no longer a threat. By 6:30 a.m. many of the Mounties on the scene at Portapique, including the staff sergeant from Bible Hill, were allowed to go home after a long, gruelling night.

Informed sources say that a new incident commander was scheduled to arrive at the scene at 10 a.m., possibly from "the Valley."

In the interim, the RCMP put out a tweet at 8:02 a.m. reiterating that a shooter was still active in the Portapique area. This made the Truro police anxious. Corporal Ed Cormier immediately called the RCMP at 8:03 a.m. looking for an update. Four minutes later, at 8:07 a.m., the RCMP responded with an updated BOLO, elaborating on their tweet: "[GW] arrestable for homicide. Advises of a fully marked RCMP car Ford Taurus. Could be anywhere in the province. Last seen loading firearms in vehicle. Vehicle photo will be sent when available."

This information reportedly came from the killer's girlfriend, who apparently came out of the woods at 6:30 a.m. However, this BOLO provided not much more information than the one at 12:58 a.m., five and a half hours earlier. It added the firearms, but any reader had to presume that GW had firearms in the earlier BOLO since he was described as a "shooter."

Still, while telling other police agencies that GW "could be anywhere in the province," so far as the public was told, GW was still in Portapique.

And the RCMP did not engage the local municipal police forces in Truro, Amherst, the New Glasgow area or even Halifax, an hour away. There are more than 900 Mounties employed in Nova Scotia in various capacities. Only a relative few of them were called in. The Mounties, however, did enlist the help of RCMP members in New Brunswick from Moncton and as far away as Fredericton, a three-hour drive at speed from Portapique.

Some expert police observers have said in interviews that the attempts to locate the killer and pursue him would have benefited from the use of a helicopter but the RCMP does not employ a helicopter in Nova Scotia. No helicopter was employed during the overnight hours, as well, to conduct a search.

"The RCMP has nine helicopters across the country, but as far as I know has never had one in Nova Scotia," said a former executive-level RCMP officer in an interview. "In renewing its contracts with the RCMP, it appears that the government of Nova Scotia has taken the position that a helicopter is an unneeded frill and dispensed with the idea. That was a big mistake. The questionable leadership of the RCMP and the questionable leadership of the government of Nova Scotia has failed to appreciate the changing dynamics of policing. The force needed a helicopter that weekend and didn't have one. Twenty-two people died. Some of those lives could have been saved."

Until 2001, the RCMP had an agreement with the provincial Department of Natural Resources, which commands four helicopters. In return, informed sources say, the DNR was allowed to use the RCMP's forensic laboratories. The RCMP denied that use in 2001, so the DNR stopped allowing the RCMP the use of the helicopters.

In the intervening 19 years, whenever the RCMP required the use of a helicopter it either negotiated with the armed forces or it paid private rental companies for one.

The relaxed attitude of the RCMP in the early morning hours of Sunday was evidenced in a video shot by CBC at the RCMP command centre at the fire hall in Great Village. Emergency response team members stand in a circle chatting away. A bored Mountie wielding a C8 rifle paces back and forth. Another Mountie helps local fire-fighters roll up some hose.

After this, things began to get even hairier.

At 5:45 a.m. surveillance cameras record GW leaving the Debert Industrial Park as he began the 40-kilometre drive to Hunter Road in Wentworth. He is believed to have arrived at the house of Sean McLeod and Alanna Jenkins at around 6:30 a.m. McLeod and Jenkins were apparently murdered in their beds. McLeod's two dogs were also killed. GW killed neighbour Tom Bagley, who had come to investigate.

For some unknown reason, the killer lingered at the McLeod property for three hours. At some point he set the house on fire and left at 9:35 a.m. according to a security camera. It is not yet known what he was doing while he lingered there.

At 9:43 a.m., the Truro police were notified by the RCMP about "a dead woman in Wentworth on the road. Advises RCMP car was seen in the area and there was a loud bang." The killer had shot retiree Lillian Hyslop, who was out for her morning walk, unaware that he was in the area because [a Tweet] had just been issued as she left the house.

The RCMP flooded the area and thought it had the killer contained, even though callers to 911 had told them that he had been seen heading eastbound on Highway 4 toward Truro. Thinking it had the killer trapped, the RCMP again failed to mobilize in an attempt to find, stop or capture him. As it had in Portapique, the RCMP did not call for help from other forces, did not set up roadblocks, call for a helicopter or track, contain or attack GW.

Instead of calling in local police for help, the Mounties relied on their own, some from far away who were entirely unfamiliar with the territory and couldn't find roads. One couldn't find the RCMP building in Bible Hill just outside Truro. Another indicated to a Truro police dispatcher that he didn't realize that there was a hospital in Truro.

Further evidence of the communications disconnect between Mounties and their commanders and between Mounties and other police forces was how messages about what was going on in Wentworth were disseminated.

At 9:46 a.m., a RCMP officer at the Colchester Regional Hospital told Truro Corporal Ed Cormier that the force believed it had the killer pinned down in Wentworth. Two minutes later Truro Constable Thomas Whidden reported that he had heard informally from the RCMP that the killer was headed to Truro. The RCMP was not formally engaging the Truro Police.

Then, at 10 a.m., RCMP Chief Supt. Chris Leather, the number two Mountie in the province and the chief of criminal operations, further added to the ball of confusion. He sent an e-mail to Truro Police Chief David MacNeil that the RCMP had the shooter pinned down in Wentworth. But that wasn't true. What Leather later told reporters is that he had meant Onslow, 30 kilometres to the south of Wentworth, an 8-minute or so drive west of Truro.

By now the killer was heading back to the Debert area, where he had spent the overnight parked behind a garage in the industrial park. Despite the fact that 13 people had been murdered, just west of there in Portapique, there were still no roadblocks or impediments to his travel.

At 9:48 a.m., GW visited the house of a couple he knew who lived on the 2900 block of Highway 4, in Debert, just north of the intersection with Highway 104. The couple hid under their bed, a gun cocked and ready. The killer backed off and continued moving south. GW left without harming them, and the couple called 911.

At 10:04 a.m. the RCMP sent out a tweet asking people to avoid the Hidden Hilltop Campground in Glenholme, which is near the couple's home. But GW wasn't there. He had moved on to Plains Road in Debert, where he killed Heather O'Brien and Kristen Beaton, two Victorian Order of Nurses who were driving in separate cars. The RCMP later said that the killer pulled them over and later still corrected that statement, saying he hadn't. The force has not yet explained what really happened.

Near Onslow, the killer passed a Mountie who was driving the other way. The unnamed Mountie, thinking that he had just seen the suspect, is reported to have turned around to pursue him, but lost sight of the killer. There was no RCMP backup in the area.

Although the killer had been spotted, the RCMP did not issue a province-wide alert or take any action to impede or stop the killer with the ultimate intention of preserving life.

The killer then headed to Truro, where he drove down Walker, Esplanade, and Willow streets between 10:16 and 10:19 a.m. and then headed south out of town toward Brookfield. The Truro police were entirely unaware that he had done that until video surfaced later that week.

Meanwhile, the RCMP finally had negotiated the use of a helicopter from the Department of Natural Resources. A source close to the DNR said that department was told that the helicopter would be used to scout the Portapique Beach Road fire scenes to ensure that the fires had not spread into the woods. The helicopter with a Mountie on board took off for Portapique. The pilot was never instructed to hunt for the killer in his readily identifiable mock RCMP cruiser—it was the only one on the road in the area that featured a push bar or ram package over its front bumper.

Back in the Truro area, more than 12 hours since the first alarm went in at Portapique Beach Road, the RCMP were still playing catch-up. At 10:21 a.m., the force tweeted that GW was in the Central Onslow and Debert area "in a vehicle that may resemble what appears to be an RCMP vehicle & may be wearing what appears to be an RCMP uniform." By then, he was long gone, but the tweet or whatever else the RCMP was saying in its internal communications may well have provoked one of the strangest known incidents that day.

Around 10:30 a.m., two Mounties emerged from a black Hyundai Elantra [actually a Nissan Altima] and started firing toward an emergency services worker outside the Onslow Belmont

Fire Brigade Fire Hall. The Mounties shot up the fire hall and just missed hitting people inside while causing considerable damage to equipment. One of the Mounties went into the fire hall for a moment and then the two left in the Hyundai.

The killer was well on the other side of Truro by then.

Five minutes earlier, at 10:25 a.m., in a well-known security video, the killer pulled into the lot of a business in Millbrook, got out of the car and changed out of a RCMP jacket into a yellow vest. He got back in the car and headed south toward Shubenacadie, where two RCMP constables, Chad Morrison and Heidi Stevenson, were driving in separate vehicles to meet up near the intersection of Highway 2 and 224.

Ten minutes after changing into the vest, the killer pulled up beside Const. Morrison, who was waiting by the side of the road for Const. Stevenson. He fired into the car, striking Morrison in one hand and the other arm.

Morrison apparently radioed for help, but the media have not been privy to that communication.

A Nova Scotia EHS tape, widely circulating on the Internet, indicates that paramedics responded to Morrison's location. In the conversation with a dispatcher, a paramedic described a "member" (the common term for a Mountie) who was shot in the foot. The paramedic says he can't transport the patient to hospital yet because he first had to recover a gun the officer had left in the woods and lock his police car. The RCMP has not confirmed any of this.

At 10:48 a.m., the killer slammed his vehicle into that of Const. Stevenson at the traffic circle connecting highways 2 and 224. The RCMP says Stevenson "engaged" the killer, but witnesses say he shot at her through the windshield and then dragged her out of her damaged vehicle. He then executed her with multiple shots as she lay on the pavement. He set his and Stevenson's vehicles on fire. When a passerby, Joey Webber, stopped to help, he was killed. The killer then dragged his guns and paraphernalia to Webber's Chevy Tracker [actually a Ford Escape] and drove off.

After the shootings were reported, the RCMP still did not get in front of the killer and stop him.

Between 11:06 and 11:23 a.m. the killer was less than a kilometre from the traffic circle where Stevenson was killed, now at the home of Gina Goulet, a fellow denturist. He shot her and her dog, changed clothes and stole her car, a Mazda 3.

The RCMP, meanwhile, was now looking for GW in Joey Webber's Chevy Tracker, issuing a Tweet to that effect at 11:24 a.m.

Unfortunately for the killer, Goulet's vehicle's gas tank may have been empty. That seems a likely reason why he pulled into the Irving station at Enfield; or, perhaps, he felt the gathering police presence around him. Instead of blocking off roads, the RCMP was going to businesses such as Sobeys and asking them to close their doors.

It was around this time that Halifax Police became engaged and began to set up a roadblock at exit 5A on Highway 102 heading [out of] Halifax, one exit south of the airport. The *Halifax Examiner* previously reported another curiosity about the lookout for the killer in that Halifax Police Chief Dan Kinsella apparently ordered his officers to attempt to capture the killer and not shoot him.

Whatever the case, the suspect was in his vehicle at the Irving station when a Mountie, reportedly a canine officer, who was stopped to fill up his vehicle recognized him. A brief confrontation ensued and the shooter was killed.

Meanwhile, the Department of Natural Resources helicopter was done with its reconnaissance of the Portapique crime scenes and was returning to Halifax. In the distance, the black smoke from the two burning cars [could be seen] at the traffic circle. Sources say the pilot was never engaged to try and hunt down the killer.

Obviously operating on a different frequency than other Mounties, the pilot was informed that the suspect was down at the Irving station at Exit 7 on the 102.

As he landed in a field near the station to let off the Mountie who was with him, the pilot received a transmission from a gruff-sounding RCMP Officer who identified himself as being "the RCMP Command Post."

What the Mountie had to tell him was that the suspect had been brought down at the Irving Station in Enfield "at Exit 11."

Exit 11, as it turns out, is in Stewiacke, approximately 25 kilometres to the north.

It was a fitting end to an epic policing failure.

I was happy to get the story on the record, even though it was all but ignored by the mainstream media. Reporters continued to write stories reinforcing the notion that the RCMP response was normal and that members heroically charged after Wortman, who, unfortunately, gave them the slip. It was evident to me that something else was going on, but what that might be, I still didn't know.

The CBC's *Fifth Estate* later fashioned a decent one-hour documentary using some of the themes I had written about. However, a one-hour documentary, excluding commercials, is merely forty-four minutes, much of it spent on tear-jerking interviews with the families of the victims. It addressed a few issues about the RCMP response but barely scratched the surface of the story.

◆

At least the YouTubers and podcasters were paying attention when the "Epic Failure" piece was published. Among the first to contact me were *Atlantic Underground* podcasters Chris Smith and Johnny MacLeod. I was naturally suspicious of them, but after a few chats I grew to like them.

Smith had emigrated to Canada from the United Kingdom after the 2008 financial crash. He described himself as a "mechanic, engineer, appraiser and the former owner of three car dealerships in England." He first resided in Hubbards on the South Shore, near where I live, and later moved to the Annapolis Valley, where he and his wife run a farm and a healing and wellness centre. His home office and library are the backdrop for his broadcasts. His partner in the enterprise is Johnny MacLeod, a friend he had met in Hubbards and who had worked for thirty years for the municipality in Halifax.

"I was always the kid reading unexplained mysteries and kind of grew up looking at the world in a questioning manner," Smith said in an interview. "I used to talk to Johnny when we saw each other in Hubbards . . . and I would always discuss world events and cover-ups with him. Eventually, he felt he had to bring the truth to the world and asked me if I would do a podcast with him. Since then, it has been an amazing journey for both of us. We started the podcast in May 2020 and have interviewed over fifty people. We maintain a group of loyal information-hungry people who we call our Truth Warriors."

The term "Truth Warrior" made me a little wary. As I got deeper and deeper into the investigation, the most unlikely people were emerging as so-called truth seekers. On a number of occasions, I had seemingly reasonable, upstanding and well-adjusted people tell me that they or their partner liked to do "deep research." Inevitably, the conversations devolved into false-flag conspiracies and the like, such as "Heidi Stevenson was executed by the Mounties at the traffic circle because she had something on the force" or "Gabriel Wortman is still alive, and they used a body double—or a mannequin." But it was publish or perish, so I cautiously stepped into the fray, ready to turn and run at the first mention of lizard people.

It worked out fine. Smith and MacLeod were anything but polished, but they asked many of the right questions and were prepared to listen. They claimed to have an audience of about 6,000, which was pitifully small by mass-media standards, but all I was aiming for was the one or two people who might know something. This was my kind of fishing. It worked.

Another person who contacted me went by the name Steve L_tt. He invited me onto a YouTube show called *Little Grey Cells*, which was based in Alberta. The title was a nod to Agatha Christie's fictional sleuth Hercule Poirot, who used a combination of logical deduction, hands-on investigation and intuition to solve the most difficult of cases. The star of the *Little Grey Cells* experience was a man who called himself Seamus Gorman. He was a somewhat mysterious and oddly religious fellow with a sonorous voice, long hair and a laconic style. He positioned himself as a paragon of honesty, morals and integrity.

Supposedly the scion of a Western Canadian family with deep roots in the legal community, he was now retired and playing the role of a shamus—an Irish detective—conducting an online investigation into the massacres through an Internet window called "The Discord." Chain-smoking as he went, and with a "non-alcoholic" beverage always at hand, he reminded me and others of the Dude, the character Jeff Bridges brought to life in the movie *The Big Lebowski*. Others saw him as a budding cult leader who had entranced his audiences and had gathered around a ferocious gang of acolytes who believed everything he said.

When I went on the show the first time, along with Seamus and Steve was a third co-host, a younger man who struck me as well versed on both the known events and the subtleties of what was going on in Nova Scotia. He went by the moniker NS Guy, and the more exchanges I had with him, the more impressed I was by how smart, shrewd and insightful he was.

Little Grey Cells had a small but fervent following, many of them family members and friends of the twenty-two murder victims. A key link between the families and the show was Tara Long, the half-sister of victim Aaron Tuck. She was a friend of Gorman, who had taken up the charge on her behalf. The show seemed an unlikely beast to generate news stories, and was largely written off by the mainstream media as a den of conspiracy theorists. There were a lot of obviously false leads, indeed, with "investigations" veering off into unlikely rabbit holes, such as a possible link between Sharpie pens being used to redact the court documents and to fill in the unit number 28B11 on Wortman's car. Another issue was that Gorman's investigations often amounted to little more than him reading reports of the day, including mine, for as much as five hours non-stop, pausing to provide his critical and often snarky commentary and insights along the way, as well as those of his audience and investigators.

I never watched a single show—I couldn't devote that much time to it—but I had spies who watched segments when needed because Gorman's long, unedited interviews with important witnesses were bringing out solid and useful information that was being ignored else-where. Even if I didn't care for his style and delivery, I needed to stay close to *Little Grey Cells*—but not too close. I had NS Guy contact me directly whenever something useful popped up.

NS Guy's real name was Chad Jones (no relation to reporter Lindsay Jones). He was thirty-three years old and a manager for a prominent Nova Scotia company. He had gotten involved as a citizen investigator partly because he had gone to high school with Kristen Beaton and partly because he was simply curious about what had really happened. One conversation led to another, and he soon confirmed my original assessment of him. He had a mind for not only the facts of the story but also the nuances and inferences that fell from them that was impressive for someone who wasn't a journalist or investigator. He could instantly recall the most obscure details in court documents, news stories and RCMP statements. He was the son I never had and the person I needed to keep going. We became like partners.

I soon came up with a nickname for him: AI—as in artificial intel-ligence—because having him at my side was like having my own personal supercomputer.

As Sun Tzu might well have put it, we were now an army of two pursuing the story.

◆

My phone rang one morning around 8:30 a.m. Sharon and I were still in bed. It was Nick Beaton on the line. I had never talked to him or any of the family members, for the reasons of journalistic distance I have already explained. From the outset of this investigation, my focus had been on the RCMP and its failings. Early on, that didn't win me many fans inside the families. Some were angry with me for being "so negative" and for "picking on the brave first responders."

"What can I do for you, Nick?" I asked.

"I just want to tell you that all the families are supporting you one hundred percent in what you are doing," he said.

"Thank you," I told him. "I'm just trying to get to the truth."

It was somewhat satisfying to have my efforts recognized, but I was under no illusion that everyone was going to be happy with me all the time. I could see where the story was headed, and I knew that the families would not be pleased about one of the routes I would have to take.

25

FAMILIES MARCH ON THE RCMP— THEN DECLARE VICTORY

On the morning of July 22, the families of the twenty-two victims and their friends and supporters began to gather in the Foodland parking lot on Pictou Road in Bible Hill. There were about 300 people, and they were angry that there was still no decision to hold a public inquiry.

"There were so many things that were done wrong, even afterwards, so we want to know why, and we want to make sure this never happens to another family again," said Darcy Dobson, a daughter of Wortman's nineteenth victim, nurse Heather O'Brien. "We want a full public inquiry with full transparency," she told Nicole Munro of the Halifax *Chronicle Herald*. "I think the people who were lost in those two days, people who were injured, our communities, everyone deserves that."

Dobson was one of the organizers of the event, along with murdered nurse Kristen Beaton's husband, Nick, who had recently called me with support for our investigation.

"When you don't have answers, your mind creates questions," Beaton told Munro, urging the Mounties to stop playing everything so close to its vest. "If they have to do it in stages, that's fine. We understand that. We don't want to jeopardize the investigation whatsoever. They are working at getting answers, but we would just like what they have to date and full transparency."

Amielia McLeod also spoke to Munro. She was a daughter of corrections officer Sean McLeod, who was murdered along with his girlfriend, Alanna Jenkins, on Hunter Road in Wentworth, making them Wortman's fourteenth and fifteenth victims.

"We want everything to come to light with what happened," Amielia said. "We want answers, and we want them now. It's been long enough. It's been three months. It's not time to hide anything anymore."

Munro also noted that while many people didn't want to speak, one who did was Nova Scotia Progressive Conservative leader Tim Houston. "There is no valid reason for this delay," Houston told Munro. "We can't wait another day. We need to start the process. It needs to start now, and it needs to start here in Nova Scotia."

Over the next year, almost nothing more was said on the subject by Houston or any other Opposition members of the Nova Scotia Legislature.

The band of protesters paraded northeast along Pictou Road, passed Stewart Auto Repair, Revana Pizza and the Village Pharmacy, then turned left on Dr. Bernie MacDonald Drive and headed to the RCMP detachment.

It was a nightmare come alive for the RCMP and its enablers. Their tried-and-true tactic of pretending to be empathetic while doing exactly what they wanted behind a curtain of perpetual secrecy had always worked before. The families had barely decamped from the Bible Hill detachment that afternoon when, as if on cue, the federal and provincial governments smartly announced that they were setting up a joint review of what had happened. It was exactly what federal public safety minister Bill Blair and Nova Scotia justice minister Mark Furey had been telegraphing for three months—and it was not going to be the full inquiry the public was demanding.

Michael Tutton of the Canadian Press described well the failings of the proposed review:

. . . little—if any—of the review announced Thursday will be con
ducted in open hearings, and lawyers for interested parties won't be
able to cross-examine witnesses.

The review panel's terms of reference don't contain provisions
to compel witnesses to speak under oath, and they specify that
information collected in the preparation of its report "shall be kept
confidential."

Despite calls from victims' relatives for the hearings to be transparent and under oath, Furey said the governments opted for a
quicker process that he said will achieve a similar result.

"We heard loud and clear that people wanted early answers,"
Furey said. Blair said the expertise of the three panel members will
provide "extraordinary capacity" to find those answers.

The press mostly reiterated Blair's glowing words for the three proposed commissioners: former chief justice of Nova Scotia J. Michael
MacDonald, former Fredericton police chief Leanne Fitch and former
federal Liberal cabinet minister Anne McLellan. I saw their "extraordinary capacity" quite differently. The esteemed panel had agreed to
conduct and put their names on a skimpy and controlled review. They
would call no witnesses. They would hold their sessions behind closed
doors. Trust them, Furey implied. They're the best of the best, Blair suggested. It didn't take much research to discover that this three-person
review panel was dragging some baggage that called into question their
so-called independence.

Former Nova Scotia chief justice J. Michael MacDonald was
related to shooting victim Andrew MacDonald, the driver wounded
in Portapique by Wortman. The former judge's first cousin, Edward,
was Andrew's father, and this wasn't disclosed to the public. Edward
is a listed owner of Maritime Auto Parts and related companies. Once
again, welcome to Nova Scotia,

Michael MacDonald had had a long and seemingly illustrious
career on the Nova Scotia bench. Like any judge, he sat through hundreds if not thousands of cases, a handful of which led critics to say
strange things happened in his courtroom. People contacted me about

some of them. No one knows what really happened behind the scenes in any of those cases, but there was one on MacDonald's docket over which the controversy has never diminished. MacDonald was the judge in the 1998 trial of former Nova Scotia premier Gerald Regan. The Liberal politician had been charged with nineteen counts of sexual offences. In what many came to see as a stunning and inexplicable decision, Judge MacDonald stayed on technical grounds the nine most serious charges. The former premier beat the others, providing fuel to the notion that it's all but impossible to put the high and mighty behind bars in Nova Scotia.

The other problem with the MacDonald appointment was that it gave the public the impression that a neutral, esteemed judge was going to be in charge. But MacDonald was not acting in the capacity of a judge, and he was not conducting a trial. This is an important distinction, because the issue of whether Wortman or someone in his circle had a special relationship with the RCMP was lurking in the background. The RCMP Operational Manual stated that the force can admit to the existence of such a relationship only to a judge—in a courtroom. If observers thought MacDonald would get to the bottom of the police response in Portapique, that was not going to happen. If a police informant or agent were involved in the case, be it Wortman or someone in his circle, the RCMP would be obliged to tell MacDonald and the panel diddly-squat.

Next was Leanne Fitch. She came from a family of police officers. Her father was a Mountie. She was one of the first openly gay women to rise to the top of a police force in Canada. Her wife, Sara McElman, was a Fredericton cop. Fitch had been deputy chief of the Fredericton Police force from 2005 to 2012, and then acting chief for a year before being affirmed in the top job in 2013. She retired in 2018.

Fitch seemed a perfect fit for the commission. She had a background in programs about intimate partner violence, and the notion that domestic violence was the root cause of the massacres was being promoted by politicians of all stripes and stature. For example, three Nova Scotia senators—Mary Coyle, Colin Deacon and Stan Kutcher—entered the fray with a joint statement: "We strongly believe that the inquiry must address the social and public safety issues which are related to this tragedy, and not just focus on the details of how the RCMP responded to the events as they unfolded," their letter stated. "A feminist lens will be critical to the inquiry's success."

For non-Canadians reading this story, I must digress for a moment and explain that senators are not elected, but appointed by the governing party to a lifetime sinecure. The Senate is supposedly the sober upper chamber of Parliament but rarely offers more than a rubber stamp to legislation. True to form, these senators were speaking like populists but acting as a team of stalking horses for the joint agenda of the federal and provincial governments, leading the public's eye away from the issues that truly contributed to twenty-two deaths in April 2020.

Feminist advocates Linda MacDonald and Jeanne Sarson, co-founders of Persons Against Non-State Torture and members of Nova Scotia Feminists Fighting Femicide, reinforced the primacy of domestic violence in this case across the breadth of the media. They demanded that there be a "feminist analysis" of the shootings, sentiments echoed in the reporting of true-believer journalists such as Jane Gerster of Global News and a host of others.

Yet even avowed feminists were contacting me to say that the murders were clearly not a question of femicide, as those who view the world through a feminist lens like to put it. More critical minds, looking at the proposed review through a feminist lens or otherwise, were seeing the forest and not just a tree or two.

There was much about Fitch's appointment to the commission that should have raised an eyebrow or two. Over the years she had established herself as a leading figure in Canadian and international policing circles, especially with her participation in various female-centric organizations such as Atlantic Women in Law Enforcement and the International Association of Women Police. Through those organizations she became close to many of the senior RCMP officers who were leading the force in Nova Scotia before, during and after the two massacres. There are photographs of her with key Nova Scotia Mounties, including RCMP white shirt Lisa Jackson, who was in charge of special

federal operations in Halifax. Jackson was a former Canadian Pacific
Railway police deputy chief. She had previously been stationed in New
Brunswick and had close ties to the upper echelons of policing in that
province. Being from the New Brunswick RCMP and in charge of
special projects in Nova Scotia made Jackson the kind of otherwise
low-profile Mountie officer whom the committee needed to scrutinize
more closely.

As Fredericton police chief, Fitch had worked hand in glove with
the Mounties in New Brunswick, especially as part of the Combined
Forces Special Enforcement Unit there. This is not an obscure point.
Gabriel Wortman was conducting criminal activities in New Brunswick
and central Nova Scotia for almost thirty years, smuggling cigarettes,
alcohol and guns over the border. Anything he was noticed doing
would have been caught on Fitch's radar. Furthermore, as her online
CV puts it, she was "the Atlantic representative on the Permanent
Working Group for Criminal Intelligence Services Canada and recent
past Chair and vice-chair of the Provincial Executive Committee for
Criminal Intelligence Services NB."

What did Fitch know about Wortman, and when did she know it?

If that was not enough to raise concerns about Fitch's apparent neutrality, in February 2020, she was photographed for the RCMP standing
beside a gleaming Assistant Commissioner Lee Bergerman. The occasion was to celebrate Fitch's appointment to the RCMP Management
Advisory Board, where she would have worked shoulder to shoulder
with Bergerman. Fitch, therefore, was conducting an investigation
into a colleague, something Blair and Furey forgot to mention in their
joint announcement of the review. Weeks later, Fitch resigned from her
RCMP management advisory role.

Finally, there was Anne McLellan, born and educated in Nova
Scotia, who was the first elected parliamentarian to serve her entire
political career as a cabinet minister, the summit of her success being
her time as deputy prime minister under Liberal prime minister Paul
Martin. She lost her seat in Parliament in the 2006 general election but
went on to practise law in Edmonton. She was a professor of law and
later a dean, as well as a director on the boards of several corporations.

In her distinguished career before and after politics, she had a reputa
tion as a Liberal problem solver and fixer.

I had studied McLellan's shrewd backroom manoeuvring while
researching my book *Dispersing the Fog*. She had been instrumental in
setting up the O'Connor Commission, which ultimately found Syrian
immigrant Maher Arar to have been the victim of RCMP incompetence and malice, leading to a public apology and $10 million. My
investigation had found many serious issues with the process that led
to that conclusion.

As I was in the midst of considering how to deal with the McLellan
appointment, I was contacted by David Herle (pronounced Her-Lee),
which gave me a little shiver. Herle invited me to go on *The Herle Burly*,
his BC-based podcast. I was told that everyone in politics tunes in
to his show. My investigation, which had begun with a conversation
with my neighbour Doug Spafford beside our big old oak tree, had
now caught the attention of those closest to the throne.

Herle had been a prominent insider in the federal Liberal Party
of Canada for decades. He was a master at creating and interpreting
public opinion polls, political strategy and candidate packaging, and
had helped elect prime ministers from Paul Martin to Justin Trudeau.
The *Toronto Star*'s Ottawa columnist Susan Delacourt described in her
2013 book, *Shopping for Votes*, how Herle was instrumental in remak-
ing Trudeau's image from a young, bumbling politician into a modern,
ethical leader who was both a feminist and someone who would bring
needed transparency to federal government dealings.

I had to ask myself if it was worth tangling with Herle, but the answer
was easy. Mainstream news was avoiding me like I was a COVID carrier. And once again, even if the audience wasn't a perfect fit, it did give
me the opportunity to speak to those close to Trudeau. Maybe even the
prime minister himself was a listener. I booked the gig.

The hour we spent chatting was enjoyable. I got to tell my story.
I thought it had gone well. Near the end, Herle asked me what I thought
about McLellan. I told him I thought she was not the right person for
the task at hand, but we were just about out of time.

"I like Anne. She's a friend of mine," Herle said. "She's highly ethical."

I believe we were off the air when I told Herle that I'd like to come back to discuss her, the Arar inquiry and why I had reservations about her being on the Nova Scotia review panel. He seemed agreeable to that.

"I really thought that was terrific and I've had a lot of great feedback," Herle e-mailed me afterwards. "Thanks for doing it. David."

Before we got to talk again, the heat had built against the review, which Furey admitted no one had "outright asked for." Five days after the review was announced, Furey and Blair appeared to bow to the public pressure and growing anger and announced that there would be a joint federal-provincial public inquiry.

"We've listened to Nova Scotians," Blair said in a statement. "This situation requires that our governments work diligently with all those affected by this tragedy to bring forward the critical answers and to ensure an event such as this will never happen again. We have heard the calls from families, survivors, advocates and the Nova Scotia members of Parliament for more transparency."

The inquiry, Blair said, "will have the power to summon witnesses and require them to give evidence orally or in writing . . . and . . . produce such documents and things as the commissioners deem requisite to the full investigation."

"I'm happy both levels of government have now recognized that a full public inquiry is what's needed to do justice to finding out what happened and to prevent this in the future," Wayne MacKay, professor emeritus of Dalhousie University's Schulich School of Law told Alexander Quon and Elizabeth McSheffrey of Global News.

The problem now was that the three commissioners were still MacDonald, Fitch and McLellan. These were the same people who had already agreed to hold a review and not call any testimony. Before I could go back on *The Herle Burly* and make my case against the trio, McLellan resigned, stating that she didn't have enough time in her schedule for a full-blown inquiry. It was a telling admission. There was no doubt that McLellan was a busy woman with numerous oars in the water, but she had signed on to conduct a review into the circumstances surrounding the murder of twenty-two people, many of whom died due to an epic failure in policing. She did so obviously believing that the review would take up only so much of her time. It spoke to the mindset of Blair, Furey and their respective governments.

Now I really couldn't wait to go back on *The Herle Burly*.

"What happened to Anne?" I e-mailed Herle. "She quit before I got to pitch."

"Ha!" he replied.

I wouldn't hear from him again.

◆

In light of the inquiry announcement, the march by the families on the RCMP detachment in Bible Hill now contained all the elements of a truly iconic moment. Their solidarity and determination had forced the government's hand. The media declared that the people had waged an epic struggle and won a monumental victory.

There was another way of looking at it, however. The announcement of the inquiry turned into a point of demarcation for just about everyone involved in the story. It was if some invisible force had pushed a cosmic mute button, silencing everyone.

The prospect of the inquiry, to be held sometime in the distant future, took the wind out of the sails of most of the exhausted and still-grieving families. What more could they possibly say? The media took the calling of the inquiry as a signal to stand down. Why waste money on getting to the truth when the inquiry would hand it to us on a platter? The RCMP now had an excuse to put a lid on any new information because, it argued, it was restricted by the inquiry from saying anything. Meanwhile, my sources were telling me the force was continuing to alter and destroy evidence it had gathered in the shootings. Nothing was being left to chance.

One of the things overlooked by almost everyone was the constitution and operations of the Serious Incident Response Team (SIRT), the independent Nova Scotia organization that investigates the police. As you will recall, SIRT was charged with investigating the Onslow Belmont fire hall shoot-up fiasco and the killing of Gabriel Wortman by Mounties at the Irving Big Stop in Enfield. SIRT did not review the entire shooting spree and the role played by the RCMP, which most experts in policing believed it should have done. The RCMP had been left to investigate itself. Inquisitive minds began to question the motivations of the relatively new director of SIRT—former judge Felix Cacchione.

Cacchione was the judge who had declared a mistrial in the murder case of notorious Hells Angels hit men Dany Kane and Aimé Simard. The RCMP had deliberately created confusion in the courtroom and destroyed the reputation of their own innocent members, all to protect the fact that Kane was a paid RCMP informant. Regardless of how they felt personally about the police response at Portapique Beach, people inside policing I'd spoken to were concerned that Cacchione had found on behalf of the SIRT that everything the Mounties had done was in good faith. They had done their best.

It took awhile, but the governments finally replaced McLellan on the commission. In her stead would be Kim Stanton, a specialist in women's issues, equality and Aboriginal rights. She had written her Ph.D. thesis on the institutional design of inquiries and was releasing a book in the fall of 2021 called *Reconciling Truths: Reimagining Public Inquiries in Canada.* Her work, including a summary of her book by publisher UBC Press, makes it clear that she envisions inquiries to be more useful as a medium to address "deep societal challenges" than as an adversarial or investigative tool:

> Whether it is a public inquiry, truth commission, or royal commission, the chosen leadership and processes fundamentally affect its ability to achieve its mandate. Kim Stanton provides in-depth critical analysis of these factors to offer practical guidance on how an inquiry can do more than have its recommendations quietly gather dust on a shelf. She argues that even if recommendations are initially ignored, holding an inquiry can create a dialogue about issues of public importance that prepares the way for attitudinal change and policy development.

At the time of her appointment, Stanton was a legal director of the Women's Legal Education and Action Fund (LEAF), as well as the Centre for Feminist Legal Studies. Stanton resigned the LEAF position when she accepted the offer to become a commissioner, although LEAF would be appearing before her during the inquiry.

It was obvious to anyone paying attention that a wall of smoke and mirrors had been constructed. Governments had been promoting the inappropriate restorative justice approach from the outset, which meant most things would be done behind closed doors, as if that's the proper way to treat the mass murder of twenty-two innocent people, a number of whom died because of the epic failure in policing by the RCMP. Investigation and transparency were not priorities.

But the collective media just yawned. In fact, *Maclean's* went so far as to name the three commissioners to its annual Power List— "50 Canadians Who Are Breaking Ground, Leading the Debate and Shaping How We Think and Live." Nick Taylor-Vaisey wrote:

> Over two horrifying days last April, 22 people in Nova Scotia were killed in a shooting spree that left communities in ruins and troubling questions about how the RCMP responded. The families of the victims demanded answers while governments in Ottawa and Halifax dithered for months on calling a public inquiry to get to the bottom of the Mounties' conduct in those fateful hours. Finally, in October, three appointed commissioners started their work.
>
> The results of their inquiry could be monumental for a national police force struggling with its underfunded rural policing model, a change-resistant culture and ongoing charges of systemic racism. Michael MacDonald, Leanne J. Fitch and Kim Stanton will face intense pressure to tell uncomfortable truths for the families, and for a police force in need of reform.

It was getting scary to watch how the rule of law was being eroded across the country and overtaken by the rule of politics. No one of stature was prepared to stand up and fight for justice. They put their faith in the government, the inquiry and the good graces of the RCMP, hoping that everything would eventually work out for the better. Faith is a double-edged sword. Those who have it say it gives them comfort to suspend their disbelief and hope for the best, even in the face of no tangible proof. That alone explains how the RCMP has survived in its present form to this day. Those who don't have such faith get their comfort from truth, provable facts and adherence to the rule of law.

At the time the inquiry was called, we still knew very little about what had really happened before, during and after the massacres. The RCMP had not even given out a convincing or conclusive timeline of events. It was withholding information, citing concerns over privacy and the potential effect on ongoing investigations, as if the murder of twenty-two people and the collapse of the police force were not more overriding concerns.

My new-found friend, citizen investigator Chad Jones, kept insisting that there was someone I should meet—Leon Joudrey. I had read about Joudrey, but I didn't know what to make of him. He was the Portapique neighbour who had taken in Wortman's girlfriend, Lisa Banfield, the morning of April 19. Jones had since befriended Joudrey and listened to his story about his run-in with Banfield. He insisted that I hear it for myself.

"You've got to go see Leon," Jones said. "There's a lot more to his story than the media is telling us. He wants to meet with you."

26
LEON JOUDREY, THE TWO LISAS AND CYNDI

We met Leon Joudrey at the Double C Truck Stop restaurant on Highway 4, about a twenty-minute drive west of Portapique. As locals often do in rural communities, they had a nickname for the place: the Chew and Choke, which was entirely unfair. The food was decent East Coast home cooking.

The four of us—Leon, Chad, Stephen Maher and me—were sitting at a table waiting for our lunch. The place was packed. The waitress was sitting on Leon's lap and they were fake flirting with each other. Her husband was across the room, barely paying attention. Welcome to the country.

Maher had spoken to Joudrey many times in the past but, like everyone else who had interviewed him, had stayed away from reporting what Joudrey had to say, worried his potentially explosive version of events was "unreliable." Chad had gone over everything written about Joudrey and could find no discrepancies in the local man's various accounts of the morning of April 19.

I wanted Maher to come along, hoping that I could convince him to wade a little deeper into the water, as it were. I even paid for the trip—car, gas and food—not wanting to be a drag on the limited budget of *Maclean's*.

In Chapter Ten, I described how Joudrey had spent that Saturday afternoon with Ron McGraw, helping Greg and Jamie Blair clean up the brush on their property. Joudrey carted it all down to the beach, where it would eventually serve as fuel for a community bonfire. Jamie made a late steak dinner for them, which they devoured at a table set up in the garage. Joudrey and his two dogs, Yzerman and Basil, were in bed by 9 p.m., which wasn't unusual.

Sitting across from me now, Joudrey, fifty-two, was intense and a little fidgety. He looked you straight in the eye when he talked to you in long, unrelenting, rapid-fire sequences. It was easy to see he was hurting and still in shock over the unfathomable loss of life, especially teenager Emily Tuck.

"She was a good girl. I really liked her," Joudrey said. "Greg, I knew him so long, it was like losing a brother. I lost eight good friends and four other neighbours. Twelve people wiped out of your life is something that you don't get over easily when you're in here [the neighbourhood]. It's all you see."

That's one reason he moved away and rented his house to someone else from the community.

He struggles with his inexplicable survival. "Why didn't he come after me?" he asked me more than once.

"Because you have lots of guns and two big dogs?" I suggested.

"That didn't stop him with other people. Many of them had guns and dogs. He just shot the dogs."

Over time and many conversations, Joudrey would strike me as having at least as strong a claim to PTSD as many of the seventy Mounties who had booked the summer of 2020 off, courtesy of taxpayers. He was a professional woodsman who worked as a forest technician for the Department of Natural Resources. He liked to hunt and had the guns to do it. He also liked to go down to the weir to fish for sea bass. Another of his favourite activities combined the two pastimes: he was always on the lookout for a new woman who might appreciate his love of hunting and fishing.

Joudrey had moved to Portapique Beach two years earlier, after his marriage had ended, purchasing a friend's house at 140 Portapique Crescent. As previously described, the road ran in a loop off Orchard Beach Drive. Joudrey's house was situated behind the Gulenchyns', which Wortman burned down, incinerating the bodies of Frank and Dawn Gulenchyn.

Joudrey said he didn't hear anything abnormal for the neighbourhood that evening. "I left Greg and Jamie's about quarter to nine, went home. Typically, I go to bed early because I'm up at four in the morning. I just went home when I heard a couple of poof poofs. Didn't know what, really, if it was a gunshot or not. People around here shoot rabbits from their porch. I turned off my phone and I fell asleep."

Joudrey was awakened by the smell of smoke at precisely 3:33 a.m. "I remember the time. I was, 'Oh geez.' I wished I could've slept for another hour, because my daughter was supposed to come that day."

He checked his cellphone and there were two messages from friends asking if he was the one doing all the shooting and starting fires. "Well, I don't know," he told them. "I just woke up. It didn't smell like a forest fire. I thought I should go investigate."

Joudrey made himself a coffee, loaded his dogs into his half-ton truck and drove out to Orchard Beach Road and then up to the intersection of Portapique Beach Road. "I didn't even notice that Frank and Dawn's place was gone."

He turned left and drove past Andrew MacDonald's house and the Portaupique Cemetery until he came to a parked RCMP armoured vehicle near the remains of Wortman's cottage at number 200. He had driven about a kilometre and had seen no other police cars or officers. Joudrey said he could see the flicker of flames around the foundation and that Wortman's cottage was a smouldering pile of ruins. "So I pulled up beside the SWAT vehicle, and I was trying to get the guy to motion to me, to talk to me. And he was screaming at me through the window. I didn't know what he was saying. I guess he couldn't roll down his window, so he turned his spotlights on me and got on the loudspeaker," Joudrey recalled. "'You in the black truck, turn around, proceed to the entrance point.'"

Joudrey ignored the order. He turned around and headed back to Orchard Beach Drive. "That's when I noticed Frank and Dawn's house burned, and that's when I knew that something didn't add up," Joudrey said. "So I flattened it as hard as I could go down the road. I looked in at Jamie and Greg's and didn't see any fire. I looked at Lisa McCully's house. Didn't see anything. I didn't look to the right at Gabriel's warehouse. I went down the road and looked into Greg's parents' place, made the loop and checked on the two old guys who lived next to Orchard Beach Crescent. Then I went back to my house and grabbed my shotgun and went into my bedroom."

Along the route he unknowingly passed the body of Corrie Ellison lying just south of the steel gates to Wortman's warehouse, which lay in ruins. Joudrey didn't notice McCully's body, hidden in the dark near her rail fence. He didn't see the Blairs, either, because at such an early hour he wouldn't enter their driveway.

"There were no police around. There wasn't a flashing light. I drove a couple or three kilometres and didn't see anything but that one armoured vehicle," Joudrey said. "Thinking about it now, if the RCMP were looking for Wortman, they weren't exactly acting like that. That guy could have cared less about who I was. If they were looking for him, why wasn't I evacuated? If these were crime scenes, why was I able to drive through them?"

Joudrey's version of events entirely contradicted the RCMP's narrative. The RCMP said, among other things, that soon after arriving its members went into formation and hunted for the gunman. As more Mounties arrived, the force said, they had gone house to house evacuating residents. Joudrey hadn't seen any of this. There were only about a dozen properties occupied that night. He wasn't evacuated. Who else wasn't evacuated, I wondered.

Joudrey's drive was briefly described by some reporters who had previously interviewed him, but none went any deeper than to say that he went for a 4 a.m. ride and saw nothing, understating what that meant to the larger story. The entire episode was astounding to me both in what Joudrey described and in that his unvarnished story was not being reported.

By 6:30 a.m. on April 19, Joudrey was in his well-lit kitchen having another coffee. The sun had begun rising about ten minutes earlier. He was still oblivious to all the horror and carnage around him. There was a knock at the door. He opened it to find Lisa Banfield standing there.

"Gabriel lost his mind," she said, which served to dislodge any remaining cobwebs in Joudrey's head.

"No shit, Lisa," Joudrey said. "He burned his own house down. What are you doing here? He hates me the most."

"I'm sorry," she said. "I'd better go."

Joudrey shut the door to stop her from leaving. He ushered her into the bathroom to hide her and called 911. It was 6:34 a.m.

"I happened to know the radio dispatcher at 911," Joudrey said. "When I got on the phone with her, I said: 'Get SWAT down here. I know they're looking for Gabriel. I want her out of my house now.'"

That Banfield's instinct was to turn and leave struck Joudrey as counterintuitive. If, as she claimed, she had been outside all night fleeing and hiding from Wortman, one would think she would be eager to find shelter with someone like the well-armed Joudrey.

"She was ready to go back out. I couldn't let her do that," Joudrey said. "So I opened the door and gave her my coat to put on and my sneakers. She was in bare feet."

Let's stop there for a moment. This may be the perfect place to revisit and update the official narrative about what allegedly happened to Banfield.

◆

Through her lawyers, Lisa Banfield has to date declined to answer any journalists' questions or to grant interviews. Her only statement about the massacres was a comment relayed to the public by the RCMP in one of the two unredacted summaries of their early interviews with her: "Lisa Banfield has had guilty feelings and wonders if Gabriel Wortman went to locations that Lisa might attend to get help and killed people as he went along. Lisa questions whether people would have died if she didn't run away."

The official RCMP narrative is largely a reconstruction of events based almost entirely on two early interviews with Banfield. One was conducted sometime on April 19 by Constable Terry Brown, who, as you may recall, was also one of the two RCMP officers who mistakenly shot up the Onslow Belmont fire hall that same day. On April 28, Banfield was subjected to a caution interview by Staff Sergeant Greg Vardy, the Nova Scotia RCMP's polygraph expert. A caution interview is conducted when police have reasonable grounds to suspect that a crime may have been committed by the person being interviewed. The RCMP said afterwards that Banfield did not take a polygraph. Vardy conducted another caution interview with her on July 28, 2020. Banfield did try to hire a lawyer on the morning she was "rescued," but we do not know whether she was accompanied by a lawyer for any of the interviews. The RCMP has never released a transcript or recording of the interviews.

At face value, the summaries of what Banfield told police portray an absolutely harrowing situation for the killer's common-law spouse. She said she and Wortman had a virtual FaceTime party that night with an unidentified couple from Houlton, Maine. The occasion was a celebration of Banfield and Wortman's nineteenth anniversary together and was held at Lisa's Bar in the warehouse. Wortman and Banfield told the other couple that the next year they were going to have "a committed party" to celebrate their twentieth anniversary.

"Don't do it," the woman from Houlton said.

Banfield was upset by the comment and decided to go home, which was about 400 metres away through the woods. Wortman was angry that she had left. Halfway home, Banfield turned around and went back to the warehouse to apologize. Wortman was so enraged by then that she returned to the cottage, stripped off her clothing and tucked herself into bed.

Not long afterwards Wortman came into the bedroom, ripped off the blankets and started to beat her up. "It's done," he told her. "Get dressed."

At one point in the summaries, Banfield said Wortman tied her hands together with what might have been the cord from a bathrobe, but the statement was vague. There was no further mention of the cord or how she became unbound.

A representative sample of what Banfield said took place next is described in documents that the RCMP kept blacked out for many months. I've interwoven three sets of statements for clarity:

Gabriel Wortman poured gasoline all inside the cottage and told Lisa Banfield to grab the gun out of the cottage. They started to walk back to the warehouse so Gabriel could burn that.

Lisa Banfield said the floor was very wet from the gas being poured on it and Gabriel Wortman told her to be careful. As they exited the cottage, Gabriel told her to look back and she could see that he started it on fire but she could not recall seeing him with matches or see him light the fire.

Lisa Banfield said that she knew things were serious as Gabriel was proud of the cottage and the warehouse and now he was burning the cottage.

"I'm done, I'm done. It's too late, Lisa, I'm done," Wortman was quoted as saying.

She remembered seeing Gabriel put gasoline on a police car that was in the driveway but can't remember if it was on fire when they left.

Gabriel Wortman told Lisa Banfield to walk in front of him and she told him she promised to walk behind him but Gabriel wouldn't allow that and ripped her shoes off her feet . . . "now you can't run, you bitch."

Lisa Banfield got loose and started running but tripped and fell. . . . Gabriel found her easily and called her an idiot and told her that he

had a flashlight. . . . Gabriel Wortman picked her up by the hair and
started pulling her towards the warehouse. Gabriel Wortman tried
to handcuff her but only got one handcuff on and then he started
shooting at the ground around her.

At the warehouse Gabriel Wortman poured gasoline on the truck
outside the warehouse. Lisa offered to move the Jeep and Gabriel
said: "Do you think I'm stupid?"

Lisa Banfield watched Gabriel walk over to the bar area and she
knew that he had guns there.

Lisa Banfield begged Gabriel Wortman not to kill her. He shot the
firearm again and then put her in the back of the police car and
then he went upstairs in the warehouse.

Lisa Banfield tried to kick the windows out and then was able to
open the glass [the silent patrolman, as the barrier between front
and back seats is known] and crawl through and escaped and ran
into the woods.

Gabriel Wortman had put all the guns on the front seat of the car.

Lisa Banfield could see smoke and heard gunshots.

Gabriel Wortman had guns like the military people have. He had
approximately 5 guns, two handguns with red lasers on them and
a military firearm that took 32 rounds.

Lisa Banfield ran and remembered running past a blue shed and
finding a truck in a grassy area and climbed inside but the inside
light went on and she was concerned that Gabriel would find her,
so she continued to run into the woods. She believed that she had a
puffy jacket on and threw it in the woods hoping the police would
find it.

Lisa Banfield heard shots and thought Gabriel might blow the truck
up and she left that hiding spot and eventually came across a tree
with an exposed root system and hid inside the cavity.

I could go on, but you get the drift by now. Banfield's statements to
the police were revealed slowly and teasingly every few weeks over
nearly a year. For the first six or eight months, just about every newspaper and television station reported each new revelation uncritically.
Eventually, Chad and I and other citizen investigators recognized
that there was rarely much new in each supposedly new reveal. It was
all the Monster and the Maiden tale and nothing about the performance of the RCMP—nor about the anomalies apparent in Banfield's
statements.

The temperature that night hovered around freezing. It was bitterly
cold, and the area was typically buffeted by strong and persistent winds
associated with the rising and falling tides. In her stories to the RCMP,
Banfield talked about running through the woods and seeing a truck
in a grassy field near a blue shed. In the absolute darkness, how could
she see colours and textures? More importantly, how could she safely
run barefoot through those tangled, mossy woods in the middle of the
night? I've been through them now a number of times—in shoes. The
woods are difficult to navigate safely even in daylight.

In the absence of anyone asking these questions, Banfield's account
of abuse meshed nicely with Brenda Forbes's report of an assault on
Banfield by Wortman. There were also a couple of second- and third-
hand reports that provided the foundation for the governments'
emphasis on domestic violence being the root cause of the massacres.
The incidents may well have happened but, to reiterate, there was no
recent or conclusive evidence of such behaviour, and no such claim
was ever made by Banfield or her family members, who were still very
much present in her and Wortman's life together.

Banfield said she was there when Wortman poured gasoline around
the cottage, covering the floors. If that were true, she likely would have
reeked of gasoline fumes. She said she saw the fire start but didn't know
how Wortman had ignited it. Fire experts uniformly agree that the

method Banfield described would result in an explosive fire and likely injury to anyone who was not well clear of the site upon ignition.

Wortman allegedly told Banfield, "I'm done. It's too late, Lisa." There was no specific timeline or context for these statements. Had he already killed someone, or was he talking about other unknown forces bearing down on him?

If Wortman was intent on killing Banfield, why did he tell her to be careful not to slip?

Banfield said Wortman smashed her cellphone and ripped off her shoes, flinging them into the woods. Did the police ever recover these shoes? Were they tested for evidence?

The RCMP never mentioned finding Banfield's puffy jacket that she "believed" she had been wearing. That statement was made only a few hours after she had been found, and she wasn't sure if she had been wearing a jacket in the freezing cold? Did the police ever find it? If so, where? Was the jacket tested for forensic evidence? If not, why not?

Banfield said there were multiple gunshots fired at or near her on at least two occasions. Did the RCMP recover the shells or casings? Did it conduct forensic testing for gunshot residue on Banfield to try to confirm that story?

Banfield's reported comments about Wortman's guns suggest that she knew more about guns than a casual observer—"a military firearm that took 32 rounds." She knew where the guns were hidden, such as near the bar and in the bedside table. Wortman allegedly asked Banfield to get a gun for him as he was burning down the cottage, which she appears to have done. Were her fingerprints on one of the guns? If she had a gun in her hand and he was threatening to kill her, did she consider using the gun to defend herself, escape or even shoot him?

Banfield told the Mounties that she was hiding close enough to the warehouse that she could hear gunshots. She said she suspected that Wortman was going house to house searching for her. She said that during the night she could hear the police but stayed in hiding because she was afraid it was Wortman continuing to stalk her. After nineteen years with him, she didn't recognize his voice—even if it was over a loudhailer?

One curious thing Banfield said was that she feared Wortman would "blow the truck up" that she was hiding in. What did that mean? She said he had guns, but she told the Mounties that she didn't know anything about explosives, such as the two cases of grenades. Was "blow up" a Freudian slip?

And then there is her story about hiding in the roots of a tree. It's a scene that seems ripped from the pages of *The Fellowship of the Ring*— Frodo and the other hobbits, Sam, Merry and Pippin, hiding from the merciless Ringwraiths under the hollow of a gnarled tree root. Has she ever identified that hiding place to police?

There is also the bizarre and suspicious coincidence of the Mounties going home at 6:30 a.m. that Sunday morning and Banfield emerging from the woods at the same time. Banfield said she noticed the lights on at Joudrey's house and found her way there. She didn't see any police, she said. By her own account she had spent about eight and a half hours outside on a bitterly cold night. She had no jacket, shoes or gloves. She had seen a blue shed at one point and had walked and crawled through the woods and along dirt and stone roads for a considerable distance, perhaps one to two kilometres or more, in the moonless black of night, without the aid of a flashlight or even a cellphone. Going to Joudrey's house seems like an unusual choice. It was a long way from where she claims to have spent the night, but it was relatively close to Highway 2, from which access could be gained to Joudrey's property through Brown Loop. Did Banfield come from the woods or the highway?

◆

Standing before Leon Joudrey in his kitchen that morning, Banfield did not look to him like someone who had run the gauntlet just described. He didn't know any of her story, other than the "Gabriel lost his mind" part. He only knew what he had heard, seen and sensed in those few minutes when she was in his house, observations that he related to the police and every reporter who interviewed him over the months ahead—all of whom dismissed his account.

Joudrey didn't see any handcuffs. He didn't smell gasoline on her. She didn't look like someone who had been pressed into the dirt of a forest floor since before midnight. "When she came to my place, she was wearing a spandex top and yoga pants, like she always did. She had no shoes on. Her makeup was perfect," Joudrey told me. "I told the police who were there that morning that I didn't believe her. I don't know what happened, but I think it isn't what she said happened. That woman did not spend the night in the woods. I don't know where she was, but she was not in the woods all night. If you're in the woods all night, the tops of your feet are going be dirty and covered in pine needles. Look at the woods around here. Look how thick they are. And I said that from the start, and I stand by it. I can picture it right in my head today how clean she was."

"Maybe she stayed warm hiding in a truck or a shed?" I speculated.

"It was freezing that night," Joudrey said. "No way. Clinton Ellison was in the woods for a couple of hours hiding from Wortman, and he was a big man dressed for the cold night. He had to go to the hospital to be treated for mild hypothermia. Lisa didn't have a scratch on her that I could see."

Chad Jones joined in: "One of the main things that [RCMP superintendent] Darren Campbell came out and said in one of the press conferences was that she was the victim of a very serious assault. Did it look to you like she may have been seriously assaulted or anything like that?"

"No, she looked like she always did," Joudrey said.

"Her eye wasn't swollen shut?" Jones asked.

"Nope," Joudrey said.

"Did she have trouble breathing?" I asked.

"Nope," Joudrey said.

"They said she had damage to her ribs," I added.

"She didn't look hurt to me," Joudrey said.

The RCMP responded to his 911 call within two or three minutes, astonishingly fast given their responses to other calls that night and the fact that the killer was still at large. What caught Joudrey's attention when they arrived at his house was the attitude of the ERT members,

how relaxed and incurious they were. "They didn't ask me any questions. They didn't even come in and search my place. When they came
in to get Lisa, my black lab, Basil, went outside. When I went out, one
of the Mounties had his gun pointed at Basil's head. I went over to him
and asked him to stop doing that," he said.

Joudrey never flinched once in telling his story over and over again.
He told it to every reporter who interviewed him, and every one of
them ignored what he was saying. It was driving him crazy. Frustrated,
he went on *Little Grey Cells* and spent more than hour with Seamus
Gorman recording a spot to be broadcast on YouTube. Gorman forgot
to hit record, so they had to do it again. Joudrey patiently redid the
interview. He wanted to get the word out.

On the other hand, Global TV's *13 Hours* podcast edited out any
perceived negative comments from Joudrey about Banfield. Even after
I published my own story calling Banfield's account into question,
Global did not redo its version of the story.

"I don't know why they would've taken that out, because it's true,"
Joudrey said. "She was clean as a whistle."

"Well," I replied, "when I talked to Sarah Ritchie [a Global News
reporter who'd appeared on the *13 Hours* podcast] about it, she said
the police said this and you said that, so they went with the police."

"Well, there you go," Joudrey said.

The more Joudrey spoke, the more questions were raised. How did
Banfield get the handcuffs off? Did she change her clothes? If so, why
did she change them and where? If she wasn't outside all night, dressed
as she was, where did she seek shelter?

The most important question of all, from both Joudrey's point of
view and mine, was why both the RCMP and the media had ignored
him. Chad and I both approached his story with skepticism but could
find no reason to doubt it. We were also confident that Maher wouldn't
be reporting it—and he didn't.

Nor was he or anyone else going to go anywhere near Joudrey's
other Lisa story.

◆

As I was piecing together the story of April 18 and 19, something about the ambiance of Portapique Beach struck me as being not my kind of place. Just about every time a news reporter lands on a tragedy in a rural area, the same trope flows from their fingertips as they try to capture the moment: "tragedy struck this tight-knit community." From what I learned, Portapique might have been tight-knit back in the days of the booming shad fishery or the dance hall, but it wasn't anymore. People who had lived there contacted me. Some loved the isolation it offered; others, like Natalie Wood (not the late actress), found the community less than enchanting. Wood grew up in a house on Highway 2 near where it intersects with one of the arms of Brown Loop. "It's an awful place to live, unlike what the vacationers will tell you," Wood told me. "Small communities are magnets for bad people."

Wood said that when she was growing up, there were so many bikers and criminals, and so much petty thievery, that it was almost impossible to get comfortable. Her description shed light on one thing Wortman used to say about his decommissioned police cars: he liked to park them on the property as a four-wheeled scarecrow to ward off burglars and bandits.

"My next-door neighbour was John Lawrence, also known as Michael John Lawrence," Wood said. "He did a hit on two Hells Angels in the Valley [Kirk Mersereau and Nancy Christensen]. The kids across the street were very shady."

There were bikers everywhere and, as we know, no RCMP service between 2 and 6 a.m.

"We had to move out of there," Wood said.

There was something else I noticed in my travels: barn stars, those tinny decorations one often finds on rural houses. A couple of houses in Portapique were adorned with them. Call me naive for my advanced age, but I didn't know until someone told me that in popular culture they are associated with swinging. Barn stars and pampas grass in the front yard, some say, are signals for swingers looking to hook up with other swingers.

I was never one for exhibitionism. Hell, I avert my gaze when I'm standing naked in front of a mirror. I can't imagine flaunting my wares and talents in front of a room filled with others evaluating and grad-ing my junk. My research, however, told me that swinging is a party sport popular with military, police and criminals, of which there were plenty in the area. There were even a couple of "lifestyle" clubs in the surrounding towns, which, I admit, I didn't check out.

It was a tawdry avenue of investigation that I couldn't ignore, espe-cially since the RCMP had already suggested that some of Wortman's victims had been his intimate acquaintances. I told Joudrey that two sources had said there used to be lots of wild parties, featuring "gor-geous" girls, local men and others who were likely police officers, maybe even Mounties. "Are you a swinger?" I asked him.

"A swinger?" he said, giving me an incredulous look. "No."

"What can you tell me about the hot-tub parties they used to have here?"

"What hot tub?" he said. "It must have been before my time. I've only been here two years."

"I hear there was a hot-tub outside one of the houses and that the female owner liked to say something like 'Come take a look at these forty-fours,'" I said, quoting what someone familiar with the hot tub and the late-night parties had told me. "I can't find that hot tub now. I hear that the owner and her forty-fours moved away, but I hear Wortman had the hots for her. They might have had a fling."

"Really?" he said. "Who told you that?"

"Somebody who knew about the hot tub. I can't tell you any more. It's not the kind of thing they want to get out."

The hot-tub diversion led to a discussion about Joudrey's love life and one of his old girlfriends in the neighbourhood: Lisa McCully.

"How did it start?" I asked him.

"She came over one day, and I had all my guns laid out on the floor," Joudrey said. "I guess that got her excited, because ten minutes later we were in the bedroom." They dated for awhile and Joudrey said he really liked her, except for a few things.

"Lisa was an outgoing schoolteacher with two kids," Joudrey said, "and she was looking for someone to marry. I had just come out of a marriage, too, and she was a hard girl to date at the same time. She was a little controlling that way. We just hung out, that kind of thing. It just wasn't my thing at the time and still isn't."

The second thing was Gabriel Wortman.

"The first time I met him he offered to buy me a flat of rum from the States—twelve bottles," Joudrey recalled. "I knew he was into something. I didn't know what. I wanted nothing to do with the guy."

McCully liked Wortman, Joudrey said. "She always spoke highly of Gabriel. I didn't get it."

It is difficult to understand the conundrum of a person like Wortman. He was a cold-blooded killer who had been an embalmer and whose business was about as unsexy as it gets—making artificial teeth to fix broken smiles. He was a promiscuous, bisexual, alcoholic, controlling, hostile and socially awkward fifty-one-year-old man who boasted about his criminal activities and bragged that he had killed people and knew how to make bodies disappear. Yet so many women were happy to see him. They were all but fighting each other to have sex with him. What was his magic? All the money? Alcohol? Street drugs? Was he an insatiable hedonist, or did he just gravitate to those circles?

In the year after his murder, it became clear that he had had affairs with an array of women, from the one depicted dancing with him on the roof of his replica police car to her daughter and several others, including at least three of his victims—Lisa McCully, Alanna Jenkins and Gina Goulet. After his death, in the face of the domestic violence focus of the RCMP, governments and media, not one of the many women with whom he'd had intimate relations stepped forward to say a bad word about him.

Getting to the truth in the story was like running an obstacle course blindfolded. There were hints here, suggestions there, and a fact or two floating about, but hardly one near the centre of the story would talk openly about anything—except for Cynthia (Cyndi) Starratt, she of the car-roof dance, and her daughter, Ocean-Mist.

Starratt, also known as Cyndi Roberts, was one of Wortman's long-time girlfriends at Portapique Beach. He was known to sometimes drop by the beach bonfires on a four-wheeler or other gatherings in the community and ask: "Anyone seen Cyndi around?" And then he would head into the woods toward her place and hunt her down. Nothing was ever planned, Starratt said, and often they would meet late at night when Wortman would show up with twelve beers in hand and knock on her door like he was a cop. As Starrratt put it at various times, Wortman carried himself like a cop, drove like a cop and, when confronted about being a cop, never entirely denied it.

In the months after Wortman's death, Starratt defended him on the *Little Grey Cells* YouTube channel and elsewhere. At one point she described him as the kind of man no woman would complain about. Then there was this thread, which I confirmed was her: "Last time I talked to Gabe he was 220 lbs, wanting to be 180 lbs!!!! Tall, nice tight shape. Can't tell with his work clothes on how inxshape [*sic*] he was!! I fit perfectly under his arm and I'm 5' 7". I've seen all kinds of sides of Gabe, but never abusive or the monster he turned into. Never have I seen him as abusive. He felt used. . . . The code he and I had was 'the gate to the warehouse was open!' I'd cut through the woods so Lisa Mac wouldn't see me."

Starratt wouldn't talk to me directly but answered some questions through a go-between, citizen investigator Wendilen Wood (no relation to Natalie from Portapique). Wortman's occasional girlfriend liked to refer to him as "the Mayor," because to her he was the most important person at Portapique. She said she worked at times for Wortman, cleaning his house and doing odd jobs. After she lost her licence for driving under the influence of alcohol, Wortman would help her out by driving her around to get groceries and water. One of the curious things she noticed about Wortman's cottage was that Lisa Banfield didn't keep any toiletries there, which she thought was odd. As many others pointed out, Banfield was an infrequent visitor, spending the majority of her time at the apartment above the clinic in Dartmouth. Starratt said she had only met Banfield twice in the six years prior to the massacre. On once occasion, Starratt showed up at Wortman's door carrying a ready-made Caesar cocktail in a can. Banfield opened the door, took the can from her and called to Wortman: "Oh, Gabriel, there's a strange woman at the door."

Starratt described her side-girl relationship with Wortman in the warmest of terms. She said they bonded over beer, hours of talking and their shared stories of childhood abuse. Wortman told her about his father making him shoot his dog and attributed a slight limp he had to the after-effects of a childhood beating. She told him that her father made her eat her pet rabbit. (Others I talked to who knew Wortman didn't notice a limp. It sounded like a wolf-in-sheep's-clothing tale.)

After her marriage had ended, Starratt wasn't looking for another partner and he was perfect—he always played the field. She liked the combination of his above-average endowment and soft personality. She sent me a video of a very effeminate and loquacious chef doing a cooking show. "That's my Gabe, except younger and with hair."

Asked if she ever spent the night with Wortman, she replied: "Oh, yah. He'd take me up and cook supper, while I bathed, run my water, start the fire!! Pour the drinks, play most of night. Early to rise and gone back home. He go back. Clean up. Then I might have not seen him for another two weeks, so I'm sure I wasn't the only one."

In fact, she said at another point that Wortman once asked her to stay with him and another of his dalliances and her two-year-old child at the cottage. She said Wortman wasn't particularly fond of the woman "because she wore cotton panties." He also told her that he couldn't stand the child and didn't like the fact that the woman was talking marriage. He didn't want to be left alone with her.

Starratt did notice, however, the dichotomous nature of Wortman's personality. "He's still not a woman beater though," she said—at least not in her personal experience with him. She added, "but I experienced his creepy side, too, hun." It went well beyond his fixation with women's underwear, dead bodies and making miniature and life-sized coffins.

Starratt later confirmed in an interview with Jordan Bonaparte of the *Nighttime* podcast that Wortman used to measure the mouths of his patients to see if he could fit his penis inside, and then would convince some of them to have sex with him. Starratt said that on one occasion she and Wortman had a threesome with one of his clients.

In Starratt's description of Wortman and his behaviour, he comes across as being almost childlike. When Wortman spoke to people, he got into their space, way too close for comfort. He was obsessed with cleanliness, especially for his sex partners. He wanted them to bathe and shower first. He was fixated on something special to him, such as women's panties. He didn't like to kiss; he preferred snuggling. He was hypersexual, a sex addict so driven that he told Starratt that he often had to masturbate between serving patients at his clinic, if he wasn't already having sex with them. He liked ejaculating into Starratt's hair, she said.

Wortman had no boundaries, it seemed. If he had an idea, he acted it out no matter what people might think. He wanted to take Cyndi to Houlton, Maine, where he suggested that she could have sex with an unnamed doctor friend of his. He would join them afterward. She declined that offer, partly out of fear of what Wortman might do to her while she was trapped in a foreign country. She didn't trust him that much.

Starratt was more than fifty years old, but Wortman told her that with her slim build and easy disinhibition she would be perfectly suited for the stripper world. He suggested putting in a stripper pole in the warehouse, where she could perform for a gang of friends. Who were these mysterious and largely invisible friends that he talked about?

Familiar as he was with Angie's Show Palace in Dieppe, Wortman said that she would be the only one in her age group to be stripping there and would have a niche market where both of them could make a lot of money. She quoted him as saying: "A lot of men would pay for your age just to pull the panties out of your ass." Cyndi declined both offers, telling him: "I'm no stripper."

Her daughter, Ocean-Mist, later said that she was unnerved by Wortman's in-your-face sexual aggressiveness and by something she saw in his warehouse, a bathroom hidden behind a sliding wall. "That night we seen the fully marked cop car [that her mother had just danced on], me and my friend had asked for the bathroom. [There was] this long narrow, cement hallway and there was a toilet like . . . in the middle of it. . . . Like, this is not normal." She described clear plastic crates filled with clothing and stuff stacked high along the walls. Who did the clothes belong to? Victims? Wortman himself? "I thought it was really weird. . . . My friend . . . said she was scared, and all I can think about was a woman being cuffed up to that toilet for weeks on end. Why does he have these secret doors to the bathroom?"

One of the most revealing insights about Wortman's life, as Starratt described it, was the state of Wortman's and Banfield's relationship. "I spent more Christmases with him than she did," Starratt said. "I spent every Christmas with him that I was here." Together Cyndi and Ocean-Mist told a story about them receiving a fruitcake from a food bank at Christmastime. Neither of them liked fruitcake, so they paid a visit to Wortman and regifted the dessert to him. "He was so happy," Ocean-Mist said, adding, "If he was in this committed relationship, why was he alone on Christmas Eve day?" A review of Banfield family Facebook pages since 2015 seemed to confirm Starratt's version of events.

In spite of all the murders and mayhem committed by Wortman, Starratt still found it impossible to condemn him.

"This is my thing with Gabe. I love Gabe as a friend. If I hate Gabe, that's going to put a wedge between me and my God. I didn't want to be one of those people who used him. I didn't want to be one of those people who mistreated him. I wanted to be a good friend and accept him for what he was," she said, before adding this: "I still love him and miss him."

All this raises an obvious question: If Wortman was such a good guy, why did he murder women he had slept with, especially Lisa McCully—or anyone, for that matter? The RCMP portrayed Wortman as an "injustice collector," but what injustice had these people ever done to him—real or perceived—that he felt the need to kill them? It just wasn't a clean fit as an explanation.

Joudrey said he and McCully socialized with Wortman and Banfield a couple of times, "but me and Gabe didn't hit it off. I just thought he was just an arrogant guy with too much money."

McCully and Banfield didn't hit it off, either, as these two excerpts from Banfield's statements to the RCMP suggest:

Lisa Banfield did not trust Lisa McCully and didn't know if she and Gabriel did anything. Lisa Banfield said that one time when having a party for Gabriel, Lisa McCully's dogs came to the yard and Lisa Banfield contacted her to get the dogs. Later that evening Lisa McCully asked her if she could come to the party and Lisa Banfield told her "no" as the party was for family and friends only. The next day Lisa McCully said that Lisa Banfield threatened her.

Lisa Banfield said that one time Lisa McCully came around the corner with beers and didn't know that Lisa Banfield was there. Lisa Banfield said that Gabriel Wortman had cheated on her many times, and that she didn't trust Lisa McCully.

There was a lot of drinking going on, and after a few drinks Wortman had a tendency to get belligerent and macho. He had done it with Aaron Tuck and countless others. He tried Joudrey on for size and challenged him to a mercy finger fight, basically arm wrestling with one hand locked onto an opponent's hand. On the mark they would test each other's strength. Joudrey was a power-saw operator and had the hand strength of Paul Bunyan. He annihilated Wortman, although the denturist never made a big deal of it afterwards, Joudrey said.

Wortman mostly avoided Joudrey until one day when the newcomer came upon the denturist sitting in his car at the gate of the warehouse. Joudrey went over to talk to him. Wortman just hit the gas, kicked up dust and sped away.

"That's the way he was," Joudrey said. "Always speeding around. He didn't care about anyone else. . . . But no one seen this coming."

Eventually Joudrey pressed McCully about why she liked Wortman so much. "I called her on it. She admitted that she had an affair with him. I told her that he was playing her. That's all he was doing. She didn't want to hear it. After that, we patched things up for a little while, but it never lasted."

Others told me that McCully had pressured Wortman about marriage, something that could not be confirmed, and that Wortman may even have given her a ring. Some or all of this may explain why Lisa Banfield told the RCMP that she knew Wortman was having affairs. She made it clear that she didn't like or trust McCully.

There was so much more to learn about Wortman and what may have motivated his killings.

After my long drive home that night from my first meeting with Joudrey, Sharon asked how it went. I told her I had learned a lot, one thing being that I now understood why people often stopped their cars outside our house and stared at it.

"Why?" she asked.

"Your pampas grass garden by the road," I said. "I suspect they think that we're swingers."

◆

The information that Chad Jones and I were gathering was great; the problem was finding a place to publish it. At *Maclean's*, Maher continued to believe that to have any chance of success in the Nova Scotia story, we needed a partnership that included a female journalist. (As a self-appointed citizen investigator, Chad wasn't the right fit for Maher.) After some discussion, I suggested Lindsay Jones, who had broken the story early on about the RCMP sending its members home from Portapique at 6:30 a.m. that Sunday morning. She was a very good reporter and writer, and had recently published in *The Walrus* magazine a long, well-executed piece about a sordid unsolved murder at Old Barns, near Truro, which was another blown RCMP investigation.

We agreed to have breakfast one day in Halifax after one of my radiation treatments at the hospital. The chosen location was the Ardmore Tea Room, a popular local hangout for university students. On the appointed morning, given the COVID restrictions, Jones, Maher and I chose to sit at a table on the sidewalk with the traffic rumbling by us on Quinpool Road. I was willing to play ball if we could have a meeting of minds. I had only one real condition: we must write about Lisa Banfield. As surprising as it might seem, Banfield's name still had not been published outside of *Frank,* and even they appeared to have run out of stories to tell.

There we were, three freelancers trying to put together an alliance to tackle the biggest story in the country, other than COVID-19. It's not the way journalism should work, but these were desperate times. As we drank our coffee and ate our breakfast, however, it soon became clear that we weren't exactly on the same page.

I believed in incremental journalism, publishing stories regularly, capturing every defensible and justifiable nuance and twist to help the reader better understand the story. Each story was a billboard advertising that I needed more information. It used to drive my mother crazy when I was a young reporter at the *Hamilton Spectator*. Just about every time I visited my parents after having a controversial story published, I would experience my own personal Groundhog Day. "I saw you had a story today in the paper," my mother, Lea, would say with her patented delivery that told you she wasn't all that happy about it.

"What did you think of it?" I'd reply.

"I just read the headline," she'd say, shaking her head. "If you keep writing stories like that, the mayor will never give you a job."

"But I have a job."

"Yeah, you have a job, alright."

Maher was a little like my mother. When I told him I was planning to report on McCully's relationship with Wortman, he asked, with a note of concern in his voice, "Are you going to clear it with the family first?"

"The family?" I asked incredulously. "Her young children? Her sister? What do you think they are going to say? I have enough proof to publish."

"I would ask them first," Maher said.

"And they're going to say no," I said. "That's how stories don't get published."

My job was to get justice for McCully, not to worry about making her blush in her grave. It was unfortunate that she'd slept with Wortman, but that was her decision—her personal responsibility. Embarrassing as it might well be to her family, it was their civic responsibility to keep nothing secret. That was the only way we might truly understand what had happened. Others in McCully's situation might ultimately recognize themselves and not make the same mistake.

This story was no different from anything else I'd ever done. I have never been afraid to speak truth to power. I have never been a public relations officer for the mayor or anyone else. I was a journalist, and Banfield's story and the RCMP's support of that story didn't pass the smell test. Maher continued to insist that his sources told him she had been seriously injured to within an inch of her life. In his mind she was lucky to be alive. My sources told me otherwise—that the attending doctor, among others, in the emergency room in Truro was surprised by her good condition.

I knew that getting Maher and Lindsay Jones onside would be an uphill battle, but Leon Joudrey was as good a starting point as any. He was the only witness left alive who had seen anything important. His observations challenged the seemingly contrived RCMP narrative.

"She had no shoes, gloves or coat and it was freezing cold," I said. "There's no way she was outside all night."

"How do you know that?" Jones asked. "Did she say it or did the RCMP say that?"

"No," I said. "I have Leon Joudrey and a reliable expert who will back him up."

"Who?"

"Dr. Science," I said. "The proof is the fact that she still has all her fingers and toes."

It seemed to me that in Maher's and Jones's view every assertion had to be balanced by comments from official sources. That kept us safe. That's what their editors wanted, and their lawyers and accountants, too, but that kind of artificial balance served only to mask the truth. And the main beneficiaries were the RCMP and governments, who could hide the truth between the lines. The losers were the families of the victims, our readers and justice.

"You're both being political," I told them a number of times, but to no discernible effect. Fear held dominion over them as if they were trapped in the *World According to Garp*, wary that some wild-eyed, tongueless Ellen Jamesian was going to rush through the door and gun each of them down for saying the wrong thing. What ever happened to critical thinking, random analysis and courage?

We kept going in circles that morning at the tiny table outside the Ardmore. If we were going to come to an agreement to work together,

I insisted that we must do a story about Banfield. Our job was to find the truth and get justice for the dead—thirteen of whom were women. I thought I was on the right side of the issue. I was doing what the story demanded.

Maher hemmed and hawed. Jones grew more and more incensed that I wouldn't back down. Finally, she popped up from her chair, looked down on me and angrily shouted: "She's a victim!"

I got the message.

Chad and I would press on together.

◆

In March 2021, almost a year after the massacres, the RCMP dumped a thousand pages or so of newly unredacted materials. It was the same old bumph, but you'd never know it by the media reaction. Once again, most of them went crazy rereporting many of the same vignettes about Lisa Banfield's terrible night.

Chad, however, pored through the documents and found something no one had reported. One word that had been blacked out was now there for everyone to see: "Lisa Banfield . . . had minor injuries."

The RCMP knew all along that Leon Joudrey was telling the truth, but it had played the media and hyped a story that at its core was not true.

Not one reporter, other than me, wrote about that single, important word—"minor"—or challenged the RCMP and the Crown about why it had been kept hidden for so long. To reset the story, the media would have had to explain that they had allowed themselves to be fooled. They weren't going to do that. The stories had been published. Podcasts had been built. They were not going to correct the record. They'd just wait for the inquiry.

I wasn't waiting. My list of questions was growing daily.

There had to be a Big Secret.

27

NEW BRUNSWICK: OUTLAW BIKERS AND DEAD INFORMANTS

We like our fiction complicated but our reality simplified. We will wade through a byzantine novel to get to the end, but we don't have the time or patience for complicated real-life stories. Just the facts! It's the way we've been trained.

Reality has other ideas.

Back on May 1, 1974, then Canadian health minister Marc Lalonde introduced into Parliament a working paper entitled "A New Perspective on the Health of Canadians." It became known as the Lalonde Doctrine. The heart of Lalonde's plan was that government combine its resources with the techniques of advertising to engineer changes in the public's behaviour. It was the beginning of the health promotion industry in Canada—for better and worse. People were convinced to use seat belts in cars but also to eat more carbohydrates. As Lalonde put it:

> The spirit of enquiry and particularly the Scientific Method, so essential to research are, however, a problem in health promotion.

The reason for this is that science is full of "ifs," "buts," and "may-
bes," while the messages designed to influence the public must be
loud, clear and unequivocal. To quote 1 Corinthians, Chapter XIV,
Verse 8: "If the trumpet gives an uncertain sound, who shall prepare himself to battle?"

It didn't take long for the dark side of the Lalonde Doctrine and its
spawn to emerge. Conspiracy theories became a cottage industry
because people sensed they weren't being told the whole truth. Even
worse, governments and the RCMP began borrowing these communications tactics for themselves. Deception in the pursuit of the Greater
Good is an accepted philosophical foundation of the rule of law. It
is the basis for undercover work. But what happens when deception,
lies and the techniques of simple storytelling are used to cover up the
government's own wrongdoings or uncomfortable truths?

The "simplest explanation" has long been one of Canadian governments' best-used weapons in misleading the public. The irony in this
case is that Ockham's razor, as we know and have interpreted it in modern times, is distorted from the concept articulated by friar William
of Ockham (1285–1347/49), a scholastic philosopher and theologian.
Ockham's "philosophical razor" for problem solving actually states
that "entities should not be multiplied without necessity," a definition
that seems applicable to our investigation of Wortman's massacres. The
domestic violence angle is way too messy—a hallmark of an imperfect story. There are too many variables, contradictions and complications. There are too many side stories that don't fit the overall narrative.
There must be a cleaner, simpler way to explain what transpired on the
evening of April 18 and the early hours of the next morning.

As a wise old Mountie—older than me, that is—once told me:
"When you see crazy and unbelievable things going on that seem to
defy logic and don't seem to make sense, and the police or criminals or
alleged terrorists are involved, think about an undercover operation.
All these situations are orchestrated and operating on a knife's edge.
It's street theatre. When things go sour, which they sometimes do, the
powers that be will come up with a barely plausible solution to explain

things away. It will be just plausible enough to capture headlines, and colourful enough to make an impression on the minds of everyday people. If I were you, I would start looking around for a blown undercover operation; try to find out what the RCMP shut down right around that time."

He wasn't the only one pushing me to think that way.

◆

RCMP staff sergeant Bruce Reid ate his gun on a baseball field on Friday, October 25, 2019, in Rothsay, New Brunswick, a suburb of Saint John. His suicide wasn't reported, but his death was: "N.B. Community Mourns Sudden Death of Long-time Mountie," as CTV News put it.

"He had some personal issues, like addiction," former staff sergeant Gilles Blinn said in an interview. "All of us suffer from PTSD after many years on the job. He didn't reach out, so it's hard to say. From what I hear, and I'm close, his suicide had nothing to do with internal struggles within the force, but only he would know, and he didn't leave a suicide note."

Law enforcement officers closer to the internal operations of the RCMP confirmed that Reid had some personal problems, but added that something going on at work was eating away at him. Reid worked out of the Hampton RCMP detachment, located between Saint John and Moncton. The detachment was a centre in the province for operations targeting outlaw bikers, organized crime and money-laundering cases. New Brunswick and Nova Scotia had become havens for outlaw bikers because there were so few police officers in rural communities. In fact, the RCMP in both provinces was stretched beyond thin due to retirements, recruiting issues and the large number of members on leave. At the time, the Mounties were asking Nova Scotia for money to hire six more officers to fight outlaw bikers.

There was also a leadership vacuum. Officers like Reid, who had operational experience and a natural feel for their caseloads, weren't the members being promoted. In addition, there was a serious and dangerous operational issue—the RCMP was desperate for informants.

It had federal government money to burn, but a dwindling pool of candidates to pay. The highly experienced Reid was disturbed by what he saw going on around him, especially with one of the informants under the control of the RCMP in New Brunswick.

As directed, I was looking for an undercover connection to Wortman's killing sprees, and Reid's suicide only months before—on turf frequented by Wortman on his smuggling runs—set off too many alarm bells to ignore. If there was any connection to be found, there had to be some kind of trail, even a faint one. If Wortman was working in some capacity with the RCMP, how and when did he start? He didn't just walk into an office and fill out a form. Something had to have happened to bring him into the RCMP fold, and it would have happened long before Reid's death.

As I reviewed everything I had learned about Wortman, his life seemed to have been trundling along in its own unusual way until the spring of 2019. He had been telling people he was thinking about retirement, but he also appeared to be rolling in cash and looking for ways to spend it. One day he landed on the doorstep of Baird's Septic Tank Pumping, on Old Tatamagouche Road in Upper Onslow, just north of Truro. Baird's had the excrement business cornered in Colchester County and much of the Maritimes, providing not only septic tank services but also colourful portable toilets for construction sites and outdoor events. The owner was looking to sell but was away on vacation. James Baxter, his right-hand man, met with Wortman, who said he was looking for a business to run when he retired from being a denturist.

"He wanted to know how much the owner wanted for the business," Baxter told me one day, as we stood outside the shop. "I told him $1.5 million and he didn't even blink an eye. It seemed to be a reasonable price for him. He said he wouldn't even need to finance it. He asked a few questions and left and said he'd be back. Never heard from him again."

Wortman was also eyeing a small strip mall in Bass River, just west of Portapique. It housed a pharmacy, a post office and a few other stores. Wortman was hoping to build a tavern and maybe a denturist shop in the mall, and install Banfield there to run the operations.

Another source reported that he was interested in a building farther along the highway in Bass River. And, as you will recall, he would soon try to buy Gina Goulet's denturist business.

Wortman seemed to be awash in cash. On December 16, 2020, eight months after the massacres, the *Halifax Examiner* reported that police found $705,000 in cash stashed in an ammunition can outside Wortman's cottage. Was the money his own, or was he setting up a front or fronts for money laundering? None of the deals ever closed, and when I tried to understand why they hadn't, I couldn't help but be suspicious about other things that were going on in Wortman's life that spring that might have helped alter the trajectory of his life.

Wortman, often accompanied by Banfield, made fifteen trips across the border to Maine over a two-year period. Five of the crossings were in the spring of 2019. Wortman was bringing back motorcycle parts and smuggling guns, among other things. According to Banfield, on one occasion, believed to be in the spring of 2019, Wortman was pulled over by the Canada Border Services Agency and searched because he was importing seventeen motorbikes into Canada. She said he was outraged because he had a NEXUS card, qualifying him as a trusted traveller. She "believed" he got an apology from the CBSA.

Banfield told an RCMP interviewer in the days after Wortman's murders that on another trip they were leaving Maine one night around 10 p.m. and Wortman had been drinking, so she drove. She hit a moose, so they returned to the house in Houlton and stayed the night. She added that Wortman snored that night and slept on the couch.

Maybe it happened that way, but some of my sources were skeptical. "To me," said Jimmy McNulty, "I would look at each of those things a little closer. It might have happened the way they said it did, or they might have had to explain away the lost time. . . . You hit a moose, you're lucky to be alive. You don't just have a sleepover and continue on. Was their vehicle damaged? Did it get repaired?"

McNulty's skepticism was well warranted. The presence of the dramatic moose story in the police documents was a red herring. The incident did take place, likely as described, but it was anything but recent. A neighbour of Wortman said it happened in 2004 or 2005, at the latest.

"The truck was a writeoff," the neighbour said, "but the strange thing was that Gabriel bought it from the insurance company and then had it towed all the way back from Houlton to Dartmouth. I helped him push it up the driveway. I don't know why he did that. It really made me wonder about what he was really up to."

Then there was the more obvious red flag—the supposed apology from the CBSA. I couldn't find anyone on either side of the border who, after being held up at the border by surly agents, complained and got an apology. That just doesn't happen in the real world. What really happened at the border? It was the perfect situation for the police to catch Wortman and/or Banfield, if she was with him, confront them with their crimes and squeeze one or both of them into becoming police informants or agents.

"Wortman was the perfect fit for what they were looking for in an informant," McNulty said. "He was a denturist with no apparent criminal record—someone that would be above suspicion."

Throughout 2019, something else was going on across Canada, another in the latest series of police operations in Ontario (Project Hobart, Project Kakia and Project Weaver, to name some) to bring down the Hells Angels and organized crime figures. In Project Weaver, police seized from the Outlaws Motorcycle Club and others the usual commodities—money, guns and drugs—and the unusual—grenade launchers and eighty-one grenades.

Around the time of his experiences at the border in the spring of 2019, Wortman's focus seems to have shifted from collecting motorbikes to buying up decommissioned police cars and collecting uniforms and other police paraphernalia. Banfield told the RCMP that he acquired his first uniform and badge around this time. Contrary to what the police suggested, Wortman's so-called obsession was not a long-time thing but had only started around the time he encountered problems at the border. He did all his "collecting" in a hurry.

Wortman bought his first decommissioned police car on March 21, 2019. On June 10, he sent an e-mail to a US company asking if it could do a custom job for him: "Are you fellows able to do a complete set for a RCMP Ford Taurus sedan?" The company declined to work with him.

Wortman acquired the decals elsewhere, and his ex-con helper, Peter Griffon, had the 2017 Taurus, acquired on June 27, decorated to look like a real Mountie cruiser by the end of July. Wortman bought another decommissioned cruiser in the meantime, on July 18, and his final one on September 5. Wortman told people that the 2017 car was a showpiece, ostensibly a tribute to the RCMP. He said the Mounties had approved of the project and that he couldn't drive it on the road but would have to trailer it.

The Mounties denied knowing about the car, but therein lies a problem. In its disclosures after the massacres, the RCMP fudged both its knowledge of the fake police car and the precise time when it was completed by Wortman and Griffon. It first suggested that the car had been finished just before the massacres. Over time, the date kept sliding backwards to July 2019. This is suspicious because many people, including Aaron Tuck, knew about the car. Some called the RCMP about it and nothing was done.

What could possibly have been going on? Why was Wortman equipping what looked like his own fake police force? A possible answer to that requires a short trip down memory lane.

Bad guys have been dressing up as police officers for decades, from the St. Valentine's Day Massacre in Chicago in 1929 to a string of armed robberies in the Toronto area in 2007 and 2008 with ties to the Hells Angels. In the Ontario case, *Toronto Star* reporter Peter Edwards described how investigators found and seized body armour marked "Police," police-style stun guns, handcuffs and illegal handguns, including one with a silencer, alongside the more typical criminal haul of money, drugs, goods and luxury vehicles. "Some of the police paraphernalia," noted Edwards, "was found hidden inside a false wall of a Richmond Hill home."

Criminals wearing police uniforms? Illegal handguns? Handcuffs? False walls? It sounded like Wortman had read the Hells Angels' script. Was he copying the bikers—even working with them to introduce something new to the East Coast underworld? Or were police using an old biker trick as part of an elaborate sting on the bikers themselves, and using Wortman as their agent? The fully decked-out replica police car would have been perfect for any number of criminal operations.

As I surveyed reports from around Nova Scotia, looking for police activity, I came across a massive raid on a biker clubhouse in Musquodoboit Harbour in 2017, where the Hells Angels were celebrating their return to Nova Scotia.

I also stumbled onto a curious story about a family fight over the estate of parents who had been murdered in September 2019. The deceased were the elderly Saulniers, whom I'd been trying to learn more about, and their murders appeared to be wrapped in court-ordered secrecy. A judge had placed an unusual publication ban on anything related to the estate. I wondered if the Saulniers could be the two people whose murders, my sources said, had helped drive Staff Sergeant Reid over the edge. I had to learn more about what happened to them, but finding the time and energy for my efforts was about to get a little more difficult.

◆

The government relaxed the COVID lockdown late in the summer of 2020, and Sharon got the call to have her next operation. She was excited about having it done. I dropped her off at the hospital in Bridgewater one Friday morning, and she walked in wheeling her travel suitcase. Visitors were not yet allowed in the hospital. I wished her good luck and made the sixty-five-minute drive to the hospital in Halifax for my daily radiation treatments.

Sharon's operation was supposed to take about two hours. Back at home that afternoon, as the hours passed, there was no word from the surgeon. I kept calling but couldn't get a straight answer. Finally, around 6 p.m., he called back. "I'm sorry," he said, explaining that near the end of the surgery he had to make a cut in a blind area. When the bleeding wouldn't stop, the doctors gave her blood transfusions that produced their own complications and aggravated the bleeding. They were pumping blood in and it was pouring out of her abdomen.

Around 7:45 p.m. the surgeon called again and told me that Sharon was now on a ventilator and was being air-lifted to Halifax, where the surgery would be completed. At 7:57 p.m. I was standing at my front door when the air ambulance flew by to the south with Sharon on board.

The operation didn't take place until Sunday at noon, and she didn't come out of recovery until Sunday evening. When I went to see her in the hospital around 10 p.m., her first words were: "Where am I?"

"In Halifax."

"How did I get here?"

"On a helicopter."

"I was on a helicopter?"

That month Sharon was admitted to the hospital on four different occasions. One positive aspect of this was that my daily radiation treatments were at the same hospital, which meant I could see her every day. And since I was an in-patient, my parking was half-price.

Nevertheless, I continued to pursue my next article. I offered it to *Maclean's*, which couldn't find the time or space to publish it. So I sent it to the *National Post*, which was going through a bout of labour problems. The story sat for weeks before appearing on October 12, 2020. I include it in its entirety because it pulls together many important findings and observations that I was continuing to gather and shows what the mainstream media had not been reporting.

'THESE TWO OLD PEOPLE WERE FED TO THE WOLVES': WHAT HAPPENED TO BERNARD AND ROSE-MARIE SAULNIER?

When the Saulniers, in their attempt to be model citizens, made the call to the police they must have thought they were serving the greater good. Then, they died

By Paul Palango

The unsolved murders of two respected Moncton-area senior citizens just over a year ago appears to have been both an act of retaliation and a warning to others about the possible dangers of calling the police on drug traffickers, according to sources in the RCMP knowledgeable about the case.

The case illustrates how dangerous it has become to work as an informant for the police, said one of the sources, a ranking RCMP officer.

"Those two old people were fed to the wolves," said the police source. "The RCMP did not do a proper risk assessment in this case."

The murders took place on Sept. 7, 2019. The victims were Bernard A. Saulnier, 78, and his wife, Rose-Marie Saulnier, 74. Their bodies were found in their bungalow on Amirault Street, a main thoroughfare running through the Moncton suburb of Dieppe. Bernard Saulnier was a local entrepreneur who was past president of Acadia Electric, past president of the Dieppe Rotary Club and past president of NB Construction. Rose-Marie Saulnier had a degree in nursing, and was a nutritionist and naturopath. She owned a business in that field—Natural Choice Health Centre.

In the months and years leading up to the Saulniers' murders, the Maritime provinces, like many places in North America, have seen a rise in the use of illegal narcotics. The region is alleged to be largely controlled by outlaw biker gangs, especially the Hells Angels. The Maritimes, with its long, largely unprotected coastline, is seen as a coveted base of operations for smuggling in drugs and distribution across North America.

The RCMP has been trying to go toe-to-toe with the bikers and shut down their operations in a never-ending and increasingly more difficult battle. One weapon the RCMP uses are informants, but turning bikers into police informants has become an overused tactic, some police observers say. In this light the RCMP has sought help from ordinary citizens, like the appeal it made in July 2018: "It is tough for us to infiltrate," RCMP Sgt. Michael Sims told Global News reporter Natasha Pace. "It is tough for us to get intelligence within these groups but we know there are people out there that can do that regularly and we certainly need them to call us and work with us."

Among those who answered the RCMP call for help, RCMP sources say, were the Saulniers. They were concerned about the activities of one of their sons, Sylvio.

A review of Sylvio Saulnier's Facebook page, where his pit bull is featured in a photo, shows connections to a number of bikers, including Hells Angels' Nomad member Robin Moulton. Believed to be in prison, Moulton has been cited recently by the RCMP as a key target in a series of anti-biker raids and arrests that have taken place in 2019 and this year in Nova Scotia and New Brunswick. Moulton's Facebook page, which he runs under the handle "Robin Angel" also features Sylvio Saulnier as a friend. His list of friends reads like a who's-who of the biker world.

When the Saulniers, in their attempt to be model citizens, made the call to the police they must have thought they were serving the greater good. "The police were raising the alarm in the community about the damage being done by the proliferation of drug use, particularly methamphetamines. The Saulniers were good people. They thought they were doing the right thing for the community by calling the police," the RCMP source said. "With the information they had, it wouldn't have been difficult for the Mounties to act on it. A couple of days of surveillance and they would be able to get search warrants."

On August 28, 2019, RCMP police forces conducted raids on five properties in Moncton, Steeves Mountain and Douglas. One of the residences raided was 204 Dominion Street in Moncton. The house was listed at the time as being owned by Sylvio Saulnier. In the raids police seized, as the CBC reported at the time, about 14.5 kilograms of suspected crystal methamphetamine, 880 grams of suspected cocaine and crack cocaine.

On Sept. 6, the day before the bodies were discovered, the RCMP announced charges against five people arrested during the raids.

The Saulniers were likely murdered that night.

While the police have not revealed what happened inside the home, an observer familiar with the investigation said the scene was "graphic." An RCMP source said the obvious intended victim was Bernard Saulnier and that his wife was likely collateral damage. "They thought they could carry on with their everyday life and then they got hit out of the blue with a bag of hammers," a police source said.

Weeks afterward, the RCMP put out an alert for two vehicles seen in the area of the Saulniers' home. One, a black BMW sedan with darkened windows, was seen on September 3 not far from their home. The occupant got out of the car and used a payphone. In the overnight hours of September 6-7, two vehicles were seen near the Saulnier home, a black BMW and an Infiniti SUV.

If the murders were in retaliation for the tip to the police, which led to the raids and arrests, police sources don't seem to think the killings were bikers. "There are Hells Angel links to this, but it's not the Hells Angels style," said a RCMP officer, whose observations were echoed by others familiar with the biker world. "The Hells Angels will kill their own members for being informers but they don't go after civilians. And they wouldn't be driving flashy cars to do a hit. In the past, Angels' hitmen preferred minivans. This sounds more like someone hired a street gang member to do the hit. It's definitely related to the bust somehow, but we just don't know how, yet."

Last December, Luc Saulnier, the deceased couple's other son, sought an order in Moncton's Court of Queen's Bench banning access to his parents' estate files. In his claim, the younger Saulnier stated that allowing details of the estate to be open to the public, as is normally the practice, could expose family members to unknown danger.

The next month, on January 16, as reported by the CBC, New Brunswick Justice Jean-Paul Ouellette issued a ban on access to the estate files. "Considering who could benefit from the estate, the circumstances of the deceased, the ongoing criminal investigation, the absence of information about the motives and identities of the murderers, publication of information could put both the beneficiaries and their family at significant risk of harm to their lives by unsavoury members of the public who could become aware of such inheritance," Ouellette stated in his written ruling.

While the Saulniers were not likely confidential informants working with the RCMP, did they say too much? Had they innocently entered into a dangerous and treacherous world by calling the police out of concern for their community?

Police sources say there is another case in Atlantic Canada where confidential informants wound up dead. "It's well-known in the criminal world that the RCMP is not a safe place for anyone to be an informant," an RCMP inside source said.

"The way the system works is that any confidential informant is identified and controlled by a handler. That handler knows everything. His supervisor may or may not know about the informant," the source said. "Only payroll knows the informant's number and the payment goes through the handler. It's a tight system. But when it comes to confidential informants, all the information about them is sent up the line to Ottawa, where all kinds of people see the information."

"You have these review groups in Ottawa where the senior person is being paid $125,000 a year and a clerk is being paid $40,000 a year and they have exactly the same access to everything," said a source familiar with the process. "They go after the ones at the lower end. That's why the government is checking out everyone's finances every year trying to see who is living above their means."

More than a year later, the New Brunswick RCMP Major Crime Unit says it is continuing to investigate the double homicide of Bernard Saulnier and Rose-Marie Saulnier. "Investigators are working diligently to identify the person or persons responsible for their deaths," said Cst. Hans Ouellette, media relations officer. "We continue to ask anyone with information related to this investigation to contact the RCMP or Crime Stoppers."

Ouellette did not respond to questions about the Saulniers being informants, whether their murders were linked to the raids in August 2019, or provide any updates on the case. He did not comment on whether the RCMP were aware of leaks in the organization at the local level or in Ottawa, and were conducting checks on employees with access to informant information. The spokesman also did not comment on the deaths of alleged confidential informants in the Maritimes.

Whatever has happened to the Saulniers, the RCMP has reacted with definitive moves in the Maritimes to shore up its efforts in dealing with biker gangs. Last November, police sources say, Assistant Commissioner Larry Tremblay, who heads New Brunswick RCMP, took control of anti-biker operations in the Maritimes. Around the same time, Chief Superintendent Chris Leather, who is considered inside the force to be an expert on undercover operations, was moved into Nova Scotia as the criminal operations officer, the second-in-command to Assistant Commissioner Lee Bergerman.

Insiders say the focus of the RCMP serious crimes units in the Maritimes is on the Hells Angels and other bikers.

The story flushed out several things. Hells Angels Nomad leaders Robin Moulton and Emery "Pit" Martin had been on my radar for months. In June 2019, I had even contacted Moulton's lawyer, former New Brunswick justice minister and attorney general Thomas Jack Burke, better known as T.J., for an interview. The former member of the US 82nd Airborne Division basically told me to pound sand.

Before long I learned from a new source that one of the people involved in the Saulnier murders—six-foot-seven Brady Sherman-Tomkins—had disappeared shortly after the killings. "He was the one who knocked on the door and got the Saulniers to open it so that the killers could get into the house," a source close to the investigation told me. "Brady had drug problems. They didn't think that he could be trusted, so he had to go."

I added Sherman-Tomkins's name to the list I was gathering of murdered and missing people in New Brunswick and Nova Scotia who might be linked to the Bruce Reid theory, that a botched operation had led to the deaths of at least two people. There was a surprisingly large number of missing persons. I was beginning to think there was a serial killer loose, and soon learned I wasn't the only one leaning that way. The idea was being kicked around on a website from New Brunswick.

While the *National Post* story was picked up by other newspapers across Canada, it was ignored in two places—New Brunswick and Nova Scotia. It was as if it never happened. The RCMP has long had ways of getting stories killed, by whispering in ears or having its Smurfs go to work undermining them, but its post-publication attack this time was unique. New Brunswick assistant commissioner Larry Tremblay issued an official RCMP communiqué that read:

I wish to address a recently published media story that attempts to make connections between several high-profile investigations involving the RCMP in New Brunswick. This story contains many inaccuracies and misinformation. More disheartening, it is an attempt to sensationalize a tragic event, and to create unnecessary fear for the sake of a "story."

Police investigations can be complex and can take time. I know people want answers when disturbing and violent acts are committed in their communities, and the RCMP is committed to releasing as much information as we can. At the same time, we must protect ongoing investigations and future court proceedings. We are also subject to legislation such as the Privacy Act, which can restrict what information we can legally release, and when.

Media play an important role in our society. They inform the public, they challenge status quo and traditional narratives, and they ignite and foster dialogue on important subjects. Our relationships with most journalists are based on mutual respect and professionalism. We know they share the same commitment we have to accountability and accuracy to the public. A story such as this undermines that foundation, and breeds misinformation and distrust.

To the members of the public, please carefully consider the stories you read, the accuracy of the information presented, and the source providing it. Most importantly, please consider what you choose to believe.

Some Mounties called me to laugh about it.

"You landed one in the bunker this time, pal," McNulty said. "You can tell by all the screeching."

The source I'm calling Bill Moreland said: "I've never seen anything like it. He claimed that someone wrote a story somewhere—we can't tell you where because you might find it—and said some things that were wrong, but we can't say what that was because of privacy legislation, but you shouldn't believe this unnamed person because he is, you know, a whacko, but we can't say that either. Believe me, you should just trust me."

And then he added: "When it comes down to it, he confirmed your story, if you really think about it. The issue is whether they were informants or not. All Tremblay had to say was that they were not informants, and your story would be sunk. But he didn't say that, did he? All the rest is incidental. I can't see what the privacy issues are in saying they were not police informants. Where's the damage to the Saulniers?"

After the Saulnier murders, Bruce Reid went into a tailspin. If he was concerned about what the RCMP was up to, his death didn't appear to make a difference. We don't yet know the details, but whatever operations were going on in New Brunswick and Nova Scotia, they continued through fall 2019 and winter 2020. And during this period, Wortman appeared to be getting crazier and more paranoid.

The *National Post* story would be my last in the mainstream media. Even the *Halifax Examiner* closed its doors to me. Around this time, Tim Bousquet took the latest unredacted information from the court documents and not only dutifully republished them, but interviewed someone about what they contained. The person he sought out (or who sought him out; we don't know) was none other than Jessica Davis, the same securities and intelligence expert who had tried to peddle information to *Maclean's* after we published the Brink's tapes. The headline over Bousquet's story said it all: "Financial expert: newly released documents show mass murderer was not an RCMP informant." He forgot to mention that his expert was an ex-CSIS agent.

Davis was continuing to argue that Wortman's $475,000 cash withdrawal from Brink's was a normal thing for a rich person to do, and Bousquet bought it, hook, line and sinker. How he considered any of this *proof* that Wortman was not an informant boggles the mind. It appears that he defied his own proud rules for investigative reporting.

None of that stopped me from pushing forward. In fact, it made my life easier now that my distant cousins in journalism had packed it in. It was as if I now had a breakaway on an open net and the freedom to do what I wanted while getting there.

28
THE WEEKS, DAYS AND HOURS LEADING UP TO THE MASSACRES

Six months after the massacres, I was standing on the concrete pad where Wortman's warehouse used to be, at 136 Orchard Beach Drive. I used an app on my iPhone to measure it. At 3,200 square feet, with a partial second floor, the warehouse had been a good-sized building. Months earlier I had met a handyman named Bill Acker, who had done some work on it for Wortman. Acker was looking to get paid for the photos he had of the warehouse and his work, mostly installing soffits and fascia.

"Are there any photos of the whole building, or even some with people in them?" I asked when we met outside a Tim Hortons in Dartmouth.

"Why would I have those?" he asked. "I'm showing you the work I did."

Like so many of Wortman's handymen, helpers and friends, Acker had more fingers on his hands than teeth in his mouth. He showed me an exchange of messages he'd had with Banfield when she was acting as Wortman's gatekeeper. "He was going to make me dentures. He was my friend. I can't believe this happened."

That sunny fall day in Portapique Beach, I was curious about a number of things, but especially something Acker had told me after I asked him if he had ever seen anything unusual on Wortman's properties. "Now that you ask," Acker said, "he had these weird little firepits all over the warehouse property. I couldn't for the life of me figure out what they were for."

Any evidence of those firepits was long gone. As soon as the RCMP had finished combing over the properties in early May 2020, it brought in heavy equipment and levelled everything except the deck, the outdoor kitchen and fireplace, and the storage area behind the cottage on Portapique Beach Road. There were still wooden crates there with markings from English companies and a Canadian military depot near Edmonton. Chad and I found an old shoebox and a shopping bag in the fireplace, but otherwise the property had been cleared.

I couldn't help but think about Wortman's boasts that he'd murdered someone in the United States and could make bodies disappear. In the short time they'd held dominion over Wortman's property, had the RCMP conducted a ground-penetrating radar search or the like to see what he might have buried? There was good reason to do so. Wortman was a man of his word. For years he had bragged that he smuggled cigarettes, drugs and guns—and he did. Why would he make up stories about being an undetected killer and body disposal expert?

Chad Jones also reminded me that early in the case, well before I knew him, something had caught his attention on the Internet, much like Kristine Kennedy's sighting of "an off-duty RC at the party" that fateful Saturday night. Jones had seen on an obscure website what he believed was Wortman calling himself a hitman, but he could never find the site again.

Was Wortman another Dany Kane, working for the RCMP by day and killing people by night? Or was he just a killer—maybe even a serial killer? The ease with which he killed twenty-two people in thirteen and a half hours seems to indicate that murder was easy for him, as if he had done it many times before. There were more than enough missing people around Nova Scotia and New Brunswick to fit a serial killer scenario. If that were the case, was Wortman the target of an investigation, and was someone close to him an informant?

One man who went missing in Truro during the summer of 2019 was thirty-five-year-old Peter Anthony (Tony) Walsh. Sporting several tattoos, including one of a diamond under his eye, Walsh was last seen on August 23 getting into a Ford pickup truck, the most ubiquitous vehicle in the country. Slightly more than a million of them were purchased by Canadians between 2012 and 2019. Wortman owned one, which is admittedly not much of a connection, but it is worth exploring.

It was well known in the Truro community that there was some kind of relationship between Walsh and the Mountain Men Rednecks motorcycle club, which operated out of Londonderry, near Portapique. Walsh reportedly owed money to the club for drugs.

Walsh's disappearance occurred the same week that the RCMP was revving up to conduct the raid that led to the murders of Bernard and Rose-Marie Saulnier. My sources had told me to look for a murder in Nova Scotia and another in New Brunswick, and I felt like I had two good candidates in Walsh and Brady Tomkins, who had knocked on the Saulniers' door.

There was a lot going on in Nova Scotia and New Brunswick, and from the outside, it looked likely that the RCMP had a massive investigation going on in both provinces. In search warrants from the biker cases, the RCMP had disclosed that an informant was involved in most, if not all, of the raids. The police were also searching for grenades, which Wortman had in inventory, and for the kind of hydraulic presses that were useful in the world of drug trafficking, and that Wortman, as a denturist, could have supplied.

As Dana Geddes had pointed out, Wortman had stopped drinking in September 2019, but by winter, just as the Walsh matter was blowing up, was back on the bottle again.

On January 20, 2020, the Nova Scotia RCMP made a splash with a press release and video saying that the force was now treating Tony Walsh's disappearance as a homicide. "We do have suspects," Corporal Jennifer Clarke said.

"We believe there are people in the community who know what happened and we need them to come forward," Sergeant Glenn Bonvie of the Northeast Nova Major Crimes Unit said in a media release.

Three weeks later, on February 12, Wortman had a very strange day. It began with him calling *Frank*. Cliff Boutilier took the call. I laid out the details in my August 10, 2020, article in the *Halifax Examiner*. In this excerpt, I have reinstated the names that were originally redacted:

> "I was off that day when Gabriel Wortman called," said *Frank* magazine editor Andrew Douglas in an interview. "Cliff took the call. Cliff said 'yeah, yeah, we're interested and took down the information, but he didn't mention anything to me for 24 hours."
>
> *Frank*, the notorious Halifax satirical magazine, is the kind of publication in the pages of which most respectable people hope never to be found. To be "Franked" is not considered to be a good thing by most, yet Wortman insisted upon it.
>
> The next day, February 13, Wortman called *Frank* again. He wanted to know what was happening with his story. Wortman promised photographs and the names of the Halifax policemen involved in the incident that Wortman wanted the world to know about.
>
> He said a grey, unmarked police vehicle was illegally parked in the fenced lot beside his denture clinic on Portland Street. When two Halifax police officers, Detective Constable Duane Stanley and Constable Tracy Longpre, showed up, clutching coffees from the Tim Hortons down the street, GW confronted them about their illegally parked vehicle. He took down their names. He had strung a heavy chain across the driveway, blocking the police officers from leaving. He even said he asked them for $20, which they refused to give him. He said the police called their office for bolt cutters and before long a small crowd had gathered and more police officers, including Staff-Sgt Tanya Chambers-Spriggs. All things were eventually resolved peacefully and Wortman allowed the police to take their car.
>
> Numerous photos of the incident and all the details, including the name of every Halifax officer at the scene, were sent to *Frank*

magazine by e-mail. It wasn't Wortman's e-mail, portapique@live.ca, however, but one belonging to his long-time companion.

"I didn't realize until after the shootings that it might have been Lisa Banfield taking the pictures or that she was the one sending them to us," Douglas said.

We don't know who did what because the girlfriend has not said a word to anyone outside her immediate family and, maybe, police since April 19. We just don't know anything about her, other than that she might have been the victim of domestic abuse, a story well propagated by both the police and activists against domestic violence.

When he called Boutilier the next day Wortman told him about something else that had happened to him, the cherry on the cake, as it were, proving the police were hounding him.

Around the time of the confrontation with Halifax police, the weather had cleared up to a degree. GW's photos show it was mostly sunny, but the meteorologists said there was still a chance of more snow. Rural roads were snow-covered with icy patches. It was a bit windy, with gusts up to 50 kilometres per hour, particularly around Truro.

In spite of the weather that Wednesday afternoon, Wortman hopped into one of his four white former police vehicles and took the one-hour-long drive to his cottage on Portapique Beach Road, about 20 minutes past Truro. There, he said, he was stopped by an RCMP officer, who gave him a speeding ticket.

On the surface, at least, it certainly appears that Wortman is truly unlucky or that the police had it in for him. Yet the question remains: what truly innocent person advertises their run-ins with the police? Who wants their name publicized and attached to a speeding ticket for all the world and insurance companies to see?

Wortman did. But why? Was there a method to his madness?

When Wortman told *Frank* magazine and Cliff Boutilier his story on February 12 and 13, the big question is: Why *Frank*? The magazine is deservedly infamous for skewering the powerful and dishing out the hidden secrets of just about anyone. In a perverse way, being Franked is a notorious badge of honour in that the "victim" is at least recognized as being someone worth writing about.

But if Wortman was hoping to get instant gratification from *Frank*, that didn't happen. The magazine didn't hit the web until February 17, in a rather long story, by *Frank* standards, with seven accompanying photos sent through GW's girlfriend's phone. The paper version of the magazine didn't come out until Wednesday, March 4.

It all looks merely quirky and innocuous until one factors in the other side of the Wortman story—suspicions that he had a special relationship with the police—specifically the RCMP and perhaps even the Halifax Police. We don't know if Wortman was a confidential informant, a police agent, or whether or not he had some other kind of special status. Policing sources have said they believe he had some kind of relationship, while the RCMP has said it could find no evidence of such a relationship. They didn't say there was no relationship. . . .

On February 12, the day of Wortman's two known and public run-ins with the police, the RCMP was in the process of making arrests of more Hells Angels and their associates in New Brunswick and Nova Scotia.

The first arrest of an unnamed biker was made on Feb. 17 in New Brunswick, the same day the *Frank* article was published about Wortman's problems with the police. The arrests continued for the next seven weeks, a highlight being a raid on the Red Devils' compound on Alma Crescent in the Halifax neighbourhood of Fairview. Not much is known about the details of that raid to date, which is unusual. If GW or anyone associated with him was suspected of being the rat, then under the Hells Angels' code his life expectancy was automatically shortened significantly.

Among the items the police and Crown focused on were the presses they found. Were the bikers getting suspicious? Attempts to find out whether GW had contacted those bikers were rebuffed by the lawyer acting for the Hells Angels.

The conjecture in policing circles is that Wortman's cover as an operative was blown and that his life was likely in danger.

If that were true, was he trying to buy back his life? On March 30, as reported in *Maclean's* magazine, Wortman mysteriously picked up $475,000 in $100 bills at the Brink's facility at 19 Ilsley Avenue in Dartmouth. The money had been routed there through CIBC Intria, which normally stocks ATM machines and provides bulk currency for other transactions. The RCMP has said it was GW's money, perhaps as part of an inheritance from an old friend, but the provenance of the money is unknown. Police sources say that if Wortman actually were a police informant or agent, the money could have been given to him by the police and, technically, at the end of the day it was in his name. The police have provided no clarity. . . .

Nevertheless, GW was given a speeding ticket that day on Portapique Beach Road by RCMP member Nicholas Andrew Dorrington, who issued it at 5:59 p.m. Wortman was charged with driving 1-15 kilometres over the speed limit. The fine was $237.50. If he wished to plead not guilty, a court date was set for April 17, 2020, at the Truro courthouse on Prince Street. Accompanying documents show that Wortman intended to plead not guilty to the charge. . . .

On its face, the Summary Offence Ticket (SOT) looks normal, but upon closer inspection there are a number of odd things about the ticket. The *Examiner* provided copies of the court document that details the ticket to a number of current and former police officers as well as other members of the law enforcement community for their analysis.

Catharine Mansley, a former Mountie who worked in Halifax County, said this: "I used to do 250 tickets a month," Mansley said. "This one was issued for 1-15 over the limit on a rural road at night. First off, 15 over is usually let go. Anything over 15 and you're playing Russian roulette. Charging someone for 1-15 is typically a reduction from a higher number, but there are no officer's notes. We don't know the basis for the charge. We are not told what the speed limit was and how fast he was going. Was the officer using LIDAR (a laser-based light detection and radar) or conventional radar? And the location is kind of suspicious: no Mountie I've ever known would be set up on a rural road in the dark enforcing speed. It just doesn't sound right to me."

Mansley's observations were echoed by others who asked not to be named. The general consensus was that the time of the ticket, the location and the lack of supporting information were suspicious. As one put it: "Six o'clock is usually shift change in a rural detachment. Nobody would be doing radar on a dirt road 30 minutes away from the detachment at that time. It just doesn't happen."

"If this was a real ticket and was knocked down from a higher speed, why would he be pleading not guilty and fighting it?" one officer said. "Presumably, the issuing officer has notes about what really happened. It doesn't make sense."

A former Crown Attorney for Nova Scotia (whom I'll describe as male) not only examined the ticket but drove to Portapique Road and conducted his own examination of the site.

"It was a Wednesday. Sunset in Portapique on February 12, 2020, was 5:37 p.m. It was about zero degrees," he said. "The ticket is not clear where the alleged offence occurred. The offence ticket states 'at or near Portapique Beach, Bible Hill.' Portapique Beach and Bible Hill are many kilometres apart. The wording makes no sense. The second point, I assume, refers to Portapique Road but that is not specified in the ticket. Does Portapique Beach refer to Portapique Beach Road or some other road in the Portapique Beach area?"

Stephen Maher doggedly pursued the issue of the speeding ticket and managed to get copies of all the tickets Constable Dorrington had written before and after the one he issued to Wortman. Maher even interviewed people who had had contact with the Mountie, including someone who had been visited by Dorrington and another Mountie, whom they believed to be Corporal Natasha Jamieson, shortly before the ticket was handed out. To Maher, Wortman's ticket looked normal, a mere coincidence, and he didn't write a story about it. I wasn't convinced. Wortman had two suspicious run-ins with the police on the same day and then advertised them. Once again, my nose detected some kind of subterfuge.

Wortman liked to work in the shadows. Now he was doing things normal people don't do. In fact, he was doing something he had only done once before in his life—bringing media attention to himself. The first time, described in Chapter Twenty, was him helping single mother Sheri Hendsbee with a set of dentures, which got him described publicly as "an angel." At the time, he was perilously close to being charged criminally. This time, there were all kinds of things going on around him, and he was once again attempting to manipulate how others saw him. Except now he wasn't trying to look like the good guy; instead, it was as if the stories about hitting a moose or border security agents sending him an apology were meant either to explain lost time or to create an image of him being unfairly harassed by the police. It looked like a show or, as Shakespeare put it in *Hamlet*: "The lady doth protest too much, methinks."

On March 6, 2020, Wortman made his last trip to Maine before the border was closed due to COVID-19. We don't know what he brought back with him, but after that he and Banfield were stuck in lockdown. Most businesses were closed by the government, including Wortman's denturist office. He and Banfield retreated to the cottage, where they would spend the last six weeks of his life, stocked up with $800 worth of gasoline and food staples to ride out the storm.

Wortman did make at least one trip to the city, when he (and Banfield, she alleged to investigators, in a separate vehicle never caught on camera) went to collect his $475,000 from the Brink's depot in Dartmouth on March 30. When he got back to Portapique, Wortman added it to the money he had stashed all over his properties. He was clearly in a mood to liquidate everything. He was in negotiations to sell his clinic property in Dartmouth, a deal that was about to close. He told others, including Cyndi Starratt, that he was considering selling the cottage and moving into the warehouse.

"Where would Lisa go?" Cyndi asked him.

"She'll find a place," Wortman told her.

Approaching Easter weekend, one week before the massacres, things were going on both inside and outside Wortman's life that may well have affected him. On April 10 the RCMP announced the last of the four arrests made between February 17 and April 9—one less than a week after Wortman's confrontation with police in the Dartmouth parking lot, the other slightly more than a week before the killings. A couple of curious things piqued my interest about the biker arrests. The first was that the RCMP went out of its way to link those arrested to Hells Angels Nomad leaders Robin Moulton and Pit Martin, although neither was charged. The second was the fact that RCMP, following some new "privacy" guidelines, did not name those charged—ever. I watched for more than a year and talked occasionally with the CBC's Karissa Donkin, who covered bikers in New Brunswick. She told me the RCMP had told her she would have to go to court, look at the dockets and figure out who had been charged.

It doesn't get more Kafkaesque than that. The RCMP seems to have forgotten why there are criminal laws and public criminal records: both deter criminal behaviour and protect the security of law-abiding citizens. The only valid explanation would be that, by hiding behind privacy laws and not publicizing the names of those charged, the RCMP could turn the people they'd arrested into informants without the biker clubs learning their identities. Not only was this strategy bad public policy, but biker bosses keep a sharp eye on everything happening around their clubs. One thing they and their lawyers couldn't help but notice was that virtually every biker-related search warrant issued around this time in the Maritimes contained three basic disclosures from the police: an informant was involved, they were looking for grenades, and they were looking for "presses." Specifically, the search warrants for the arrests announced on April 10 referred to a hydraulic press in which a camera had been hidden. The bikers would have immediately gone hunting for whoever had fobbed off that piece of equipment on them.

A couple of other things may have happened around April 10, 2020, a week before the massacres. There were unconfirmed rumours that

Wortman purchased a motorcycle from a person associated with the seemingly defunct but still active Mountain Men Rednecks MC. That was the funny thing about Wortman: just about everyone in Nova Scotia seemed to know him, yet so much of his business was conducted unbeknownst to authorities.

A reliable source came forward to me with a tale I could not confirm, but if true, it would provide a crucial connecting piece to this puzzle. The source overheard the end of a phone call. The person speaking didn't realize my source was there. The speaker was well acquainted with Wortman and said he had told them that, about a week to ten days before the massacres, he had "acted as a facilitator for a $1 million transaction between the Hells Angels and another unknown group."

I approached the person who had reportedly said this and asked if it was true. They denied it, but in the opinion of those who saw the video of our conversation, the denial was unconvincing.

Was Wortman's cover blown? Was that transaction, if it indeed took place, the final act that led to him being identified as a police agent? Or, conversely, was Wortman the target of a sting and someone close to him an informant? Perhaps the RCMP used a "Mr. Big" sting, for which it is so infamous. In a Mr. Big sting, the RCMP uses undercover operators to create a scenario that will lure a target into confessing their crimes. Mr. Big is purportedly the boss of a criminal network and will allow new members to join his gang only if they tell him everything they've ever done. The controversial technique is considered entrapment and banned in many jurisdictions.

I ran that possibility by my police sources. The consensus was that whatever happened with Wortman, it was not likely a Mr. Big sting, because such projects usually require lots of travel and many moving parts. The target of the investigation is typically made to go far out of their comfort zone. In Wortman's case, there could be no travel because of the COVID lockdown. However, that does not negate the possibility that a Mr. Big scenario had been under way, only to be interrupted by the lockdown. If so, it is plausible that the RCMP had tried to pull off the sting even without the disorienting travel component, during which Wortman got wise to what was really going on and the likelihood that he was headed to jail.

Whatever was going on inside Wortman's life and head that weekend, it didn't go entirely unnoticed.

◆

Other than Banfield's family members, three people were actively involved with Wortman during his final week. Six days before the massacre, on Easter Sunday night—April 12—Portapique neighbour Dana Geddes and his wife, Brenda, paid a visit to Wortman's cottage to "check in" on Gabriel and Lisa.

"I go to the door, and he says, 'We're playing checkers,' he says. 'Pandemic games.' He was talking to me and then Lisa come out and she said: 'Gabriel, get over here. Get your mask on.' He went over to get a mask and come back over talking to me."

Both Dana and Brenda thought something was bothering Banfield that night. "She seemed quite odd. She seemed different that night to me," Geddes said. "She had a lot of makeup on. I got thinking after, was the makeup covering bruises? You know, afterwards, you're thinking. She just seemed out of sorts. It wasn't Lisa. Usually she says, 'Hi, Dana.' Usually she has a big smile, but she was not happy."

The couples had a couple of drinks and were together for more than an hour, Geddes remembered. "We had a long conversation. It was over an hour, and Gabriel was drinking some," Geddes said. "He said this COVID stuff, this pandemic, was freaking him out bad, bad, bad. He says: 'I got lots of food here, and if I run out of food, I got a gun here and bullets. There's lots of deer running around. I'll get something to eat.'"

"That doesn't sound like COVID panic," I interjected. "He's just got a plan. Or am I wrong?"

"When he went to the cottage at the first of March, Gabe told me: 'This is a chance for me to see what retirement will be like. I'll stay over there till it's over.'"

The other thing that happened that week was that Geddes's lifelong buddy Eddie Creelman ran an errand for Wortman. After Wortman learned that Creelman, a trucker, was still doing runs to Ontario during the Atlantic lockdown, Wortman asked Geddes about getting Creelman to drive motorcycle parts to his friend Kevin von Bargen. In return, Wortman would knock $500 off a set of dentures for Creelman. "'Sure, no problem,' I says," Geddes recalled. "'You put it in a crate,' and he did. I looked at it. It was just a motor. I took it to Buddy [Creelman] and we loaded it inside the back of his truck so that it was out of the way when he was loading his stuff. He took it up to [von Bargen] and brought a bunch of stuff back."

A sole practitioner, von Bargen continued to be listed on search engines as the general counsel and corporate secretary of Brookfield Residential Property Services (the federal government's and RCMP's relocation company), although that job appears to have ended many years ago. Despite earlier offering an interview to Stephen Maher for cash, von Bargen has not replied to my requests for interviews. In this matter, he has declared a solicitor-client relationship with Lisa Banfield.

It wasn't an easy delivery for Creelman to make. Von Bargen's house was on the eastern edge of the Greater Toronto Area, near the Lake Ontario shoreline, Creelman recalled. "I had to unhitch my trailer and drive my rig to his house," Creelman said. "He gave me a box with a gas tank and a fender, and there was a little cog, and I hauled it back for him."

When Creelman got back to Nova Scotia with the pieces from von Bargen, he had hoped to meet with Wortman on the morning of April 18. Geddes was the go-between, and when he called Wortman he was told there was no hurry. "Keep it all there. We'll come down and get it Tuesday or Wednesday," Wortman told Geddes. "I told Gabriel that I was looking like a Scottish sheepdog. We couldn't get a haircut or nothing. I was looking horrible. Gabe said: 'Lisa was a hairdresser for years. She'll cut your hair, too, and Brenda's if you like.' Perfect! We'll do that."

But like a lot of things Wortman was planning to do after that weekend, the haircuts never happened.

✦

Among the items that the RCMP convinced Judge Laurel Halfpenny MacQuarrie to black out in the court documents were statements Banfield made about what she and Wortman had done earlier that Saturday. It was their nineteenth anniversary, and she said they had gone for an eerie drive around the Portapique Beach area, passing places owned by people that Wortman would target or kill in the second massacre.

When the section was unredacted for the media to see, five months after the massacres, it was construed as a prelude to the killings, as if Wortman was walking through his plans for what would happen that night and the next day. But Banfield's statements about that morning were vague and inconclusive. She talked about them driving the back roads northwest toward Springhill and looping back to Portapique. At one point, Wortman was said to have stopped by a denturist's home somewhere twenty minutes west of Portapique, but the denturist was never identified. This led the *Halifax Examiner*, for example, to declare that it obviously wasn't murder victim Gina Goulet, who resided in the opposite direction, in Shubenacadie.

The *Examiner* was right and wrong. They were right about Wortman visiting another denturist. A source in the denturist community who did not want to be identified would later emerge with a story about how Wortman wanted to sell off all his denturist equipment because he said he was "heading in another direction." What did that mean? Retirement? Witness protection? A murder spree?

The *Examiner* was wrong about Wortman seeking out Gina Goulet. Banfield had told the RCMP that Wortman *had* driven past Goulet's cottage, which apparently shocked Banfield, who said she didn't understand why Wortman knew where it was located, since Goulet was her friend, not his. As we now know, Goulet and Wortman were at odds and, for whatever reason, Wortman was determined to kill her—his twenty-second and final victim.

Banfield also said that another stop Wortman made was near the Diefenbunker, where he would hide out later that night after the first thirteen murders in Portapique Beach. He was intrigued and comforted by the facility, Banfield said. As the court documents put it: "Gabriel Wortman commented on a building that had asbestos that he could have purchased for $70,000. They drove to a building where planes were and saw some people there and Gabriel commented that they were not properly social distancing." The RCMP did not provide video evidence of the apparent visit, which was likely available since security cameras were mounted in the area.

The most telling stop, however, was outside the walls of the Springhill federal penitentiary, where his uncle Glynn had served time after stabbing his own father. "Gabriel commented that he could never go in there," Banfield told the police. Again, there was no video confirmation provided to the public.

In the context of what was to follow only hours later, Wortman's reported comment suggests he may have felt the police closing in on him and that he was facing jail time. Was he between a rock and a hard place, with the Hells Angels on one side and the RCMP on the other? If he was an agent with his cover blown, had he formulated a plan to go out with a bang rather than be on the run for the rest of his life?

Once they arrived back at the Portapique Beach Road cottage, Banfield said that she and Wortman found Peter Griffon doing yardwork around the property. Griffon told the RCMP he went back to his shack in the woods around 5 p.m. Wortman, meanwhile, always looking for something to keep himself busy, cleaned and shined up his Jeep. At 6 p.m. he and Banfield went to the warehouse for their anniversary party.

All hell broke loose three hours later.

More than a year later, Chad Jones, my document ferret, found a little nugget buried deep inside one of the dozens of unredacted documents, on page 78 of 143 pages: "FBI Agent Raymond Goergen [reported that he] could not find proof of a phone call or FaceTime call with Lisa and Gabriel [on April 18, 2020]."

Now it looked like the virtual party was a myth, too. What else wasn't true?

◆

The more research we did, the clearer it was becoming evident that this was no conspiracy theory, as my detractors would have it, but rather a bona fide conspiracy. I needed to keep searching for information that would lead me closer to the truth. The biggest problem I faced was that the media were no longer covering the story. My appearances on *The Rick Howe Show* were getting farther and farther apart and would soon end. Howe eventually went off the air for a planned eight weeks to have surgery. Once recovered, he chose to retire rather than return.

My only option was *Frank*.

I called Andrew Douglas and told him I had a couple of stories for him that needed a home, but I had to be allowed to report and write them in my style, not *Frank*'s.

"It's a deal," Douglas said.

Others in my immediate circle thought I should have been aiming higher, at the *Globe and Mail* or the CBC or, dare I say it, *Maclean's*. They didn't understand that this story was old news to those outlets, incomplete as they had left it.

Stephen Maher damned me with faint praise: "I guess *Frank* would be a better fit for you."

No one could have appreciated at the time just how good a fit it would be.

29
TRANSPARENCY, ONE LEAF AT A TIME

Six months after the massacres, few of the facts you already know from this story were disclosed or known to the public. Everywhere I turned, I met with a wall of secrecy. It was certainly not the optimal route to justice for those who had died. I had to start somewhere. Chad Jones and I went back to Portapique Beach to go over the RCMP timeline one more time. I tried to put myself in the heads of everyone involved—Wortman, Banfield and the Mounties.

Standing on Wortman's expansive cottage deck at 200 Portapique Beach Road, I could imagine how proud he had been. I could also see some of his fear. He had built a double barrier to protect his property from the destructive tides. The lot was relatively small and getting smaller. The ocean was coming for him and his beloved cottage—more than a metre every year—as the tides ate up the mud banks.

If Banfield's story to the police about Wortman splashing gasoline around the cottage and setting it alight was true, then I had to wonder how they got from there to the warehouse, 400 metres through the woods. Did he drag her all that way by the hair? Or did they drive the one and a half kilometres around to 136 Orchard Beach Drive? I couldn't get into Banfield's head. She said she had run into the woods and hid, but that looked improbable, if not impossible. The woods were filled with scrubby saplings. The forest floor was rocky and covered with slick green moss. She was barefoot and underdressed. It was pitch dark. I found it too incredible that she'd spent eight and a half hours in that freezing tangle of muck, pine needles and dense brush and emerged clean, unharmed and in no apparent distress from the cold.

Both Leon Joudrey and Dana Geddes had told me I should speak with Judy Myers, a bookkeeper who lived with her husband, Doug, near the bottom of Orchard Beach Drive. The Myers, along with the Tucks and Bonds on Cobequid Court, were the only permanent residents in that corner of the neighbourhood.

Before retiring to Portapique Beach, Judy and Doug Myers had made their living in the hospitality industry, travelling around Canada, running motels in obscure places from coast to coast to coast. The first thing that leapt out at me about their property was the many feral cats, each of whom lives in its own little house along the fence line, on the porch, under the porch and even inside the house. Judy takes part in a feline shelter program.

It was now approaching winter at the end of 2020, and no one in the media had talked to the Myerses. The couple had had a few dealings with Wortman. The image of him racing up and down the road on his side-by-side was etched into their memories. "It was a nice ride," Doug said. "Didn't see him much on motorbikes."

Doug and Judy first met Wortman face to face when he ran an errand for Dana Geddes. "Judy is my bookkeeper's sister," Geddes said. "Actually, one time, Gabriel was here, heading down [to Portapique], and I forgot to give her some important paper for, let's say, October's statement for HST. I said: 'Will you take these down to Judy for me?' He said: 'Okay.' I told him they are really nice people, very good people."

Judy Myers remembered Wortman arriving at her front door. "I know the face, but I don't know who you are," Judy recalled saying.

"You've been served!" Wortman said, handing her a bag containing the paperwork.

After a pregnant pause, as Judy tried to understand why someone was suing her, Wortman dropped his ruse: "No, Dana sent this with me." He laughed, then turned and left: "See ya."

Doug Myers was another one of Wortman's satisfied denture clinic customers. "I got his name from Dana," Doug said. "He made my top denture. He said the price would be $900, but then he came back and said: 'Seeing as you're a neighbour—$600. How's that? Does that sound better?'" Doug was more than pleased. "Gee, that's not a bad guy, man."

Doug added that one of the things he and Judy liked about Wortman was that, although he obviously had a ton of money and "a gorgeous cottage," Wortman was not ostentatious about it. "He doesn't flaunt his wealth like he's some 'I'm a little better than you' kind of thing."

But another dealing with Wortman left them somewhat more suspicious about him. Their son was looking to buy a place to live near his parents. "He likes it here," Doug said. "There's a lot of freedom here. You can walk up and down the street with a bottle of beer in your hand because it's private. It's that kind of a feel. You don't make an idiot of yourself, but you have fun." Their son met Wortman at one of the beach parties and they talked about a property that was for sale, but the son didn't have the financial wherewithal to pull off the deal.

"Well, I can help you," Wortman told him. "We can get that together. And then you can live there, and then you can pay the mortgage to me."

The deal didn't get done because Wortman wanted the price to go lower and someone else snapped up the property, which didn't entirely displease the Myerses.

"We didn't like the sounds of it," Doug said. "We're fortunate that we didn't go along with him."

On the Saturday night of the first massacre, the Myerses were going through their typical routine. Doug was in the bedroom getting ready for the night, while Judy was watching television, waiting for the CTV regional news at 11:30 p.m. "I heard some gunshots—three then two," Judy recalled. "It was 11:28 p.m. I remember the exact time because the CTV [national] news was almost over. I was getting ready to watch *The Honeymooners*. That's what I do every Saturday night. It comes on at midnight."

Judy's recollection didn't fit the RCMP timeline, but it did fit with what other witnesses had said. In the court documents were statements to the police made by Alan and Peter Griffon, who each talked about the sounds of gunshots and explosions happening at around that time. The Griffons said someone came to their door at around 11:30 p.m., but they didn't answer it. But the police say Wortman had left the area before 11:28 p.m.

Judy said she awoke around 4 a.m. after hearing cats fighting in her yard. She went outside and didn't hear any commotion or smell any fires. It was peaceful. When she awoke in the morning, she was shocked to find out on Facebook what had taken place around her.

Around 9 a.m., she said, an RCMP ERT vehicle turned around in her driveway, and fifteen minutes later another pulled in and stopped. Officers in their tactical gear came to her door. They asked her if she was safe and whether they could search her sheds and trailer. They looked under the tonneau cover of their pickup. One of the Mounties then returned to their front door. "You need to leave," the combat-ready policeman said. "And if you don't have a place to go, you can go to the Onslow fire hall."

It was almost 9:30 a.m. when the Myerses left their home, Judy said. "When they told us to leave, we just grabbed a couple of things," she explained. "I fed the cats, put food out, jumped in the car, drove straight out Orchard Beach Drive, which is the way we go out. Doug's driving, I'm in the front seat. As he's driving by Gabe's on this side [and] Lisa's on the right side, I see this yellow tarp beside Gabe's driveway. It was Corrie Ellison."

"I stopped," said Doug.

"There's a leg," Judy recalled saying. "There's a leg sticking out from underneath the tarp."

"Yeah, there was a leg," Doug said. He wondered, "What the hell is going on?"

Then they looked over toward Lisa McCully's front yard. "I saw a yellow tarp in her yard," Judy said. "It was out close to the fence in the middle of the lawn. There were no police there. There was nobody guarding it. No yellow tape. Nothing."

"I was going to get out and look to see if they were all right, or what was happening," said Doug. "It was just a reflex."

"I said, 'Don't do that,'" Judy recalled. "'We've got to get out of here.' When we passed Frank and Dawn's house, it was burned down."

When they got up to Highway 2, they recalled, they saw a Mountie there, maybe a couple—but certainly no army. On the Highway 104 expressway, near the exit to Highway 102, the Myerses encountered a lone Mountie conducting traffic stops of vehicles heading south toward Halifax or east toward Cape Breton. "He just looked in the back seat of our truck and said 'Okay,'" Judy said. "There was one vehicle that almost didn't stop because he was over in the other lane. But he did stop because the Mountie waved at him."

This was around the time that Wortman was fleeing from the Fishers' house in nearby Glenholme and on his way back to Debert, where he killed Kristen Beaton and Heather O'Brien.

Ignoring readily available municipal officers in nearby Truro, Amherst, Halifax, New Glasgow and Stellarton, the RCMP was calling for help from its own members in New Brunswick, up to three hours away. When I tried to imagine what the Mounties might have been thinking, it certainly looked like they didn't want to get any other force involved. The Mounties on Portapique Beach Road that Saturday night seemed to have been preoccupied with something very big, to the exclusion of everything else, including saving lives. Once again, what was the Big Secret?

◆

A good starting point was Lisa Banfield, the mystery woman at the heart of the story. I had written a lengthy feature about her and submitted it to *Maclean's* and, after they sat on it for a long while, to the *National Post*, which did the same. I finally sent it to Andrew Douglas at *Frank*, who was more than happy to have it. We intended to publish it on Monday, December 7. But then strange things began to happen.

On the afternoon of December 4, the RCMP made a dramatic announcement: Lisa Diana Banfield, now fifty-two, her brother James Blair Banfield, sixty-four, and her brother-in-law Brian Brewster, sixty, had been charged under Section 101 of the Criminal Code for providing ammunition to Gabriel Wortman that he used during his rampage. Suddenly, the media that had spent almost eight months assiduously avoiding naming Banfield were blaring her name. She had been charged with transferring .223-calibre Remington cartridges and .40-calibre Smith & Wesson cartridges to Wortman between March 17 and April 18, 2020.

My friend Scott Anderson from the CBC called me. He had covered the Mayerthorpe massacre and had produced a solid documentary on Dennis Cheeseman and Shawn Hennessey, who were convicted of giving shooter James Roszko a ride to the farm where he ended up killing four Mounties on March 3, 2005. "In the Mayerthorpe investigation and inquiry, the Mounties controlled everything from behind the scenes," Anderson said. "It was impossible to find out anything. It's the old Mountie bag of tricks. Delay and deflect."

That's a perfect description of what was going on in Nova Scotia. Everyone I talked to in law enforcement described the charges against Banfield as little more than a speeding ticket. "It looks like a stall," McNulty told me. "She'll likely never see a day in court, and the case could be used to block her testifying at the inquiry."

Douglas was poised to hit the publish button and make *Frank* the first media outlet to run a profile of Banfield, but the RCMP stole that distinction away from him. We published the story anyway, which included much of what you have read here.

The media found itself twisted into an impossible logic knot. No one had named Banfield because she was "a victim." But now that the police had charged her with a two-bit crime, she was fair game—but only regarding the charges. No one dared express a word of skepticism about her alleged abuse at her common-law husband's hands. The *Toronto Star*, for example, expressed outrage at the charges, calling the charges "pure cruelty." Meanwhile, most media outlets were still not naming Wortman, using only euphemisms or initials to describe him. Meanwhile, several days after Banfield and her relatives were charged, the *Halifax Examiner* published its story about Wortman leaving behind $705,000 in cash on his property. It appeared to me that the Mounties were doing everything they could to promote their preferred Monster narrative about Wortman.

What I didn't yet appreciate was that something else was going on in the background, and it required the RCMP's media-manipulation skills to make sure no one else noticed either.

◆

Back in May 2020 my first Deep Throat tipster had told me that the force was hiding, altering and destroying evidence in the Wortman case. Along the way others, like Jimmy McNulty, had told me much the same thing ("pasteurizing evidence," he had called it, while wondering aloud at the absence of 911 tapes or any other electronic evidence).

I believed my sources and regularly solicited help from my audience. When I appeared on *The Rick Howe Show* or elsewhere, I always mentioned the destruction of evidence, even if it made me sound like my tinfoil hat was on a little too tight. Finally, Chad Jones gave me a call and told me that *Little Grey Cells* had something. It was a leaked RCMP internal document, and Jones quickly got his hands on it.

Although Andrew Douglas and I were planning to wait until after Christmas to begin publishing our stories, this one couldn't wait. On a Sunday morning and afternoon, we got the story together, complete with photographs of the documents. The screaming headline was in 52-point bold typeface.

MONTHS TOO LATE?

RCMP ordered moratorium on Wortman evidence destruction in October

By Paul Palango

The RCMP issued an order seven weeks ago to its members involved in the investigation in the Nova Scotia massacres to stop destroying evidence in the case, according to internal RCMP documents obtained by *Frank* magazine.

The trigger for the moratorium on destruction of evidence appears to be a Canada Labour Code investigation undertaken by Employment and Social Development Canada into the matter.

The four-page document is dated October 15, 2020. It appears to come from an internal RCMP web page and is headlined: "MD-218—Moratorium on the destruction of information involving Gabriel Wortman pertaining to the investigation of the mass shooting in Nova Scotia on 2020-04-18 and 2020-04-19." The URL for the web page is: http://infoweb.rcmp-grc.gc.ca/manuals-mauels/national/moratorium-moratoire/md-218-.

The last bit of information is missing from the photocopy.

The document first was sent anonymously to *Little Grey Cells*, a YouTube channel, which operates out of Alberta. The show's host, Seamus Gorman, has been discussing it for the past few days in his broadcasts as part of a group called The Discord. It is comprised of 380 citizen investigators who have banded together since the massacre to dig up information.

The timing and wording of the memorandum strongly suggests that the RCMP has been destroying documents and data in the case. Since May, multiple anonymous sources close to the investigation have suggested the RCMP was destroying or altering paper and electronic evidence. This has previously been reported in the *Halifax Examiner* and on the Halifax talk show hosted by Rick Howe. The RCMP has not commented on the allegations to date.

The order commands the RCMP to collect, protect and retain every kind of evidence in the case, including paper documents, electronic data, 911 calls and radio communications.

To date the RCMP has resisted releasing any information or answering any questions about what it did and didn't do before, during and after the shootings on April 18 and 19.

In the new documents the RCMP is ordered to collect and retain "all records, documents, and information pertaining to communications and dealings with Gabriel Wortman, and all occurrences linked or related to Gabriel Wortman, including intelligence reports, citizen reports, calls for service and occurrence reports."

The RCMP has been told to collect and retain "all occurrence reports, briefing notes, SITreps, taskings and regular members' notes of the incidents, including notes or regular members who responded from 'H' Division," which is Nova Scotia. . . .

In recent months a current RCMP member has been quoted on numerous occasions in the *Halifax Examiner* and elsewhere as saying that the RCMP was attempting to "pasteurize" the evidence in the case. The member said there are ways the force can alter electronic files and data, "or even make it disappear."

Another current member said in an interview that the biggest problem from a public interest point of view is that the RCMP data management system, known by its acronym PROS, can be manipulated by senior officers.

"There has never been an audit conducted on the integrity of data in the PROS system," the ranking officer said. "The force has had six months to play with the evidence. Now, these investigators aren't going to take 'the dog ate my homework' for an answer. They will demand answers to their questions."

A third former RCMP officer who is familiar with the current inner workings of the force said this in an interview: "This is the nightmare for the force that I've been expecting. They have been doing everything they can to hide information. They have likely been trying to scrub the database to get rid of anything incriminating." . . .

A former executive-level officer in the RCMP says the revelation of this memo is devastating to the organization.

"It shows how corrupt the force is, and how it has to be disbanded," the former officer tells *Frank*.

"They use the word 'moratorium'? That means not preserving evidence is a regular thing. That means they're gonna continue to do it all the time."

Meantime, a former member of the judiciary says they are "really surprised" that a moratorium is required.

"Especially in this case where they would have known there was going to be at least a SIRT inquiry, evidence should have been retained."

Royal Canadian Gendarmerie royale
Mounted Police du Canada   Canadä

National Home > RCMP Manuals > Moratoriums > MD-218 – Moratorium on the destruction of
information involving Gabriel Wortman pertaining to the investigation of the mass shooting in Nova
Scotia on 2020-04-18 and 2020-04-19

MD-218 – Moratorium on the destruction of information involving Gabriel Wortman pertaining to the investigation of the mass shooting in Nova Scotia on 2020-04-18 and 2020-04-19

Published: 2020-10-15

1. General

1. 1. Pending resolution of a federal/provincial inquiry and the civil proceedings against the
Government of Canada involving individuals named in sec. 1.1.2., and the Canada Labour Code
investigation undertaken by Employment and Social Development Canada (ESDC), until further
notice, retain all information involving Gabriel Wortman related to the mass shooting in Nova
Scotia (NS) on 2020-04-18 and 2020-04-19.

1. 1. 1. This includes, but is not limited to:

1. 1. 1. 1. all records, documents, and information pertaining to communications and dealings
with Gabriel Wortman, and all occurrences linked or related to Gabriel Wortman, including
intelligence reports, citizen reports, calls for services, and occurrence reports;

1. 1. 1. 2. all records, documents, communications and dealings with respect to the response to
and the investigation of the events of 2020-04-18 and 2020-04-19 in Nova Scotia involving the
deceased shooter Gabriel Wortman, including occurrence reports, briefing notes, SitReps,
taskings and regular members' notes of the incidents, including notes of regular members who
responded from "H" Division or elsewhere;

1. 1. 1. 3. all medical, employment, and training files of Cst. Heidi Stevenson, Cst. Chad
Morrison, and other individuals injured or involved;

1. 1. 1. 4. information related to current and previous policies, processes, procedures, code
guidelines, initiatives, protocols, trainings, and best practices programs, including pending
changes to policies and procedures post-incident regarding:

1. 1. 1. 4. 1. media relations, including processes for releasing information to the media,
public, and relatives of the victims; and

1. 1. 1. 4. 2. uniforms, including any records related to the disposal of RCMP kit and clot
items and the revocation of authorization for retired regular members to wear the unifo

http://infoweb.rcmp-grc.gc.ca/manuals-manuels/national/moratorium-moratoire/md-218-

It looked like a pretty solid case. It gave me the opportunity to address for the first time the issue of the vulnerability of data in the PROS (Police Reporting and Occurrence System). I made a point of sending copies of the story to my distant cousins in the mainstream media. In my considerable experience with such stories back in the stone age of journalism, the appearance of a document like this screamed cover-up. Douglas and I then waited for something to happen.

Four days later, RCMP corporal Lisa Croteau provided a 709-word response to Douglas, which read:

Hi Andrew,

Yes, the Moratorium on the destruction of information was published to the RCMP intranet on October 15, 2020.

TBS [Treasury Board of Canada Secretariat] policy requires the destruction of information once the associated retention period has elapsed. As per these requirements, the RCMP does not keep personal information longer than necessary.

All information has an expiry date. At some point it loses validity or needs to be managed appropriately due to the sensitivity of the information. In some cases, there are legal requirements which govern minimum or maximum amounts of time an institution can keep information. RCMP retention periods are created by reviewing the criminal code, applicable acts and regulations, applicable policies and directives and finally business considerations. Based on all requirements, a retention is set indicating how long a file is to be kept. Once the retention period elapses, disposition takes place.

It is important to note that disposal/disposition means the act of disposing of information resources which no longer provide value to the RCMP, either by destroying them, transferring them to the Archives Management Section, Library and Archives Canada, or a non-Government of Canada organization.

There are few exemptions permitting departments to retain information longer than the associated retention period and a moratorium is one such exception. The publication of a moratorium is part of the RCMP's process to inform employees of the organization not to destroy information relating to a moratorium. As all information has a retention period, this ensures information that exists is kept until Legal Services lifts the hold on destruction.

The RCMP started working on the moratorium once the appropriate information was received from Legal Services. As part of the moratorium publishing process, details are requested to ensure the ability to find all relevant information. The publishing process requires coordination between relevant stakeholders and can take several weeks. While this process was underway, key stakeholders were contacted to apply a legal hold on the relevant information to ensure information was not destroyed.

Any information relating to this incident would be considered under investigation and therefore cannot be deleted. Files are only destroyed once a case is closed. When it comes to retention periods, orders are not given to destroy, rather they are destroyed once a specific pre-identified period of time has elapsed or if there is a court order to do so.

A file needs to be concluded before we apply a retention period. Files can only be concluded once all associated or anticipated activities have been completed. Purge dates, also known as disposition dates, are applied based on the end of the retention period associated to the concluded file. During the disposition phase (purge date review), Information Management functional specialists or their delegated authority perform a review of files and information of business value once the retention period has elapsed and they have to determine if:

A. The information still has business value based on specific criteria, in which case the retention period is extended

B. The information is considered historical, in which case files/ information resources are sent to Archives Management Section (AMS) and eventually Library and Archives Canada

C. The information no longer has business value, in which case it is destroyed as per security criteria

D. The information no longer has business value to the organization however we were assisting another policing partner, in which case we communicate with the policing partner to determine if they want to have the information returned to them, if not, information is destroyed as per security criteria.

From the outset of the H-Strong investigation, the RCMP committed to keeping victim's families informed as well as providing the public and media with the facts related to H-Strong, while maintaining the integrity of the investigation.

The RCMP's commitment to transparency and accountability includes publicly reporting on our activities to help achieve those objectives and we have done so since April 19, 2020.

The RCMP recognizes the need to provide the factual account of what transpired this past April. With the public inquiry now ongoing, the most appropriate and unbiased opportunity to do so is with our full participation in the inquiry.

The inquiry is underway and RCMP is fully cooperating. The RCMP will respectfully refrain from further commenting on these matters outside of the inquiry.

Take care,
Lisa

Croteau was saying that the information being destroyed was no longer of use to the investigation—which hadn't been completed—and was extraneous to it. How could that possibly be? Afterwards, I learned from a new source that the encrypted communications were slated to be destroyed but weren't. The hard drives were being stored in Dartmouth and New Brunswick, I was told. Mounties from New Brunswick had been called to Nova Scotia, but it raised the question, once again, about whether the entire operation had been run out of New Brunswick, as some of my other sources had suggested. The Mounties seemed hell-bent on bending and twisting the rule of law to their own benefit.

The rest of the media ignored the *Frank* story. That sent a message to the RCMP and its enablers that anything we said, no matter how many facts we had to back it up, wasn't going to be treated seriously. So I decided to jab away at the Mounties and show them a little disrespect, hoping that my bravado would inspire others. After the Brink's story in June, Superintendent Darren Campbell had described my work as "a fairy tale." Six months later, I decided to actually give him one.

As you may recall, during the interlude between the massacres Wortman had allegedly hidden overnight behind Brian MacDonald's welding shop next to the Diefenbunker in Debert. The RCMP later found various items strewn among the bushes: ammo packing, a metal holder and bracket, RCMP high brown boots, a Sam Browne belt and holster, a restraint control module, a municipal unit radar and antenna, and a coat hanger. But one thing caught my eye most of all: a pair of slippers.

Here is a condensed version of my fairy tale:

A PAIR OF NUKNUUKS,
AND ALL KINDS OF QUESTIONS

There are many mysteries and unknowns about what actually happened during the two Nova Scotia massacres—13 people killed at Portapique on April 18 and nine more murdered the next day well after the RCMP had been called, responded and knew that Gabriel Wortman was the killer.

One piece of evidence that has gone unnoticed has a Cinderella quality about it. It's a pair of Nuknuuk slippers. The question is: who do they fit?

Nuknuuks are Canadian-designed sheepskin-lined slippers that are a popular item at Costco. They sell for about $55 a pair, sometimes more. The pair in question was listed as a piece of evidence on page 87 of the contested Information to Obtain a warrant documents (ITOs), in which various news organizations have spent a king's ransom trying to find out what the police are hiding under the swimming pools of black ink. . . .

On page 87, the RCMP details items it found behind 123 Ventura Road, as it is erroneously described at that point in the ITOs. It's actually Venture Drive, and is corrected elsewhere, but it is still one of the surprising number of errors and misstatements found in the official police documents about the incident. The site is next to the Debert Diefenbunker, a tourist attraction that is a monument to the Cold War era. It was one of two nuclear fallout shelters constructed by then prime minister John Diefenbaker. . . . Apparently, Wortman was fascinated with the structure and the notion of crawling into a hole and riding out a conflagration. . . .

Then there is the footwear. That's really curious.

When he started in Portapique, what shoes was he wearing? It seems highly unlikely he initiated his killing spree wearing riding boots or Nuknuuks. Wortman got rid of the riding boots. After all, he would have looked a little silly going around murdering people in a nostalgic cavalry costume. If he had to run, those boots were not for anyone who needed to be fleet of foot.

Next is the pair of Nuknuuks. Why was he toting Nuknuuks around on his killing spree? Were they men's or women's Nuknuuks? What size? If they were his, was he planning a sleepover somewhere?

The presence of the Nuknuuks in the evidentiary materials raises all kinds of potentially disturbing questions. If they weren't his, who did they belong to?

Were they, perhaps, a present he may have given his common-law wife, Lisa Banfield, for their 19th anniversary together, which they had celebrated the night before? In the outdoor fireplace at Wortman's cottage at 200 Portapique Road, there was an empty Romika shoe box and a Winners bag. Did the RCMP really find Nuknuuks or are they using it as a catch-all for that kind of slipper, like all tissue paper is called Kleenex?

The fact that the Nuknuuks were linked to the replica police car takes us back to the presumed beginning of the story. Eight months later, exactly what happened has never been clearly articulated by either the RCMP or Banfield, who refuses through a lawyer to speak to the media. Most of what is publicly known is a series of unsupported conflicting rumours.

According to one of the earliest renditions, Banfield had gone to bed around 9 p.m., an incredibly early hour, one would think. She was reportedly awakened by an enraged Wortman and tied or restrained or handcuffed allegedly in the back of a decommissioned police car—not the replica police car—from which she reportedly escaped.

Banfield's story seems to be that she ran terrified into the woods, discarding her jacket so that searchers could find her. Did she throw away her footwear, too? She reportedly moved around the woods all night, ignoring calls of "this is the police" because, apparently, after 19 years of being together, she wasn't sure if the voice calling was Wortman's.

It is impossible to believe that Wortman would let her go barefoot outside on such a bitterly cold night, especially since the official documents have him warning her to be careful not to slip on the gasoline he was pouring on the floor of his cottage before he set it alight. . . .

Banfield arrived barefoot at Leon Joudrey's house and wasn't suffering from hypothermia or frostbite. As far as we know, all her toes and fingers are still attached.

If the Nuknuuks were Banfield's, that suggests she may have been in the replica police car that night. If not, where else could she have been?

The questions remain:

What size were those Nuknuuks? Were they men's or women's?

It is imperative that the RCMP or Banfield give us, for lack of a better word, a franker explanation for this . . . and everything else.

By now I was well past caring whether the mainstream media were interested in what I was doing. The skepticism and lack of interest from competitors came with the territory. I didn't realize it at the time, but a series of unlikely events and new sources would soon lead me a little closer to the truth.

◆

Jordan Bonaparte worked for TD Insurance by day, although during the COVID lockdown, he was on reduced hours—ten hours a week. The pandemic had turned him into a stay-at-home dad for his two children—ages eight and three. Six years earlier, the affable Bonaparte had taken up podcasting, narrowcasting from his basement. His first story was about his grandfather's alleged experience with a UFO. It was typical podcast fare, and he was good at it. He did two more shows on his grandfather and then began to branch out. As the blurb for his *Nighttime* podcast puts it: "Join us for true crime, mysteries and a celebration of Canada's weird and wonderful people, places, and events." Eventually, he veered off into a video component to the show and started drifting into subjects like weird guitars and ugly forks—and me.

Bonaparte had read the online version of my *Frank* story challenging the RCMP timeline, and he was intrigued. I had done his show once the previous summer after the Brink's story, and now he wanted me back. It was five days before Christmas, which was going to be a quiet one for us. No visitors thanks to COVID, which was good because Sharon was back on the long road to recovery from another surgery three weeks earlier.

Bonaparte and I taped the show using Zoom on a Sunday night beginning around 10:20 p.m. His style was to point the microphone and let his guests run, allowing me the time to explore and detail the obvious holes in the RCMP's narrative. The Mounties had pretended that they were on top of things, but I could show that they hadn't found the Tucks' bodies until 6 p.m. the next night. When Judy and Doug Myers were evacuated Sunday morning, bodies were still lying by the side of the road as they left the community. The RCMP said it had followed normal police procedures, but it obviously hadn't.

I sought help from Bonaparte's audience, but even as I asked for it, I was yawning and trying to stay awake. When it was over, around 11:30 p.m., I went to bed wondering why I continued to do this. It was the Christmas weekend. Who could possibly be listening to such an obscure channel at such a fringy hour?

As it would turn out, there was a Santa Claus, after all.

30

A SNORING HUSBAND
LEADS TO RCMP SECRETS

Laura Thomas Graham was a regular listener to Jordan Bonaparte's *Nighttime* podcast. A mother of two, she lived in Orangeville, Ontario, northwest of Toronto, almost 2,000 kilometres from my home office. As I was fighting to stay awake that Sunday night, December 20, Graham saw me and heard what I was saying. Something clicked.

Over the next ten days, she ruminated about a strange and disturbing event from eight months earlier and wondered whether it was connected to what I was talking about. Finally, on the morning of December 30, she sent me a message on Facebook: "Hey Paul, regarding Nova Scotia Rampage. Has anyone spoken to you about what they may have heard that evening through police scanner? I was listening that night from approx 11-2amish."

"Sure," I replied. "You didn't tape it did you?"

"No," she wrote. "Little embarrassed that I listen to be honest, but I have a husband that likes to snore LOL. Anyways, I typically keep it to local stuff, but that night I came across dispatch for that area, and it was an utter gong show."

Graham explained that when she turns on her scanner application, the busiest active communications are ranked. "On most nights, all the action is in the big US cities like Chicago or St. Louis," said Graham, who had grown up on the South Shore of Nova Scotia. "That night, Pictou Nova Scotia was at the top of the list. I thought I'd go to that channel and find out what was going on."

If she was looking for something to lull her to sleep, Graham was in for a shock. The story unfolding as she lay eavesdropping while her husband, Jon, snored the night away was chilling.

Graham continued: "So glad you are speaking up about this because what I did hear was not matching up with what I heard on the news etc. I was on around 11 pm till about 2 am. Just dispatch talking to officer in command. At first all I could figure out was dispatch was talking to the fellow who was hiding in the woods. And dispatch was relaying the info to command. He was basically saying he was hiding, he thought he was being chased and had found a spot by an old cabin to hide behind. He was begging for support, but command kept saying they weren't going in to help, and he had to come out by himself. That went on for hours and at one point it felt like the cops thought he was the person committing the crime. They spent a lot of time surrounding that area of the woods. Meanwhile calls were coming in of shots being fired and I specifically remember command saying ignore just probably propane tanks. It must have been around 2 a.m., there was an officer patrolling and he reported into command that he had found two bodies in an area, but he was not sure where he was. He was told to make note of the coordinates and keep moving on. They then brought everyone in to a meeting spot, I think it was a fire hall, to re-group. I turned off at that point as I was a little freaked out to what I was hearing. I woke my husband to tell him, he said I was dreaming and go back to sleep . . . I didn't go back onto dispatch for the rest of the weekend, and I was a little distressed. Anyhow I guess what I'm trying to say is I agree with your theories. . . . I believe it was not handled correctly. I don't think they realized what a big deal it was until it was too late. Thank you for speaking up for the families."

Throughout the day Graham and I went back and forth and agreed to chat again after New Year's Day. She didn't appear to be a crank.

"Now, my head is flipping inside out," Graham wrote. "All dispatch calls are recorded, will this not come out at some point? Can't this be public knowledge if there is any sort of inquiry?"

"It should be, but they are hiding it," I replied. "Wonder why?"

"At the end of the day, the families deserve to know the truth," Graham said. "I will make notes tonight. I only know what I heard. It's been nine months but will do my best if it's going to help the families get closure in any way. Take care."

Some might dismiss her story. She was recalling details of an incident eight months earlier. But her recollections seemed to parallel what had taken place in Portapique Beach that Saturday night and early Sunday morning. The person hiding in the woods was likely Clinton Ellison, who claimed that after finding his brother dead by the side of the road on Orchard Beach Drive he had fled into the woods and hid from a man with a flashlight. The dead bodies might have been those of Lisa McCully and Ellison's brother, Corrie. But the timing was way off the RCMP narrative, which held that members had rushed to the scene following the first call to 911, evacuated residents, saved the four children in McCully's basement and so on. Graham's story, if true, suggested a very different reality.

I had to find a way to prove what Graham thought she'd heard. Unlike in the United States, where 911 calls are considered public information, in Canada the privacy of individuals and institutions are given priority over public disclosure. As a journalist, I'd always found access-to-information programs all but useless for accessing 911 recordings, and I didn't have a clue how to find a record of the RCMP communications.

As Superintendent Campbell had mentioned in his first press conference, the RCMP's communications in Nova Scotia (like most police communications in Canada) are conducted on encrypted channels that are not possible to hear on a standard scanner. Old-fashioned analog channels typically used by fire departments and road crews are still accessible to the public. After I downloaded the app Graham had been using (called, of all things, Police Scanner), I tried to narrow down which channel she might have been listening to. The only one that made sense was the Pictou County Public Safety channel. Pictou was an hour's drive east of Portapique. Why would the RCMP be using an open channel from so far away?

One of the citizen investigators who had been working on the massacres from the beginning was Pete Stevens, whom I had never met in person. He was prolific in posting his evolving thoughts about the massacre online, as well as curating thousands of photographs and videos about the massacres. He was the one who had taken my appearances on *The Rick Howe Show* and elsewhere, set them to a driving video and published and archived them on YouTube and elsewhere.

"Are police audiotapes archived somewhere?" I asked Stevens.

It took him twenty minutes to find out.

"They are stored on Broadcastify," Stevens said.

My world was getting bigger every day. I bought a subscription to Broadcastify, a US-based website that rebroadcasts and archives analog 911 calls. Chad Jones, Stevens and I immediately downloaded the recordings and individually began listening to them, making notes and transcribing the important bits. It was a miracle. Graham's recall was dead-on. I could now hear for myself what had been etched into her memory. I wrote three different stories about the recordings, each touching on a different critical issue.

The first was that the tapes revealed the name of the previously unknown Mountie who had been placed in charge of the entire operation as the critical incident commander.

PORTAPIQUE TAPES: 'ALL MEMBERS STAND BY, ALLOW RISK MANAGER TO DISPATCH'
By Paul Palango

The incident commander who was put in charge of the RCMP operation at Portapique Beach in the early morning hours of April 19 was a staff sergeant who for the past several years has been Nova Scotia's head of traffic services, *Frank* magazine has learned.

It was after midnight when Staff-Sgt. Jeffrey West took over the operation at the command centre which had been set up at Great Village fire hall around 10:30 p.m. the night before. Great Village is about a seven minute or so drive east of Portapique Beach Road. The information is contained in a recording of the switchover obtained by *Frank* this week.

Staff-Sgt. West's first announcement that he was now in command went out on an encrypted radio channel, but the RCMP was having problems with reception on those channels that night.

Steve Halliday, another staff sergeant at the scene, radioed to West: "Can you re-announce your command? You were digital. No one copied."

West then replied on an analog channel, known as Pictou County Public Safety, that the Mounties began using about 30 minutes earlier.

"All units on Portapique call. Staff sergeant Jeff West on scene at the Great Village fire hall and I'm taking over command and control of this matter at this time. Staff sergeant West on scene and is now in control of this matter."

The message still didn't get through to everyone, including the Emergency Response Team (ERT) leader known as Hotel One, who asked West, now using the moniker Oscar Charlie:

"Oscar Charlie . . . have you taken control of this yet?"

"I *am* in control," West said, cockily emphasizing the "am," somewhat reminiscent of a similar infamous assertion from U.S. Secretary of State Alexander Haig after President Ronald Reagan was shot in March of 1981.

"Do you have a better radio there?" West was asked. "You are in and out."

By the time West was appointed, it is believed that gunman Gabriel Wortman had long been gone from the scene. . . .

It is not known who appointed West as the incident commander. He was not the only staff sergeant at the scene. Others included Addie MacCallum from Pictou, Al Carroll and Brian Rehill from Bible Hill, Andy O'Brien, who was a traffic specialist like West, as well as another one from New Minas, name unknown, who arrived

a few hours before dawn. The order likely came from the top of
the force from either Assistant Commissioner Lee Bergerman,
Chief Superintendent Chris Leather or Superintendent Darren
Campbell.

According to those at the scene, Campbell was the only "white
shirt" or commissioned officer to go to the scene, which he did on
the morning of April 19. Leather is the CROPs officer for Nova
Scotia, which means he is in charge of all criminal operations. He
has been effectively mute since April 19, when he and Bergerman
held a press conference to attempt to explain what had happened.
As for Bergerman, she has largely remained out of sight, although
she did make an appearance on Remembrance Day, placing a
wreath at Grand Parade in Halifax. She was accompanied that day
by one other Mountie dressed in red serge—Staff-Sgt. West.

That a long-time traffic cop should be tasked with running
what would turn out to become one of the biggest criminal cases in
Canadian history comes as no surprise to many critics both inside
and out of the force. . . .

But one former RCMP executive, who has been actively monitoring the matter, is horrified by what he's hearing. . . .

"That's not how anyone would expect such a major investigation to be handled. If this was in a major city in Ontario, an experienced crack investigative squad with experienced detectives would
be in charge. From what I've seen in this case, they have corporals
acting as commanders and doing it badly. Where were the white
shirts? How are they earning their keep?" . . .

The ex-Mountie's mention of "corporals" refers to earlier stories
in the *Halifax Examiner* and *Frank* about the first minutes of the
Portapique investigation.

The third or fourth officer to arrive at the scene was Corporal
Natasha Jamieson. For many years she was the RCMP's co-ordinator
for human trafficking investigations. In that capacity she did
numerous public relations stints for the force and was the public
face when charges were laid in human trafficking cases. Recently,
she was assigned to the Millbrook First Nations detachment.

Jamieson is a card-carrying member of the Mi'kmaq nation, according to published entries on her Facebook page.

One of the critical and pressing issues at the time Corporal Jamieson arrived on the scene was that four children were hiding in the basement of Lisa McCully's house at 135 Orchard Beach Drive. . . . They called 911 and were being kept on the line. That would last for two hours as the RCMP dithered.

At the front lines near the top of Portapique Beach Road Jamieson refused to allow any Mounties to attempt a rescue of the children. One of them was Constable Jeff Stevens, a tactical officer from Cole Harbour.

"If you go down that road, it will be your last shift in the RCMP," officers familiar with what happened quoted Jamieson as saying.

Eventually, Sergeant Dave Lilly appeared. He overrode the orders, put together a squad and they went by foot, a considerable walk, down to 135 Orchard Beach Drive, where they rescued the children and took them to the hospital in Truro.

The Risk Manager

To be fair to Corporal Jamieson, there was another important influence on how the RCMP response played out—the risk manager.

In light of previous high-profile disasters in which Mounties were killed in Mayerthorpe, Alberta and Moncton, the RCMP is extremely cautious about exposing its members to danger. The force was fined $540,000 for work code violations after it failed to implement recommendations made after Mayerthorpe which were found to have led to the murder of three Mounties at Moncton.

The first risk manager at Portapique appeared to be Staff Sergeant Brian Rehill from the Bible Hill detachment.

What played out on the recordings *Frank* has acquired was a virtual tug of war between the troops in the field, the incident commander and the risk manager.

At one point in the early morning hours, officer Nicholas Dorrington volunteered to check out something with two other officers, when an unidentified voice from the command centre interjected.

"All members stand by, allow the risk manager to dispatch. Go ahead, please. Risk manager go ahead. We're on scene at Great Village firehall . . . (breaks up) . . . control centre . . . (breaks up).

A voice interjects: "You're completely visible whoever is speaking to me."

That was a warning from the field that whoever was speaking should be careful because they were speaking on a channel that could be monitored by scanners.

"Staff Rehill," the risk manager said, identifying himself, "Don't offer up services until risk manager dispatches them."

Now, the world can begin to understand some of what happened that night and early morning in Portapique.

My second story focused on what time the RCMP found the bodies of Corrie Ellison and Lisa McCully. The Mounties had said they initially went down the road and discovered dead bodies somewhere between 10:26 p.m., when the first officers arrived, and midnight at the latest, since the Mounties had gone along with the story revealed in McCully's obituary that the four children in her basement had spent just two hours there. The Pictou recordings put the lie to that timeline:

An exchange between an Emergency Response Team officer and the RCMP incident commander in Portapique is one of several chilling moments to come across an open analog communications channel in the overnight hours of April 18 and 19.

"Oscar Charlie, Hotel One . . . We've just stopped here on the road, ah, we're going to do a quick vitals on this deceased person on the side of the road just to make sure he's deceased and not still alive."

It was more than four and a half hours after the RCMP received the first call that something was amiss in Portapique. The ERT officer, going by the call sign Hotel One, is addressing Staff-Sgt. Jeff

West (Oscar Charlie), the long-time head of traffic services for the RCMP in N.S., who was in command on the scene.

"Yah, confirmed, deceased," the Mountie said of Corrie Ellison, 34 seconds later.

"What road was that on, Jim?" a Mountie believed to be West asked.

Jim didn't know. There are only three main roads in the survey and a couple of side roads, but the Mounties were having extreme difficulty finding their way throughout the night. Since he couldn't describe where the body was, the Mountie marked it with GPS coordinates.

"N 45.397153," Jim said. "W 063.703527."

The Mountie then walked across the road to where Lisa McCully's body was lying on the front lawn. In earlier conversations the ERT members acknowledged that the first call to 911 came from "the teacher's house" which they were now standing in front of.

At 3:04 a.m., the Mountie reported to control: "Going to do a second vital on a second body out by the fence . . . over by the other body."

"Okay," the supervisor said. "Oscar Charlie copy."

Thirty-six seconds later, the Mountie announced the coordinates "for the second body."

A little over an hour earlier, at 1:50 a.m., another Mountie did an initial, quick examination of a body believed to be Corrie Ellison's.

"Hotel One to risk manager.

"Go Hotel One," said risk manager Staff Sgt. Brian Rehill, who was located at the makeshift command centre at the Great Village firehall, about a seven minute drive away.

"The father of these two (garbled) . . . they approached (garbled) to check out the fire. . . . He shot one of them in the head. It's a 40-calibre Smith and Wesson."

The Mounties did not tape off the scene or protect it any other way. Hours later, neighbour Judy Myers drove by the bodies, now covered by a yellow tarp, on her way out of Portapique that Sunday morning.

My final story about the tapes dealt with the four children trapped in the basement of Lisa McCully's house. Her obituary had stated that the children were on the line with the Mounties for two hours before they were rescued. The tapes showed it was *three* hours. Not only that, but the RCMP rescued criminal Peter Griffon and his family between 11:30 p.m. and midnight, more than an hour before they saved the children. Here is a condensed version of the story:

SAVE THE KIDS OR SAVE THE EX-CON?
By Paul Palango

On that terrible night in Portapique, the RCMP faced what on the surface, at least, seemed like a no-brainer of a situation: rescue four children hiding in a basement after their parents had been murdered by Gabriel Wortman, or save a convicted drug trafficker with ties to a Mexican drug cartel and his parents. Save the kids or save the con. An easy choice, you'd think.

Yet, the RCMP chose to evacuate convicted drug trafficker Peter Griffon and his parents, Alan and Joanne Griffon, an hour or so before attending to the children. The cavalry showed up at the Griffon house at 4 Faris Lane sometime around midnight.

Meanwhile, since 10:01 p.m. on April 18, four terrified children, two aged 12 and two aged 10, had been on the line with a 911 operator for about two hours, hunkered in the basement of slain schoolteacher Lisa McCully's house at 135 Orchard Beach Drive. Some half a kilometre away from the Griffon residence, as the crow flies.

Two of the boys were the children of Greg and Jamie Blair. A boy and a girl were McCully's children. The Blair children had taken their dead father's cell phone from his pocket, run over to the McCully house and woke the children there. Outside, McCully was already lying dead on the front lawn.

The Mounties left the children there until around 1 a.m., a total of three hours, according to RCMP communications recordings obtained recently by *Frank* magazine.

What does it mean, that the RCMP chose to save a relatively recent parolee over four frightened children?

The Portapique Comms do not provide a complete record of what the RCMP was doing that night because some officers were using encrypted channels, cell phones or both. However, the recordings, combined with information already on the public record and information from new witnesses, raise major questions, perhaps none more serious than why the RCMP was so invested in protecting the Griffons.

Who evacuated the Griffons, and why?

Alan and Joanne Griffon were friends with Wortman and his common-law wife, Lisa Banfield. They had moved in 15 years earlier.

In the RCMP's unredacted documents, Alan Griffon reported seeing Wortman's cottage at 200 Portapique Beach Road on fire that Saturday night. He said he called 911 at 9:15 p.m.

Peter Griffon saw Wortman's warehouse at 136 Orchard Beach Drive on fire around the same time. In the same documents, the RCMP rebut the Griffons' version of events, stating that the call to 911 was at 10:39 p.m.

The exact time when Wortman started the fires has never been clear.

Great Village Fire Chief Larry Kinsman said in a recent interview that he was called by Bass River Fire Chief Alfred Grue sometime after 10 p.m. but before 10:30 p.m. and told about a number of fires at Portapique. He said the RCMP had already ordered the Bass River department to stand by. Kinsman said he was told that Great Village should be ready but not respond.

"A few minutes after I hung up with Grue, the RCMP called and said they wanted to use the hall as a command centre," Kinsman said in the interview.

Alan and Peter Griffon provided two other important time references.

On page 65 of the unredacted ITOs, Alan Griffon is quoted as saying: "Around 23:15 he noted that the house across from his was not on fire and approximately 15 minutes later a set of headlights came into his yard. Alan Griffon heard knocking and banging on his door and the person was there for a solid five minutes. The person did not yell out anything and was knocking on the door and ringing the doorbell."

Who was knocking at the Griffons' door? Was it Wortman? Lisa Banfield? Or was someone else in the neighbourhood who hasn't been identified?

Even more curious is the statement that the Griffons wouldn't answer the door. We can only speculate, because the Griffons are refusing to talk to media, but why wouldn't they come to the door? If it was because they were frightened, what did they know?

Alan Griffon also stated in the ITOs that "around midnight they [Alan, Joanne and Peter] were evacuated from their house by the RCMP and they left the area."

Who in the RCMP rescued them?

Over the past nine months, it has been made abundantly clear and repeatedly reported that the first responders to Portapique were held in check at the intersection of Portapique Beach Road and Highway 2. The RCMP has never disputed this.

It has also been made abundantly clear and repeatedly reported that the first Emergency Response Team members did not arrive until well after midnight.

We also know that four children hid in the McCully basement while on the line with a 911 operator for what was initially described as two hours. (The Portapique Comms confirm that the children were left in place for *three* hours or more.)

The RCMP had a choice. Some of its officers were chomping at the bit to rescue the children but were being held back, yet the Griffons were rescued before them? It's precisely the opposite of what 99.9 percent of police officers would normally do in such a situation.

Why were the Griffons such a priority?

Orchard Beach Drive

It appears that all regular members, the men and women in marked patrol cars, were kept on the outside of the crime scenes south of Highway 2. Many of them were manning road blocks west of Portapique all the way to Bass River, a distance of about eight kilometres. Wortman escaped to the east along Highway 2.

The only time any of the Mounties appeared to venture into the neighbourhood was after 1 a.m. when a foray was finally mounted to rescue the four children at 135 Orchard Beach Drive. At that time the bodies of the Blairs, McCully and Corrie Ellison were likely discovered by Mounties, but apparently from a distance.

The tight control by commanding officers on the RCMP members on the ground could be heard in the following seemingly innocuous transmission.

Constable Stuart Beselt was reported to be the first officer to arrive at the scene that night at 10:26 p.m. He met neighbour Andrew MacDonald, who was trying to escape from Gabriel Wortman, who had just fired two shots at him and his wife. Around 1 a.m., Beselt went on the rescue mission of the children, headed by Sgt. Dave Lilly.

After the children were evacuated from Lisa McCully's house in a Tactical Armoured Vehicle (TAV), Beselt and a few others were left behind to "hunker down" on the dark and freezing-cold night.

At 1:50 a.m. Beselt radioed the incident commander, likely Staff-Sgt. Jeff West: "Looking to see if we can walk out, if it's going to be a lot longer."

Eventually a TAV was sent to pick up the Mounties after 2 a.m.

Clinton Ellison was hiding in the woods 150 metres or so to the south of McCully's property. The Mounties made no attempt to allow the members already near him to go find him. They didn't get to him for another 40 minutes, for reasons that are unclear.

The Mounties had finally inserted themselves into the neighbourhood but were ordered to immediately retreat. For reasons that are likewise unclear. Armed with Colt C8 rifles—an AR-15-like semi-automatic weapon—they were told to do nothing but defend themselves, if need be.

"That's an unnatural thing for the police to do," said one expert police observer who reviewed the tapes.

"They had established a beachhead. They appear to have found multiple victims. There were more of them than the killer. There were ERT units there to lead the charge. But then they were told to retreat and not investigate . . . Something's missing in the story."

Throughout all this, there appears to be no attempt to do anything proactive on Orchard Beach Drive even after daylight arrived.

The RCMP has stated in the past that much of its time was devoted to going house to house "clearing" the area. There was no evidence of such action on the tapes. Residents in the neighbourhood say the RCMP did nothing of the kind.

That Saturday night and well into the day on Sunday, the RCMP seemed obsessed with keeping regular members away from nine crime scenes at Portapique Beach, even after the threat had been neutralized.

Nobody bothered to do a wellness check on the Tucks, for one small example, until seven hours after Gabriel Wortman's rampage was finally brought to an end in Enfield. Why?

And on the previous night, why was the safety of three grown adults—an ex-con among them—prioritized over that of four scared pre-teen children?

With the Pictou recordings I had now uncovered key clues, facts, names and more insights about what had actually taken place in the hours immediately after the Portapique Beach massacre. Andrew Douglas couldn't wait to publish it in *Frank*, but before we did, I alerted all the major television news departments, as well as a number of newspapers, about the existence of the recordings. I hoped they would produce their own stories. I didn't want to see recordings disappear the moment the Mounties saw what we had.

The information contained on the Pictou recordings appeared to prove that one of two things had happened that night as regards the RCMP response: there was either Olympic-calibre incompetence or a clumsy, improvised cover-up. Established procedures and protocols were violated at every turn.

Once again, our stories and the tapes landed with a thud in local and national newsrooms. Global TV made use of the recordings but didn't have the courtesy to acknowledge how they'd gotten them, other than to say they had come from another reporter covering the story.

The RCMP was silent. It had either forgotten that the calls were on an open channel or didn't think anyone would find the recordings. In fact, had someone monitored the Pictou County Public Safety channel that night between 10 p.m. and midnight, they would have heard a lot of dead air. It appears that the RCMP used only encrypted channels at first and then, for some unknown reason, partially switched over to the old analog channel for a couple of hours. They were still using at least a half dozen other encrypted channels and cellphones.

The RCMP had made a point of not putting any names on the public record. I was doing the opposite. By reporting who was there and what they might had been doing, I was intentionally making it difficult for anyone at the receiving end of a public inquiry or a civil or criminal action to hide behind intransigence, privacy laws or any other phony shield.

A final twist in this episode came not from the mainstream media, the RCMP or their enablers, but from the alternative blogosphere. After I released the communications recordings to everyone, "Seamus Gorman" (actual name Paul Ragona) began speculating on *Little Grey Cells* that I had made the entire story up. Accusing me of inventing Graham, whose name I had not revealed as per her wishes at the time, Gorman told his followers that the story I described smelled like an RCMP misdirection campaign. Some of his listeners took the bait and suggested that I was secretly in league with the RCMP—a scenario that, I'm certain, would shock the Mounties.

So on one side the mainstream and alternative media were largely ignoring us or demeaning us as amateurs and conspiracy theorists, while on the other side the conspiracy theorists were accusing us of working with the police. It was beyond crazy.

31

SPRING HAS SPRUNG AND A ROBIN IS CAUGHT—A BUTCHER, TOO

As the one-year anniversary of the massacres approached in April 2021, it was abundantly clear to a growing number of people that a massive cover-up was under way, one that tested the natural laws of conspiratorial physics. Chad Jones and I were determined to expose more weak spots in the official narrative, which meant re-examining facts and incidents, and reinterviewing people who had seen or heard things that might have been too quickly dismissed by other media.

One of the people we revisited was Nathan Staples. As you may recall, Staples was purported to be on Wortman's "hit list," which the RCMP later admitted didn't exist. Staples had competed against Wortman at a government auction, where he bid him up on an RCMP Zodiac boat. On the night of the shootings, Staples and his wife, Lavona, were in what he called "the she shed," a glass-walled greenhouse/party centre next to the garage at the top of their driveway. Their home is about a fifteen-minute drive east of Portapique. They were entertaining themselves with a karaoke machine and were entirely unaware of what was happening, though at one point Staples noticed a long procession of police cars racing west along Highway 2 toward Great Village.

"We saw police car after police car go by," he said. "I lost count at thirty-five or so."

At 12:35 a.m., Staples said, he was fiddling with a power cord or "messing with the speaker" when he heard Lavona trying to get his attention over the music.

"Nathan. Nathan," she said.

"She gives me, like, the death stare," Staples said. "And I turned around and looked and here's this RCMP guy in brown. He didn't have his helmet on, but he had his headset on. He had the big C8 carbine. He asked me my full name. I said: 'Nathan Luke Staples.' He didn't ask me for ID."

The Mountie did ask Staples if the decommissioned police car in his yard had moved that night. Staples told him he hadn't moved it.

"And you're here by yourself?" the Mountie asked.

"Yes," Staples said.

"There's no one else on your property?"

"No."

"There's five more of us here on the ground," the Mountie said. "You won't see us or hear us, but we're here."

"Then he turned and walked away. I didn't see his vehicle. He disappeared as quick as he came in."

As described in one of my *Frank* stories, what happened next smacked of significance.

Two days later, on April 21, Staples had another RCMP visitor. He was working in his garage. One of his friends was there, as well. It was around 5 p.m.

"I heard scuffling coming up the driveway and I turned around and there was this heavyset guy in a suit," Staples said.

"He opened the inside of his jacket and showed me his gun in a holster. He told me he was from the RCMP and that his name was Sgt. Bill Raaymakers.

"He came to apologize to me for the ERT guy scaring me," Staples recalled. "He told me that 'the wife'—he didn't name her by name—had told the Mounties about people that Wortman didn't like. I don't know why he wouldn't like me. It might be because of what happened at [the] government auction." . . .

Staples described Raaymakers as being embarrassed and possibly distressed about what the RCMP had done at Portapique.

"He told me that the RCMP cars responding to Portapique passed Wortman going the other way and didn't know it at the time," Staples said.

"He handed me his business card and said: 'This is good for eight more days and then I am out of here.'"

Raaymakers then left the property and Staples never heard anything else from him. When he retired, the lead investigator's job was assigned to Corporal Gerard Rose-Berthiaume from Pictou.

Raaymakers's interaction with Staples left behind dozens of questions which have not been answered. Foremost among them: if Lisa Banfield didn't have any communication with police until she emerged from the woods at 6:30 a.m. on April 19, why is it that the Emergency Response Team paid Staples a visit six hours earlier?

It should also be said that Raaymakers's description of Wortman's escape from Portapique makes more sense than those in the ever-changing official RCMP versions of events. In the past it has said that Wortman left the area by 10:35 through Brown Loop, a dirt road east of Portapique Beach Road. Later, it changed that to 10:45. Lately, it has suggested that Wortman didn't leave then, either, but at another time and by another route.

Frank magazine has identified a witness who was in Brown Loop from 10:38 p.m. on and who did not see any vehicle come up the hidden laneway next to a blueberry field, which was Wortman's supposed route of escape. That witness has asked not to be identified at this time but has phone records proving his story.

All this raises more serious questions about what was actually going on that night.

The story didn't end there for Staples. A few days later, two more Mounties came to see him. One wasn't identified to him, but the other was Sergeant Angela Hawryluk. I wrote in *Frank*:

> In her 28 years with the RCMP Hawryluk spent much of her time in federal operations involving outlaw bikers, drugs and confidential informants. In June 2019, as the RCMP in the Maritimes narrowed its focus even more on those areas, Hawryluk was transferred to the Legal Applications Support Team in Halifax.
>
> After Wortman's rampage, Hawryluk was the point person who compiled statements and swore an affidavit in support of the ITOs filed with the court to obtain search warrants. Those documents have been heavily redacted, and the media has been forced to fight in court—inch by inch—to find out what is hidden under the black ink.
>
> Hawryluk has previously stated that she didn't expect the contents of the documents to ever see the light of day.
>
> "I was shocked that she was the [person who swore the affidavit]," said a law enforcement official familiar with Hawryluk over the years.
>
> "Her background in bikers and CIs makes me really suspicious about what is going on."
>
> Nathan Staples also was a little flummoxed by both Hawryluk's visit and her attitude while she was there.
>
> "I don't know why she was the one who came to see me," Staples said.
>
> "To my way of thinking, she's way up there. With all that was going on that week you'd think she'd have more to do than come all the way out here."
>
> Staples said the entire conversation was not what he would expect from police investigators in that situation. He is no virgin in this territory. He has two relatives who are Mounties.
>
> He said Hawryluk's unnamed assistant, whom he described as "her finger puppet," was sarcastic and largely disbelieving of

anything Staples had to say. At a number of points, he said, Hawryluk felt compelled to signal to her fellow Mountie to "zip it up," as Staples put it.

"When I told her what Raaymakers said," Staples told me, "she said: 'He's old. He's retired. There was probably some miscommunication there.'"

Staples said Hawryluk listened to him for a while and then told her assistant that they wouldn't even bother filing a report about their interview.

"Let's go. There's no meat and gravy here," Staples quoted her as saying as she left, not even leaving her business card behind.

"It really made me mad," Staples said. "I really don't trust the Mounties, now."

This really smelled. I tried to contact Raaymakers, but to no avail. For those aficionados, as it were, of RCMP and government cover-ups from the past, Staples's tale provided abundant clues pointing to something untoward going on. There was a ready consensus among my law enforcement sources that the appointment of Sergeant Raaymakers to head the investigation was a sure sign that the RCMP was not prepared to conduct a serious investigation.

"Appointing someone who has a week left before retiring is an old trick," said one former RCMP deputy commissioner. "He opens the file and then leaves a few days later. There is no continuity in the case, and that is by design. That's really disturbing. Then they put a lowly corporal in charge of it all. Where are all the white shirts in this?"

◆

Andrew Douglas asked me to write a one-year-after piece for *Frank*. I was swamped by then writing this book and conducting the investigation, working the two mediums in tandem with appearances on the *Nighttime* podcast to drive the story forward and find new evidence. It had all begun to mesh into a formidable information-gathering-and-distribution machine.

I told Andrew that I didn't want to do the typical heart-wrenching anniversary piece, but one that sketched out the most important findings from the past year to clearly show the cover-up in progress. My preamble summed up what I had to say:

One year after Gabriel Wortman's murder sprees on April 18/19, thousands of unanswered questions about what really happened then and afterward continue to linger.

The most transparent thing about the RCMP investigation is its lack of transparency.

What did the RCMP do and not do before, during and after the rampage that left 22 innocent people dead, scattered across mainland Nova Scotia?

The RCMP, the Crown and the provincial and federal governments have sown so much confusion it is all but impossible for casual observers and, sadly, the majority of professional journalists, to see the forest for all the trees.

From the earliest days, the powers that be have tried to reduce this entire matter down to a domestic violence situation gone horribly wrong. If that was indeed the case, why is it that a year later we are still searching for basic information?

Why have the police, Crown and government thrown so many obstacles in the path of clarity? Wouldn't it have been easier and more helpful to just lay everything out on the table?

By any measure this is a massive and complicated subject. I am going to break it down into some of its more easily digestible components.

The "digestible components" were labelled: Two Separate Incidents: The First Massacre, The Second Massacre; The Initial Response and Misinformation; Shifting Timelines; Why Were the Griffons Evacuated First?; Chasing Flashlights; The Encrypted Police Communications vs. the Analog Ones; The Serious Incident Response Team; SIRT: The Incident at Onslow Belmont Fire Hall; Police in Private Vehicles; SIRT: The Killing of Wortman; Did Wortman Have a Police Radio?;

Lisa Banfield; The Destruction of Evidence; The Disappearing Faces; The Public Inquiry; and finally A Plea to Potential Deep Throats.

There might not have been many people reading and listening to what I was writing and saying, but those who were included key players in every corner of the story, and their numbers were growing.

My appeal to potential Deep Throats began by reminding any readers in the force that new members swear an oath to the RCMP, not to the country it is meant to protect, and continued from there:

> I would ask you to take a look at yourself in the mirror. I want you to ask yourself this: "Am I a Canadian first or a Mountie first?"
>
> If you are a Canadian first, I have a proposition for you. I know there's the pension and the gold-plated benefits at risk, but 22 people were murdered that weekend. Thirteen of them died at Portapique Beach while the Mounties dithered in their response. We don't really know yet, and may never know, how many of them might have been saved by prompt, courageous police officers doing what police normally do—preserving life.
>
> On April 19, nine more innocent people were murdered, including Constable Heidi Stevenson. Those deaths are due to what appears to be some mixture of incompetence, reckless behaviour or even criminal negligence by the RCMP.
>
> Drop a dime on us or any other reporter and tell them what really happened. Name names. Show us documents. Point us in the right direction.
>
> That's what a great Canadian would do.

◆

In the year since she had witnessed the two Mounties' wild and crazy shoot-up of the Onslow Belmont fire hall from her kitchen window, Sharon McLellan had continued to wonder how the incident would be handled by police watchdogs.

SIRT director Felix Cacchione, former judge of hit-man Dany Kane fame, had already tendered an official report in which he found that the Mounties had done nothing wrong at the fire hall. SIRT findings are final and cannot be appealed. I pointed out in my anniversary piece that Cacchione "must have got lost in the subject matter because he missed several obvious points." I elaborated on that sentiment in my report on the SIRT findings:

1. There was not a word in Cacchione's report about Wortman being in the immediate area. He was caught on camera passing by fourteen minutes earlier. The real Mountie's vehicle and Wortman's were in the same frame. Did Wortman do something to trick the Mounties into firing on one of their own? Did he have a radio?

2. The two Mounties who shot up the fire hall said they thought the other Mountie, who was dressed in a safety vest, resembled Wortman and that he didn't obey their commands. Did they not notice that the Mountie's cruiser was parked behind three safety cones? Did they think a spree killer on the run would do that?

3. One of the shooters was Constable Terry Brown. He was also involved that day with interviewing Lisa Banfield. There were 1,000 Mounties in Nova Scotia, so why was Brown multi-tasking that day? On the surface, at least, it appears that the RCMP may have been limiting knowledge about what was really going on to a tight circle. That is suspicious.

4. The Mounties fired their guns, did a rudimentary check to see if anyone was injured and then raced from the scene without identifying themselves, none of which is proper RCMP procedure.

If Cacchione and the RCMP hoped they could bury what had really happened at the fire hall, their bold misdescription of events and their attempts to micromanage the obvious cover-up resulted in unintended consequences.

As you will recall, when the unmarked police car pulled up at the Onslow Belmont fire hall back on April 19, 2020, and the officers opened fire, there were more witnesses than Sharon McLellan. There was also the driver of a Toyota Prius, who drove up to the officers and then around them. He was followed a few seconds later by someone in a half-ton pickup truck.

The Prius driver was Jerome Breau, a fifty-one-year-old machinist at Pratt & Whitney at Halifax Stanfield International Airport. After reading Cacchione's findings, Breau approached Deputy Chief Darrell Currie at the fire hall, who contacted me.

Chad Jones and I soon met with Breau and retraced his trip that day from his home in the community of Valley to the Onslow Belmont fire hall and back. What he saw and had to say was illuminating, to say the least.

"I didn't want to say anything before because of what happened to all the families. I didn't want to irritate anyone," Breau said, explaining what changed his mind. "After I read the SIRT report, I couldn't believe what they said. What was particularly hard for me to digest is him saying that nobody else would have acted differently in this kind of situation. I am not trained as an RCMP officer, and I'm not trained with weaponry. I am not trained about the criminal mind. The police are supposed to have the upper hand when dealing with a difficult situation. . . . That didn't happen."

Breau was a typical Nova Scotian that Sunday morning. Wortman was killing people, and the RCMP was tweeting out vague messages about what was going on. Breau didn't use Twitter, and the news reports weren't much more enlightening. He went for a drive.

As I then described in *Frank*:

We know from surveillance cameras capturing Breau's movements that he met [a real] police car on Highway 2 at about 10:17 a.m. He had just missed Wortman, who had taken that very route and at that moment was actually driving through Truro. He had been captured driving on the Esplanade at 10:16 a.m., passing a pair of unaware strangers walking on the sidewalk to his right. Wortman headed south from that point and soon killed his last three victims: RCMP Constable Heidi Stevenson, Good Samaritan Joey Webber and fellow denturist Gina Goulet.

Breau drove for seven more kilometres west on Highway 2. At that point was a large building on his left: McLellan Machine Shop. On his right was the Onslow Belmont firehall, which was being used at that point as an emergency shelter for three people evacuated from Portapique the night before, including Corrie Ellison's father, Richard. Up ahead, Breau noticed something unusual.

"I saw this unmarked Ford Taurus come over the crest of the hill. When it got about 800 feet in front of me, it went over the centre line and took about 40 per cent of my lane and came to a stop," Breau said.

Thinking it was a traffic stop, Breau eased his car up to near where the police car was stopped. He rolled down the window, expecting it was a routine traffic stop.

"The two guys got out of the car and were dressed in dark SWAT gear," Breau said. "They both put their rifles on top of the door and were looking through their scopes."

He thought the two Mounties were aiming their weapons at him.

"I knew that they were looking for a bald guy like me, but I was driving a Prius. I knew that was not what they were looking for," he said. "I put my hands up, but then I realized that they were looking past me into the firehall parking lot. I could see an RCMP car there and someone standing near the car."

Breau said the two Mounties then retreated briefly behind the car, where they seemed to be conferring, perhaps on the radio with someone. Breau had his window down, expecting to be questioned by the police. He couldn't hear what they were saying, but more importantly, he didn't hear them shouting out any commands or, for that matter, anything else. He was about to try to edge by the police car and get out of harm's way, when one of the Mounties waved him to pass by and the two of them began running toward the firehall.

"While they were running, they started firing their guns," Breau said. "One guy fired three times while he was running and then, I think, the other one fired three times. I was close enough that I could feel the percussion from the guns in the car. No wonder they missed everything because they were running and shooting at the same time." . . .

Breau continued on his way . . . and decided to head home via Highway 104. With all the turmoil going on, he didn't see a Mountie vehicle until he came to an emergency vehicle turnaround lane just west of Exit 15, the only exit to Truro, Halifax and the South Shore. . . .

"I said to one of the cops, 'Hey, look, there a shootout at the firehall," Breau recalled. "I'm basically talking right through him. He's listening to me but he's not really listening. Hey, buddy, there's a shooting at the firehall. They were all strung out. I got the sense they didn't know what was going on and they were very disorganized. Then I heard on his radio a message: 'He's in a grey Mazda.' They all got in their cars and were making U-turns and headed to the ramp toward Halifax."

Breau wasn't sure what he had seen or if it was even all that import-ant in the grander scheme of things, but that night he was contacted by an investigator for SIRT who had obviously been told by one of the Mounties about his presence at the scene. A former police officer working as a SIRT investigator visited him the next day at work.

"He immediately started downplaying the situation. He asked me where I was driving, how many shots, that sort of thing. I'd say he spent maybe fifteen minutes with me, including all the chit-chat in between. He wrote some things down. It was all very brief. Pretty non-chalant."

Breau said the SIRT investigator indicated that there wasn't much of anything special in what he had witnessed: 'Yeah, that's pretty well what everybody saw.'"

Soon afterwards, another Mountie investigator from British Columbia showed up and invited Breau to the Bible Hill detachment office. This Mountie was from the Hazardous Occurrence Investigation Team.

"It seemed to me that they were more like damage-control people," Breau remembered. "They were asking me about my mental health. They asked about where the officers' hands were that day and questions like: 'Did you hear them speak?' They were adamant about whether I heard them screaming orders (to those in the fire hall parking lot), but I told them I had my window down and they didn't scream nothing. They were all but insinuating that these two guys had screamed 'Stop' to the other guys at the fire hall."

With Breau idling in his all-but-silent Prius hybrid with the window open and surrounded by only the tiny country village early on a Sunday morning, he'd surely have heard two officers right outside his car yelling orders at a suspected mass murderer several dozen metres away.

Next came an investigator working for a law office. Where they got Breau's name from was unknown. This investigator was a former Mountie—a common practice. Other investigators working for lawyers involved in the civil action were former police officers, many of them Mounties, including one who had spent thirty-nine years in the RCMP. It's modern legal thinking at its worst, and there are a number of problems associated with it. Ex-police involved in an investigation of their former colleagues or associates are all too often protective—an obvious conflict that is usually ignored. The perception among litigators and in the justice system is that the only good investigators are police and ex-police, which is not necessarily true. As I've reported in previous books, there are investigators in a variety of fields, from tax to insurance to journalism, who are equally as thorough. In some ways they are even better, as former police officers tend to see the world through a single lens: what evidence will go undisputed in court. This attitude sometimes creates a closed-minded approach to investigations. At Onslow Belmont, much of this came into play.

"That investigator was telling me that it appeared that the police officer who was being shot at had fired back at the two officers and had hit the LED sign," Breau said.

That didn't happen. Constable Dave Gagnon didn't fire a shot. He got out of his cruiser and had his hands in the air while hiding behind the car. Having been shot at by his fellow RCMP members, Gagnon never recovered from the event and has apparently left the force.

The efforts by the RCMP and the investigators from SIRT, the supposedly independent police watchdog agency, seemed to have one goal in mind—to find a way to discredit or dismiss witnesses or convince them that what they'd seen was all perfectly reasonable under the circumstances.

Breau wasn't the only new witness, as it turned out. While Jones and I were at the fire hall, another one emerged: the man in the half-ton truck. He lived down the highway. His name was Charlie Hoyt. A sixty-nine-year-old retiree, he was driving to Tim Hortons to grab a Sunday coffee that morning. He was about twenty seconds behind Breau, according to the CCTV cameras at the fire hall.

Although McLellan, Breau and Hoyt had somewhat different versions of events, the one thing they all agreed on was that the RCMP shooters had stopped their car west of the fire hall. That was important because it revealed as a lie the story that the Mounties had stumbled onto the marked police car at the scene. It also explained why the LED sign was hit by a bullet.

How the LED sign got hit has long been a conundrum. It sits on the western edge of the fire hall property, seemingly out of the line of fire. Figuring out what happened to the sign seems key to unravelling the true story.

Enter Deputy Fire Chief Darrell Currie.

When we told him our findings, he suggested that Jones, Breau and I go for a drive and approach the fire hall from the west, like Constables Brown and Dave Melanson did that morning, and see for ourselves what they could see. So we did.

We drove east down Highway 2, past a farm field and two houses, and then suddenly, out of nowhere, the fire hall appeared, having been hidden by a large hedgerow and the LED sign.

Here's what the SIRT report by Cacchione stated about the actions of the two officers (SO1 and SO2):

> As they neared the Onslow Fire Hall, they saw [the EMO worker], a man wearing a yellow and orange reflective vest standing by the driver's side door of a fully marked RCMP vehicle parked in front of the fire hall. Attempts made by SO2 [Melanson], using both the mobile and portable radios, to notify other officers of what SO1 [Brown] and SO2 were seeing were unsuccessful due to the heavy volume of radio traffic. When SO1 identified themself as police and ordered [the EMO worker] to show his hands, [he] did not do as ordered but instead ducked behind the police vehicle and then popped up before running into the fire hall.

As Currie had suggested, that description of events was impossible. There was no way that the two officers driving down Highway 2 could have recognized the situation that quickly. The RCMP cruiser was backed up to a door and surrounded by safety cones. If one stopped at the neighbour's driveway to the west of the fire hall, one had a clear line—through a gap in the LED sign's structure—to see the police car parked in front of the garage door.

Did the Mounties try to fire through that gap, miss and hit the LED sign?

Another thing that went largely unnoticed in Cacchione's report was that the two Mounties had been told what colour vest Wortman was wearing. As Cacchione put it in his February report, they knew "through a statement given to SO1 by the killer's intimate partner, that the killer was wearing an orange vest."

There are a few problems with that. Of all of the almost 1,000 Mounties in Nova Scotia, Constable Terry Brown purportedly interviewed Wortman's common-law wife, Lisa Banfield, when she allegedly came out of the woods at 6:30 a.m., and she told him that Wortman was wearing an orange vest. And now Terry Brown was hunting down Wortman, too? Why weren't all the Mounties on Highway 104 being asked to do more? Also, how did Banfield know what Wortman was wearing that day? She'd told the Mounties she hadn't seen him since 10 p.m. the night before.

A last point about the EMO worker's vest before we move on: it was green, not orange.

"It was lime green," said Sharon McLellan. "There was so little orange on it, you couldn't possibly see it."

The two Mounties said they happened upon what they believed was Wortman, but did they? It seems clear that something else happened. They stopped short of the fire hall. The LED sign was between them and the real RCMP cruiser. They made no attempt to get close to the man whom they thought was Wortman.

They shot from far away like snipers.

It raises the question of whether a shoot-to-kill order was in effect, as well as another important issue. If the two Mounties couldn't possibly have come upon the police car at the fire hall, recognized the situation and stopped in time, that means someone had *told* them that Wortman was in the police car at the fire station. The only person who might have done that would have been Wortman himself. He had passed by the fire hall only moments earlier. But the RCMP continues to deny that Wortman had either a cellphone or a police radio.

Meanwhile, the Mounties have been doing everything they can to suppress evidence, including behaving in what can only be described as a surreptitious manner.

◆

Sharon McLellan was not the giving-up type and continued to be skeptical about what the Mounties and the government were really up to. Into this scene walked RCMP chief superintendent John Robin, who, along with another Mountie, paid a visit to McLellan one afternoon, around the time I published my appeal for new inside sources. After a seemingly aimless and harmless conversation, Robin and the other Mountie left, but first, Robin handed McLellan one of his shiny new official business cards. She was stunned by what she read on it:

JOHN ROBIN
CHIEF SUPERINTENDENT
CONTRACT AND INDIGENOUS POLICING
RCMP NATIONAL HEADQUARTERS
NOVA SCOTIA MASS CASUALTY COMMISSION

McLellan called me and sent me the card. Although the inquiry had been announced the previous summer, neither of us knew its formal name. It was something of a shock to see it printed on an RCMP business card.

"Do you know who John Robin is?" I asked McLellan.

"It says he's a chief superintendent with the Mass Casualty Commission," she said. "How can that be? It's supposed to be an independent commission."

"I've been waiting for Robin to surface for the past year," I told her. "He's married to the head of the RCMP in Halifax County, and his last job, as far as I know, was director of Covert Operations in Ottawa."

"Should we be afraid?" McLellan asked. "What does he want with me?"

It seemed like a sign that the RCMP was going out of its way to make sure the lid was being kept sealed on its official narrative. Why else would a senior officer be paying courtesy calls to potential witnesses?

I had just prepared a story on all of the RCMP couples who were in positions of power in Nova Scotia, and now I could finally add Robin to the mix. Following is an excerpt from the story, published in *Frank*:

A CLIQUE OF MARRIED COUPLES WITH
B.C. CONNECTIONS RUN THE RCMP IN N.S.,
AND WHY THAT'S A PROBLEM

A high-ranking RCMP officer who was in charge of national covert operations at the force's headquarters in Ottawa has been quietly working for the Nova Scotia Mass Casualty Commission as an investigator.

Chief Superintendent John Robin is married to Chief Superintendent Janis Gray, who has been the officer in charge of the RCMP in Halifax County since October of 2019.

As the officer in charge of covert operations from late 2019 until the fall of 2020, Robin likely would have been aware of all RCMP undercover operations, including the use of confidential and other informants and agents, knowledgeable sources inside the RCMP said in interviews.

This is pertinent because police sources have been indicating since soon after Gabriel Wortman murdered 22 innocent people on April 18 and 19, 2020, that he or someone in his immediate circle may be RCMP informants. The RCMP has denied such a relationship, but the sources continue to insist that the force is not being truthful.

There are also questions about the possible role played by the Combined Forces Special Enforcement Unit, which is comprised of RCMP, Halifax Regional Police and members from some other agencies. If there, in fact, was a covert operation either involving Wortman or targeting him, the CFSEU would likely have had a hand in it. That would mean that Chief Supt. Gray would have had some kind of role.

On its website page, the Nova Scotia Mass Casualty Commission lists its "Commission Team," including its investigators: Dwayne King, Joel Kulmatycki, Christoper Lussow, Elizabeth Montgomery, Scott Spicer and Paul Thompson. There is no mention of Robin.

At the time of posting, nobody from the Mass Casualty Commission was answering questions about him.

Robin's link to the Mass Casualty Commission was first revealed on *Little Grey Cells*, a YouTube channel. *Frank* obtained three different copies of Robin's business card after I put out an appeal to the audience on the *Nighttime* podcast with Jordan Bonaparte.

On April 12, Robin and another unidentified officer, who said he didn't have a business card, paid a visit to Sharon and Tim McLellan. They live across from the Onslow Belmont firehall. On April 19, 2020, Sharon witnessed two Mounties mistakenly shoot

at another Mountie and an Emergency Management Office officer who were standing in the parking lot. Wortman had driven by
moments earlier. Some of the shots went through the wall of the
firehall and narrowly missed some people inside. Total claimed
damage to the firehall was almost $40,000.

"He came to our workshop and asked me and Tim if we could go
somewhere quiet to talk," Sharon McLellan recalled in an interview.
"He said he just came by to see how we were doing. He didn't take
any notes or anything. It was just talking. He said he had just come
back from Europe in September, and that he had worked in Ottawa
for a while. He didn't say what he was doing. He did say that his wife
worked as a police officer in the HRM. He left us his business card."

For the McLellans, who hadn't heard from the Mounties for
more than a year, Robin's visit was the second from the force in
two days. The first one was from Corporal Kyla Lounsbury, whose
business card states that she worked for the major crimes section in
the "special project unit/Adhoc Interview Team." She was accompanied by another unidentified Mountie without a business card.

The McLellans repeated their well-known story about what they
saw and didn't see that morning at the firehall.

McLellan found the subsequent visit by Robin to be somewhat
odd. After Robin and his sidekick had left, she and her husband
were scratching their heads about why he was there. . . .

Both McLellans were left with the impression that Robin's
unnamed wife was with Halifax Regional Police, rather than her
actual job as commander of the RCMP in Halifax County.

Robin's until now hidden secondment to the Mass Casualty
Commission appears, among other things, to raise questions about
the neutrality of the entire enterprise.

"This is a clear conflict of interest," said a Mountie familiar with
both Robin's career and the internal workings of the force.

After my story was published, the Mass Casualty Commission leapt
into high dudgeon. Robin was not attached to the commission, it
declared. "The Mass Casualty Commission has been made aware that

a business card is providing confusion," Emily Hill, a lawyer for the commission, said in a written statement. "We want to provide clarity. The Mass Casualty Commission is an independent inquiry. The Commission does not employ anyone from the RCMP. We are asking the RCMP to clarify the card to avoid further confusion."

The RCMP took a couple of days to respond and then came up with this, as reported by Chris Lambie in the Halifax *Chronicle Herald*: "A Mountie spokesman said Wednesday that 'Robin is the officer in charge of co-ordinating the RCMP's responses to the Nova Scotia Mass Casualty Commission. He is responsible for ensuring that the Mass Casualty Commission is provided with information they require from the RCMP, in order to conduct their examination and provide answers to the victim's families and the public.'" Lambie added that both the RCMP and the commission had confirmed that Robin did not work for the Mass Casualty Commission.

Of the 19,000 regular members and 10,000 civilians in the force, why would the RCMP call upon Robin, of all people, for this job? His wife, Chief Superintendent Gray, was clearly, as the police themselves might put it, "a person of interest" in any thorough investigation of Wortman's possible relationships with police prior to the massacres.

Days later, Andrew Douglas got another tip from inside the RCMP related to the Robin story. Someone else *Frank* should be looking at, Douglas was told, was former RCMP staff sergeant Mike Butcher. He was the husband of the boss in the province, Assistant Commissioner Lee Bergerman. Butcher, a former undercover specialist, had been hired by the force to work alongside Robin to vet documents that might be disclosed to the commission or to health and safety investigators.

On May 29, Elizabeth McMillan of the CBC followed up our story about Robin's visit to McLellan by digging up government e-mails that showed Bergerman had gone to the province seeking additional funds to hire her husband.

> CBC News obtained correspondence between Mark Furey, who was the province's justice minister at the time, and Assistant Commissioner Lee Bergerman, the commanding officer of the

RCMP in Nova Scotia, through freedom of information laws.

The records show that in the summer and fall of 2020, Bergerman wrote to Furey asking for financial support to help pay for an "issues management team" being set up in the wake of the mass shootings.

"As you may appreciate, public perception of the province fully funding the RCMP to respond to inquiry demands would not be favourable," Furey wrote in a Dec. 11 letter to Bergerman.

Like McMillan's earlier story about seventy Mounties taking the summer off on stress leave, this one also raised important points that would be ignored by other media. It showed that even Minister of Justice Mark Furey, the former RCMP staff sergeant, was finally standing up to his alma mater. What about the Portapique case could be so seriously dividing the province and the federally run police force?

I could sense something on the horizon. I started receiving strange overtures. A soon-to-be-ex-Mountie offered me ten uniforms and other paraphernalia for sale. He said he couldn't think of anyone else who would want them. I passed. A pretty, long-haired woman wanted to study at my knee and learn the ins and outs of investigative journalism. I'd seen and rejected that move in my mid-twenties—and many times since. Other Mounties, former Mounties and apparently ordinary citizens were keen to meet me for one reason or another.

What was more intriguing were the e-mails and blocked calls from people I didn't know asking whether I was worried about surveillance. Typically, I would tell them that, yes, I felt like I was being surveilled, and every so often I would interrupt a call by mockingly asking into the phone: "Did you catch that, Corporal? Do I need to repeat it for you?"

My go-to method of sharing information has always been the same. We live in a world of e-mails and instant messaging and encryption, all of which may or may not be compromised by the authorities or hackers. I have a simple solution: put it in an envelope and mail it to me, but not to my normal address. I'll give you one that nobody knows. And one other thing . . . don't lick the stamp.

32

TRUE BLUE AND THE 911 TAPES

The wall of denial continued to be unwaveringly bolstered by what might have appeared to be an unlikely alliance: the RCMP, the federal and provincial governments, the mass media and some alternative media, many of the families and friends of the victims, and a large chunk of the general public. Everybody *said* they wanted answers, but in the grand tradition of Nova Scotia politics, from the Donald Marshall case to the Westray mining disaster to the acquittal of former premier Gerald Regan, it was obvious that backroom deals were being made and almost everyone was prepared to acquiesce to the RCMP's silence and just shrug.

It was hard on innocents like Leon Joudrey, who had taken in Lisa Banfield that Sunday morning and didn't believe her story. He was the one being doubted by the intrepid keyboard warriors and Internet trolls. Some were even suggesting that he was party to the murders. Others proposed that he and Banfield must have had a hidden relationship. None of these accusations appeared to have any basis in reality. They were a vivid manifestation of the arrogance of the ignorant—their certainty undiminished by facts to the contrary.

Joudrey had agreed to be interviewed by anyone who called. He was that kind of guy. He looked you straight in the eye and let her rip.

His story is clear and concise. Perhaps the best example of how the system helped the police to hide the truth was what happened when Joudrey was interviewed for Global TV's podcast *13 Hours*. Absent from the Global story was anything in Joudrey's statement that might be seen as impugning Banfield and contradicting the possibility that the Portapique killings were anything but a case of domestic violence gone wrong. The omissions did not go unnoticed by viewers on social media, who directly questioned Global about it. One, who operated under the name of mizzfoxx902, recounted what Joudrey had actually said, and added: "This is an important fact and a 'feminist lens' should have nothing to do with that . . . the truth about her NOT being in the woods all night directly relates to every other person (man, woman and child) being murdered that night/morning. Please don't suppress such important information. Please inform your superiors, who may be telling you not to write these things, that any and all Nova Scotians involved or related to this case want the truth and nothing else because Lisa survived and the others didn't and there's no reason to choose her over everyone else."

Another person who contacted Global went by the moniker Truthbetold and published a social media conversation with news director Rhonda Brown. The exchange was soon removed from the Global Instagram account, but not before I got a copy of it.

"How in the name of God did SHE [host Sarah Ritchie] leave out the full testimony of Leon Joudrey?"

Brown was quoted as saying: "I can tell you this . . . conversation about the Leon Joudrey testimony went to the highest levels of Global News. We were advised that parts of his testimony may not be verified. And the police had a different account."

After everything the RCMP has done, Global was concerned about their story dovetailing with the police account. Comparing Banfield's "victimhood" with Joudrey's, I wrote this in *Frank*:

> All this has come down hard on Leon Joudrey. This is not his world. He'd rather be in the bush or down at the weir fishing. He didn't ask for anything. The nightmare landed on his doorstep one morning.

"I lost 13 neighbours that weekend and some of them were my good friends," he lamented to me recently.

Just before Christmas he cracked up. He had been in a running dispute with his bosses over what he believed was possible corruption in the department. He had survived the massacre and always wondered why. More pressure came from keyboard warriors on social media, whackadoodles hiding in the ether who were speculating that Joudrey was in on the whole thing—maybe he and Lisa Banfield had something going on. It was a ridiculous notion, but it was all driving him crazy. He finally lost it and mentioned his guns in a social media exchange. His employers reported him to the police and circulated his photo and credentials on social media—a violation of privacy, one would think. He was arrested and placed in a psychiatric ward at Colchester Hospital for 30 days over Christmas and New Year's. His guns were taken away.

"It was all taken out of context," Joudrey says. "I would never hurt anyone. I was just so upset."

He's feeling better now, but you can bet your bottom toonie that the entire episode will be used in an attempt to discredit his story when and if the time comes.

That's the terrible state we're in. The real victims, the dead, their families and bystanders like Leon Joudrey are largely being ignored by the media. Meanwhile, a perceived domestic violence victim is declared to be a bona fide victim and off-limits without any real proof because the collective media is viewing this through a "feminist lens" or whatever. The police and the government go along with this because it serves their own interests in keeping a lid on what really might have happened. As I've said before, the most transparent thing about all this is that it is obvious that something big is being hidden.

The bottom line is that the corporatized media has allowed itself to become politicized and, in doing so, has failed in its duty to hold the government and police accountable.

Joudrey's experience with Global TV alone illustrated how deep in bed—unwittingly or otherwise—the media were with the powers that be. Who was going to leak information to the networks or newspapers when those same organizations would immediately run with it to the police or government? If someone was going to leak anything to the media, the only honest broker left on this story, unlikely as it might have seemed to many, appeared to be *Frank*. And that's exactly what happened.

◆

My appeal to a Great Canadian to step out of the shadows—or at least to let us shine a light on what was being hidden—worked better than I imagined. A new source emerged who claimed to be bursting with insider information. I'll use the pronoun "he" to describe the source.

He told us that the Mass Casualty Commission was designed as a sham, with no plan to investigate anything. He said the commission had been given no information about Lisa Banfield other than her driver's licence and one other government record. He told us that the Province of Nova Scotia was being blocked by the federal government from finding out anything of substance. He said the RCMP and the federal government had a team of sixty lawyers and investigators inserted between them and the commission, determined to prevent anything of substance from getting out. He also had audio and video recordings.

On Sunday evening, May 30, 2021, Jordan Bonaparte and I did another *Nighttime* podcast. I told the audience that I had a new, important source and that his stories promised to be (and I deliberately understated it) "very interesting." Over the next few days all kinds of nicknames for the source were offered up—the Red Swerve, the Honest Horseman, Red Serge, Truth Squad, Coaster Connection. I didn't want to call him Deep Throat, but I didn't like any of the suggestions. One night, as I was thinking about it, I rolled over in bed and looked into Sharon's beautiful green eyes. She said: "True Blue." That was it.

In the wake of the new leaks, we convened a meeting at *Frank*'s offices on Lower Water Street in Halifax. Present were Andrew Douglas, Chad Jones, Jordan Bonaparte, me and a film crew for the documentary I was now helping to make. We filmed Andrew going over the situation on the phone with his corporate lawyer, David Hutt at Burchells LLP, who gave us the go-ahead to proceed with capturing this key moment on camera.

I knew roughly what was on the recordings we were about to hear and watch, having listened to some of the audio over the telephone. The audio was of 911 calls from the night of April 18. The video was of Wortman's death.

For Bonaparte, this was all very difficult. He had started out podcasting as a hobby and entertainment vehicle, and now he was at the heart of one of the most controversial moments in Canadian journalism. My first instinct was to publish two of the 911 tapes, but not the one involving a call from the four trapped children, and everyone agreed.

Listening to the other two tapes was draining. Poor Jamie Blair. What she experienced was horrifying. As she was being stalked and eventually murdered by Wortman, her last seconds were spent dealing with a feckless 911 operator who seemed more interested in ticking off procedural boxes than listening to what she had to say. In the other tape, gunshots can be heard, but the 911 operator seemed oblivious to all that was going on at the time on Orchard Beach Drive.

After listening to those two tapes, we had a duty to hear the third one. The recording was four minutes and twenty-two seconds long, during which the twelve-year-old son of Jamie and Greg Blair calmly and heroically tried to call for help, only to be confronted by another 911 operator who seemed lost at the end of his leash.

It was a clear case of the public interest versus privacy considerations. There was no doubt what we were going to do. And for its part, the RCMP was going to do what it always does in such situations: use the victims as pawns behind whom it could hide while whipping up public sympathy and anger.

Sitting beside Bonaparte, I could all but hear his heart pounding. This was going to get scary, people were going to be upset, and we all knew it. We decided first to publish a transcript of the tapes for people who didn't have the stomach to listen.

"If we run just the transcripts, the RCMP will say they are wrong and shouldn't be believed," I said.

"If we only run the transcripts, then people will doubt that we actually have the tapes," Douglas said. "We'll publish it all and let the chips fall where they may."

"Either way, we're going to get hammered," I said. "But we really have no choice."

Around this time my cellphone rang. It was Robert Pineo, the lawyer for the families in a class-action suit launched against the RCMP and the governments.

Pineo was in a difficult position. Some of the families did not want him to talk to me, but he knew that what I was doing was valuable for their case. I told him about the 911 tapes and what was on them. I asked him to contact the families involved and warn them about what was coming. Before hanging up, I also told him that we had videos of Wortman's demise.

Everyone in the room agreed, and we moved forward with the first story. Douglas decided that everything would be published outside of *Frank*'s paywall, because he didn't want to give anyone the opportunity to claim that he was trying to make a dime off the 911 tapes. Douglas published a warning that the content of the tapes and the transcripts was disturbing. The story was published around 6 p.m. on June 2, 2021—409 days after Wortman had been shot.

EXCLUSIVE: PORTAPIQUE 911 CALLS REVEAL WHAT RCMP KNEW FROM THE START

By Paul Palango

In a 25-minute span on April 18, 2020, near the beginning of Gabriel Wortman's murderous rampage in which he killed 22 people, three people called 911 for help. One was a desperate Jamie Blair, who had less than 2 minutes left in her life. Another was her 12-year-old son, [Alex], who calmly and heroically tried to tell the operator what was happening. The third was from Andrew MacDonald, who, along with his wife, Katie, was ambushed by Wortman.

All three told the 911 operators that the shooter was Gabriel Wortman.

All three said he was driving what appeared to be a marked RCMP cruiser.

The RCMP has said from the outset that it didn't know that Wortman was driving a marked cruiser until told so by his common-law wife, Lisa Banfield, who purportedly had emerged from a night of hiding in the nearby woods.

The information is contained in 911 audio tapes provided to *Frank* magazine and the *Nighttime* podcast with Jordan Bonaparte by a confidential informant we are naming True Blue.

The time-stamped tapes are heart-wrenching and disturbing to hear, but each one contains valuable information about what the RCMP knew at the time and strongly suggests that the force has been attempting to cover up that fact for reasons that are currently unknown.

Frank has decided to both report on the tapes and publish them online because it deems the content contained in them to be in the public interest. We acknowledge that the recordings are graphic, but in their entirety, they raise serious issues about the performance and accountability of 911 operators and police and fire dispatchers.

We encourage anyone who is squeamish not to listen to the tapes.

The first call to 911 appears to have been placed at 10:01 p.m., as the RCMP admitted, but it wasn't from the children. It was from 40-year-old Jamie Blair (JB) just before Wortman came upon her and murdered her. The call was time-stamped at 22:01:13. In producing the transcript, some words were garbled and difficult to make out. We have done our best to be as accurate as possible. Where appropriate I have inserted a brief description of what could be heard in the background.

Jamie Blair's call to 911
911: 911. What is your emergency?

JB: (*inaudible*) my neighbour . . . (*garbled*) . . . been shot."

911: I'm sorry, I can't make out what you are saying.

Jamie tries to calm down and get the tremble out of her voice

JB: My neighbour is . . . (*inaudible*). I think he just shot my husband.

911: You think your husband's been shot?

JB: Yes!

911: Okay. Do you have a home phone or land line to that location . . .

JB: I know . . . talking over . . .

911: Where are you? What is your civic address?

JB: 123 Orchard Beach Drive in Portapique.

911: 123 Orchard Beach Drive in Portapique. Is your husband injured?

JB: I don't know, he is laying on my deck, I don't know what the fuck is going on, there is a police car in the fucking driveway.

911: There are police cars in the driveway?

JB: There's a police car, but he drives . . . he a denturist and he drives . . . those police cars—

The 911 operator cuts Jamie off. She's frantic.

911: I'm sorry, did you say there was a police car in your driveway?

JB: There is an RCMP . . . it's labeled RCMP . . . I don't know if it's not a police car . . .

She can be heard moving around and is likely trying to hide her two sons, Alex, 12, and Jack, 10.

911: Listen, you're at 123 Orchard Beach Drive in Portapique, Colchester County? You called from 902 --- ----.

JB: Yes.

911: Is your husband injured?

JB: I don't know.

Blair is obviously frustrated.

911: Can you see him?

JB: He is lying face down on the deck.

911: Okay. Has he moved?

JB: I went back out to check on him and the man was coming back up on the deck with a big gun.

911: Stay on the line and we're going to the police. Don't hang up.

RCMP: RCMP, *bonjour.* Hull-oh-oh, can you see your husband from where you are?

The tape cuts off at this point. We do not know what is on the RCMP part of the tape.

It was around this point that Wortman returned to the house, found Blair and shot her numerous times in the face. It raises the question about whether Wortman had a radio or scanner in his car. Did he hear Jamie calling 911? Is that why he returned and shot her?

After he killed her, Wortman fired a number of shots at Blair's children, who were hiding behind a locked bedroom door. One of those bullets narrowly missed one of the boys. According to a source close to the family, Wortman yelled at the boys, words to this effect: "She should have died the first time." It suggests that he had already shot Jamie Blair and thought she was dead, although Blair makes no mention of being shot in the 911 call.

In the aftermath, bullet holes could be found around the house, through various windows and walls, in the soffit outside and in a garage door. Wortman pulled some burning logs out of the fireplace and placed them on the floor in a feeble attempt to burn down the house and possibly incinerate Jamie Blair. Wortman then left the scene. The Blair children came out of hiding to find their mother overkilled—horribly mutilated and unrecognizable.

They put the logs back into the fireplace and then went outside, where their father was lying dead face down on the porch. Their family dog, Zoey, a nine-year-old miniature pinscher, had also been shot, but would survive after being rushed to a veterinarian in Truro hours later.

One of the boys dug into their dead father's pants pocket and pulled out his cell phone, before they both gingerly made their way over to the McCully property, through a path in a patch of woods to the south. During this period, it has been previously reported, it appears that Wortman circled by the house twice, but didn't see the boys.

McCully ushered the children into the basement with her daughter and son and then went to check what was happening. It was then that she likely came across Wortman, who shot her in the head on her front lawn.

The next call to 911 was logged in at 10:16:30. It was from Alex Blair. He and Lisa McCully's 12-year-old daughter, also named Alex, were in the basement. Their younger brothers had left the house and gone outside.

Blair took charge of the situation. In a clear and composed tone of voice, he heroically attempted to explain the gravity of the

situation to a male 911 operator who couldn't seem to focus on the situation or the possible perils facing the four children.

Alex Blair's call to 911
AB: *(garbled)* Oh my!!

911: Hello?

AB: Um, there is a crazy man, and he is burning down his own garage, he came over to our house, killed both our parents, and is burning down our house!

911: Ma'am, where are you at right now? Do you know the address?

AB: Yes, we are at our neighbour's house in, in between . . . we are at . . . what's your address *(asking Alex)*?

911: Are you in Portapique?

AB: Yes, Portapique! *(inaudible)*

911: Miss, Miss, Miss. I understand we already got calls in for this area, you say there is a fire there now?

AB: Yes! There is a huge fire.

911: Do you know what house you are at there in Portapique?

AB: YES! 135 Orchard Beach Drive. Do you know where Portapique Drive is? You take a left and then you take a right on the first one.

911: Is that where the fire is?

AB: YES!

911: Just stay on the phone for me, okay?

AB: Yes, that's where we are and . . .

911: Miss?

AB: The fire is right across . . .

911: The fire is across the street?

AB: Yes.

911: So, at 136?

AB: Yes. Or 135 Orchard Beach Drive.

911: That's where you are at, right now?

AB: Yes.

911: Okay, where is the fire at? Is it across the street?

AB: Yes, my house and my little brother's house is 123 Orchard Beach Drive, right beside it.

911: 123, okay. And the fire is at 123?

AB: He came in, he shot my father ten times. My mom was calling [911] and he came in and he killed her.

911: Where is she at? Is she still in the house?

AB: She's (*voice lowering*) dead, in her room.

911: In her room. Okay.

AB: And she is burned. Her head is on fire.

911: Okay, where is the guy who did this?

AB: We don't know. He pulled out of the driveway and left.

911: Did you see what kind of vehicle?

AB: It was a police car. I couldn't find, uh, I couldn't find the, uh, the licence.

911: Okay. Did you see anything else about the vehicle? You said it was a police car?

AB: Yes, it was.

911: It was.

AB: Like a police car.

911: Okay, alright, we got police on the way. For the other part of this I'm going to put you in contact with fire. Okay, we have 135 Orchard Beach Drive in Portapique.

AB: OH, and he shot our dog, and half of our dog is missing.

911: Okay, 135 Orchard Beach Drive in Portapique, Colchester County. Right?

AB: Yes.

911: Do you have a cellphone number or a number we can get you?

AB: No. Alex, what's your phone number?

AM: I don't have a phone.

AB: We don't have one. Her mom went over there, and she hasn't come back.

911: Okay.

AB: And we don't know where our little brothers are. They went outside, I guess.

911: Okay, you don't have a phone number or anything?

AB: No, we don't.

911: Okay, just stay on the phone for me, okay? I'm going to put you through to fire for a second. Okay?

AB: Okay.

FIRE DISPATCHER: Operator.

911: It's 911 Truro for Bass River Fire. Alright, so we got a fire across the street from 135 Orchard Beach Drive in Portapique.

AB: (*interrupting*) Yes! And it is huge!

911: Miss, Miss, just let me talk to her for a second, okay?

AB: It's a sir.

BASS RIVER FIRE: 135 Orchard Beach Drive where?

911: In Portapique, in Colchester County. She doesn't have a call-back number. Uhhh, there was an incident there with a shooting and everything involved, so there are police and ambulance going there as well, but the house was also lit on fire.

AB: (*interrupting*) And there are more bullets . . . (*garbled and crosstalk*)

911: (*sternly cutting Alex off*) Miss, Miss . . . one moment, please!

BASS RIVER FIRE: Is it secure there for fire to go ahead?

911: Not at this point. We are still getting all the other resources together.

BASS RIVER FIRE: Once it's secure, we can send fire over.

911: Okay. Perfect. Will do. Hi, ma'am, you still there?

AB: Sir, it's a sir.

911: Okay. Just one second. Okay? I'm going to put you through to fire . . . er, to police. One second. Okay?

AB: Yes.

Telephone rings.

RCMP (male): Hello. RCMP. Hi!

Afterward the RCMP said it rushed to the scene, scoured the area for Wortman and went door to door evacuating people. That didn't happen on Orchard Beach Drive and vicinity, where 11 of the 13 people murdered at Portapique Beach that night were shot. Nobody was evacuated. The RCMP told McCully's family that the children were on the phone for two hours with RCMP members and support staff before they were rescued. In fact, previous communications tapes obtained by *Frank* showed that the children were left in the house for three hours before being rescued. It was at that time that their dog, Zoey, was taken to a veterinarian in Truro for surgery, which she survived.

The RCMP also told the McCully family that the children were safe because the RCMP had members hidden around the house protecting them at all times. It was the same line that the force used with Nathan Staples, who was on Wortman's purported hit list, as well as at least one other person, who asked not to be identified. There is no proof that the RCMP actually did such a protective maneuver, but the McCully family, for one, continues to believe that they did.

Back to that Saturday night in Portapique. About 4½ minutes after Alex Blair was transferred over to the RCMP, another 911 call came in.

Andrew and Katie MacDonald had a cottage at the intersection of Portapique Beach Road and Orchard Beach Drive. They had noticed the raging fire burning at Wortman's warehouse/man den at 136 Orchard Beach Drive and decided to check it out. As they drove toward the blaze, they were on the phone with 911. They then noticed that there was also a fire burning in the kitchen of Frank and Dawn Gulenchyn's house. They saw a police car parked in the driveway of the Gulenchyns'. They passed the Gulenchyn house, turned around and were heading back to it, still talking to 911. As they approached the house, the RCMP cruiser approached them door-to-door. Here is the transcript, some of which was barely decipherable, in which AM is Andrew and KM is Katie MacDonald. The call was logged at 10:25:31 p.m.:

Andrew MacDonald's call to 911
911: 911, what's your emergency?

AM: I am calling from Portapique, there, as there is a house on fire down the road from our house. I don't know if someone called already?

911: Yup, so you can see the house on fire?

AM: Yeah.

911: So, what's the address?

AM: It's . . . I don't know the exact address, but it's on Orchard Beach Road.

911: Okay, yeah, we got a few calls there, so Orchard Beach Road, Portapique, Colchester County.

AM: Yup.

The operator repeats the caller's phone number, and he replies with an affirmative.

911: . . . and you see the house on fire?

AM: Yeah, we just drove down the road to check it out. It's like a big garage. It's one of our neighbours, so he is probably not there.

911: Okay, just one moment. I'm going to connect you to fire.

AM: Yeah.

911: (*calling fire department*) Hi. Dispatch. Hi, calling for a fire call for Bass River Fire, you got the call there. I think it's 123 Orchard Beach Road? Oh my god . . . yeah, it should be close to that area, Orchard Beach in Colchester County?

AM: There's another house on fire here!

911: Do you see two houses on fire?

AM: Yeah, we just drove by another house, and their whole kitchen is on fire. There is a police officer in the driveway.

In the background, someone in MacDonald's car says, "What the fuck?"

FIRE DISPATCHER: RCMP, are you aware of the situation that is going on—on that road?

911: Yeah, he's saying there are two houses on fire, so . . . just thought we would update you there.

FIRE DISPATCHER: Are the two houses beside each other, sir?

AM: No, they are down the road. The police officer is parked at the driveway, so I don't know what . . . like, he is coming around. I don't know if he is going to talk to me or what?

911: Is it safe for you to be on that road right now?

AM: Hi . . . hi.

Loud gunshot.

911: Sir?

KM: Oh God . . . (*screaming*) . . . oh God!

911: Sir?

Sound of vehicle accelerating.

AM: I've been shot. I've been shot.

911: Fire, are you aware there are possibly a second fire?

KM: What the fuck is happening?

AM: It's my neighbour Gabe, he just shot me in the arm.

KM: Please help us . . . 911!

The MacDonalds raced up Orchard Beach Drive and then came into contact with the first RCMP officer on the scene, Constable Stuart Beselt. They relayed to him what had happened and, as previously reported, Beselt apparently radioed his dispatcher the information about Wortman being dressed as a police officer and driving a RCMP car.

The 911 tapes do not tell the whole story, obviously, because we haven't yet seen the RCMP side of the story. That being said, the performance of the 911 operators was, at best, questionable.

"They are staying calm and controlled, so calm and controlled that they aren't listening to the situation," said one senior police officer who listened to the tapes. "You can see them checking off a list entirely unaware that some children are trapped in a basement and that a demonic killer is not that far away from them. He could come back at any time. By the time the kids called, they already knew that people had been murdered next door. There's no sense of urgency."

The tapes strongly suggest that the RCMP has not been forth-right. From Jamie Blair's call at 10:01, the RCMP appeared to do everything it could to downplay any information about Wortman, his police uniform and his RCMP lookalike cruiser.

For example, it didn't issue its first Tweet about the incident until a full one hour and 31 minutes after Jamie Blair's call—at 11:32 p.m.

#RCMPNS is responding to a firearms complaint in the #Portapique area. (Portapique Beach Rd, Bay Shore Rd and Five Houses Rd.) The public is asked to avoid the area and stay in their homes with doors locked at this time.

The next morning the RCMP stated that it first learned that Wortman had a replica police car after his underdressed common law wife, Lisa Banfield, emerged after 8½ hours or so in the woods and told them so.

At 8:54 a.m.—almost 11 hours after Jamie Blair's description was given to them, supported by the other two 911 calls—the RCMP issued this Tweet:

51-year-old Gabriel Wortman is the suspect in our active shooter investigation in #Portapique. There are several victims. He is considered armed & dangerous. If you see him, call 911. DO NOT approach. He's described as a white man, bald, 6'2-6'3 with green eyes.

The RCMP, once again, forgot to mention that Wortman was dressed as a Mountie and driving a vehicle that looked exactly like a RCMP cruiser.

It wasn't until 10:17 a.m.—a full 12 hours after Blair's first call—that the RCMP admitted how Wortman was dressed and what vehicle he was driving.

#Colchester: Gabriel Wortman may be driving what appears to be an RCMP vehicle & may be wearing an RCMP uniform. There's 1 difference btwn his car and our RCMP vehicles: the car #. The suspect's car is 28B11, behind rear passenger window. If you see 28B11 call 911 immediately.

Still there was no public alert, no roadblocks, and three more people would end up dying—RCMP Constable Heidi Stevenson, Good Samaritan Joey Webber and Wortman's fellow denturist Gina Goulet, with whom he had had an affair.

One would think that all this would be the subject of the upcoming Mass Casualty Commission's work, but True Blue is skeptical about the intentions of the commission, calling it "a scam. They're not going to do anything."

True Blue said that part of their motivation for coming forward is their personal frustration with the stonewalling by the RCMP, not only in this matter, but also in other cases in Nova Scotia in the past.

Finally, the 911 calls strike at the heart of the RCMP narrative that it only knew about Wortman and the police car from Lisa Banfield.

The RCMP story is patently false, therefore, which raises serious questions about the force's relationship with and coddling of Ms. Banfield.

She was, apparently, the last person to see Wortman alive. She, her brother and brother-in-law have been charged with providing Wortman with ammunition. She has claimed that she had spent the night in the woods—hiding in a tree hollow, among other things—on a blistering cold night. The RCMP has called her "a victim" from the first week.

Now that we know a little bit about what really happened that night without the interference, deflection and deceptions of the RCMP clouding the issue, one can only wonder what more there is to know.

Finally, there is this. Over the past 14 months the RCMP have played games with the timeline, comically so in the first few days. It had problems nailing down when the first call had come in. At one point it was 10:15. At another it was 10:01. They even suggested that the children in the basement had made the first call at 10:01, without ever actually saying that. They allowed the timing of Alex Blair's call to be conflated with Jamie Blair's call—effectively making her and her tragic story disappear.

The use of conflation is an old RCMP trick to hide evidence. It's something that we will see again in our next story.

◆

Bonaparte and I were teed up to do an "emergency podcast" on the story, which we did.

Bonaparte even allowed the audience to read the story first before we started talking about it. The audience was stunned in a good way. The anger wasn't far behind.

By the time I got off the podcast, around 7:30 p.m., the first calls were coming in from some of the family members, tearing a strip off me.

"I'm here to help you," I told one man.

"Nobody asked for your help," he replied. "We just want to be left alone."

One man threatened my health and well-being in a fevered voice and graphic terms. After he said that he or some evil associate of his would pay me a visit and bring me some pain and hurt, I casually replied: "You can do that, but you don't know who I know, do you?" After that, he swore at me, hung up the phone and posted on the Internet that I was threatening family members, leaving out his own preamble. Pineo moved quickly to calm him and others down, which I appreciated.

The next day RCMP assistant commissioner Lee Bergerman put out a message denouncing *Frank* and me, without naming us, of course:

> Publishing the audio recordings demonstrates a disgraceful disregard for the victims and their families. This publication has chosen to make public the darkest time in these families' lives, with no regard for how it must feel to have to relive that tragedy in the public eye.
>
> We have spoken to victims' families through our family liaison and are assuring them that we will be investigating the source of the recordings and any related offences that may have occurred with respect to unauthorized release, possession and subsequent publishing.

It was amazing. Bergerman didn't seem to notice or dare acknowledge that the RCMP was caught in a series of lies. The RCMP published her statement on Twitter, where the force got slammed for the next couple of days. As one witty poster put it: "You're releasing this on Twitter? You can't stop making the same mistakes, can you? RCMP will never learn. What are you hiding?"

New Nova Scotia justice minister Randy Delorey said he was "concerned" about the publication. "The release of specific Nova Scotians' names and information that came as part of the disclosure, that would be something where we're evaluating the circumstances, kind of preliminary, to see if it's appropriate to refer to the privacy office for an investigation."

The Mass Casualty Commission decried *Frank* in the following statement: "The Commission does not support the publication of these recordings and requests that the magazine remove the content immediately. We are extremely concerned for the privacy of those affected by the content, especially the child."

Most of the media did its usual thing in such a situation and piled on, too. One would think that shooting the messenger wouldn't be their first instinct, but all too often, these days, that's what they do. With the notable exception of Chris Lambie in the Halifax *Chronicle Herald*, who grasped the message of the story, the media latched onto the "outrage" of the "poor children" story.

It was easier to do that than address the obvious issues, among them that the twelve-year-old Blair boy had told the 911 operator all the details and that two ten-year-old boys were wandering around outside while Wortman was right there. Then there was the additional fact that the RCMP didn't rescue those children for another three hours—a chilling point that most of the media had been ignoring for 409 days.

It was alarming to watch how willing so many people were to attack *Frank* and me.

Dr. Stephen Ellis, a medical doctor, was running as a Conservative for federal public office, and couldn't wait to harness the dramatic and misplaced outrage to attack on behalf of his "future constituents." He urged them to speak out against *Frank*. How deep and thoughtful, doctor. He later won election to the House of Commons. Three local Colchester County councillors, Tom Taggart, Marie Benoit and Lisa Patton, pressured local businesses and Sobeys supermarkets not to carry the magazine anymore and urged constituents not to buy it. Taggart, a former bankrupt, later ran for the provincial legislature in the August 2021 election and won.

Free speech isn't such a valued commodity in Canada. The campaign was effective, as store after store stopped carrying *Frank*, including Atlantic News, a major news outlet in the south end of Halifax. It continued to carry satirical magazines like France's *Charlie Hebdo*, but *Frank* hit a little too close to home.

Nova Scotia Conservative Party leader Tim Houston, trapped in a "pro police" policy environment, jumped on the outrage train, too, along with politicians from every political stripe. Everyone was running against *Frank* magazine in that election. Nobody wanted to talk about the issues we'd exposed—the epic failure in policing, the lies of the RCMP, the collusion within the system and the dire implications from all that. Houston was later elected premier of Nova Scotia for his efforts.

It took a couple of days for the media to come around—but only a bit.

On June 13, CBC reporter Michael Gorman's online dispatch finally acknowledged the evident gap between the RCMP's claims and reality.

MEDIA LAW EXPERTS SAY DECISION TO PUBLISH 911 CALLS NOT A MATTER FOR INVESTIGATION

Iain MacKinnon, a Toronto-based lawyer and president of the Canadian Media Lawyers Association, said it is not the role of the RCMP to be looking into the leak, particularly given that it casts doubt on their own actions.

"It's somewhat outrageous for them to be pursuing this when really what should be under the microscope is the RCMP's accountability and whether they were negligent in the way they acted and if they acted appropriately and quickly enough based on the information that they had," he said in an interview.

Lisa Taylor, an associate professor at Ryerson University's journalism program, said it may make sense for Delorey, as an elected official, to look into something if he's getting a large volume of requests from the public.

But if he finds nothing, Taylor said, Delorey should make that clear given his public statements.

The province's Emergency 911 Act refers to the requirement for calls to remain confidential, but it says nothing about a media outlet publishing them should they be leaked. 911 calls often become public in courtroom settings.

As for the RCMP, Taylor said the force's statement amounts to "self-interested dealing." She sees it as a police force that's on the hot seat trying to deflect attention to somewhere else, in this case the outlet that published the recordings.

"The conflict here is so huge that I would count on a sixth grader being able to identify it."

We rode out the storm that week. The 911 recordings story created a schism inside the families' group, where Charlene Bagley, the McLeod family, and members of the Gulenchyn and Webber families were among many to fully back what we had done.

Tammy Oliver-McCurdie expressed her support for *Frank* and me, and because of that was attacked by other families, who threatened to have her removed from their online chat groups: "I stand behind and with you. . . . Doing what I can to change the perspective within. I am just not a coward and will speak the truth (and) not be a follower because of bullying, cause [sic] that is what is happening within. Them threatening to remove me is more than sad and disappointing but it is clear bullying for having a different perspective."

◆

While all that was going on, a trove of information arrived from a different direction. In June 2020 Robert Pineo and fellow lawyer Sandra McCulloch had filed a class-action suit against the RCMP and the federal attorney general on behalf of the families. It alleged a host of wrongdoing by the RCMP, including short staffing, inadequate response and general incompetence and negligence. One of the stunning revelations in the lawsuit was that the RCMP had returned Heather O'Brien's car to her family with human remains and shell casings still inside the vehicle. It wouldn't be the first such horror story.

It was later revealed that the RCMP did not remove Joey Webber's body from the back seat of Wortman's burned-out replica police car but towed the vehicle away with his remains still inside—but not to the coroner's office. The vehicle was taken first to the RCMP detachment in Bible Hill. Why? It raised speculation that the RCMP was intent on removing anything from Wortman's vehicle that might have been incriminating—like an encrypted police radio. If Wortman indeed had one in his vehicle, as seems possible from the numerous unexplained calls during the rampage that seemed to throw the RCMP off his back, he either obtained it illegally from an RCMP source or had been given the use of it while co-operating in some capacity with the force. It's easy to see why police would consider it desirable to "pasteurize" evidence of either possibility.

"We think that there's a great deal of importance of this proceeding," McCulloch told the CBC's Carolyn Ray. "This has grander implications for Nova Scotia and our country as a whole. There's been a lot of questions that have arisen since the events of April 18 and 19. A lot more questions than answers, and some of the answers that have come out have been less than satisfactory."

The RCMP, represented by the federal attorney general, ignored the suit for a year until ordered by the court to respond. Coincidentally, the timing of this order put the force's canned version of events up against the reality of the 911 recordings, which were fresh on the minds of the public, having been released the night before.

The centrepiece of the RCMP's defence was an affidavit by Superintendent Darren Campbell signed on June 3, 2021, one day after the 911 recordings had been published. There is no mention of the recordings in Campbell's nine-page statement. The contents of the court documents finally surfaced eleven days later and, as if on cue, many in the media immediately took the tried-and-true RCMP bait. For example, on June 14, 2021, the *Toronto Star* went wild with this headline: "N.S. Mass Shooter Intended to Kill at Least Five Others. Court Documents Lay Out Massacre from RCMP's Perspective."

Here we were, approaching fourteen months since the massacres, and the RCMP was still winning huge headlines from information—the hit list that never was—purportedly handed to them by Lisa Banfield after she had emerged from the woods. No matter how much evidence was thrown in their faces, most reporters still hadn't caught on that by now no RCMP statement could be taken at face value.

Campbell's new version of events laid out a timeline that, on the surface, seemed plausible, but that on closer inspection raised even more skepticism about the RCMP's evolving narrative. In paragraph fifty-eight of the affidavit, for example, Campbell stated: "To my knowledge, at the time of the events, no police force in Canada had used a provincial emergency alert in relation to an active shooter event." The system was rolled out on March 31, 2015, but had never been used by the police in Nova Scotia.

In describing what had happened in Portapique that Saturday night, Campbell stated that officers in tactical formation went down Orchard Beach Drive at 10:49 p.m. and found a deceased victim by the side of the road. They saw someone with a flashlight, who ran and hid in the woods, and then they found a second body. The obvious problem with that story is that the Mounties knew that two children were hiding in the basement of McCully's home and were on the phone with the RCMP, and that two ten-year-old boys were outside wandering around. Why did the Mounties not go into McCully's house to either protect and comfort the children or rescue them? A rescue effort wasn't mounted for another two hours.

The larger problem with Campbell's timeline is that it doesn't quite mesh with what we had published months earlier from the communications found on the Pictou County Public Safety channel. At that time, Staff Sergeant Andy O'Brien was captured saying: "Clinton Ellison called us at 22:59 or the father [Richard] called us at 22:59 indicating that his other son, Corrie Ellison, was shot. . . . We're trying to relate back to where the other son is. We understand that he could be in the woods hiding out somewhere."

If the RCMP found Corrie Ellison's body at 10:49 p.m. (22:49), one would expect that they would linger for a few minutes at least. The Mounties said they saw someone approaching with a flashlight who they suspected was the killer. If so, why didn't they confront him?

Clinton Ellison managed to get to where his brother lay dead and identify him before running into the woods. It would have taken him a couple of minutes to find a hiding place. He was reluctant to make any noise, but eventually called his father, told him what was happening and asked him to call 911, which Richard Ellison did at 10:59. What were the Mounties doing during those ten minutes?

Campbell said that the Mounties then discovered McCully's body. If so, why didn't they check her vital signs, declare her dead, call for more police and secure the crime scenes?

The Mounties knew that two children were in the basement and two were running around the property. They did not go into the house, and don't appear to have searched for the children. Instead, they retreated. That's not normal police procedure.

Campbell's comments were reported in a story in the Halifax *Chronicle Herald* that caught the attention of Clinton Ellison. He was refusing to talk to the media, but he posted this on Facebook:

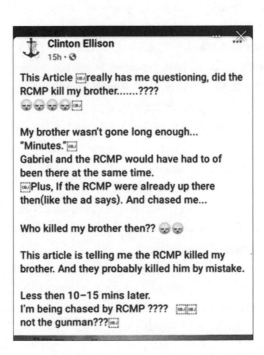

Ellison said in his post: "My brother wasn't gone long enough . . . 'Minutes.' Gabriel and the RCMP would have had to of been there at the same time."

Ellison's timing issue demanded closer examination. He had left his father's place, likely around 10:30, and walked up the gravel road several hundred metres toward Wortman's burning warehouse. That would have taken him several minutes.

But the Pictou County tapes revealed other timing discrepancies, if you will recall.

After the four children, all back together in McCully's basement, were finally rescued at around 1 a.m., some Mounties were left to "hunker down" around the property, waiting for a ride out from the RCMP ERT to the highway.

At 1:50 a.m., another Mountie did a quick initial examination of a body believed to be Corrie Ellison's. The Mountie reported: "The father of these two (garbled) . . . they approached (garbled) to check out the fire. . . . He shot one of them in the head. It's a .40-calibre Smith & Wesson."

If the Mounties found Corrie Ellison's body at 10:49 p.m., they re-found it three hours later at 1:50 a.m. and did nothing before retreating from the area.

After Clinton Ellison was rescued from his hiding place in the woods just after 2:30 a.m., RCMP officers found the bodies of Ellison and McCully again. It was by then shortly after 3 a.m. You may recall the conversation from Chapter Thirty in which unidentified Mounties say: "Oscar Charlie, Hotel One . . . We've just stopped here on the road, ah, we're going to do a quick vitals on this deceased person on the side of the road just to make sure he's deceased and not still alive."

The Mounties soon confirmed that Ellison and then McCully were dead and noted the GPS coordinates for each body because they didn't know exactly where they were.

The question raised by Ellison is a valid one: Did the RCMP accidentally shoot Corrie Ellison? It's not a question the Mounties are going to answer, but it requires an independent investigation by someone other than the RCMP. That's an impossibility in Eastern Canada.

The Mounties are the federal and provincial police, and operate in some municipalities, too. All the independent municipal forces have working agreements and memoranda of understanding with the RCMP. They depend on the RCMP for a multitude of functions, including crime labs. There really is no possibility of an independent investigation by another local police force. The next alternative is Nova Scotia's police watchdog, the Serious Incident Response Team. It could be called in if there is evidence that the police were involved in the shooting, but the RCMP did not conduct such an investigation. It put all the blame on Wortman, and no one even thought of questioning it at the time.

Elsewhere in his affidavit, Campbell declared that he had first been contacted at 10:46 p.m. that Saturday night by an unnamed on-call critical incident commander to approve "the full Critical Incident Program to respond to Portapique."

Campbell stated that at 11:10 p.m. the RCMP called for aerial support with forward-looking infrared radar capabilities from RCMP Air Services in Moncton but were told that the RCMP helicopter was down for maintenance. "As a result, additional inquiries to secure air support were made with the Joint Rescue Coordination Centre—Canadian Forces and Canadian Coast Guard as well as the Nova Scotia Department of Natural Resources," Campbell said.

It was somewhat satisfying to read this. In my own reporting in the *Halifax Examiner* almost a year earlier, I had pointed out that the Department of Natural Resources helicopter was never engaged in locating or chasing Wortman. Campbell had told the CBC's Elizabeth McMillan that any stories I was publishing that ran contrary to the RCMP narrative were "fairy tales." Now who was telling fairy tales? I wanted to rush into print and point out some of the obvious errors in Campbell's claims, but on June 16 Brian Hill and Sarah Ritchie of Global News beat me to it, revealing further cracks in the media's faith in the RCMP:

> It wasn't until 6 a.m. the following morning—more than eight hours after the first 911 calls were received—that the RCMP had any kind of air support. This was a drone operated by officers at the scene.

Global News has previously reported that the RCMP didn't ask the Canadian Armed Forces for air support to assist with the manhunt. This was according to a response to questions sent by Global News to the Department of National Defence (DND).

Campbell's affidavit suggests the RCMP did request air support from the military.

"Additional inquiries to secure air support were made with the Joint Rescue Coordination Centre—Canadian Forces and Canadian Coast Guard," the affidavit said.

Global News asked DND to clarify whether the RCMP requested air support to assist with the manhunt.

In a written statement, the department said it can't comment because of the proposed class-action lawsuit against the RCMP and the government.

But a source familiar with communication between the RCMP and DND on the weekend of the shooting spree told Global News that RCMP didn't make an official request for air support to help with the manhunt.

Instead, the RCMP contacted the military to inquire about its "capabilities" to mount a search operation, the source said. These inquiries didn't include any formal submissions or requests for air resources to assist with the search.

Campbell confirmed a number of things in his statement, including that the critical incident commander assigned to Portapique took over at 1:24 a.m., as was revealed in the Pictou County tapes. Campbell didn't identify that officer as Staff Sergeant Jeff West, the head of traffic operations in Nova Scotia, who had cockily declared at 1:24 a.m., "I *am* in control."

Another of Campbell's matter-of-fact claims was that at 12:49 a.m. the first RCMP ERT members arrived at the scene in Portapique, at the same time that "J" Division, the RCMP in New Brunswick, advised that one of its police service dog and handler teams was en route to Portapique. That begged a couple of questions. Who were the ERT members who visited Nathan Staples at 12:35 a.m. and told him they were there to protect him? And why were the New Brunswick RCMP being called in at such an early stage when there was help more readily available from the Truro, Amherst and Halifax municipal police?

Campbell said that around 1 a.m. the RCMP was using infrared imaging to scour the woods around Portapique. If so, how did they miss Clinton Ellison, who spent four hours in the woods, or Lisa Banfield, who was purportedly there for over eight hours?

All in all, Campbell's new timeline described a situation in which the RCMP was overwhelmed, confused and the victims of much erroneous and misleading information from witnesses. If that was what really happened, the sympathetic public would have given the RCMP a pass once again. But instead of admitting to the shortcomings of its response during a chaotic situation, the force was doing everything it possibly could to delay and deflect attention away from its own failures and misdeeds. In the grand tradition of the Mounties, it looked like they were also getting ready to sacrifice one of their own.

Campbell's affidavit read:

The RCMP members on the Portapique scene included members who had stopped and issued a summary offence ticket for speeding to Gabriel Wortman . . . on February 12, 2020. At the time of the traffic stop, the gunman was driving a white 2013 Ford Taurus decommissioned police cruiser with reflective tape on the rear bumper. At that time, one of the RCMP members took a photo of the gunman's driver's licence, vehicle and the speed radar reading.

"When witnesses described that the gunman was driving a car that resembled a police car, the member recalled the traffic stop, and circulated the photograph of the gunman's licence, speed and the rear of his Ford Taurus vehicle. Shortly after midnight, this photo was provided to some RCMP members on scene as well as the Critical Incident Commander.

The officer was Constable Nicholas Andrew Dorrington, who played many roles that night in Portapique. At one point, the former soldier was part of a team assigned to chasing reports of flashing car lights and flashlights and conducting searches several kilometres west of Portapique. Later in the evening, Dorrington took the Blairs' severely injured dog, Zoey, to a veterinarian in Truro. Along the way he ran into a deer and had to stop at the Great Village fire hall with his damaged cruiser.

Here was Campbell now, swearing on June 3 in an official court document that the force had relied on Dorrington's photo as a guide to identify the vehicle that Wortman was driving. The 911 tapes, published the night before, showed clearly that the force had heard from three callers between 10:01 p.m. and 10:26 p.m. that the shooter was Wortman and that he was driving an RCMP cruiser. The RCMP instead relied on Dorrington's photo and put out a BOLO for a car with a "Canada decal" on it.

Lawyer Robert Pineo was astounded by how little of substance there was in the RCMP's filings with the court. "They offered nothing," he said. "We are shocked."

He shouldn't have been all that surprised. The RCMP was determined to double down on its original narrative, but that had been all but destroyed by the release of the 911 recordings. We had proven that the RCMP had been lying about many things, most importantly when they were told that Wortman was the shooter and that he was dressed as a police officer and driving what appeared to be an RCMP cruiser.

The tide had turned. Now that the dust was settling from the 911 recordings story, it was time to drive home the point about the RCMP deceptions with the next bombshell, courtesy of the courageous True Blue.

33

THE EXECUTION OF GABRIEL WORTMAN

"He went into the gas station on one side of the highway and saw all the cops, so he went across to the other side of the highway. Wortman pulled into the pumps and some cops were there filling up. One of them thought he recognized him, but the others weren't so sure. I think there was a bit of an argument, mainly because Wortman was driving a different car than the one they said he had. Eventually, the canine guy and an ERT member confronted him and shot him."

—*Doug Spafford, Chester Basin, Nova Scotia, April 19, 2020.*

Gabriel Wortman was lying dead on the pavement of the Irving Big Stop in Enfield when my neighbour, Doug Spafford, told me that story, which you first read in Chapter Three. It was colourful and detailed—remarkable considering that Wortman had been dead for only a few minutes. Others later told me the same story. It had spread like wildfire through the policing community.

In my first interviews about the massacres, I had referred to that version of events, only to be slapped down by a critic or two who pointed out that at Enfield there was no service station on the west side of Highway 102. I checked the maps. They were right. In my mind's eye I had mistaken the site of the gas station. It was in Elmsdale, one exit away, where there were service stations on either side of the highway. I should have realized right then that something was wrong with the official story.

When Felix Cacchione, director of the Serious Incident Response Team, put out his report on Wortman's shooting just before Christmas 2020, he seemed to clear this all up. All the elements of Spafford's version of events were contained in the report, but there was just one service station—the Irving Big Stop.

There was much about Cacchione's underwhelming final report that didn't sit right with me and many other observers. Eyewitnesses had reported contemporaneously on social media a much different story. On the *Nighttime* podcast and elsewhere, I laid out my concerns about the differences. I pointed out repeatedly that this is the kind of situation that leads to the flourishing of so-called conspiracy theories. "What we need," I told Jordan Bonaparte and his audience, "is proof of death." To some, it seemed a ghoulish and macabre position to take, but it was the only way I could think of to kill the rumours and get to the truth. It appeared to a growing number of people, including me, that the RCMP and its enablers were not being entirely forthright. Among them, True Blue heard my call for help and answered it by providing us with video from two service stations—the Petro-Canada at Exit 8 in Elmsdale and the Big Stop at Exit 7 in Enfield.

As Douglas, Jones, Bonaparte and I viewed the videos for the first time, we couldn't help but recognize that the original narrative and the one unfolding before our eyes were indeed not the same. The Mounties had lied about when they'd first learned that Wortman was the killer, a falsehood exposed by the 911 recordings. Now they were lying about how they had accidentally happened upon him, shot and killed him.

DID THE RCMP EXECUTE GABRIEL WORTMAN?
LEAKED GAS STATION SECURITY TAPES
CAST DOUBT ON SIRT REPORT
By Paul Palango

Security tapes from two service stations obtained by *Frank* magazine that depict the last few minutes of Gabriel Wortman's life and his shooting by two RCMP officers appear to contradict findings made by the police oversight body known by its acronym SIRT.

Copies of the tapes were provided to *Frank* by a source we've dubbed True Blue.

In the first tape, Wortman is seen standing beside a Mazda 3 next to a gas pump at the Petro-Canada station on the west side of Exit 8 on Highway 102. Wortman had stolen the vehicle after murdering Gina Goulet, his 22nd and last victim minutes earlier at her home/office on Highway 224 in Shubenacadie.

After killing fellow denturist Goulet, Wortman loaded the guns, ammunitions and other items into the back seat of Goulet's car. When he drove away, however, he must have noticed that her car was running on empty. Goulet was notorious for driving her car down to the fumes before adding more gas.

When he arrived at the Petro-Canada station, Wortman pulled into the wrong service lane. He is shown unsuccessfully trying to stretch the filling hose over the car to reach the fuel door.

A black RCMP vehicle is at the bay right next to Wortman. We can't see him yet, but an RCMP officer is standing on the other side of the pump, fuelling up just a few feet away from Wortman.

Wortman wasn't wearing the same clothing or driving a Chevy Tracker as described in the most recent RCMP Tweets from that morning. In fact, he was never driving a Chevy Tracker, but rather a Ford Escape. The erroneous description was given to the RCMP by a witness at the cloverleaf traffic circle in Shubenacadie, where Constable Heidi Stevenson and Good Samaritan Joey Webber had been killed by Wortman. Wortman escaped in Webber's Ford Escape.

According to True Blue, Wortman drove for about one kilometre to Goulet's house, broke through a glass door window and cut his arm in the process. He shot Goulet's protective German Shepherd, Ginger, twice. Wortman dripped blood through the house before smashing down a bathroom door and shooting Goulet. He changed out of the RCMP clothing that he had been wearing into pants and a white t-shirt.

Back at the Petro-Canada station in Elmsdale, a Mountie dressed in tactical gear appears at the rear of the RCMP vehicle, just as Wortman places the gas nozzle back on the pump and gets back in the car. The Mountie was obviously curious about Wortman, who had a contusion on his forehead, likely as a result of the crash with Stevenson.

Wortman then wheels away to a pump in the next bay, where he pulls up and sits in the car for a few seconds. By now, he may or may not have realized that the pumps had been shut down by the police at the gas stations on either side of the highway as part of a lockdown. (Actually, the pumps were shut down just after the Mountie had filled up.) In a few frames of the video, the two tennis balls impaled on the rear roof antenna of Goulet's car are evident.

Meanwhile, the curious Mountie was still eyeballing Wortman while turning to talk to his partner, who we now have a partial view of as well. As for the other Mountie who is clearly in view, his attention is clearly trained on the bald man in the Mazda 3.

During the final few seconds of the 28-second clip, we have a partial view of a third Mountie standing near the front of the RCMP vehicle.

Without getting out of the Mazda 3, Wortman drove away and headed back into the southbound lanes of Highway 102.

'I was right behind them'

Halifax *Chronicle Herald* photographer Tim Krochak was close on the tail of RCMP vehicles that followed Wortman to Enfield.

"I was near Stewiacke, and I hear on the radio that Wortman was last seen in the Brookfield area. That's, like, the next exit. Right then over in the southbound lane I can see a convoy of eight RCMP cars and an armoured car heading south toward Halifax. I turned around and started following them as fast as I could."

Krochak then got another call from another photographer: "Dude, it's going down in Shubenacadie."

"As we got near Shubie, there was a fire call for two RCMP cars burning. I could see a tall thing of smoke from the highway, but the convoy didn't go that way. They drove right past Shubie and they all got off at Exit 8 in Elmsdale. They pulled up at the Superstore [near the Petro-Canada station]. I was right behind them. A couple of them got out of the car and started talking. I couldn't see what was going on at the pumps. Then they ran back to their vehicles. I got the sense that they thought they had gone to the wrong place. They got back on the highway and headed toward Halifax."

The Irving Big Stop at Enfield was 7.7 kilometres away, about a four-minute drive at normal speeds. The convoy was right behind Wortman. They had him in their sights.

Early on in the investigation a blurry photo was released purportedly showing Wortman passing a Government of Nova Scotia inspection station. The RCMP said the time was 11:23 a.m., although the clock read otherwise. From that location, it would have taken Wortman at least 90 seconds to get to the Big Stop and pull up to the pump.

In the second and third Big Stop clips—different security camera angles—Wortman can be seen leaning across the seats and possibly into the back seat, where rifles were lying under a crocheted blanket. It's not clear whether Wortman was reaching for a gun or ducking for cover. In all, there were 10 bullet holes in the windshield—all on the passenger side of the car.

The time stamp of the overhead security camera view reads 11:25 when the shooting starts.

An accompanying photo provided by True Blue showed ammunition scattered on the front passenger seat of the car and a plastic jug of milk, less than half-full.

A synopsis of the autopsy, also provided by True Blue, showed that Wortman had bullet wounds to the head, arms, neck and torso. A total number of shots is not recorded.

The report also said that Wortman had blunt injuries to the head, various bruises and abrasions, had an enlarged heart and a spot on his lung.

'They just executed him'

Two highly experienced police officers who reviewed the shootings each voiced their concerns about what exactly happened.

"It appears that the Mounties made no attempt to arrest him," said a former high-ranking Mountie. "They appeared to know exactly who he was when they pulled up and they simply executed him. You can see why they don't want people to see that. It raises all kinds of questions about what was really going on."

The second policeman said that in his view this was what police manuals refer to as "a barricaded suspect."

"They had overwhelming numbers at the scene," the former officer said. "It would have been no problem for them to box him in. He was going nowhere. They made no attempt to negotiate. There is an entire protocol for barricaded suspects. They didn't do that. They just executed him. That might have made a lot of people happy, but it wasn't right. It's as if they had a do not apprehend, shoot-on-sight order."

The information contained in the videos confirms what eye-witnesses saw and posted on social media at the time of Wortman's shooting.

Witness Glen Hines was driving by the Big Stop with his wife and was one of the first witnesses to go before television cameras. "I just happened to drive by the Irving and I seen this SWAT team come in and park beside the pumps and the fellow got out of the passenger side and he just went right out in front of the car with his gun and just opened up right through the windshield of the car. All I could hear was gunshots," Hines told CTV News.

Recall that Halifax resident Alex Fox was there, too, and posted this on his Facebook page·

> . . . I decided to stop [at the Big Stop in Enfield]. After I used the ATM I stopped near the front doors to warm my hands up for a minute and put away my wallet. When I walked out the front door the parking lot and pumps were mostly deserted. There was only a small silver car at the pumps across from my motorcycle. As I'm walking along the sidewalk to my bike, a white truck pulls up at high speed to the opposite side of the gas pump from the car and two men in green tactical gear (thought they were soldiers at the time) got out and aim assault rifles at the car. They shout something like "Show us your hands!" There's a brief pause before they both open fire on the vehicle from close range. (I later read they shot ten times which I would believe). I am roughly parallel to this entire event and about 60' away according to Google Earth.

AUTOPSY FINDINGS

1. Gunshot wounds of the head
2. Blunt injuries of the head
3. Gunshot wounds of the neck
4. Gunshot wounds of the chest
5. Gunshot wounds of the abdomen
6. Gunshot wounds of the right arm
7. Bruise of the right elbow
8. Gunshot wound of the left arm
9. Abrasions of the left arm
10. Abrasions and bruises of the anterior thighs
11. Cardiomegaly
12. Pleural adhesions, right pleural space

Summary of the findings of Gabriel Wortman's autopsy (credit: True Blue)

The investigation by SIRT, the Serious Incident Response Team, was supposed to take three months but Director Felix Cacchione did not deliver a report until December 15, 2020. As you shall see, Cacchione makes no mention of most of this, including the eye-witnesses.

The following paragraphs are taken directly from Cacchione's thin final report. I have substituted Wortman for the acronym AP (Affected Person) used by Cacchione.

Compare the video information and other reporting above to what Cacchione wrote:

> . . . Wortman then set fire to both the RCMP officer's police vehicle and the mock police vehicle he had been driving and drove away in the civilian's Chevrolet Tracker.
>
> Unbeknown to the police, Wortman then drove a short distance to the residence of an acquaintance where he entered the residence and killed the acquaintance. Wortman then changed out of the RCMP clothing he had been wearing and into civilian clothes. Wortman then drove away in his latest victim's grey Mazda 3 vehicle leaving behind the Chevrolet Tracker and the discarded RCMP clothing.
>
> Wortman was headed toward Halifax-Dartmouth when he stopped for gas at the Irving Big Stop in Enfield. SO1 [1st Mountie] and SO2 [2nd Mountie] were travelling together and unaware that Wortman was no longer driving the Chevrolet vehicle when they pulled in to refuel at the same Irving Big Stop. SO1 was driving the police vehicle and stopped at a pump adjacent to a pump where a grey Mazda 3 vehicle was parked. SO1 exited the vehicle to begin re-fueling and as he looked across to the adjoining pump he observed a male with a noticeable hematoma and some blood on his forehead.

SO1 recognized this person as Wortman from photographs he had seen at the command post. SO1 drew his service weapon and alerted SO2 that Wortman was in the vehicle parked next to theirs. SO2, a member of the Emergency Response Team, left the vehicle and moved across the front of the police vehicle. Wortman then raised the pistol he had stolen from the RCMP officer he killed approximately 30 minutes earlier. SO1 and SO2 then began firing their service weapons. Wortman died at the scene.

RCMP spin team leaks 'the inside story' . . .
When the SIRT report hit the streets, the RCMP spin team then went into action, "accidentally" leaving the name of dog handler Constable Craig Hubley uncovered long enough for Halifax *Chronicle Herald* reporter Chris Lambie to stumble into, as the headline put it: "The inside story of how an RCMP dog handler shot N.S. mass murderer."

Lambie quoted an unidentified "police source" as describing Hubley as a "hard worker, diligent, tactically sound, committed and probably one of the best dog handlers that I know."
Lambie went on to write:

> Hubley recognized the mass killer, who was exhibiting "the 1,000-yard stare" as he gassed up within a few metres of the Mounties at the Irving Big Stop, said the source.
>
> "He stops to get fuel in his dog truck and he has the wherewithal to be standing there watching his surroundings and he sees the guy," said the police source.
>
> "They spotted him and their training immediately kicked in and they challenged the guy. And boom, they're heroes. They stopped the man who killed 22 people, including one of their own." . . .

The mass murderer appeared to be "making a threatening move," when the two officers shot him, said the source. "They were concerned for their safety."

Hubley's observation skills are unique, said the source.

"A lot of people wouldn't have spotted him, and he would have slipped away and gone on killing," the source said of the dog handler's observational skills.

"That alone speaks volumes to the kind of officer he is. He's smart. He's just switched on, to use one of our phrases. He's just squared away. He's got a big police brain."

The gas station tapes, once again, show that the RCMP, the Crown and governments have been playing fast and loose with the facts since last April.

A final note: In January of this year, Goulet's bullet-riddled car was towed to Andrew MacDonald's Maritime Pick a Part in Cow Bay, before it went to the John Ross & Sons scrapyard in Goodwood and destroyed. MacDonald, as you may recall, was wounded by Wortman outside Frank and Dawn Gulenchyn's burning house that fateful Saturday night.

Felix Cacchione's first move was to totally ignore a series of pertinent questions presented to him by Andrew Douglas prior to our publication of the above story. Did Cacchione have access to the Petro-Canada recordings? Did he talk to the RCMP members at Elmsdale? Why did he choose to hear only the stories of the police officers at the scene and not the civilian eyewitnesses?

"Please share with us what evidence you had that led you to believe this was a lawful takedown, and not a calculated execution," Douglas asked. "If you had access to the security tapes at the Petro-Canada in Elmsdale, did you purposely conflate the encounters in Elmsdale and Enfield for the purposes of your report? If so, why?"

Perhaps the most important question of all was this: If the RCMP had not positively identified Wortman at Elmsdale, how were they so certain that it was him when they immediately opened fire on him at the Irving Big Stop?

Witness Jerome Breau, who you will recall was on the scene at the Onslow Belmont fire hall when two Mounties opened fire on one of their own and an EMO worker, saw and heard something else that day. After leaving the scene, he eventually found his way up to Highway 104, where a group of heavily armed Mounties were congregating at a highway turnaround. He pulled over and tried to tell one of the Mounties what he had seen back at Onslow Belmont.

"I said to one of the cops, 'Hey, look, there a shootout at the fire hall,'" Breau recalled. "I'm basically talking right through him. He's listening to me but he's not really listening. Hey, buddy, there's a shooting at the fire hall. They were all strung out. I got the sense they didn't know what was going on and they were very disorganized. Then I heard on his radio a message: 'He's in a grey Mazda.' They all got in their cars and were making U-turns and headed to the ramp toward Halifax."

When I interviewed Breau in September 2021, after he finally came forward, he recounted the story about the grey Mazda and said he didn't think much of the comment because he didn't think that Wortman was driving such a vehicle. But he was. It was Gina Goulet's, which he had stolen after murdering her at her house near Shubenacadie. The timing was also right. Breau stopped to talk to the police at around 11:15 a.m., give or take a minute or two. It was around this time that police had come across Wortman trying to fill Goulet's car with gasoline at the Petro-Canada station in Elmsdale.

Dashcam video from firefighter Steve Currie [no relation to Darrell Currie] showed Wortman driving Goulet's car on Highway 214 away from the Petro-Canada station as he was about to take a right turn onto the ramp to Highway 102 toward the Irving Big Stop a few minutes away in Enfield. The video does not show any vehicles behind Wortman, which seems to indicate the RCMP were not in hot pursuit, although, as photographer Tim Krochak pointed out, they did take off after him eventually.

Cacchione wouldn't talk to us, but he did agree to answer questions from others, including the CBC's Elizabeth McMillan, who wrote:

SIRT's director, Felix Cacchione, said video from the Petro-Canada was part of the materials he reviewed, but he didn't draw any conclusions from it beyond that it showed the suspect had changed out of a police uniform and was driving the car he stole from Gina Goulet, the last person he killed.

Cacchione said he found no evidence that RCMP officers followed the gunman from the Petro-Canada to the Big Stop about 7.5 kilometres away.

"There was no indication in any of the radio transmissions that indicated he had been recognized and a broadcast made that he was driving a grey Mazda 3 vehicle. There was nothing like that. The officers didn't know—the officers at the Petro-Can—that it was him," said Cacchione.

One of the videos Frank Magazine posted shows that three seconds after opening his door, an officer had his gun drawn. It's not clear at what point he started firing.

Cacchione disputed the suggestion that the officer, a dog handler, got out of the vehicle intending to shoot. He said it only took seconds for the officer to spot a bruise on the gunman's forehead and realize it was the man wanted for murdering several people.

"Getting out of the vehicle, [the officer] would have been looking directly at the affected party and that's when he recognized him. There was no indication that he recognized him while he was in the police vehicle," said Cacchione.

"The quality [of video] we viewed was excellent, it was not grainy. It was typical of surveillance footage but it was not blurry," he said. "What I see on screen from Frank Magazine is very condensed compared to what I saw."

He said viewing snippets of video can change the appearance of the events. However, Cacchione said he could not release the full videos and said SIRT handed over its files to the public inquiry that is now examining the events of April 18 and 19, 2020.

"I would rather that the entire footage be posted than to pick and choose portions," he said.

It was entirely laughable. Cacchione was essentially saying that *Frank* should be ashamed of publishing such a poor-quality video when he had a much better version of the cover-up, which, unfortunately, he couldn't show to McMillan. The RCMP, unsurprisingly, said it couldn't comment because of ongoing lawsuits and its commitment to participating in the Mass Casualty Commission sometime in the future.

The federal and provincial governments were rendered speechless. The RCMP across Canada had been accused of atrocities and poor behaviour over the decades, and it had always dodged the opprobrium it so rightfully deserved. The uncovering and publication of the 911 tapes and the gas station videos proved that the force had been lying at both the beginning and end of the Portapique debacle. I couldn't help but wonder how the RCMP could successfully prosecute so much as a speeding ticket after all this.

The videos brought into focus what the Mounties were likely doing from the moment they arrived on scene that Saturday night in Portapique and throughout the next Sunday morning as Wortman roamed around killing nine people. If there was a shoot-on-sight order, issued from on high, it might well explain a number of incidents that had seemed so incongruous.

First was the shooting of Corrie Ellison. From the 911 tapes we know that the first callers told the RCMP about Wortman, yet the force acted like it didn't have this information. Were arriving officers issued an execution order and, nervous about the implications of that order, did they mistakenly shoot the first person they saw? Based on the RCMP's sketchy narrative, that is clearly within the realm of possibility.

The shoot-up of the Onslow Belmont fire hall by two Mounties was written off by Cacchione as entirely lawful. He said there was no harm done and no criminal intent. As with his later report about Wortman's demise, Cacchione ignored citizen witnesses such as Sharon McLellan, Jerome Breau and Charlie Hoyt. His findings did not fit the facts, although he protested to the contrary. "Just read my report," he told one woman who got him on the phone and complained to him about what he had done. She taped the conversation and allowed me to hear it.

If the Mounties were operating with a shoot-to-kill order, that helps to explain why the two officers jumped out of their unmarked Nissan Altima and began firing without warning at one of their colleagues and an EMO worker. There was no intent to arrest Wortman. Somebody wanted him dead.

If there was such an order, who issued it, when and why?

An execution order would also explain why the RCMP didn't forewarn the Truro Police Service that Wortman was headed their way. The Truro police were given a heads-up only after Wortman had passed through the town. If they had captured or engaged Wortman, then they would have had their own file on him. From the RCMP's actions then and subsequently, it is abundantly clear that the force wanted to keep any record of its pursuit of Wortman in-house. Therefore, it was prepared to accept the risk of letting Wortman travel through Truro, hoping he wouldn't kill anyone there or get caught in the town. He didn't.

Finally, there was the curious order from the Halifax Regional Police to its officers, reported by Tim Bousquet of the *Halifax Examiner*. The Halifax police were told by the RCMP to set up a roadblock but not to kill Wortman—just capture him. Why? Once again, the RCMP did not want Halifax to open a criminal file. If Wortman was arrested by the Halifax police, the RCMP would just take the case over as part of its provincial or federal mandate—or both. But if Halifax shot and killed him, it would necessitate a separate investigation.

All of this, of course, begs the question of why the RCMP made everything so complicated. We still don't have an answer for why the Mounties, after having shot Wortman dead, tried to claim for the next three and a half hours that he was "in custody," as the force put it on Twitter. A reasonable inference is that someone was trying to come up with a suitable explanation for how he had been killed. Once again, the RCMP's behaviour was not normal.

After the *Frank* story about the videos was published, someone close to the investigation stepped forward and told me something they had witnessed that raised further concerns about what happened at the Irving Big Stop. "When Wortman was pulled out of the car, he was placed on his stomach and his hands were tied behind his back with a shoelace," the source said. As a precaution, police sometimes handcuff an apparently dead suspect in case they suddenly resurrect. "Nobody wanted to put their handcuffs on him. Why not? It's as if they were already thinking about not being linked to whatever had gone down."

It wasn't even worth asking the question of the RCMP. The force had already proven that it would just ignore inconvenient questions about its narrative and was happy to leave them to the Mass Casualty Commission to answer. The way things were unfolding, it was a reasonable assumption that the commission would be more interested in jeremiads than in uncovering wrongdoing.

The name of Craig Hubley, the Mountie who shot Wortman, was quickly forgotten, as was likely the grand plan. He didn't step forward for an interview and melted back into anonymity. A few months later, I received a tip about Hubley indicating that he was no ordinary police officer. It didn't take long to figure out his story. As it turned out, he was not quite a nobody in Nova Scotia. Like so many Mounties in this story, his father, Carl, had been a long-time member of the force, before retiring as corporal in 2009. When Craig was a teenager, his father and mother went through a messy divorce. His father went on to marry a Halifax lawyer named Deborah K. Smith. She eventually was appointed a family court judge and then, in September 2019, Prime Minister Trudeau named her Chief Justice of the Supreme Court of Nova Scotia. Was that why Hubley was kept in the shadows? Suffice to say, the unusual connection was never raised by the local or national media, but certainly added another ounce of intrigue.

The revelations about the 911 tapes and Wortman's death were leading the public away from the police narrative that domestic violence was the sole impetus for Wortman's murder sprees. That didn't mean the powers that be wouldn't continue to try to hide behind it, but the public had a little more context with which to assess what was really going on.

Together, however, Douglas, Jones, Bonaparte and I took comfort in the fact that we had cracked open the door enough to let some light shine in on the truth. It might take years and a lot of luck to finally get to the whole truth, but we were all confident that the rest of the story would come tumbling out eventually.

◆

The next Friday night we left the *Frank* office and drove across the bridge to Dartmouth. Along the way we went up Portland Street and passed Gabriel Wortman's former denturist office. The toothy sign was long gone. The windows were boarded up. Someone had tagged the stone wall next to the driveway with spray paint. The property had been sold and was going to be redeveloped. Ashes to ashes.

We ended up at the Boondocks, a fried-fish restaurant with a large patio at Fisherman's Cove. It was a cold evening, sitting out by the water. Andrew Douglas and Peggy, Chad Jones and Caroline, and Sharon and I were all there. Jordan Bonaparte couldn't make it. He had a family commitment and was still getting over the shell shock of watching *Frank* magazine, Douglas and me fending off the vicious attacks over the 911 tapes.

All was good, at least for now.

We raised our beers and Caesars to toast those who had brought us together. One by one we named them: Jamie Blair, Greg Blair, Lisa McCully, Corrie Ellison, Frank Gulenchyn, Dawn Gulenchyn, John Zahl, Elizabeth Joanne Thomas, Peter Bond, Joy Bond, Aaron Tuck, Jolene Oliver and young Emily Tuck—the victims of the first massacre.

Then we toasted those who died in the second, entirely avoidable massacre: Alanna Jenkins, Sean McLeod, Tom Bagley, Lillian Hyslop, Kristen Beaton and her unborn baby, Heather O'Brien, Constable Heidi Stevenson, Joey Webber and Gina Goulet.

It was a solemn and tearful moment, but it wasn't entirely without satisfaction. The night before I'd had an idea and, with the help of my daughter Katie and some strangers, managed to get it all together just in time. I had brought a cardboard box to the dinner, which I said was filled with gifts I'd had made for everyone, but especially Douglas.

Without him we wouldn't have been there. I asked him to close his eyes while I took his present out of the box.

When he opened his eyes, he was momentarily stunned, and then he broke out in a long burst of laughter. It was a white T-shirt embossed with the *Frank* logo and a tinfoil hat. The message above read: "I'm a conspiracy theorist & I can prove it."

34

A MASSACRE?
WHAT COVER-UP?

Much had transpired over the previous fourteen months.

I walked into the local pharmacy in Chester Basin one Friday afternoon to pick up a prescription for the usual maladies affecting someone of my advancing age. The thirtyish pharmacy assistant knew a little bit about me from the pharmacists, who knew a lot about what I had been doing.

"I hear you're writing a book," she said. "What's it about?"

"Gabriel Wortman," I said.

"Who?" she asked, raising an eyebrow.

"The Nova Scotia massacres," I responded. Noting that she was still drawing a blank, I added, "The shootings last year."

"Someone got shot?" she asked with a look of both astonishment and concern.

At the building supply store in Chester, Nick Langille, one of the warehousemen, told me he couldn't believe how many people weren't paying attention to what had taken place and was continuing to happen.

As we were filming for the documentary at the offices of *Frank* magazine, the sound technician was gobsmacked by what he was hearing through his headphones. "What's this story all about?" he asked. He hadn't been out of Nova Scotia since before COVID and the massacres, and he still didn't have a clue what had taken place.

It was a modern twist on the whodunnit—a whodunwhat, as it were—courtesy of the police, the government and the self-censoring media. Instead of finding out at the end of the story who the murderer is, we never find out what happened and are left in a perpetual state of suspension.

In an often-quoted observation from his 1994 book *The Prosperous Few and the Restless Many*, the American linguist and philosopher Noam Chomsky described the phenomenon well: "The general population doesn't know what's happening and it doesn't even know that it doesn't know." The pharmacy assistant and the soundman aren't alone. Many people don't pay for cable or a serious news site (let alone an actual newspaper or magazine) or keep up with current events. They get their news from Netflix or social media feeds tailored to please or nonsensically outrage. Plugged in as people are, they live off the grid with respect to news, each in their own dogmatically de-stressed, "positive" world of free, oversimplified or harmless news—too often crafted devoid of history, civics or philosophy. And so the pharmacy assistant, the soundman and their ilk remain, wanting all the benefits of citizenship with none of the costs. This kind of wilful ignorance makes it easy to shoot the messenger rather than deal with the problem.

Over the last fourteen months, I had been sworn at, ridiculed, lambasted and threatened with violence. It's what happens to anyone, nowadays, who tries to do an honest job that might involve telling people things they don't want to hear. Far too many of us are entrenched, defensive, hypervigilant—and thin-skinned. Hell, the CBC announced in June 2021 that it was no longer going to allow comments on its Facebook page because of the trauma being inflicted on its employees. Fearful reporters are not what the world needs right now.

One Mountie told my source McNulty this: "That Palango is worse than the plague."

I asked McNulty to relay this message to the Mountie: "Thank you."

After part of an interview with me was broadcast on the CTV network, former RCMP staff sergeant Stephen Mills played the Smurf and wrote this comment online on behalf of the RCMP Veterans' Association:

I note you had Paul Palango on CTV News Atlantic on June 9th.

This is the same man who said the shooter from Portapique was an informant with a "licence to kill."

This is the same man who said that the shooter collected $475,000 from Brinks as a payment from the RCMP when in fact he simply cashed out his RRSPs and that is the standard procedure that Banks utilize to handle this type of large cash transaction. This is the same man who claimed a Staff Sergeant in Tantallon refused to authorize overtime because it would affect his non-existent performance pay. Palango knows that none of this is true. There are many other examples of Palango's ethical standards but at the root of the problem are his "sources." They are typically anonymous, if they exist at all, and his stories generally morph into what has accurately been described as fairy tales.

And now Palango and Frank Magazine have stooped to an unbelievable new low by publishing a leaked 911 tape from a 12-year-old boy and two other victims. Whomever leaked these recordings will hopefully be held to account but, in a race to the bottom of incivility with no regard whatsoever for their families, Palango and Frank Magazine have managed to lower the bar to another level. He also had the unmitigated gall to criticize the families of the victims for being outraged. Its [sic] despicable.

If that wasn't enough Palango and Frank Magazine now report that RCMP members executed the shooter and CTV News ran with that story. Anyone with an ounce of policing experience would dispute everything he says about these latest video clips. Even your own policing expert, Chris Lewis, pounded holes in the accusation and yet CTV News continues to give Palango a platform. Why?

Palango has been on a life long rant about the RCMP and the tragedy of Portapique and not allowing the Commission to do their work without distraction. This tragedy was the most unprecedented and horrible event in Canadian history and there is no chance the response would have been done perfectly in any jurisdiction. Some tough lessons will be learned but it is imperative that the Commission and only the Commission be the only credible source for all answers in regard to Portapique. Not Palango. Not Frank Magazine. Not CTV News or anyone else.

Charlene Bagley, the daughter of murder victim Tom Bagley, replied on social media: "The truth hurts some time. Just like it hurt when I found out my father was shot and killed 11.5 hours after GW was first identified. These weren't just little mistakes you made. My father would still be here today if it wasn't for your mistakes. The only so-called fairy tale I can see is the story you are trying to convince the public that happened."

The attack by former Staff Sergeant Mills was typical of those I had seen over the years. Words were attributed to me that I had never spoken or written, and I was castigated for having motives I do not have. I didn't take on this story to make friends, but I made many along the way. I didn't do it for fame and fortune but to get justice for the dead, to bring accountability to the RCMP and its enablers, and to stop yet another tawdry Canadian cover-up. I most certainly didn't start out with the intention of writing another book about the RCMP.

As you will recall, this all began when I was fortunate enough to have *Maclean's* publish my thoughts about the Nova Scotia massacres. The headline read: "The Nova Scotia Shooting Encapsulates All That's Wrong with the RCMP." I severely understated the problem. In the last lines of that column, I wrote this:

There are a thousand horrible questions for which answers are needed.

But Nova Scotians and Canadians must get over suspending their disbelief and their fond memories of the Musical Ride to do the hard work of addressing this very important issue.

The time has come for recriminations.

This book was a first step in highlighting and distributing those recriminations.

One of the thorniest issues for politicians is that no matter how dysfunctional and broken the RCMP appears to be, it is a recognized symbol of Canada—anyone who dares criticize it is construed as attacking the country. Time and time again the public and their governments have let the Mounties get away with circumventing the dictates of propriety or the rule of law. They have never faced any serious recriminations because it has never been the right time to level them. As a result, the insidious rot inside the force and the justice system has continued to spread.

Even after twenty-two Nova Scotians were murdered by Gabriel Wortman on April 18 and 19, 2020, and it was obvious that some combination of RCMP shortcomings, miscalculations and misdeeds were involved, it would be fair to say that most Canadians were reluctant to challenge the RCMP's version of events. For far too many, there was no room or place for recriminations. That's just not what's done in much of Canada.

After the release of the tapes and the videos, even with the damaging evidence contained within them, governments were still content to let the RCMP remain in control. Outside police forces were not called in to conduct a rigorous investigation. Instead, the RCMP was asked to investigate itself. When, in July 2021, the Mounties finally called in an outside police force, the Ontario Provincial Police, it was to look into who leaked the 911 tapes to *Frank*—"the Halifax gossip and satire magazine," as the Canadian Press reported. Five months later, the OPP team had still not delivered anything.

The mainstream media were reduced to reporting only what official sources were telling them, often filled with inaccuracies, making me and others wonder who was perpetuating the gossip. It was all so satirical.

The mainstream and much of the alternative media played a significant role in helping the RCMP and the governments spray confusion
and a thick layer of opacity over the fallout from the Portapique killings. The media love to say they abide by the KISS rule: keep it simple,
stupid. But they don't understand their own definition of "simple."
I can't count the number of journalists who have told me, often with a
heavy dose of smugness, that they rely on Ockham's razor as a guide.
They don't understand what Ockham's razor really describes: the
simplest answer is the one that encompasses all the variables. There
should be no dangling threads, knots or chunks of rope. The mis-
guided and misinterpreted KISS rule merely encourages intellectual
and journalistic laziness.

In early July 2021, news was leaked that Assistant Commissioner
Bergerman had decided to retire, which would take effect three weeks
before the Mass Casualty Commission's sittings. One would think it
would be a major news story that the top police officer in Nova Scotia
was stepping down in the midst of such controversy. There was some
television coverage, but the Halifax *Chronicle Herald* didn't publish a
story or even an editorial comment about it. Two weeks later, it did
mention her retirement after reports that her husband, Mike Butcher,
and Chief Superintendent John Robin had been quietly removed from
their proposed roles as liaisons between the RCMP and the Mass
Casualty Commission.

A provincial election in Nova Scotia was held in August 2021.
During the campaign, none of the three major party leaders breathed
a word about the RCMP or the massacres. Nor did any of the can-
didates during the federal election that followed in September. On
November 5, Brad Johns, the latest Justice Minister, rose in the Nova
Scotia Legislature to call for a motion to thank Lee Bergerman for her
"many years of distinguished service to Canadians and Nova Scotians."
The motion passed unanimously.

Nothing about the massacres is more upsetting than the murders
of those twenty-two people, but there are nonetheless moments that
occurred in their wake that didn't get the media attention they rightfully deserved. When it was revealed that the RCMP was destroying

evidence in the case, the mass media yawned. When one of their own, the CBC's Elizabeth McMillan, reported that seventy Mounties had taken the summer off, claiming they were stressed, the rest of the media yawned again. The fact that the province of Nova Scotia was forced to pay $3.75 million dollars for replacement officers brought in from across the country wasn't news. The "sick" Mounties got full pay and lounged around their vacation properties, many posting photos on social media.

Another story that was glossed over was Judge Laurel Halfpenny MacQuarrie's ruling that the sixteen names contained in the Information to Obtain search warrants would be kept secret because it would be a "serious risk" to name these people, who were "simply conduits of information to the police and nothing more."

"You see that story about the sixteen people?" one of the sixteen asked me, laughing. "That's me and . . . and a bunch of other people I know." I can't name the person without violating the court order, even though the person is willing to be identified.

Among the sixteen were many people who were near Wortman or had dealings with him right up until that weekend. Why were their names being kept hidden? It was counterintuitive but par for the course, police sources said.

Why would anyone close to Wortman not be examined? The government and the courts are doing nothing to foster public confidence by donning a mask of concern and care for individuals. It's in the public interest that we are told everything about Wortman and what transpired—everything.

The media have a serious problem when reporting on police. "We journalists can start with reforming how we talk about policing," Karen Attiah wrote in the *Washington Post* on November 4, 2021. "There have long been calls for the media to stop unquestioningly treating police narratives as if they are established fact, when case after case has shown that police can and do distort the truth." Attiah was talking about media, race and policing in the United States, but the point holds in Canada, too. "Lie 'til you die," is the unofficial credo of Mounties, said many members to me, including prominent former member and former CEO of Paladin Security, Leo Knight. Over the years the RCMP has been caught so many times lying and destroying inconvenient evidence in active cases across the country that it doesn't fight back anymore. It knows that the media will soon forgive and forget. That can't continue.

Judges and justices of the peace, bureaucrats, police and cabinet ministers are paid by citizens to uphold the rule of law. They have a duty to protect the public, not to be hollow men and women caught up in self-interest, gender politics, wokeism and cancel culture—more afraid of trolls online than of failing in their duty to bring justice to the dead. They mustn't allow themselves to conspire to protect the RCMP or culpable individuals, as they have done in this and other cases in Nova Scotia. That's wrong and worrisome. There must be accountability. Some individuals might suffer in the process of pursuing the truth, but if those in power are not held accountable, all of society suffers. This is not the time for squeamishness from powerful people who are inclined to lead from behind, doing only what the polls tell them is safe to do. We need leadership, but when faced with confronting the massive and established problem that is the Royal Canadian Mounted Police, our leaders continue to be willfully deaf, blind and mute. No matter what it does, the unaccountable RCMP is considered untouchable.

In late September, Lisa Banfield launched a lawsuit seeking to protect her interest in Wortman's estate, which pitted her against the families of the victims in the fight over Wortman's assets. Banfield had been named the executor of Wortman's estate but had renounced that position a month after the massacres. She had been named the sole beneficiary of the net proceeds of the estate. She was in hiding but still had her eye on the money. Prosecutors seemed to be in no rush to bring her to court to face the charge of providing ammunition to Wortman that was laid ten months earlier. The timing and substance of the suit made it look like just another obstacle being thrown up to shield Banfield from future scrutiny.

As this book was in its final revisions, the Mass Casualty Commission was about to begin its first hearings, in October 2021. As that date approached, the Commission made a stunning announcement on October 13 that it was delaying its first hearings until the end of January 2022. It said it had new evidence to digest. New evidence? Did the members just start reading *Frank* or listening to the *Nighttime* podcast? By design, it appeared to be the ultimate possible expression of the rule of politics. Almost everyone involved in its operation, from its advisory board to the commissioners to the investigators themselves, appeared to have been chosen with political considerations. Even the lead investigator, former Toronto police officer Scott Spicer, came to the task as a representative of the all-powerful Privy Office, which oversees the bureaucracy and policy implementation of the federal government. It describes itself as: "the department [that] helps the government in implementing its vision, goals and decisions in a timely manner." The Privy Council Office has long been the invisible hand in Canadian politics. What ever happened to true independence and disinterested investigations? The rule of politics has superseded the rule of law—and few seem to care.

Even though the book was written, I kept digging, and new twists were emerging at a surprising pace. In spite of the undeniable proof that police watchdog Felix Cacchione had published two flawed and misleading official reports about the incidents, he not only was allowed to continue in his role as SIRT director but also was given expanded responsibilities. In October 2021, SIRT was hired by the province of New Brunswick to be its police watchdog, as well.

Shortly afterward, the RCMP announced the convictions of various outlaw bikers in trials that had gone unreported. In doing so, the Mounties finally revealed the names of the two projects that were concluded just before the massacres: J-Thunder and J-Thunder-struck. Three days later, on October 19, before I could muster inquiries about whether there was a connection between the projects and Wortman, CBC reporter Jacques Poitras dropped a bombshell story. Poitras reported that in July 2021 New Brunswick public safety minister Ted Flemming had invoked a codicil in the province's contract with the RCMP to have Assistant Commissioner Larry Tremblay removed from his position as head of the RCMP in that province. In a letter to RCMP Commissioner Lucki, Flemming said Tremblay "no longer commands my confidence" and that his removal was "an urgent necessity."

Flemming cited two matters in his letter, Poitras wrote: the RCMP was resisting the government's desire to make illegal drug crime and crimes driven by drugs its top priority; and Flemming also wanted to "reverse the trend of diminishing RCMP accountability to local government leaders."

Flemming's actions were unprecedented. No previous RCMP provincial police chief anywhere in the country had been removed from office in such a public and unceremonious fashion. "I have never heard of something like this ever happening," said a former RCMP deputy commissioner who asked for anonymity. "It speaks volumes about the current state of the RCMP. It's another sign that the force needs to be torn down. In my opinion it can't be fixed."

The Opposition parties in the New Brunswick legislature, however, immediately chastised Premier Blaine Higgs for taking such daring action against the RCMP. Meanwhile, the rest of the media ignored the story.

"The word is that this is all about what happened in Portapique," my source, McNulty, said. "The heat is rising to the top and everyone is ducking."

All this took place as I was closing in on a new story about Tremblay, who had gone out of his way a year earlier to slag me to the media with a curiously oblique communique (see page 430) impugning my credibility over the murders of the Saulniers in Dieppe. It had now taken me two months to wheedle out of my sources the threads of this new story. I finally had enough to publish it in *Frank* on Halloween 2021.

When Wortman was buying decommissioned RCMP vehicles from GC Surplus, the arm of the Canadian Government that liquidates used and surplus equipment, he had an unlikely competitor who was also a frequent flyer at the auctions: RCMP Assistant Commissioner Larry Tremblay.

Wortman made 44 purchases from GC Surplus, Tremblay made 77. Both had accelerated their purchasing in the year and a half prior to GC Surplus shutting down its operations on March 11, 2020, due to Covid-19 restrictions. Each man made his final purchase that day. It was not known if they ever met at the site in Dartmouth's Burnside Business Park, but their crossing paths so frequently is curious enough to warrant further investigation.

"We began to wonder if GC Surplus was being used as a meeting place between Tremblay and confidential informants or agents," a source said. "We had no proof that this was the case or whether Tremblay or Wortman met there, but in light of what happened with Wortman, it seemed like a possibility."

After the story was published, tips began pouring in about Tremblay, who had grown up in the same Riverview suburb of Moncton as Wortman. The Mountie was a few years older, but the co-incidences, the new things I was learning about Tremblay and the possible implications were more than a little intriguing. I would have to add it all to the list of the many unanswered questions about the massacres. Why did the RCMP in Nova Scotia rely so heavily upon their counterparts in New Brunswick and not upon other local police forces in Nova Scotia? There are still so many unanswered questions about the massacres.

Wortman seemed to have a plan that he was about to put in motion. He was negotiating the sale of his properties on Portland Street in Dartmouth. He was already looking to sell off all the equipment because he was "heading in another direction," as the denturist told me. Wortman had withdrawn $475,000 through Brink's and had a total of $705,000 hidden outside. Was there a plan for him or someone he trusted to come back and get it after the fires? Did that plan change because something unknown had gone wrong and set him on his murderous course?

Why did the RCMP rely so heavily on Lisa Banfield's statements when it knew, or ought to have known, that they were problematic?

Why was evacuating convicted drug trafficker Peter Griffon more important than rescuing four children?

Was Wortman an informant or the target of an informant-driven investigation?

With the uncovering of the 911 tapes, the gas station videos and a more complete version of the story surrounding the Onslow Belmont fire hall shoot-up, we now know that the RCMP has been lying since the beginning of Wortman's rampage. Is it lying about what was going on beforehand, perhaps, between the force and the killer? We still don't know what the inciting incident really was that sparked Wortman's rage, nor exactly what happened after the shooting started. From the outset, there was reasonable speculation that Wortman dressed up as a Mountie and used a replica RCMP cruiser in his rampage as a perverse way of punishing the RCMP for a perceived wrongdoing.

We don't know whether the RCMP dispatched Wortman because he was a liability to the force. Dead men can't talk. In fact, much is still unknown, and it doesn't take a genius to figure out that some of it has been kept deliberately hidden. That can be readily inferred from the fact that the RCMP felt compelled to lie and deceive in the first place, which begs a single, pointed question:

What's the Big Secret?

A NOTE ON SOURCES

As readers may have already deduced, in my approach to researching, gathering evidence and writing this book I deliberately did not adopt a traditional format for sourcing non-fiction. In part because printing lengthy books in the era of COVID-19 is an unreliable enterprise, I've avoided dozens of pages of largely redundant endnotes and have chosen instead to incorporate enough identifying details about published materials I've cited that anyone could find the underlying documents online by using a search engine.

From the earliest days in April 2020, it was obvious to me that the RCMP and various levels of government involved in dealing with the Nova Scotia massacres were gaslighting the public in an effort to cover up what had really led to the killings and the RCMP handling of them. Unfortunately, many in the mainstream and alternative media were all too eager to play along. This created a journalistic schism, as it were. During the time I was writing this book, it became clear to me that media viewed me as an enemy rather than a competitor. When I sought permission from Doreen Coady to republish an excerpt from her book, *100 Moms, 1000 Tips, 1 Million Reasons*, she was delighted to have me do that. When I sought permission from a major news outlet to reprint a portion of one of their reports, I was told by a spokesperson that the outlet did not want to be referred to or quoted at all in the book.

Any news outlet ought to know that no institution has the right to go unmentioned in a significant public-interest story in which they are involved. One of the running threads of this book is the media's choices of subject matter and tone, as well as their deferential behaviour towards the RCMP. I have quoted from and highlighted various outlets' work to show what they were comfortable reporting, in contrast to my own work and analysis. In that way, I believe that readers might better understand the important differences.

Next came the issue of sourcing. Many in the mainstream media and general public have taken the position that the only credible sources are those who will allow their real names to be used. In my opinion as a long-time journalist, author and even former editor at a national newspaper, that approach is journalism as conceived and practiced by ivory-tower purists, accountants, lawyers and their insurers. In the real world, investigative journalism isn't and can't be conducted in such a neat and tidy fashion. It is the duty of any experienced reporter to be able to judge the credibility of the source, the context of the situation and the quality of the information. Time will tell whether I have judged the viability of my sources well. Since I began writing this book, many things told to me off the record, such as the RCMP's destruction of evidence, have since been revealed to be factual. I am confident that other unnamed sources in this book will prove similarly prescient and invaluable.

In recent years, there has been a popular move in journalism towards stories being double- or even triple-sourced. The accepted wisdom is that if two or three people agree something happened, it is most likely to be true. Reality doesn't always play along. Sometimes there are not two or three people involved in or witness to a situation, and, all too often I suspect, even when there are multiple sources, the second and third sources are merely agreeable people. Such requirements for overreporting would make it almost impossible to ferret out deep, well-protected stories.

Many of the sources in this book were law enforcement and government insiders who felt they had much to lose by speaking with me. Many feared being ostracized by friends and family. Many feared for their jobs, a few for their lives.

To attract sources, I showed in my radio appearances and published articles that I could write and publish stories that were incremental, on point and in which I always protected my sources. I also made it clear that I could keep sources truly anonymous, and allowed them to either deal with me directly or use cut-outs or go-betweens. This system worked very well. For example, I had a vague idea of who True Blue was in real life, but never had direct contact with him or her. The proof of their credibility was in what was provided to us and the public—the 911 tapes and the video of the shooting of Gabriel Wortman.

Pseudonyms were adopted for a number of sources for the same reasons. They needed to be protected, especially from the RCMP and its enablers in government who have proven to be extremely vindictive and even vicious when dealing with so-called whistleblowers (recall the experiences of Catherine Galliford and Cathy Mansley). The information and direction these sources provided was much more valuable than the public knowing who they are.

Finally, I relied upon citizen investigators, ordinary, everyday people who became invested in the story. Some of them were named but others asked to remain in the background. I know who they each are in their everyday lives. Their collective desire could be summed up this way: all they wanted was justice for the dead, accountability and the defense of the rule of law.

ACKNOWLEDGEMENTS

I never thought I'd write another book, but my old friend and colleague Steve Jarrett, who was at my side for my three previously published books, insisted that this story was mine for the telling. I brushed him off repeatedly, but he persisted, and pushed me over the edge. Thank you, once again, to Steve and to his wife, my long-time friend Paula Jarrett.

Circumstances and serendipity propelled me forward. The person who acted as the catalyst for this project was journalist Stephen Maher, who helped get my first piece published in *Maclean's* magazine. Early on we worked together, but we eventually parted ways over what were ultimately incompatible views of how to approach the story. Thank you, Stephen.

In the formative stages of my investigation, Tim Bousquet of the online *Halifax Examiner* gave me the space to publish my findings and opinions, which led to the development of new contacts and leads.

Halifax talk-show host Rick Howe was an important cog. He gave me time to not only describe what I was learning but also openly solicit for new information, which proved incredibly important in challenging the official narrative. Howe used the power of his show to perform a much-needed and important public service. After he retired, his successor, Todd Veinotte, kept putting me on the air. Thanks to both of you.

Freelance reporter Lindsay Jones was a close confidant in the early stages and kept watch over me when it was clear that the RCMP and many of its former members were not at all happy with what I was doing. She even introduced me to a top Halifax criminal lawyer, who was placed on standby in the event I needed such help.

After so many years away from journalism, I re-entered to find a barely familiar world of podcasts and bloggers and tweets. One blogger, Michael Marshall of *40 Gallons and a Mule*, proved to be an invaluable guide to the inner workings and characters of Halifax, old Dartmouth and Nova Scotia in general. Thank you, Michael— you were so helpful, and I really enjoyed talking to you. As the story gained momentum, it was well served by Paul Ragona (a.k.a. Seamus Gorman) of *Little Grey Cells*, Chris Smith and Johnny MacLeod of the *Atlantic Underground* podcast, Laura-Lynn Tyler Thompson, David Herle, and Jesse Brown's *Canadaland*.

It was my great fortune to meet Jordan Bonaparte of the *Nighttime* podcast. Over time we became a solid team committed to getting to the bottom of the story with our regular late Sunday night YouTube shows and podcasts. Thank you, Jordan, for all you did. I know I scared you a couple of times, but you have been a great storytelling partner.

It was through this medium of podcasts that I met Chad Jones, a thirty-three-year-old manager for a major Nova Scotia company. In his spare time he doubled as an intrepid and dogged citizen investigator—and a great one, at that. Working independently and with me, he provided a wealth of information and understanding of the characters and issues. As described in the book, I nicknamed Chad "Artificial Intelligence." We talked multiple times a day, and having him by my side was akin to having my own personal supercomputer. I could ask him anything and he could usually come up with the answer off the top of his head. He assisted me in almost every stage of the investigation and was one of my readers as I wrote the book. The book would have been considerably less detailed if not for him. Thank you, Chad, and a special thank you to his patient and brilliant partner, Caroline Kuepers.

When I needed someone to publish my long and often complex stories, Andrew Douglas of *Frank* magazine in Halifax stepped up and gave me a home. Until the late fall of 2020, I had no idea who he was. Once we had met, Andrew provided the unlikely engine that helped me drive this story. Like an old-time editor and publisher, he did not allow himself to be entirely constrained by either format or subject matter. He was flexible, always professional and absolutely dedicated. He proved to be an astute editor, committed to uncovering and reporting the truth. Thank you to Andrew and to his sidekick, the invaluable Cliff Boutilier.

This was, naturally, a traumatic event for the families of the victims. I wish to extend a special thank you to them for being so kind, understanding and gracious, particularly Charlene Bagley; Scott, Chris and Dale McLeod; Tammy Oliver-McCurdie; Crystal Mendiuk; Ryan Farrington; Daniel Zahl and Peter Bond.

My sources and supporters throughout this project came from a cross-section of society and the political spectrum. They ranged in age from their late teens to energetic and committed senior citizens. Everyone who legitimately offered their information, insights or labours was heard and had an impact on the final story.

Because the subject matter involved policing, it should come as no surprise that many were such right-wing conservatives that "they dragged sand," as my late former colleague Trent Frayne liked to put it. There were others who were so far to the left that they could only see the centre with a telescope. Thankfully, the majority were in the middle.

Most were exemplary citizens who never had been in trouble. Others were rabblerousers, ardent conspiracy theorists or anti-vaxxers, the kind of people not considered by the mainstream and most alternative media as being credible. A surprising number had moral or legal blemishes on their reputations. Several had spent time in prison, while a few others appeared to be headed that way. Almost all of them good, tainted and otherwise were allergic to public controversy, leaving that part of the game to me. I tried to listen to them all, and each of them contributed something to my investigation. I cancelled no one.

The glue that united this unlikely coalition was that we all had three things in common: we were concerned citizens who cared about where we lived and the fate of our neighbours, we were determined to seek justice for those who had died, and we wanted to hold accountable those in government and policing who caused or allowed this terrible tragedy to happen.

Along the way, many current and former law enforcement officers contributed their knowledge and insights to my investigation. The vast majority asked not to be named, but you, and in some cases your partners, know who you are. Others who were willing to be quoted on the record included Edgar MacLeod, Michael Gregory, Tom Juby, Leo Knight, Cathy Mansley, Calvin Lawrence, Tim Kavanagh, Pete MacIsaac and Gilles Blinn. Thank you all.

Other journalists and editors who helped me included Tim Krochak, Chris Lambie, Scott Anderson, Dan Donovan, Parker Donham, Elizabeth McMillan, Karissa Donkin, Deborah Stokes, Peter Edwards and Enzo DiMatteo.

Portapique and Nova Scotia residents who were touched by the story and opened up to me included: Doug Spafford, Leon Joudrey, Nathan Staples, Autumn Natasha Doucette, Jennifer Sampson, Holly Grue, Natalie Wood, Sharon and Tim McLellan, Darrell Currie, Jerome Breau, Charlie Hoyt, Jeff Crawford, Judy and Doug Myers, Cindy and Carlyle Brown, Angie Anjoul, Tammy Mercier, Kaitlyn Keddy, Craig Vanderkooi, Janie Andrews, Dana and Brenda Geddes, and Wes Robinson.

I must give a special shout-out to Laura Thomas Graham and her husband, Jon, in Orangeville, Ontario. If not for his snoring, we would know much less than we now do.

A special thank you to lawyer Rob Pineo, and then to others who asked not to be named. There was Jimmy McNulty and Bill Moreland, my original "Deep Throat" and the hero of the story "Deep Blue." Others included V.M., JackVegas, True Blue and Dave B. Your contributions were much appreciated and helped shape the story.

Citizen investigators and others who contributed significantly to this book in one way or another were: Pete Stevens, William Roy, Barry Renouf, Anne Calder, Wendilen Wood, Matty Rhind, Tim Kirkwood and Brandon Svenningsen. Dozens of other went by pseudonyms like Miss Foxx and ec120guy. And then there was June, a self-proclaimed senior citizen investigator, who hounded every official and journalist she could find and kept everyone on their toes.

I had been out of the writing business for a long while and had lost my connections. When I needed an agent, my real estate agent, Piers Baker, put me in touch with his friend, film director Jason Buxton. Jason set me on a path that led to Samantha Haywood of the Transatlantic Agency. She listened to my terribly incomplete story and hooked me up with Rob Firing.

I didn't arrive at their door entirely empty-handed, however. While this was all going on, like others in the early stages of the story, I had been approached by a number of documentary producers from around the world. One who came late to the game was Patrick McGuire from London, England. "Don't sign anything until we get back to you," he said, and I didn't. Eventually, Patrick was joined by Michael Kronish in Montreal and Allyson Luchak, and together we began working on a documentary, which, if all goes well, will be completed sometime in the future. They all read the manuscript as I was writing it, and their continuing support and encouragement was fundamental in moving this project along, since I'm terrible at doing book proposals.

Speaking of book proposals, Rob Firing helped me craft a decent one and it attracted some attention, which surprised me. Thank you, Rob.

Senior editor Craig Pyette of Random House Canada took charge of the project, and from our first Zoom conversations we were clearly on the same page. Craig asked me how much of the story I knew at the time of the proposal. I told him, "Sixty percent. By the time I finish the book, I expect to be ninety percent or so along the way." I think I got there. Yes, there's still more to do. Thank you, Craig, for rolling the dice and for your faith in me. I really appreciated the confidence you showed. It made things much easier for me. A special thank you to copy editor Sue Sumeraj for wading through all this with such care and insight.

I wrote the first draft in 140 continuous days between January and early June 2021, which would have been physically impossible without the regular massage therapy I received from therapist Cynthia Lohnes.

My other readers and critics included my daughter, Lindsay, who has been doing that off and on since she was fifteen. My stepdaughter, Katie Gorman, was magnificent not only in that capacity but also as my supporter and guard dog and, occasionally, as a sleuth in her own right. My brother, David Palango, provided his typically wicked observations and commentary, which are always useful. Thank you, thank you, thank you for your time, patience and contributions.

It would be remiss of me to not mention an old friend, the late Anne McCaffery, with whom I reconnected during this process after many decades apart. Her wry humour, observations and witty comments kept my spirits up even as she was suddenly but gracefully fading away.

Last, but certainly not least, is my beautiful and talented wife, Sharon McNamara. She went through a living hell for two years, physically and emotionally, due to health issues, but no matter how much she was suffering, she encouraged me to continue standing up for those who had been murdered. That's what I tried to do. There were threatening phone calls, attempts at intimidation, dozens of frightening moments and seconds of self-doubt here and there, but she never flinched. She helped make me strong. You can understand why I love her so.

Paul Palango
December 2021

INDEX

PAUL PALANGO is a veteran investigative journalist. He started his career at the *Hamilton Spectator*, his hometown newspaper. In 1977, he joined the *Globe and Mail* as a reporter, and between 1983 and his resignation in 1990, he served successively as its sports editor, metro editor and, eventually, national editor. During his tenure at the *Globe*, Palango's reporters swept the Centre for Investigative Reporting Awards in five consecutive years. In 1989, he accepted the Michener Award for disinterested public service journalism on behalf of the *Globe*. He is the author of three previous books: *Dispersing the Fog: Inside the Secret World of Ottawa and the RCMP*, *The Last Guardians: The Crisis in the RCMP ... and in Canada*, and *Above the Law: The Crooks, the Politicians, the RCMP and Rod Stamler*.